Gailun

# 语言学概论

（第3版）

教育部教学改革重点项目
——文化原典导读与本科人才培养 成果

教育部新文科研究与改革实践项目
——文史哲拔尖创新人才培养创新与实践 成果

刘 颖 主 编

刘春卉 李宇凤 杜晓莉 副主编

（按章节编写顺序排序） 编 委

朱 姝 郑春兰 韩江华

李 果 谷 丰 何 倩

汉语言文学专业系列教材　　重庆大学出版社

# 内容提要

本书是语言学理论教材,适合汉语言文学、外国语言文学、对外汉语等专业的本科生教学使用。本书分为八章,分别介绍语言学的概念、语音、语义、语法、文字、语言的发展和语言学流派等。本书以"回到原典"为教学宗旨,书中精选大量语言学研究中的经典文献,并通过对这些经典的适当解读,引导学生通过独立思考掌握语言学的基础知识和理论。

**图书在版编目(CIP)数据**

语言学概论/刘颖主编.--3 版. —重庆:重庆
大学出版社,2023.4
汉语言文学专业系列教材
ISBN 978-7-5689-3791-7

Ⅰ.①语… Ⅱ.①刘… Ⅲ.①语言学—高等学校—教
材 Ⅳ.①H0

中国国家版本馆 CIP 数据核字(2023)第 047133 号

## 语言学概论
### YUYANXUE GAILUN
(第 3 版)

刘 颖 主编
刘春卉 李宇凤 杜晓莉 副主编
责任编辑:李桂英 版式设计:林佳木
责任校对:邹 忌 责任印制:张 策

\*

重庆大学出版社出版发行
出版人:饶帮华
社址:重庆市沙坪坝区大学城西路 21 号
邮编:401331
电话:(023)88617190 88617185(中小学)
传真:(023)88617186 88617166
网址:http://www.cqup.com.cn
邮箱:fxk@ cqup.com.cn(营销中心)
全国新华书店经销
重庆升光电力印务有限公司印刷

\*

开本:787 mm×1092 mm 1/16 印张:26.5 字数:666千
2023 年 4 月第 3 版 2023 年 4 月第 9 次印刷
印数:12 401-15 400
ISBN 978-7-5689-3791-7 定价:66.00 元

高等院校汉语言文学专业系列教材

# 编委会

# 总序

这是一套以原典阅读为特点的新型教材,其编写基于我担任教育部教学改革重点项目——"文化原典导读与本科人才培养"和教育部新文科研究与改革实践项目——"文史哲拔尖创新人才培养创新与实践"的理论探索与长期的教学实践。

大学肩负着文化传承与创新、人才培养、科学研究、社会服务、国际交流合作的重要使命。近年来,我国高等教育取得长足进步,已建成世界最大规模的高等教育体系,2021年在学总人数超过4430万人。然而,尽管高校学生数量在世界上数一数二,但是人才培养质量仍然不尽如人意,拔尖人才、杰出人才比例仍然严重偏低。半个多世纪以来,中国在人才培养质量上没有产生一批堪与王国维、鲁迅、钱锺书、钱学森、钱三强等人相比肩的学术大师。

钱学森提出"为什么我们的学校总是培养不出杰出人才?"这个著名的"钱学森之问",体现的问题是当代教育质量亟待提高。其根本原因就是学生基础不扎实,缺乏创新的底气和能力。人才培养的关键还是基础,打基础很辛苦,如果不严格要求,敷衍了事,小问题终究会成为大问题。基础不牢,地动山摇;基础精通,一通百通。基础就是学术创新的起点,起点差,就不可能有大造化、大出息,就不可能产生真正的学术大师。怎样强基固本,关键就是要找对路径,古今中外的教育事实证明,打基础应当从原典阅读开始,一步一个脚印地扎扎实实前进。中华文化基础不扎实的现象不仅仅体现在文科学生上,我国大学的理、工、农、医科学生的文化素养同样如此。

针对基础不扎实的问题,基于培养一批拔尖创新人才的教学理念,我主编了这套以原典阅读为特点的新型教材,希望能够弥补教育体制、课程设置、教学内容、教材编写等方面的不足,解决学生学术基础不扎实、后续发展乏力这个难题。根据我的观察,目前高校中文学科课程设置的问题可总结为四个字:多、空、旧、窄。

所谓"多",即课程设置太多,包括课程门类多、课时多、课程内容重复多。不仅本科生与硕士生,甚至与博士生开设的课程内容也有不少重复,而且有的课程如"大学写作""现代汉语"等还与中学重复。而基础性的原典阅读反而被忽略,陷入课程越设越多、专业越分越窄、讲授越来越空、学生基础越来越差的恶性循环。其结果就是,不仅一般人读不懂中华文化原典,就连我们的大学生、研究生和一些学者的文化功底也堪忧。不少人既不熟悉中华文化原典,也不能用外文阅读西方文化原典,甚至许多大学生不知道十三经(《周易》《尚书》《诗经》《周礼》《仪礼》《礼记》《春秋左传》《春秋公羊传》《春秋穀梁传》《论语》《孝经》《尔雅》《孟子》)是哪十三部经典,也基本上没有读过外文原文的西方文化经典。就中文学科而言,我认为对高校中文学科课程进行"消肿",适当减少课程门类、减少课时,让学生多一些阅读作品的时间,改变中文系本科毕业生读不懂中华文化原典、外语学了多年仍没有读过一本原文版的经典名著的现状,这是我们进行课程和教学改革的必由之路与当务之急。

所谓"空",即我们现在的课程大而化之的"概论""通论"太多,具体的"原典阅读"较少,导致学生只看"论",只读文学史便足以应付考试,而很少读甚至不读经典作品,即使学经典的东西,学的方式也不对。比如,《诗经》、《论语》、《楚辞》、唐诗宋词,我们多少都会学一些,但这种学习基本是走了样的,不少课程忽略了一定要让学生直接用文言文来阅读和学习这样一种原典阅读的规律,允许学生用"古文今译"读本,这样的学习就与原作隔了一层。因为古文经过"今译"之后,已经走样变味,不复是文化原典了。以《诗经·周南·关雎》为例:"关关雎鸠,在河之洲。窈窕淑女,君子好逑。"余冠英先生将这几句诗译为:"水鸟儿闹闹嚷嚷,在河心小小洲上。好姑娘苗苗条条,哥儿想和她成双。"余先生的今译是下了功夫的,但无论怎样今译,还是将《诗经》译成了打油诗。还有译得更好玩的:"河里有块绿洲,水鸭勒轧朋友;阿姐身体一扭,阿哥跟在后头。"试想,读这样的古文今译,能真正理解中国古代文学,能真正博古吗?当然不可能。诚然,古文今译并非不可用,但最多只能作为参考。这种学习方式不仅导致空疏学风日盛,踏实作风渐衰,还会让我们丢失了文化精髓。不能真正理解中华文化原典,也就谈不上文化自信。针对这种"空洞"现象,我们建议增开中华文化原典和中外文学作品阅读课程,减少文学概论和文学史课时,真正倡导启发式教育,让学生自己去读原著、读作品。在规定的学生必读书目的基础上,老师可采取各种方法检查学生读原著(作品)的情况,如课堂抽查、课堂讨论、诵读、写读书报告等。这样既可养成学生的自学习惯,又可改变老师"满堂灌"的填鸭式教学方式。

所谓"旧",指课程内容陈旧。多年来,教材老化的问题并没有真正解决。例如,现在许多大学所用的教材,包括一些新编教材,还是多年前的老一套体系。陈旧的教材体系,不可避免地造成了课程内容与课程体系陈旧,学生培养质量上不去的严重问题,这应当引起我们的高度重视。

"窄",也是一个亟待解决的问题。自20世纪50年代以来,高校学科越分越细,专业越来越窄,培养了很多精于专业的"匠人",却少了高水平的"大师"。现在,专业过窄的问题已经引起了教育部的高度重视。教育部提出"新文科",就是要打破专业壁垒和限制,拓宽专业口径,加强素质教育,倡导跨专业学习,培养文理结合、中西相通、博古通今的高素质通才,"新文科"正在成为我国大学人才培养模式的一个重要改革方向。中文学科是基础学科,应当首先立足于培养基础扎实、功底深厚、学通中西的高素质拔尖人才。只要是基本功扎实、眼界开阔的高素质的中文学科学生,我相信他们不但适应面广、创新能力强,而且在工作岗位上更有后劲。

基于以上形势和判断,我们在承担了教育部教学改革重点项目——"文化原典导读与本科人才培养"和教育部新文科研究与改革实践项目——"文史哲拔尖创新人才培养创新与实践"的教学改革实践和研究的基础上,立足原典阅读,着力夯实基础,培养功底深厚、学通中西的高素质拔尖人才,编写了这套原典阅读新型教材。本系列教材特色鲜明,立意高远、汇集众智,希望能够秉承百年名校的传统,再续严谨学风,为培养新一代基础扎实、融汇中西的高素质、创新型中文拔尖人才贡献绵薄之力。

本系列教材共18部,分别由一批学科带头人、教学名师、著名学者、学术骨干主编及撰写,他们是:四川大学文科杰出教授、教育部社会科学委员会委员、四川大学"985"文化遗产与文化互动创新平台首席专家项楚教授,四川大学文科杰出教授、欧洲科学与艺术院院士、"长江学者"特聘教授、国家级教学名师曹顺庆教授,原伦敦大学教授、现任四川大学文学与新闻学院符号学-传媒学研究所所长赵毅衡教授,四川大学文学与新闻学院院长、国家万人计划哲学社会科学领军人才李怡教授,"长江学者"特聘教授、国家万人计划哲学社会科学教学名师傅其林教授,著名学者冯宪光、周裕锴、阎嘉、谢谦、刘亚丁、俞理明、雷汉卿、张勇(子开)、杨文全,以及干天全、刘荣、邱晓林、刘颖等教授。需要特别指出的是,本系列教材在主编及编写人员的组织遴选上不限于四川大学,而是邀请国内外高校中一些有专长、有影响力的著名学者一起编写。如韩国又松大学甘瑞媛教授、四川师范大学文学院李凯教授、西南交通大学艺术与传播学院徐行言教授、西南民族大学文学院徐希平教授、西南大学文学院肖伟胜教授、成都理工大学传播科学与艺术学院刘迅教授、西南财经大学国际教育学院邓时忠、成都信息工程大学人文学院廖思湄教授等。

本系列教材自出版以来,被多所高校选作本科生、研究生的教材,或入学考试的参考用书,读者反响良好。在出版社的倡议和推动下,我们启动了这 18 部教材新版修订编写工作。此次修订编写依然由我担任总主编,相信通过这次精心的修订,本系列新版教材将更能代表和体现"新文科"教学的需要,更好地推进大学培养优秀拔尖创新人才的教学实践。

　　路虽远,行则将至。事虽难,做则必成。是为序。

2022 年 12 月于四川大学新校区寓所

# 第三版前言

　　这本《语言学概论》由四川大学文学与新闻学院语言学及应用语言学教研室诸位同仁共同编写,自 2010 年首版以来,得到读者的广泛关注和应用,时时收到各种意见。作为语言学相关专业的教材,其读者既包括颇富经验的教学研究者,也有相关专业的研究生,还有初涉语言学的本科生。他们的真诚意见让我们十分感动,因为有关语言学概论的教材、专著实在太多,其中不乏大家之作,没想到我们这本小书还能在众多读者中引起一些注意,迎来第三版的修订。

　　十二年前,我们教研室在给四川大学汉语言文学相关专业授课时发现,学生在上"语言学概论"这门课程时总有不少困难,究其原因,不外乎以下两点:一是这门课程主要涉及语言学基本理论,如果学生对实际语料及语言现象缺乏有意识的关注和了解,则会感到内容抽象难懂;二是语言学领域与其他学术领域一样也有诸多术语,学界的翻译和解释并不统一,翻译也可能带来误解和混淆,这让学生进一步产生困惑。语言学作为一门既古老又年轻的学科,和我们的日常生活息息相关,其研究对象却又如我们赖以生存的空气,让人感觉不到其存在。因此,"语言学概论"作为这门学科的入门课,其目标应当是通过这门课程让学生对语言现象产生真正的兴趣,对语言学学科理论及发展有基本了解,从而有意愿进一步深入了解、学习或研究。我们教研室当时以年轻人为主,或许是初生牛犊不怕虎,或许是因为对语言学及教学工作满腔热情,我们决定针对这些情况编撰一本不同以往的《语言学概论》教材。彼时四川大学文学与新闻学院正在进行"文化原典导读与本科人才培养"等教学项目的探索,我们对原典阅读的意义深有感触,因此决定将这本教材按照"内容阐述+原典阅读"的方式编排起来。我们希望探索一条既不同于以理论阐述为主的传统思路,也不同于以经典导读为主的编撰方式的新道路。我们的想法是按照不同章节选取与学科内容相关的语言学经典,将原典作为教材的一部分,与系统学科内容相辅相成;让学生在接触学科基本框架的同时,直接"聆听"大师的教诲。此外,我们在教材中尽量增添了多种语言实例,并与汉语相对照,引导学生有意识地关注语言现象,以求让学生更直观地理解理论。

尽管这本教材还有一些问题(比如有些内容表述仍有争议、原文非英语的原典代以英汉译本等),事实证明这种直引经典的方式让学生受益匪浅。在教材应用过程中,学生们普遍认为,原典部分读起来难,一旦啃下来效果却立竿见影。汉语看不明白的问题一对照原文就迎刃而解。此外,原典与学科内容的结合,展现了不同学者、学派的观点,拓宽了学生的眼界,也提高了他们的思辨能力。近年来,我国语言学的发展取得了长足进步,我们不仅需要能掌握具体语言的应用型人才,也需要能进行理论研究的学术型人才,语言人才的培养可谓任重道远。因此,当编辑告知我们将进行第三版修订时,我们一方面感到欣慰,另一方面也深感责任重大。经过再三考虑,我们决定在原有版本基础上,修改、增添部分内容,选补一些原典,并拓展数字资源。由于本书框架定于一纪以前,难免有所疏漏,我们尽力而为,也希望读者继续支持、指正。各章节都有一定修改,主要新增以下内容:

第六章增加第三节"语言接触与语言的发展"一节,由杜晓莉撰写。

第七章增加第七节"认知语言学",由韩江华撰写;原第七节改为第八节,并增加"韵律语法学"相关内容,由李果撰写。

第八章增加第七节"语言学和神经科学",由谷丰撰写;第六节"语言学和语言教学"由何倩作了较多修改。

此外,其他原有章节,分别由刘颖、朱姝、刘春卉、李宇凤、杜晓莉等一一作了校订与修改,并感谢重庆大学出版社编辑对原典部分重新进行了校订。

刘颖

2022 年 1 月于望江

# 前言

　　"语言学概论"是中国语言文学、外国语言文学、对外汉语等专业的必修课程之一,该课程一般开一学期,占 3 个学分,用 54 学时。和其他专业课相比,该课程理论性较强,涉及内容广,讲授起来有一定难度。

　　本教材的编写主要有以下几个特点:

　　(1)内容具有系统性。语言本身即为系统,各个部分紧密相连。因此,本书力图系统地讲述语言及语言学基础理论与概念,逻辑清晰,章节明确,充分揭示语言的全貌。

　　(2)语言深入浅出。语言学理论和概念比较抽象,因此阐述、解释时应清晰准确。本教材用语明白晓畅,生动易懂,举例时尽量涉及多种语言,如英语、法语、日语等,为不同语种的学生提供更直观的教学语料。

　　(3)贴近现实,目光前瞻。语言学理论不断发展,本教材撰写时非常注意学科前沿问题,阐述时不拘于传统,并对最新观点适当进行介绍。举例尽量使用与当今社会紧密相关的真实语料和案例。

　　(4)富有启发性。教材最重要的目的是为学生提供学习的蓝本,同时也为教师提供讲课的大纲,因此应富有启发性。本教材编写时结合理论,谈实际问题,培养学生的创新能力。每小节后附复习题和思考题,既考查学生对基本概念的掌握情况,又启发学生在课后进行延伸思考。

　　(5)注重原典,以原典代替部分阐述。这是本教材最重要的特色。教材每一章的内容分为两部分:内容阐述和原典引用。过去的语言学教材基本上是理论阐述到底,虽然会介绍一些重要的语言学流派及相关理论,但很少直接使用原典。本教材直接将语言学大师的原典搬到教材中,原典以语言学经典理论为主,凡是原文为英文的文献都尽量采用原文,为方便学生阅读,其他西文文献也采用经典英文译文。有成熟的汉译本的文献尽量附上汉语译文。此外,本教材还选用了一些中国古代典籍中有关语言的论述及少量和现代汉语有关的语言学经典文献。将原典选段作为教材的重要内容,不但能直接展现经典原貌,减少转介时产生的不必要的误读,还能培养学生对相关领域原典的阅读能力,引导学生进入风光绮丽的语言学之林。

　　本教材共分八章,由四川大学文学与新闻学院语言学及应用语言学教研室成员共同编写。分工如下：

第一章"总论"、第七章"当代语言学流派及理论概述"、第八章"语言学和其他学科的关系"由刘颖编写。

第二章"语音"由朱姝编写。

第三章"语义"由刘春卉编写。

第四章"语法"由李宇凤编写。

第五章"文字"由郑春兰编写。

第六章"语言的发展"由杜晓莉编写。

此外，还要特别感谢语言学及应用语言学专业的硕士研究生郑佳佳、蒋珠铸、郝力、曾智、周攀、罗然等同学，他们为教材的编写和资料整理作出了重要的努力。

四川大学文学与新闻学院
语言学及应用语言学教研室
2010.8

因时间仓促，本教材所引用的某些文章及译文未及时与著作人联系，见书后，请有关著作权人与重庆大学出版社或重庆市版权保护中心联系。

# 目　录

# 第一章 总 论

## 第一节 什么是语言学

### 一、语言学的性质及研究对象

语言学,英文为 Linguistics,顾名思义,就是关于语言的一门学问,是以人类的语言为研究对象的一门科学。也许有人会说,语言我们每天都在用,再熟悉不过了,有什么好研究的呢? 正常人都掌握了至少一门语言,有的人甚至还掌握了两种以上的语言。然而,我们每个人对语言本身都有理性的认识吗?

语言学的基本任务,是研究语言基础理论,揭示其性质、功能、结构以及其发展变化的规律,使人们对语言系统有更深入的了解,懂得关于语言的理性知识,从而更好地学习和使用语言。其内容首先包括语言的结构,即语言由哪些要素组成,如何组成,有什么规律等;其次是语言的功能、作用,以及这些作用如何发挥;再次是语言的本质,包括语言的定义、形成过程,以及人获得语言能力的途径、方式;最后是语言的意义,意义的产生、表达和接受等。这些都是语言学要解决的问题。

我们认为,语言学是一门科学。首先,它的研究对象是科学的,它们大多可以观察和验证,使用的材料也是客观、全面而真实的。其次,语言学的研究方法遵循科学化的原则。它注重全面分析人类语言中的各种现象,关于现象的推论与演绎合乎逻辑,前后连贯;对语言的描写也客观、简明,没有艺术化的修饰。

那么,语言学属于社会科学还是自然科学呢? 语言是人类最重要的交流工具,是社会活动的产物,具有社会属性。就其功用与性质而言,它属于人类社会科学的范畴。在研究方法上,语言表现出一些自然科学的特点,如语言研究材料的客观真实,采用数据归纳、推理或演绎等方法,又呈现出数学和逻辑学的特点。语言的研究涉及人类生理和心理的各个领域,又与计算机技术、机器翻译等相关联。因此,语言学成为社会科学中的领先学科,同时与自然学科有所交叉。

## 二、从"语文学( Philology )"到"语言学( Linguistics )"

从有语言文字开始,人类就必然出现有关语言与文字的思考。随着人类思想的逐步繁荣,人们在文化遗产的积累和传承中难免因字形、语音、语义等问题产生分歧或讨论,最早的"语文学"开始萌芽了。渐渐地,零星知识不再能满足人们的需求,一些有影响的著作逐渐形成,人们对语言的探索逐步系统化。一开始,语言研究不是作为一门独立的学科被提出,而是依附于哲学、经学或其他学科而存在。人们对语言的认识还不甚清楚,研究语言主要不是为了科学地认识语言本身,而是出于实用目的。如为古代留传下来的哲学、宗教、历史、文学等经典作注解,"随文释义",解决文献阅读中的困难,帮助童蒙学习语言文字,有时作者也借此阐发个人的思想。这在中国形成"小学"传统,是围绕汉字的字形、字音、字义应运而生的,集文字学、音韵学、训诂学为一体。类似地,在西方对经典文献进行阐释和注解的过程中,也产生了与学科及文献相关的语言问题研究,一般称为"语文学"。

很长一段时间以来,世界上对语言的研究以"语文学"为主。直到 18 世纪末、19 世纪初,语言学研究才进入一个新的时期。希腊—罗马传统与印度传统的结合,产生了以历史比较语法为标志的历史比较语言学(早期的比较语法),这使人类语言的研究进入了一个新的科学的轨道。研究对象由古典文献的书面语开始转向口语,研究任务从研究单一的语言结构规律转向探索语言共性的结构原理和语言演变的历史规律,为现代语言学的确立奠定了基础。

19 世纪中期,语言学家开始关注人类语言的一般规律,普通语言学诞生了。德国的洪堡特与瑞士的索绪尔被公认为普通语言学的奠基者。20 世纪初,索绪尔出版了《普通语言学教程》一书,并明确提出语言学的研究对象是语言本身及其规律,区分了语言和言语、共时和历时、内部语言学和外部语言学、组合关系和聚合关系等概念。此时,语言学才完全摆脱了哲学、经学的附庸,正式作为一门独立的学科成立起来,开始了语言学史的新纪元。索绪尔也因此被称为"现代语言学之父"。

### 三、语言学的分类

语言学作为一门独立的学科逐渐成熟发展以后,由于研究目的、材料、方法的不同,形成了许多分支。从不同的角度,可以把语言学划分为不同的类别。

(一)历时语言学、共时语言学和比较语言学

索绪尔在《普通语言学教程》中运用"二分法"的思想,把语言分为历时和共时,为语言学的划分奠定了基础。从研究方法来看,语言学可分为历时语言学、共时语言学和比较语言学。历时语言学,也叫历史语言学,是用历史的方法对某种语言不同时期的历史演变方式进行研究,如把一种语言的语音、词汇、语法等的发展演变放在历史中,研究它古今变化的原因、结构和规律,是动态的研究。例如汉语史、蒙古语史、斯拉夫语史等。共时语言学研究语言的横断面,即语言在某一阶段的状态、特点,是静态的研究。共时研究通常以描述为主,要求语言学家重视客观现实的语言材料,避免对某种具体的话语形式下主观的判断,特别强调实地调查和客观分析。例如,描述先秦两汉时期文言文的古代汉语,以现代汉民族共同语为主要研究内容的现代汉语等。比较语言学是采用比较的方法,从不同语言的语音、词汇、语法等方面进行比较研究,寻找它们之间的异同及规律。例如,对同源自拉丁语的法、西、意、葡等亲属语言进行相互比较,找出它们的异同及规律;或者进行不同语系语言间的比较等。

(二)具体语言学和普通语言学

根据研究对象不同,可以将语言学分为具体语言学和普通语言学。以具体的语言为研究对象的叫具体语言学。例如汉语语言学、蒙古语语言学、维语语言学等。而以研究语言的本质、普遍现象为己任,为语言研究提供基本的概念、理论和方法的,称为普通语言学,又叫作一般语言学,是关于语言的普遍性的理论。普通语言学的分支学科还有"普通语音学""普通语法学"等。一般情况下,我们所说的"语言学"主要指"普通语言学"。

(三)理论语言学和应用语言学

从研究的角度来看,语言学又可分为理论语言学和应用语言学。理论语言学着重研究语言的一般理论和共同规律。研究如何用理论来解决实际问题的,则称为应用语言

学。应用语言学有广义与狭义之分。狭义的应用语言学主要是对语言教学理论和方法的研究；而广义的应用语言学扩展到了更多的领域，如机器翻译、实验语音学、人工智能、信息传达处理、失语症的治疗等，由此也就产生了计算机语言学、神经语言学、心理语言学等学科。

### （四）宏观语言学和微观语言学

从研究范围上，语言学可分为宏观语言学和微观语言学，有时也称外部语言学和内部语言学。宏观语言学主要研究与语言现象有关的问题，从综合的角度研究语言与其他学科的关系，如语言与人工智能、社会心理等。微观语言学则侧重研究语言结构本身。我们现在所讨论的语言学大多数属微观语言学的范畴。例如一般语言或某种语言的结构特点等。

总的来说，语言学概论主要涉及普通语言学和理论语言学方面的内容，同时又以个别的、实际应用的语言研究为基础，具有明显的交叉性。因此，我们在学习这门课程时，既要注意理解语言学的基础理论，又要联系实际，留心观察身边的语言现象，学会分析语言事实。

## 四、学习语言学的意义

### （一）语言学的研究对象——语言，是人类最重要的信息交流工具

一个人出门在外，无论做什么，懂当地语言都要方便很多。人们借助语言进行思维，表达自己的思想、感情。人类的语言能以有限的单位组合出无限的句子，表达复杂的意思。每一次成功的对话过程，也是信息交流的过程，而语言是这个过程中不二的载体和工具。语言学通过对语言本质、规律等的研究，能帮助人们更好地实现信息交流的过程，并拓展语言这一交流工具的作用。

### （二）语言学能更好地促进外语学习，推动我国语言文字工作的研究和发展

在已经掌握了一门外语后再学习第二外语时，需要的周期往往更短，学习起来也更容易，因为他们已经有了一些外语学习的经验。而这些经验，就是语言的规律。例如第一外语为英语的人，在学习第二外语西班牙语时，可以比较两种语言在语音、词汇、语法上的异同，总结出规律，从而指导西班牙语的学习。语言学是以语言及其规律为研究对象的科学，让人对语言有理性的认识。因此，语言学对外语学习和教学研究来说非常有益。例如，我国的语言文字工作，包括文字改革、推广普通话、少数民族语言教学以及汉

语国际推广等,都是建立在正确的语言学理论基础之上的。

(三)语言学与科技现代化相结合,在更多领域有更为广泛的应用

语言学的范围由微观的研究语言本身,扩大到宏观的研究语言及其相关领域。科技现代化,不断把语言研究带向新的领域。与计算机相关的机器翻译、人工智能、信息传达处理、情报自动检索等,与现代医学相关的听障人士学话、口吃矫正、失语症治疗等工作,都需要运用语言学。由此,应用语言学领域产生了计算机语言学、医学语言学、心理语言学等衍生学科,对语言学的需求也更加多样化。

# 第二节 语言和言语

## 一、语言和言语的定义

要想知道"什么是语言学",首先要了解"什么是语言"。那什么是语言呢? 对此,最广泛的回答可能是"语言就是人们平时所说的话"。也有人说"语言是一种人与人之间交流沟通的工具。没有语言人类就无法正常生活"。还有人回答:"语言就是书写的文字和口头的言语的结合。"那么,这些回答准确吗? 去过云南的人应该知道纳西族的东巴文,这是中国古老的象形文字的典型。如今这种文字却成了一种没有语音,只有字形的文字,已很少有人能读懂它的意义了。如此看来,东巴文还成其为语言吗? 同样地,在北美的一些印第安部落里也存在着只有语音没有文字的土著语,这些能称为语言吗? 这些问题,只有在我们弄清楚什么是语言后才能回答。

对普通人来说,说话就是语言,但从语言学的角度来看,说话与语言虽密切相关,却不尽相同。说话是一种复合活动,至少包括三部分内容:一是张口说话的动作,也就是发音的过程;二是说话所用的代码,包括语言符号及其组合的规则等,比如同一句话用汉语、英语、日语来说,其词汇、语法规则不同,代码也不同;三是说出来的话。通常在语言学上我们称第一部分为"言语动作",第二部分为"语言",第三部分为"言语作品"。

由此看来,言语动作是说话者个人的具体行为过程,其发生与否及发生方式均取决

于个人的意志。言语作品是言语动作产生的结果,不论是口头的还是书面的,都是个人的创作,可以打上说话者(作者)的标记。语言则是在漫长的历史过程中逐渐形成的、由社会约定俗成的社会产物。人一出生就处在某种语言体系所构成的网络中,习得并使用语言。个人只有遵守这种社会的约定来说话,才能与他人沟通。言语活动以语言体系为基础,同时语言又客观地存在于言语之中。语言学家要研究语言,必须以具体的言语活动和作品为材料,从中总结规律,概括出语言体系。

语言(langue)和言语(parole)的区分最早由瑞士语言学家索绪尔明确提出。他认为研究语言学的第一步就是区分语言和言语。所谓言语,包括了前面讲到的"言语动作"和"言语作品"两部分,即个人说话(写作)的行为和结果,是人们对语言的运用。语言则是具体言语赖以存在的音义结合的符号系统,人们遵照这个规则的系统来使用它。

## 二、语言和言语的对立统一

在语言学研究中,语言和言语有着本质的区别;另一方面,语言和言语犹如光影,密不可分。

语言和言语都是音义结合体,并互为前提。言语要被人所理解,必须以语言为基础;要建立语言,也必须有言语作为事实。但是,二者的区别也十分明显:第一,语言系统是社会约定俗成的交际工具,是所有社会成员共同遵循的交际规则,因此具有相对的稳定性和静止性;言语是人们运用语言工具的具体行为和结果,各单位的结合比较自由,具有动态性质。比如说,我们中国人说普通话,总是遵循一定的语法规则,主谓宾顺序及语法结构等相对来说是不变的、静止的;但是同一个内容可以有不同的表达方式,可用不同的句式,选择不同的词汇,这些内容则是动态的。第二,语言系统是社会的产物,因此具有社会性;言语是个人运用语言工具说(写)的行为和结果,因此除了社会因素外,还受个人因素影响。同是说英语的国家,英国、美国、澳大利亚的语言体系不论语音、词汇还是语法的运用上都有差异;反过来看,尽管三国的语言运用有细微的差异,我们还是认为他们都是英语国家,这主要和社会因素相关。同处一个社会,由于个人的成长环境、教育背景、性格等因素的影响,不同的人有各自特殊的表达习惯、写作风格等,因此说话或写作的过程和结果都有区别。同是中国的小说家,沈从文与老舍一南一北,遣词造句就绝不相同;张爱玲与白先勇一女一男,风格也迥然各异。个人因素对言语的影响是非常明显的。第三,稳定的语言系统虽具有一定张力,一旦形成却相对封闭,其结构成分受一定限制。但是人们利用这些有限的规则却能产生无限的言语过程和言语结果。因此语言系统相对来说封闭有限,言语则是无限开放的。

在二者的区别中不难看出,语言和言语实际上是相互依存的。语言存在于言语之中,从具体的言语中概括而来。没有言语,就没有语言。所有词汇和抽象的语法规则都存在于人们说的话或写的作品中,如果他们不再出现于言语作品中,也就从语言中消失了。如果新的词语和语法规则频繁出现于言语作品中,就有可能成为语言的构成部分。也正因为如此,语言学家的研究总是从言语材料入手的。同样言语也离不开语言,没有语言,就没有说话写作的章法,就像断了线的珍珠项链再也不是项链了。

# 第三节 语言的功能

人类的生活处处有语言。我们谈话时,必须借助语言来表达自己的想法;我们写作时,必须通过语言来叙述故事、描述风景或分析问题;即使我们独处一隅默默思考,语言仍在发生作用。可以说,人类的意识活动时时刻刻处在语言的包围中。语言是人类独有的交际工具和思维工具。

## 一、语言的交际功能

语言是社会现象,是在人类的社会生活中逐渐形成的。关于语言的起源,有人根据现代语言中尚存的拟声词,认为语言是原始人模仿大自然的声音来称呼客观事物而逐渐产生的。但是,现代语言中拟声词的比例并不大,许多客观事物的命名另有起因,而且不是所有的事物都能发声,因此这种说法难以成立。有人认为原始人因感受而产生交换、感叹,这些自发的声音逐渐形成语言。比如我国古代典籍《毛诗序》中说说:"情动于中而形于言,言之不足故嗟叹之……",《礼记·乐记》中亦有言:"凡音者,生人心者也,情动于中,故形于声;声成文,谓之音。"但是叹词同样很少,而且叹词可以表达感情,却难以名万物。有人认为原始人制定契约,规定各种事物的名称,如《圣经》中上帝让亚当给万物命名。但是在人类没有语言之前,用什么来制定契约呢? 还有人认为原始人最早用身体语言来传递信息,语言起源于原始人的手势。可是,声音是自发的,无论从速度还是表现力来说,都比手势更有优势。事实上,世界上任何一个民族,不论其发展程度如何,都有自己的有声语言。马克思主义认为,语言是在人类形成时,在集体劳动的过程中为了满足交际的需要而产生的,而且从一开始就是有声的,也就是说"劳动创造人,也创造了语言"。远古时期,原始人为了生存,不得不依靠集体的力量。集体协作中,人类越来越迫切地需要交流的工具,共同性的劳动决定了产生语言的需要。语言的诞生反过来又进一步促进人类的交际活动,使社会经验的积累、传承成为可能。

事实上,不论是哪种语言起源说,最后都落到语言的重要社会功能——交际功能上。语言因人们的交际需要而产生;反过来,人们的一切活动都要用语言工具来交流思想。语言诞生之后,要么发展完善,要么逐渐消亡,其命运与其社会价值特别是交际价值息息相关。一种语言具有实际的交际价值,就能存在,乃至发展;反之则可能逐渐退出社会舞台。比如汉语在世界不少国家和地区得到使用,适用人群较多,学习的人也越来越多,相关的理论专著、教学用书也频频出版,汉语就能得到更好的发展。有的语言彻底消亡,不但人们不再使用这种语言说话、写文章,连那些用这种语言创作的文献也丢失了。有的语言虽然不再被人应用,但相关的文献还存世,可看作假性消亡。如梵语因大量佛教文献而存在于人们的视野中,在一定条件下还具有交际价值。另外,一些少数族群可能只有口头语言,缺少书面文字,其语言在主流文化的冲击下很容易逐渐失去交际价值而被替代,从而走向消亡。为了保持各种群的多样性,国家、政府有时候会干预语言的发展,采取措施保护少数种群语言的发展。我国对许多少数民族的语言就采取了类似的态度。

人类的交际工具极其繁多,除语言之外,还有文字、符号语、体态语等。文字帮助人们记录语言;符号语在特定环境下能起到辅助交际的作用,如机场地勤人员、铁道工人使用的旗语,航海中的灯光语,电报,密码等;体态语用途广泛,但仍然容易受到条件的限制。总的来说,人类的语言是所有交际工具中最重要的一种。

同时,语言又是人类独有的交际工具。我们知道,动物之间也有许多特殊的交流工具,包括声音、气味、行为动作等。可是,无论是有声还是无声,动物的交际方式与人类的语言是不同的。首先,人类语言是社会的产物,具有社会属性、心理属性和自然属性,其中社会属性是最根本的。语言在人类社会发展的各个阶段都是全民的交际工具,协调人们的共同活动,促进人们的社会生产。同时,语言又因使用者的特殊社会身份而有所不同。而动物的"语言"仅仅是为了适应自然而引发的生理现象。其次,人类的语言发展到一定阶段就具有了系统性。人类的语言有明确的单位,有一套可以用语音、语义、词汇、语法等要素来规范的体系。动物的"语言"则无法明确分析。最后,人类的语言是不断发展变化的。语言虽有着一套相对稳定的体系,但是人们运用这个体系能产生出无限多的句子。同时,语言在历史进程中随着交际的需要而不断发展,词汇不断丰富,语义也不断变化。如行业习惯语可能在某些场合泛化为全民共享的词汇,有些词语在不同的历史条件下获得新意义,有些词汇随着社会生活的进步而被创造出来等。动物的"语言"相对来说是固定的、有限的,一千年前的蜜蜂之舞和现在的蜜蜂之舞可能不会有什么区别。另外,人天生具有特殊的语言能力,但是必须靠后天的学习才能真正掌握某种语言。而且,人类通过学习可以掌握多种语言,还能模仿动物的声音。所谓的动物"语言"大多数是与生俱来的①,而且动物无法学会人类的语言。智商极高的黑猩猩在科学家的训练下能够掌握一些单词,运用字母来表达一些意思,但并不能真正掌握语言。因此,语言不但是人类最重要的交际工具,也是人类独有的交际工具,是人和动物的根本区别之一。

## 二、语言的思维功能

思维是人脑对客观事物间接、概括的反映,是认识的高级形式,包括形象思维和逻辑思维。狭义的思维主要指逻辑思维。一般来说,思维表现为三种主要形式:概念、判断、推理。概念是人脑对事物的一般特征和本质特征的反映,判断是对事物之间关系的反映,推理是从一个或几个已知判断中推出新的判断,三者密切相关。思维的认知加工方式包括分析、综合、比较、抽象、概括、具体化与系统化等,每一种方式都是认知过程中的重要内容。不论从思维的表现形式还是认知方式来看,语言是思维必不可少的要素,没有语言,思维活动难以发生;没有语言,思维表现无法定形;没有语言,思维内容难以得到表达。

**信息的传递与存储离不开语言。**信息的交流过程分为编码—发送—传递—接受—解码五个阶段。人为了表达信息,首先要将信息转化为编码,按照规则排列起来。这个编码一般就是语言。语言编码通过发音发送出去,并经由空气或其他介质传递到听话人耳中。听话人接受到表现为语音的语言编码后进行解码,还原信息并理解内容。语言作为信息的载体时刻参与这个过程,将信息存储在编码中。没有语言,信息的编码和解码过程就难以完成。人思考问题时,不断从大脑中提取必要的信息,并对信息进行处理。这个过程相当复杂,至今难以得到科学的解释。但是,哪怕是潜意识的思维活动,也离不开信息的存储和传递。有时我们脑海中闪过一束思维的火花,但似乎无法捕捉。这一点灵感要得到清晰的整理和表达,必须通过有条理的语言来组织。因此,人们常发现通过写作更容易理清自己的思路。事实上,我们想问题时也常常在脑海中自言自语。

随着信息化时代的来临,科技的发展要求人们更好地开发语言的功能。语言研究的内容从自然语言延伸到通信、自动化、计算机技术等领域。以计算机为例,计算机在许多方面越来越多地替代人脑,成为人类思维的延伸。人机沟通时,人向计算机发出指令,计算机接受指令进行操作,并将结果告诉人。此时也需要信息的载体——语言。最初计算机无法理解人的自然语言,人为了和计算机沟通,必须通过编写程序,采用二进制,设计

---

① 有些动物"语言"同样需要学习。据科学家研究,一些鸟类在不同场合会唱出不同的歌声,父母必须向幼仔传授这些"歌唱方式",比如求偶的歌声、觅食的歌声等。如果幼仔失去父母的照顾,将学不会这些特殊的鸣叫声。

出计算机能够识别的逻辑语言。自然语言先转化为机器语言，发出指令，计算机识别后进行操作，产生的结果再从机器语言转化为自然语言。如今计算机技术不断革新，如何解决人机对话，是计算机开发的关键。早期使用计算机，必须懂得一定的计算机语言。现在计算机界面越来越友好，不懂计算机语言的普通人也可以轻松学计算机，并用自然语言来完成基本操作。这说明，技术的发展使计算机识别和处理人类语言的能力越来越强，语言作为信息载体的功能被逐渐开发出来。当然，随着社会生活的进步，语言功能在其他领域中的应用还会进一步被人们认识、发掘。

**人们认识世界离不开语言。**人们认识客观世界后，必须将认识的成果存储起来。人们认识世界的成果通过语言符号存储、固定，并代代累积和传承，由此才形成人类文明。

由于生存环境、发展进程等的差异，每个民族认识世界的方式和结果也有所不同，这些差异往往从相应的语言、词汇中得到反映。比如说，汉语中表示亲属关系的词很多，可是在英语中对应的词就没有那么精确。如汉语中的堂兄、堂弟、表兄、表弟、堂姐、堂妹、表姐、表妹在英语中都对应一个词 cousin，必要时只有通过特别的说明或上下语境才能分辨清楚，比如通过姓氏来判断。很显然，汉语中将堂（表）兄弟（姐妹）分得如此清楚，跟中国人的宗族观念紧密相关。再比如一般人看来，雪就是白色的，但爱斯基摩人根据雪的状态、位置、大小等有若干种形容雪的"颜色词"。彩虹在讲汉语的人看来是赤橙黄绿青蓝紫等七种色彩，而讲英语的只有少部分人会用七种颜色来形容彩虹，更多的人则从小就认为彩虹是六种颜色。

由于这样一些有趣的现象，一些人认为语言能够决定人的思维。美国人类学家、语言学家萨丕尔和他的弟子沃尔夫就持此种观点，认为所有高层次的思维都倚赖于语言，语言背景决定一个人的思维方式。英国作家奥威尔也认为语言能够决定思维，因此在他的小说《1984》中，政府为了限制人们的思想自由，编写意义简单、狭隘的"新话字典（Newspeak）"，使人们的语言变得贫乏，思想也逐渐退化。语言对思维当然是有影响的，但是片面地认为思维由语言决定显然是错误的。实际上，客观世界先于思维，语言体系并不能决定人们对世界的认识。说同一种语言的人可能有不同的世界观，说不同语言的人对世界的看法也许出奇一致。人们的社会实践决定人们的思维方式，语言根据需要是可以不断变化的。尽管汉语中没有爱斯基摩人那么多种形容雪的词汇，但是我们还是可以理解他们的意思，必要时也可使用词的组合来表达类似的意思。语言此时正可以起一个桥梁作用，伴随我们不断加深对世界的认知。

总之，我们不能过分夸大语言对思维的作用，但也不可否认语言是思维的重要工具。

### 三、语言的其他功能

除了交际功能和思维功能,语言还有许多其他附属功能。

语言的交流涉及人类社会活动的方方面面,同时又可世代相传,成为记录社会文化的重要工具。每一个民族的历史、文化、社会变迁都可通过该民族的语言直接记录下来,此外,人们还能从其表现形式及演变过程等窥测古代文化的风貌及历史的变迁。比如汉语中"货币"的"货"字从贝,化声,古字形僷,由这个词可推测古时候人们曾用贝壳作为交换物品的货币。英语中的 paper(纸)一词来自拉丁语 papyrus,原指生长于尼罗河流域的一种类似芦苇的植物,古埃及人用其制作莎草纸。由这个词我们可以看到西方造纸工艺的发展和我国古代的造纸术并不相同。又如汉语的佛教语言有许多借自梵语,唐朝时期的音乐用语很多来自西亚语言,"五四"时期许多西方术语又通过日语的转译进入汉语,现在的汉语中更是增加了许多外来词,这些都表明中华民族和其他民族文化之间的交流。所以,语言不仅是学习和了解不同时期、不同国家文化的工具,它本身就承载着民族的历史、文化,反映不同文化之间的交流,记录历史的痕迹。

语言记录着不同民族的历史文化,也反映不同人群的差异,因此还具有特殊的标记功能。不同时期的人语言不同,不同地区的人语言不同,判断一个人来自何处,最直观的就是方言。湖南人、四川人、浙江人、东北人等地区的人往往一开口,人们就能辨出其家乡的印记。不同行业、不同文化程度的人群语言也不同。教师和学生的用语有差别,农民、工人、小贩等都有各自的语言特色。正因为语言是说话者身份的重要标记,文学创作者在创造人物时必须要使人物的语言与其身份相配,才能使人物鲜活起来。另外,当人们进入新的群体时,为了获得他人的认同,也常常通过语言的变化来增加自己的亲和力、凝聚力。

语言在人类的社会生活中不可缺少,其功能也在不断拓展。除了交际和思维等重要功能之外,还有其他许多功能等待挖掘。

# 第四节　语言学的研究范围

　　语言学是研究人类语言的科学。语言学的任务是由语言的性质和它的社会地位、人类研究语言的目的和所处的社会历史条件决定的。一般来说,语言学的主要研究范围是研究语言的结构和功能,追溯语言发展演变的历史以及研究语言和其他相关现象的关系。在语言的研究中,由于研究的目的、研究的角度和研究方法等因素的影响,形成了形形色色的语言学分科。从研究的范围来看,语言学大体上分为两大类:内部语言学和外部语言学。语言学的研究范围基本囊括在内部语言学和外部语言学之内。

## 一、内部语言学

　　内部语言学又称微观语言学,它主要研究语言的内部结构。对于语言系统内部结构要素及其在系统中的地位,语言学界有不同的看法。20 世纪 50 年代以前,我国语言学者一般将语言看作是由语音、语法、语汇构成的。语音是语言的形式,语汇是语言的建筑材料,语法是词的组成和变化以及组词成句的规则。20 世纪 50 年代以来,尤其是转换生成语法出现以后,很多学者认为语言系统的内部结构是由语义、句法、语音构成的,他们认为语言符号由声音(sound)和意义(meaning)两部分组成,并且通过句法(syntax)组织起来。

　　目前对内部语言学的研究主要分为语音、语义、语汇、语法等几个研究部分。比如说,可以从共时的角度对这些部分进行描写,描写它们在某一时期断代的情况,或者是从历时的角度来探索它们的历史演变过程,或者是进行一定范围内的语际间的比较从而探索分析史前的演变过程。通过这些研究,我们可以了解到语言各要素演变的规律和方式,有助于我们对语言的进一步理解和认识;同时我们也可了解语言各要素的历史模样,从而有助于加深对古代文献的理解;我们还可以了解哪些因素推动了语言的发展,这些因素彼此如何作用,他们之间有何规律等。对语言的各个方面加以研究,形成了语言学的各个分支学科,每一个分支学科都是语言学的研究对象,这些研究对象就是语言学要研究的范围。研究语音的可以笼统地称为"语音学(phonetics)",从生理和物理的角度对语言进行研究,就产生了"生理语音学"和"声学语音学";从语言功能的角度研究语音结构体系的称为"音位学";专门研究某一种语言语音的称为"个别语音学",如"汉语语音学""英语语音学";研究多种语言语音的一般性质和规律的称为"普通语音学"。研究语义的称为"语义学(semantics)",传统研究曾经把语义看作是词汇学的研究内容。研究语言里各单位的分类及其组合的层次和次序的称为"语法学(grammar)",语法学通常包括"形态学"(即词法学 morphology)和"句法学(syntax)"两部分,转换生成语法诞生后,grammar 已被用来指整个内部语言学,包括语音学、语义学、语法学。也有人认为内部语言学应该包括语音学、语义学、语汇学和语法学。除此以外,"词源学""方言学""文字学"等也是语言学的分支学科,也在内部语言学的研究范围之中。

内部语言学的研究范围相对于外部语言学来说是狭窄的,语言学的核心当然是"本体语言学",即研究语言的语音、语汇、语法结构,研究语言的演变规律,研究语言之间的共性和语言的类型等,这些研究是语言学的基础,但是这些研究是远远不够的,语言系统的产生、演变和发展无不和语言之外的许多其他因素有着互动的关系。

## 二、外部语言学

外部语言学又称宏观语言学,主要研究语言与其他领域的相互关系,常包含一些与语言学相关的交叉领域,如社会语言学、心理语言学、文化语言学、人类语言学、地理语言学、神经语言学、实验语言学、计算语言学等。语言学和其他学科的关系,其范围随着语言功能的不断开发而日益扩大。语言学的传统伙伴绝大多数是人文科学,包括文学、社会学、历史学、地理学、考古学、心理学、哲学、逻辑学等。语言学和人文科学结合产生了许多交叉学科,如文化语言学、人类语言学、地理语言学;语言学和社会科学结合产生了社会语言学、法律语言学、政治语言学、伦理语言学、商业语言学等,这些交叉学科赋予语言学新的生命力。而今,语言学的关系网又在向科技方向拓展,同数学、信息论、电子学、医学、符号学、情报学、通信技术、计算机科学、自动化技术等发生密切的联系。在 20 世纪,许多新的语言学分支已经诞生,这既是语言学理论发展的必然,更是社会的需要。有学者把语言学这种特点称为"交缘性",并指出语言学的交缘性具体体现在它与社会科学的其他学科、与自然科学以及与思维科学的密切联系上[①]。

学术领域是互动的,在历史比较语言学中我们看到了达尔文进化论的影子,在结构主义语言学中我们感受到了物理主义的精神,转换生成语言学则明明白白地用现代数学的方法在思考,用现代数学的方法来表达。几乎所有重大理论的创新都来自学科的交

---

① 刘富华,孙炜.语言学通论[M].北京:北京语言大学出版社,2009:15-17.

叉,交叉点则是新思想的源泉。比如说数学、计算机科学和语言学的结合,它们从理论上探索语言的数理性质和运作机制,还可指导机器翻译、人机对话、资料检索、语音合成、语音识别等实用系统。

语言学和其他学科的联系建立了一系列的新兴交叉学科,主要有:

社会语言学:用社会学的方法研究语言与社会多方面关系的学科。它从不同的社会科学,诸如社会学、人类学、民族学、地理学、历史学等角度去考察语言,进而研究在不同社会条件下产生的语言变异。

人类语言学:综合运用语言学和文化人类学的理论和方法,研究语言结构、语言变化和社会文化结构的关系,也就是研究语言所反映的民族文化及其演变情况。

心理语言学:研究语言活动中的心理过程的学科,它涉及人类个体如何掌握和运用语言系统,如何在实际交往中使语言系统发挥作用,以及为了掌握和运用这个系统应具有什么知识和能力。

神经语言学:研究产生、接收、分析和储存语言的神经机制以及这一机制与语言的关系,观察大脑功能在言语过程中的影响,可应用于分析失语症、阅读障碍等语言机能失调问题。

实验语言学:实验语言学是应用其他学科技能,如物理学、心理学、生理学的方法、技术、原理来测定语言的物理、心理或生理的变化与定位。20 世纪后,实验语言学所运用的机器包括录音机、X 光机、声谱仪、气压气流器、颚位图等,且利用机器产生的数据来对各种语言的研究作比较与描述。

计算语言学:通过建立形式化的数学模型来分析、处理自然语言,并在计算机上用程序来实现分析和处理的过程,从而达到以机器来模拟人的部分乃至全部语言能力的目的。

以上所列的是有关语言学的主要新兴交叉学科,虽然不能穷尽当前所有与语言学相关的交叉学科,但毫无疑问能让我们看到,众多交叉学科的发展必然会扩大语言学的社会影响,与此同时,这些交叉学科也给语言学提供新的课题,给语言学的发展提供内在动力。

## 思考与练习

一、名词解释

1.语言和言语

2.内部语言学

3.外部语言学

二、思考题

1.蜜蜂的舞蹈、海豚的呼叫、猩猩的动作、婴儿的呓语、成人的语言有什么异同?

2.谈谈学习语言学的意义。

3.谈谈你对语言学方法论的认识。

## 【原典阅读】

# 1.Introductory:Language Defined
## Sapir

SPEECH is so familiar a feature of daily life that we rarely pause to define it.It seems as natural to man as walking,and only less so than breathing.Yet it needs but a moment's reflection to convince us that this naturalness of speech is but an illusory feeling.The process of acquiring speech is,in sober fact,an utterly different sort of thing from the process of learning to walk.In the case of the latter function,culture,in other words,the traditional body of social usage,is not seriously brought into play.The child is individually equipped,by the complex set of factors that we term biological heredity,to make all the needed muscular and nervous adjustments that result in walking.Indeed,the very conformation of these muscles and of the appropriate parts of the nervous system may be said to be primarily adapted to the movements made in walking and in similar activities. In a very real sense the normal human being is predestined to walk,not because his elders will assist him to learn the art,but because his organism is prepared from birth,or even from the moment of conception,to take on all those expenditures of nervous energy and all those muscular adaptations that result in walking. To put it concisely,walking is an inherent,biological function of man.

Not so language. It is of course true that in a certain sense the individual is predestined to talk, but that is due entirely to the circumstance that he is born not merely in nature,but in the lap of a society that is certain,reasonably certain,to lead him to its traditions. Eliminate society and there is every reason to believe that he will learn to walk,if,indeed,he survives at all. But it is just as certain that he will never learn to talk,that is,to communicate ideas according to the traditional system of a particular society.Or,again,remove the newborn individual from the social environment into which he has come and transplant him to an utterly alien one.He will develop the art of walking in his new environment very much as he would have developed it in the old.But his speech will be completely at variance with the speech of his native environment.Walking,then,is a general human activity that varies only within circumscribed limits as we pass from individual to individual. Its variability is involuntary and purposeless. Speech is a human activity that varies without assignable limit as we pass from social group to social group,because it is a purely historical heritage of the group,the product of long-continued social usage. It varies as all creative effort varies—not as consciously, perhaps, but none the less as truly as do the religions, the beliefs, the customs, and the arts of different peoples. Walking is an organic, an instinctive, function ( not, of course, itself an instinct); speech is a non-instinctive, acquired, "cultural" function.

There is one fact that has frequently tended to prevent the recognition of language as a merely conventional system of sound symbols, that has seduced the popular mind into attributing to it an instinctive basis that it does not really possess. This is the well-known observation that under the stress of emotion, say of a sudden twinge of pain or of unbridled joy, we do involuntarily give utterance to sounds that the hearer interprets as indicative of the emotion itself. But there is all the difference in the world between such involuntary expression of feeling and the normal type of communication of ideas that is speech. The former kind of utterance is indeed instinctive, but it is nonsymbolic; in other words, the sound of pain or the sound of joy does not, as such, indicate the emotion, it does not stand aloof, as it were, and announce that such and such an emotion is being felt. What it does is to serve as a more or less automatic overflow of the emotional energy; in a sense, it is part and parcel of the emotion itself. Moreover, such instinctive cries hardly constitute communication in any strict sense. They are not addressed to any one, they are merely overheard, if heard at all, as the bark of a dog, the sound of approaching footsteps, or the rustling of the wind is heard. If they convey certain ideas to the hearer, it is only in the very general sense in which any and every sound or even any phenomenon in our environment may be said to convey an idea to the perceiving mind. If the involuntary cry of pain which is conventionally represented by "Oh!" be looked upon as a true speech symbol equivalent to some such idea as "I am in great pain," it is just as allowable to interpret the appearance of clouds as an equivalent symbol that carries the definite message "It is likely to rain," A definition of language, however, that is so extended as to cover every type of inference becomes utterly meaningless.

The mistake must not be made of identifying our conventional interjections( our oh! and ah! and sh!) with the instinctive cries themselves. These interjections are merely conventional fixations of the natural sounds. They therefore differ widely in various languages in accordance with the specific phonetic genius of each of these. As such they may be considered an integral portion of speech, in the properly cultural sense of the term, being no more identical with the instinctive cries themselves than such words as "cuckoo" and "killdeer" are identical with the cries of the birds they denote or than Rossini's treatment of a storm in the overture to "William Tell" is in fact a storm. In other words, the interjections and sound-imitative words of normal speech are related to their natural prototypes as is art, a purely social or cultural thing, to nature. It may be objected that, though the interjections differ somewhat as we pass from language to language, they do nevertheless offer striking family resemblances and may therefore be looked upon as having grown up out of a common instinctive base. But their case is nowise different from that, say, of the varying national modes of pictorial representation. A Japanese picture of a hill both differs from and resembles a typical modern European painting of the same kind of hill. Both are suggested by and both "imitate" the same natural feature. Neither the one nor the other is the same thing as, or, in any intelligible sense, a direct outgrowth of, this natural feature. The two modes of representation are not identical because they proceed from differing historical traditions, are executed with differing pictorial techniques. The interjections of Japanese and English are, just so, suggested by a common natural prototype, the instinctive cries, and are thus unavoidably suggestive of each other. They differ, now greatly, now but little, because they are builded out of historically diverse materials or techniques, the respective linguistic traditions, phonetic systems, speech habits of the two peoples. Yet the instinctive cries as such are practically identical for all humanity, just as the human skeleton or nervous system is to all intents and purposes a "fixed", that is, an only slightly and "accidentally" variable, feature of man's organism.

Interjections are among the least important of speech elements. Their discussion is valuable mainly because it can be shown that even they, avowedly the nearest of all language sounds to instinctive utterance, are only superficially of an instinctive nature. Were it therefore possible to demonstrate that the whole of language is traceable, in its ultimate historical and psychological foundations, to the interjections, it would still not follow that language is an instinctive activity. But as a matter of fact, all attempts so to explain the origin of speech have been fruitless. There is no tangible evidence, historical or otherwise, tending to show that the mass of speech elements and speech processes has evolved out of the interjections. These are a very small and functionally insignificant proportion of the vocabulary of language; at no time and in no linguistic province that we have record of do we see a noticeable tendency towards their elaboration into the primary warp and woof of language. They are never more, at best, than a decorative edging to the ample, complex fabric.

What applies to the interjections applies with even greater force to the sound-imitative words. Such words as "whippoorwill", "to mew", "to caw" are in no sense natural sounds that man has instinctively or automatically reproduced. They are just as truly creations of the human mind, flights of the human fancy, as anything else in language. They do not directly grow out of nature, they are suggested by it and play with it. Hence the onomatopoetic theory of the origin of speech, the theory that would explain all speech as a gradual evolution from sounds of an imitative character, really brings us no nearer to the instinctive level than is language as we know it today. As to the theory itself, it is scarcely more credible than its interjectional counterpart. It is true that a number of words which we do not now feel to have a sound-imitative value can be shown to have once had a phonetic form that strongly suggests their origin as imitations of natural sounds. Such is the English word "to laugh". For all that, it is quite impossible to show, nor does it seem intrinsically reasonable to suppose, that more than a negligible proportion of the elements of speech or anything at all of its formal apparatus is derivable from an onomatopoetic source. However much we may be disposed on general principles to assign a fundamental importance in the languages of primitive peoples to the imitation of natural sounds, the actual fact of the matter is that these languages show no particular preference for imitative words. Among the most primitive peoples of aboriginal America, the Athabaskan tribes of the Mackenzie River speak languages in which such words seem to be nearly or entirely absent, while they are used freely enough in languages as sophisticated as English and German. Such an instance shows how little the essential nature of speech is concerned with the mere imitation of things.

The way is now cleared for a serviceable definition of language. Language is a purely human and noninstinctive method of communicating ideas, emotions, and desires by means of a system of voluntarily produced symbols. These symbols are, in the first instance, auditory and they are produced by the so-called "organs of speech." There is no discernible instinctive basis in human speech as such, however much instinctive expressions and the natural environment may serve as a stimulus for

17

the development of certain elements of speech, however much instinctive tendencies, motor and other, may give a predetermined range or mold to linguistic expression. Such human or animal communication, if "communication" it may be called, as is brought about by involuntary, instinctive cries is not, in our sense, language at all.

I have just referred to the "organs of speech." and it would seem at first blush that this is tantamount to an admission that speech itself is an instinctive, biologically predetermined activity. We must not be misled by the mere term. There are, properly speaking, no organs of speech; there are only organs that are incidentally useful in the production of speech sounds. The lungs, the larynx, the palate, the nose, the tongue, the teeth, and the lips, are all so utilized, but they are no more to be thought of as primary organs of speech than are the fingers to be considered as essentially organs of piano-playing or the knees as organs of prayer. Speech is not a simple activity that is carried on by one or more organs biologically adapted to the purpose. It is an extremely complex and ever-shifting network of adjustments—in the brain, in the nervous system, and in the articulating and auditory organs—tending towards the desired end of communication. The lungs developed, roughly speaking, in connection with the necessary biological runction known as breathing; the nose, as an organ of smell; the teeth, as organs useful in breaking up food before it wan ready for digestion. If, then, these and other organs are being constantly utilized in speech, it is only because any organ, once existent and in so far as it is subject to voluntary control, can be utilized by man for secondary purposes. Physiologically, speech is an overlaid function, or, to be more precise, a group of overlaid functions. It gets what service it can out of organs and functions, nervous and muscular, that have come into being and are maintained for very different ends than its own.

It is true that physiological psychologists speak of the localization of speech in the brain. This can only mean that the sounds of speech are localized in the auditory tract of the brain, or in some circumscribed portion of it, precisely as other classes of sounds are localized; and that the motor processes involved in speech (such as the movements of the glottal cords in the larynx, the movements of the tongue required to pronounce the vowels. lip movements required to articulate certain consonants, and numerous others) are localized in the motor tract precisely as are all other impulses to special motor activities. In the same way control is lodged in the visual tract of the brain over all those processes of visual recognition involved in reading. Naturally the particular points or clusters of points of localization in the several tracts that refer to any element of language are connected in the brain by paths of association, so that the outward, or psycho-physical, aspect of language, is of a vast network of associated localizations in the brain and lower nervous tracts, the auditory localizations being without doubt the most fundamental of all for speech. However, a speech sound localized in the brain, even when associated with the particular movements of the "speech organs" that are required to produce it, is very far from being an element of language. It must be further associated with some element or group of elements of experience, say a visual image or a class of visual images or a feeling of relation, before it has even rudimentary linguistic significance. This "element" of experience is the content or "meaning" of the linguistic unit; the associated auditory, motor, and other cerebral processes that lie immediately back of the act of speaking and the act of hearing speech are merely a complicated symbol of or signal for these "meanings," of which more anon. We see therefore at once that language as such is not and cannot be definitely localized, for it consists of a peculiar symbolic relation—physiologically an arbitrary one—between all possible elements of consciousness on the one hand and certain selected elements localized in the auditory, motor, and other cerebral and nervous tracts on the other. If language can be said to be definitely "localized" in the brain, it is only in that general and rather useless sense in which all aspects of consciousness, all human interest and activity, may be said to be "in the brain." Hence, we have no recourse but to accept language as a fully formed functional system within man's psychic or "spiritual" constitution. We cannot define it as an entity in psycho-physical terms alone, however much the psycho-physical basis is essential to its functioning in the individual.

From the physiologist's or psychologist's point of view we may seem to be making an unwarrantable abstraction in desiring to handle the subject of speech without constant and explicit reference to that basis. However, such an abstraction is justifiable. We can profitably discuss the intention, the form, and the history of speech, precisely as we discuss the nature of any other phase of human culture—say art or religion—as an institutional or cultural entity, leaving the organic and psychological mechanisms back of it as something to be taken for granted. Accordingly, it must be clearly understood that this introduction to the study of speech is not concerned with those aspects of physiology and of physiological psychology that underlie speech. Our study of language is not to be one of the genesis and operation of a concrete mechanism; it is, rather, to be an inquiry into the function and form of the arbitrary systems of symbolism that we term languages.

I have already pointed out that the essence of language consists in the assigning of conventional, voluntarily articulated, sounds, or of their equivalents, to the diverse elements of experience. The word "house" is not a linguistic fact if by it is meant merely the acoustic effect produced on the ear by its constituent consonants and vowels, pronounced in a certain order; nor the motor processes and tactile feelings which make up the articulation of the word; nor the visual perception on the part of the hearer of this articulation; nor the visual perception of the word "house" on the written or printed page; nor the motor processes and tactile feelings which enter into the writing of the word; nor the memory of any or all of these experiences. It is only when these, and possibly still other, associated experiences are automatically associated with the image of a house that they begin to take on the nature of a symbol, a word, an element of language. But the mere fact of such an association is not enough. One might have heard a particular word spoken in an individual house under such impressive circumstances that neither the word nor the image of the house ever recur in consciousness without the other becoming present at the same time. This type of association does not constitute speech. The association must be a purely symbolic one; in other words, the word must denote, tag off, the image, must have no other significance than to serve as a counter to refer to it whenever it is necessary or convenient to do so. Such an association, voluntary and, in a sense, arbitrary as it is, demands a considerable exercise of self-conscious attention. At least to begin with, for habit soon makes the association nearly as automatic as any and more rapid than most.

But we have traveled a little too fast. Were the symbol "house"—whether an auditory, motor, or visual experience or image—attached but to the single image of a particular house once seen, it might perhaps, by an indulgent criticism, be termed an element of speech, yet it is obvious at the outset that speech so constituted would have little or no value for purposes of communication. The world of our experiences must be enormously simplified and generalized before it is possible to make a symbolic inventory of all our experiences of things and relations; and this inventory is imperative before we can convey ideas. The elements of language, the symbols that ticket off experience, must therefore be associated with whole groups, delimited classes, of experience rather than with the single experiences themselves. Only so is communication possible, for the single experience lodges in an individual consciousness and is, strictly speaking, incommunicable. To be communicated it needs to be referred to a class which is tacitly accepted by the community as an identity. Thus, the single impression which I have had of a particular house must be identified with all my other impressions of it. Further, my generalized memory or my "notion" of this house must be merged with the notions that all other individuals who have seen the house have formed of it. The particular experience that we started with has now been widened so as to embrace all possible impressions or images that sentient beings have formed or may form of the house in question. This first simplification of experience is at the bottom of a large number of elements of speech, the se-called proper nouns or names of single individuals or objects. It is, essentially, the type of simplification which underlies, or forms the crude subject of, history and art. But we cannot be content with this measure of reduction of the infinity of experience. We must cut to the bone of things, we must more or less arbitrarily throw whole masses of experience together as similar enough to warrant their being looked upon—mistakenly, but conveniently—as identical. This house and that house and thousands of other phenomena of like character are thought of as having enough in common, in spite of great and obvious differences of detail, to be classed under the same heading. In other words, the speech element "house" is the symbol, first and foremost, not of a single perception, nor even of the notion of a particular object, but of a "concept," in other words, of a convenient capsule of thought that embraces thousands of distinct experiences and that is ready to take in thousands more. If the single significant elements of speech are the symbols of concepts, the actual flow of speech may be interpreted as a record of the setting of these concepts into mutual relations.

The question has often been raised whether thought is possible without speech; further, if speech and thought be not but two facets of the same psychic process. The question is all the more difficult because it has been hedged about by misunderstandings. In the first place, it is well to observe that whether or not thought necessitates symbolism, that is speech, the flow of language itself is not always indicative of thought. We have seen that the typical linguistic element labels a concept. It does not follow from this that the use to which language is put is always or even mainly conceptual. We are not in ordinary life so much concerned with concepts as such as with concrete particularities and specific relations. When I say, for instance, "I had a good breakfast this morning," it is clear that I am not in the throes of laborious thought, that what I have to transmit is hardly more than a pleasurable memory symbolically rendered in the grooves of habitual expression. Each element in the sentence defines a separate concept or conceptual relation or both combined, but the sentence as a whole has no conceptual significance whatever. It is somewhat as though a dynamo capable of generating enough power to run an elevator were operated almost exclusively to feed an electric doorbell. The parallel is more suggestive than at first sight appears. Language may be looked upon as an instrument capable of running a gamut of psychic uses. Its flow not only parallels that of the inner content of consciousness, but parallels it on different levels, ranging from the state of mind that is dominated by particular images to that in which abstract concepts and their relations are alone at the focus of attention and which is ordinarily termed reasoning. Thus the outward form only of language is constant; its inner meaning, its psychic value or intensity, varies freely with attention or the selective interest of the mind, also, needless to say, with the mind's general development. From the point of view of language, thought may be defined as the highest latent or potential content of speech, the content that is obtained by interpreting each of the elements in the flow of language as possessed of its very fullest conceptual value. From this it follows at once that language and thought are not strictly coterminous. At best language can but be the outward facet of thought on the highest, most generalized, level of symbolic expression. To put our viewpoint somewhat differently, language is primarily a pre-rational function. It humbly works up to the thought that is latent in, that may eventually be read into, its classifications and its forms; it is not, as is generally but naïvely assumed, the final label put upon the finished thought.

Most people, asked if they can think without speech, would probably answer, "Yes, but it is not easy for me to do so. Still I know it can be done." Language is but a garment! But what if language is not so much a garment as a prepared road or groove? It is, indeed, in the highest degree likely that language is an instrument originally put to uses lower than the conceptual plane and that thought arises as a refined interpretation of its content. The product grows, in other words, with the instrument, and thought may be no more conceivable, in its genesis and daily practice, without speech than is mathematical reasoning practicable without the lever of an appropriate mathematical symbolism. No one believes that even the most difficult mathematical proposition is inherently dependent on an arbitrary set of symbols, but it is impossible to suppose that the human mind is capable of arriving at or holding such a proposition without the symbolism. The writer, for one, is strongly of the opinion that the feeling entertained by so many that they can think, or even reason, without language is an illusion. The illusion seems to be due to a number of factors. The simplest of these is the failure to distinguish between imagery and thought. As a matter of fact, no sooner do we try to put an image into conscious relation with another than we find ourselves slipping into a silent flow of words. Thought may be a natural domain apart from the artificial one of speech, but speech would seem to be the only road we know of that leads to it. A still more fruitful source of the illusive feeling that language may be dispensed with in thought is the common failure to realize that language is not identical with its auditory symbolism. The auditory symbolism may be replaced, point for point, by a motor or by a visual symbolism (many people can read, for instance, in a purely visual sense, that is, without the intermediating link of an inner flow of the auditory images that correspond to the printed or written words) or by still other, more subtle and elusive, types of transfer that are not so easy to define. Hence the contention that one thinks without language merely because he is not aware of a coexisting auditory imagery is very far indeed from being a valid one. One may go so far as to suspect that the symbolic expression of thought may in some cases run along outside the fringe of the conscious mind, so that the feeling of a free, nonlinguistic stream of thought is for minds of a certain type a relatively, but only a relatively, justified one. Psycho-physically, this would mean that the auditory or equivalent visual or motor centers in the brain, together with the appropriate paths of association, that are the cerebral equivalent of speech, are touched off so lightly during the process of thought as not to rise into consciousness at all. This would be a limiting case—thought riding lightly on the submerged crests of speech, instead of jogging along with it, hand in hand. The modern psychology has shown us how powerfully symbolism is at work in the unconscious mind. It is therefore easier to understand at the present time than it would have been twenty years ago that the most rarefied thought may be but the conscious counterpart of an unconscious linguistic symbolism.

One word more as to the relation between language and thought. The point of view that we have developed does not by any means preclude the possibility of the growth of speech being in a high degree dependent on the development of thought. We may assume that language arose pre-rationally— just how and on what precise level of mental activity we do not know—but we must not imagine that a highly developed system of speech symbols worked itself out before the genesis of distinct concepts and of thinking, the handling of concepts. We must rather imagine that thought processes set in, as a kind of psychic overflow, almost at the beginning of linguistic expression; further, that the concept, once defined, necessarily reacted on the. life of its linguistic symbol, encouraging further linguistic growth. We see this complex process of the interaction of language and thought actually taking place under our eyes. The instrument makes possible the product, the product refines the instrument. The birth of a new concept is invariably foreshadowed by a more or less strained or extended use of old linguistic material; the concept does not attain to individual and independent life until it has found a distinctive linguistic embodiment. In most cases the new symbol is but a thing wrought from linguistic material already in existence in ways mapped out by crushingly despotic precedents. As soon as the word is at hand, we instinctively feel, with something of a sigh of relief, that the concept is ours for the handling. Not until we own the symbol do we feel that we hold a key to the immediate knowledge or understanding of the concept. Would we be so ready to die for"liberty,"to struggle for"ideals,"if the words themselves were not ringing within us? And the word, as we know, is not only a key; it may also be a fetter.

Language is primarily an auditory system of symbols. In so far as it is articulated it is also a motor system, but the motor aspect of speech is clearly secondary to the auditory. In normal individuals the impulse to speech first takes effect in the sphere of auditory imagery and is then transmitted to the motor nerves that control the organs of speech. The motor processes and the accompanying motor feelings are not, however, the end, the final resting point. They are merely a means and a control leading to auditory perception in both speaker and hearer. Communication, which is the very object of speech, is successfully effected only when the hearer's auditory perceptions are translated into the appropriate and intended flow of imagery or thought or both combined. Hence the cycle of speech, in so far as we may look upon it as a purely external instrument, begins and ends in the realm of sounds. The concordance between the initial auditory imagery and the final auditory perceptions is the social seal or warrant of the successful issue of the process. As we have already seen, the typical course of this process may undergo endless modifications or transfers into equivalent systems without thereby losing its essential formal characteristics.

The most important of these modifications is the abbreviation of the speech process involved in thinking. This has doubtless many forms, according to the structural or functional peculiarities of the individual mind. The least modified form is that known as "talking to one's self" or "thinking aloud." Here the speaker and the hearer are identified in a single person, who may be said to communicate with himself. More significant is the still further abbreviated form in which the sounds of speech are not articulated at all. To this belong all the varieties of silent speech and of normal thinking. The auditory centers alone may be excited;or the impulse to linguistic expression may be communicated as well to the motor nerves that communicate with the organs of speech but be inhibited either in the muscles of these organs or at some point in the motor nerves themselves; or, possibly, the auditory centers may be only slightly, if at all, affected, the speech process manifesting itself directly in the motor sphere.There must be still other types of abbreviation. How common is the excitation of the motor nerves in silent speech, in which no audible or visible articulations result, is shown by the frequent experience of fatigue in the speech organs, particularly in the larynx, after unusually stimulating reading or intensive thinking.

All the modifications so far considered are directly patterned on the typical process of normal speech. Of very great interest and importance is the possibility of transferring the whole system of speech symbolism into other terms than those that are involved in the typical process.This process, as we have seen, is a matter of sounds and of movements intended to produce these sounds.The sense of vision is not brought into play. But let us suppose that one not only hears the articulated sounds but sees the articulations themselves as they are being executed by the speaker.Clearly, if one can only gain a sufficiently high degree of adroitness in perceiving these movements of the speech organs, the way is opened for a now type of speech symbolism—that in which the sound is replaced by the visual image of the articulations that correspond to the sound.This sort of system has no great value for most of us because we are already possessed of the auditory-motor system of which it is at best but an imperfect translation, not all the articulations being visible to the eye.However, it is well known what excellent use deaf-mutes can make of "reading from the lips" as a subsidiary method of apprehending speech.The most important of all visual speech symbolisms is, of course, that of the written or printed word, to which, on the motor side, corresponds the system of delicately adjusted movements which result in the writing or typewriting or other graphic method of recording speech.The significant feature for our recognition in these new types of symbolism, apart from the fact that they are no longer a by-product of normal speech itself, is that each element (letter or written word) in the system corresponds to a specific element (sound or sound-group or spoken word) in the primary system. Written language is thus a point-to-point equivalence, to borrow a mathematical phrase, to its spoken counterpart. The written forms are secondary symbols of the spoken ones—symbols of symbols-yet so close is the correspondence that they may, not only in theory but in the actual practice of certain eye-readers and, possibly, in certain types of thinking, be entirely substituted for the spoken ones.Yet the auditory-motor associations are probably always latent at the least, that is, they are unconsciously brought into play.Even those who read and think without the slightest use of sound imagery are, at last analysis, dependent on it. They are merely handling the circulating medium, the money, of visual symbols as a convenient substitute for the economic goods and services of the fundamental auditory symbols.

The possibilities of linguistic transfer are practically unlimited.A familiar example is the Morse telegraph code, in which the letters of written speech are represented by a conventionally fixed sequence of longer or shorter ticks. Here the transfer takes place from the written word rather than directly from the sounds of spoken speech.The letter of the telegraph code is thus a symbol of a symbol of a symbol.It does not, of course, in the least follow that the skilled operator, in order to arrive at an understanding of a telegraphic message, needs to transpose the individual sequence of ticks into a visual image of the word before he experiences its normal auditory image. The precise method of reading off speech from the telegraphic communication undoubtedly varies widely with the individual. It is even conceivable, if not exactly likely, that certain operators may have learned to think directly, so far as the purely conscious part of the process of thought is concerned, in terms of the tick-auditory symbolism or, if they happen to have a strong natural bent toward motor symbolism, in terms of the correlated tactile-motor symbolism developed in the sending of telegraphic messages.

Still another interesting group of transfers are the different gesture languages, developed for the use of deaf-mutes, of Trappist monks vowed to perpetual silence, or of communicating parties that are within seeing distance of each other but are out of earshot. Some of these systems are one-to-one equivalences of the normal system of speech; others, like military gesture-symbolism or the gesture language of the Plains Indians of North America ( understood by tribes of mutually unintelligible forms of speech) are imperfect transfers, limiting themselves to the rendering of such grosser speech elements as are an imperative minimum under difficult circumstances. In these latter systems, as in such still more imperfect symbolisms as those used at sea or in the woods, it may be contended that language no longer properly plays a part but that the ideas are directly conveyed by an utterly unrelated symbolic process or by a quasiinstinctive imitativeness. Such an interpretation would be erroneous. The intelligibility of these vaguer symbolisms can hardly be due to anything but their automatic and silent translation into the terms of a fuller flow of speech.

We shall no doubt conclude that all voluntary communication of ideas, aside from normal speech, is either a transfer, direct or indirect, from the typical symbolism of language as spoken and heard or, at the least, involves the intermediary of truly linguistic symbolism. This is a fact of the highest importance. Auditory imagery and the correlated motor imagery leading to articulation are, by whatever devious ways we follow the process, the historic fountain-head of all speech and of all thinking. One other point is of still greater importance. The ease with which speech symbolism can be transferred from one sense to another, from technique to technique, itself indicates that the mere sounds of speech are not the essential fact of language, which lies rather in the classification, in the formal patterning, and in the relating of concepts. Once more, language, as a structure, is on its inner face the mold of thought. It is this abstracted language, rather more than the physical facts of speech, that is to concern us in our inquiry.

There is no more striking general fact about language than its universality. One may argue as to whether a particular tribe engages in activities that are worthy of the name of religion or of art, but we know of no people that is not possessed of a fully developed language. The lowliest South African Bushman speaks in the forms of a rich symbolic system that is in essence perfectly comparable to the speech of the cultivated Frenchman of a rich symbolic system that is in essence perfectly comparable to the speech of the cultivated Frenchman. It goes without saying that the more abstract concepts are not nearly so plentifully represented in the language of the savage, nor is there the rich terminology and the finer definition of nuances that reflect the higher culture. Yet the sort of linguistic development that parallels the historic growth of culture and which, in its later stages, we associate with literature is, at best, but a superficial thing. The fundamental groundwork of language—the development of a clear-cut phonetic system, the specific association of speech elements with concepts, and the delicate provision for the formal expression of all manner of relations—all this meets us rigidly perfected and systematized in every language known to us.Many primitive languages have a formal richness, a latent luxuriance of expression, that eclipses anything known to the languages of modern civilization.Even in the mere matter of the inventory of speech the layman must be prepared for strange surprises.Popular statements as to the extreme poverty of expression to which primitive languages are doomed are simply myths. Scarcely less impressive than the universality of speech is its almost incredible diversity.Those of us that have studied French or German, or, better yet, Latin or Greek, know in what varied forms a thought may run.The formal divergences between the English plan and the Latin plan, however, are comparatively slight m the perspective of what We know of more exotic linguistic patterns. The universality and the diversity of speech lead to a significant inference. We are forced to believe that language is an immensely ancient heritage of the human race, whether or not all forms of speech are the historical outgrowth of a single pristine form.It is doubtful if any other cultural asset of man.be it, the art of drilling for fire or of chipping stone, may lay claim to a greater age.I am inclined to believe that it antedated even the lowliest developments of material culture, that these developments, in fact, were not strictly possible until language, the tool of significant expression, had itself taken shape.

(*language*. New York：Harcourt, brace and company, INC)

译文：

# 引论：什么是语言

### 陆卓元, 译

　　说话是日常生活里太熟习的事情了,我们难得会踌躇一下来给它下个定义。人说话,和走路一样,是自然而然的,只是比呼吸略次一点儿。然而只要稍加思索,我们就会相信:人自然就会说话,这不过是一种幻觉。学说话的过程其实是和学走路的过程绝不相同的。学走路时,文化,或者说社会习惯的传统,不起什么重要作用。小孩子天生具有我们叫做生物遗传的一套复杂因素,能做出走路所必需的一切肌肉、神经适应。这些肌肉和神经系统的相应部分的配备,可以说本是特别适宜于做出走路和类似的动作的。实在说,一个正常的人先天就注定要走路,并不是因为大人帮助他学会这种技术,而是因为从出生起,甚至于从受胎起,他的机体就准备好承担起走路这件事的一切神经机能消耗和一切肌肉适应。简括地说,走路是人类的遗传的生物的功能。

　　语言不是这样的。自然,在某种意义上,说一个人先天注定要说话,也是对的。但这完全是由于他不只出生在自然界里,同时也出生在社会怀抱之中,而社会一定会,大概一定会,领导他走向社会传统。没有了社会,如果他还能活下去的话,无疑他还会学走路。但也同样可以肯定,他永远学不会说话,就是说,不会按照某一社会的传统体系来传达意思。要不然,把一个刚生下来的人从他出生的社会环境迁移到完全另外一个社会环境里去。在新环境里,他会发展走路的技术,差不多像在老环境里一样。然而他的言语会和他本土环境的言语全然不同。那么,走路是一种普遍的人类活动;人和人之间,走路的差别是有限的。这种差别是不自主的,无目的的。言语这一人类活动,从一个社会集体到另一个社会集体,它的差别是无限度可说的,因为它纯然是一个集体的历史遗产,是长期相沿的社会习惯的产物。言语之有差别正如一切有创造性的事业都有差别,也许不是那么有意识的,但是正像不同民族之间,宗教、信仰、习俗、艺术都有差别一样。走路是一种机体的、本能性的功能(当然它不是一种本能);言语是一种非本能性的、获得的、"文化的"功能①。

有一件事往往叫人不会认识语言只是声音符号的习惯系统,而引起通俗的想法,以为语言具有某种它实在没有的本能基础。这就是大家都看到的,在情绪激动之下,譬如说在剧痛或是狂欢时,我们会不由自主地发出声音来。听到的人以为这声音就是情绪的表达,但是这样的不由自主的感情表现和传达意思的正常方式(也就是言语)天差地远。前者实在是本能的,不是符号性的。换句话说,疼痛的声音、喜欢的声音本身并不表达情绪,它并不像是自己站在一旁,宣称某种情绪正在被感觉到。它所做的只是叫情绪的力量多少自动地流露出来,从某种意义上说,它只是情绪本身的一部分。并且,严格地说,这种本能的喊叫也难以说是传达。它们并不是对任何人发出的。如果有人听到的话,也只不过是偶然听到,就像听到狗叫、行近的脚步声或风的淅淅声一样。如果这也对听者传达了某些意思,那只是就最广泛的意义说的,环境中任何声音以至任何现象都可以说对观察到的人传达了意思。要是把不由自主的呼痛声(通常用"噢"来代表)看做真正的语言符号,和"我很疼"那样的意思等同起来,那么也就可以把出现云彩看做等同于"看来要下雨了"这样的传递确定信息的符号了。语言的定义假若扩展到包括一切这样的推想,就变得毫无意义了。

千万不要犯这样的错误,以为我们惯用的感叹词("噢!"、"啊!"、"歇!")就是本能的喊叫。这些感叹词不过是自然声音的习俗的定型,所以在各种语言里,它们按着各该语言的语音特性而有很大差别。这样,就语言这个名称的确切的文化上的含义来说,感叹词可以算是语言本身的一部分。它们不等于本能的喊叫,就像 cuckoo、killdeer② 不等于真的鸟叫,罗西尼(Rossini)在《威廉泰尔》歌剧序曲里描拟的风暴不就是风暴。换句话说,正常语言里的感叹词、象声词和它们的自然原型的关系,正像是艺术和自然的关系,而艺术纯粹是社会的或文化的。也许有人会反对说:从一种语言到另一种语言,感叹词虽然略有区别,但又突出地相似,像一家人一样,所以可认为是从一个共同的本能基础上成长起来的。但是这种情况跟绘画表现上的民族风格没有什么不一样。日本画画山和现代欧洲画画同样的山,既相同又不相同。二者都受到同一自然形象的启发,都是"摹拟"它。二者又都不是这自然形象本身,也不能用任何让人能了解的话把它们说成是这自然形象所直接产生的。这两种表现风格不一样,因为它们出自不同的历史传统,是用不同的绘画技术来处理的。日语和英语的感叹词也正是这样,都是同一自然原型,本能喊叫,所启发的,所以不能不是彼此互相启发的。它们有时差得很大,有时差得极小,因为它们是由这两个民族历代沿袭下来的不同资料或不同技术所构成的。这不同的资料或不同的技术就是这两个民族各自的语言传统、语音系统和说话习惯。然而,整个人类的本能喊叫本身是差不多完全相同的,就像人的骨骼或神经系统总不过是人体组织的"固定"部分,只能稍有"偶然的"变异而已。

语言成分中,感叹词属于最不重要的部分。它们所以值得讨论,主要是因为可以用它们来说明:即使是它们,肯定是所有语音中最接近本能喊叫的,也只在表面上具有本能性质。所以,即使我们能证明整个的语言,在它原始的历史和心理基础上,都可以追溯到感叹词,我们仍然不能说语言是一种本能活动。何况事实上企图这样来解释语言起源都是徒然的。没有任何可以抓得住的证据——历史的或其他的——足以说明语言成分和语言程序大体上是从

---

① 译按:"本能"是 instinct,"本能性的"是 instinctive。这里反映本世纪初年美国心理学上的一种争论。

② cuckoo 是鹧鸪的叫声在英语里的语言定型,killdeer 是一种美洲小鸟的叫声在英语里的语言定型,是这两种鸟的名字。——译者

感叹词演化来的。感叹词只是语言词汇中极小的和功能上最不重要的一部分;在任何时候,在有记载的任何语言领域中,都没有看到它们有组成语言基本经纬的明显趋势。它们从来就至多不过是这块宽阔而复杂的织品上的装饰花边而已。

感叹词是这样,象声词更是这样了。Whippoorwill、to mew、to caw① 这一类的词都不是人本能地或自动地响应自然的声音。它们实在是人脑的创作,想象力的发挥,和语言里任何其他东西一样。它们并不直接从自然里生长出来,只是自然所启发的,与自然游戏而已。所以语言的象声起源说,就是认为一切言语都是从摹拟性的声音逐渐演化出来的,并不能使我们达到比我们今日所认识的语言更为接近本能水平的地步。至于这种学说本身,它也不见得比感叹词起源说更可信些。诚然,有些词我们今天虽然已经不感到它们有摹拟声音的意味,可以证明曾经有过一种语音形式,很有力地暗示着它们的起源是摹拟自然声音的,例如英语的 to laugh(笑)②。即便如此,也不可能证明,并且没有内在的理由足以叫人设想,语言成分,除去微不足道的部分,是从象声起源的,或是语言的形式机构上的任何东西是从象声起源的。不管我们在一般原则上怎样有意强调摹拟自然声音在原始人的语言里的基本重要性,事实上这些语言对摹拟词并不显出特殊的爱好。马更些(Mackenzie)河上的阿萨巴斯根(Athabaskan)部落是美洲土著最原始的一种,他们的语言里几乎没有或者全然没有象声词;而在英语、德语这样自以为文明的语言里却随便使用象声词。这个例证可以说明语言的根本性质和单纯摹拟之间,关系是何等微弱。

上文已经廓清了道路来给语言下一个可用的定义。语言是纯粹人为的,非本能的,凭借自觉地制造出来的符号系统来传达观念、情绪和欲望的方法。这些符号首先是听觉的符号,是由所谓"说话器官"产生的。不管本能表现和自然环境能给某些语言成分的发展多大刺激,不管本能的趋势(运动的或其他的)在多大程度上规定了语言表达的范围和方式,人类语言本身并没有可以觉察到的本能基础。人或动物用不由自主的、本能的喊叫来进行的交际(如果可以叫做交际的话),根本不是我们所谓语言。

我刚谈到了"说话器官",乍一听,这好像等于承认说话本身是一种本能的、由生理决定的活动。不要被这个名词引入歧途。确切地说,并没有说话器官,只是有些器官碰巧对发生语音有用罢了。肺、喉头、上腭、鼻子、舌头、牙齿和嘴唇都用来发音,但它们不能认为主要地是说话器官,正像手指不能认为主要地是弹钢琴的器官,或膝盖主要地是祈祷的器官。说话并不是一种简单的活动,不只是由一个或几个生理地适应于这用途的器官来进行的。它是一张极端复杂、经常变动的调节网(在脑中,神经系统中,以及发音和听觉器官中),用以满足交际的要求。肺大致可说是为了所谓呼吸这一必需的生物功能而发展起来的,鼻子是嗅觉器官,牙齿是为了嚼碎食物以备消化。这些器官以及其他器官经常在说话时被利用,那是因为任何器官一经存在,只要能自主地控制,人就会叫它服务于第二重目的。从生理方面说,说话是一种上层的功能,或者更恰当些说,是一群上层的功能。它叫神经、肌肉的器官和功能尽可能地为自己服务,而这些器官和功能却是为了另外的目的而存在的。

诚然,生理心理学家会谈到语言在脑中的位置。这只能这么理解:语音是位于脑的听觉神经路中,或位于它的某一限定的部分中的,就像非语音的声音也位于那里一样;说话所包含的运动过程(如喉头中声带的动作、发元音所必需的舌头动作、发某些辅音所必需的嘴唇动作

----

① Whippoorwill 是一种美洲猫头鹰的叫声在英语里的语言定型,就是这种鸟的名字。mew、caw 是猫叫声和乌鸦叫声的语言定型:to mew、to caw 是这两个词的动词形式。——译者

② 译按:指盎格鲁-撒克逊 hlehhan,参考古日耳曼 hlabhan 等。

等等)是位于运动神经路中的,就像其他一切特殊运动的神经冲动也位于那里。同样,阅读这动作所包含的那些视觉认识过程,它们的神经控制也位于脑的视觉神经路中。当然,跟任何语言成分有关的各神经路中的各个位置点,或各丛位置点,都由脑中的联合路线连接起来;所以语言的外观方面,或是心理-物理方面,是由脑中的联合位置和下导神经路所组成的一张大网,而其中听觉位置无疑地是最基本的。但是,位于脑中的一个语音,即使已经和发这个语音所必需的"说话器官"的一定动作联合起来了,也还远不能成为一个语言成分。它必须进一步和人的经验的某个成分或某些成分(例如某个或某类视觉印象,或对外物的某种关系的感觉)联合起来,否则不可能具有起码的言语意义。这个经验"成分"就是一个语言单位的内容或"意义"。在说话这动作和听话这动作的直接背景上,有互相联合着的听觉的、运动的和其他大脑的过程,而这些过程不过是这些"意义"的复杂符号或标记,下面就要讨论这一点①。可见语言并没有,也不可能有一定位置,因为语言是一种特别的符号关系,一方面是一切可能的意识成分,又一方面是位于听觉、运动和其他大脑和神经线路上的某些特定成分;从心理上说,这关系是一种任意关系。如果要说语言是一定地"位于"脑中的,那也只是在一般的并且没有多大用处的意义上说的,即意识的一切方面,人类的一切兴趣和活动,都可以说是"在脑中"的。那么,我们没有别的办法,只有承认语言是在人的心灵或"精神"结构中充分形成的功能系统。我们不能把语言当做单只是一件心理-物理的事来给它下定义,虽然这心理-物理基础是很必需的,否则语言不能在人身上发生作用。

从生理学家或心理学家的观点来看,我们研究语言这一门学问,而不经常或者明明白白地谈到这基础,好像是无理地说得那么抽象。但是这样的抽象说法正是可以辩解的。我们大可以从语言的作用、形式和历史来讨论它,正像我们可以把人类文化的任何其他方面——譬如说艺术或宗教——只当作一桩制度上的或文化上的事情来讨论,抛开背后的生理的和心理的机构不谈,把它们看做是当然有的事情。所以必须明确了解:这本语言研究绪论就是不谈作为语言基础的生理学和心理学方面的事。我们的语言研究不是有关某一具体机构的产生和作用的研究;它不如说是为了讨论所谓语言这个任意性符号系统的功能和形式。

我已经指出语言的本质就在于把习惯的、自觉发出的声音(或是声音的等价物)分派到各种经验成分上去。"房子"这个词,如果所指的只是组成它的辅音和元音,按着一定的次序说出来,而在耳朵产生音响效果,那不是语言;发出这个词的运动过程和触觉也不是语言;听者对这发音动作的视觉也不是语言;对写在或印在纸上的"房子"这个词的视觉也不是语言;书写这个词的运动过程和触觉也不是语言;对这些经验的任何一种或全部的记忆也不是语言。只有当这些,可能还有其他的,联合的经验自动地和一个房子的印象联合起来时,才具有一个符号,一个词或一个语言成分的性质。但是仅仅这样联合起来还是不够的。一个人可能在某一所房子里,在一种感人的情况下,听到过某一个词,以至于这个词和这个房子的印象在这个人的意识中总是共同出现,缺一不可。这样的联合并不构成语言。联合必须是纯粹符号性的。换句话说,这个词必须指出这个印象,标出这个印象,并且每当需要而且合适的时候,能

---

① 译按:本节下文原文晦涩。如不能读,跳过也不妨。那个时代的语言学者都知道一些神经生理学以及当时流行的所谓机能心理学,特别像作者提到"关系的感觉",那是詹姆斯(James)的看法。本节所说,大致不过是:语言活动以及所凭借的神经生理这方面,和个人经验(就是意识)这方面的关系是符号性的关系,符号性的关系,即语音和经验的关系,是偶然建立起来的。作者说:"语言是在人的心灵或'精神'结构中充分形成的功能系统",这也不能解释为二元论或是"并行论"。作者是受了克罗齐(Croce)的《精神哲学》的影响的,并且当时的机能心理学又把意识当做一种神经机能。

用作这个印象的筹码①，而不作别用。这样地联合起来——自主地，而且在某种意义上说只是任意地做的——需要高度运用自觉注意。至少开始的时候要这样，因为习惯很快就会叫这种联合变得几乎像任何联合一样地自动，而且比其中绝大多数运用得更为迅速。

但是我们又走得太快一点了。如果"房子"这个符号——不管是听觉的、运动的，或是视觉的经验或印象——只是附着于某次看到的某一所房子的个别印象，那么，泛泛地说，它是可以叫做一个语言成分。可是显而易见，这样组成的言语在交际上很少有价值或者全没有价值。必须把我们的经验世界大事简化和一般化，才可能给我们所有的对事物、对关系的经验开一个清单，这个清单是我们传达观念时所必需的。语言成分，标明经验的符号，必须和整组的经验，有一定界限的一类经验相联合，而不只是和各个经验相联合。只有如此才可能交际，因为单个的经验位置在个人的意识中，严格地说是不能传达的。要想传达，它必须归入一个社团所默认的共同的类。这样，我对某一房子的个别印象就必须和我对它的所有其他印象参同起来。更进一步，我对这所房子的一般化的记忆或我对这所房子的"意念"，必须和所有看见过这所房子的人对它的"意念"融合起来。原来的那个个别经验到此已扩展开来，包括了凡有感觉的人对这所房子形成的或可能形成的一切感觉或印象。这样初步把经验简化，是一大类语言成分的基础。这一大类即所谓专名词或各人各物的名字。这样的经验简化，主要地也是历史和艺术所依托的，是形成它们的素材的。但是我们还不能满足于把无穷的经验仅仅这样简化。我们必须深入到底，必须多少有点任意地把一堆堆相似的经验归在一起，认为它们是相似到足以看做是相同的——这样做是错误的，但正是方便的。这所房子和那所房子以及成千累万性质相似的其他现象，尽管细节上有很大的和显著的差别，还是被认为足够相像，可以归为同一项目。换句话说，"房子"这个语言成分主要不是单个知觉的符号，甚至也不是对某一事物的意念的符号，而是一个"概念"的符号；或者说，是一个可以顺手把思维包装起来的胶囊，包括着成千累万不同的经验，并且还准备再接纳成千累万的。如果说语言的单个有意义的成分是概念的符号，那么实际上联串的言语就可以认为是把这些概念安排起来，在它们中间建立起相互关系的记录。

常有人提到这个问题：没有语言，思维是否可能。或者进一步问：语言和思维是否不过是同一心灵过程的两个方面。这个问题到处逢到误解，以致更加变为难题。不如首先指出，不管思维是否需要符号（也就是语言），联串的言语并不总是表示思想的。我们已经看到，一个典型的语言成分标明一个概念。但是并不能由此引申说，语言的使用永远或主要地是概念的。日常生活中，我们并不怎么关心概念，反而更关心具体的东西和特殊的关系。例如我说："今天早晨的一顿饭很不错"，显然我并没有苦苦思想，我所要传达的只不过一种愉快的回忆，用符号把它顺着常轨表现出来。

句中的每一成分指定单个的概念或是概念的关系，或是概念和关系联合起来，但整个句子没有概念的意味。这就有点像一个能供给足够的电力来开动电梯的发电机只用来专门供给一个电铃。这样比拟，乍一看没多大意思，其实不然。可以把语言看成一架乐器，能奏出不同高度的心灵活动。语言的流动不只和意识的内在内容相平行，并且是在不同的水平面上和它平行的，这水平面可以低到为个别印象所占据的心理状态，也可以高到注意焦点里只有抽象的概念和它们的关系的心理状态，就是通常所谓推理。可见，语言只有外在的形式是不变的；它的内在意义，它的心灵价值或强度，随着注意或心灵选择的方向而自由变化，不消说还随着心灵的一般发展而自由变化。从语言的观点来看，思维的定义可以是：言语的最高级的

---

① "筹码（Counter）"指"合符"，"代表"。——译者

潜在的(或可能的)内容,要达到这内容,联串的言语中的各个成分必须具有最完满的概念价值。由此可知语言和思维不是严格地同义的。语言最多也只有在符号表现的最高、最概括的水平上才能作为思维的外表。稍微改变一下角度来看,语言主要地是一种先理性的功能。它逐渐接近思维。思维先只是潜伏在语言的分类法中和形式中,而最终才可以从语言中看出思维。语言并不像一般的但是肤浅的想法那样,是贴在完成了的思维上的标签。

大多数人,如果你问他能否不用言语来思想,大概会回答:"能,但要我这样做不容易,然而我知道是能的。"语言只不过是一件外衣!但如果语言不怎么像一件外衣,而更像是一条现成的路或是车辙,那又怎么样呢?非常可能,语言本是一种在概念水平以下使用的工具,而思维是把语言的内容精炼地解释了之后才兴起的。换句话说,产品随着工具而改进。正像数学推理非借助一套适当的数学符号不能进行一样,没有语言,思维的产生和日常运用未必更能想象。没有人相信数学命题,即使是最难的,注定要依靠一套任意性的符号;但是不可能设想,没有符号,人的心灵会得出这个命题或把它掌握住。作者本人颇以为许多人觉得能不用语言来思想,甚至推理,只是一种错觉。这种错觉似乎是由好几个因素造成的,其中最简单的是没有能区分印象和思维。事实上,只要我们试一试叫一个印象和另一个印象在意识上发生关系,就会发现自己默默地说了一连串的词了。思维可能另是一个自然领域,不同于人为的言语,但是就我们所知,言语似乎是通向思维的唯一途径。还有一个原因更会叫人幻想思维可以抛弃语言,那就是一般不理解语言并不等于它的听觉符号。听觉符号可以用运动符号或视觉符号一个对一个地来代替(例如许多人能够纯粹凭视觉来阅读,即不需要从印刷或书写的词引起一连串相应的听觉印象作为中间环节),或用其他一些更隐微,更难以捉摸,以至不容易确指的转移作用来代替。所以,仅仅因为一个人不觉得有听觉印象同时存在,就硬说他不用语言来思维,那绝不是合理的。甚至可以猜想思维的符号表达有时会跑出意识边缘之外,所以就某种类型的人的心理来说,会感觉到一种自由的、非语言的思维之流,这倒是相对地可以辩护的(但也只是相对地)。从心理-物理的角度来看,这句话的意思就是:言语在大脑中的相应部分,即脑中的听觉中枢,或相应的视觉或运动中枢,以及和这些中枢适应的联合路线,在思维过程中只被轻微地触动,以致全没有进入意识。这是一种极端的情况,思维不和语言手拉手地颠簸着,而只轻飘飘地骑在潜伏的语言的顶峰上。现代心理学给我们指出符号在无意识心理中起着多么有力的作用①。所以现在比二十年前更容易了解,最清虚的思维可能只是无意识的语言符号的有意识的对应物。

让我就语言和思维的关系再略谈几句。上文发挥的观点一点也不排除这样一种可能:语言的成长要充分依赖思维的发展。我们可以假定语言是先理性地兴起的——至于如何兴起,确切地在哪样的心理活动水平上才会兴起,我们不知道——但是我们绝不能想象一个高度发展的语言符号系统会在明确的概念和思想(即概念的安排)起源之前自己发达起来。我们宁可设想,几乎在语言表达开始的时候,思维过程像是一种精神泛滥,就渗进来了;并且,一个概念一经确定,必然会影响到它的语言符号的生命,促使语言的进一步成长。我们确实看到这种语言和思维相互作用的复杂过程在我们眼前进行着。工具使产品成为可能,产品又改良了工具。一个新概念的产生总是在旧语言材料的使用多少有点勉强的时候或是扩大了的时候预示出来;这个概念在具有明确的语言形象之前是不会获得个别的、独立的生命的。在绝大多数情况下,这个概念的新符号是用已经存在的语言材料,按照老规矩所制定的极端严格的方式造成的。有了一个词,我们就像松了一口气,本能地觉得一个概念现在归我们使用了。

---

① 译按:"现代心理学"原文作"the modern psychology",指弗洛伊德(Freud)的精神分析论。

没有符号,我们不会觉得已经掌握了直接认识或了解这个概念的钥匙。假如"自由"、"理想"这些词不在我们心里作响,我们会像现在这样准备为自由而死,为理想而奋斗吗?但是我们也知道词不只是钥匙,它也可以是桎梏。

语言主要地是一个听觉符号系统。因为它是说出来的,它也是一个运动系统。但是语言的运动方面显然比听觉方面次要。在正常的人,语言的冲动首先发生在听觉印象的范围,然后再传送到控制发音器官的运动神经。运动过程和相伴的运动感觉可也不是终点。它们只是一种手段、一种制约,引起说话的人和听话的人的听觉。说话的目的是交际,只有当听者的听觉翻译成适当的和预期的一串印象或思维,或二者兼有,交际才算成功。所以就语言作为纯粹的外表工具来说,它的循环起始于并且终结于声音的领域。起始的听觉印象和终了的听觉知觉互相对应了,这个过程才得到社会的印证,算是成功了。正如我们已经看到的,这个过程的典型程序可以受到无穷的修改,或转移成别的相当的系统,而不丧失它主要的形式特征。

种种修改之中,最重要的就是思想时语言过程的紧缩。随着各人的心理结构或心理功能的特点,这种紧缩无疑会有多种形式。修改得最少的形式是所谓"自言自语"或"出声思想"。这里,说话者和听话者变为同一个人,可以说是自己对自己交际。更有意思的是进一步紧缩的形式,它根本不发出语音来。各种各样的默语和正常思想都属于这一类。只有听觉中枢受到了激动;或者是语言表达的冲动虽然传给了跟发音器官相通的运动神经,而被抑制在这些器官的肌肉中或运动神经本身的某点上;再不然是听觉中枢只稍稍受到影响,或根本没有受到影响,言语过程直接在运动范围中显现出来。一定还有其他类型的紧缩。默语时虽然听不见声音,看不见发音动作,但是运动神经的兴奋却是常有的。例如在阅读非常动人的读物之后或深思之后,发音器官,特别是喉头,往往会感到疲乏,这就证明运动神经的兴奋。

以上所说的一切修改法都是以正常言语的典型过程做底子的。还有非常有趣而且重要的事,就是把整个言语符号系统转移到典型过程所不包括的其他范围里去的可能性。典型过程只涉及声音和用来发出声音的动作。视觉并没有参与。但是我们可以假设一个人不仅听见声音,并且看见说话者的发音器官的动作。显然,人观察说话器官的动作,只要能灵敏到足够的程度,就给一个新类型的语言符号开辟了道路,和声音相应的动作所引起的视觉印象就代替了声音。对绝大多数人,这样的一个系统没有多大用处,因为我们已经有了听觉-运动系统,而视觉系统最多也不过是把它不完全地翻译一下,不是一切发音动作都是眼睛看得见的。不过大家都知道聋哑人如何巧妙地利用"念嘴唇"来作为了解言语的辅助方法。在一切视觉语言符号中,最重要的自然是书写或印刷的字。在运动方面与此相应的是有精细调节的动作系统,它形成手写、打字,或其他记录语言的书写方法。从这些新类型的符号里,我们除了认识到它们已经不再是正常语言的副产品,还认识到一件有意思的事,那就是新系统中的每一个成分(字母或书面的词)相应于原本的系统中的一个特殊成分(单音或音组或口头的词)。借用一个数学术语来说,书面语和口语是点对点地相等的。书面形式是口语形式的第二重符号——符号的符号,但是它们对应得如此严格,以致不仅在理论上而且在某些专用眼睛读书的人的实践上,又可能在某些类型的思想里,书面形式可以完全代替口语形式。不过听觉-运动的联合大概至少总还是潜伏在内的,就是说它还是在下意识里起作用。即使那些在阅读或思想时绝不用声音印象的人,分析到底,还是要靠它的。基本听觉符号好比是商品和服务,而视觉符号是流通媒介,是货币,这些人只是为了方便而掌握了货币。

语言转移的可能性实际上是无限的。一个大家熟悉的例子就是摩尔斯(Morse)电码,书面语的字母用约定俗成的一串串长短不同的滴滴声来代表。这里,转移由书面的词形成,而不是直接由口语的声音实现的。所以电码字母是符号的符号的符号。自然,一个熟练的电报员要了解电文,并不需要把一串串的滴滴声先翻成词的视觉印象,然后才能体验到正常的听觉印象。每个人实在怎么从电报交际中念出言语来,那无疑是有很大差别的。甚至可以想象(虽然未必实有其事),就思维过程的纯粹可意识的部分来说,某些电报员可能学会了直接用滴滴的听觉符号来思想;或者碰巧他们对运动符号有很强的自然倾向,会直接用发送电讯所引起的相应的触觉-运动符号来思想。

另一类有趣的转移是各种手势语,例如聋哑人用的、发誓永不说话的脱拉毕斯脱(Trappist)教派的修道士用的,或是能互相看见而不能互相听到的两方交际人用的。这些系统之中,有的是和正常言语系统点对点地相等的,有的,像军用手势符号或北美洲平原印第安人的手势语(语言互不相通的部落都懂得),是不完全的转移,仅限于在困难情况下传递必不可少的、比较粗糙的言语成分。也许有人会争辩说,在这后两种系统里,还有在海上或森林里使用的更不完全的符号里,语言实在已经不起作用、观念是直接由跟语言决然无关的符号过程传达的,或是由半本能的摹仿来传达的。这样的解释未免错了。这些较模糊的符号所以能了解,不是因为别的,还是因为把它们自动地、默默地翻译成了更完备的词句。

我们可以毫不犹豫地做出这样的结论:除了正常言语之外,其他一切自主地传达观念的方式,总是从口到耳的典型语言符号的直接或间接的转移,或至少也要用真正的语言符号做媒介。这是非常重要的事。听觉印象和与之相关的引起发音的运动印象,是一切言语和一切思想的历史渊源,不管追溯它的过程是怎样的曲折。还有一点更为重要。语言符号能容易地从一种官能转移到另一种官能,从一种技术转移到另一种技术,可见单只语音并不是语言的基本事实;语言的基本事实毋宁说在于概念的分类、概念的形式构造和概念的关系。再说一次,语言,作为一种结构来看,它的内面是思维的模式。我们所要研究的,与其说是言语的物理事实,不如说是这抽象的语言。

有关语言的一般现象中,最叫人注意的无过于它的普遍性。某个部落是否有足以称为宗教或艺术的东西,那是可以争论的,但是就我们所知,没有一个民族没有充分发展的语言。最落后的南非布须曼人(Bushman)用丰富的符号系统的形式来说话,实质上完全可以和有教养的法国人的言语相比。不用说,在野蛮人的语言里,较为抽象的概念出现得不那么多,也不会有反映较高文化水平的丰富词汇和各种色彩的精密定义。然而,语言和文化的历史成长相平行,后来发展到和文学联系起来,这至多不过是浮面的事。语言的基础规模——清晰的语音系统的发展、言语成分和概念之间的特定联合,以及为种种关系的形式表达做好细致准备——这一切在我们所知的每一种语言里都已经完全固定了和系统化了。许多原始的语言,形式丰富,有充沛的表达潜力,足以使现代文明人的语言黯然失色。单只清算一下语言的财富,就会叫外行人大吃一惊。通俗的说法以为原始语言在表达方面注定是非常贫乏的,这简直是无稽之谈。语言的多样性也给人深刻的印象,不见得次于它的普遍性。我们学过法语或德语的,更好是学过拉丁语或希腊语的,都知道同一种想法可以采取多少不同的形式。但是英语的规模和拉丁语的规模,在形式上的分歧还是比较小的,只要看一看我们所知的更陌生的语言格局就知道了。语言的普遍性和多样性引出一个很有意思的推论。我们不得不相信语言是人类极古老的遗产,不管一切语言形式在历史上是否都是从一个单一的根本形式萌芽的。人类的其他文化遗产,即便是钻木取火或打制石器的技艺,是不是比语言更古老些,值得怀疑。我倒是相信,语言甚至比物质文化的最低级发展还早;在语言这种表达意义的工具形成以前,那些文化发展事实上不见得是一定可能的。

(节选自《语言论》,商务印书馆,2017)

# 2.荀子·正名篇·第二十二(节选)

后王之成名:刑名从商,爵名从周,文名从礼,散名之加于万物者,则从诸夏之成俗曲期;远方异俗之乡,则因之而为通。散名之在人者:生之所以然者谓之性。性之和所生,精合感应,不事而自然谓之性。性之好、恶、喜、怒、哀、乐谓之情。情然而心为之择谓之虑。心虑而能为之动谓之伪。虑积焉、能习焉而后成谓之伪。正利而为谓之事。正义而为谓之行。所以知之在人者谓之知。知有所合谓之智。智所以能之在人者谓之能。能有所合谓之能。性伤谓之病。节遇谓之命。是散名之在人者也,是后王之成名也。

故王者之制名,名定而实辨,道行而志通,则慎率民而一焉。故析辞擅作名以乱正名,使民疑惑,人多辨讼,则谓之大奸;其罪犹为符节、度量之罪也。故其民莫敢托为奇辞以乱正名,故其民悫。悫则易使,易使则公。其民莫敢托为奇辞以乱正名,故壹于道法而谨于循令矣,如是则其迹长矣。迹长功成,治之极也,是谨于守名约之功也。

今圣王没,名守慢,奇辞起,名实乱,是非之形不明,则虽守法之吏,诵数之儒,亦皆乱也。若有王者起,必将有循于旧名,有作于新名。然则所为有名,与所缘以同异,与制名之枢要,不可不察也。

异形离心交喻,异物名实玄纽,贵贱不明,同异不别。如是,则志必有不喻之患,而事必有困废之祸。故知者为之分别制名以指实,上以明贵贱,下以辨同异。贵贱明,同异别,如是,则志无不喻之患,事无困废之祸,此所为有名也。

然则何缘而以同异?曰:缘天官。凡同类同情者,其天官之意物也同;故比方之疑似而通。是所以共其约名以相期也。形体、色、理,以目异;声音清浊、调竽奇声,以耳异;甘、苦、咸、淡、辛、酸、奇味,以口异;香、臭、芬、鬱、腥、臊、洒、酸、奇臭,以鼻异;疾、养、沧、热、滑、铍、轻、重,以形体异;说、故、喜、怒、哀、乐、爱、恶、欲,以心异。心有征知。征知,则缘耳而知声可也,缘目而知形可也,然而征知必将待天官之当簿其类然后可也。五官簿之而不知,心征之而无说,则人莫不然谓之不知,此所缘而以同异也。

然后随而命之:同则同之,异则异之;单足以喻则单;单不足以喻则兼;单与兼无所相避则共,虽共,不为害矣。知异实者之异名也,故使异实者莫不异名也,不可乱也,犹使异实者莫不同名也。故万物虽众,有时而欲徧举之,故谓之物。物也者,大共名也。推而共之,共则有共,至于无共然后止。有时而欲徧举之,故谓之鸟兽。鸟兽也者,大别名也。推而别之,别则有别,至于无别然后止。名无固宜,约之以命,约定俗成谓之宜,异于约则谓之不宜。名无固实,约之以命实,约定俗成谓之实名。名有固善,径易而不拂,谓之善名。物有同状而异所者,有异状而同所者,可别也。状同而为异所者,虽可合,谓之二实。状变而实无别而为异者,谓之化;有化而无别,谓之一实。此事之所以稽实定数也。此制名之枢要也。后王之成名,不可不察也。

"见侮不辱","圣人不爱己","杀盗非杀人也",此惑于用名以乱名者也。验之所以为有名而观其孰行,则能禁之矣。"山渊平","情欲寡","刍豢不加甘,大钟不加乐",此惑于用实以乱名者也。验之所缘无以同异而观其孰调,则能禁之矣。"非而谒楹,有牛马非马也。"此惑于用名以乱实者也。验之名约,以其所受悖其所辞,则能禁之矣。凡邪说辟言之离正道而擅作者,无不类于三惑者矣。故明君知其分而不与辨也。

夫民易一以道而不可与共故,故明君临之以埶,道之以道,申之以命,章之以论,禁之以刑。故其民之化道也如神,辨埶恶用矣哉!今圣王没,天下乱,奸言起,君子无埶以临之,无刑以禁之,故辨说也。实不喻然后命,命不喻然后期,期不喻然后说,说不喻然后辨。故期、命、辨、说也者,用之大文也,而王业之始也。名闻而实喻,名之用也。累而成文,名之丽也。用丽俱得,谓之知名。名也者,所以期累实也。辞也者,兼异实之名以论一意也。辨说也者,不异实名以喻动静之道也。期命也者,辨说之用也。辨说也者,心之象道也。心也者,道之工宰也。道也者,治之经理也。心合于道,说合于心,辞合于说,正名而期,质请而喻。辨异而不过,推类而不悖,听则合文,辨则尽故。以正道而辨奸,犹引绳以持曲直;是故邪说不能乱,百家无所窜。有兼听之明,而无奋矜之容;有兼覆之厚,而无伐德之色。说行则天下正,说不行则白道而冥穷,是圣人之辨说也。诗曰:"颙颙卬卬,如珪如璋,令闻令望。岂弟君子,四方为纲。"此之谓也。

辞让之节得矣,长少之理顺矣,忌讳不称,祆辞不出;以仁心说,以学心听,以公心辨;不动乎众人之非誉,不治观者之耳目,不赂贵者之权埶,不利传辟者之辞:故能处道而不贰,吐而不夺,利而不流,贵公正而贱鄙争,是士君子之辨说也。诗曰:"长夜漫兮,永思骞兮。大古之不慢兮,礼义之不愆兮,何恤人之言兮。"此之谓也。

君子之言,涉然而精,俛然而类,差差然而齐。彼正其名,当其辞,以务白其志义者也。彼名辞也者,志义之使也,足以相通则舍之矣;苟之,奸也。故名足以指实,辞足以见极,则舍之矣。外是者谓之讱,是君子之所弃,而愚者拾以为己宝。故愚者之言,芴然而粗,啧然而不类,诪诪然而沸。彼诱其名,眩其辞,而无深于其志义者也。故穷借而无极,甚劳而无功,贪而无名。故知者之言也,虑之易知也,行之易安也,持之易立也;成则必得其所好而不遇其所恶焉。而愚者反是。诗曰:"为鬼为蜮,则不可得;有靦面目,视人罔极。作此好歌,以极反侧。"此之谓也。

凡语治而待去欲者,无以道欲而困于有欲者也。凡语治而待寡欲者,无以节欲而困于多欲者也。有欲无欲,异类也,生死也,非治乱也。……

无稽之言,不见之行,不闻之谋,君子慎之。

(节选自《荀子简注》,上海人民出版社,1974)

## 【推荐阅读】

索绪尔.普通语言学教程[M]. Roy Harris,译.北京:外语教学与研究出版社,2001.

# 第二章　语　音

## 第一节　语音的属性

语音是语言的物质外壳,一般而言,具有四大属性,即物理属性、生理属性、心理属性和社会属性。

### 一、语音的物理属性

语音是一种声音,因此,它首先具有和自然界其他声音一样的基本特点,即物体受外力的作用而发生振动,并推动周围的空气形成声波,当声波传到人的耳朵里,引起鼓膜的振动,刺激听觉神经而使人感觉听到了声音。我们把这种特点叫作物理属性。

从物理学的角度来看,可以从声音的高低、强弱、长短和声音的本色几个方面来分析声音,同样,我们也可以从这四个方面来分析语音,由此得到语音的四要素:音高、音强、音长和音色。

（一）音　高

简单地说，音高就是声音的高低，这是由物体振动的频率决定的。所谓频率是指物体每一秒内震动的次数，次数越多，频率越高。频率同音高成正比，振动频率高的声音高，振动频率低的声音低。

是什么影响和决定了物体振动的频率呢？不同物体具有不同的形状和质地，因而具有不同的振动频率。举个例子，儿童说话的声音一般都比老人说话的声音高，这是因为儿童的声带更短、更窄、更薄。男人说话的声音浑厚，女人说话的声音尖细，也是因为男人的声带长、宽、厚，相比之下，女人的声带短、窄、薄。所以，大的、长的、粗的、厚的发音体振动慢、频率低，发出的声音也低；而小的、短的、细的、薄的、紧的发音体振动快、频率高，发出的声音也高。同一个人说话，通过控制声带的松紧，也可以发出高低不同的声音。

音高在一些语言中有区别意义的作用，比如汉语当中的声调，就具有这样的作用，同一个音节，不同的音高构成不同的声调，分别联系不同的意义。比如坡（pō）和破（pò）的不同是由音高的不同形成的，而在英语、法语、德语中，音高则不具备区别意义的作用。同时，音高在任何语言中都是语调的主要构成要素，语调可以用来表达说话人的语气以及说话人的态度和情绪等。

（二）音　强

音强指声音的强弱。它取决于发音体振动幅度的大小，实际上就是发音体振动时离开其平衡位置的距离的大小。发音时用力强，物体振动的幅度就大，声音就强；发音时用力弱，物体振动的幅度就小，声音就弱。所以，语音的强弱决定于发音时用力的程度和气流量的大小。声音的强弱和音高没有关系，主要看作用力的大小。

在具体的分析中，要注意区分音强和响度这两个概念。这二者关系密切，但并不是一回事。比如我们说话时把嗓门压得比较低，即使用了很大的力气来发音，听上去还是不怎么响亮；相反，如果提高嗓门，即使不用那么大的力气说话，发出的声音也会响亮得多。因此，一个强度较大的音听起来不一定比一个强度较小的音更响亮，这是因为除了音强之外，音高等因素也会对声音的响度产生影响。

音强在许多语言中都具有区别意义的作用。如汉语中，"地道"这个词，如果"道"读作轻声，意思是正宗的、纯正的、符合标准的；如果"道"读作原调，则是指地下的通道。

（三）音　长

音长指声音的长短。它取决于发音体振动持续时间的长短。振动时间长，声音就长,反之则短。音长变化在许多语言中有区别意义的作用,如在英语和日语中,都有互相对立的长短元音,如英语中的 not［nɔt］(不)和 naught［nɔːt］(零)。日语中的おばあさん(祖母、外祖母)和おばさん(大娘、大婶)。在汉语一些方言中,音长也有区别意义的作用。

(四)音 色

音色就是音质,也就是声音的本质,是一个声音区别于其他声音的个性、特色,它由声波的形式决定。声波不同,我们听到的语音就不同。发音体不同,发音方法不同,共鸣器的形状不同,音质就不同,这和音高、音强、音长没有关系。举个例子,钢琴和小提琴,是两个不同的发音体,所以音色不同。同样是小提琴,用琴弓拉出来的声音和用手指拨出来的声音是不同的,这是因为发音方法不一样。同样,我们也可以通过改变小提琴的共鸣腔而获得发音时完全不同的效果。

## 二、语音的生理属性

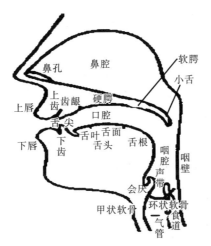

语言和自然界的其他声音一样,都是物体振动引起的物理现象,同时,它又有不同,语音是人的发音器官发出的。语音是由人的发音器官协同动作而产生的,人的发音器官及其运动是语音的生理基础,决定着语音的生理特性。

根据发音器官在语音形成中的作用,发音器官可以大致分为三个部分:

(一)动力部分:肺、隔膜、气管、支气管

这一部分器官是人的呼吸器官,人体通过这些器官进行氧气和二氧化碳的交换,同时,它们也是人发出语音时的动力装置,为语音的发出产生气流并传送。具体来说,肺、隔膜是语音发音的动力制造体,气管、支气管是传送管道。气流由肺呼出,经气管输送到声带。多数语音是在呼出时发出的,只有少数的个别语音是在吸气时发出的,如人在疼痛时发出的"咝"和汉语中表示称赞时发出的"啧"就属于吸气音。

### (二)发音部分:喉头、声带

喉头的外表是喉结,当中有声带。它由软骨构成,上通咽腔,下连气管。声带是两片很小的平行弹性薄膜,前后两端黏附在软骨上,可以打开或闭拢,其间的通路叫声门。肺呼出的气流经气管输送到声带,声带在气流的冲击下产生振动,发出声音,这种声音我们把它叫作浊音。所有的元音发音时声带都要振动。有一部分辅音发音时声带也要振动,这些辅音叫浊辅音。而发另一些辅音的时候,声带不振动,我们把发音时声带不振动的语音称为清辅音。

### (三)共鸣部分:口腔和鼻腔

口腔、鼻腔是语音的共鸣腔。了解口腔的构造,对于学习语音有着非常重要的作用。口腔的最前端是上唇和下唇,往里是上齿和下齿。齿的根部分别是上腭和下颚,上腭的前部是硬腭,后面柔软的部分是软腭,小舌的根部连接着软腭;下颚的上下活动造成了口腔的开合。口腔中最灵活的器官是舌头,它在发音中作用重大。舌头又可分为舌尖、舌叶、舌面三个部分,最前端的部分是舌尖,在发音时又分为舌尖前、舌尖中、舌尖后,舌头平放时,相对于齿龈的部分是舌叶。舌叶后面的部分是舌面,也可分为舌面前、舌面中、舌面后,习惯上又把舌面后称为舌根。舌头的运动快速灵活,使得人类可以发出的音的种类很多。元音在口腔中受到调节,不同的共鸣腔形成了不同的元音。辅音在口腔或鼻腔中受到阻碍,因阻碍部位不同而形成不同的辅音。

## 三、语音的心理属性

人的听觉感知具有很强的选择性和概括性,比如汉语中 o 和 e 两个元音,我们在发音和听音时,关注的都是唇形不同带来的变化。实际上,不同的人发出的同一个音是有差别的,同样是发 o 这个音,人与人之间的圆唇度有区别,不同人的声音大小、高低、音质不同,这些因素都会导致这个具体的音的物理属性发生变化。但是,人的听觉器官和大脑听觉中枢对语音的发音和声波的感知,会认为这个音就是元音 o,也就是说,语音声学要素的变化不一定都能在听觉上得到对等的感知。所以,我们可以说,语音的心理属性就是主观化了的声音。

同时，人类的发音也是个复杂的心理过程。各种发音器官能在瞬间协同合作，发出所需的音来，不仅需要一定的生理基础，还需要大脑中枢指挥协作，这是一个复杂的心理过程。

## 四、语音的社会属性

不论是物理属性、生理属性还是心理属性，其实都是语音的自然属性，决定语音本质的还是它的社会属性，这是使语音从根本上与一般声音区别开来的本质属性。

语音的本质是一种社会现象，主要表现在以下几个方面：首先，语音是和语言的意义联系在一起的，而什么样的语音表达什么样的语义，什么样的语义由什么样的语音表达出来，并不是天然的。就像莎士比亚的名作《罗密欧与朱丽叶》中的台词说的那样："名字是什么？玫瑰就算换了名字，也依旧芬芳。"这就形象地说明了语音和语义的联系是社会约定俗成的。其次，语音具有民族性。任何民族的语言都有自己独特的语音系统，这种系统是在特定的社会中形成的，是特定社会独特选择的结果。比如，当中国人听到 rén（人）这个音时，知道这个语音表达"能制造工具并使用工具进行劳动的高级动物"的意思，但是，若换成不懂汉语的外国人来听这个音，或许他的母语中也有这个音，他会以为是别的意思，或许他的母语里根本就没有这个音，他完全不明白。因此，rén 这个语音形式并不是天然就有这种功能，而是说汉语普通话的人共同约定、认可的。另外，语音还具有地域性。同一语言在不同的地方可能有不同的语音系统，使用不同的语音，赋予语音不同的功能和价值。俗话说的"十里不同俗，百里不同音"，就是对语言地域性特征的生动表述。

# 第二节　音响和发声

## 一、音　响

和各种声音一样，语音也是发音体振动的结果，从物理属性上看它包括了音高、音强、音长和音质四个要素。语言学家最关心的是音质,音素是从音质角度划分出来的最小的语音单位。我们可以从音响的角度对语音音质加以分析和归类。

像音叉的振动简单而有规则,有固定的振动频率,它产生的就是单调的纯音;像各种乐器振动复杂而有规则,所发出美妙的音就是乐音。而复杂又不规则的振动产生的就是噪音了。在语言中,元音都是乐音,辅音多是噪音。

对于乐音来说,它是由不同频率的纯音构成的。频率低的为基音,其他的为陪音,陪音的频率是基音的整数倍。基音决定音的基调,陪音区别音的类别。乐音音质的不同,是陪音数量、频率和强度不同的结果,而陪音的不同则与发音体的共鸣腔有很大关系。人类的发音器官也像是精密的乐器,发音体是声带,共鸣腔有咽腔、鼻腔、口腔。

对语音进行研究的实验语音学,可以借助仪器和软件对音响进行更加科学详尽的分析,常用的有脑电仪、眼动仪、气流计、声门仪等,以及基于计算机系统的专业语音分析软件。

## 二、发　声

关于发声的生理基础我们在"语音的生理基础"部分已经做了详细的介绍。

对于学习语言的人来说,了解发声机制的重要性不仅在于可以指导我们的理论研究,还在于它对实践的促进作用。我们要学习语言,需要大量地使用发音器官,比如喉、声带等,如何用得更好、更科学,如何让发出的语音不仅准确而且动听,可以从播音发声学中得到借鉴。

"气乃音之帅",气流冲击声带产生振动而发声。简单来说,喉和声带是最重要的发音器官,喉是振动发音的"房子",喉室内的声带处在不同的状态。发声时,两条声带边缘接近,也就是声门关闭,这时气流冲出而发声。

不同的表达需求,对嗓音的使用是不同的。日常谈话时的声音,以中音区的发音和口腔共鸣为主,主要靠声带本身的张力完成,它要求喉头稳定,唇舌有一定力度,下巴不能松弛,这样才能吐字清晰有力。具体来说,嗓音的使用应遵循以下原则:

(一)保持喉头稳定

喉头可以上下运动,活动范围过大是不利于发声的。如果用力喊叫或下巴过分用力、仰脖,喉头就会上移,共鸣腔相对变窄,声带也易疲劳,声音就不够洪亮、圆润,如果保持喉头稳定而松弛就利于音响共鸣。

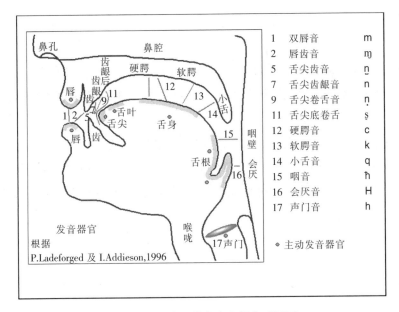

发音器官及常见辅音发音部位对照图

| 1 | 双唇音 | m m̥ |
| 2 | 唇齿音 | m̩ |
| 5 | 舌尖齿音 | n̪ |
| 7 | 舌尖齿龈音 | n ṇ |
| 9 | 舌尖卷舌音 | ṇ̊ |
| 11 | 舌尖底卷舌 | ṣ |
| 12 | 硬腭音 | c |
| 13 | 软腭音 | k |
| 14 | 小舌音 | q |
| 15 | 咽音 | ħ |
| 16 | 会厌音 | H |
| 17 | 声门音 | h |

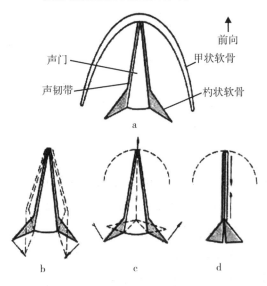

声带动作示意图

a.正常呼吸时状态　b.用力呼吸的外展作用

c.假嗓及耳语时的中央压紧状态　d.说话时全部关闭状态

## (二)气流要饱满

发音要响亮、悦耳,除了要控制喉头,还应从控制气流上下功夫。利用气流巧妙发声,保持其平稳、充足,既可以加强喉头的稳定性,又能减轻声带的压力,延长声带寿命。

（三）注意发音姿势，保护嗓音

正确的发音姿势是发声悦耳的前提。发声时要求头要正，两眼平视，下巴稍向里收拢，两肩自然下垂，胸部放松。这样既不会使声腔变形，也有利于声道通畅、气流深入、声带自由振动。

发音器官是我们每个人宝贵的财富，它精密但也脆弱，在日常用嗓中要学会呵护它。用嗓要有度，发音练习或喊叫过度都会使声带疲劳和嗓子沙哑；伤风感冒也会使发音器官充血、发炎，有损发音；吃过冷、过热或者强刺激性的食物和嗜烟酗酒等恶习都不利于嗓音的保护。

# 第三节　音　素

## 一、音素概说

在实际的语言表达中，我们听到的是语流，我们可以从听觉上，把一串语流切分成一个个的小片段，比如，sìchuāndàxué（四川大学）这一串，可以从听觉上切分为 sì-chuān-dà-xué 这样几个片段，这些片段在语言学上叫作音节。在此基础上，我们还可以做进一步的切分，上面这串语流还可以分为 s-i-ch-u-ɑ-n-d-ɑ-x-u-e，这些小的片段就不能再往下分了，它们即是语音研究的最小单位——音素，这是从音质上切分出来的最小语音片段。

结合前面提到的语音的心理属性，我们知道，同一个人在不同的情况下发同一个音也是有差别的，他们发音时间的长短、声带用力的大小等都导致这些音有所不同，但是除非专门用仪器或软件测量，否则，我们的大脑会认为都是同一个音。因此，音素的概念也是具有概括性的，忽略了细小差别的。

## 二、国际音标

每一个音素在语流中停留的时间非常短，只能在头脑中形成看不见也摸不着的心理印象,这种心理印象在人们心中保留却难以交流。为了方便研究,人们把每一个音素都使用一个书面符号记录下来,这种符号就是音标,换句话说,音标其实就是音素的文字。

音标的种类很多,采用的记音方法不同,所用符号也不同。目前最通行的音标是国际音标。第一版国际音标(国际音标表)发表于1888年8月,它的特点是:每一个独特的语音都用一个不同的字母与之对应,相同的符号出现在任何语言的记录中都表示相同的发音;音标符号尽可能采用拉丁字母,只有在确实需要的情况下才使用新造字母和附加符号。这样,音素和音标一一对应,不存在含混不清的情况。国际音标在使用时都要加上[ ],以区别于字母。国际音标由于有众多优点,得到了各国语言学界的广泛认可。

## 三、元音和辅音

音素可以分为元音和辅音两大类。

### (一)元　音

从物理属性来看,元音的主要成分是乐音。发元音时,气流在声门的状况是一样的,元音与元音之间的不同主要是由口腔的不同形状决定的。口腔形状的变化,主要取决于三个条件:一是嘴张得大还是小,二是舌头往前伸还是往后缩,三是嘴唇噘拢或者平展。其实,只要我们自己体会一下就知道,嘴张得大,舌头的位置就低一些;嘴张得小,舌头位置就高一些。因此,总结起来,这三个因素是:舌头的高低、前后和嘴唇的圆展。依据这三个因素,我们知道,舌位最高的是高元音,根据舌位的高低依次是:高、次高、半高、中、半低、次低、低。舌位前的是前元音,舌位后的是后元音,舌位在中间的是央元音。嘴唇圆的是圆唇元音,嘴唇不圆的是不圆唇元音。任何一个元音都可以从这三个方面来描写。

根据共鸣腔运用的情况,元音可以分为口元音和鼻元音两类。口元音又可依据发音时舌头的状态分为舌面元音、舌尖元音和卷舌元音三类。我们具体来介绍。

1.舌面元音

舌面元音发音时调节气流要靠舌面和硬腭部分,每一个舌面元音同样的也受上文提到的三个因素决定,我们可以根据出现频率把舌面元音分为基本元音和次基本元音两类。

(1)基本元音

基本元音通过国际音标中的元音图来表示,由八个常见的元音组成,是一套人为确定的、固定的元音音质。这八个元音是人类发音器官发出的最基本的元音,在许多语言中都常被使用,因此可以为实际中出现的众多元音提供一个参照的框架。

# 国际音标表(2005 年修订)

© 2005 国际语音学会

**辅音(肺气流)**

| | 双唇音 | 唇齿音 | 齿音 | 齿龈音 | 齿龈后音 | 卷舌音 | 硬腭音 | 软腭音 | 小舌音 | 咽音 | 声门音 |
|---|---|---|---|---|---|---|---|---|---|---|---|
| 爆破音 | p b | | | t d | | ʈ ɖ | c ɟ | k g | q ɢ | | ʔ |
| 鼻音 | m | ɱ | | n | | ɳ | ɲ | ŋ | N | | |
| 颤音 | B | | | r | | | | | R | | |
| 触音或闪音 | | ⱱ | | ɾ | | ɽ | | | | | |
| 擦音 | ɸ β | f v | θ ð | s z | ʃ ʒ | ʂ ʐ | ç ʝ | x ɣ | χ ʁ | ħ ʕ | h ɦ |
| 边擦音 | | | | ɬ ɮ | | | | | | | |
| 近音 | | ʋ | | ɹ | | ɻ | j | ɰ | | | |
| 边近音 | | | | l | | ɭ | ʎ | ʟ | | | |

符号成对出现时,右侧符号代表带声音。阴影处表示发音被判断为不可能。

**辅音(非肺气流)**

| 吸气音 | | 带声内破音 | | 挤喉音 | |
|---|---|---|---|---|---|
| ʘ | 双唇音 | ɓ | 双唇音 | ʼ | 如: |
| ǀ | 齿音 | ɗ | 齿音/齿龈音 | pʼ | 双唇音 |
| ǃ | 齿音(后)音 | ʄ | 硬腭音 | tʼ | 齿音/齿龈音 |
| ǂ | 腭龈音 | ɠ | 软腭音 | kʼ | 软腭音 |
| ǁ | 齿龈边音 | ʛ | 小舌音 | sʼ | 齿龈擦音 |

**其他符号**

| ʍ | 不带声唇软腭擦音 | | ɕ ʑ | 齿龈硬腭擦音 |
|---|---|---|---|---|
| w | 带声唇软腭通音 | | ɺ | 带声齿龈边闪音 |
| ɥ | 带声唇硬腭通音 | | ɧ | 同时发 ʃ 和 x |
| ʜ | 不带声会厌擦音 | | | |
| ʢ | 带声会厌擦音 | | | |
| ʡ | 会厌破裂音 | | | |

塞擦音和双重发音必要时可以表示为两个符号用连弧连接。k͡p  t͡s

**元音**

| | 前 | 央 | 后 |
|---|---|---|---|
| 闭 | i y | ɨ ʉ | ɯ u |
| 闭中 | e ø | ɘ ɵ | ɤ o |
| 开中 | ɛ œ | ɜ ɞ | ʌ ɔ |
| 开 | a ɶ | | ɑ ɒ |

(ɪ ʏ / ʊ / ə / ɐ / æ 为图中间符号)

符号成对出现时,右侧符号代表圆唇元音。

**超音段**

| ˈ | 主重音 | |
|---|---|---|
| ˌ | 次重音 | ˌfoʊnəˈtɪʃən |
| ː | 长 | eː |
| ˑ | 半长 | eˑ |
| ̆ | 特短 | ĕ |
| \| | 次(音步)群 | |
| ‖ | 主(语调)群 | |
| . | 音节间断 | ɹi.ækt |
| ‿ | 连系(无间断) | |

**变音符** 下拉符号可将变音符放在符号上面,如 ŋ̊

| ̥ | 不带声 | n̥ d̥ | ̤ | 呼气带声 | b̤ a̤ | ̪ | 齿 | t̪ d̪ |
|---|---|---|---|---|---|---|---|---|
| ̬ | 带声 | s̬ t̬ | ̰ | 嘎吱带声 | b̰ a̰ | ̺ | 舌尖 | t̺ d̺ |
| ʰ | 送气 | tʰ dʰ | ̼ | 舌唇 | t̼ d̼ | ̻ | 舌叶 | t̻ d̻ |
| ̹ | 更圆 | ɔ̹ | ʷ | 唇化 | tʷ dʷ | ̃ | 鼻化 | ẽ |
| ̜ | 更展 | ɔ̜ | ʲ | 硬腭化 | tʲ dʲ | ⁿ | 鼻除阻 | dⁿ |
| ̟ | 较前 | u̟ | ˠ | 软腭化 | tˠ dˠ | ˡ | 边除阻 | dˡ |
| ̠ | 较后 | e̠ | ˤ | 咽化 | tˤ dˤ | ̚ | 无可闻除阻 | d̚ |
| ̈ | 央化 | ë | ̴ | 软腭化或咽化 | ɫ | | | |
| ̽ | 中央化 | ě | ̝ | 升高 | e̝ (ɹ̝ =带声齿音擦音) | | | |
| ̩ | 成音节 | n̩ | ̞ | 降低 | e̞ (β̞ =带声双唇擦音) | | | |
| ̯ | 非音节 | e̯ | ̘ | 舌根前伸 | e̘ | | | |
| ˞ | 儿化 | ɚ a˞ | ̙ | 舌根后缩 | e̙ | | | |

**声调和词重读**

| 平调 | | | 曲拱调 | | |
|---|---|---|---|---|---|
| e̋ 或 ˥ | 特高 | | ě 或 ˩˥ | 升 | |
| é ˦ | 高 | | ê ˥˩ | 降 | |
| ē ˧ | 中 | | e᷄ ˧˥ | 高升 | |
| è ˨ | 低 | | e᷅ ˩˧ | 低升 | |
| ȅ ˩ | 特低 | | e᷈ | 升降 | |
| ↓ | 降阶 | | ↗ | 整体升 | |
| ↑ | 升阶 | | ↘ | 整体降 | |

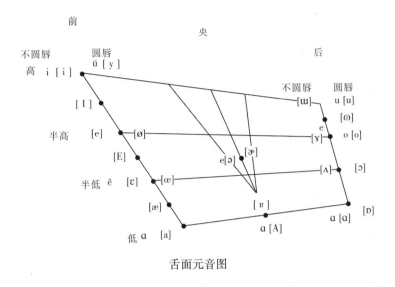

舌面元音图

舌面元音图中以[a]、[ɑ]、[i]、[u]四个音为极点构成一个不规则四边形,左右两条线表示舌位的前后,上下两条线表示舌位的高低,竖线左右表示嘴唇的圆展,左侧为展唇,右侧为圆唇。而把从[i]到[a],从[u]到[ɑ]三等分,又可以得到[e]、[ɛ]、[o]、[ɔ]四个元音。

我们依次描写这八个基本元音:

[i]前高不圆唇元音

北京话　mi　米　　英语　big[big]　大　　蒙古话　pi　我

[e]前半高不圆唇元音

成都话　khe　客　　英语　bed[bed]　床　　朝鲜语　pe　粗布

[ɛ]前半低不圆唇元音

上海话　sɛ　色　　英语　hair[hɛr]　头发

[a]前低不圆唇元音

北京话　an　安　　苗语(湘西)　ta⁵⁴　真

[ɑ]后低不圆唇元音

上海话　kaka　家家　　英语　guitar[giːtɑː]　吉他　　土族语　ɑs　牲畜

[ɔ]后半低圆唇元音

安化语　lɔ　老　　英语　dog[dɔg]　狗　　英语　sock[sɔk]　短袜

[o]后半高圆唇元音

武昌话　koko　哥哥　　土族语　modo　裤子

[u]后高圆唇元音

北京话　bugu　布谷　　英语　book[buk]　书

(2)次高次低元音;央、中元音

[I]前次高不圆唇元音

[æ]前次低不圆唇元音

[ə]不圆唇央元音

2.舌尖元音和卷舌元音

由舌尖起主要作用形成的元音就是舌尖元音。由舌尖、舌面同时起作用形成的音就是卷舌元音。

(1)舌尖元音又分为舌尖前元音和舌尖后元音

舌尖前元音[ɿ][ʮ]。发前一个音时舌尖向前上抬,接近上齿龈前部,如汉语普通话中的资[tsɿ]、疵[ts'ɿ]、思[sɿ]。发后一个音时,只需把嘴唇变圆,其他部位不变,如宁波话的书[sʮ]

舌尖后元音[ʅ][ʯ]。发前一个音时舌尖向上翘起,靠近上齿龈后部、硬腭前部,比如汉语普通话中的知[tʂʅ]、吃[tʂ'ʅ]、狮[ʂʅ]。发后一个音,其他部位不变,把嘴唇变圆,如湖北应山话须[ʂʯ]。

(2)卷舌元音

卷舌元音[ər],舌面抬平、舌尖同时向硬腭方向翘起。舌面元音多是由一个舌面元音加上一个[r]来标写,如普通话中的儿[ər],花儿 huār。

(二)辅　音

从心理属性上看,有一类和元音相对的音素,不如元音响亮,也不那么悦耳,这一类音素,气流要克服发音器官的某一阻碍才能发出音来,这就是辅音。同时,气流要克服发音器官的某一阻碍,这也是所有辅音发音时的共性。语音学上,我们把气流受到阻碍的这个位置称为发音部位;把形成阻碍、排除阻碍的方式,气流的强弱,声带的振动与否称为发音方法。辅音的不同就是由发音位置和发音方法的不同造成的。分别依据发音部位和发音方法,我们可以对辅音进行分类。

1.按发音部位分类

发音部位是指气流在发音器官中形成阻碍和克服阻碍的部位,因此根据发音部位可以把辅音分成十三类:

(1)双唇音:上下唇紧闭形成阻碍,然后除去阻碍而发出的音,如[p]、[p']、[m]。

(2)唇齿音:上齿和下唇的内侧接近而形成阻碍发出的音,如[f]、[v]。

(3)齿间音:舌尖抵在上下齿之间而发出的音,如[θ][tð]。

(4)舌尖前音:舌尖抵住上齿背发出的音,如[ts]、[ts']、[s]。

(5)舌尖中音:舌尖抵住上齿龈发出的音,如[t]、[t']、[n]、[l]。

(6)舌尖后音:舌尖抵住上齿龈后部发出的音,如[tʂ]、[tʂʻ]、[ʂ]、[ʐ]。

(7)舌叶音:舌面与前腭节制气流发出的音,如英语中的 chinese[tʃaɪˈniz]和 shot[ʃɔt]中的[tʃ]、[ʃ]。

(8)舌面前音:舌面前部与中腭作用发出的音,如[tɕ]、[tɕʻ]、[ɕ]。

(9)舌面中音:舌面中部和软腭作用发出的音,如英语 year[jəː]中的[j]。

(10)舌面后音:舌根和软腭成阻再除阻发出的音,如[k]、[kʻ]、[x]。

(11)小舌音:小舌和舌面后作用发出的音,如[R]。

(12)喉壁音:喉头紧缩,舌根往后接近喉壁,摩擦气流发出的音,如[ʔ]

(13)喉门音:声门先紧闭再突然打开,如[h]。

2.按发音方法分类

辅音的发音方法是指气流在发音器官内形成阻碍和克服阻碍的方式,分为四个方面:

(1)清与浊:根据发音时声带是否颤动,可以分为清音和浊音两类。声带不颤动的叫清音,颤动的叫浊音。现代汉语语音中浊辅音只有[m]、[n]、[ŋ]、[l]、[ʐ],其他都是清辅音。

(2)送气与不送气:发音部位除阻后,气门有很强的气流呼出的叫送气音,如[pʻ]、[tʻ]、[kʻ]。气流比较弱的叫不送气音,如[p]、[t]、[k]。一般来说,因为只有塞音和塞擦音有完全阻塞的成阻阶段,所以只有塞音和塞擦音有送气和不送气的区别。

(3)塞与擦:根据气流除阻的方式的不同,可分为塞音与擦音。发塞音时气流在发音器官内成阻和持阻时被完全阻塞,先是两个发音部位紧密接触,然后突然打开闭塞,受阻的气流爆发而出,因此塞音又叫爆破音,如[p]、[t]、[k]。发擦音时两个发音部位靠近而形成一条缝隙,气流从缝隙中擦挤而出,如[f]、[v]。所谓的塞擦音就是把塞与擦结合起来,先塞后擦而发出的音,如[ts]、[tsʻ]、[tʂ]、[tʂ]、[tɕ]、[tɕʻ]。

(4)口与鼻:根据气流是从口腔还是鼻腔而出,可分为口音与鼻音。口音如[s]、[t],鼻音如[m]、[n]。

因此,辅音一般按发音方法分为:塞音、擦音、塞擦音、边擦音、鼻音、边音、颤音、闪音。

任何一个辅音的描写,都必须结合发音方法和发音部位。例如[p]的发音特征就是双唇不送气清塞音,[t]的发音特征是舌尖中不送气清塞音。反过来,我们只要知道了某一个辅音的发音部位和发音方法,就能够确定这个辅音并发出它。比如知道了舌尖前音、不送气音、清音、塞擦音这四个特征,就能够确定这是辅音[ts]。

(三)元音和辅音的区别

从发音角度看,元音和辅音的主要区别是:

第一,气流是否受阻。发元音时,气流带动声带振动,并且在口腔中不受阻碍;而发辅音时,气流要克服发音器官某个部位受到的阻碍,只有克服了这种阻碍才能发出音来。气流是否受阻,这是元音和辅音最主要的区别。

第二,肌肉紧张程度不同。发元音时,发音器官的各个部位保持均衡紧张;而发辅音时,只有形成阻碍的那部分器官是紧张的。

第三,气流强弱不同。发元音时,气流呼出畅通无阻,因而气流较弱;而发辅音时,呼出的气流要克服某种阻碍才能通过,因而气流是更强的。

第四,声带振动情况有差别。发元音时,声门紧闭,气流从声门缝隙中挤出,声带振动发声。发辅音时,浊辅音要振动声带,清辅音不振动声带。

第五,响亮度有区别。发元音时,因为声带振动和共鸣腔的共同作用,声音响亮而且可以延长。辅音是在克服了阻碍的一瞬间发出的,因此不如元音响亮,而且大多数辅音也不能延长。

# 第四节　音　位

从社会功能的角度分析语音,得出的最小单位就是音位。研究语言中音位系统的学科是音位学。要理解"音位",必须先搞清"语言的声音"和"言语的声音"的区别。在现实的语言交际中,每一个人说话都有自己的特点,我们把每个人说出的话语的声音叫作"言语的声音"。不同人的嗓音特点、发音习惯等都是不一样的,因此,"言语的声音"是具体特定的。然而,我们之所以可以进行言语的交流,是因为我们共同认同这不同之中的相同之处,那就是我们可以把声音和意义结合起来,这样就可以进行交际了,这种声音的共性,就是我们说的"语言的声音"。这实际上和我们已经了解的语言和言语之间的关系是一致的,"语言的声音"存在于"言语的声音"当中。我们从"言语的声音"入手,最终的研究对象是"语言的声音"。

音位是从社会功能角度划分出来的具有区别意义作用的语音单位。音位的这种区别意义的作用叫作"辨义功能"。音位是具有辨义功能的最小的语音单位,所谓"最小的",是指从中不能再切分出更小的语音单位了。音位是由一组彼此的差别没有辨义作用而音感上又相似的音素而概括成的音类;音位是从辨义功能的角度划分出来的语音单位,这种划分只关注那些与意义的区别有关的语音差别,而对那些与意义的区别无关的音质上的细微差别则可以忽略不计。

## 一、音位和音位变体

我们知道,从自然属性划分出来的语音的最小单位是音素。从物理属性的角度看,人类可以发出的音素是无穷的,每种语言只使用了其中的一部分。虽然在实际的语言运用过程中,未被选用的音素也会出现,但是并不会影响人们对语言的理解和交流,原因在于这些音素在语言中的地位是不相同的。音素和音素间的差别有两种不同性质:一种差别是能够区别语素的语音形式和意义,例如汉语普通话中两个语音 dà(大)和 tà(踏)的区别,是由辅音音素的不同造成的,这种差别叫作对立性差别。判断两个音素是否对立,要找一个语音位置,然后把这两个音素放这个位置上,看是否能产生两个不同的词 ,如果可以,那么这两个音素就是对立的。音素和音素间的另一种差别是不区别语素,也不区别词的形式和意义,如汉语普通话中的 tā(她)、xiā(虾)、diān(颠)、gāng(刚)四个音节中的 α 的实际发音都是不一样的,用国际音标记录下来分别是[A][a][æ][ɑ],但是它们在汉语普通话中没有区别意义的作用,这种差别叫作非对立性差别。这几个音素互补而且语音相似,那么我们就可以把它们归并为一个音位。音位是一类音的概括形式,这些被概括在一类音里的一个个具体的音,就叫作音位变体。比如我们前面例子中的[A][a][æ][ɑ]就是/a/音位的变体。

因此,音位是非对立性区别的若干音的概括,而音位变体则是音位的具体表现形式,我们一般几个音位变体中选取一个符号来做音位的标记,用/ /表示。至于具体选择哪一个符号,是约定俗成的。音位和音位变体之间的关系,可以理解为一个类别和它的成员间的关系,一个类别是由它的成员组成的,成员的数目可以是不确定的。

每种语言都有自己的音位系统,不同的语言,音位系统不同,比如汉语中的元音音位[y],在英语、俄语中就没有;英语和俄语中的[d]音位,在汉语中没有。另外,不同语言中或许有共同的音素,但不一定都做音位。所以,音位是属于一定语言的,离开了具体的语言就无法确定一个音是不是音位。

音位理论的基本原理是根据音素是否具有辨义功能,可以将具体语言或方言里数目繁多的语素归纳为一套为数有限的音位,从而使语音系统的结构特征得以呈现。

## 二、音质音位和非音质音位

音位可以分为音质音位和非音质音位(也可称为音段音位和超音段音位)。

(一)音质音位(音段音位)

音素是从音质角度切分出的最小单位。以音素为材料,从音质角度进行分析得出的音位叫作音质音位。每个音质音位内部的各个音位变体之间音质接近,也没有区别词性和词义的作用。如[A][a][æ][ɑ]就是/a/。而不同音质音位之间可以区别意义,音质也不同。这些音位内部可以进行线性排列,因此又叫音段音位。

(二)非音质音位(超音段音位)

在音质音位相同的条件下,音高、音长、音强也可能具有区别意义的作用,这种有区别意义作用的音高、音长、音强就叫作非音质音位。

语言里的音节都具有一定的音高,有些语言就是靠音高的变化来区别意义,这些有区别意义作用的音高变化就是声调,由声调充当的非音质音位叫调位。汉语就是声调语言,不同方言的声调情况不一样,北京话有四个调位,上海话有五个调位,广州话有九个调位。普通话有四个声调,同样的音质音位,因为搭配不同的声调而具有了区别意义的作用,比如"巴""拔""把""坝"四个词,音质音位都是一样的,所不同的正是它们各自的声调。由此,我们知道,声调具有区别意义的作用,也应该看成是音位。当然,调位也存在变体的情况,比如汉语普通话中的上声,在不同情况下会出现变体。英语、日语、俄语等不属于声调语言,音位、音高不起区别词形和意义的作用。

音强是相连的音节中某个音节发音突出的现象,这样使得音节具有区别词形的作用,成为重位,表现为词重音。比如英语中的 instinct [in'stiŋkt](活跃的)和 instinct ['instiŋkt](本能)就是靠重音来区别的。语言学中把这种能区别词的语音形式的重音叫作重位。

音长作用于一定的音节,使之具有区别词形和意义的作用,称为时位。比如日语中的おじいさん(爷爷)和おじさん(叔叔)。汉语中没有时位,因为汉语音节中元音没有长短音的区别。

调位、重位、时位都是非音质音位,其数目和包含的具体内容在各种语言或方言中是不一样的。

## 三、音位的区别特征

音位和音位之间彼此对立,能够区别词的语音形式,从而区别意义。音位之间能够形成对立并区别意义,一定是音位在语音特征上有差别。比如英语中的 tot(幼儿)和 dot(点)是靠 / t / 和 / d / 来区别意义的, / t / 和 / d / 的唯一区别就是前者送气和而后者不送气,送气与不送气这两个语音特征使 / t / 和 / d / 形成对立,从而把这两个音位区别开来。再比如,汉语普通话中的两个音节 mɑi(卖)和 dɑi(代)是靠 / m / 和 / t / 来区别的, / m / 和 / t / 的不同是靠双唇或舌尖、鼻音或塞音来区别的。我们把这些能够把音位区别开来的语音特征叫作区别特征。音位之间的对立表现在一对或两对语音特征上,并不是在所有语音特征上。

我们研究一个音位的区别特征,需要在音系中把这个音位和其他音位进行对比。我们以汉语普通话为例:

| / p / | 双唇 | 塞音 | 清音 | 不送气音 |
| / pʻ / | 双唇 | 塞音 | 清音 | 送气音 |
| / m / | 双唇 | 鼻音 | | |
| / t / | 舌尖 | 塞音 | 清音 | 不送气音 |
| / k / | 舌根 | 塞音 | 清音 | 不送气音 |

如果我们以 / p / 为比较基点,它与 / pʻ / 形成对立是因为一个是送气音一个是不送气音;与 / m / 形成对立是因为一个是塞音一个是鼻音;与 / t / 形成对立是因为一个是双唇音一个是舌尖音;与 / k / 形成对立是因为一个是舌尖音一个是舌根音。经过这样的比较,我们可以归纳出 / p / 的区别特征是双唇、塞、清、不送气, / pʻ / 的区别特征是双唇、塞音、清音、送气, / m / 的区别特征是双唇、鼻, / t / 的区别特征是舌尖、塞、清、不送气, / k / 的区别特征是舌根、塞、清、不送气。所以,我们还可以说,音位是区别特征的总和。

音位的区别特征可以从发音方面来确定,以上我们的比较就是从发音上来决定的,同时,还可以从音响方面来决定,这就要依据声谱的图形特点来决定。

人类语言中的音素是很多的,国际音标记录语音的符号有 200 个左右,区分这些音素的语音特征有几十个。因为不是所有的语音特征都是区别特征,所以人类语言中的区别特征要比语音特征少得多。

从发音特征的角度,汉语普通话的音位系统大体可以用 9 对区别特征加以描写,分别是:有阻/无阻;鼻音/口音;唇音/舌音;舌尖/舌面;塞/擦;送气/不送气;前/后;高/低;圆/展。

# 第五节　语音组合

## 一、音　节

人们在说话时总是伴随着发音器官肌肉的松紧变化,在听感上形成了一个个的语音片段,这种在听感上最容易感觉到的最小语音片段就是音节,音节也是音位组合的最小结构单位。汉语中,通常一个汉字就对应一个音节,日语中也大多是一个假名代表一个音节。一个音节既可以由若干个音质音位构成,也可以只由一个音质音位构成。

事实上,各种语言的音节结构都有自己的特点,很难找到一种适用于各种语言通用的划分音节的方法。比如俄语中 pyka(手)的音节划分是 py-ka,而词的形态结构划分是 pyk-a。音节的划分不完全与意义相联系,这是印欧语系的特点。而在东方的部分语言中,比如汉语、泰语等,这些语言中的词是由音节构成的,绝大多数音节和一定的意义相联系,在这些语言中,音节不仅是重要的语音单位,也是词的表现形式之一。

## 二、音节的种类

### (一)开音节和闭音节

以元音结尾的音节叫开音节,比如汉语中的 ma(妈),英语中的 he(他)。

以辅音结尾的音节叫闭音节,比如汉语中的 tan(摊),英语中的 like(喜欢)。

汉语普通话音节的一般特点是:开音节占大多数;没有辅音连缀的情况;音节中必须出现元音;有声调。英语音节的一般特点是:闭音节占大多数;有辅音连缀的情况;响亮的辅音也可构成音节;有重音但没有声调。通过这组特点的比较,我们知道,不同语言的音节结构是不同的,各有自身的特点。

我们通过了解一种语言的音节结构和特点,可以进一步认识这种语言的结构特点和规律。

（二）复元音和复辅音

在一个音节内部，元音和元音组合起来构成了复元音。两个元音结合的叫二合元音，三个元音结合的叫三合元音。

与单元音相比，从发音方式看，复元音的音质变化是连续不断的，比如我们发汉语普通话中的 ai 这个复元音，并不是先发完 a 再发 i，发音过程是舌位逐渐抬高，口腔开合度逐渐变小，音质也随之逐渐发生变化，这个过程中出现了很多过渡音，既非 a 也非 i。可以想象，如果没有这些过渡音，先发完 a 再发 i，就变成了两个音节，而不是复元音了。

与单元音相比，从发音响亮度看，复元音发音时，其中各个元音的音长和音强不是完全相等的，比如前面例子中的 ai，听感上我们可以辨别，a 比 i 要响亮得多。

复辅音是指在同一音节内同处在起音和收音位置上的辅音的组合。复辅音在印欧语系的语言里很常见。与复元音不同的是，复辅音中的各个辅音都有自己的发音过程，音质变化有明显界限，不像复元音发音时有音质的连续变化。汉语、日语等没有复辅音。

## 三、语流音变

语言中的每一个词语都有一个固定的读音，但有些词单独念时是一种读法，在一连串的语流中，其读音要发生相对的变化，这种变化叫作语流音变。这种变化有时来自前后音的影响，有时是受到说话高低、快慢的影响。

语流音变只是在语流中发生的变化，或者说是在言语交际时才发生的，它并不会改变这个音本来的或单独使用时的读音，也不会改变一个语言单位在一段时间内的相对稳定的读音。这种现象非常普遍，各种语言中都有。但是由于语音体系不同，语流音变的具体情况也是不同的。归纳起来，语流音变主要有以下几种。

（一）同 化

原来两个不相同的音在组合时相互影响，变得相同或部分相同，这种变化就是"同化"。如英语的 ribbon（带子）本读作 ['ribn]，但有人读作 ['ribm]，舌尖音 [n] 被唇音 [b] 同化为唇音 [m]；bacon（咸肉）本读作 ['beikn]，常读作 ['beikŋ]，舌尖音 [n] 被舌面音 [k] 同化为舌面后音 [ŋ]。又如德语 haben（有）本读作 ['haːbn]，但常被读成 ['haːbm]，舌尖音 [n] 被唇音 [b] 同化为唇音 [m]。现代汉语普通话中"兜肚" [tou$^{55}$tu$^{214}$]，在北京口语里读作 [tou$^{55}$tou$^3$]，"山门" [ʂan$^{55}$mən$^{35}$] 读作 [ʂam$^{35}$mən$^{35}$]。

（二）异　化

为了避免发音的拗口，将原本相同或相近的音在语流中变为不相同或不相近的音，这种变化叫语音的"异化"。如现代汉语普通话中两个上声相连，前一个上声调值变得接近35。"想起"［çiaŋ²¹⁴tç'i²¹⁴］变作［çiaŋ³⁵tç'i²¹⁴］。在拉丁语中，l 和 r 是比较难发的音，如果音节前后有两个 r，有的在英语里异化成了 l 和 r。例如 turtle（甲鱼）来自 turtur，marble（大理石）来自 marmor（这两个词的后面的 r 异化为 l，第二个词的第二个 m 又异化为 b）。

（三）弱　化

在语流中，有的发音用力减少，音强减弱，音程缩短，引起音质改变，不那么清晰，这种变化就叫"弱化"。弱化可能表现在辅音上，也可表现在元音或声调上。如希腊语字母 β 在古代读作［b］，在现代读作［v］，是辅音弱化的结果。北京话"回来"［xui lɛ］（"来"［lai］弱化为［lɛ］）；"笑话"［çiao xuə］（"话"［xua］弱化为［xuə］）；"打扮"［ta pən］（"扮"［pan］弱化为［pən］）。这些都是元音的弱化。又如，"尾巴"［wei²¹⁴pa⁵⁵］在口语中弱读为［wei²¹⁴ba］，这是声调和辅音的同时弱化。

（四）脱　落

一连串音连续发出时，有时会发生音素脱落的情况。脱落往往是弱化的结果。比方北京话的"你们"［ni mən］常发成［nim］，"我们"［womən］常发成［wom］。英语 cupboard（碗橱）［'kʌpbəd］常读作［'kʌbəd］，castle（城堡）［kaːstl］常读作［kaːsl］，kindness（亲切）［'kaindnis］常读作［'kainnis］，各失落一个辅音。

（五）增　音

有些音连用时增加了一个原来没有的音。增音有时是为了方便，避免发音部位过快变化。如英语 dreamt（做梦—过去时），本读作［dremt］，但常被读成［drempt］，［p］出现在［m］［t］之间。这是因为发完［m］音之后应该把发音部位和方法同时调整到［t］的发音部位和方法，但当双唇还没有来得及分开的时候，软腭已上举闭住气流到鼻腔的通路，就产生了一个双唇塞音，这个双唇塞音可能是［b］，也可能是［p］，不过因为后面［t］的影响，发完［m］以后，声带就停止颤动，所以增加的音是［p］。汉语普通话中语气词"啊"［A］跟前面音节连读时会随着前面韵尾的不同而增加一个相同部位的音，如"美啊"读成［mei²¹⁴ia⁴］，增［i］音，［A］因同化移前成［a］。

## (六)换　位

在语流中,有的音可以互换位置。有时是为了在发音时避免两个相似音过分接近,使其中一个和别的音调换位置。如北京话"言语一声"[iɛnjy i ʂɤŋ]常常说成[yɛnji i ʂɤ],其中"言语"一词的[i][y]换位。有时存在偶然的换位,这是说话人紧张造成的,如英语 well-oiled bicycle(上好油的脚踏车)说成 well-boiled icicle(煮沸过的冰柱子)等。

## (七)合　音

两个音或两个音节在语流中合成一个音或一个音节的现象叫合音。如北京话中"两个"[liaŋ kə]读作[lia²¹⁴],文字上写作"俩";"三个"[san kə]读作[sa⁵⁵],文字上写作"仨";"不用"[pu³⁵ iuŋ⁵¹]读作"甭"[pəŋ³⁵]。

以上就是几种语流音变的简介,在实际的语流中,往往不止一种变化,而是多种变化一起发生。

## 思考与练习

一、填空题

1.从物理属性看,语音具有_____、_____、_____、_____四个要素。

2.音素可以分为_____和_____两大类,其区别的根本点是发音时气流在口腔中是否_____。

3.音位是从_____角度划分出来的具有_____作用的语音单位。

二、名词解释

1.音素

2.音标

3.元音

4.辅音

5.音位

6.音位变体

7.语流音变

三、简答题

1.音高和音强在汉语中具有区别意义的作用吗？请举例说明。

2.请说明音位和音位变体之间的关系。

3.请说明音位与音素的区别。

4.简要回答语音的本质属性表现在哪些方面。

## 【原典阅读】

# 1.语音的物理成素
### 赵元任

言语学中所论的语音同语音的单位(叫音素)都不是简单的现象,例如取一个 m 音,通常以为是一个简单不能再分析的音素,其实这 m 的为物是很复杂的。第一:发生 m 音所用的生理作用,就是把唇闭起来,把咽头(velum)垂下,让鼻腔通气,把声带的口缩小,让肺中气出来鼓动声带成乐音。这些作用的生理作用与其生出的各部的触觉都是 m 的生理成素,这是生理的语音学所应研究的。第二:m 音在听的人的耳朵里所发生的反应也是 m 音的一部分。m 音虽似简单,但是因为成年人听起各种声音来(尤其言语的声音)没有不带出许多联想的,所以在听者耳朵里收了 m 音进去同时又发生唇喉等部的发音的感觉或意象。这类联想的成分在实用言语的时候占很重要的地位。——言语的义意完全是语言的连带作用;但是要用科学的方法研究语音不能不单就发出来的声音追根的分析,换言之,就是从纯粹物的观点分析语音。我并不是说作了这种研究就好了,就可了事了,并不是说各种联想作用不用研究,或不要紧,不过就是说语音的物理成素的研究也是要紧的就是了。

科学的语音学从生理的语音学始,这不过是近百年以内的事,后来实验的语音渐兴,但也不过是以发音的生理作用,作实验的材料。至于物理的语音学(或叫声学的语音学)到近年来才有东一个人西两个人稍微研究研究,所以本篇所论的没有什么成绩可言,不过是把物理的常识应用到语音现象上看有些什么问题发生就是了。

平常论语音的常以为天下的语言不外乎元音(vowel)辅音(consonants)两个成素,没有第三种成素。还有人这么辩:说你随便说一句哪国的话,里头一个一个音不是辅音就是元音,不是元音就是辅音,所以不会有别的。这话非常不通,同样我能说明天下的人只能做两样事情,因为不是醒着就是睡着,不是睡着就是醒着,决不会有第三种事情。其实醒不光是醒,同时又做许多别的事情,睡也不光是睡,同时也会呼吸,循环做梦等等。同样,语音的成素也有种种同时并存的各方面。大旨说起来,一个语音有以下的音学的成素:

①时间的长度,

②强度,

③基本音高(pitch of fundanental),

④陪音(或附音)(overtones),

⑤噪音(noice)。

这几种成素不恰恰和语音学的名词相当,这是因为语音学中一向用的观念不是以物理学的观念发生的,所以不同物理的分析一一相当。现在举些例来解释解释:

1.时间的长度。 凡音都有长度,这是很明白的。例如在中国南方,入声字音同别种字音不同点之一就是入声最短。在英文 horrid 的 o 比 nor 的 o 短。misstate 的 ss 比 missing 的 ss 长一倍。

2. 强度。 语音的物理的强度同主观的语音强度大致并行,但不恰恰并行,这是什么缘故呢?因为主观的强度同发音时所用的劲有联想关系,听者听见了一个音,晓得是要用劲的,这音就是不很响也觉得很响。反之,不大用劲的虽响,也会估量的太轻(以为不响)。例如用一样大劲读乌、阿两音,若是给一个没有物理或心理实验的训练的人听,就好像一样响似的,但照这么读的乌、阿两音,后者比前者可听得远,可见得后者比前者物理的强度大。最明白的例就是有的音素在语音上是要紧的音素,在物理方面是没有声音,或是零度的强度,而听者觉得是有强度的。例如广东入声字用不破裂的 p⌐、t⌐、k⌐收声,这三个东西在语音学里也叫做"音",其实是停止声音的作用。其所以听得出 ip、it、ik 的不同,乃是因为 i 音将完时变到 p 音的片刻的流音、变到 t 的流音与变到 k 的流音,三者不同,因此,听得出区别来。在英文 sharp pain coattail 的 tt,thick coat 的 kc,都是一种延长的静止作用,在物理方面完全是一个常时间的零强度,但发音者同听者的心理生理方面都是有强度的长辅音,可以算是一种"此时无声胜有声"的作用。

3. 基本音高。 语音当中有两大部,一部是带音的,就是发音时声带近关闭的位置,被肺中空气鼓动成乐音的,一部是不带音的,就是(a)声带半开或大开,不颤动成乐音,或(b)全闭也不颤动。平常用语音时能除打喳喳(whisper)全不用带音的语音外,大半总是带音的。在带音的音,声带的颤动的每秒次数(frequency)就定这音的音高。因为语音除声带颤动的音高外,还有别种的附属的音高,所以把这主要的音高特名为基本音高(pitch of the fundamental)。语音的基本音高在多数欧洲之语不占重要地位。(最古时有音高的辨别 pitch accent,现在已失去。)在中国言语,基本音高非常要紧。例如在重庆方音"衣"字音高高,"移"字音高低。但中国言语的声调,多数是音高同时间的函数关系,所以这一层等到下节再论。

4. 陪音。 陪音有两种,一种是和谐的陪音,一种是不和谐的陪音。例如一根弦子全体颤动每秒 256 次,得物理中的 C 音,这是弦子的基本音高。这弦子同时又分为两截,每截又以 312 次数颤动发生 C 音。同时这弦子又分为三截四截等等,成各种和谐的陪音。乐器的各种音彩(法文叫 timbre),就是各种和谐陪音的成素的不同与比较的强度的不同的结果。科学实验所用的调音叉声音淡暗而无色彩,是因为最近于纯音的基本音,而几乎没有陪音的缘故。

不和谐的陪音在乐器里间或有之。例如钟类乐器的陪音同基本音,并不是 2、3、4、5 等简单比例,所以听起来不如别种乐器纯和。

陪音在语音上占最重要的部分。从前解释元音各音色的学说都是以和谐陪音来解释。例如"衣"是基本音加若干强度的二倍陪音,若干强度的三倍陪音,等等。"乌"音又是一种"处方"配的,"阿"音又是一种"处方"配的,等等。照这说每个元音的特性,全靠陪音及基本音的相对音高定的。假如读音的基本音高上下,陪音也跟着改变。这学说出来不久就被打破了。后来就有人说"衣"的所以为"衣"、"乌"的所以为"乌"等等,是因为喉腔鼻腔口腔等部的应声作用(resonance)生出固定绝对音高的陪音,与声带发生的基本音高完全没有和谐的关系(除碰巧成简单比例外)。例如把舌前提高近牙,咽头提上关闭鼻腔。这种位置就是一种"衣"音的应声器(resonator)。无论声带颤动作高(soprano)音低(bass)音,或呼气作打喳喳音(whisper),或吃气,或在嘴跟前戳破一个涎子泡,或放一个电火星,结果总是一种有"衣"音意味的应声。这学说似乎有一种难处,就是小孩子头小嘴小,怎么也能发大人甩的种种元音,这疑难有两层答法。第一,小孩子说话确不同大人一样。例如小孩子的"呵"音,因为口腔小,张到最大,还是只抵到大人读浅"呵"音的应声尺寸,因此小孩子叫"妈"字的音,不像大人说

"妈"音那么深而像法文 ma(=我的)音的浅"呵"音似的,仿佛在英文 mama 的 ma 同 mat 的 ma 之间。第二层解答是小孩到三四岁能说话的时候,身体虽小,初发音的发育已经长到这超过别部分的比例。据 Otto Jespersen 的统计,初会说话的小孩子的下颚骨长已经有大人的十分之七八了。

这学说出来过后,英国有一个姓 Lloyd① 的又做了些实验,他的说法是说舌前舌后(喉舌间)成两个应声腔(resonating chamber)。凡是元音的特性,都是这两个应声腔的绝对陪音音高所定的。更古怪的,就是这两个音高虽然合声带上的基本音高毫不相干,而多数听得清说得准的元音的两个陪音都成简单的比例。例如 i=39∶1,e=19∶1,a=5∶1,u=1∶1,这人的学说可惜还没有别人证明,但元音性质是靠陪音的绝对音高,而不靠陪音与声带基本音的相对的音高,这是已经可以倚靠得住的结果了。那么声带的基本音高既然和元音的性质全不相干,研究元音的时候最好是用打喳喳声音(whisper)作阿也厄衣恶乌迂等音,令观察者好听出要紧的陪音,使耳朵不为不相干的喉部基本音所搅混,这是现在研究语音常用的法子。

不和谐的陪音非但是元音的要素,而且也是辅音的要素。因为有许多辅音本没有基本音(不带音),所以不必"陪音"这种名词,径称作应声(resonance),显示得是有独立音高的声音。假如念ㄅ、ㄆ两音的纯音(换言之,就是不加元音作成ㄅㄜ、ㄆㄜ)让音后的破裂作用发出,就可以听得出ㄅ的破裂的音高高,ㄆ的音高低。这是因为读ㄅ时声带几乎全闭,应声的内孔从口到喉为止,读吐气的ㄆ时,声带大开,从口到肺管成很深的应声腔,所以应声很低。又如德文的[x,ʃ,s,ç]四音(例如在 ach、fisch、es、ich 的尾音)所成的应声差不多成 do、mi、sol、do¹ 四个音高的关系。(中国南方人读西方 ʃ 音太近 ç,这么着应声的音高太高,所以一定要读得很准,才能成那四音的调呢。)

5.噪音。 凡是声音,其颤动不成周期的,就是噪音。但自然界中同言语中所用的音,大多数都是乐音噪音相混的,看那一部分强(多)就算那一类。如上言不带音的辅音也有应声的音高,似乎是自相矛盾的话,其实所谓不带音,就是喉头声带不作乐音的意思,别部仍有微弱的乐音。噪音在语音中最要紧的功用就是变各种辅音的特性。例如空气在上下唇间生出时摩擦的噪音就成ɟ音,同时声带颤动就成 υ 音,舌根抵住上颚忽然放开让空气出来就成破裂的 k 音,声带大半开让空气出来在喉部生摩擦就成 h 音等,这类作用的大旨非常明白容易懂,细节不是非常复杂。现在辅音的物理比元音物理还幼稚得许多,所以这上头也没有话讲了。

以上说的,是从物理方面分析语音的各成素的。现在看这些成素复起来怎么成语音中种种现象。

1 同 2。 时间与强度。 说话句句不是一样响,音音不是一样响,这是谁都晓得的。句中的各大部的轻重大概都是看意思的轻重而定。至于一个词里的各音节(svllables)那个轻那个重,这现象甚复杂。除用历史的解释外大都无规则可言。所以在多数言语中(如英文、希腊文、北京话)初学者须硬记重音(stress accent)的所在。例如北京话"老子"两音节并重是人名,"老"重"子"轻是俗语的"父亲";"北京"两音节并重,但"南京"是"南"重"京"轻。英文 ′label,la′pel,′aspect,re′spect。

在一个音节里强度也大都以时间而变。如"哀"音[ai]前部比后部响,"鸦"音[ia]就是先轻后响。英文的 hear、tear、mere、dear 等等,在美国东北读[-iə]先强后轻(i 比 ə 也长些),在英国南部就先弱后强(i 轻短,几成 j 音)。

就是在一个单纯音的强度,也常有时变。例如北京赏声字纯音字如"椅"、"五"、"两"等

---
① R.J.Lloyd:Speech Sounds,Their Value and Causation.

等的强度,先半强,中强,最后轻。在英文 misspell 的 ss 是一个两头重、中部轻的长 s 音。

　　1、2 同 4。　时间、强度同陪音。　这三种相互的关系就发生音节的问题来 (syllabication)。无论那种言语都可分成一个一个的音节。这音节同音节的分界是拿什么做标准呢?在中国言语大概一个字是一个音节,但也有例外的。例如说"你去看戏阿?""阿"字说的很轻而且音含糊,近中性(ə)音,所以"戏阿"虽是两个汉字写的,可是只是一个音节[çiə],仿佛美国东北部 hear 读[hiə]似的。北京,南京,常把"儿"字加在字后成一个音节,例如"花儿"。但杭州也用"儿"字,却不同前字混成一个音节。这区域分析起来究竟是什么性质?这不是可以随口解答的问题。在英文平常分音节法有种种的规条,要晓得结果,查字典可以晓得每个词怎么分节,但这些规条完全是预备印书写字时在行底破字用的,一点也没有学理的根据,一点不能作客观的标准。

　　现在分音节最通用的科学的定义,就是拿听觉主观响度超作的最高点(maximum of auditory sonority)当一个音节的中心,拿一个最高点到下个最高点中间的最低点当音节的分界;用物理的话头,就是在强度时间的曲线上拿浪峰当音节的中心,拿浪谷当音节的分界。为什么要说分节的问题又包括陪音的成分呢?这是因为主观的强弱看音的色彩怎么样,各种陪音会有不同的主观的影响。在语言中辅音没有元音响,所以有多少主要元音就有多少音节,元音同元音当中的辅音恰恰分节的界限。在中国言语多数字音是辅音起头,元音或异高的辅音收尾,所以大多数是一个字一个音节。但音节不尽与元音辅音相当。假如一串辅音中有一个高出来独成一个浪峰的,也可以成一个音节。例如德文有许多-en 收尾的辞 e 母不读音;hatten[hat*n*]的音素是 h 轻,a 响,t 轻,n 又响,所以 n 又成一个音节的中心。在英文有人念"verv little"念的极含糊起来几乎就是 vrrll 三种音,但听起来系四个音节,因为一个长 r 当中轻两头重(成马鞍形强度曲线),一个长 l 也是如此。所以 very little 仿佛是"$_v$r,r l,l"似的,仍旧保存四音节四浪峰的条件。同样,有时连 s 音都能成音节的主音。例如 velocity 有人不读 i,把四个音读成[ vi-,′lɔ-s-tɪ](s 音特别读长而重,不同前 lo 并在一个浪峰里)。

　　非但一串辅音可另成音节,就是一串元音也不一定合成一音节的结合韵母。在各元音中主观的响度的次序大约是 a o e i y(迂)u。假如有 iai 三音相连,除非特别费力把 i、i 念响,a 音念轻,造成两峰一谷,才成两个音节。若是平平的念过去 iai 是天然的中部最响,所以成一个音节,例如崖字读"iai"。反之,aia 的天然曲线是马鞍式,所以是两个音节,例如"阿呀"两字读 aia。浪谷既然是音节的分界,那么怎么测定是在哪里呢?这个在各国言语各有不同的习惯。在英文的最低点大多数在辅音的正中,例如 lover 两个音节的分界也不在 *v* 前,也不在 *v* 后,乃在 *v* 中间。在德文、法文大多数在辅音前(但也有些例外的),例如 lie-ber,a-ma-teur。中国话除尾音 *n*、*ng*、*m* 同南方入声 *p*、*t*、*k* 外音节的分界都在辅音前(如德、法)。

　　1 同 3。　时间同基本音高。　言语的基本音高同时间所生的函数关系就成言语的腔调 (intonation)。没有一国言语没有特别的腔调。例如有经验的在老远听人说话,虽然一个字听不出,可听得出说的是法国话、德国话、英国话(英美腔调很不同)。腔调在古希腊语。近代东方几处之语,非洲之语,同中国之语,除表示口气外,又作字义的成素的功用。例如"衣移椅意一",因为腔调不同,表五个风马牛不相及的字。这种用法的腔调用在希腊语叫 pitch accent,用在东方言语叫声调(古名"声",北京四声、南京五声等等,英文 tones)。字调的性质是很明白的,不懂声学的说字调是高低、长短、强弱等等,都是隔靴搔痒。最主要的就是时间和音高的函数关系就是了。[①]

---

　　①　详细的讨论,见《科学》第七卷第九期著者的"声调的实验法"。

2 同 3。　　强度同基本音高。　　强度同音高没有必要的关系。但在自然的言语中,强高弱低比强低弱高的例多的多,换言之,音高同强度的统计的配合率(coefficient of statistical correlation)很高,因此在多数人心里中常常把高低同强弱相混。例如通常说"你声音太高,说低一点。"英语也有这习惯,说"He never, *raises* his voice, but always speaks in a *low* voice",应该说"He never speaks *louclly*, but always uses a *soft* voice",善做戏的,在戏台上说话有时说的像很小的声音(例如说情话),又须给全园几千人听得真,他的诀窍就是用低而响的声音说话,人听见音低,所以由统计的联想作用觉得声似轻似的。

结　语

声学在物理上的位置有一点偏僻,比不上元量论、相对论的那么占基本重要的位置,但在应用的物理上,声学非常要紧。大凡纯粹的科学有两种截然不同的应用法:——一种是应用到人生的物质的方面。例如算学应用到记油盐柴米,物理应用到汽车电话,这类应用是他们敬仰科学代表的人的所应许,而心中实在看不起的。还有一种应用的性质完全不同。就是譬如算学应用到天文物理,物理应用到种种别的学问,这是各种学问互相贯通的作用,而且是学问进步的一个大机会。我常遇见研究语音的,研究音乐的,研究听觉的心理的,同研究物理的声学的会谈起来(可惜很少会谈),往往所问非所答,所驳非所辩,名辞不正,说话不顺,我想这是近代学术分专科过甚的一个征状。读者晓得近几十年来物理学化学的最大的进步就是统一的进步胜过各科细节的进步,以致现在理化中心的学理的能一贯全部胜过无论哪一时代哪一门实验科学的状况。近来心理学同生物学的进步也有统一社会科学、人种学、言语学等的趋势和希望。但论起成绩来,还是希望多,趋势少,同物理还是望尘不及。本期虽然是数理化专期,但本报不是数理化专报,所以我用物理学学生同言语学学生的双名义作这一篇语音的物理成素。如前所说,这一门的研究的成绩还很幼稚。这篇文章是开开一扇门,请大家看看科学界中是有这么一门有兴趣而要紧的问题在那儿。

(节选自《赵元任语言学论文集》,商务印书馆,2001)

# 2. Types of Phonetic Change

## Leonard Bloomfield

21.1　Phonetic change, as defined in the last chapter, is a change in the habits of performing sound-producing movements. Strictly speaking, a change of this kind has no importance so long as it does not affect the phonemic system of the language; in fact, even with perfect records at our command, we should probably be unable to determine the exact point where a favoring of certain variants began to deserve the name of a historical change. At the time when speakers of English began to favor the variants with higher tongue-position of the vowels in words like *gōs* ' goose ' and *gēs* ' geese, ' the dislocation was entirely without significance. The speakers had no way of comparing the acoustic qualities of their vowels with the acoustic qualities of the vowels which their predecessors, a few generations back, had spoken in the same linguistic forms. When they heard a dialect which had not made the change, they may have noticed a difference, but they could have had no assurance as to how this difference had arisen. Phonetic change acquires significance only if it results in a change of the phonemic pattern. For instance, in the early modern period, the Middle

English vowel [ɛː], as in *sed* [sɛːd] 'seed', was raised until it coincided with the [eː] in *ges* [geːs] 'geese,' and this coincidence for all time changed the distribution of phonemes in the forms of the language. Again, the Middle English short [e] in a so-called "open" syllable—that is, before a single consonant followed by another vowel, as in *ete* ['ete] 'eat'—was lengthened and ultimately coincided with the long vowels just mentioned. Accordingly, the phonemic structure of modern English is different from that of medieval English. Our phoneme [ij] continues, among others, these three older phonemes; We may note, especially, that this coincidence has given rise to a number of homonyms.

Old and Middle English [eː] has changed to modern [ij] in *heel*, *steel*, *geese*, *queen*, *green*, *meet* (verb), *need*, *keep*.

Old and Middle English [ɛː] has changed to modern [ij] in *heal*, *meal* ('taking of food'), *cheese*, *leave*, *clean*, *lean* (adjective), *street*, *mead*('meadow'), *meet* (adjective).

Old and Middle English [e] has changed to modern [ij] in *steal*, *meal*('flour'), *weave*, *lean* (verb), *quean*, *speak*, *meat*, *mete*, *eat*, *mead* ('fermented drink').

On the other hand, the restriction of this last change to a limited phonetic position, has produced different phonemes in forms that used to have the same phoneme: the old [e] was lengthened in Middle English *were* <*weave*, but not in Middle English *weft*<*weft*. In the same way, a phonetic change which consisted of shortening long vowels before certain consonant-clusters has produced the difference of vowel between *meadow*(<Old English ['mɛːdwe]) and *mead*, or between *kept*(<Old English ['keːpte]) and *keep*.

A few hundred years ago, initial [k] was lost before [n]: the result was a change in the phonemic system, which included such features as the homonymy of *knot* and *not*, or of *knight* and *night*, and the alternation of[n-]and [-kn-] in *know*, *knowledge*: *acknowledge*.

21.2   The general direction of a great deal of sound-change is toward a simplification of the movements which make up the utterance of any given linguistie form. Thus, consonant-groups are often simplified. The Old English initial clusters [hr, hl, hn, kn, gn wr] have lost their initial consonants, as in Old English *hring>ring*, *hlēapan>leap*, *hnecca>neck*, *cnēow>knee*, *gnagan>gnaw*, *wringan>wring*. The loss of the[h] in these groups occurred in the later Middle Ages, that of the other consonants in early modem time; We do not know what new factor intervened at these times to destroy the clusters which for many centuries had been spoken without change. The[h]-clusters are still spoken in Icelandic; initial[kn] remains not only in the other Germanic languages (as, Dutch *knie* [kniː], German *knie*[kniː], Danish [knɛːʔ]Swedish[kneː]), but also in the English dialects of the Shetland and Orkney Islands and northeastern Scotland. The [gn]persists almost as widely—in English, more widely;[wr-], in the shape of [vr-], remains in Scandinavian, the northern part of the Dutch-German area, including standard Dutch, and in several scattered dialects of English. As long as we do not know what factors led to these changes at one time and place but not at another, we cannot claim to know the causes of the change—that is, to predict its occurrence. The greater simplicity of the favored variants is a permanent factor; it can offer no possibilities of correlation.

Simplificaition of final consonant-clusters is even more common. A Primitive Indo-European* [peːts] 'foot' (nominative singular)appears in Sanskrit as [paːt] and in Latin as pes[peːs]; a Primitive Indo-European* ['bheronts] 'bearing' (nominative singular masculine) appears in

Sanskrit as ['bharan], and in Latin as *ferens* ['ferens], later ['fere:s]. It is this type of change which leads to habits of permitted final(§ 8.4) and to morphologic alternations of the type described in § 13.9. Thus, a Primitive Central Algonquian *[axkehkwa] 'kettle,' phiral *[axkehkwakil, reflected in Fox [ahko:hkwa, ahko:hko:ki], loses its final vowel and part of the consonant-cluster in Cree [askihk, askihkwak] and in Menomini [ahke:h, ahke:hkuk], so that the plural-form in these languages contains a consonant-cluster that cannot be determined by inspection of the singular form. In English, final [ŋg] and [mb] have lost their stop; hence the contrast of *long*; *longer* [lɔŋ—'lɔŋgr], *climb* : *clamber* [klajm — 'klɛmbr].

Sometimes even single final consonants are weakened or disappear. In pre-Greek, final [t, d] were lost, as in Primitive Indo-European*[tod] 'that,' Sanskrit [tat]: Greek [to]; final [m] became [n], as in Primitive Indo-European *[ju'gom] 'yoke,' Sanskrit [ju'gam]: Greek [zu'gon]. The same changes seem to have occurred in pre-Germanic. Sometimes all final consonants are lost and there results a phonetic pattern in which every word ends in a vowel. This happened in pre-Slavic, witness forms like Old Bulgarian [to] 'that,' [igo] 'yoke.' It is a change of this sort that accounts for morphologic situations like that of Samoan(§ 13.9); a Samoan form like [inu] 'drink' is the descendant of an older*[inum], whose final consonant has been kept in Tagalog [i'num].

When changes of this sort appear at the beginning or, more often, at the end of words, we have to suppose that the languages in which they took place had, at the time, some phonetic marking of the word-unit. If there were any forms in which the beginning or the end of a word had not the characteristic initial or final pronunciation, these forms would not suffer the change, and would survive as sandhi-forms. Thus, in Middle English, final [n] was lost, as in *eten>ete* 'eat,' but the article an before vowels must have been pronounced as if it were part of the following word—that is, without the phonetic peculiarities of final position—so that the [n] in this case was not lost (like a final [n]), but preserved (like s medial [n]): *a house* but *an arm*. Latin *vōs* 'ye 'gives French *vous* [vu], but Latin phrase-types like *vōs amātis* 'ye love' are reflected in the French sandhi-habit of saying *vous aimez* [vuz eme]. Latin est 'he is' gave French *est* [ɛ] 'is,' but the phrase-type of Latin *est ille*? 'is that one?' appears in the French sandhi-form in *est-ill*[ɛti?] 'is he?' In the same way, a Primitive Indo-European*['bheronts] is reflected not only in Sanskrit ['bharan], above cited, but also in the Sanskrit habit of adding a sandhi [s] when the next word began with [t], as in ['bharās 'tatra] 'carrying there.'

21.3 Simplification of consonant-clusters is a frequent result of sound-change. Thus, a pre-Latin*['fulgmcn] 'flash (of light-ning)' gives a Latin *fulmen*. Here the group [lgm] was simplified by the change to [lm], but the group [lg], as in *fulgur* 'flash,' was not changed, and neither was the group [gm], as in *agmen* 'army.' In describing such changes, we speak of the conditions as *conditioning factors* (or *causing factors*) and say, for instance, that one of these was absent in cases like *fulgur* and *agmen*, where the [g], accordingly, was preserved. This form of speech is inaccurate, since the change was really one of [lgm] to [lm], and cases like *fulgur*, *agmen* are irrelevant, but it is often convenient to use these terms. The result of a conditioned change is often a morphologic alternation. Thus, in Latin, we have the suffix-*men* in *agere* 'to lead': *agmen* 'army' but *fulgere* 'to flash': *fulmen* 'flash (of lightning).' Similarly, pre-Latin [rkn] became [rn];

beside *pater*'father' :*paternus* ' paternal,' we have *quercus* ' oak ' : *quernus* 'oaken.'

Quite commonly, clusters change by way of *assimilation*: the position of the vocal organs for the production of one phoneme is altered to a position more like that of the other phoneme. The commoner case is *regressive* assimilation, change of the prior phoneme.

Thus, the voicing or unvoicing of a consonant is often altered into agreement with that of a following consonant; the [ s ] of *goose* and *house* has been voiced to [ z ] in the combinations *gosling*, *husband*. This, again, may give rise to morphologic alternations. In the history of Russian the loss of two short vowels (I shall transcribe them as [ ɪ ] and [ ʋ ]) produced consonant-clusters; in these clusters a stop or spirant was then assimilated, as to voicing, to s following stop or spirant. The old forms can be seen in Old Bulgarian, which did not make the changes in question. Thus * [ ˈsvatɪba ] 'marriage' gives Russian [ ˈsvadba ]; compare Russian [ svat ] ' arranger of a marriage.' Old Bulgarian [ otʋbe:ʒati ] ' to run away' appears in Russian as [ odbeˈʒat ]; compare the simple Old Bulgarian [ otʋ ] ' from, away from ': Russian [ ot ]. On the other band, Old Bulgarian [ podʋkopati ] 'to undermine ' appears in Russian as [ potkoˈpat ]; contrast Old Bulgarian [ podʋ igo ] ' under the yoke' : Russian, [ ˈpod igo ].

The assimilation may affect the action of the velum, tongue, or lips. If some difference between the consonants is kept, the assimilation is *partial*; thus in pre-Latin [ pn ] was assimilated to [ mn ], as in Pmnitive Indo-European * [ ˈswepnos ] ' sleep ', Sanskrit [ ˈsvapnah ]: Latin *somnus*. If the difference entirely disappears, the assimilation is *total*, and the result is a long consonant, as in Italian *sonno* [ ˈsɔnno ]. Similarly, Latin *octō* ' eight' >Italian *otto* [ ˈɔtto ]; Latin *ruptum* ' boken' > Italian *rotto* [ ˈrotto ].

In *progressive* assimilation the latter consonant is altered. Thus, pre-Latin * [ kolnis ] ' hill' gives Latin *collis*; compare Lithuanian [ ˈka:lnas ] ' mountain.' Our word *hill* underwent the same chang [ ln ] > [ ll ] in pre-Germanic; witness Primitive Indo-European * [ pl:ˈnos ] ' full ', Sanskrit [ pu:rˈnah ]. Lithuanian [ ˈpilnas ]: Primitive Germanic * [ ˈfollaz ], Gothic *fulls*, Old English *full*, or Primitive Indo-European * [ wl:na: ] ' wool,' Sanskrit [ ˈu:rna: ], Lithuanian [ ˈvilna ]: Primitive Germanic * [ ˈwollo: ], Gothic *wulla*. Old English wull.

......

21.8 Some changes which superficially do not seem like weakening or abbreviations of movement, may yet involve a simplification. In a good many languages we find an intermediate consonant arising in a cluster. A Primitive Indo-European [ sr ] appears as [ str ] in Germanic and in Slavic; thus, Primitive Indo-European * [ srow- ] ( compare Sanskrit [ ˈsravati ] ' it flows ' ) is reflected in Primitive Germanic * [ ˈstrawmas ] ' stretan,' Old Norse [ strawmr ], Old English [ stre:am ], and in Old Bulgarian [ struja ] ' stream.' English, at more than one time, has inserted a [ d ] in the groups [ nr, nl ] and a [ b ] in the groups [ mr, ml ]: Old English [ ˈθunrian ] > ( *to* ) *thunder*; Old English [ ˈalre ] ( accusative case ) > *alder*; Gothic has [ ˈtimrjan ] ' to construct' as well as [ ˈtimbrjan ], but Old English has only [ ˈtimbrian ] and [ jeˈtimbre ] ' carpentry-work,' whence modern *timber*; Old English [ ˈθymle ] > *thimble*. These changes involve no additional movement, but merely replace simultaneous movements by successive. To pass from [ n ] to [ r ] , for instance, the speaker must simultaneously raise his velum and move his tongue from the closure position to the trill position:

$$[\,n\,] \qquad\qquad [\,r\,]$$

velum lowered →velum raised

dental closure→trill position

If with a less delicate co-ordination, the velum is raised before the change of tongue-position, there results a moment of unnasalized closure, equivalent to the phoneme [ d ]:

$$[\,n\,] \qquad\qquad [\,d\,] \qquad\qquad\qquad [\,r\,]$$

velum lowered→velum raised

dental closure →trill position

The second of these performances is evidently easier than the first.

In other cases, too, an apparent lengthening of a form may be viewed as lessening the difficulty of utterance. When a relatively sonorous phoneme is non-syllabic, it often acquires syllabic function; this change is known by the Sanskrit name of *samprasarana*. Thus, in sub-standard English, *elm* [ elm ] has changed to [ 'elm ]. This is often followed by another change, known as *anaptyxis*, the rise of a vowel beside the sonant, which becomes non-syllabic. Primitive Indo-European *[ agros ] 'field' gives pre-Latin *[ agr ]; in this the [ r ] must have become syllabic, and then an anaptyctic vowel must have arisen, for in the historical Latin form *ager* [ 'ager ] the *e* represents a fully formed vowel. Similarly Primitive Germanic forms like *[ 'akraz ] 'field,' *[ 'foglaz ] 'bird', *[ 'tajknan ] 'aign,' *[ 'majθmaz ] 'precious object' lost their unstressed vowels in all the old Germanic dialects. The Gothic forms [ akrs, fugls, tajkn, majθms ] may have been monosyllabic or may have had syllabic sonants; anaptyxis has taken place in the Old English forms [ 'ɛker, 'fugol, 'ta: ken, 'ma: ðom ], though even here spellings like *fugl* are not uncommon.

Another change Which may be regarded as a simplification occurs in the history of some stress-using languages: the quantities of stressed vowels are regulated according to the character of the following phonemes. Generally, long vowels remain long and short vowels are lengthened in "open" syllables, that is, before a single consonant that is followed by another vowel; in other positions, long vowels are shortened and short ones kept short. Thus, Middle English long vowels remained long in forms like *clene* [ klɛ: ne ] > *clean*, *kepe* [ 'ke: pe ] > *keep*, *mone* [ 'mo: ne ] > *moon*, but were shortened in forms like *clense* > *cleanse*, *kepte* > *kept*, *mon* ( *en* ) *dai* > *Monday*: and short vowels were lengthened in forms like *weve* [ 'weve ] > *weave*, *stele* [ 'stele ] > *steal*, *nose* [ 'nose ] > nose, but stayed short in forms like *weft*, *stelth* > *stealth*, *nos* ( *e* ) *thirl* > *nostril*. In some languages, such as Menomini, we find a very complicated regulation of long and short vowels according to the preceding and following consonants and according to the number of syllables intervening after the last precedinig long vowel.

The complete loss of quantitative differences, which occurred, for instance, in medieval Greek and in some of the modern Slavic languages, makes articulation more uniform. The same can be said of the abandonment of distinctions of syllable-pitch, which has occurred in these same languages; similarly, the removal of word-accent uniformly to some one position such as the first syllable, in pre-Germanic and in Bohemian, or the next-to-last, in Polish, probably involves a facilitation.

In the same sense, the loss of a phonemic unit may be viewed as a simplification. Except for English and Icelandic, the Germanic languages have lost the phoneme [ θ ] and its voiced development [ ð ]; the reflexes coincide in Frisian and in Scandinavian largely with [ t ], as in

Swedish *torn* [toːṛn] : *thorn*, with the same initial as *tio* [tiːe] : *ten*, and in the northern part of the Dutch-German area with [d], as in Dutch *doorn* [doːṛn] : *thorn*, with the same initial as *doen* [duːn] : *do*. Old English [h] before a consonant, as in *niht* 'night,' or in final position, as in *seah* '(I) saw,' was acoustically doubtless an unvoiced velar or palatal spirant; in most of the English area this sound has been lost or has coincided with other phonemes.

21.9　Although many sound-changes shorten linguistic forms, simplify the phonetic system, or in some other way lessen the labor of utterance, yet no student has succeeded in establishing a correlation between sound-change and any antecedent phenomenon: the causes of sound-change are unknown. When we find a large-scale shortening and loss of vowels, we feel safe in assuming that the language had a strong word-stress, but many languages with strong word-stress do not weaken the unstressed vowels; examples are Italian, Spanish, Bohemian, Polish. The English change of [kn-, gn-] to [n-] seems natural, after it has occurred, but why did it not occur before the eighteenth century, and why has it not occurred in the other Germanic languages?

Every conceivable cause has been alleged: "race," climate, topographic conditions, diet, occupation and general mode of life, and on. Wundt attributed sound-change to increase in the rapidity of speech, and this, in turn, to the community's advance in culture and general intelligence. It is safe to say that we speak as rapidly and with as little effort as possible, approaching always the limit where our interlocutors ask us to repeat our utterance, and that a great deal of sound-change is in some way connected with this factor. No permanent factor, however, can account for specific changes which occur at one time and place and not at another. The same consideration holds good against the theory that sound-change arises from imperfections in children's learning of language. On the other hand, temporary operation of factors like the above, such as change of habitat, occupation, or diet, is ruled out by the fact that sound-changes occur too often and exhibit too great a variety.

The *substratum theory* attributes sound-change to transference of language: a community which adopts a new language will speak it imperfectly and with the phonetics of its mother-tongue. The transference of language will concern us later; in the present connection it is important to see that the substratum theory can account for changes only during the time when the language is spoken by persons who have acquired it as a second language. There is no sense in the mystical version of the substratum theory, which attributes changes, say, in modern Germanic languages, to a "Celtic substratum"—that is, to the fact that many centuries ago, some adult Celtic-speakers acquired Germanic speech. Moreover, the Celtic speech which preceded Germanic in southern Germany, the Netherlands, and England, was itself an invading language: the theory directs us back into time, from "race" to "race", to account for vague "tendencies" that manifest themselves in the actual historical occurrence of sound-change.

Aside from their failure to establish correlations, theories of this kind are confuted by the fact that when sound-change has removed some phonetic feature, later sound-change may result in the renewal of just this feature. If we attribute some particular character to the Primitive Indo-European unvoiced stops [p, t, k]—supposing, for the sake of illustration, that they were unaspirated fortes— then the pre-Germanic speakers who had begun to change these sounds in the direction of spirants [f, θ, h], were doubtless incapable of pronouncing the original sounds, just as the English-speaker of today is incapable of pronouncing the French unaspirated [p, t, k]. At a later time, however,

Primitive Indo-European [ b, d, g ] were changed in pre-Germanic to unvoiced tops [ p,t,k ]. These sounds did not coincide with those of the first group: the sounds of the first group had no longer the [ p,t,k ] character, having changed to aspirates or affricates or perhaps already to spirants; the sounds of the second group, on the other hand, were not subjected to the same change as those of the firs group, because, as we say, the sound-change of [ p,t,k ] to [ f,θ,h ] was *past*. More accurately, we should say that the sound-change of [ p,t,k ] was *already under way*: the new [ p,t,k ] constituted a different habit, which did not take part in the displacement of the old habit. In time, the new [ p,t, k ] became aspirated, as they are in present-day English; so that, once more, we are incapable of pronouncing unaspirated unvoiced stops.

The English sound-changes that are known under the name of "the great vowel-shift," are of a type that has little effect beyond altering the acoustic shape of each phoneme; the long vowels were progressively shifted upward and into diphthongal types:

MIDDLE ENGLISH>EARLY MODERN>PRESENT-DAY

| | | |
|---|---|---|
| [ 'na:me ] | [ ne:m ] | [ nejm ] *name* |
| [ dɛ:d ] | [ di:d ] | [ dijd ] *deed* |
| [ ge:s ] | [ gi:s ] | [ gijs ] *geese* |
| [ wi:n ] | [ wejn ] | [ wajn ] *wine* |
| [ stɔ:n ] | [ sto:n ] | [ stown ] *stone* |
| [ go:s ] | [ gu:s ] | [ guws ] *goose* |
| [ hu:s ] | [ hows ] | [ haws ] *house* |

Another theory seeks the cause of some sound-changes in formal conditions of a language, supposing that forms of weak meaning are slurred in pronunciation and thereby permanently weakened or lost. We have met this doctrine as one of those which deny the occurrence of purely phonemic changes (§ 20.10). We have no gauge by which we could mark some formal features of a language as semantically weak or superfluous. If we condemn all features of meaning except business-like denotations of the kind that could figure in scientific discourse, we should have to expect, on this theory, the disappearance of a great many forms in almost every language. For instance, the inflectional endings of adjectives in modern German are logically superfluous; the use of adjectives is quite like the English, and a text in which these endings are covered up is intelligible.

In fact, sound-changes often obliterate features whose meaning is highly important. No grammatical difference could be more essential than is that of actor and verbal goal in an Indo-European language. Yet the difference between the Primitive Indo-European nominative in *[ -os ], as in Sanskrit [ 'vrkah ], Greek [ 'lukos ], Latin *lupus*, Primitive Germanic *[ 'wolfaz ], Gothic *wulfs*, and the accusative in *[ -om ], as in Sanskrit [ 'vrkan ], Greek [ 'lukon ], Latin *lupum*, Primitive Germanic *[ 'wolfan ], Gothic *wulf*, had been obliterated by the weakening of the word-final in pre-English, so that the two cases were merged, even in our earliest records, in the form *wulf* 'wolf'. In Old English a few noun-types, such as nominative *caru* : accusative *care* 'care,' still had the distinction; by the year 1,000 these were probably merged in the form [ 'kare ], thanks to the weakening of unstressed vowels. In the same way, sound-change leads to all manner of homonymies, such as *meet*: *meat*; *meed*: *mead* ('meadow'): *mead* ('drink'), *knight*: *night*. The classical instance of this is Chinese, for it can be shown that the vast homonymy of the present-day languages, especially of North Chinese, is due to phonetic changes. Homonymy and *syncretism*, the merging of inflectional categories, are normal results of sound-change.

The theory of semantic weakness does seem to apply, however, to fixed formulas with excess slurring (§ 9.7). Historically, these formulas can be explained only as weakenings far in excess of normal sound-change. Thus, *good-bye* represents an older *God be with ye*, *ma'm* an older *madam*, Spanish *usted* [u'sted] an older *vuestra merced* ['vwestra mer'θed], and Russian [s], as in [da s] 'yes, sir,' an older ['sudar] 'lord.' In these cases, however, the normal speech-form exists by the side of the slurred form. The excess weakening in these forms has not been explained and doubtless is connected in some way with what we may call the sublinguistic status of these conventional formulae. In any event, their excess weakening differs very much from ordinary phonetic change.

Since a sound-change is a historical happening, with a beginning and an end, limited to a definite time and to a definite body of speakers, its cause cannot be found in universal considerations or by observing speakers at other times and places. A phonetician tried to establish the cause of a change of the type [azna > asna], which occurred in the pre-history of the Avesta language, by observing in the laboratory a number of persons who were directed to pronounce the sequence [azna] many times in succession. Most of the persons—they were Frenchmen—yielded no result, but at last came one who ended by saying [asna]. The phonetician's joy was not clouded by the fact that this last person was a German, in whose native language [z] occurs only before syllabics.

It has been suggested that if a phoneme occurs in a language with more than a certain relative frequency( § 8.7), this phoneme will be slurred in articulation and subjected to change. The upper limit of tolerable frequency, it is supposed, varies for different types of phonemes; thus, [t] represents in English more than 7 per cant of the total of uttered phonemes, and in several other languages (Russian, Hungarian, Swedish, Italian) the unvoiced dental stop runs to a similar percentage, while the type [d], on the other hand, with a lower relative frequency (in English it is less than 5 percent) would in any language suffer sound-change, according to this theory, before it reached a relative frequency like that of English [t]. The relative frequency of a phoneme is governed by the frequency of the significant forms that contain it; thus,[ð] in English is evidently favored by the high frequency of the word *the*. The frequency of significant forms is subject, as we shall see, to unceasing fluctuation, in accordance with changes in practical life. This theory, therefore, has the merit of correlating sound-change with an ever present and yet highly variable factor. It could be tested if we could determine the absolute upper limit for types of phoneme, and the actual frequency of a phoneme at a stage of a language just before this phoneme was changed— as, say, of [v] in English just before the change *havok > hawk*. We should then still have to account for the specific nature of the change, since phonemes of any one general type have changed in different ways in the history of various languages. Against the theory we must weigh the great phonetic difference between languages and the high frequency, in some languages; of what we may call unusual phonetic types; [ð], which plays such a great part in English, was at one time eliminated (by a pre-West-Germanic change to [d]) and has remained so in Dutch-German, later it was re-introduced into English by a change from [θ] to [ð]:

21.10 Certain linguistic changes which are usually described as sound-change, do not come under the definition of phonetic change as a gradual alteration of phonemic units. In various parts of

Europe, for instance, the old tongue-tip trill [r] has been replaced, in modern times, by a uvular trill. This has happened in Nortb-umbrian English, in Danish and southern Norwegian and Swedish, and in the more citified types of French (especially in Paris) and Dutch-German. Aside from its spread by borrowing, the new habit, in whatever times and places it may first have arisen, could have originated only as a sudden replacement of one trill by another. A replacement of this sort is surely different from the gradual and imperceptible alterations of phonetic change.

Some changes consist in a redistribution of phonemes. The commonest of these seems to be *dissimilation*: when a phoneme or type of phoneme recurs within a form, one of the occurrences is sometimes replaced by a different sound. Thus, Latin *peregrinus* 'foreigner, stranger' is replaced in the Romance languages by a type *pelegrīnus*, as in Italian *pellegrino*, and in English *pilgrim*, borrowed from Romance: the first of the two [r]'s has been replaced by [l]. In the languages of Europe, the sounds [r, l, n] are especially subject to this replacement; the replacing sound is usually one of the same group. Where the replacement occurs, it follows quite definite rules, but we cannot predict its occurrence. The change, if carried out, would produce a state of affairs where recurrence of certain sounds, such as [r] and [l], was not allowed within a word—the state of affairs which actually prevails in the modern English derivation of symbolic words, where we have *clatter*, *blubber*, but *rattle*, *crackle* (§14.9). Probably this type of change is entirely different from ordinary phonetic change.

There is also a type of dissimilation in which one of the like phonemes is dropped, as when Latin *quinque* ['kwi:nkwe] 'five' is replaced, in Romance, by a type *['ki:nkwe]*, Italia *cinque* ['tfinkwe], French *cinq* [sɛ̃k].

There are several other kinds of phonetic replacement which cannot properly be put on a level with ordinary sound-change. In *distant assimilation* a phoneme is replaced by another of related acoustic type which occurs elsewhere in the same word. Thus, Primitive Indo-European *['penkʷe]* 'five,' Sanskrit ['panca], Greek ['pente] appears in Latin not as *['pinkwe]*, but as *quinque*. In pre-Germanic this word seems to have suffered the reverse assimilation, to *['pempe]*, for we have Primitive Germanic *['fimfe]* in Gothic and Old High German *fimf*, Old English *fif*, and so on. Sanskrit has [ç—ç] in words where we expect [s—ç]。

*Metathesis* is the interchange of two phonemes within a word. Beside the expected *āscian* 'ask,' Old English has also *ācsian*. In Tagalog some morphologic alternations seem to be due to changes of this kind; thus, the suffix [-an], as in [a'sin] 'salt': [as'nan] 'what is to be salted,' is sometimes accompanied by interchange of two consonants that come together: [a'tip] 'roofing': [ap'tan] 'what is to be roofed'; [ta'nim] 'that planted': [tam'nan] 'what is to have plants put into it.' In the languages of Europe distant metathesis of [r-l] is fairly common. To Old English *alor* 'alder' there corresponds in Old High German not only *elira* but also *erila* (>modern *Erle*). For Gothic ['werilo:s] 'lips,' Old English has *weleras*. Latin *parabola* 'word' (a borrowing from Greek) appears in Spanish as *palabra*.

When a phoneme or group of phonemes recurs within a word, one occurrence together with the intervening sounds, may be dropped; this change is known as *haplology*. Thus, from Latin *nūtriō*, 'I nourish' the regular feminine agent-noun would be *nūtrī-trix* 'nurse,' but the form is actually *nūtrix*. Similarly, the compound which would normally have the form *stīpi-pendium* 'wage-payment' appears actually as *stīpendium*. Aucient Greek [amphi-pho'rews] 'both-side-carrier' appears also as [aspho'rews] 'amphora.' Changes like these are very different from those which are covered by the assumption of Sound-change; it is possible that they are akin rather to the types of linguistic change which we have still to consider—analogic change and borrowing.

*(Language. George Allen & Unwin Ltd.1955)*

译文：

# 语音演变的类型

### 袁家骅,赵世开,甘世福,等译

21.1 语音演变,如上章所述,是发音动作的习惯起了变化。严格地说,这类变化如果并不影响语言的音位系统,就是无关紧要的;事实上,纵使我们掌握了完善而无缺陷的记录,我们也还是不可能确切地指出某些变体的流行的起点,认为是名副其实的历史演变的开始。说英语的人们在 gōs(goose)和 gēs(geese)这些词里头倾向于采用舌位较高的元音变体,开始时候发音位置的变动是毫无所谓的。他们所发这些元音的音响性质,同不多几个世代以前,先人们在同样的语言形式里所发元音的音响性质,他们无从比较。他们要是听见一个方言没有发生这种变化,也许会注意到差别,但是他们无法肯定这种差别是怎样产生的。语音演变只在引起了音位模式的变化才会获得意义。例如,在现代英语的初期,中古英语元音[ɛː],如 sed[sɛːd](seed(种籽)),舌位提高了,以至跟 ges[geːs]中的[eː]合而为一,这样的合并在语言的所有形式中完全改变了音位的分布。再有,中古英语的短[e]在所谓开音节里——就是,后面的单辅音紧跟着另一个元音,如 ete['ete]('eat'吃)——音量延长了,终于跟刚才提到的长元音合流。因此,现代英语的音位结构跟中世纪的英语是不同的。现在的[ij]音位在整个系统中继承了这样三个古老的音位;特别值得注意的是,这样的合并产生了一批同音词。

古和中古英语[eː]变成了现代的[ij],如 heel(脚跟),steel(钢),geese(鹅,复数),queen(皇后,女王),green(青,绿),meet(遇见),need(需要),keep(保持,持有)。

古和中古英语[ɛː]变成了现代的[ij],如 heal(治疗),meal(餐),cheese(奶酪),leave(离开),clean(清洁),lean(消瘦),street(街道),mead(草原),meet(相遇,合适)。

古和中古英语[e]变成了现代的[ij],如 steal(偷),meal(面粉),weave(织),lean(倚靠),quean(妇人),speak(说),meat(肉食),mete(度量,分配),eat(吃),mead(蜜酒)。

另一方面,末一项变化受到一定语音位置的限制,因而原来具有同样音位的形式现在却有不同的音位:古英语[e]变长了,如中古英语 weve> weave,但中古英语 weft> weft '纬线'却没有变。同样地,另一种音变使某些辅音丛前面的长元音变短了,因而引起了元音的不同,如 meadow '草原'(<古英语['mɛːdwe])和 mead 之间,或 kept '保持了'(<古英语['keːpte])和 keep 之间的差异。

几百年前,英语丢了词首[n]前面的[k]:结果是音位系统中起了变化,包括下面的特征,即同音词 knot 和 not,或 knight 和 night 的产生,以及[n-]和[-kn-]的交替,如 know(知道),knowledge(知识):acknowledge(承认,认识)。

21.2 大多数音变的一般倾向是任何特定语言形式的发音动作的简化。辅音丛就是往往这样简化了的。古英语的词首辅音丛[hr,hl,hn,kn,gn,wr]丢掉了头一个辅音,如古英语 hring>今 ring((指)环,(铃)响),hlēapan>leap(跳跃),hnecca> neck(颈子),cnēow> knee(膝头),gnagan>gnaw(咬),wringan>wring'扭,拧'。这些词群里[h]的消失发生在中世纪的晚期,其他辅音的消失发生在现代的早期;我们不知道这些时候闯进来了什么新因素帮助消除这些曾经经过好些世纪活在人民口头的辅音丛。[h]音丛还保存在冰岛语里;词首[kn]不但还留在旁的日耳曼语言里(如荷兰语 knie[kniː],德语 knie[kniː],丹麦语[krɛːʔ],瑞典语[kneː],英语 knee[nij]),并且也见于设得兰和奥克尼群岛①以及苏格兰东北部的英语方言。[gn]差不多同样广泛地持续不变——在英语里更加广泛;[wr-]改读[vr-]还留存在斯堪的纳维亚语,荷德语区的北部(包括标准荷兰语),和好些分散的英语方言。我们既然不知道什么因素在某个时候和地方,而不在另一个时候和地方,导致了这些变化,我们就不敢自信以为知道了变化的原因——就是说,不能预言音变的发生。被爱好的变体较为平易单纯,这是一个永恒的因素;可以匹比的类似的可能性是找不到的。

词尾辅音丛的简化就更普通了。原始印欧语*[peːts]'脚',(主格单数)出现在梵语里是【paːt】,在拉丁语里是【peːs】;原始印欧语*[bheronts]'负担,携带'(主格单数阳性)出现在梵语里是['bharan],在拉丁语里是 ferens['ferens],后来变作['fereːs]。就是由于这一类型的变化,产生了实际容许的尾音习惯(§8.4)和§13.9 所描述的形态变换类型。同样,原始中央阿耳贡金语*[ax-kehkwa]'锅,镬',复数*[axkehkwaki],反映在福克斯语里是[ahkoːhkwa,ahkoːhkoːki],在克利语[askihk,askihkwak]和美诺米尼语[ahkɛːh,ahkɛːhkuk]丢了末尾的元音和辅音丛的一部分,所以这些语言里的复数形式含有一种辅音丛,从单数形式的审察上是看不清楚的。英语里尾音[ŋ]和[mb]丢掉了最后的塞音;因而出现这样的对照,long:longer[lɔŋ—'lɔŋgə](长:更长),climb:clamber[klajm—'klɛmbə]('攀登':'爬,攀')。

有时候甚至词尾单辅音也会弱失或消失。前希腊语丢掉了尾音[t,d],如原始印欧语*[tod]'那',梵语[tat]:希腊语[to];尾音[m]变为[n],如原始印欧语*[ɟu'gom]'轭',梵语[ju'gam]:希腊语[zu'gon]。同样的变化似乎也曾发生在前日耳曼语里。有时候所有的词尾辅音都丢了,结果出现了一种语音模式,其中每一个词都以元音结尾。前斯拉夫语里发生过这种变化,请看古保加利亚语的形式[to]'那',[igo]'轭'。正是这一类的变化才能说明萨摩亚语的形态现状(§13.9);萨摩亚语[inu]'喝,饮'这个形式是古*[inum]的后裔,末尾辅音还保存在塔加洛语[i'num]里。

这类变化既然是出现在词首或者更常见的是出现在词尾,我们就得假定那些发生这种变化的语言当时关于词的单位大概具有某种语音标志。假使有些形式,其中词的开头和结尾并没有起止的发音特点,那么这些形式就不会受到这种变化的感染而按照连读形式继续保存下去。比如,中古英语尾音[n]丢掉了:eten>ete'eat',但是冠词 an(一个)在元音前面必然是完全发音的,仿佛是后面跟着的那个词的一部分——就是说,没有结尾位置的语音特点——所以在这种情形之下[n]并没有丢掉(如尾音[n]),反而被保存了(如词内部的[n]):a house'一所房屋',但是 an arm'一支手臂'。拉丁语 vōs'你们'变为法语 vous[vu],但是拉丁语短句 vos amātis'你们爱'反映在法语的连读习惯却说成 vous aimez[vuz eme]。拉丁语 est'他是'变成法语 est[ɛ],但是拉丁语短句 est ille?'是那个么?'出现在法语的连读形式里是 est-il?[ɛti?]'是他么?'按同样方式,原始印欧语*[bheronts]不但反映在梵语['bharan]里(见上引),并且也按照梵语连读的习惯,增加一个连读嵌音[s],如果后面的那个词以[t]开头,如['bharãs 'tatra]'携带到那儿去'。

**21.3** 辅音丛的简化是常见的音变结果。比如,前拉丁语*['fulgmen]'闪(电)'出现在

---

① 设得兰(Shetland)英国苏格兰东北一群岛郡,盛产羊毛。奥克尼(Orkney)在苏格兰北的岛郡。——译者

拉丁语里是 fulmen。这儿[lgm]音群简化了，变为[lm]，但是 fulgur'闪亮'中的音丛[lg]没有变，agmen'军队'中的音丛[gm]也没有变。我们描写这样的音变时，把有关的条件称为条件因素（或导致因素）；比如说，fulgur 和 agmen 这些例子缺少这样一个因素，所以其中的[g]给保留了。这种说法是不很恰当的，因为这儿所谈的变化实际上只是[lgm]简化为[lm]，跟 fulgur, agmen 等例子并不相干，但是利用这些术语往往也有方便。条件音变的结果时常是形态上的替换。就像拉丁语的后缀-men 见于 agere'指挥，引导'：agmen'军队'，但是 fulgere'闪耀'：fulmen'闪（电）'。同样，前拉丁语[rkn]变作[rn]；除 pater'父亲'：paternus'父亲的'以外，我们还有 quercus'橡树'：quernus'橡树的'。

辅音丛因同化作用而发生变化，是很寻常的：发一个音位的器官位置稍稍改变，使更接近另一个音位的部位。较常见的是逆同化，前面音位受后面音位的影响。

比如，辅音的浊化或清化往往随着后面的辅音性质变为一致；英语 goose 和 house 的[s]在 gosling, husband 的辅音组合里浊化为[z]。这也会引起形态上的替换。在俄语的历史上，两个短元音（下面标写为[ɪ]和[ʊ]）消失的结果产生了一些辅音丛；这些音丛里的塞音或擦音后来被紧跟着的塞音或擦音在清浊上同化了。古保加利亚语没有发生这儿所说的变化，还看得出古老的形式。例如*['svatɪba]'婚姻'出现在俄语里是['svadba]；比较俄语[svat]'媒人'。古保加利亚语[otubeˈʒati]'逃走'出现在俄语里是[odbeˈʒat]；比较古保加利亚语的简单形式[otu]'离开，去'：俄语[ot]。另一方面，古保加利亚语[podukopati]'摧毁'出现在俄语里是[potkoˈpat]；对比古保加利亚语[poduˈigo]'在轭下'：俄语[ˈpod igo]。

同化作用可以影响软颚、舌头、或嘴唇的动作。假使前后辅音还保持差异，同化只是部分的；如前拉丁语[pn]同化为[mn]，原始印欧语*['swepnos]'睡眠'，梵语[ˈsvapnah]：拉丁语 somnus。假使差异完全消失了，同化就是全部的，结果是一个专辅音，如意大利语 sonno [ˈsɔnno]。同样，拉丁语 octō'八'>意大利语 otto[ˈɔtto]；拉丁语 ruptum'打破了的'>意大利语 rotto [ˈrotto]。

顺同化是后一个辅音的改变。比如前拉丁语*[kolnis]'小山'在拉丁语里是 collis；比较立陶宛语[ˈkaːlnas]'山'。英语 hill（小山）在前日耳曼语里经历了同样的变化[ln]>[ll]；请看原始印欧语*[plˈnos]'满'，梵语[puːrˈnah]，立陶宛语['pilnas]：原始日耳曼语*[ˈfollaz]，哥特语 fulls，古英语 full，或原始印欧语*[ˈwlːnaː]'羊毛'，梵语['uːrnaː]，立陶宛语[ˈvilna]：原始日耳曼语*[ˈwolloː]，哥特语 wulla，古英语 wull（今 wool）。

......

**21.8** 有些变化表面上看来并不像发音动作的放松或缩减，其实倒也许含有简化作用。我们在好些语言里发现辅音丛中产生一个过渡辅音。原始印欧语[sr]出现在日耳曼语和斯拉夫语里是[str]；例如原始印欧语*[srow-]（比较梵语[ˈsravati]'它流'）反映在原始日耳曼语是*[ˈstrawmaz]'溪流'，古北欧语[strawmr]，古英语[streːam]，和古保加利亚语[struja]'溪流'。英语不止一次在[nr, nl]音群中嵌进一个[d]，在[mr, ml]音群中嵌进一个[b]：古英语[ˈθunrian]>(to) Thunder'打雷'；古英语[ˈalre]（宾格）>alder'赤杨'；哥特语有[ˈtimrjan]'构造'（动词），同时还有[ˈtimbrjan]，但是古英语只有[ˈtimbrian]和[jeˈtimbre]'木工'，从而有了现代的 timber（木材）；古英语[ˈθymle]>thimble（顶针，针箍）。这些变化并不包含额外增加的动作，仅仅是用连续动作代替了同时并举的动作。比方说，从[n]过渡到[r]，说话人必需同时抬起软颚并且把舌头从堵塞位置移到颤动位置：

$$
\begin{array}{cc}
[n] & [r] \\
\end{array}
$$

软颚下降——→软颚抬起
舌齿堵塞——→舌尖颤动

假使动作的配合不是那么恰好,舌位改变以前就抬起软颚来,结果来了非鼻音化的舌头堵塞的瞬息,就等于发[d]这个音位:

$$[n] \qquad\qquad [d] \qquad\qquad [r]$$

软颚下降——→软颚抬起

舌齿堵塞　　　　　——→舌尖颤动

第二种动作显然要比第一种容易些。

在旁的情况下,一个形式似乎拉长了,也可以认为是减轻了发音的困难。一个相对响亮的音位本来是非领音性的,往往会获得领音作用;这种变化按梵语叫作领音化(samprasarana)。比如,次标准英语 elm[elm](山榆)读作[ˈelm]。这往往会跟来另一种变化,叫作嵌音(anaptyxis),就是一个响音又变得非领音性的了,旁边产生出一个元音来。原始印欧语 *[agros]‘田地’递给了前拉丁语 *[agr];这里面的[r]大概曾经是领音性的,后来又产生了一个中嵌元音,因为有历史记载的拉丁语形式 ager[ˈager],其中 e 代表一个完全形成了的元音。同样地,原始日耳曼语形式如 *[ˈa-kraz]‘田地’, *[foglaz]‘鸟’, *[tajknan]‘记号’, *[ˈmajθmaz]‘珍贵物品’,在所有的古日耳曼语方言里都丢掉了轻元音。哥特语形式[akrs, fugls, tajkn, majθms]也许是单音节的,或者也许含有领音的响音;古英语形式里却产生了嵌音[ˈɛker, ˈfugol, ˈtaːken, ˈmaːðom],虽然 fugl 这样的拼写法在这儿也还是很普通的。

另一种变化也可以当作简化看待,发生在某些利用重音的语言的历史里:重元音的音量按照随后音位的性质加以调整。一般说来,在“开”音节里,就是在一个单辅音跟着另一个元音的前面,长元音仍然是长的,短元音也延长了;倘在旁的位置,长元音缩短,短元音还是短的。比如,中古英语的长元音在有些形式里依然是长的:clene[ˈklɛːne]>clean(清洁),kepe[ˈkɛːpe]>keep(持有),mone[ˈmoːne]>moon(月亮),但是在旁的形式里却缩短了,如 clense>cleanse[klenz](洗净),kepte>kept(保持了),mon(en)dai>Monday(星期一);短元音在有些形式里延长了,如 weve[ˈweve]>weave(织),stele[ˈstele]>steal(偷),nose[ˈnose]>nose(鼻子),但是在旁的形式里依然不变,如 weft(纬线,织物),stelth>stealth(偷窃行为,秘密),nos(e)thirl>nostril(鼻孔)。在有些语言里,如美诺米尼语,我们发现长短元音的调整非常复杂,要看前后的辅音情况,还要看最后一个长元音后面嵌有多少音节的数目。

音量区别的完全消失使发音更加单纯一致,曾经发生在,举例说,中古希腊语和某些现代斯拉夫语言。这些语言也抛弃了音节声调的区别,可以说收到了同样效果;同样地,词重音位置的移动,如前日耳曼语和波希米亚语一律移到第一个音节,波兰语一律移到倒数第二个音节,可能使发音更加省力。

在同样的意义上,一个语音单位的消失可以看作是一种简化。除英语和冰岛语以外,日耳曼诸语言都丢了[θ]音位和与之相应而发展起来的浊化[ð];这两个音在弗里斯兰语和斯堪的纳维亚语里大都同[t]合并了,如瑞典语 torn[toːrn]:英语 thorn(荆棘),词首音同 tio[ˇtiːe]:英语 ten(十),而在荷德语区的北部则与[d]合流,如荷兰语 doorn[doːrn]:英语 thorn,词首音同 doen[duːn]:英语 do。古英语辅音前的[h],如 niht(night),或词尾的[h],如 seah((I) saw),实际音值无疑是后颚或前颚清擦音;在英语区的绝大部分,这个音已经消失了,或者同旁的音位合并了。

**21.9** 虽然许多音变缩短了语言形式,简化了语音系统,或者用旁的方式减轻了说话的劳动,可是还没有一个学者能在音变和某种先行的现象之间成功地建立一种相互关系:音变的原因是不知道的。当我们发现大规模的元音缩短和消失时,我们敢于大胆假设这种语言有很强的词重音,但是许多有强重音的语言并没有弱化它的不带重音的元音;意大利语,西班牙语,波希米亚语,波兰语就是例证。英语[kn-,gn-]变为[n-],发生以后现在看来是很自然的,但是这一音变为什么没有发生在十八世纪以前,又为什么没有发生在旁的日耳曼语言里呢?

任何能以想象的原因都提过了:"种族",气候,地理条件,饮食,职业和一般的生活方式,以及其他。冯特认为音变由于说话速度的增加,而这又由于社会文化和一般智慧的进步。这样说是很安全的,就是,我们说话要求尽量地快,尽量地少费气力,几乎经常达到交谈人请我们非得重复一遍的限度,许多音变跟这个因素都有某种联系。然而找不到一种永恒的因素能以说明特种音变发生在某个时间和地点,而不在另一个时间和地点。依据同样理由,音变起于儿童学习语言存在缺陷的说法是站不住的。另一方面,上面所说居住地区,职业或饮食习惯的变动,这些因素的暂时作用也得勾消,因为事实上音变发生得太经常了,表现的花样也太繁多了。

底层说把音变的原因诿之于语言的转递:一个社团采用一种新的语言,说得不完善,带有自己母语的发音特点。语言的转递我们随后还要讨论;这儿有关重要的是,应该看到底层说只能解释人们学习使用第二种语言时才会出现的那些变化。底层说故弄玄虚,比方说,把现代日耳曼诸语言中的变化归因于"凯尔特"底层——就是说,许多世纪以前,操凯尔特语的成年人学会了日耳曼语:这又说明什么呢。并且,凯尔特语在日耳曼语来到以前就出现在德国南部,荷兰,和英格兰,本身也是一种入侵的语言:底层说叫我们回顾往古,从"种族"到"种族",企图说明历史上实际发生的音变事例中表现出来的隐约模糊的"倾向"。

这一类的理论除了不能建立相应关系以外,而且还被下面这个事实难倒了,就是当一个音变已经抹掉了某种语音特征时,后来的音变也许正好恢复了这个特征。假使我们认为原始印欧语的清塞音[p,t,k]具有某种特性——为了说明方便,假定这些是不送气的强音——那么使用前日耳曼语的人们已经开始把这些音逐渐改变为擦音[f,θ,h]的时候,无疑地就不能发出原来的音了,就好像今天说英语的人们不能发法语不送气的[p,t,k]似的。然而往后一个时期,原始印欧语的[b,d,g]变成了前日耳曼语里的清塞音[p,t,k]。这些音并没有同第一组的音合流:第一组的音不再保留[p,t,k]的性质,已经变为送气音或塞擦音,甚至可能早已变成擦音了;另一方面,第二组的音没有受第一组音的演变所感染,因为,照我们的说法,[p,t,k]转为[f,θ,h]的音变已经过时了。我们应该更正确地说,[p,t,k]的音变早已上了路了:新的[p,t,k]组成了另一种风尚,并没有参与那个旧风尚的改革。新的[p,t,k]到了一定时期也变成送气音了,好像今天英语里的发音一样;所以,我们又一度不能发非送气的清塞音了。

英语音变称为"元音大转移"的,除了改变每个音位的音值以外没有旁的多大影响;长元音步步向上移动,变成了复元音:

| 中古英语 | 现代初期 | 今　天 |
|---|---|---|
| [ˈnaːme] | [neːm] | [nejm]name(名字) |
| [dɛːd] | [diːd] | [dijd]deed(事情) |
| [geːs] | [giːs] | [gijs]geese(鹅(复数)) |
| [wiːn] | [wejn] | [wajn]wine(酒) |
| [stɔːn] | [stoːn] | [stown]stone(石头) |
| [goːs] | [guːs] | [guws]goose(鹅) |
| [huːs] | [hows] | [haws]house(房屋) |

另一种理论是要在语言的形式方面寻找某些音变的原因,假定意义微弱的形式在发音时

轻轻掠过,因而永远弱化或消失了。这一类主张否认纯音位变化的事例,前面已经谈过(§20.10)。我们没有衡量的标准能以指出一种语言的某些形式特征在意义上是微弱的或多余的。假使我们认为除了那些能够出现在科学论著中的干巴巴的表述以外都算不得重要的意义特征,那么,按照这个理论,我们就自然料想到差不多任何语言会有许许多多的形式要消失了。例如,现代德语形容词的屈折变尾从逻辑上说是多余的;形容词的用法很像英语,一篇德文把这些变尾掩盖起来还是看得懂的。

事实上,音变时常磨灭了意义十分重要的一些特征。在印欧语系的一种语言里,施事(行为者)和受事(动词目的)的区别也许比任何语法区别都重要。可是原始印欧语以 *[os] 表示的主格,如梵语['vrkah],希腊语['lukos],拉丁语 lupus,原始日耳曼语 *['wolfaz],哥特语 wulfs,和以 *[-om] 表示的宾格,如梵语['vrkam],希腊语['lukon],拉丁语 lupum,原始日耳曼语 *['wolfan],哥特语 wulf,二者的区别在前英语里由于词尾的弱化被磨灭了,所以在最早的英语记载里,两个格合并为一个形式 wulf(今 wolf '狼')。古英语里有少数几个名词类型,如主格 caru:宾格 care(操心,关怀),仍然保持区别;到了公元 1000 年,大概由于轻元音的弱化,二者合并为['kare]这个形式。按照同样方式,音变导致了各式各样的同音词,如 meet(遇见):meat(肉食);meed(报酬):mead(草原):mead(蜜酒);knight '武士':night '夜'。汉语是这方面的古典范例,因为今天的汉语方言,特别是北方话,能够被指出大量的同音现象,都是音变造成的。同音现象和屈折范畴的混合是音变的正常结果。

然而意义微弱的理论作为固定的公式,的确似乎适用于某些在特别地含糊其词的地方(§9.7)。从历史上看,这些公式只能解释为远远超过了正常音变的弱化。比如,英语 good-bye(再见)代表较古的 God be with you(上帝伴随保佑您),ma'm 代表较古的 madam(夫人),西班牙语 usted [u'sted] 来自较古的 vuestra merced['vwestra mer'θed]'先生,您呐',俄语[da s]'是的,先生'中的[s]来自较古的['sudar]'老爷'。可是在这些例子里,正常的言语形式跟简略形式平行并存。这些形式的极端弱化并没有得到解释,无疑地多少牵涉到我们不妨称之为俗套的半语言形式。无论如何,这些形式的过分弱化同平常的音变是大不相同的。

因为音变是一种历史事件,有始有终,限于一段明确的时间和一个具体的人群,所以一个音变的原因要是依靠普遍的考虑或者观察其他时间和地点的说话的人群,是找不到的。一位语音学家企图建立[azna>asna]这个曾经发生在阿维斯达语史前时期的音变类型的原因,在实验室里观察一些人,请他们发[azna]这一串音,连续发好几遍。大多数人——他们是法国人——没有得出结果,但是最后来了一位,终于说出[asna]来了。这位语音学家的高兴并没有受蒙蔽,因为事实是,这最后一位是德国人,德语里[z]只出现在领音前面。

有人曾经暗示说,一个音位出现在一种语言里要是出于一定的相对频率(§8.7),就会含糊起来,容易发生变化。据说,相当大的频率的较高限度随着音位的不同类型而有所不同;比如,[t]在英语代表话语里的音位数量占百分之七以上,在好些旁的语言里(俄语,匈牙利语,瑞典语,意大利语)舌尖清塞音达到相近的百分比,可是另一方面,[d]类型的相对频率要低些(英语里低于百分之五),那么,按照这个理论,在它达到近似英语[t]的相对频率以前,在任何语言里会发生音变的。一个音位的相对频率是由包含这个音位的重要形式的出现频率决定的;例如英语里的[ð]由于冠词 the 的高度频率而显然处于优越地位。重要形式的频率,按照实际生活的变迁,会不断地发生波动的,这问题下面我们还要谈到。所以,这个理论有个优点,就是把音变同始终出现而又变动无常的因素互相联系起来。假使我们能够确定各种类型的音位的绝对高限,和一个音位刚要发生变化以前在该语言阶段中的实际频率,那么这个理论是可以进行测验的——不妨举个例，英语[v]在 havok>hawk（鹰）这一变化刚要发生以前。可是我们还得说明这种变化的特殊性质，因为任何普通类型的音位在不同语言的历史里变化情况各不相同。针对这个理论，我们必须衡量语言间的巨大语音差别和某些语言中我们也许认为不寻常的语音类型的高频率；[ð]在英语里占有如许重要的地位，在一个时期被剔除了（前西日耳曼语变为[d]），至今在荷德语里还是如此；后来重新引入英语，又由[θ]转为[ð]的变化。

21.10　有些语言变化，常常被描写为音变的，并不属于音变范围，因为所谓音变是语音单位的逐渐改变。例如欧洲有好些地方，古来的舌尖颤音[r]近代被小舌颤音替代了。这现象发生在英语诺森伯利方言，丹麦语，南挪威语和瑞典语，法语城市化了的话（特别是巴黎话），以及荷德语。这种新习惯的传布除借用以外，不论最初是在什么时间和地点兴起的，只能产生于一种颤音突然地被另一种所替代。这一类的替代的确不同于逐渐的、不知不觉的语音演变。

有些变化构成音位的重新分布。最普通的一种就是异化作用：一个音位或者一个音位类型一再出现在某个形式里，其中的一次出现有时被一个不同的音替代了。比如，拉丁语 peregrīnus‘外人，生人’到了罗曼诸语言给 *pelegrīnus 替代了，如意大利语 pellegrino 和借自罗曼语的英语 pilgrim（朝圣者，香客）；头一个[r]给[l]替代了。欧洲语言里，[r,l,n]这些音最容易接受这样的替代；替代者常常就是其中的一个。发生替代的地方，遵循着很明确的规则，但是我们不能预言它的发生。这种变化要是贯彻实现了的话，就会导致一种情况，就是某些音，如[r]和[l]，不容许再次出现在同一个词里头——这个情况实际上支配了现代英语中象征性的派生词，如一面是 clatter（辟拍作响，喋喋不休），blubber（号哭），而另一面是 rattle（戛戛作响，喋喋不休），crackle（爆裂声，破碎声）（§14.9）。这一类型的变化似乎完全不同于平常的语音演变。

也有一种异化现象，相似音位之一给丢掉了，如拉丁语 quinque['kwiːnkwe]‘五’到了罗曼语被 *['kiːnkwe]代替了，如意大利语 cinque['tʃinkwe]，法语 cinq [sɛ̃k]。

还有好几种语音替代不能恰当地同平常的音变相提并论。在远距离的同化作用中，同一个词里头一个音位被另一个并不相连的音值近似的音位所替代。比如，原始印欧语 *['penkʷe]‘五’，梵语['panca]，希腊语['pente]，出现在拉丁语里不是 *[pinkwe]，而是 quinque。前日耳曼语里这个词似乎经过了相反的同化，变作 *['pempe]，因为我们遇见的是原始日耳曼语 *['fimfe]，如哥特语和古高德语 fimf，古英语 fif，等等。梵语有些词里头我们预期[s—ç]，偏偏出现[ç—ç]。

换位是一个词内部两个音位交换地位。古英语除所预期的 āscian（‘ask’问）以外，还有 ācsian。塔加洛语里有些形态上的替换似乎是这类变化所造成的；如后缀[-an]，见于[aˈsin]‘盐’：[asˈnan]‘放了盐的东西’，有时两个紧连的辅音互相调换：[aˈtip]‘盖（屋）顶’：[apˈtan]‘盖了顶的（房屋）’；[taˈnim]‘栽的（植物）’：[tamˈnan]‘预备栽下植物的（东西）’。欧洲语言里，(r-l)远距离的换位是相当常见的。与古英语 alor‘赤杨’相对应，古高德语不仅有 elira，并且还有 erila(>现代 Erle)。哥特语[ˈweriloːs]‘唇’（复数），古英语却是 weleras。拉丁语 parabola‘词’（借自希腊语）出现在西班牙语里是 palabra。

一个或一组音位重复出现在一个词里头，其中之一连同介于其间的音素可能给丢了：这种变化叫作节略（haplology）。比如，从拉丁语 nūtriō‘我抚养’派生正规阴性行为名词应该是 *nutrī-trīx‘保姆’，但是实际形式是 nūtrīx。同样，复合词正规形式应该是 *stīpi-pendium‘发付工资',实际出现为 stīpendium。古希腊语[amphi-pho'rews]'双肩挑者'也出现为[ampho'rews]('amphora'双耳盛(酒)器)。这些变化跟音变假设所包括的内容很不相同;这类情况倒也许更接近我们还要讨论的类推变化——类推和借用。

(节选自《语言论》,商务印书馆,1980)

# 第三章　语　义

    语言是音义结合的符号系统,语义正是构成语言符号的所指方面。语素、词、短语、句子等各级语言单位都有意义,各级各类语义的组合与聚合就构成了一个语言的语义系统。

## 第一节　语义的定义和分类

    语义是个含义非常广泛而复杂的概念,它是哲学、逻辑学、心理学、文艺学、语言学等诸多学科都关心的问题,只要涉及人类语言交际活动,就一定涉及"语义"。作为语言学术语,语义指的是语言符号的意义内容。

    语义作为所指跟语形共同构成语言符号,"义"是"形"的内容,"形"是"义"的载体。"义"和"形"的关系是十分复杂的,一义一形、同形异义、同义异形都普遍存在。"同形异义"是形式相同意义不同,也是多义现象,而"同义异形"则是形式不同意义相同,属于同义现象。这里的"形"可指书写形式、语音形式、词语和句子的结构方式,"义"则可指词汇意义、结构意义(语法意义)、语义关系,也可指比喻义、引申义和各种修辞用法,还可指和客观事物特定的对应关系以及话语的内容(说写者的思想感情)等。

    语义从不同的角度可以分为不同的类型。比如,根据语言符号的不同层级,语义可以分为语素义、词义、短语义、句义等;根据语义的特点,可以分为理性意义、语法意义和色彩意义三类;根据语义跟语境的关系,可以分为语言意义和言语意义两大类。语素义、词义、短语义、句义是根据语言单位所作的分类,比较容易理解。下面着重介绍后面两种分类。

## 一、理性意义、语法意义与色彩意义

理性意义、语法意义与色彩意义共同构成语义内容的整体,这三种语义内容的统一表现于词义中,也同样体现于短语义、句义中。

(一)理性意义

理性意义又指概念意义、指称意义或逻辑意义,是概括、反映客观存在及其关系的本质属性和一般属性而形成的一种意义。对词而言,它的理性意义就是语音所表示的对客观存在的反映。例如"书",它所表示的理性意义就是"装订成册的著作"。

理性意义以概念为基础,它一方面反映了客观对象的本质特征,另一方面又反映了人们对客观对象的理性认识。它是构成词义的基本成分,也是语言交际中所表达的最基本的意义,没有这种概念意义就无法进行语言交际。

理性意义与概念既有联系,又有区别。概念属于思维范畴,理性意义属于语言范畴。概念的职能在于认识和反映客观世界,所以它要求反映得全面、深刻。语义的职能在于交际,只要能使人们达到相互理解,能反映出把此事物和彼事物区分开来的特征也就可以了。所以,不应把语言的理性意义和概念看成是一种东西。

在现实生活中,不同的人,由于年龄、职业、文化程度、生活条件等方面的差别,对于概念和词义的认识是不同的。有的认识深刻些,有的肤浅些,有的比较全面,有的则不够全面。例如"人"这个词,没有文化的人、小孩等对它的理解可能只是会说话、穿衣服、直立行走等外部整体的形象特征,这些足以把人和其他动物区分开来,也可以用这个词进行交际,但是他们绝不可能懂得"人是由类人猿进化而成的,能制造和使用工具进行劳动,并能运用语言进行思维的动物"这些更深刻的内容。

虽然不同的人,由于不同的条件,对概念和词义(理性意义)的掌握程度不同,但是对于同一个人来说,他对概念和词义这两种事物的认识程度却永远是一致的。当一个人掌握了完整的概念,那么他所掌握的词义也达到了完整的高度;如果一个人所认识的词义是个不完全的内容,那么他所掌握的概念也是一个不完全的概念。如对"电"的认识,物理学家是一个样子,小孩或普通人又是另一个样子。但是他们各自掌握的关于"电"的概念和词义却是一致的,即概念和词义在一个人身上是永远统一的。

词义本身无所谓错误和正确之分,但词义对客观对象来说,有些就是一种错误的、歪曲的反映。例如"鬼""神""天堂""魔鬼""仙女""龙王"等词所表示的事物都是现实中不存在的东西。这些词的词义都是人们对客观存在进行了错误认识的结果。在科学不发达的年代里,人们在社会实践中遇到了一些无法解释的现象和克服不了的困难,于是就产生了这些错误的反映,出现了"鬼""神"之类的词。这些词的意义往往带有主观想象的成分,有些还寄予了人们的希望和幻想。但是这类虚幻的词义也并非完全出于人们的主观虚构,它们也有自己的客观基础,如果没有客观依据,也不能形成词义。如"魔鬼""仙女"等词所表示的事物形象往往是在凡人形象的基础上虚构而成的。《西游记》中有许多鬼怪、妖精,它们的基本形象也都是人的形象,或者把人的形象和其他动物的形象混合在一起而形成的。所以说,它们仍然有着得以产生的客观依据。

可见,词义的产生,无论是基于人们对客观存在的正确认识,还是基于错误的认识,都是在客观存在的基础上形成的。这就是词义的客观性。

此外,有不少词的理性意义还具有一定的模糊性。词义的模糊性是指一个概念所指对象的范围是不明确的,如"中年""青年""老年"等。客观事物错综复杂,许多事物之间的界限并不分明,因此许多相关概念的外延相互交叉重叠,界限不明。比如"大"与"小"、"深"与"浅"、"高"与"低"、"美"与"丑"等概念所反映的事物性质都是相对而言的。如果我们不考虑科学术语的话,模糊性实际上是大多数语词的一个性质,因为词语所代表的各类事物和各类现象之间是有过渡状态的,这些过渡状态反映在语言当中就体现为语义的模糊性。不过,我们不要片面地认为模糊性是不好的,其实词义的模糊性在人们的交际过程中起着相当重要的作用。人们在传递信息、交流思想时,一般只要把不同事物相互区别开来,明确这个词所指称的事物的大致范围就可以了。这样,人们就能根据交际的需要,在不同的场合灵活地选择与运用词语来表达特定的思想内容,使语言成为方便而灵巧的交际工具。在特定的场合中词义的模糊性还可以作为特殊的手段加以运用。

语言是社会的产物,因此语义还具有社会性、民族性等特征。

(二)语法意义

语法意义是指词进入语法组合后由语法结构所赋予的关系意义。词典的释义所说明的一般都是词的词汇意义,而词语组合成语法结构以后,整个结构的意义总是大于结构中各词意义的总和,这里增加的就是符号和符号之间的语法关系意义。语言中的虚词就只有语法意义而没有词汇意义,英语的形态变化也大多表示的是语法意义。

语法意义的概括程度高于词的理性意义。如"人"和"树"等词本身就是一种概括,它们分别概括了所有的人和所有的树的本质特点,这种概括表现为词的理性意义;但

"人"和"树"等词又有相同的地方,即它们都表示客观事物的名称,"人""树"等一大批表示客观事物名称的词再加以抽象概括,就称为"名词",因此,名词的概括性又进了一步。对名词等词类的语法功能再进一步概括,可以得出主语、宾语等概念,名词是一种类聚,主语等也是一种类聚。语言中的每一个词都存在于某种语法关系的类聚和概括之中,所以每一个词都有语法意义。如"伟大",它的语法意义就是"形容词,可作谓语、定语等";"并且"的语法意义是"连词,可以连接并列的动词、形容词、副词和小句"。对语法意义的认识可以指导人们更好地理解语言,使用语言,无论是对母语学习还是外语学习都有很大帮助。

语法意义总是通过一定的语汇意义或依附于一定的语汇意义而实现的。这样,语法意义虽然不同于语汇意义,却和语汇意义有千丝万缕的联系,并且相互影响,相互制约,所以语法意义可能会由于受不同的语汇成分的语汇意义的影响而呈现出种种差异。

(三)色彩意义

色彩意义是词语的附加意义,主要包括感情色彩、语体色彩、联想色彩和形象色彩等。

**1.感情色彩**

感情色彩就是说话人对所谈对象的主观感情评价和态度。语言单位的感情色彩是历史形成、全民公认的。例如,对老年妇女的呼称,"老太太"带尊敬色彩,属于褒义;"老太"带中性色彩;"老太婆、老东西、老不死"则含贬义。

感情意义指的是言语社团对某一客观对象的主观评价或态度。正面感情如表示赞扬、喜爱、尊敬、礼貌等,负面感情如贬斥、厌恶、轻蔑等。我们平常所说的词义的褒贬,就是这种主观评价的反映。

直接表示人的情感态度的词,如"喜欢—讨厌、诚实—虚伪、高尚—卑劣、聪明—愚蠢"等,它们所包含的感情成分并不是附加的,而是理性意义的主要组成成分,即表示人的喜好、性格、品质等。

词义的感情色彩虽然表示的是人的主观态度,但它不是个人随意规定的,而且在理性意义的基础上历史地形成的。

**2.语体色彩**

语体色彩是指某个领域里使用的语言的特点。从词汇分类来分,一般分书面语色彩和口语色彩两大类。常用于书面写作、某些特定的文体或某些庄重的交际场合的词有书面语色彩,比如,"爸爸"和"父亲"分别具有比较亲切的口语色彩和比较庄重的书面语色彩。我们在使用这两个词时,应该根据交际环境的不同而有所选择。假如一个小孩在家里总是称呼他的爸爸为"父亲",会使人感到非常别扭。再如"吝啬"与"小气"也同样存在书面语体与口语体的对立。不过,大多数词都是既用于书面语也用于口语的通用词。

语体色彩也是历史形成的。交际场景复杂多样,为了适应不同的对象与文体,人们在使用语言的过程中创造或区分出了一些适合不同交际环境的词语。人们在使用语言时通常要根据交际场景的不同选择一些与之相适应的词语,不能在正式的外交场合使用谈家常所使用的话语,也不能在与亲朋好友拉家常时使用外交辞令。

### 3.联想色彩

联想色彩也是一种附加意义,它是在词语理性意义的基础上产生的,而且往往和客观事物的本性和特点相联系。比如在汉语中"猪"常带有"肮脏、贪吃、懒"等联想色彩,说某人是一只猪,就可能是说某人很脏、很贪吃或者很懒等。"狐狸"与"羔羊"则分别带有"狡猾"和"温顺"等联想色彩。

需要指出的是联想色彩是不稳定的,它可以因人而异,也可能因社团、国家、民族或时代而异。例如"狗"的联想色彩在不同民族中就存在差异。

### 4.形象色彩

形象色彩就是指能引起人们某种形象联想的词义成分。词语的形象色彩以视觉形象居多,也有听觉形象、嗅觉形象与味觉形象等。比如"金钱豹、仙人岭、凤尾竹、象鼻山"等均具有十分鲜明的形象感。再如"稀里哗啦""叮叮咚咚"等给人以鲜明的听觉形象,"香喷喷""甜丝丝"则带有很强烈的味觉形象,等等。

形象色彩是词语中客观存在的,而且有不少形象色彩鲜明的词语在构词法上具有很强的修辞意味,比如上述"金钱豹、仙人岭、凤尾竹、象鼻山"等就是通过比喻构词而形成的。此外,由比喻用法而形成的比喻义也往往具有鲜明的形象感。比如,"堡垒、潮流、包袱、饭碗、帽子、棍子"等词的比喻义与原有事物形象之间的联系十分密切,"丢了饭碗"的说法也比"失业"要形象生动得多。

除了感情色彩、语体色彩、联想色彩与形象色彩外,色彩意义还包括风格色彩、地方色彩、民族色彩等。

词汇意义、语法意义、色彩意义是词义内容的重要组成部分,但三者在词义中的地位也不是平等并列的,其中词汇意义是词义内容的核心,语法意义和色彩意义都是在词汇意义的基础上产生的,没有词汇意义也就无所谓语法意义和色彩意义,而且在交际中词义的主要交际功能也是由词汇意义来承担的。


## 二、语言意义与言语意义

语言意义是客观对象以及对象之间的关系在人们意识中抽象概括的反映,它是抽象的、概括的和相对稳定的。语言意义是语义的核心部分,是语义学研究的主要对象。语言意义是语言系统的"字面上的意义",它是客观世界在一个社会集团的集体意识中的概括反映,可以脱离语境而独立存在,词典中的义项就是词语语言意义的分项列举。

言语意义是指特定交际环境中具体言语片段的意义,它是在语言意义的基础上产生的说写者或听读者所表达或理解的特定的意义,它是具体的、个别的、复杂多变的。言语意义包括各种语言单位由于交际环境的影响而产生的临时意义。由于言语意义与具体语境密切相关,所以它是临时的、相对不稳定的,必须结合语境才能存在。

语言意义与言语意义之间存在着相互依存的关系。语言意义是言语意义的综合与概括,而言语意义又是语言意义的个别体现与具体运用。二者既有区别又有联系,这些区别和联系主要体现在如下几个方面。

（一）语言义具有概括性和概念对应性;言语义具有具体事物对应性

语言义是对客观对象的概括反映,具有概括性。它概括了某一类客观对象所共有的特点,而舍弃了个别事物的个别特点,即使专有名词也如此。例如"北京"就概括了历史上的北京,现在的北京以及它的人口、地理、风土人情等各方面的情况。

语言义具有概念对应性特征。以词义为例,当词作为词汇的组成单位存在于语言符号系统之中的时候,也就是当词作为静态语言单位的时候,词义体现为语言义,它所反映的绝不会是某一个具体的客观对象,而是某一类客观对象及其特征,即词义和概念是相对应的。比如,"人"作为语言系统当中的一个语言单位,它概括了所有"能制造工具,使用工具,能思维,有语言"的高等动物,而不指向某个特定的人,没有年龄、性别、肤色、身高、体重、衣着、发型等具体特征。

当词作为动态单位出现在交际中的时候,词义体现为言语义,它就有了具体事物对应性,指向某一个具体事物。言语义不是在任何情况下都存在的,而只能在一定语境中跟具体事物相联系时才能体现出来。言语义的具体事物对应性是在语言义的概念对应性的基础上产生的,但它又和语言义的概念对应性不同。比如说"前面来了一个人"。其中的"人"的词义不仅和"人"的上述概念相对应,而且它还指向特定的某个人,有特定的年龄、性别、肤色、身高、体重、衣着、发型等,所以它同时又具有了具体事物对应性。

具有具体事物对应性的言语义要比具有概念对应性的语言义要丰富得多。比如说"我穿的这双鞋是青岛产的"中的"鞋"的词义除了"穿在脚上,走路着地的东西"外,还增加了一些和具体事物相对应的意义内容,如"黑色的、皮的、系带的、高跟的"等。

（二）语言义具有客观性,相对比较稳定;言语义具有较强的主观性和临时性

语言义具有客观性。仍以词的语言义为例加以说明。词的语言义是客观事物、现象及其关系的概括反映,客观存在的事物、现象及其关系是形成词义的基础。理性意义、语

法意义与色彩意义都有这种客观基础。所以,词的语言义具有客观性。例如"鸟"是"带翅膀、有羽毛、卵生、具有角质两足的自然动物",这种意义的形成是以客观存在的"鸟"的特征为根据的。没有客观存在,就无从产生词的语言义,这就是语言义的客观性。

在这里,我们还应该明确这样一个问题,即词的语言义有客观性,但它并不等于客观事物。词的语言义反映客观世界是通过人们的认识而起作用的。人们的认识有全面的认识,也有不全面的认识;有正确的认识,也有错误的认识。这就使词义和它所反映的客观事物之间并不完全对应,即词义对客观存在的反映有正确的,也有不全面的或歪曲的。例如"鬼""神""天堂""魔鬼""仙女""龙王"等词所表示的事物都是现实中不存在的东西。这些词的词义都是人们对客观存在进行了错误认识的结果。在科学不发达的年代里,人们在社会实践中遇到了一些无法解释的现象和克服不了的困难,于是就产生了这些错误的反映,出现了"鬼""神"之类的词。这些词的意义往往带有主观想象的成分,有些还寄予了人们的希望和幻想。但是这类虚幻的词义也并非完全出于人们的主观虚构,它们也有自己的客观基础,如果没有客观依据,也不可能形成词义。如"魔鬼""仙女"等词所表示的事物形象往往是在凡人形象的基础上虚构而成的。《西游记》中有许多鬼怪、妖精,它们的基本形象也都是人的形象,或者把人的形象和其他动物的形象混合在一起而形成的。所以说,它们仍然有着得以产生的客观依据,而且就词义本身来看,无所谓错误和正确之分。

可见,词义的产生,无论是基于人们对客观存在的正确认识,还是基于错误的认识,都是在客观存在的基础上形成的,具有较强的稳定性。

词语在具体运用中会表现出不同程度的主观差异,即个人可以赋予词不同的意义和色彩,这些主观性就是词语在不同的语境中的言语义。例如"能干",我们可以说"这个人一看就很能干"。这里的"能干"就是"能力强"的意思,含有一种褒扬的色彩。但有时也可以说反话,例如有个人把东西摔坏了,我们说"你真能干",这里的"能干"显然被说话者赋予了另一种意义内容,即"笨"的意思,是反语,感情色彩也发生了变化,由褒扬变为贬斥。这就是言语义所表现出来的主观性。

此外,言语义是在共时状态下运用语言义的结果,不同的人可以有不同的主观发挥,这种主观发挥在没有得到全体社会成员普遍承认之前,只是一种临时意义。例如用"你真聪明"挖苦某人做了蠢事时就只是一种修辞用法,"聪明"表示"蠢"是一种临时言语意义,依附于特定言语环境,并没有被固定下来进入语言义中。同样地,阿Q忌讳"光、亮、灯、烛"正是因为他怕别人谈及头上的癞疮疤这一特定的心理语境所产生的言语义。再如,曹操的口令"鸡肋"在当时语境中也具有特定的言语义,即食之无味,弃之可惜,暗示他对于汉中之地,欲收不能,欲罢不甘。所有这些言语义的产生都带有很强的主观性和临时性,一旦脱离具体的语言听说者以及当时的言语场景,相关言语义便不复存在。所以言语义一般不会作为词语的义项被词典收录,它只是具体交际中的一种"随机应变",并不具有规约性,是临时的、短暂的。

(三)语言义和言语义的互相转化

语言义是相对稳定的,但它也不是一成不变的。社会的发展、客观事物以及人们认识的发展变化,都会在词义中有所反映。例如"兵"过去指"武器",今天指"战士";"走"过去指"跑",现在指"行走";"江"过去指"长江",现在是江的通称。有的从单义词变成了多义词,有的从这种意义变成另外一种意义,都说明词义是发展的。

在同一时代,词义也有发展。例如"污染"原指空气、水源等混入有害物质的现象,如"空气污染""水源污染"等,现在这个词也可以指某种抽象事物的污染,如"精神污染","污染"的词义增加了新义项,这个新义项是在现代汉语阶段出现的。可见,词义无论是在历时阶段,还是在共时阶段,都会变化发展。

这里所说的语言义的发展都是言语义转化为语言义的结果。因为有的言语义经过多人多次的运用,可能会被规约固定下来,从而成为全体社会成员普遍承认的意义,此时这个言语义也就转化成了语言义。例如"宰"这个词,本来的语言义是"杀(动物)",后来在具体运用中,有人用来形容"商家向顾客索要高价",成为临时性的言语义,由于采用这种说法的人越来越多,最后被约定俗成,转化为语言义。

因此,言语义与语言义有着非常密切的关系。言语义虽然是临时获得的意义,但是这种创造性用法一旦得到社会的普遍认同,大家都这样使用,言语义往往就从临时义变成词语的固定义项,成为词的语言意义,换句话说,已经为公众广泛接受的言语义往往会固化为词语约定俗成的语言义。其实,词语语言义的发展,即由本义发展出引申义,由单义变成多义,在很大程度上都是在言语义的基础上形成的。词的创造性运用形成言语义,而言语义又因被越来越多的人接受而逐渐变成一般性的用法。任何一个词义义项,特别是引申义,都不是突然产生的,都是在言语义使用的基础上逐渐固定在词中的。语言在运用中发展,语言义也是在不断的运用中通过吸收言语义而逐步发展的。

总之,语言义和言语义是既有区别,又有联系的。语言义来自言语义,是从既有的无数言语义中抽象概括而来的;固定下来的语言义又是言语义的基础,言语义正是对语言义的具体运用,是语言义在动态中产生的无数个变体。

## 思考与练习

简答题

1.什么是语义?语法意义与理性意义有什么区别与联系?

2.什么是理性意义的客观性?

3.举例说明语义的模糊性,如何辩证地看待语义的模糊性?

4.色彩意义有哪些? 请分别举例说明。

5.语言意义和言语意义有何不同?

6.为什么说言语义具有较强的主观性和临时性?

# 第二节　语义的聚合和组合

一个语言系统中各级各类语言单位的意义都可以按照一定的关系聚合起来或组合起来,这些语义的聚合与组合就构成了该语言的语义系统。

## 一、语义的聚合

语义的聚合关系是根据语义间的关系而确定的。由于语义关系的多样性和层级性,语义的聚合也有多种表现,其中语义场是语义聚合最典型的表现。

语义场是借用物理学中"场"的概念而来的,是含有某个共同义素的义位构成的语义系列,是基于词义和词义之间的共同点或相互之间的某种关系形成的词义类聚。如"父亲""母亲""儿子""女儿"因共同含有"亲属"义素,从而形成"亲属语义场"。"教师""学生"之间因含有教育和被教育的关系,组成"师生关系语义场"。

语义场的存在体现了词汇的系统性。语义场是通过不同词之间的对比,根据词义的共同特点或关系划分出来的语义范围。语义场重视词与词之间的语义关系及它们之间的相互影响,强调每个词都跟同一语义场中的其他词在语义上存在着密切的联系。同一语义场的词语互相规定、互相制约、互相作用,只有通过比较、分析词与词之间的语义关系,才能确定这个词真正的内涵。

同一语义场内的成员因为共同义素的存在彼此连接在一起,同时又因为不同义素的存在而互相区别。依据对共同义素的分析角度不同,语义场相应地区分为不同的类别,如同义义场、反义义场、分类义场、关系义场等。

需要指出的是,这些语义场分类并不能反映语义聚合关系的全部情况,而且由于其划分标准不统一,其中有交叉跨类现象。尽管归纳出的这些类型并不十分全面严密,但区分这些类型仍然有助于我们从不同角度去理解语义场的构成方式,深化对语义场的认识。

(一)类属义场

类属关系,实际上就是一般和个别的关系,即属概念和种概念的关系。属概念是指一般的大类概念,种概念是指具体的小类概念。基于类属关系建立的语义场就是类属义场,类属义场中各成员称为类属词。

类属词表示的概念必须是上下级的类属关系,既不能处在同级,也不能跨越几级,必须是紧紧相连的上下级层次。如"家具-床-沙发-衣柜""衣服-裤子-短裤"等。

"菊花"和"桃花"在同一层次,是对义词而不是类属词,"菊花"与"植物"虽然不在同一层次,但依然不能形成类属词的关系,因为类属词表示的是最直接的类属概念,而它们不是最直接的种类关系。此外,类属义场中的词语所表示的概念是整体和成员的关系,而不是整体和构件的关系,如"大衣-袖子""房子-窗户"都不构成类属义场。

类属词的类属关系可以是一对多的关系,也可以是一对一的关系。"花"与"菊花、桃花"等一系列的词形成类属关系,也与其中的每一个词分别形成类属关系。

类属关系也叫上下位关系,上位概念是属概念,下位概念是种概念,所以语言中具有类属关系的类属词也叫上下位词。如"颜色"与"红、黄、蓝、白、黑"形成类属词的关系,"颜色"是属概念,"红、黄、蓝、白、黑"是"颜色"的种概念。再如,"金属"与"金、银、铜、铁、锡"、"年龄"与"老年、中年、青年、少年、童年、幼年"、"花"与"菊花、桃花、玫瑰花、杜鹃花"等都属于类属词,是基于类属关系的意义类聚。

上下位词的意义呈现一定的规律性,越是下位词,它的意义越丰富、具体;越是上位词,它的意义越概括、抽象。

(二)顺序义场

顺序义场是基于数量、时间、程度、等级等方面的顺序建立起来的语义场。比如"春、夏、秋、冬"分别是一年中的四个季节,次第出现;"学士、硕士、博士"是学位的三个等级,前后承接。

顺序义场的各成员都是按照某种固定的顺序排列的,如"大学、中学、小学""January、February、March、April、May、June、July、August、September、October、November、December"等。

如果义场中包含的成员很多,可以在前面或后面加上数词表示序数的表示,如"一月、二月、三月""一楼、二楼、三楼""一等、二等、三等""星期一、星期二、星期三"等。

顺序义场中的成员必须根据它在序列中所处的相对位置来理解,顺序是这些成员的一个义素,其中成员的增减会影响到其他成员,比如,在由"大尉、上尉、中尉、少尉"所构成的顺序义场中,"上尉"处于尉官第二级,但有些军队不设大尉,上尉就成了"上尉、中尉、少尉"尉官顺序义场中的第一级了。

有些顺序义场是封闭型的,可以周而复始,可以叫做"循环义场"。比如,"春夏秋冬",冬去春来,持续循环。再如,"星期一、星期二、星期三……星期日",星期日之后又是星期一,不断循环,周而复始。有些顺序义场则是非封闭型的,不可以循环,如"小学、初中、高中、大学"就是单向的,不可能周而复始。

### (三)同义义场

同义义场是由意义相同或相近的一组义位构成的语义场。义位是词义存在的基本形式,是语义系统中的基本单位。一个词有一种意义,就有一个义位。有的词有多种意义,其中能够独立运用的一种意义,就是一个义位。

同义义场中义位的主要义素都相同,次要义素有差异。如"父亲-爸爸"构成一个同义义场,可以分析出以下义素:[+直系亲属][+长辈][+男性][±书面语色彩],其中,前三个反映了词义本质特征的主要义素都相同,只有色彩义显示了两者的区别。再如,"推翻-颠覆"理性意义相同,只是存在感情色彩的褒贬对立。

同义词之间的语义关系复杂多样,一般分为等义词和近义词两大类。理性意义和附加意义都相同的同义词叫等义词,略有差异的叫近义词。

等义词数量不是很多,如"卷心菜-包头菜""嫉妒-妒忌""互相-相互""演讲-讲演"等。等义词意义相同,在语言运用中大都可以互相替换。不过,等义词是词汇系统的冗余成分,从历时的角度看,它们要么发生意义分化,要么一方被另一方淘汰,一般不会有绝对的等义词长期共存。

近义义场各义位之间的义素大同小异。同主要表现为基本义相同或部分相同,异主要表现为基本义略有不同、色彩义不同或者基本义与色彩义都略有差异。

基本义有同有异的很多:"交流、交换",但"交流"搭配的对象大都是意义较抽象或所指范围较大的词,如"思想""经验""文化""物资"等;"交换"搭配的对象大都是意义较具体的或所指范围较小的词,如"礼物""意见""资料""产品"等。"轻视-蔑视""优异-优秀""渴望-希望"语义轻重不同;"边疆-边境""事件-事故"词义范围不同,都是前者范围较大,后者范围较小;"河流-河""书籍-书"是具体与概括不同,前者表示集体的、概括的事物,后者表示个别的、具体的事物。

基本义相同而色彩义不同的情况也很常见。例如:"生日-诞辰"理性意义相同,只语体色彩有别,前者适用于口语语体,后者适用于书面语体。"成果-结果-后果"感情色彩不同,"成果"指取得的成就,是褒义词;"后果"指不好的结局,是贬义词;"结果"则没有什么褒贬的意义,是中性词。"维生素-维他命"中前者有民族色彩,后者有外来色彩。

基本义与色彩义都略有不同的近义词也不少,比如:"煽动-鼓动",在理性意义上,前者指"促使人去做坏事情",后者指"促使人去做好事情",二者具有一定差别,在色彩意义上,前者是贬义词,后者是褒义词,二者感情色彩也不同;"粗俗-粗鄙"在理性意义上都是指作风格调或言谈举止的粗野庸俗,但"粗鄙"中还含有性质低下的意思,在色彩义上,"粗鄙"有书面语体色彩,"粗俗"则通用于口语和书面语。

需要指出的是,由于多义词的干扰,同义词有时候并不是词和词的关系,而只是词和义项的关系或者义项和义项的关系。如果义同的双方都是单义词,那么,两者形成的同义关系是纯粹的同义词关系。如果义同的双方一方是单义词,另一方是多义词,那么,两者构成的是词与义项之间的同义关系。如果义同的双方都是多义词,那么,两者形成的同义词关系表现为义项之间的同义关系。

(四)反义义场

反义义场是意义相反或相对的义位构成的语义场,如"construction-destruction""战争-和平"等。反义义场中各义位既有共同的义素,又有对立的义素。共有的义素表明了义位之间的统一关系,对立义素则显示了义位之间相反或相对的关系。如:

君子:[+人][+人格高尚]　　　　小人:[+人][+人格卑下]

相同的义素"人"代表了"君子"和"小人"属于同一个意义范畴,而"人格高尚"和"人格卑下"两个相互对立的义素则构成了它们之间的意义对立关系。

反义义场分为互补反义义场和极性反义义场。互补反义义场中的两个义位中的能显示区别性特征的义素是建立在客观事物矛盾关系的基础上的,表现为截然相反的关系,肯定义素甲就否定了义素乙,否定了义素甲就肯定了义素乙,肯定了义素乙就否定了义素甲,否定了义素乙就肯定了义素甲,甲和乙之间没有中间概念存在。如:

生:[+生命][+存在]　　　　死:[+生命][+消失]

"存在"和"消失"反映的是客观对象的矛盾关系,两者之间不存在中间概念,即没有"既非存在也非消失"的中间状态。所以"生""死"构成了互补反义义场。

客观世界中存在的大量互补对立现象在语言当中也大多体现为互补反义义场,如"动-静""死-活""男-女""这-那""男人-女人""真实-虚假""战争-和平""全面-片面""永远-暂时"等都是互补反义义场。对于这些反义义场的两个义位而言,非此一定是彼,非彼必然是此,亦此亦彼是不可能的。

处于互补反义义场中的反义词也叫绝对反义词,两个词表示的意义永远矛盾对立、互相排斥,其间没有中间状态存在,否定一方就意味着肯定另一方。

极性义场中显示区别性特征的义素建立在客观事物对立关系的基础上,表现为肯定义素甲就否定了义素乙,肯定了义素乙就否定了义素甲,但是,反过来,否定了义素甲却不能肯定义素乙,否定了义素乙也不能肯定义素甲,甲和乙之间存在中间概念。如在"老"和"少"之间还有"青年""中年"等中间状态存在,两者不能形成非此即彼的关系,它们构成极性反义义场。再如"大"与"小",rich 与 poor 形成两极,但也存在"不大不小"及 neither rich nor poor(不富也不穷)这样的过渡地带。

因此,处于极性义场中的反义词并是矛盾对立的,否定一方并不意味着肯定另一方。这类反义义场很多,如"穷-富""老-少""大-小""爱-恨""深-浅""轻-重""美-丑""重视-轻视""先进-落后""积极-消极""自大-自卑""快乐-痛苦""天才-傻瓜""懦夫-勇士""伟大-渺小"等等都构成极性反义义场。

不过,由于词义本身存在多义性等复杂的情形,反义词并不是词与词之间的整齐对应,而是呈现词与词之间、词与义项之间、义项与义项之间等反义对应的复杂情形。一般情况下,一个多义词只要其中一个意义与另一个词的某个意义构成反义关系,我们就可以把这两个词叫作反义词。

反义词虽然反映了客观世界中的矛盾对立关系,但反映这种关系的并不都是反义词,只有用词表示这种关系的才是反义词。如"大-不大"就不构成反义义场,因为后者是词组,不能跟形容词"大"构成一对反义词。

反义词是以词义的相反相对关系为连接点所形成的词义类聚,它们是客观事物中存在的矛盾对立现象在语言中的反映。反义词在语言应用中常常以对举的形式出现,用以揭示事物现象之间的矛盾对立。

除了上述几种语义场之外,还有关系义场。关系义场中的义位主要反映人与人、人与事物及事物与事物之间的关系,其中有二元的,如"老师-学生""丈夫-妻子""exit-entrance";有多元的,如"敌军-友军-我军""哥哥-姐姐-弟弟-妹妹"。关系义场跟其他义场一样具有民族性,在不同语言中体现不同,比如"哥哥-姐姐-弟弟-妹妹"这一义场在英语中却是二元的,由 brother 和 sister 两个成员构成。

## 二、语义的组合

词语是语言的备用单位,要实现语言的实际职能,必须把词语组织成话语。因此,把词语义组合成话语义是交际过程的中心环节。

### (一)语义组合的制约条件

词语组合除了要受语法规则支配外,还要受到语义条件的制约。例如,"人吃饭"可以接受,因为它反映了客观现实中的真实存在,而"饭吃人"则不能被接受,虽然在语法结构上它跟"人吃饭"一样,都符合汉语语法规则。"饭吃人"不能成立是因为其中各成分的语义不能组合,"吃"这个动词要求与之组合的施事者是有生命的人或动物,它的受事者应是非液体状态的可食之物,而"饭吃人"不符合这样的语义组合条件。

从理性义上看,词语搭配组合主要看它们的语义是否相融,能相融的就可以搭配组合;不相融的则不能搭配组合。例如,虽然"烟""酒""肉"都是名词,但是只有"酒"可以与动词"喝"组合成"喝酒",而"喝烟""喝肉"都不能被人接受。这是因为"喝"这个动词要求它所关涉的对象具有【+液体】义素,"酒"具有这一义素,所以"喝酒"成立,"烟"和"肉"均不具有这一义素,因而都不能与"喝"搭配组合。

从色彩义上看,词语搭配组合的语义条件是风格协调。褒义词适用于肯定、褒扬的人和物,贬义词语适用于否定、贬斥的人和物,否则,语义组合就不能被人接受。比如,"伟大的诗人""伟大的祖国"很自然,但"伟大的流氓""伟大的叛徒"就不能被接受。再如,"敌人勾结在一起"可以说,"人民勾结在一起"就不能说。此外,常用于口语的词和常用于书面语的词一般不应在同一场合夹杂使用,否则会造成风格失调,像"吃过晚饭,我们几个老头常在校园里溜达"很自然,如果将"溜达"改成"徜徉",风格则极不协调。

当然,语义组合规则在不同方言中可能有不同表现。例如,现代汉语普通话中不能说"吃烟""吃酒"等,而在许多方言中"吃烟""吃酒"都是成立的,这是因为不同方言的语义系统稍有差异,相关词语的语义跟普通话是不对等的。

(二)语义组合关系

组合在一起的词语不仅具有结构关系,而且还具有复杂的语义关系。语义组合关系是一定现实关系的概括反映。词语组合的结构关系可以概括出有限的类型和模式,同样地,语义组合关系也可以概括出若干类型。词语组合的语义关系复杂多样,很难穷尽列举,这里列举一些比较常用的类型。

(1)施动关系:施事是动作动词表示的动作或行为的发出者,施动关系就是施事与动作的关系。如"小王看过了"中的"小王"为施事,"看"是"小王"发出的动作。再如"我先说""兔子跑了"中的"我"和"兔子"分别跟"说"和"跑"构成施动关系。

(2)受动关系:受事与施事相对,是动作动词表示的动作或行为的承受者,是施事发出的动作所直接影响的现成的客体事物。受动关系就是受事与动作的关系。如"饭吃完了"中的"饭"是接受"吃"这一动作行为的受事。再如"砍了一棵树""洗了两件衣服"中的"一棵树"和"两件衣服"分别与"砍"和"洗"构成受动关系。

(3)动作结果关系:动作与动作行为所产生的结果的关系。如"妈妈正在打毛衣"中的"毛衣"是动作行为"打"的结果。再如"盖房子""写论文"中的"房子"和"论文"分别是动作"盖"和"写"的结果。

(4)动作时间关系:动作与动作行为发生或持续的时间的关系。如"他昨天走的"中的"昨天"是动作行为"走"发生的时间;"这本书我读了两天"中的"两天"是动作行为"读"持续的时间。

(5)动作处所关系:动作与动作行为发生或涉及的处所的关系。如"在上海读书""衣服放在箱子里""飞往桂林"中的"上海""箱子里"和"桂林"分别是"读书""放"和"飞"相关的处所。

时间和处所根据动词或相关介词的语义特征还可以细分为起点、经由和终点,如"火车从广州(起点)出发经过武汉(经由)去西安(终点)""会议自两点(起点)开始到五点(终点)结束""演讲比赛过了三点(经由)才开始"等。

(6)动作工具关系:动作与动作行为所使用的工具的关系。如"我用毛笔写字""吃大碗"中的"毛笔"和"大碗"分别是动作行为"写字"和"吃"所使用的工具。

(7)动作方式关系:动作与发出该一动作行为所采取的方法、手段或形式的关系。如"他通过互联网寻找相关信息"和"用银行卡付款"中的"互联网"和"银行卡"分别是动作行为"寻找"和"付款"的方式手段。再如"唱美声""存活期""考口试""游蝶泳"等中的"美声""活期""口试""蝶泳"等都是表示相关动作行为的方式。

名词性成分之间的关系比较常见的有领属关系、限定关系、同指关系等,如:

领属关系:领有者与被领有者的关系。如"她的裙子很漂亮"中的"她"是"裙子"的领有者,"裙子"为"她"所拥有,是被领有者。

限定关系:限定者与被限定者的关系。如"这是一本语言学教材"中的"一本"和"语言学"分别从数量与性质上限定"教材","一本"和"语言学"是限定者,"教材"是被限定者。

同指关系:在组合中表示相同对象的不同词语之间的语义关系是同指关系。如"中国的首都北京"中"中国的首都"与"北京"所指相同,二者的语义关系是同指关系。

需要说明的是,词语组合的语义关系并不限于上述语义关系类型,语义组合关系远比词语组合的结构关系复杂多样。

有些语义组合关系跟结构关系有一定的对应和联系,如语义上是领属关系和限定关系的,结构上一定是偏正关系。以"学习材料"为例,如果它是限定关系,结构上就是偏正关系,如果是受动关系,结构上就是动宾关系。不过,语义组合关系与结构关系是从内容和形式两个方面考察词语的组合,性质根本不同,通常不相对应。例如,语义上是受动关系的词语组合,结构上可以是主谓关系,如"书被卖了";也可以是动宾关系,如"卖书"。再如,"鸡不吃了"结构上是主谓关系,但"鸡"和"吃"可能是施动关系,也可能是受动关系。

**思考与练习**

简答题

1.什么是语义场？为什么说语义场体现了词汇的系统性？

2.语义场有哪些类型？请举例说明。

3.请举例说明同义义场与反义义场的各种类型。

4.什么是同类义场？什么是类属义场？二者有什么区别与联系？

5.什么是顺序义场？什么是关系义场？请分别举例说明。

6.请举例说明语义组合的制约条件有哪些。

7.语义组合关系有哪些类型？语义组合关系跟句法结构关系有什么区别与联系？

# 第三节　词汇和词义

## 一、词义及其性质

　　词义是客观对象在人们意识中的抽象概括反映。词义的形成还要受词汇语义系统的制约,同一词汇系统中的成员相互依存、相互利用,某个词的意义通常不是由该词自己规定的,而是由同一系统中别的相关词给它规定的,同一语义场内的词语的词义相互制约的关系尤其明显。例如,汉语中"哥哥、弟弟、姐姐、妹妹"四个义位并存,所以既分性别又分长幼。英语只有"brother""sister"两个义位,因此只分性别不分长幼。古汉语中"父亲的兄弟"有时根据排行用"伯父、仲父、叔父、季父"等义位区分父辈兄弟,其中"伯父"只指父辈兄弟中的老大,"叔父"则指老三。现代汉语只有"伯伯、叔叔"两个义位,"伯父"指"父亲的哥哥","叔叔"指"父亲的弟弟",语义范围变宽了,变化的原因就是同一语义场中的成员数量发生了增减。

　　词义的性质主要体现为客观性、概括性和民族性。客观性指客观存在的事物是词义形成的基础,即使是一些以虚幻的事物、现象为基础形成的词义依然有其客观性。概括性指词义在客观反映事物的过程中它要舍弃同类客观对象中不同个体的具体特征,从中抽象出共同的本质的特征,即使是专有名词也不例外。如"黄河"专指一条河流,但它的意义却概括了黄河的发源、流域、水质、水量等各个方面不同的特点以及黄河的历史、现状等情况,所以"黄河"的词义依然是概括的。语言中所有词的意义都具有概括性特点。民族性指不同民族在用语言标记客观世界的过程中,由于民族思维、语言系统等方面的差异,决定了词义出现民族性的差异。这种差异主要表现在选择不同的语言单位概括相同的事物现象或者选择不同数量的词来概括相同的事物现象,等等。此外,词义的民族性在色彩意义方面尤其是感情色彩方面也有着鲜明的表现。

根据词语意义的单一与复杂,可以分为单义词与多义词两大类。

## 二、单义词

单义词只有一个意义。如"语言学""辅音""语素""北京""西瓜""藕""氧""葡萄""纳米""原子"等。

单义词主要有以下几类:常见事物的名称,如汽车、飞机、大米、西红柿;专有名称,如马克思、鲁迅、北京、黄河;科技术语,如原子、元素、行星、克隆;等等。语言中单义词是最便于理解和记忆的。用单义词表示常见事物名称、专有名词,便于明确指称。而科技术语意义的单一性是保证科技术语科学性的必要条件。

词语刚刚产生的时候往往都是单义的,在发展演变的过程中可能增加新义项,由单义词发展为多义词。例如,"流产"最初的意义是指"怀孕后胎儿未满28周就产出"。在语言运用和发展的过程中,该词又增加了一个新的意义,即"比喻事情在酝酿或进行中遭到挫折而不能实现",从而由单义词演变为多义词。

单义词的产生还可能有另外一种情况,即词义在发展过程中由多义变成单义,即多义词的一些意义在发展过程中消失,只剩下其中的一个意义。

## 三、多义词

多义词包含几个既有联系又有区别的意义。如"跑"就具有"两只脚或四条腿迅速前进"、"逃走"、〈方〉"走"、"为某种事务而奔走"、"物体离开了应该在的位置"、"液体因挥发而损耗"六项互相有联系但又各不相同的意义。

多义词的义项是对多义词意义的分项说明。前面所举"跑"的六项意义即是该词的六个义项。再如,"剪影"有两个义项,一个义项是"照着人脸或人体的轮廓的剪纸成形",另一个义项是"比喻对于事物轮廓的描写",这两个意义既有区别,又有联系。

有些词典在解释各项词汇意义的同时还附带提及词的色彩意义。凡义项中带有

〈方〉、〈书〉、〈口〉等标记的,都显示了该项意义同时具有方言色彩、书面语色彩或口语色彩。"跑"含有的"走"的义项从色彩意义的角度分析,蕴含了方言色彩,用〈方〉字标出。

(一)多义词的义项分类

多义词的多个义项可以从不同角度分类,最常用的分类方式有两种,一是根据意义的产生时间分为本义和转义;二是根据各义项的使用频率分为基本义和非基本义。

一个词的一组意义中最早出现的意义叫本义,它是派生新意义的基础,一个词后来产生的意义一般都是在其基本义的基础上直接或间接转化而来的。转义又叫引申义或派生义,是在本义或基本义的基础上产生的意义。例如,"树"的本义是"木本植物的通称",其后产生的"种植;栽培""树立;建立"等意义就是在本义基础上派生而来的转义。再如,"兵器"是"兵"的本义,"军队"是它的转义。

基本义指的是词在现代最常用的意义。如"老"的基本义是"年纪大",其他几个意义如"陈旧的""原来的""很久以前就存在的"等则是非基本义。如果从历史发展的角度看,多义词的基本义可能不止一个,但是从共时方面来看,多义词在某一发展阶段上只能有一个基本义。

词语产生之初大都是单义的,本义就是基本义。在词义的发展过程中,有些词的本义还是基本义,有的词则可能发生变化,转义变成基本义,如"走""兵"等。所以,一个词的本义不一定是它的基本义,在这一问题上我们必须把历时和共时的情况区分开来。

多义词虽然有若干意义,但进入言语环境后语义通常就会单一化。所以正确理解话语中多义词的含义必须依赖言语环境。

(二)转义的派生方式

多义词转义的派生方式或产生途径非常复杂,辐射式、连锁式和结合式是词义派生最常见的三种方式。

**1.辐射式**

辐射式引申是以本义为中心向不同的方向派生出数个直接引申义的词义引申脉络,即由本义发展出几个平行的无直接联系的派生意义。如"老"的本义是"年纪大",由此派生出来的"历时长久"(老建筑)、"陈旧"(老机器)、"原来的"(老习惯)、"经常"(老迟到)、"很"(老远)等意义都是由本义往不同方向引申而来,这些引申义之间并没有派生关系。再如:

$$
竹节
\begin{cases}
草木节(草木)\\
关节(动物)\\
季节(时令)\\
节拍(音乐)\\
气节(道德)\\
礼节(社会)\\
节约(用度)
\end{cases}
$$

"节"的本义是竹节,由此派生出"木节""骨头等的分节""时节""节奏""法度""节操""节制"七个意义,这些派生义都是由本义派生出来的,只是引申方向不一样,这些转义之间没有派生关系,属于辐射式引申。

### 2.连锁式

意义连锁派生是以本义为起点,向着同一方向次递派生出几个意义,即由本义引申出甲义,又由甲义引申出乙义,再由乙义引申出丙义,这样一环套一环,形成一个词义系列。从这些引申义跟本义的关系看,除了甲义是由本义直接引申而来外,其他意义都是间接引申。如"鄙"本义是"边邑",由此以连锁式次第引申出"质朴"(地处边远,民性质朴)、"见识浅陋"(质朴而见闻不广)、"轻视"(因见识浅被看不起)三个意义。再如"要"的本义是"腰",后来在此基础上依次发展出其他引申义。

①腰:昔楚灵王好细要。(《墨子·经说》)

②中间:是王之地一经两海,要绝天下也。(《战国策·秦策》)

③拦截:吴人要而击之,获邓廖。(《左传·襄公三年》)

④要挟:虽曰不要君,吾不信也。(《论语·宪问》)

"要"的意义引申脉络如下:

①腰(人体的中间部分)→②中间(事物的中间部分)→③拦截(迫使他人中途停止前进)→④要挟(迫使他人改变意向)

### 3.综合式

很多多义词义项的产生既有辐射式,又有连锁式,两种引申方式共同构成多义词复杂的意义发展体系。如"信"的本义是"言语真实",后来通过辐射式引申和连锁式引申发展出了多个不同义项。

①言语真实:信言不美,美言不信。(《老子》)

②诚信:与朋友交,能不信乎?(《论语·学而》)

③相信:人谓子产不仁,吾不信也。(《左传·襄公三十一年》)

④的确:舜其信仁乎?(《韩非子·难一》)

⑤信物:用为符信,上书自陈。(《史记·外戚世家》)

⑥信使:诗好几时见?书成无信将。(杜甫《寄彭州高三十五使君适虢州岑二十七长史参》)

⑦音信:自可断来信,徐徐更谓之。(《孔雀东南飞》)

⑧书信:不忍拈将等闲用,半封京信半题诗。(元稹《书乐天纸》)

"信"的语义发展脉络如下:

①言语真实 ⎰ ②诚信
　　　　　 ⎱ ③相信
　　　　　 　 ④的确
　　　　　 ⎱ ⑤信物→ ⑥信使→ ⑦音信→ ⑧书信

可见,"信"的第②、③、④、⑤义项都是直接引申义,由本义到这几个义项的关系是辐射式的,第⑥、⑦、⑧等几个义项则是以引申义⑤为基础的连锁式引申,所以"信"的词义发展体现为复合式的引申。

(三)词义派生的规律

词义的派生规律主要体现为三个方面,一是由具体到抽象或由个别到一般;二是由抽象到具体或由一般到个别;三是由甲类事物到乙类事物。

(1)由具体到抽象或由个别到一般。如:

道:道路(会天大雨,道不通)→途径、方法、措施(治世不一道)→规律、道理(天有常道)

响:回声→响声

色:脸色→颜色

(2)由抽象到具体或由一般到个别。如:

子:孩子(不分男女)→男孩儿

朕:自身→皇帝自称

臭:气味→难闻的气味

丈夫:男子→女性的配偶

(3)由甲类事物到乙类事物。

"府"原指"收藏文书、钱财的地方",后指"管理财物的官名",再后来指"官府",而"收藏文书的地方"一义消失了。再如:

走:跑→行走

脚:小腿→足

狱:案件官司→监狱

（四）多义词与同音词的区别与联系

多义词是一个形式表示几个意义,但它不同于同形同音词。同形同音词在意义上没有联系,只是声音形式相同而已,如"开花"与"花钱"中的"花"语义毫无关联,它们是两词同音,不是一词多义。所以,多义词和同音词的区别主要在于意义上有没有联系。如果意义上有联系,就是多义词,否则就是同音词。

多义词意义之间如果失去联系也会变成同音词。如古汉语中"管"有"钥匙"和"管理"两义,是多义词,因为掌握钥匙（管状）就意味着掌握权力。现代汉语中,钥匙不再称为"管","管"这个词的"管状物"和"管理"两个意义失去联系,因而变成了语义没有联系的同音词。

**思考与练习**

简答题

1.什么是词义? 它具有什么性质特征?

2.本义与基本义有什么区别与联系? 请举例说明。

3.单义词主要有哪几类? 为什么?

4.多义词意义的派生方式有哪些?

5.词义派生的规律主要体现在哪些方面?

6.举例说明多义词与同音词的区别与联系。

# 第四节　句　义

句义可以分为词汇意义和关系意义两大部分。词汇意义句中词语的意义是组成句义的基础,理解一个句子的意义,首先要懂得句中词语的词汇意义,但句义不是词汇意义的简单相加。关系意义是由句内词语间的结构关系所赋予的意义。词汇意义是词语本身所具有的意义,一个词语即使孤立存在,也会具有一定的词汇意义,而关系意义则是词语进入组合之中才产生的意义,它只存在于一定的句法结构之中,孤立的词语是没有关系意义的。

## 一、句子的语言意义

句子的语言意义可以分为语法关系意义和语义关系意义两大类。语法关系意义是语法结构关系所赋予的意义,如主谓、动宾、偏正等。语义关系意义则是词语组合时产生的语义上的关系,比如动作受事(吃苹果)、动作施事(大鱼吃小鱼)、动作工具(吃大碗)、动作处所(吃食堂)等关系,这种关系是对现实关系的概括反映。

任何一个句子都具有语法关系意义和语义关系意义,比如,"小王买书"所包含的语法关系意义有"小王"和"买书"之间的"陈述"的意义以及"买"与"书"之间的"涉及"的意义,而这句话所包含的语义关系意义则是"买"和"小王"之间存在的"动作"和"施事"的意义以及"买"和"书"之间的"动作"和"受事"的意义。

句中词语的关系意义有很多种,其中语义角色和语义指向是最常用的分析语义关系的手段或方法。

### (一)语义角色

句法结构中的语义关系多种多样,在各种语义关系中,名词性成分担任了一定的语义角色,如"施事""受事""与事""工具""方式""目的""原因""时间""处所"等。

语义角色实际上揭示的是名词性成分跟谓词性成分之间的语义关系。例如,"他向同学们挥了挥手""你得跟父母好好商量商量""老张对老李很有意见"中的"同学们""父母"和"老李"是动作行为的与事;"救火""打扫卫生""公司派老王跑材料""为了挽救落水老人张华献出了生命"中的"火""卫生""材料"和"挽救落水老人"是动作行为的目的;"会议因地震而延期""小王在家养病""乡亲们在躲避敌机的空袭""老王又在操心儿子的婚事"中的"地震""病""敌机的空袭"和"儿子的婚事"是动作行为的原因;等等。

名词的语义角色实际上还有好多种,它可以跟动作直接组合,也可以靠介词引入。语义角色具有很强的解释力,建立起语义关系的类型,就可以合理解释句法结构内部的复杂情况。动词同名词性词语之间的语义关系是由它们双方共同决定的,同一个动词,与不同的名词性词语搭配就可能产生不同的语义关系。例如:

    吃面条(动作——受事)  吃大碗(动作——工具)  吃食堂(动作——处所)
    吃包月(动作——方式)

同一个名词性词语,与不同的谓词搭配也可能产生不同的语义关系。例如:

    买毛衣(动作——受事)  织毛衣(动作——结果)
    打人(动作——受事)    来人(动作——施事)

语义角色主要是名词和谓词性成分的语义关系,其实名词之间的语义关系也很复杂多样,它们也是构成句义的重要组成部分。如领属关系(我的书)、来源关系(北京的烤鸭)、质料关系(全棉外套)、比喻关系(历史的车轮)等。

(二)语义指向

语义指向是句子中某一成分跟句中或句外的一个或几个成分在语义上的直接联系。句中某个成分的语义指向可以同句法结构关系一致,也可以不一致。比如"我吃完了"中的补语"完"指向"吃",表示动作结束,而同样是动补结构的"我吃饱了"中的补语"饱"则指向"我"。再如:

砍光了　　砍累了　　砍钝了　　砍快了　　砍疼了　　砍坏了

从格式上看,以上各例都是"动+形+了"述补结构。但是,其补语成分的语义所指仔细分析起来会发现它们各不相同:

砍光了[补语"光"在语义上指向"砍"的受事,如"树砍光了"。]

砍累了[补语"累"在语义上指向"砍"的施事,如"我砍累了"。]

砍钝了[补语"钝"在语义上指向"砍"的工具,如"这把刀砍钝了"。]

砍快了[补语"快"在语义上指向"砍"这一动作本身。]

砍疼了[歧义结构:补语"疼"语义可指向"砍"的受事,也可指向"砍"的施事。]

砍坏了[歧义结构:补语"坏"语义可指向"砍"的受事,也可以指向"砍"的工具。]

以上分析的只是补语语义指向的不同,可见,语义指向揭示的是句中成分语义关系,跟句法结构关系并不直接相关,有些句法成分语义指向一个对象,而有些句法成分在语义上却可能指向不止一个对象,如:

小王撞倒了一棵大树。

上海队打赢了山东队。

你穿好衣服走。

第一例中的补语"倒"在语义上指向后面的宾语"大树",第二例中的补语"赢"的语义指向前面的主语"上海队"。第三例中的谓语动词后面的"好"既可以直接与它前面的谓语动词"穿"发生语义关系("穿好"即穿戴整齐),也可以和它后面的名词"衣服"发生语义关系(好衣服)。前者构成述补结构,后者构成定中结构。

可见,在不同的语境中,有的句法成分可能只跟一个其他成分发生语义关系,也可能跟两个或两个以上的成分发生语义关系。

语义指向具有很强的解释力。有些句法结构的情况比较复杂,语义指向可以合理解释句子成分之间的关系,而且某些歧义现象也可以借助于语义指向分析得到合理解释。例如:

小王最喜欢游泳。

她又买了一件毛衣。

第一例如果是针对"许多人都喜欢游泳"这一情境来说的,那么"最"语义指向"小王";如果这句话是针对"小王喜欢许多项运动"这一情境来说的,那么"最"语义指向"游泳"。

第二例情况更为复杂,我们可以通过设置语境的方法来加以分析:

　　a.我买了一件毛衣,她又买了一件毛衣。("又"语义指向"她")

　　b.她已借了一件毛衣,她又买了一件毛衣。("又"语义指向"买")

　　c.她已买了两件毛衣,她又买了一件毛衣。("又"语义指向"一件毛衣")

　　d.她已买了一件皮衣,她又买了一件毛衣。("又"语义指向"毛衣")

## 二、多义句

多义句是指同一形式的语言符号序列可能表达不同意义的现象。造成句子多义的原因有很多种,比较常见的有以下几类。

### (一)同音词、多义词与兼类词造成歧义

你先别上。("别"既可以理解为动词,也可以理解为副词。)

他的包袱很重。("包袱"既可以指用布包起来的包,也可以指某种负担。)

他的房间都没有锁。("锁"既可以理解为名词,也可以理解为动词。)

### (二)结构层次不同造成的歧义

他是我前几天刚认识的李娟的哥哥。("前几天刚认识的"可能是"李娟",也可能是"李娟的哥哥"。)

部分男生和女生参加了调查。(可能是"部分/男生和女生",可能是"部分男生/和女生"。)

### (三)结构关系不明造成的歧义

他喜欢进口汽车。("进口汽车"可以理解为偏正结构,也可以理解为动宾结构。)

学生家长都来了。("学生家长"可以理解为并列结构,也可以理解为偏正结构。)

### (四)指代不明造成的歧义

小张看到王老师正和自己的同事热烈地交谈着。("自己"指代不明)

小张扶着一位老人走下车来,他手里提着一个黑色皮包。("他"指代不明)

(五)动词的施受对象不明造成的歧义

刚转学过来的张明谁都不认识。(可能是张明不认识别人,也可能是别人不认识张明。)

最担心的还是家人。(可能是"家人担心",也可能是"担心家人"。)

(六)动词或介词的支配范围不明造成的歧义

记者否认外星人的存在是有根据的。(动词"否认"的宾语不明确,可以理解为"外星人的存在",也可以是"外星人的存在是有根据的"。)

对厂长的意见,我没什么好说的。(介词"对"的宾语可以是厂长,也可以是"厂长的意见"。)

(七)介词或连词词性不明造成的歧义

这是历史学家与文学家争论不休的问题。("与"可做连词理解,也可做介词理解。)

她上周跟同事去了趟北京。("跟"可以理解为连词,也可以理解为介词。)

这里只是列举了多义句形成的部分原因,总的来说,多义句的形成可能是由于相同的词语之间的句法结构关系不同,也可能是由于词语间的语义结构关系不同。

需要指出的是,这里讨论的多义句主要是就口语中的句子而言的,没有包括书面语。结构层次不同所造成的多义短语一般不会造成多义句,这类作为语言备用单位的歧义短语一旦进入作为交际单位的句子当中,其意义就会变得单一明确,因为作为语言应用单位的句子会用语音停顿等手段对这类多义加以取舍,使之能够明确表义。如"他们三个人一本书""三个学校的领导都来了"等包含了多义短语的句子在具体使用过程中一般不会产生歧义,除非它们出现在书面上。

## 三、句子的言语意义

受交际语境、说话人语气语调以及重音等的影响,句子还经常会产生字面组合之外的言语意义或言外之意。例如,当爸爸严厉训斥做错了事的孩子时,爷爷对爸爸说"他还是个孩子"。就语言意义而言,这句话是对"他"(孩子)这个主体的断定,指明他尚未成年的属性。就言语意义而言,这句话实际上是说孩子年龄小不懂事,容易做错事,做了错事大人应该原谅,用不着大动肝火。

在特定的上下文中,很多句子都会产生一些与句子的字面意义不一致的言外之意或

言语意义,由于这类意义常在会话中产生,所以也叫会话含义。如:

　　甲:你昨天去开会了吗?

　　乙:我昨天上了一整天的课。

　　乙的话语表示"昨天没有去开会",但这种意思不是句子"我昨天上了一整天的课"字面上就有的,而是在特定的话语组合中产生的。只有问句是"你昨天去开会(或除"上课"之外的其他什么事)了吗"时,"我昨天上了一整天的课"才会有这样的会话含义,如果问话是"你昨天干什么了"或"你昨天上课了吗",回答"我昨天上了一整天的课"就不会有上面的会话含义。语言单位会有什么样的会话含义取决于它所在的会话环境。再如:

　　A:明天的同学聚会老张会来吗?

　　B:我听说小赵要来。

　　这个对话言外之意的推理就比较复杂,必须要了解老张与"我"、与小赵或与其他参加者之间错综复杂的关系,才能使例中 B 的答话与谈话主题"来不来参加明天的同学聚会"关联起来而形成它的言外之意。

　　对于"小李去过四川吗?"这个问句,肯定的回答方式可以有很多种,如"去过""他是四川大学毕业的""他老婆是四川人""他们公司去年才从成都搬到南京"等,除了第一个回答是直接肯定之外,后面三种回答都是通过言外之意传达出来的。

　　句子言语意义的确定建立在对语境全面把握的基础上,比如交际对象、交际意图、交际场景、前言后语或上下文等。如果只有孤零零的一句话或者发话者突然转换话题却没有任何语言提示,受话者就只能依据他对其他相关语境的了解来推断言语义。

　　人们为什么要选择具有言外之意的说话方式呢? 这是因为人们经常需要追求某种特殊的交际效果,例如有时羞于启齿,有时难以言传,有时为了委婉含蓄,有时为了留有余地,有时是想使话语含讥带讽,有时则是想让话语活泼变化……言外之意可以使语言的表达方式更加丰富多彩。

　　一旦确定话语具有言外之意之后,受话者是如何进行推理以准确把握住这个言外之意的呢? 在实际的语言交际中,当受话者接受了一个语句之后,如果发现它缺乏关联性而认定语句的语言意义并没有直接表达发话者的真正意图,他就会进行推理以探求具有最佳关联性的言外之意。这一推理一般以话语的语言意义为起点,虽然它缺乏关联性,但只要受话者坚信发话者是有说话诚意的,他就会进一步认为发话者不是随意说出这句话的,从这句话的语言意义中一定能发现某种因素,使这句话最终具有关联性。

　　受话者首先就会琢磨发话者是在什么样的语境条件下说出这句话来的,受话者必须在这些跟语言意义相关的很多语境因素中进行选择。尽管推理而来的言语义并没有固定的语言形式,但它所传递的信息却正是发话者说这句话的真正意图,与当时的谈话主题具有最佳关联性,受话者只有真正理解了对方话语的言语意义,交际才算真正成功。

言外之意的把握需要借助于语境从语言意义推测揣摩出发话者真正的语用意图。很多言外之意都是通过违反某种交际原则产生的,如数量原则、质量原则、合作原则、礼貌原则等。此外,语言交际活动中还有许多其他类型的言外之意,如双关、委婉等。充分认识交际中人们如何运用言外之意来传情达意,对提高语言交际效果至关重要。

## 思考与练习

简答题

1.句义包括哪两部分? 它们有什么区别与联系?

2.举例说明句义构成中的语法关系意义和语义关系意义。

3.什么是语义角色? 常见的语义角色有哪些? 请分别举例说明。

4.举例说明什么是语义指向。

5.造成句子多义的原因主要有哪些? 请举例说明。

6.什么是句子的言语意义? 如何正确推测句子的言语意义?

# 第五节　语篇义

语篇义同样存在语言义和言语义的对立。语言义是"言内"的,即语句组合本身的字面意义,也包括可能产生但尚未被采用的潜在意义。言语义是"言外"的,并不能由语言要素本身直接推知,比如,诗歌的比兴寄托就主要受语言外因素(如物理、文化、心理等)的制约,同基于字面组合的语言义具有本质的不同。每一个有比兴寄托的诗歌文本都相当于修辞学中隐喻的喻体,本体是隐藏的与之具有某种相似性的对象。由于同一个喻体可能指向很多本体,后人难以在众多的本体中确定作者的写作缘起,所以有些诗歌的解读常常会出现争议。比兴寄托义属于语篇的言语义,同基于语句组合的语言义具有明显不同。

比兴寄托是中国古典诗歌的一个优良传统,这在咏物诗中表现得特别明显,杜甫的不少咏物诗都被认为是有所寄托的,如《天河》:

常时任显晦,秋至辄分明。纵被微云掩,终能永夜清。

含星动双阙,伴月落边城。牛女年年渡,何曾风浪生。

对这首诗,仇兆鳌《杜诗详注》认为"此直咏天河,而寓意在言外。篇中微云掩、风浪生,似为小人谗妒而发"。其他如《萤火》一诗"腐草喻腐刑之人,太阳乃人君之象,比义显然"(幸因腐草出,敢近太阳飞。未足临书卷,时能点客衣。随风隔幔小,带雨傍林微。十月清霜重,飘零何处归。);《归燕》(不独避霜雪,其如俦侣稀。四时无失序,八月自知归。春色岂相访,众雏还识机。故巢傥未毁,会傍主人飞。)则用以表达"身虽弃官、心犹恋主"的情怀。

比兴寄托不只是咏物诗的常用表现手法,叙事或抒情诗中也经常暗含比兴寄托,把政治追求寄托于男女情事的诗歌传统就是一个很明显的表现,如张籍的《节妇吟》和朱庆余的《闺意献张水部》都是很成功的典范。

诗歌的比兴寄托属于语篇的言语义,既不同于其显性语言义,也不同于潜性语言义。王希杰早在20世纪80年代就提出了潜性语言和显性语言的理论。按照潜显理论,潜和显的对立体现在语言交际的各个方面,但在语言世界里,任何潜性语言现象都是在特定语言规则的基础上形成的,否则任何演绎和预测都将变得根本不可能,词语潜义也不例外。如"婚龄""学龄"本来表示时点,即法定的允许结婚的年龄和适宜于儿童入学读书的年龄,而汉语中还有"-龄"表示时段的用法,如"工龄""教龄"等,以后者的语义组合模式作为基础,"婚龄""学龄"也可以挖掘出"结婚后的年限""入学之后的年数"等表示时段的潜义;"东坡肉"这一具有特定含义的词语根据汉语偏正短语组合成义的一般规则可能具有"东坡身上的肉"这种潜在意义,那在表义上与"唐僧肉"一样自然而然;"小老婆"在中国文化中早已有了特定含义,但仍可能按照汉语规则产生出它作为自由短语的一般意义,即"年龄小(或个头小)的老婆"等。可见,语言学上的潜显意义是指某一话语或话语片段根据语言学的一般组合规则可能产生的意义总和,尽管人们只根据需要开发出了其中的某一个或几个意义,但其他的意义在适当的情况下也是可以很自然地发掘出来使之显化的,有不少相声和笑话就是巧妙地利用了这一点挖掘词语潜义来达到某种幽默效果。如:

老师:"你能用'特长'造个句子吗?"

学生:"我姐姐的头发和指甲都特长!"

所以,话语的潜性意义应该是在词汇意义和语法意义的基础上形成起来的,它是话语中词语组合时按照一定的语法规则能够产生的各种可能意义关系的总和减去已使用的显性意义。如"鸡不吃了""三个工厂的领导""咬死了猎人的狗"等歧义句就都存在着与表达者实际意图不同的潜性意义。而比兴寄托义则不是在诗歌语言意义的基础上产生的,与词语之间的组合关系和组合层次没有任何联系,它不是建立在文本文字组合关系的基础之上,而是以文本的整体意义作为喻体,通过某种相似性联想与对应的本体联系起来形成隐喻。而且这种相似性联想大多是基于语言外的物理或文化心理世界的,甚至可能具有很强的个人色彩,因为同一事物从不同的角度可能挖掘出不同的相似点,对咏物诗而言,诗的题目是喻体,相似点体现在诗歌文本的语句中,所以通过不同的语句可能开发出不同的甚至截然相反的相似点。如历来作为富贵华丽象征的牡丹到了李商隐《僧院牡丹》一诗中就有了完全不同的寓意:

　　　薄叶风才倚,枝轻雾不胜。开先如避客,色浅为依僧。

　　　粉壁正荡水,缃帏初卷灯。倾城惟待笑,要裂几多缯。

　　解读这类作品是由喻体出发寻找本体,而在创作过程中二者顺序正好相反,因为作者是先有自己的真正想法或写作缘起(即本体),然后再为它寻找可以把这种想法传达出来的媒介(即喻体)。而且由于某种想法不便直说或难以言传,常常促使诗人借助具有相似特征的物或事来含蓄表达或暗示透露特定的比兴寄托义。但诗歌两重意义间的这种基于相似性的关系与语言本身存在的多义性是有本质不同的。

　　诗歌的比兴寄托,不论是"比方于物",还是"托事于物",其实质上都是一种比喻——隐喻,即只出现喻体不出现本体的比喻。

　　对于比喻,根据潜显理论,任何一个本体都可能基于某种相似性与无数个喻体联系起来,同理,任何一个喻体也可能基于不同的相似性指向很多个本体。因此,孤立地看作为喻体的诗歌文本,它在理论上就可能与多个本体联系起来。但按照知人论世的原则,究竟哪一个更符合作者真实的创作动机,或者说他的写作缘起究竟是什么,这是人们苦苦探求的目标。然而由于事物间的相似性是非常复杂的,可能从很多不同的侧面或角度找到不同的相似点与不同的事物联系起来,也可能在同一个相似点上与很多事物联系起来。所以有时会感觉到某个诗歌文本作为喻体,虽然它所选择的相似点(即文本描述的内容)是确定的,但它的寄托却是非常隐蔽模糊、飘忽不定的,或者说有些诗歌难以明确解读是因为基于同一相似点的对象(即本体)太多,难以确定,而不是通常认为的相似关系过于模糊含混。这在李商隐的无题诗和咏物诗中表现得尤为突出。如他的《落花》就分别被解为"悼亡""身世之感"与"寂寞之景",它们都与落花之情态具有相似性,也正是由于相似关系的多种可能性决定了同一喻体对应于多个主体,甚至作者也许正是利用这多种可能来表达他复杂的情思,因为人的感情往往不是单一明确的,而是交错含混难以言传的。

　　好的咏物诗一定有某种精神理想的感悟或期许,但这种感悟或期许一定不是很明白地表现在字面的表层,不是作为诗的语言意义直接表达出来的,而是作为一种若有若无、若隐若现、可体味却不能确定、可感悟而难以明言的"本体"甚至"本体群"暗藏在诗歌所描述的相似点中。杜甫的很多咏物也都巧妙地做到了这一点,但并不能也不应该生硬地把某种精神作为比兴寄托义外加于这些咏物诗,那样只会破坏它的和谐与完美,如果一味执着于诗歌的具体所指或确切的寄托,就一定会出现众说纷纭的局面。另外,如果不把某首咏物诗看作是有所寄托的，即排除了它作为喻体具有"言外之义"（即本体）的可能性之后，它也会成为一首单纯的咏物诗。黄庭坚就反对穿凿附会地把杜甫的每一首咏物诗都看作是有寓意、有寄托的。如《大雅堂记》"子美诗妙处，乃在无意为文……彼喜穿凿者，弃其大旨，取其发兴于所遇林泉、人物、草木、鱼虫，以为物物皆有所托，如世间商度隐语者，则子美之诗委地矣"。可见，好的咏物诗不只是有所寄托，更重要的是诗本身的完美精妙。

相似性不只是存在于物与物之间，事与事之间或感觉与事物之间也往往会具有某种相似性，有不少歇后语就是基于事件之间的相似性而创造出来的。如"黄鼠狼给鸡拜年——没安好心"，这一歇后语中"黄鼠狼给鸡拜年"就是一个事件喻体，可以基于"（貌似做好事，实际）没安好心"这一相似点把它与很多本体联系起来，或者说可以把很多相似事件用这同一个喻体表现出来。所以，在古典诗歌中，比兴寄托不只是出现在咏物诗中，还可以出现在其他类的叙事或抒情诗中，古诗把政治追求寄托于男女情事的传统就是一个很明显的表现。如唐人张籍的《节妇吟》既可以当作一个喻体来表达各种场合下的委婉回绝，如作者本人就是用它委婉地表明自己对朝廷的忠贞，对李师道的拒绝，也可以不把它看作比喻，而直接从字面上理解为一首纯粹的爱情诗。如少妇也完全可以用《节妇吟》的显性意义达到委婉地回绝其他异性追求的目的：

> 君知妾有夫，赠妾双明珠。感君缠绵意，系在红罗襦。妾家高楼连苑起，良人持戟明光里。知君用心如明月，事夫誓拟同生死。还君明珠双泪垂，恨不相逢未嫁时。

由于诗中所用的能指符号全是属于爱情题材的词语，连一个政治词语也没有，因此人们在脱离当时政治背景的情况下读其诗，就只能领悟到它是一首纯粹的男女情事之诗，只是写节妇的忠贞守节，而很难挖掘出它的比兴寄托义。虽然就作者原意来说，它是一首不折不扣的政治诗。所以，对这些有比兴寄托的文学作品而言，语言意义和寄托意义之间只是有条件的暂时的联系，即话语的比兴寄托并不是由词语组合必然产生的，而是由语境赋予的。比如男性作者也可以借助诗以女人的口吻来表达一定的政治目的，此时只有联系写作背景才能体会到这一层。同样，单看诗歌的话语本身，朱庆余《闺意献张水部》中的"妆罢低声问夫婿，画眉深浅入时无"生动地描写了新妇拜见公婆前的忐忑不安，并没有什么比兴寄托。所以说，比兴寄托不是话语本身固有的意义，而是由特定语境生发出来的。虽然这些比兴寄托与语言意义之间没有必然联系，但不可否认它们之间具有某种相似性，只是由于相似性有很多方面，使得同一话语在不同语境下会产生各不相同的比兴寄托罢了。所以，即使抛开所有的比兴寄托，显性意义仍是自足的，人们完全可以在一定语境下仅仅利用显性意义很好地达到交际目的，如少妇用《节妇吟》表达拒绝，新妇用《闺意献张水部》中的诗句表达紧张不安的心情，而任何人都可以用《酬朱庆余》中的诗句表达对一位才艺双全的女子的赞美。因此，比兴寄托同语言意义是游离的，它们只是有条件地暂时地联系在一起。

在这一意义上,《闺意献张水部》和《酬朱庆余》等诗歌中的政治寄托不应看作是话语的潜义,因为这些政治寄托义不是由文本中的词语组合按照汉语语法规则可能生发出来的,而是以话语意义为基础,由相似性联想产生出来的。它们之间的关系完全不同于"婚龄"可以挖掘出"结婚后的年限"这一表示时段的潜义,因为汉语中有"党龄""教龄"等语义组合模式作为基础;也不像"东坡肉"与"小老婆"这些在中国文化中早已有了特定含义的词语仍可能按照汉语规则产生出它作为自由短语的一般意义。语言学上的潜义是根据语言组合规则所可能产生的意义,而诗歌的比兴寄托不是建立在文字组合的基础之上,而是以文本的整体意义作为喻体,通过某种相似性与对应的本体联系起来形成的隐喻。所以已经被研究者所挖掘出的比兴寄托只是一个个显性的本体,仍有一些同样跟喻体具有某些相似性的可能本体尚未被挖掘出来,可以称之为潜本体,这些潜在的本体在适当的时机完全可以很自然而贴切地与作为喻体的文本联系起来。这种基于相似性的联想并非话语的潜义,因为它不是属于语言本身的可能性,而是属于物理世界、文化世界或心理世界的潜在可能。

诗歌的比兴寄托可以看作是隐藏在作为喻体的文本背后的本体,它的多解性体现的是隐喻的多指向性,因为基于相似性的比喻所连接的两个对象是有多种可能性的,在理论上,同一个喻体在不同的方面可能与很多事物(即本体)具有一定的相似性,那么也就可能形成无数个比喻。如果用语言学的潜显理论来解释这一现象,那就是同一个喻体存在着无数个潜本体,这些潜本体都通过一定的相似性与作为文本的喻体联系起来。

基于相关性的语境义也不能看作是话语的潜义。如"真冷"在一定的条件下可能指"请关上窗户"或"请打开空调"等意思,这些言外之义对当时的说话环境的依赖性很大,不是话语本身可以生发出来的。所以把这些临时意义处理为话语潜义是不科学的。它们是话语的语境义,由于同一话语所出现的语境有多种可能性,除了已经运用于其中的显语境之外,还存在着很多可能的潜语境,那么自然也对应地存在着很多潜在的语境义,它们作为一种库存可能随时被某种特定的语境激活而显化,这种受制于语言外因素的潜语境义跟语言世界内部的话语潜义是有本质不同的。

此外,诗歌的情感基调也不属于语篇的潜性意义。因为作为语言意义的潜义和显义是直接面对话语字面本身的意义组合可能性的,是存在预测可能的,而作品的情感基调则是首先要联系作者或主人公身世遭遇的,单从字面上是难以准确捉摸的,欢乐背后也可能暗藏忧伤。如杜甫《饮中八仙歌》的基调就曾引起过争论:

> 知章骑马似乘船,眼花落井水中眠。汝阳三斗始朝天,道逢曲车口流涎,恨不移封向酒泉。左相日兴费万钱,饮如长鲸吸百川,衔杯乐圣称避贤。宗之潇洒美少年,举觞白眼望青天,皎如玉树临风前。苏晋长斋绣佛前,醉中往往爱逃禅。李白一

斗诗百篇,长安市上酒家眠,天子呼来不上船,自称臣是酒中仙。张旭三杯草圣传,脱帽露顶王公前,挥毫落纸如云烟。焦遂五斗方卓然,高谈阔论惊四筵。

这历来被认为是一首带有浪漫和欢快基调的诗篇,然而程千帆先生却根据成诗的年代,结合"八仙"各自的特殊身世,从诗中读出了郁闷和无奈。前者是脱离时代背景就语言本身的意义而言的;后者是结合了时代背景以及作者和诗中人物的身世遭遇而得出的结论,它脱离了诗歌字面意义本身,不能看作话语潜义。

总之,语篇的潜义是"言内"的,即是从词语组合本身可能产生尚未被采用的意义,而诗歌的比兴寄托是"言外"的,不是能够从词语意义组合的可能性推断出来的,因此把它看作是话语的潜义是不正确的,在语言学上应该把有比兴寄托的诗歌看作隐喻,每一个这样的文本就是一个喻体,由于从不同的角度它可能同很多事物或事件具有相似性,所以同一个文本(喻体)可能指向很多本体,这些基于诗歌总体意义的相似性联想所可能沟通的所有本体中,有已经被使用的显本体,也有尚未被发现的潜本体,与同一个喻体相联系的这众多的本体混在一起就常常造成解读的困难或争议。因为和喻体相联系的这众多的本体中究竟哪一个或几个符合作者真正的创作意图很难判断,所以有争议的或费解的诗往往不是由于喻体和本体之间的联系过于含混,而是由于难以在众多的本体中明确选择出原始本体。而且由于相似性的选择主要受物理世界和文化心理世界的制约,而不是受语言规则的制约,所以,话语的比兴寄托义并非话语潜义。同理,话语行为意图取决于特定的语境,诗歌的感情基调对作者或主人公的身世背景依赖性很大,它们都不是话语潜义。如果要分别为它们定性的话,应该把话语潜义看作是话语意义内容的组成部分,而把比兴寄托或感情基调看成是话语的思想内容,正如方光焘所言:在言语作品中,言语的意义内容是在词汇意义和语法意义的基础上形成起来的。言语作品就是借助它的帮助来表达、暗示、反映和透露思想内容。当然根据潜显理论,作为话语思想内容的比兴寄托也是有潜显之分的,作者已经表现出来的或已经被读者解读出来的是显性的比兴寄托,可能具有但还没被发掘出来的比兴寄托是潜性的,但从内容上看它们是依附于话语意义之上的思想情感的潜和显,从修辞的角度看是隐喻本体的潜和显,而不是语篇的语言意义本身的潜和显。

因此,分析文学语篇或交际话语时,一定要深入考察各种意义之间的联系机制,而不能把"言外之意""象征""神韵"等所指宽泛的概念一股脑推给语义,而不加具体分析,这种把语义当作垃圾桶而逃避科学分析的做法似乎还挺普遍。虽然语义有时的确是不可言传或过于微妙,难以分析,但也不能反过来把所有精细微妙的蕴涵或关系都归入语言学的语义,这样只会使语义学这一语言学中最复杂的部门更加混乱,更难实现科学化。

# 第六节 语义和修辞

语义和修辞的关系十分密切。首先，修辞是同义手段的选择过程，而正是语义场中的同义义场为之提供了选择比较的空间，如果没有同义义场的存在，也就没有选词炼字的必要性和可能性了；其次，借助于一定的修辞手段构成的词语在语义上往往带有很强的形象色彩，它们使相关意义的表达生动有趣；再次，语义的发展演变离不开带有修辞色彩的言语活动，正是这些带有修辞色彩的言语活动使词语突破了原先的语言义，生发出临时性的言语义，而这些临时性的言语义为语义的发展提供了可能。

## 一、"炼字"与修辞

中国古代文论家特别讲究"炼字"。所谓"炼字"，其实就是从同义义场中选择更适合表情达意的词语。强调对词语的选择锤炼古今中外皆然，同义语义场正好为此提供了广阔的选择空间，所以有人把修辞活动看作是同义手段的选择过程。

以汉语表示"死亡"的同义语义场为例，它包括很多理性意义相同的成员，但这些成员的色彩意义或适用对象各不相同。比如"驾崩"用于皇帝；"香消玉殒"用于有地位、有才学、有姿色的妇女；"老成凋谢、驾鹤西游"等用于老者；"夭折"用于未成年人；"涅槃、羽化、圆寂"等带有佛教色彩；"牺牲、杀身成仁、以身殉国"带有褒义；"玩完儿、翘辫子、上西天、见阎王"则带有贬义；"呜呼哀哉、一命呜呼"等也含贬义，但与前一组相比有文白之别。再看两个英语例子：

Genius is one percent of inspiration and ninety-nine percent of perspiration.（天才是百分之一的灵感，百分之九十九的汗水。）

与例中 perspiration（汗水）语义相同的至少还有 sweat，如果把同义的抽象词汇也考虑进来，还可以包括 diligence 及 industriousness 等。但 perspiration 与 inspiration 有相同的词根和后缀，二者不仅语音和谐，而且还可以造成相映成趣的效果。

Disease：ill, pill, bill and sometimes will.（患病、吃药、付账单，有时因治不好而写遗嘱。）

以 pill 的选取为例,与它在同一语义场内的有 medicine、drug、remedy、medication、curative agent 等。唯独选用它,其目的是维持四个名词押尾韵的共同特征。

同义语义场中的同义词从不同的角度表达基本相同的概念,它们为交际者提供了广阔的选择空间,从而有助于传情达意更加准确、精细、严密。如鲁迅先生在小说《伤逝》中描写子君的神情先后用了三个词"凄然""凄苦""凄惨",当子君知道涓生被辞退之后,用的是"凄然",当子君饲养的油鸡因生活所迫被吃掉之后,用的是"凄苦",当子君心爱的小狗阿随被迫丢掉之后,用的是"凄惨",三者都具有"凄凉、悲伤"的核心意义,意义相近,但它们在表义程度上轻重有别,由轻到重,准确、细腻地反映了涓生和子君生活境况日趋窘迫的情状。

同义语义场中的同义词在同一个语境中共现,往往可以强化某种意义或情感。例如:

你骂了我,你挖苦我! 你侮辱我,哦,你还瞧不起我! (大声地)现在我快活极了! 我高兴极了! 明天早上我要亲眼看着你的行里要挤兑,我亲眼看着付不出款来,我还亲眼看着那些十块八块的穷户头,(低声恶意地)也瞧不起你,侮辱你,挖苦你,骂你,咒你,——哦,他们要宰了你,吃了你呀! (曹禺《日出》)

例中的"快活""高兴"是同义连用,"骂""咒"也是同义连用,前者强化了李石清在潘月亭破产时极度幸灾乐祸的心情,后者则显示了李石清对潘月亭极度憎恨的感情。

选择同义语义场中的同义词来表示大致相同的意思还可以避免重复呆板,使语言富于变化。如"谈天说地""谈古论今",其中的"谈"与"说","谈"与"论"都是同义词,而且在此特定语境中应用,不是为了显示其意义上的细微差异,而是利用其义同的特点寻求语言表达上的变化和丰富。

可见,同义词的作用是表现在多个方面的。无论是意义的细小差异,还是意义的相同、相近,都有可能为同义词发挥相应的作用提供某种基础或条件。

## 二、修辞造词与词义的形象性

在语义上带有很强形象色彩的词语往往是借助于一定的修辞手段构成的,比喻、摹声是最常用的修辞手段。

### (一)比喻构词与词义的形象性

比喻造词分为全喻、半喻两种类型。全喻指的是参与构词的成分以整体比喻的方式反映客观对象,如"佛手、画眉、黑锅、碰壁"等。半喻指的是参与构词成分中一个是喻体,一个是本体,如"梯田、瓜分、火红、碑林"等。

全喻式构词是指每个词素都不能单独表示比喻,各个词素组合为一个整体才表示比喻的一种造词方式。它往往是在一般词组的基础上压缩凝结而成。例如:

龙眼:原是一般词组,指龙的眼睛。后来人们着眼于事物相似性的关系,将这一词组压缩凝结为一个新词,指代"形如龙眼"的水果——桂圆。

半喻式构词根据喻指成分的位置可以分为前喻式复合词与后喻式复合词。喻体位置在前的是前喻式复合词,如"冰糖、蜂拥、雪白"等。喻指成分位置在后的是后喻式复合词,如"碑林、笑柄"等。

前喻式复合词的比喻性词素在前,对后面表示本体的词素起修饰、限制作用。

如:兽行 梯田 烟雨 虎将 波动 龟缩 囊括 风行 奴役 鼠窜 蚕食
　　席卷 瓜分 火速 冰凉 笔挺 笔直 银白 火红 金黄 草绿 雪亮

在前喻式复合词中,喻体都是修饰限定成分,本体修饰中心成分。喻体通常喻指事物的形状、色彩、位置、功能、性质等方面的特点,相关词语的语义通常具有很强的形象色彩。比如,"狼狗、冰糖、月饼、臼齿、叶轮、卵石、蚕豆、扇贝、凤尾竹"等词是以形状进行比喻;"锦鸡、金橘、银幕、霜鬓、茶镜、墨菊、火鸡、鸡血石"等词是以色彩进行比喻;"耳房、脚灯、腋芽、颔联、颈联、云梯"等词是以位置进行比喻;"母机、植物人"等词是以功能进行比拟;"虎威、玉颜、兽心、牛性、海碗、胶泥、萍踪、草民、水酒"等词是以性质进行比喻,所有这些词语的语义都带有鲜明的形象色彩。

后喻式复合词的比喻性词素在后,表示本体的词素在前。

如:油田 熊猫 石笋 糖衣 茶砖 冰山 钢筋 火舌 雨丝 雪花 火苗
　　焊枪 熨斗 喷嘴 铣床 热浪 干冰 温床 哑铃 血洗 舌耕 笔耕

可见,汉语中用比喻的方法构成的复合词很多,其构成方式也多种多样,但所有这些词语的语义上都具有鲜明的形象色彩。

此外,还有一些短语由于经常在其原有字面意义的基础上用作隐喻,久而久之就固化为词,称为具有形象色彩的比喻式复合词,如"墙头草、绣花枕头、过街老鼠、落水狗、低谷、迷雾、苦水、绿帽子、破鞋、虎穴"等。

(二)摹声造词与词义的形象性

摹声词,又叫拟声词、象声词、状声词,是模仿自然声音构成的词。摹声词是世界上所有语言都具备的成分。准确使用摹声词能使语言的生动性与形象性大大增强。摹声词数量很多,构词方式也多种多样,以汉语为例,有单音节的、双音节的,还有多音节的。

单音节摹声词如"唰、哗、轰、嘭、砰、嘘、啾、飕、哗、当"等。这些单音节摹声词都有可能构成双音节或多音节摹声词。

双音节摹声词包括 AA 式与 AB 式两种,前者如"啦啦、哗哗、汪汪、咚咚、咚隆、呀呀、呼呼、沙沙、吱吱"等,后者如"扑哧、扑通、喀嚓、滴答、咻溜、哗啦、噼啪、轰隆、吱呀"等。

多音节摹声词的构成方式更加复杂,有叠音式的,也有非叠音式的。如:

叮叮当　滴滴答　扑通通　哗啦啦

叮叮咚咚　叽叽喳喳　咕咚咕咚　轰隆轰隆

叽里咕噜　噼里啪啦　叽里呱啦

这些摹声词都是运用摹状修辞格造出来的,其语义生动形象,对真实地再现相关情景具有很强的表现力。

## 三、修辞与语义的发展

修辞是人们为了达到一定表达效果对语言所进行的运用。修辞为词义发展创造了常规或超常规的环境,在一定程度上是词义发展的动因。汉语有着十分丰富的修辞手法,汉语词义的发展和修辞手法的运用有着深刻的联系,而且在词义发展演变的过程中,修辞起到了不可忽视的作用。

多义词产生义项的手段大都是修辞的手法。例如,"包袱"引申义的产生就是由于修辞的需要,尽管"负担"一词早已存在,"思想负担"的说法也早已有之,但"思想负担"说成"思想包袱"更加形象生动。当"思想包袱"这个说法为社会约定俗成之后,"包袱"就产生了"负担"的义项。比喻和借代是多义词语义发展的最重要的两种方式。

### (一) 比喻与语义的发展

比喻义是借用一个词的基本义来比喻另一个事物所产生的意义。比喻法则着重于形象方面的联想,这种意义发展方式在很多语言中都普遍存在。如汉语的"压力"与英语的"pressure"本义均指物体所承受的与表面垂直的作用力。汉语中在此基础上发展出了意义相对抽象的"施加压力",英语中同样可以说"put pressure upon one",二者的意义发展理据都是比喻。

此外,即使语言系统中已经有了相关的词或短语来表达相关事物或现象,但不够形象生动,说话者需要一个比现成词更恰当的词以增强话语的表达力,这也可能会造成词义发展。如汉语中可以说"吃得多但无用的人",但为了增强语言表达的效果,人们选用"饭桶"来表达同一概念,形象而生动。类似的例子举不胜举,如"狐狸精、里程碑、烙印、万金油、桥梁、悲剧、尾巴、草包、筹码、窗口、环节、诱饵、油水、熔炉"等。

引起词义发展的比喻一般是以相似性为基础的。相似性有很多种体现:形貌性状相似,如"斗"由酌酒器引申为斗星;功能作用相似,如"关"由门闩引申为关卡;方式情态相似,如"奋"由鸟展翅引申为举起、扬起;等等。

比喻所引起的词义发展在各类词中都普遍存在,这里分别以名词、动词和形容词为例加以说明。

(1)捷径,原型指近路:这条小路是~

隐喻较快地达到目的的巧妙手段:学习没有~。

(2)奠基,原型指打下建筑物的基础:人民英雄纪念碑是1949年9月30日~的。

隐喻给事物一个坚实的开头:鲁迅是中国新文学的~人。

(3)干净,原型指没有尘土、杂质等:把屋子打扫~

隐喻a.一点不剩:把敌人消灭~;b.来路正、正派:这钱来得~。

(二)借代与语义的发展

借代义是基于相关性而引起的词义发展,如"请喝茶"中的"茶"表示"茶水"意义就是由借代造成的词义。这类新义项的产生是基于相关性的借代引起的。相关性有很多类型:甲事物对乙事物具有标志作用,借甲代乙,如"齿"由门牙、牙齿引申为年龄;借形状特点指代事物或人,如"刚"由坚硬引申为金属钢;借方位处所指代事物或人,如"陵"由大土山引申为帝王的坟墓;等等。

借代转义使本义与新义项之间的语义关系非常复杂多样。"漆、网、策、锄、磨、锯、锤、锉、锁、犁"等词语的原义是表示具有一定功能的工具,新义项表示凭借该工具的动作行为。"指、顶"等原义表示人体部位,新义项表示该部位发出的动作。"经理、董事、导演、编辑、裁判、领导、调度、翻译"等原义表示动作行为,新义项表示发出该动作行为的主体。"鼓、囚"原义表示动作行为,新义项表示受该动作行为影响的客体。"刷、通知、证明、报告、报道"等原义表示动作行为,新义项表示该动作行为所凭借的事物。"画、建筑、计划、设计、组织、发明、总结、记录"等原义表示动作行为,新义项表示该动作行为所产生的结果物。"鬼、油、典型、标准、道德"从主体转指性状。"香、先进、秘密"由性状转指主体。"松、紧、热、稀罕"由性状转指能够致使该性状发生的动作行为。

(三)通感与词义的发展

"通感"不仅是一个常用修辞格,而且是一种十分普遍的语义转移手段。各种语言的词汇里的通感式语义转移以及由此产生的大量"通感词"具有极大的相似性。汉语的"苦"与英语的"bitter"原型都是"味道苦",同时它们又都可以表示"痛苦"。汉语中有"甜甜的声音""柔和的音乐"之说,英语有"sweet music"和"soft voice"之说。总之,很多语言中听觉、视觉、味觉、触觉、嗅觉之间相互联通、相互投射的情况都普遍存在。

通感可以使人们借助于某种更为熟悉或更为直接的感觉来形象准确地表达另一种

感觉。在各种表达感觉的汉语词语中,许多词都是通过某一感觉领域向另一领域的转移而构成的,如"尖锐、苦涩、辛酸、辛苦、痛苦、寒酸、热闹、冷静、温柔、冷淡"等。

需要指出的是,尽管人体各个感受器对同一外来刺激的生理和心理反应,虽然并不因民族而异,但不同民族由同一外来刺激所引起的相似联想,却并非总是一致。以味觉为例,"酸""辣""苦"对于不同民族来说,都是一种令人不快的刺激,这类感官感受所引起的也是令人不快的相似联想,不过,具体的联想对象及其联想过程却不尽相同。譬如"酸"在汉语中与"嫉妒"等心理感受具有共通之处,如:

听到被表扬的不是自己,她心里有些酸溜溜的。(《现代汉语词典》)

这里的"酸溜溜"表示"嫉妒"。然而,日语的"酸"却没有相应的通感转义和通感构词。此外,汉语"酸"可表"悲痛",故有"悲酸""心酸"之类的通感造词。但英语中的"sour"并无此类通感联想,因此汉语说"辛酸的眼泪",英语并无"sour tears",而是"bitter tears"(苦味的眼泪);俄语也说"горькиеслёзы"(苦泪)。汉语"苦"可转指"不辞烦劳、反复恳切地说",例如"苦口相劝""苦口婆心";但日语"苦"(にが)却没有这一通感转义,日语一般用"酸"表示相关意思,如:

(1)口(くち)を酸(す)っぱくして言(い)う

(2)老婆心(ろうばしん)から酸(す)っぱくして忠告(ちゅうこく)すること

可见,修辞是词义发展的重要方式,多义词义项的产生有很多都是修辞运用的结果。尽管具体词语的义项发展具有一定的民族差异,但各种语言词义发展的方式仍然具有很大的共性。不过,需要指出的是,新义项的产生是在长期的言语实践中逐渐凝固和稳定的结果,只有那些在言语活动中被重复使用、广泛接受的修辞词义变体可以进入词义发展演变的范畴,从而由言语义发展为语言义,成为词语的新义项。

此外,修辞与语义发展是互相促进的。一方面,修辞运用打破了词义既有的规范,促进了词义的发展;另一方面,词义的发展又为修辞活动提供了更为广阔的空间,因为有了更多更好的同义手段可供选择。

## 思考与练习

简答题

1.语义跟修辞有什么关系?

2.为什么说同义义场为"炼字"提供了广阔的选择空间?

3.举例说明比喻造词的方式及其语义特点。

4.举例说明通感造词在不同语言中的共性与差异。

5.举例说明比喻与语义发展的关系。

6.举例说明借代与语义发展的关系。

7.为什么说修辞与语义发展是互相促进的?

## 【原典阅读】

# 1.Seven Types of Meaning

## G. Leech

Some people would like semantics to pursue the study of meaning in a wide sense of 'all that is communicated by language'; others (among them many modem writers within the framework of general linguistics) limit it in practice to the study of logical or conceptual meaning in the sense discussed in Chapter 1. Semantics in the former, wider sense can lead us once again into the void from which Bloomfield retreated with understandable misgivings—the description of all that may he the object of human knowledge or belief. On the other hand, we can, by carefully distinguishing types of meaning, show how they all fit into the total composite effect of linguistic communication, and show how methods of study appropriate to one type may not be appropriate to another.

On this basis, I shall break down 'meaning' in its widest sense into seven different ingredients, giving primary importance to logical meaning or (as I shall prefer to call it) CONCEPTUAL MEANING, the type of meaning I was discussing earlier in connection with 'semantic competence'. The six other types I shall consider are connotative meaning, social meaning, affective meaning, reflected meaning, collocative meaning, and thematic meaning.

Conceptual Meaning

CONCEPTUAL MEANING (sometimes called 'denotative' or 'cognitive' meaning) is widely assumed to be the central factor in linguistic communication, and I think it can he shown to be integral to the essential functioning of language in a way that other types of meaning are not (which is not to say that conceptual meaning is the most important element of every act of linguistic communication). My chief reason for assigning priority to conceptual meaning is that it has a complex and sophisticated organization of a kind which may be compared with, and cross-related to, similar organization on the syntactic and phonological levels of language. In particular, I would like to point to two structural principles that seem to lie at the basis of all linguistic patterning: the principle of CONTRASTIVENESS and the principle of STRUCTURE. Contrastive features underlie the classification of sounds in phonology, for example, in that any label we apply to a sound defines it *positively*, by what feature it possesses, and also by implication *negatively*. by what features it does not possess. Thus the phonetic symbol /b/may be explicated as representing a bundle of contrastive features + bilabial, + voice, + stop, −nasal; the assumption being that the distinctive sounds or phonemes of a language are identifiable in terms of binary, or largely binary, contrasts. In a similar way, the conceptual meanings of a language can be studied in terms of contrastive features, so that (for example) the meaning of the word *woman* could be specified as +HUMAN, −MALE,

+ADULT, as distinct from, say, *boy*, which could be 'defined' +HUMAN, +MALE, −ADULT.

The second principle, that of structure, is the principle by which larger linguistic units are built up out of smaller units; or (looking at it from the opposite point of view) by which we are able to analyse a sentence syntactically into its constituent parts, moving from its *immediate constituents* through a hierarchy of sub-division to its *ultimate constituents* or smallest syntactic elements. This aspect of the organization of language is often given visual display in a tree-diagram:

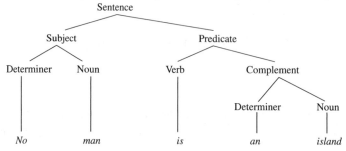

Or it can be represented by bracketing:

{(No)(man)} {[(is)] [(an)(island)]}

It has long been taken for granted that the syntax of a language is to be handled in such terms. But it is now also widely accepted that the semantics of natural language has its own counterpart of syntactic structure, or (to use in many ways a closer analogy) of the systems or symbolic logic devised by mathematicians and philosophers (see Chapters 8 and 9).

The two principles of contrastiveness and constituent structure represent the way language is organized respectively on what linguists have termed the PARADIGMATIC (or selectional) and SYNTAGMATIC (or combinatory) axes of linguistic structure. It will be my main aim in the latter part of this book (Chapters 6-17) to explore as fully as I can the application of these principles to semantic analysis, and so to show how methods of study devised for other levels of language can bring precision and insight to conceptual semantics.

In this discussion, I have taken for granted a third generally acknowledged principle of linguistic organization, which is that any given piece of language is structured simultaneously on more than one 'level'. At least the three following levels, in the pictured order, seem to be necessary for a full account of the linguistic competence by which we are able to generate or understand linguistic utterances:

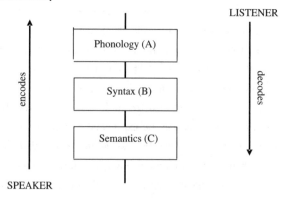

And this means that for the analysis of any sentence, we need to establish a 'phonological representation', a 'syntactic representation' and a 'semantic representation', and the stages by which one level of representation can be derived from another. The aim of conceptual semantics is to provide, for any given interpretation of a sentence, a configuration of abstract symbols which is its 'semantic representation', and which shows exactly what we need to know if we are to distinguish that meaning from all other possible sentence meanings in the language, and to match that meaning with the right syntactic and phonological expression. The ability to match levels operates in one direction ( A→B→C on the diagram) if we are DECODING, i. e. listening to a sentence and interpreting it; and in the opposite direction (C→B→A) if we are ENCODING, i.e. composing and speaking a sentence. From this account it will be clear that conceptual meaning is an inextricable and essential part of what language is, such that one can scarcely define language without referring to it. A 'language' which communicated by other means than by conceptual meaning (e.g. a 'language' which communicated solely by means of expletive words like *Oh! Ah! Oho! Alas!* and *Tally ho!*) would not be a language at all in the sense in which we apply that term to the tongues of men.

Connotative Meaning

More of what is distinctive about conceptual meaning will appear when we contrast it with CONNOTATIVE MEANING. Connotative meaning is the communicative value an expression has by virtue of what it *refers to*, over and above its purely conceptual content. To a large extent, the notion of 'reference' overlaps with conceptual meaning. If the word *woman* is defined conceptually by three features ( + HUMAN, − MALE, + ADULT), then the three properties 'human', 'adult', and 'female' must provide a criterion of the correct use of that word. These contrastive features, translated into 'real world' terms, became attributes of the referent (that which the word refers to). But there is a multitude of additional, non-criterial properties that we have learnt to expect a referent of *woman* to possess. They include not only physical characteristics ('biped', 'having a womb'), but also psychological and social properties ('gregarious', 'subject to maternal instinct'), and may extend to features which are merely *typical* rather than *invariable* concomitants of womanhood ('capable of speech', 'experienced in cookery', 'skirt-or-dress-wearing'). Still further, connotative meaning can embrace the 'putative properties' of the referent, due to the viewpoint adopted by an individual, or a group of people or a whole society. So in the past woman has been burdened with such attributes ('frail', 'prone to tears', 'cowardly', 'emotional', 'irrational', 'inconstant') as the dominant male has been pleased to impose on her, as well as with more becoming qualities such as 'gentle', 'compassionate', 'sensitive', 'hard-working'. Obviously, connotations are apt to vary from age to age and from society to society. A hundred years ago. 'non-trouser-wearing' must have seemed a thoroughly definitive connotation of the word *woman* and its translation equivalents in European languages, just as in many non-western societies today womankind is associated with attributes foreign to our own way of thinking. It is equally obvious that connotations will vary, to some extent, from individual to individual within the same speech community: to an English-speaking misogynist *woman* will have many uncomplimentary associations not present in the minds of speakers of a more feminist persuasion.

It will be clear that in talking about connotation, I am in fact talking about the 'real world' experience one associates with an expression when one uses or hears it. Therefore the boundary

117

between conceptual and connotative meaning is coincident with that nebulous but crucial distinction, discussed in Chapter 1, between 'language' and the 'real world'. This accounts for the feeling that connotation is somehow incidental to language rather than an essential part of it, and we may notice, in confirmation, that connotative meaning is not specific to language, but is shared by other communicative systems, such as visual art and music. Whatever connotations the word *baby* has can be conjured up (more effectively, because the medium is directly representational) by a drawing of a baby, or an imitation of a baby's cry. The overlap between linguistic and visual connotations is particularly noticeable in advertising, where words are often the lesser partners of illustrations in the task of conferring on a product a halo of favourable associations.

A second fact which indicates that connotative meaning is peripheral compared with conceptual meaning is that connotations are relatively unstable: that is, they vary considerably, as we have seen, according to culture, historical period, and the experience of the individual. Although it is too simple to suggest that all speakers of a particular language speak exactly 'the same language', it can be assumed, as a principle without which communication through that language would not be possible, that on the whole they share the same conceptual framework, just as they share approximately the same syntax. In fact, some recent semanticists have assumed that the same basic conceptual framework is common to all languages, and is a universal property of the human mind.

Thirdly, connotative meaning is indeterminate and open-ended in a sense in which conceptual meaning is not. Connotative meaning is open-ended in the same way as our knowledge and beliefs about the universe are open-ended: any characteristic of the referent, identified subjectively or objectively, may contribute to the connotative meaning of the expression which denotes it. In contrast, it is generally taken as fundamental to semantic theory that the conceptual meaning of a word or sentence can be codified in terms of a limited set of symbols (e.g. in the form of a finite set of discrete features of meaning), and that the semantic representation of a sentence can be specified by means of a finite number of rules. This postulate of the finiteness and determinateness of conceptual content is modelled on the assumptions that linguists generally make when analysing other aspects of linguistic structure. Such assumptions are to some extent over-simplified, but without them it would be difficult to uphold the view of language as a finite and coherent system.

Social and Affective Meaning

We turn now to two aspects of communication which have to do with the situation in which an utterance takes place. SOCIAL MEANING is that which a piece of language conveys about the social circumstances of its use. In part, we 'decode' the social meaning of a text through our recognition of different dimensions and levels of style within the same language. We recognize some words or pronunciations as being dialectal, i.e. as telling us something of the geographical or social origin of the speaker; other features of language tell us something of the social relationship between the speaker and hearer: we have a scale of 'status' usage, for example, descending from formal and literary English at one end to colloquial, familiar, and eventually slang English at the other.

One account (Crystal and Davy, *Investigating English Style*) has recognized, among others, the following dimensions of socio-stylistic variation (I have added examples of the categories of usage one would distinguish on each dimension):

*Variation according to:*

DIALECT ( The language of a geographical region or of a social class )

TIME ( The language of the eighteenth century, etc. )

PROVINCE ( Language of law, of science, of advertising, etc. )

STATUS ( Polite, colloquial, slang, etc., language )

MODALITY ( Language of memoranda, lectures, jokes, etc. )

SINGULARITY ( The style of Dickens, of Hemingway, etc. )

Although not exhaustive, this list indicates something of the range of style differentiation possible within a single language. It is not surprising, perhaps, that we rarely find words which have both the same conceptual meaning and the same stylistic meaning. This observation has frequently led people to declare that 'true synonyms do not exist'. If we understand synonymy as complete equivalence of communicative effect, it is indeed hard to find an example that will disprove this statement. But there is much convenience in restricting the term 'synonymy' to equivalence of conceptual meaning, so that we may then contrast conceptual synonyms with respect to their varying stylistic overtones:

$$
\left\{
\begin{array}{l}
\text{steed ( poetic )} \\
\text{horse ( general )} \\
\text{nag ( slang )} \\
\text{gee-gee ( baby language )}
\end{array}
\right.
\qquad
\left\{
\begin{array}{l}
\text{domicile ( very formal, official )} \\
\text{residence ( formal )} \\
\text{abode ( poetic )} \\
\text{home ( general )}
\end{array}
\right.
$$

$$
\left\{
\begin{array}{l}
\text{cast ( literary, biblical )} \\
\text{throw ( general )} \\
\text{chuck ( casual, slang )}
\end{array}
\right.
\qquad
\left\{
\begin{array}{l}
\text{diminutive ( very formal )} \\
\text{tiny ( colloquial )} \\
\text{wee ( colloquial, dialectal )}
\end{array}
\right.
$$

The style dimension of 'status' is particularly important in distinguishing synonymous expressions. Here is an example in which the difference of status is maintained through a whole sentence, and is reflected in syntax as well as in vocabulary:

(1) They chucked a stone at the cops, and then did a bunk with the loot.

(2) After casting a stone at the police, they absconded with the money.

Sentence (1) could be said by two criminals, talking casually about the crime afterwards; sentence (2) might be said by the chief inspector in making his official report. Both could be describing the same happening, and their common ground of conceptual meaning is evident in the difficulty anyone would have in assenting to the truth of one of these sentence, and denying the truth of the other.

In a more local sense, social meaning can include what has been called the ILLOCUTIONARY FORCE of an utterance: for example, whether it is to be interpreted as a request, an assertion, an apology, a threat, etc. The function an utterance performs in this respect may be only indirectly related to its conceptual meaning. The sentence *I haven't got a knife* has the form and meaning of an assertion, and yet in social reality ( e.g. if said to the waiter in a restaurant ) it can readily take on the force of a request such as 'Please bring me a knife'.

From this it is only a small step to the consideration of how language reflects the personal feelings of the speaker, including his attitude to the listener, or his attitude to something he is talking about. AFFECTIVE MEANING, as this sort of meaning can be called, is often explicitly conveyed through the conceptual or connotative content of the words used. Someone who is addressed: 'You're a vicious tyrant and a villainous reprobate, and I hate you for it!' is left in little doubt as to the feelings of the speaker towards him. But there are less direct ways of disclosing our attitude than this: for example, by scaling our remarks according to politeness. With the object of getting people to be quiet, we might say either:

(3) I'm terribly sorry to interrupt, but I wonder if you would be so kind as to lower your voices a little.

or:

(4) Will you belt up.

Factors such as intonation and voice-timbre—what we often refer to as 'tone of voice' —are also important here. The impression of politeness in (3) can be reversed by a tone of biting sarcasm; sentence (4) can be turned into a playful remark between intimates if delivered with the intonation of a mild request.

Affective meaning is largely a parasitic category in the sense that to express our emotions we rely upon the mediation of other categories of meaning— conceptual, connotative, or stylistic. Emotional expression through style comes about, for instance , when we adopt an impolite tone to express displeasure( as in (4) above) ,or when we adopt a casual tone to express friendliness. On the other hand, there are elements of language (chiefly interjections, like *Aha*! And *Yippee*!) whose chief function is to express emotion. When we use these, we communicate feelings and attitudes without the mediation of any other kind of semantic function.

Reflected and Collocative Meaning

Two further, though less important types of meaning involve an interconnection on the lexical level of language.

First, REFLECTED MEANING is the meaning which arises in cases of multiple conceptual meaning, when one sense of a word forms part of our response to another sense. On hearing, in a church service, the synonymous expressions *The Comforter* and *The Holy Ghost*, both referring to the Third Person of the Trinity, I find my reactions to these terms conditioned by the everyday non-religious meanings of *comfort* and *ghost*. *The Comforter* sounds warm and 'comforting' (although in the religious context, it means 'the strengthener or supporter'), while *The Holy Ghost* sounds awesome.

One sense of a word seems to 'rub off' on another sense in this way only when it has a dominant suggestive power either through relative frequency and familiarity (as in the case of *The Holy Ghost*) or through the strength of its associations. Only in poetry, which invites a heightened sensitivity to language in all respects, do we find reflected meaning operating in less obviously favourable circumstances:

Are limbs, so *dear*-achieved, are sides,

Full-nerved-still warm-too hard to stir?

In these lines from *Futility*, a poem on a dead soldier, Wilfred Owen overtly uses the word *dear* in the sense 'expensive(ly)', but also alludes, one feels in the context of the poem, to the sense 'beloved'.

The case where reflected meaning intrudes through the sheer strength of emotive suggestion is most strikingly illustrated by words which have a taboo meaning. Since their popularization in senses connected with the physiology of sex, it has become increasingly difficult to use terms like *intercourse*, *ejaculation*, and *erection* in 'innocent' senses without conjuring up their sexual associations. This process of taboo contamination has accounted in the past for the dying-out of the non-taboo sense of a word: Bloomfield explained the replacement of *cock* in its farmyard sense by *rooster* as due to the influence of the taboo use of the former word, and one wonders if *intercourse* is now following a similar path.

COLLOCATIVE MEANING consists of the associations a word acquires on account of the meanings of words which tend to occur in its environment. *Pretty* and *handsome* share common ground in the meaning 'good-looking', but may be distinguished by the range of nouns with which they are likely to co-occur or (to use the linguist's term) collocate:

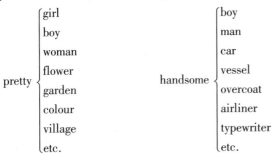

|          | pretty     |          | handsome   |
|----------|------------|----------|------------|
|          | girl       |          | boy        |
|          | boy        |          | man        |
|          | woman      |          | car        |
|          | flower     |          | vessel     |
|          | garden     |          | overcoat   |
|          | colour     |          | airliner   |
|          | village    |          | typewriter |
|          | etc.       |          | etc.       |

The ranges may well, of course, overlap: *handsome woman* and *pretty woman* are both acceptable, although they suggest a different kind of attractiveness because of the collocative associations of the two adjectives. Further example are quasi-synonymous verbs such as *wander* and *stroll* (*cows* may *wander*, but may no *stroll* or *tremble* and *quiver* (one *trembles* with *fear*, but *quivers* with *excitement*). Not all differences in potential co-occurrence need to be explained as collocative meaning: some day be due to stylistic differences, others to conceptual differences. It is the incongruity of combining unlike styles that makes 'He *mounted* his *gee-gee*' or 'He *got on* his *steed*' an improbable combination. On the other hand, the acceptability of 'The donkey *ate hay*', as opposed to 'The donkey *ate silence*', is a matter of compatibility on the level of conceptual semantics (on such 'selection restriction',). Only when explanation in terms of other categories of meaning does not apply do we need to invoke the special category of collocative meaning: on the other levels, generalizations can be made, while collocative meaning is simply an idiosyncratic property of individual words.

Associative Meaning: a Summary Term

Reflected meaning and collocative meaning, affective meaning and social meaning: all these have more in common with connotative meaning than with conceptual meaning; they all have the same open-ended, variable character, and lend themselves to analysis in terms of scales or ranges, rather than in discrete either-this-or-that terms. They can all be brought together under the heading of ASSOCIATIVE MEANING, and to explain communication on these levels, we need employ nothing more sophisticated than an elementary 'associationist' theory of mental connections based upon contiguities of experience. We contrast them all with conceptual meaning, because conceptual meaning seems to require the postulation of intricate mental structures which are specific to language and to the human species.

Associative meaning contains so many imponderable factors that it can be studied systematically only by approximative statistical techniques. In effect, Osgood, Suci and Tannenbaum proposed a method for a partial analysis of associative meaning when they published their ambitiously titled book *The Measurement of Meaning* in 1957. Osgood and his coauthors devised a technique (involving a statistical measurement device, the Semantic Differential) for plotting meaning in terms of a multidimensional semantic space, using as data speakers' judgements recorded in terms of seven-point scales. The scales are labelled by contrasting adjective pairs, such as *happy-sad*, *hard-soft*, *slow-fast*, so that a person may, for example, record his impression of the word *bagpipe* on a form in the following way:

|  | 3 | 2 | 1 | 0 | 1 | 2 | 3 |  |
|---|---|---|---|---|---|---|---|---|
| good | ___: | ___: | × : | ___: | ___: | ___: | ___ | bad |
| hard | ___: | × : | ___: | ___: | ___: | ___: | ___ | soft |
| passive | ___: | ___: | ___: | ___: | ___: | ___: | × | active |

etc.

Statistically, the investigators found that particular significance seemed to lie in three major dimensions, those of evaluation (*good-bad*), potency (*hard-soft*), and activity (*active-passive*). It is clear, even from this very brief sketch, that the method can provide no more than a *partial* and *approximate* account of associative meaning: *partial* because it entails a selection from indefinitely many possible scales, which in any case would only provide for associative meaning in so far as it is explicable in scalar terms; *approximate* because of the statistical sampling, and because a seven-point scale constitutes a cutting-up of a continuous scale into seven segments within which no differentiation is made—a process similar in its crudity to that of cutting up the spectrum into seven primary colours. This is not to disparage the Semantic Differential technique as a means of quantifying associative meaning: the lesson to be learned is, in fact, that it is only by such relatively insensitive tools as this that associative meaning can be systematically studied: it does not lend itself to determinate analyses involving yes-no choices and structures of uniquely segmentable elements.

Another important observation about the Semantic Differential is that it has been found useful in psychological fields such as personality studies, 'attitude measurement', and psychotherapy, where differences in the reactions of individuals are under scrutiny, rather than the common core of reactions that they share. This upholds what I said earlier in particular reference to connotative meaning: that whereas conceptual meaning is substantially part of the 'common system' of language share by members of a speech community, associative meaning is less stable, and varies with the individual's experience.

Thematic Meaning

The final category of meaning I shall attempt to distinguish is THEMATIC MEANING, or what is communicated by the way in which a speaker or writer organizes the message, in terms of ordering, focus, and emphasis. It is often felt, for example, that an active sentence such as (1) has a different meaning from its passive equivalent (2), although in conceptual content they seem to be the same:

{ (1) Mrs Bessie Smith donated the first prize.
{ (2) The first prize was donated by Mrs Bessie Smith.

Certainly these have different communicative values in that they suggest different contexts: the active sentence seems to answer an implicit question 'What did Mrs Bessie Smith donate?', while the passive sentence seems to answer an implicit question 'who was the first prize donated by?' or (more simply) 'Who donated the first prize?'. That is, (1), in contrast to (2), suggests that we know who Mrs Bessie Smith is (perhaps through a previous mention). The same truth conditions, however, apply to each: it would be impossible to find a situation of which (1) was an accurate report while (2) was not, or vice versa.

Thematic meaning is mainly a matter of choice between alternative grammatical construction, as in:

(3) A man is waiting in the hall.
(4) There's a man waiting in the hall.

(5) They stopped at the end of the corridor.
(6) At the end of the corridor, they stopped.

(7) I like Danish cheese best.
(8) Danish cheese I like best.
(9) It's Danish cheese that I like best.

But the kind of contrast by ordering and emphasis illustrated by (1) and (2) can also be contrived by lexical means: by substituting (for example) *belongs to* for *owns*:

(10) My brother owns the largest betting-shop in London.
(11) The largest betting-shop in London belongs to my brother.

In other cases, it is stress and intonation rather than grammatical construction that highlights information in one part of a sentence. If the word *electric* is given contrastive stress in (12):

(12) Bill uses an *electric* razor.
(13) The kind of razor that Bill uses is an electric one.

The effect is to focus attention on that word as containing new information, against a background of what is already assumed to be known (viz. that Bill uses a razor). This kind of emphasis could have been equally achieved in English by the different syntactic construction of (13). The sentences bracketed together above obviously have, in a sense, 'the same meaning'; but all the same, we need to acknowledge that their communicative value may be somewhat different; they will not each be equally appropriate within the same context.

Demarcation Problems

I have now dealt with the seven types of meaning promised at the beginning of the chapter, but I do not wish to give the impression that this is a complete catalogue, accounting for all that a piece of language may communicate. One might, for example, have added a category for the physiological information conveyed by an act of speech or writing: information about the sex of the speaker, his age, the state of his sinuses, and so on.

A further caveat about the seven types of meaning: there are always problems of 'demarcation', and more especially, problem of separating conceptual meaning from the more peripheral categories. The difficulty of delimiting conceptual from connotative meaning, noted earlier, is paralleled in other borderline areas, such as that between conceptual meaning and socio-stylistic meaning:

(1) He *stuck* the key in his pocket.

(2) He *put* the key in his pocket.

We could argue that (1) and (2) are conceptually synonymous, and that the difference between the two is a matter of style (sentence(2) is neutral, while (1) is colloquial and casual). On the other hand, we could maintain that the shift in style is combined with a conceptual difference: that *stick* in a context such as (1) has a more precise denotation than (2) and could be roughly defined as 'to put carelessly and quickly'. There is support for the second explanation in the slight oddity of the following sentences:

?* He stuck the key slowly in his pocket.

?* He stuck the key carefully in his pocket.

[The preceding asterisk, according to a convention of linguistics, signals the unacceptability of a sentence.]

Often, in fact, the solution to a problem of delimitation is to conclude that quasi-synonyms differ on at least two planes of meaning.

As a second illustration, we may take a case on the border between conceptual and collocative meaning, that of the verbs *smile* and *grin*. Do these words have different conceptual meanings, or is it just that the range of expressions with which they habitually combine is different? Few would hesitate over which of the two words to insert in:

The duchess ——ed graciously as she shook hands with her guests.

Gargoyles ——ed hideously from the walls of the building.

But the question is whether such differences in collocation spring from different conceptual and connotative content: whether, for example, a *grin* can be defined as a broader, toothier and more potentially hostile expression than a *smile*, and is more likely to be found on the face of a gargoyle than that of a duchess for that very reason. This is a particularly complex case in that differences of social and affective meaning are also clearly implicated. In fact, as already observed, affective meaning is a category which overlaps heavily with style, connotation, and conceptual content.

Intended and Interpreted Meaning

It may be wondered why I have avoided making a distinction between the INTENDED meaning, that which is in the mind of the speaker when he is framing his message, and the INTERPRETED meaning, or that which is conveyed to the mind of the listener when he receives the message. I have equated meaning in its broad sense with 'communicative effect', and 'communication' usually means transfer of information from a source (A) to a target (B). On this basis, one might argue that communication has only taken place if we know that what was in mind (A) has been transferred to, or copied in, mind (B). It is natural, then, that studies of meaning (particularly in philosophy) should have devoted much attention to the vexed question of the relation between meaning, intention, and interpretation. In spite of this, a linguist may feel entitled to ignore the difference between the intention of a message and its effect, because he is interested in studying the communication system itself, rather than what use or misuse is made of it. He is interested in studying the semantic aspect of the language which we may assume to be common to the minds of (A) and (B), and this includes, incidentally, studying ambiguities and other aspects of language (e.g. variability of associative meaning) which give scope for miscommunication. But the important point is that meaning, for semantics, is neutral between 'speaker's meaning' and 'hearer's meaning'; and this is surely justifiable, since only through knowing the neutral potentialities of the medium of communication itself can we investigate difference between what a person intends to convey and what he actually conveys.

All normal use of language, of course, implies some intention on the part of the speaker; but in so far as meaning implies an intention, the intention is only recoverable from the meaning itself. In other words, intentions are private but meaning is public. This applies even to social meaning: a matter to which I shall return in Chapter 16, in discussing the relation between semantics and pragmatics.

Summary

As this chapter has introduced quite a range of terms for types of meaning, it is fitting that it should end with a summary, and a suggestion or two for simplifying terminology:

SEVEN TYPES OF MEANING

|  | | 1.CONCEPTUAL MEANING or *Sense* | Logical, cognitive, or denotative content. |
|---|---|---|---|
|  | ASSOCIATIVE MEANING | 2.CONNOTATIVE MEANING | What is communicated by virtue of what language refers to. |
|  | | 3.SOCIAL MEANING | What is communicated of the social circumstances of language use. |
|  | | 4.AFFECTIVE MEANING | What is communicated of the feelings and attitudes of the speaker/ writer. |
|  | | 5.REFLECTED MEANING | What is communicated through association with another sense of the same expression. |
|  | | 6.COLLOCATIVE MEANING | What is communicated through association with words which tend to occur in the environment of another word. |
|  | 7.THEMATIC MEANING | | What is communicated by the way in which the message is organized in terms of order and emphasis. |

I have here used SENSE as a briefer term for 'conceptual meaning', (or 'meaning' in the narrower sense), and will feel free to use it for clarity and convenience from now on. For 'meaning' in the wider sense which embraces all seven types listed, it is useful to have the alternative term COMMUNICATIVE VALUE.

( *Semantics*: *The Study of Meaning* (2nd edn.). Penguin Books Ltd. ch. 2, 1981. pp. 9-23.)

译文：

# 七类不同的意义

### 李瑞华,王彤福,杨自俭,穆国豪,译

有些人希望语义学从广义上,即从"通过语言进行的一切交际"这个意义上去对意义进行研究。另外一些人(包括大多数从事普通语言学研究的现代著作家)实际上则把语义学限制为对逻辑意义或理性意义的研究,这一点在第一章里已作了论述。前者,即广义的语义学可能会再一次把我们引入使 Bloomfield 望而生忧,最终只能退离的那个空泛的境地,因为这种广

义语义学旨在描述人类的一切认识或信仰。另一方面,我们可以通过精心区分不同类型的意义,来说明这些不同类型的意义如何适从于语言交际的总体效果,同时说明适用于一类意义的研究方法不一定适用于另一类意义。

据此,我将把最广义的"意义"划分为七种不同的类型,并将重点放在逻辑意义或(我喜欢把它称为)**理性意义**上,这类意义我在前面结合"语义能力"已谈到过。我还将谈到的其他六类意义是内涵意义、社会意义、情感意义、反映意义、搭配意义和主题意义。

理性意义

人们普遍认为**理性意义**(有时叫做"外延"意义或"认知"意义)是语言交际的核心因素。我认为可以证明在某种意义上理性意义对语言的基本功能来说是不可缺少的,而其他类型的意义却并非如此(这并不是说理性意义总是语言交际行为中最重要的因素)。我优先考虑理性意义的主要理由是它有一种复杂的结构,这种结构可以同语言的句法层次和音位层次上类似的结构相比,并且与之交叉相关。我特别要指出,在所有的语言模式结构中似乎都存在两条结构原则:**对比**原则和**结构**原则。对比特征是音位学中对语音进行分类的基础;例如,我们应用于语音的任何标记都是根据语音所具有的特征来确定的,它所具有的特征用正号表示,它不具有的特征用负号表示。比如可以说音标/b/代表了这样一组对比特征:+双唇、+浊音、+爆破音、-鼻音;其出发点是:一种语言中的不同音或音位可以通过两项对比或大体上通过两项对比来识别。同样,语言的理性意义也能够根据对比特征进行研究。例如:woman(女人)这个词的意义可以说包含了+HUMAN(人)、-MALE(非男性)、+ADULT(成人)这几个特征,因此它就有别于boy(男孩)这样一个词,boy可以被"解释"为+HUMAN(人)、+MALE(男性)、-ADULT(未成年)。

第二是结构原则。按照这条原则,较大的语言单位由较小的语言单位组成,或者说(从相反的角度来看这个问题),根据这个原则,我们可以把一个句子在句法上分析成它的各个组成部分;这种分析从句子的直接成分开始,按层次逐步进行,直到它的最终成分,即最小的句法成分。语言结构的这个侧面常用树形图形象地加以表示:

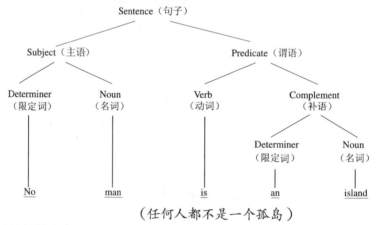

(任何人都不是一个孤岛)

或者可以用括号来表示:

{ (No) (man) } { [ (is) ] [ (an) (island) ] }

以这种方式来分析语言的句法结构,人们早已习以为常;但是现在很多人也已接受了以下这种观点:自然语言的语义层有其本身与句法结构相对应的成分,或者说(用一个在许多方面更加接近的类比)有与数学家及哲学家所建立的符号逻辑体系相对应的成分(参看第八、九两章)。

　　对比和成分结构这两条原则分别说明了语言是如何在被语言学家称作语言结构的**聚合**（即选择性的）轴和**组合**（即组合性的）轴上组织起来的。在本书的后面部分（第6—17章）我的主要目的将是尽力探索如何把这些原则应用于语义分析，从而说明为语言的其他层次所设计的研究方法如何能促进概念语义学向更精确、更深入的方向发展。

　　在这一讨论中，我把被普遍接受的语言结构的第三条原则看作是不言而喻的。这条原则是，任何一个语言片断都是同时在一个以上的"层次"上组织起来的。如果要对我们赖以生成和理解话语的语言能力进行充分描写，那么至少需要下列三个按图表顺序的层次：

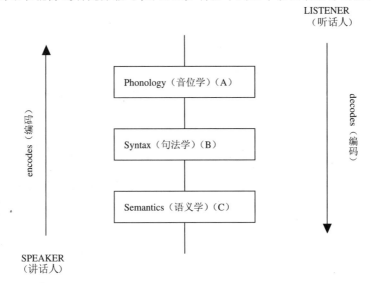

　　这个图表告诉我们，对任何句子进行分析，都需要进行"音位表达"、"句法表达"和"语义表达"，以及确定从一个层次的表达派生出另一个层次的表达所需要的步骤。概念语义学的目标就是为一个句子的任何特定解释提供一套抽象的符号，即这个句子的"语义表达"。这套抽象符号要能确切地表明，如果我们要把该句的意义与语言中可能存在的其他一切句子意义区分开来，并使该句的意义与一定的句法和音位表达方式对应，那么我们需要知道些什么。假若我们在**解码**，即我们在听并且在理解一个句子，这种与层次相符的能力就沿着上面图表所表示的（A→B→C）方向发挥作用；如果我们在**编码**，即在编排并且讲出一个句子，这种能力就沿着相反的方向（C→B→A）发挥作用。由此可见，理性意义是语言不可缺少的基本组成部分；如果不提理性意义，就几乎无法说明什么是语言。一种不依靠理性意义而依靠其他手段进行交际的"语言"（例如只靠像Oh！（哦！）Ah！（啊！）Oho！（哦嗬！）Alas！（哎呀！）Tally ho！（嗬！）之类的感叹词进行交际的"语言"）就根本不是我们所谈的语言。

　　内涵意义

　　当我们将理性意义与**内涵意义**加以对比时，就会发现理性意义更多的区别性特征。内涵意义是指一个词语除了它的纯理性内容之外，凭借它所指的内容而具有的一种交际价值。在很大程度上，"所指"这个概念与理性意义相重叠。如果 woman 这个词从概念上按照三个特征（+HUMAN、-MALE、+ADULT）确定其含义，那么"human"，"adult"和"female"这三个特征就一定会提供一个正确使用这个词的标准。这些对比特征一经转为"真实世界"中使用的词语就成为所指事物（这个词所指的事物）的特征。但是我们知道，woman 这个词所指的事物还应包含很多附加的、非标准的特性。它们不仅包括躯体特征（"双足"、"有子宫"），而且包括心理和社会特征("爱聚群"、"有母性本能"),还可以进而包括仅仅是典型的而不是女性所必具的特征("善于词令"、"善于烹调"、"穿裙子或连衣裙")。再进一步,由于某一个人或一部分人或整个社会的看法,内涵意义可包含所指事物的"公认特性"。过去居于支配地位的男子喜欢把"脆弱"、"易流眼泪"、"懦怯"、"好动感情"、"缺乏理性"、"反复无常"这些形容词强加于女子头上,当然,也把她们描述为具有像"文雅"、"富有同情心"、"敏感"和"勤勉"这些比较符合其性格的品质。显然,内涵是随着时代和社会的变化而变化的。一百年以前,"无权当家"这个概念,无疑是英语和欧洲各种语言中女子这个词完全确定的内涵,今天在许多非西方社会中,女子这个词仍具有许多在我们看来是陌生的含义。同样,十分明显,在某种程度上内涵在同一言语社团中是因人而异的。对一个讲英语的厌恶女子的人来说,woman 一词会引起许多不好的联想,但这种联想不会出现在具有较多男女平等思想的人的头脑中。

很清楚,在讨论内涵的时候,我实际上谈的是人们在使用或听到一个词语时,这个词语使人所联想到的"真实世界"中的经验。因此理性意义和内涵意义的界限是与第一章中讨论过的"语言"和"真实世界"之间的那种模糊不清但又十分重要的界限相一致的。这就是为什么人们感觉到内涵对语言来说是附带的,而不是语言的基本组成部分的原因。我们可以注意到,内涵意义并非为语言所特有,而是为视觉艺术和音乐之类的其他交际体系所共有的,这也证实了内涵意义不是语言的基本组成部分,而仅是附带的。不管婴儿这个词有什么样的内涵,都可以凭着一张婴儿的图画或模仿婴儿的哭声更有效地想象出来(因为使用了直接的表达手段)。语言内涵和形象内涵之间的重叠在广告中特别值得注意,在竭力宣传赞美某一产品的广告上,文字的作用往往不及画面的作用大。

与理性意义相比,内涵意义比较不稳定,这也表明了内涵意义的附属性。正像我们已经看到的,内涵意义经常随着文化、历史时期和个人经历的变化而发生很大的变化。虽然说所有讲一种特定语言的人都使用"同一种语言"讲话,这种说法未免太简单化了,但可以认为,正像讲那种语言的人都使用大体上相同的句法一样,他们大体上也都具有同样的概念体系。这是一条重要的原则,否则就不可能用那种语言进行交际。实际上,现在有一些语义学家认为,所有的语言都具有同样的基本概念体系,这个基本概念体系是人类思维的一种普遍特征。

再次,在某种意义上说内涵意义是不明确的、无限的,而理性意义却不是如此。正如我们对宇宙的认识和看法具有无限性一样,内涵意义也同样具有无限性:主观上或客观上认识到的所指事物的任何特点,都对表示该所指事物的那个词的内涵意义有一定作用。对比之下,人们一般认为以下两点认识构成语义理论的基础:(一)一个词或一个句子的理性意义可以通过一套有限的符号来表示(例如采用一套有限的、互不重复的意义特性);(二)通过有限的规律可以表达一个句子的语义。对理性内容的有限性和限定性作这种假设是以语言学家分析语言结构的其他方面时一般所作出的设想为根据的。这样的设想在某种程度上过于简单,但是如果没有这种设想,人们就难以把语言说成是一个有限的连贯的体系。

社会意义和情感意义

现在我们来讨论与产生话语的环境有关的交际的两个方面。**社会意义**是一段语言所表示的关于使用该段语言的社会环境的意义。某一语言的文体有不同的侧面和层次,我们部分地通过对这些不同的侧面和层次的辨认,来对一个语段的社会意义进行"解码"。我们说一些词或发音具有方言性质,就是说这些词或发音在告诉我们说话人所生活的地理环境和社会环境;语言的其他特征向我们表明讲话人和听话人之间的社会关系。我们可以在用法方面分成一系列不同的"等级",例如,最高的等级是正式英语和文学英语,较低的等级是口语和熟稔用法,最后是俚语。

Crystal 和 Davy 在《英语文体探讨》一书中区分了社会——文体变异的若干方面(我对各个方面的用法范畴补充了一些例子):

根据以下诸方面产生变异

**方言**(某一地理区域或社会阶段的语言)

**时间**(如:十八世纪的语言)

**使用域**(如:法律语言、科学语言、广告语言)

**等级**(如:礼貌语言、口语、俚语)

**语气**(如:便函语言、讲演语言、笑话语言)

**特性**(如:狄更斯风格、海明威风格)

上表虽然不是详尽无遗,但表明了在一种语言中可能区分的语体的范围。我们很难找到理性意义和语体意义完全等同的两个词,这一点恐怕并不奇怪。因此,人们往往认为"真正的同义词是不存在的"。如果我们把两个同义词之间的关系理解为两者的交际效果完全相同,那真是很难找到反驳这个意见的例证。但是如果把"同义关系"这个术语限制在理性意义等同这个范围之内,那就会方便得多,这样我们就可以比较概念同义词之间不同的语体含义:

马 { steed(诗歌用语) / horse(一般用语) / nag(俚语) / gee-gee(儿语) }

住宅 { domicile(很正式的公文用语) / residence(正式用语) / abode(诗歌用语) / home(一般用语) }

掷抛 { cast(文学用语,圣经用语) / throw(一般用语) / chuck(较随便的用语,俚语) }

小 { diminutive(很正式的用语) / tiny(口语) / wee(口语的,方言用语) }

"等级"这一语体侧面在区别同义词时特别重要。在下面的例子中,可以看到等级差别贯穿全句,这种差别不仅反映在词汇上,也反映在句法上:

(1)They chucked a stone at the cops, and then did a bunk with the boot.(他们用石头扔了警察,拿着抢来的东西逃跑了。)

(2)After casting a stone at the police, they absconded with the money.(他们以石头掷了警察之后,就带着钱潜逃了。)

句(1)可能是两个犯罪分子在事后随便谈起抢劫行为时说的;句(2)大概是探长在正式报告中使用的语言。两者可描述发生的同一件事。任何人都很难既肯定其中一个句子的真实性又否定另一个句子的真实性,可见这两个句子的理性意义显然有其共同之点。

从比较狭隘的意义来说,社会意义能包括一段话语的**言外之意**:例如,这句话是否应解释为请求、陈述、道歉或威胁等等。一段话语在这方面所起的作用与其本身的理性意义可能只有间接的关系。句 *I haven't got a knife.*(我没有小刀。)具有陈述的形式和意义,但在社会现实中(例如,在餐馆里对服务员说这样一句话)这个句子就很容易有像"Please bring me a knife."(请拿给我一把餐刀。)这样的请求的意思。

由此我们很容易考虑到语言如何反映讲话人的个人感情,包括他对听者和他所谈事物的态度。这一类意义可以叫做**情感意义**,它经常通过所用词的理性内容或内涵内容明确地表达出来。当有人对某个人说:"你是个凶恶的土霸王,可耻的堕落者,为此我非常恨你!",说话人对他的感情是无庸置疑的了。但是我们也可以用不这么直接的方式来表达我们的态度:例如我们可以根据礼貌的需要而采用不同的措词。要让人安静些,我们或许可以说:

(3)I'm terribly sorry to interrupt, but I wonder if you would be so kind as to lower your voice

129

a little.(打扰您我十分抱歉,不过不知您是否能把声音稍放低一点。)

或者说:

(4)Will you belt up.(你快点住嘴!)

被我们经常称之为"语气"的语调和音色这些因素在上述情况下也是很重要的。句(3)若用了讽刺挖苦的语气,那温文尔雅的口吻就烟消云散了;句(4)如果用一种温和的请求的语调来表达,那就可以变为知己之间的嬉笑之词。

情感意义基本上是依附性的,因为为了表达情感,我们要依赖意义的其他范畴(即理性意义、内涵范畴或语体范畴)。例如当我们采用不礼貌的语气表示不愉快(像在上面的句子(4)中那样)或采用较随便的语气表示友好的时候,情感的表达都是通过语体来实现的。另一方面,有一些语言成分(主要是感叹词,如 Aha!〔表示得意、嘲弄、惊奇等〕和 Yippee!〔表示欢欣鼓舞的欢呼声〕),其主要功能就是表达情感,在我们使用这些语言成分时,即使没有任何其他种类的语义功能作媒介,也能表示情感和态度。

反映意义和搭配意义

虽然这两类意义不那么重要,但它们包含着语言词汇层次上的一种相互联系。

首先,在存在多重理性意义的情况下,当一个词的一种意义构成我们对这个词的另一种意义的反应的一部分时,便产生**反映意义**,在教堂做礼拜时一听到同义词 The Comforter(圣灵)和 The Holy Ghost(圣灵)(两者均是基督教中圣父、圣子、圣灵三位一体的第三人称提法),我就觉察到我对这两个词的反应受 comfort(安慰)和 ghost(幽灵)这两个词的日常的、非宗教意义的影响。听到 The Comforter 这个词使人感到温暖和"安慰"(虽然在宗教这种语境中,Comfortor 这个词意味着"给人以力量或支持"),而 The Holy Ghost 听起来却使人敬畏。

一个词的意义只有由于出现的频率较高,并且人们对它较为熟悉(例如 The Holy Ghost 中的 ghost),或者通过联想的力量,而且有很强的启示能力的时候,才能以上述方式"扯"到另一种意义上去。只有在使人们对语言的各个方面高度敏感的诗歌中,我们才能看到反映意义在不太显眼的情况下所起的作用:

Are limbs, so *dear*-achieved, are sides,

Full-nerved—still warm—too hard to stir?

(战士如此珍贵的四肢,

他那密布神经依然温热的两肋,

难道已僵直得动弹不得?)

这两行诗句摘自一首描写阵亡士兵的诗《无益》,作者 Wilfree Owen 在字面上用 dear 这个词表达了"珍贵的"这个意义,但人们感到在诗的上下文中,他也用这个词来暗指"可爱的"这个意思。

反映意义通过情感联想突出地表现出来,这种情况可以用带有禁忌意义的词语清楚地加以说明。由于 intercourse、ejaculation、erection 这些词有关性生理的意义(分别指"性交"、"射精"、"勃起"),变得越来越为人们所熟知,所以要在不发生性的联想,在"毫无邪念"的意义上使用它们,使人日益感到困难。禁忌词语这一污染过程已说明了一个词所含的非禁忌意义为什么会渐渐消失:Bloomfield 解释过为什么 cock 这个词在养鸡场的意义上要用 rooster(雄鸡)来代替:是因为 cock 一词受到它的禁忌用法(指"阴茎")的影响。或许 intercourse 这个词现在正发生着类似的变化。

**搭配意义**是由一个词所获得的各种联想构成的,而这些联想则产生于与这个词经常同时出现的一些词的意义,pretty(漂亮)和 handsome(俊美)在"好看"这个含义上有其共同点,但两

130

者可以通过与一系列名词同现或（用语言学家的术语来说）"搭配"来加以区别：

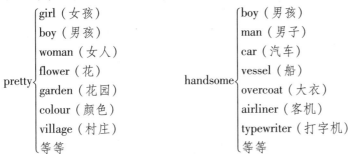

当然这两个搭配范围很可能重迭：虽然 *handsome woman*（端庄美貌的女子）和 *pretty woman*（漂亮的女人）由于这两个形容词的搭配关系表明了不同类型的"美"，但两者都是可以接受的。还可以再举一些准同义动词为例，例如 *wander*（蹓跶）和 *stroll*（散步）——*cows*（母牛）可以 *wander* 但不能 *stroll*；再如 *tremble*（发抖）和 *quiver*（颤动）——人们由于害怕而发抖（*tremble with fear*），但因为激动而颤动（*quiver with excitement*）。不必把可能同现的一切差别都解释为搭配意义：有些可能是由于语体的差别而引起的，另外一些也可能因为概念的差异而相异。"He mounted his gee-gee"或者"He got on his steed"，这两句之所以搭配不当，是因为在这两个句子中把一些语体不同的词语不协调地结合在一起了。另一方面，"The donkey ate hay"（驴吃了干草）这个句子可以接受，而相比之下，"The donkey ate silence"（驴吃了沉默）这句话则不能接受。这是一个相容性的问题，属于观念语义学这一层次。只有在按照意义的其他范畴都解释不通的时候，我们才需要求助于搭配意义这个特殊范畴；其他类型的意义具有普遍性，而搭配意义却是各个词具有的特异性。

联想意义：一个概括性的术语

反映意义、搭配意义、情感意义和社会意义这四个意义与内涵意义之间比它们与理性意义之间具有更多的共同之处：它们都具有同样的不限定、可变化的特性，并且都能作程度和范围的分析，而不能用那些孤立的"不是这个便是那个"的方式进行分析。这五种意义都可以用**联想意义**这一名称来概括。为了说明这五种意义层次上的交际作用，我们不需要很深奥的理论，只需要浅近的"联想"理论——以经验的相互关联为基础说明思维之间联系的理论。我们所以把这五种类型的意义都与理性意义加以对比，是因为理性意义似乎需要以人类所特有的语言和复杂的思维结构为前提。

联想意义含有很多无法正确估计的因素，以至于只能用近似统计的方法对它进行系统的研究。实际上，Osgood，Suci 和 Tannenbaum 在 1957 年出版他们那本题目涉及范围很大的著作《意义的衡量》时，就提出一种对联想意义部分地进行分析的方法。Osgood 和他的合作者设计了一种从多面语义空间去测定意义的方法（牵涉到一种叫做"语义鉴别法"的统计度量），他们根据七项阶记录下说话人的判断，用来作为研究资料。这些阶是通过比较成对的形容词，例如，*happy-sad*（愉快的—悲哀的）、*hard-soft*（坚硬的—柔软的）、*slow-fast*（迟缓的—迅速的）来作标记的。这样，就可以用下面的方法把一个人对 *bagpipe*（风笛）这样一个词的印象记录在一张图表上：

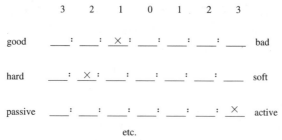

从统计的角度看,研究者发现三个主要方面特别重要:一是评价(优—劣),二是效验(坚硬的—柔软的),三是活动(主动的—被动的)。甚至从这个很简单的图上也可以清楚地看到,这个方法只能为联想主义提供一种部分的和近似的描写:之所以只能是部分描写,是因为它需要从无数个可能存在的阶中加以选择,而只有在用阶分的术语可能解释的范围内,才能用这种阶来解释联想意义;之所以只能是近似描写,是因为只能作抽样统计,同时因为七项阶把一个连续的阶分割成七段,在每段中就不再作进一步的区分,这就像把光谱分割成七种原色一样粗略。这不是要贬低作为度量联想意义的一种手段的语义鉴别法,实际上,要引起注意的是,只有依靠像上面说的那种比较迟钝的工具,才能系统地研究联想意义,因为它不适合于那种在"是""非"之间作选择、并只能以独特方式对结构进行分割的确定的分析方法。

关于语义鉴别法的另一个重要方面,是已经发现这种方法在像个性研究、"态度度量"和心理治疗之类的心理学领域里极其有用。在这些领域中,需要详尽调查的是人们反应的差别,而不是他们反应中的共同之处。这一点和我前面关于内涵意义的论述是一致的:即理性意义实质上是言语集团的成员所共有的语言"共同体系"的一部分,联系意义则不那么稳定,可以因个人经历的不同而变化。

主题意义

我试图区分的最后一个意义范畴是**主题意义**,这种意义是说话者或写文章的人借助组织信息的方式(语序、强调手段、信息焦点的安排)来传递的一种意义。例如我们经常感觉到,虽然下面句(1)和句(2)在理性内容上似乎相同,但像句(1)这样的主动句和与之对等的被动句句(2)却有不同的意义:

(1)Mrs. Bessie Smith donated the first prize.(贝西·史密斯夫人捐赠了一等奖。)
(2)The first prize was donated by Mrs. Bessie Smith.(一等奖由贝西·史密斯夫人捐赠。)

无疑这两个句子具有不同的交际价值,因为它们使我们联想到不同的上下文:主动句似乎隐含着这个问题"What did Mrs. Bessie Smith donate?"(贝西·史密斯夫人捐赠了什么?),而被动句似乎回答了以下的问题"Who was the first prize donated by?"(一等奖由谁捐赠?)或更简单地说,"who donated the first prize?"(谁捐赠了一等奖?)。这就是说,与句(2)比较,句(1)表明我们知道贝西·史密斯夫人是谁(可能因为前面已提到过)。然而两个句子具有同样的真实性:句(1)和句(2)都精确地描述了同一情景。

主题意义主要涉及在不同的语法结构之间进行选择的问题,如:

(3)A man is waiting in the hall.(一个男人正在大厅里等着。)
(4)There's a man waiting in the hall.(有一个男人在大厅里等着。)
(5)They stopped at the end of the corridor.(他们在走廊的一头停下。)
(6)At the end of the corridor, they stopped.(在走廊的一头,他们停下了。)
(7)I like Danish cheese best.(我最喜欢丹麦乳酪。)
(8)Danish cheese I like best.(丹麦的乳酪我最喜欢。)
(9)It's Danish cheese that I like best.(我最喜欢的是丹麦乳酪。)

但是句(1)和句(2)所表明的通过语序和强调来达到的对比,也可以凭借词汇手段来获取,例如可以用 *belongs to*(属于)来替换 *owns*(拥有):

　　(10)My brother owns the largest betting-shop in London.(我兄弟拥有伦敦最大的赌场。)
　　(11)The largest betting-shop belongs to my brother.(伦敦最大的赌场为我兄弟所有。)

在其他情况下,是通过重音和语调而不是通过语法结构来强调句子中某一部分的信息。在句(12)中如果给 *electric*(电的)这个词加上对比重音:

　　(12)Bill uses an *electric* razor.(比尔使用电剃刀。)
　　(13)The kind of razor that Bill uses is an electric one.(比尔用的那种剃刀是电剃刀。)

结果就把注意力集中在这个词上,把它看作是包含新信息的一个词,从而和假设是已知的情况(即比尔使用剃刀)形成对比。在英语中这样强调的目的同样可以通过句(13)这种不同的句法结构来达到。从某种意义上说,上面每个大括号中的一组句子显然都具有"相同的意义";但我们仍然必须承认它们的交际效果可能稍有差别;在同样的上下文中,并不是每个句子都合适的。

　　分界问题

　　现在我已经论述了在本章开始时提出的七种不同类型的意义,但我不希望给人这样的印象:这些就是全部的意义类型,能说明一段话所传递的一切意义。还可以增添一个通过言语行为或文字来传递生理方面信息的范畴,比方说,关于讲话人的性别、年龄、器官状态等方面的信息。

　　关于意义的七种类型还有一点需要说明:它们之间总是存在着一些"界限"问题,尤其是理性意义和附带意义之间的"界限"问题。前面已经提到的划定理性意义和内涵意义之间界限的困难也存在于其他的一些范畴之间,例如存在于理性意义与社会语体意义之间:

　　(1)He *stuck* the key in his pocket.(他把钥匙塞进口袋。)
　　(2)He *put* the key in his pocket.(他把钥匙放进口袋。)

我们可以说句(1)句(2)在理性上是同义的,但在语体上是不同的[句(2)属于中性语体,而句(1)属于口语和较随便的语体]。另一方面我们可以认为,语体的变化是与概念的差别结合在一起的:就是说 *stick*(塞进)这个词在句(1)这样的上下文中,比句(2)具有一个更明确的外延,可以大致解释为"迅速而粗率地放"。后一种解释可以从下面这两句有点奇怪的句子中得到进一步的证实:

　　?* He stuck the key slowly in his pocket.(他把钥匙慢慢地塞进他的口袋。)
　　?* He stuck the key carefully in his pocket.(他把钥匙细心地塞进他的口袋。)

　　[根据语言学的一个规约,句子前边的星号表示该句是不可接受的。]

实际上,要解决划界问题,我们必须承认准同义词之间至少在意义的两个平面上是不同的。

　　我们还可以以动词 *smile*(微笑)和 *grin*(露齿而笑)为例,来说明理性意义和搭配意义之间的界限。这两个词的区别仅仅在于它们具有不同的理性意义还是习惯性搭配的词语范围不同?几乎人人都能毫不犹豫地把上述两个动词分别填入下边两个句子的空格中去:

　　The duchess _____ed graciously as she shook hands with her guests.(公爵夫人与客人握手时谦和地_____。)

　　Gargoyles _____ed hideously from the walls of the building.(奇形怪状的滴水嘴从墙边上狰狞地_____。)

然而问题在于搭配中的这种差别,是不是出自不同的理性内容和内涵内容:例如与 *smile* 相比,*grin* 这个词可否解释为人笑时嘴张得更大,牙齿露得更多,并带有敌意。正因为这个原因,*grin* 这个词所包含的内容在奇形怪状的脸上比在公爵夫人的脸上更加可能看到。这是一种特别复杂的情况,因为社会意义和情感意义的差别也清楚地包含在里面。实际上,我们已经看到,情感意义在很大程度上是一个与语体、内涵和理性内容重叠的范畴。

要表达的意义与被理解的意义

**要表达的**意义是指讲话者在组织他的信息时头脑中考虑的那种意义;**被理解的**意义则指听话者接受信息时传递到他头脑中的那种意义。可能有人要问我为什么不把这两者加以区别。我已把广义的意义和"交际效果"这个概念等同起来,而"交际"通常指把信息从其来源(A)传送到它的目标(B)。根据这一点,我们可以说如果我们知道(A)头脑中的信息已传到或印在(B)的头脑中,我们才可以断定交际过程已经发生。于是,研究意义(特别在哲学领域研究意义)应该特别注意意义本身——要表达的意义——被理解的意义之间的关系这一令人头痛的问题。尽管如此,语言学家可能认为信息的目的与效果之间的差别可以不必考虑,因为他们的兴趣在于交际体系本身,而不在于交际体系的正确使用或误用。语言学家感兴趣的是语言的语义侧面,我们认为,对来源和目标来说,语义侧面是共同的。对语言的语义侧面的研究包括歧义和会给交际带来困难的其他方面的问题(如联想意义的变异),但重要的是,就语义学而言,语义在"说话者的意义"和"听话者的意义"之间是中性的;这样说是确实有道理的,因为只有通过理解交际手段本身的中性潜力,我们才能研究一个人准备传递和实际传递的两种信息之间的区别。

当然,语言的一切正常使用都意味着讲话者带有某种目的,但是只要语义本身隐含着目的,这种目的就只能通过意义才能领会到。换言之,想要表达的意思是私下的,而意义是公开的。这甚至也适用于社会意义:我将在十六章讨论语义学和语用学之间的关系时对此作进一步的论述。

小结

由于这一章介绍了一系列有关意义类型的术语,所以在结束此章时应该加以归纳,并提出一两点有关简化术语的建议。

意义的七种类型

| 1.理性意义(或意义) | | 关于逻辑、认知或外延内容的意义。 |
|---|---|---|
| 联想意义 | 2.内涵意义 | 通过语言所指事物来传递的意义。 |
| | 3.社会意义 | 关于语言运用的社会环境的意义。 |
| | 4.情感意义 | 关于讲话人/写文章的人的感情和态度的意义。 |
| | 5.反映意义 | 通过与同一个词语的另一意义的联想来传递的意义。 |
| | 6.搭配意义 | 通过经常与另一个词同时出现的词的联想来传递的意义。 |
| 7.主题意义 | | 组织信息的方式(语序、强调手段)所传递的意义。 |

我在这儿使用了**意义**(sense)这个词作为一个比较简短的术语来代替"理性意义"这个术语(即狭义的"意义"),并且从现在开始,为了清楚和方便起见,我将使用这个术语。对于包含上述七种意义的广义的"意义",另一个术语——**交际价值**( communicative value)是很有用处的。

(节选自《语义学》,上海外语教育出版社,1987:13-33)

## 2. On Sense and Reference

### Gottlob Frege

Equality[1] gives rise to challenging questions which are not altogether easy to answer. Is it a relation? A relation between objects, or between names or signs of objects? In my *Begriffsschrift*[1] I assumed the latter. The reasons which seem to favour this are the following: $a = a$ and $a = b$ are obviously statements of differing cognitive value; $a = a$ holds *a priori* and, according to Kant, is to be labelled analytic, while statements of the form $a = b$ often contain very valuable extensions of our knowledge and cannot always be established *a priori*. The discovery that the rising sun is not new every morning, but always the same, was one of the most fertile astronomical discoveries. Even today the identification of a small planet or a comet is not always a matter of course. Now if we were to regard equality as a relation between that which the names 'a' and 'b' designate, it would seem that $a = b$ could not differ from $a = a$ (i.e. provided $a = b$ is true). A relation would thereby be expressed of a thing to itself, and indeed one in which each thing stands to itself but to no other thing. What is intended to be said by $a = b$ seems to be that the signs or names 'a' and 'b' designate the same thing, so that those signs themselves would be under discussion; a relation between them would be asserted. But this relation would hold between the names or signs only in so far as they named or designated something. It would be mediated by the connexion of each of the two signs with the same designated thing. But this is arbitrary. Nobody can be forbidden to use any arbitrarily producible event or object as a sign for something. In that case the sentence $a = b$ would no longer refer to the subject matter, but only to its mode of designation; we would express no proper knowledge by its means. But in many cases this is just what we want to do. If the sign 'a' is distinguished from the sign 'b' only as object (here, by means of its shape), not as sign (i.e. not by the manner in which it designates something), the cognitive value of $a = a$ becomes essentially equal to that of $a = b$, provided $a = b$ is true. A difference can arise only if the difference between the signs corresponds to a difference in the mode of presentation of that which is designated. Let $a$, $b$, $c$ be the lines connecting the vertices of a triangle with the midpoints of the opposite sides. The point of intersection of $a$ and $b$ is then the same as the point of intersection of $b$ and $c$. So we have different designations for the same point, and these names ('point of intersection of $a$ and $b$', 'point of intersection of $b$ and $c$') likewise indicate the mode of presentation; and hence the statement contains actual knowledge.

It is natural, now, to think of there being connected with a sign (name, combination of words, letter), besides that to which the sign refers, which may be called the reference of the sign, also what I should like to call the *sense* of the sign, wherein the mode of presentation is contained. In our example, accordingly, the reference of the expressions 'the point of intersection of $a$ and $b$' and 'the point of intersection of $b$ and $c$' would be the same, but not their senses. The reference of 'evening star' would be the same as that of 'morning star', but not the sense.

It is clear from the context that by 'sign' and 'name' I have here understood any designation representing a proper name, which thus has as its reference a definite object (this word taken in the widest range), but not a concept or a relation, which shall be discussed further in another article. The designation of a single object can also consist of several words or other signs. For brevity, let every such designation be called a proper name.

The sense of a proper name is grasped by everybody who is sufficiently familiar with the language or totality of designations to which it belongs;[2] but this serves to illuminate only a single aspect of the reference, supposing it to have one. Comprehensive knowledge of the reference would require us to be able to say immediately whether any given sense belongs to it. To such knowledge we never attain.

The regular connexion between a sign, its sense, and its reference is of such a kind that to the sign there corresponds a definite sense and to that in turn a definite reference, while to a given reference (an object) there does not belong only a single sign. The same sense has different expressions in different languages or even in the same language. To be sure, exceptions to this regular behaviour occur. To every expression belonging to a complete totality of signs, there should certainly correspond a definite sense; but natural languages often do not satisfy this condition, and one must be content if the same word has the same sense in the same context. It may perhaps be granted that every grammatically well-formed expression representing a proper name always has a sense. But this is not to say that to the sense there also corresponds a reference. The words 'the celestial body most distant from the Earth' have a sense, but it is very doubtful if they also have a reference. The expression 'the least rapidly convergent series' has a sense but demonstrably has no reference, since for every given convergent series, another convergent, but less rapidly convergent, series can be found. In grasping a sense, one is not certainly assured of a reference.

If words are used in the ordinary way, what one intends to speak of is their reference. It can also happen, however, that one wishes to talk about the words themselves or their sense. This happens, for instance, when the words of another are quoted. One's own words then first designate words of the other speaker, and only the latter have their usual reference. We then have signs of signs. In writing, the words are in this case enclosed in quotation marks. Accordingly, a word standing between quotation marks must not be taken as having its ordinary reference.

In order to speak of the sense of an expression 'A' one may simply use the phrase 'the sense of the expression "A"'. In reported speech one talks about the sense, e.g., of another person's remarks. It is quite clear that in this way of speaking words do not have their customary reference but designate what is usually their sense. In order to have a short expression, we will say: In reported speech, words are used *indirectly* or have their *indirect* reference. We distinguish accordingly the *customary* from the *indirect* reference of a word; and its *customary* sense from its *indirect* sense. The indirect reference of a word is accordingly its customary sense. Such exceptions must always be borne in mind if the mode of connexion between sign, sense, and reference in particular cases is to be correctly understood.

The reference and sense of a sign are to be distinguished from the associated idea. If the reference of a sign is an object perceivable by the senses, my idea of it is an internal image,[3] arising from memories of sense impressions which I have had and acts, both internal and external, which I have performed. Such an idea is often saturated with feeling; the clarity of its separate parts varies and oscillates. The same sense is not always connected, even in the same man, with the same idea. The idea is subjective: one man's idea is not that of another. There result, as a matter of course, a variety of differences in the ideas associated with the same sense. A painter, a horseman, and a zoologist will probably connect different ideas with the name 'Bucephalus'. This constitutes an essential distinction between the idea and the sign's sense, which may be the common property of many and therefore is not a part of a mode of the individual mind. For one can hardly deny that mankind has a common store of thoughts which is transmitted from one generation to another.[4]

In the light of this, one need have no scruples in speaking simply of *the* sense, whereas in the case of an idea one must, strictly speaking, add to whom it belongs and at what time. It might perhaps be said: Just as one man connects this idea, and another that idea, with the same word, so also one man can associate this sense and another that sense. But there still remains a difference in the mode of connexion. They are not prevented from grasping the same sense; but they cannot have the same idea. *Si duo idem faciunt, non est idem.* If two persons picture the same thing, each still has his own idea. It is indeed sometimes possible to establish differences in the ideas, or even in the sensations, of different men; but an exact comparison is not possible, because we cannot have both ideas together in the same consciousness.

The reference of a proper name is the object itself which we designate by its means; the idea, which we have in that case, is wholly subjective; in between lies the sense, which is indeed no longer subjective like the idea, but is yet not the object itself. The following analogy will perhaps clarify these relationships. Somebody observes the Moon through a telescope. I compare the Moon itself to the reference; it is the object of the observation, mediated by the real image projected by the object glass in the interior of the telescope, and by the retinal image of the observer. The former I compare to the sense, the latter is like the idea or experience. The optical image in the telescope is indeed one-sided and dependent upon the standpoint of observation; but it is still objective, inasmuch as it can be used by several observers. At any rate it could be arranged for several to use it simultaneously. But each one would have his own retinal image. On account of the diverse shapes of the observers' eyes, even a geometrical congruence could hardly be achieved, and an actual coincidence would be out of the question. This analogy might be developed still further, by assuming A's retinal image made visible to B; or A might also see his own retinal image in a mirror. In this way we might perhaps show how an idea can itself be taken as an object, but as such is not for the observer what it directly is for the person having the idea. But to pursue this would take us too far afield.

We can now recognize three levels of difference between words, expressions, or whole sentences. The difference may concern at most the ideas, or the sense but not the reference, or, finally, the reference as well. With respect to the first level, it is to be noted that, on account of the uncertain connexion of ideas with words, a difference may hold for one person, which another does not find. The difference between a translation and the original text should properly not overstep the first level. To the possible differences here belong also the colouring and shading which poetic eloquence seeks to give to the sense. Such colouring and shading are not objective, and must be evoked by each hearer or reader according to the hints of the poet or the speaker. Without some affinity in human ideas art would certainly be impossible; but it can never be exactly determined how far the intentions of the poet are realized.

In what follows there will be no further discussion of ideas and experiences; they have been mentioned here only to ensure that the idea aroused in the hearer by a word shall not be confused with its sense or its reference.

To make short and exact expressions possible, let the following phraseology be established:

A proper name (word, sign, sign combination, expression) *expresses* its sense, *stands for* or *designates* its reference. By means of a sign we express its sense and designate its reference.

Idealists or sceptics will perhaps long since have objected: 'You talk, without further ado, of the Moon as an object; but how do you know that the name "the Moon" has any reference? How do you know that anything whatsoever has a reference?' I reply that when we say 'the Moon,' we do not intend to speak of our idea of the Moon, nor are we satisfied with the sense alone, but we presuppose a reference. To assume that in the sentence 'The Moon is smaller than the Earth' the idea of the Moon is in question, would be flatly to misunderstand the sense. If this is what the speaker wanted, he would use the phrase 'my idea of the Moon'. Now we can of course be mistaken in the presupposition, and such mistakes have indeed occurred. But the question whether the presupposition is perhaps always mistaken need not be answered here; in order to justify mention of the reference of a sign it is enough, at first, to point out our intention in speaking or thinking. (We must then add the reservation: provided such reference exists.)

So far we have considered the sense and reference only of such expressions, words, or signs as we have called proper names. We now inquire concerning the sense and reference for an entire declarative sentence. Such a sentence contains a thought.[5] Is this thought, now, to be regarded as its sense or its reference? Let us assume for the time being that the sentence has reference. If we now replace one word of the sentence by another having the same reference, but a different sense, this can have no bearing upon the reference of the sentence. Yet we can see that in such a case the thought changes; since, e.g., the thought in the sentence 'The morning star is a body illuminated by the Sun' differs from that in the sentence 'The evening star is a body illuminated by the Sun.' Anybody who did not know that the evening star is the morning star might hold the one thought to be true, the other false. The thought, accordingly, cannot be the reference of the sentence, but must rather be considered as the sense. What is the position now with regard to the reference? Have we a right even to inquire about it? Is it possible that a sentence as a whole has only a sense, but no reference? At any rate, one might expect that such sentences occur, just as there are parts of sentences having sense but no reference. And sentences which contain proper names without reference will be of this kind. The sentence 'Odysseus was set ashore at Ithaca while sound asleep' obviously has a sense. But since it is doubtful whether the name 'Odysseus', occurring therein, has reference, it is also doubtful whether the whole sentence has one. Yet it is certain, nevertheless, that anyone who seriously took the sentence to be true or false would ascribe to the name 'Odysseus' a reference, not merely a sense; for it is of the reference of the name that the predicate is affirmed or denied. Whoever does not admit the name has reference can neither apply nor withhold the predicate. But in that case it would be superfluous to advance to the reference of the name; one could be satisfied with the sense, if one wanted to go no further than the thought. If it were a question only of the sense of the sentence, the thought, it would be unnecessary to bother with the reference of a part of the sentence; only the sense, not the reference, of the part is relevant to the sense of the whole sentence. The thought remains the same whether 'Odysseus' has reference or not. The fact that we concern ourselves at all about the reference of a part of the sentence indicates that we generally recognize and expect a reference for the sentence itself. The thought loses value for us as soon as we recognize that the reference of one of its parts is missing. We are therefore justified in not being satisfied with the sense of a sentence, and in inquiring also as to its reference. But now why do we want every proper name to have not only a sense, but also a reference? Why is the thought not enough for us? Because, and to the extent that, we are concerned with its truth value. This is not always the case. In hearing an epic poem, for instance, apart form the euphony of the language we are interested only in the sense of the sentences and the images and feelings thereby aroused. The question of truth would cause us to abandon aesthetic delight for an attitude of scientific investigation. Hence it is a matter of no concern to us whether the name 'Odysseus', for instance, has reference, so long as we accept the poem as a work of art.[6] It is the striving for truth that drives us always to advance from the sense to the reference.

We have seen that the reference of a sentence may always be sought, whenever the reference of its components is involved; and that this is the case when and only when we are inquiring after the truth value.

We are therefore driven into accepting the *truth value* of a sentence as constituting its reference. By the truth value of a sentence I understand the circumstance that it is true or false. There are no further truth values. For brevity I call the one the True, the other the False. Every declarative sentence concerned with the reference of its words is therefore to be regarded as a proper name, and its reference, if it has one, is either the True or the False. These two objects are recognized, if only implicitly, by everybody who judges something to be true—and so even by a sceptic. The designation of the truth values as objects may appear to be an arbitrary fancy or perhaps a mere play upon words, from which no profound consequences could be drawn. What I mean by an object can be more exactly discussed only in connexion with concept and relation. I will reserve this for another article. But so much should already be clear, that in every judgment,[7] no matter how trivial, the step from the level of thoughts to the level of reference (the objective) has already been taken.

One might be tempted to regard the relation of the thought to the True not as that of sense to reference, but rather as that of subject to predicate. One can, indeed, say: 'The thought, that 5 is a prime number, is true.' But closer examination shows that nothing more has been said than in the simple sentence '5 is a prime number.' The truth claim arises in each case from the form of the declarative sentence, and when the latter lacks its usual force, e.g., in the mouth of an actor upon the stage, even the sentence 'The thought that 5 is a prime number is true' contains only a thought, and indeed the same thought as the simple '5 is a prime number.' It follows that the relation of the thought to the True may not be compared with that of subject to predicate.

Subject and predicate (understood in the logical sense) are indeed elements of thought; they stand on the same level for knowledge. By combining subject and predicate, one reaches only a thought, never passes from sense to reference, never from a thought to its truth value. One moves at the same level but never advances from one level to the next. A truth value cannot be a part of a thought, any more than, say, the Sun can, for it is not a sense but an object.

If our supposition that the reference of a sentence is its truth value is correct, the latter must remain unchanged when a part of the sentence is replaced by an expression having the same reference. And this is in fact the case. Leibniz gives the definition: '*Eadem sunt, quae sibi mutuo substitui possunt, salva veritate.*' What else but the truth value could be found, that belongs quite generally to every sentence if the reference of its components is relevant, and remains unchanged by substitutions of the kind in question?

If now the truth value of a sentence is its reference, then on the one hand all true sentences have the same reference and so, on the other hand, do all false sentences. From this we see that in the reference of the sentence all that is specific is obliterated. We can never be concerned only with the reference of a sentence; but again the mere thought alone yields no knowledge, but only the thought together with its reference, i.e. its truth value. Judgments can be regarded as advances from a thought to a truth value. Naturally this cannot be a definition. Judgment is something quite peculiar and incomparable. One might also say that judgments are distinctions of parts within truth values. Such distinction occurs by a return to the thought. To every sense belonging to a truth value there would correspond its own manner of analysis. However, I have here used the word 'part' in a special sense. I have in fact transferred the relation between the parts and the whole of the sentence to its reference, by calling the reference of a word part of the reference of the sentence, if the word itself is a part of the sentence. This way of speaking can certainly be attacked, because the whole reference and one part of it do not suffice to determine the remainder, and because the word 'part' is already used in another sense of bodies. A special term would need to be invented.

The supposition that the truth value of a sentence is its reference shall now be put to further test. We have found that the truth value of a sentence remains unchanged when an expression is replaced by another having the same reference: but we have not yet considered the case in which the expression to be replaced is itself a sentence. Now if our view is correct, the truth value of a sentence containing another as part must remain unchanged when the part is replaced by another sentence having the same truth value. Exceptions are to be expected when the whole sentence or its part is direct or indirect quotation; for in such cases, as we have seen, the words do not have their customary reference. In direct quotation, a sentence designates another sentence, and in indirect quotation a thought.

We are thus led to consider subordinate sentences or clauses. These occur as parts of a sentence complex, which is, from the logical standpoint, likewise a sentence—a main sentence. But here we meet the question whether it is also true of the subordinate sentence that its reference is a truth value. Of indirect quotation we already know the opposite. Grammarians view subordinate clauses as representatives of parts of sentences and divide them accordingly into noun clauses, adjective clauses, adverbial clauses. This might generate the supposition that the reference of a subordinate clause was not a truth value but rather of the same kind as the reference of a noun or adjective or adverb—in short, of a part of a sentence, whose sense was not a thought but only a part of a thought. Only a more thorough investigation can clarify the issue. In so doing, we shall not follow the grammatical categories strictly, but rather group together what is logically of the same kind. Let us first search for cases in which the sense of the subordinate clause, as we have just supposed, is not an independent thought.

The case of an abstract noun clause, introduced by 'that', includes the case of indirect quotation, in which we have seen the words to have their indirect reference coinciding with what is customarily their sense. In this case, then, the subordinate clause has for its reference a thought, not a truth value; as sense not a thought, but the sense of the words 'the thought, that...,' which is only a part of the thought in the entire complex sentence. This happens after 'say', 'hear', 'be of the opinion', 'be convinced', 'conclude', and similar words.[8] There is a different, and indeed somewhat complicated, situation after words like 'perceive', 'know', 'fancy', which are to be considered later.

That in the cases of the first kind the reference of the subordinate clause is in fact the thought can also be recognized by seeing that it is indifferent to the truth of the whole whether the subordinate clause is true or false. Let us compare, for instance, the two sentences 'Copernicus believed that the planetary orbits are circles' and 'Copernicus believed that the apparent motion of the sun is produced by the real motion of the Earth.' One subordinate clause can be substituted for the other without harm to the truth. The main clause and the subordinate clause together have as their sense only a single thought, and the truth of the whole includes neither the truth nor the untruth of the subordinate clause. In such cases it is not permissible to replace one expression in the subordinate clause by another having the same customary reference, but only by one having the same indirect reference, i.e. the same customary sense. If somebody were to conclude: The reference of a sentence is not its truth value, for in that case it could always be replaced by another sentence of the same truth value; he would prove too much; one might just as well claim that the reference of 'morning star' is not Venus, since one may not always say 'Venus' in place of 'morning star'. One has the right to conclude only that the reference of a sentence is not *always* its truth value, and that 'morning star' does not always stand for the planet Venus, viz. when the word has its indirect reference. An exception of such a kind occurs in the subordinate clause just considered which has a thought as its reference.

If one says 'It seems that ...' one means 'It seems to me that ...' or 'I think that ...' We therefore have the same case again. The situation is similar in the case of expressions such as 'to be pleased ', 'to regret', 'to approve', 'to blame', 'to hope', 'to fear'. If, toward the end of the battle of Waterloo, Wellington was glad that the Prussians were coming, the basis for his joy was a conviction. Had he been deceived, he would have been no less pleased so long as his illusion lasted; and before he became so convinced he could not have been pleased that the Prussians were coming— even though in fact they might have been already approaching.

Just as a conviction or a belief is the ground of a feeling, it can, as in inference, also be the ground of a conviction. In the sentence: 'Columbus inferred from the roundness of the Earth that he could reach India by travelling towards the west,' we have as the reference of the parts two thoughts, that the Earth is round, and that Columbus by travelling to the west could reach India. All that is relevant here is that Columbus was convinced of both, and that the one conviction was a ground for the other. Whether the Earth is really round and Columbus could really reach India by travelling west, as he thought, is immaterial to the truth of our sentence; but it is not immaterial whether we replace 'the Earth' by 'the planet which is accompanied by a moon whose diameter is greater than the fourth part of its own.' Here also we have the indirect reference of the words.

Adverbial final clauses beginning 'in order that' also belong here; for obviously the purpose is a thought; therefore: indirect reference for the words, subjunctive mood.

A subordinate clause with 'that' after 'command', 'ask', 'forbid', would appear in direct speech as an imperative. Such a clause has no reference but only a sense. A command, a request, are indeed not thoughts, yet they stand on the same level as thoughts. Hence in subordinate clauses depending upon 'command', 'ask', etc., words have their indirect reference. The reference of such a clause is therefore not a truth value but a command, a request, and so forth.

The case is similar for the dependent question in phrases such as 'doubt whether', 'not to know what'. It is easy to see that here also the words are to be taken to have their indirect reference. Dependent clauses expressing questions and beginning with 'who', 'what', 'where', 'when', 'how', 'by what means', etc., seem at times to approximate very closely to adverbial clauses in which words have their customary references. These cases are distinguished linguistically [ in German ] by the mood of the verb. With the subjunctive, we have a dependent question and indirect reference of the words, so that a proper name cannot in general be replaced by another name of the same object.

In the cases so far considered the words of the subordinate clauses had their indirect reference, and this made it clear that the reference of the subordinate clause itself was indirect, i.e. not a truth value but a thought, a command, a request, a question. The subordinate clause could be regarded as a noun, indeed one could say: as a proper name of that thought, that command, etc., which it represented in the context of the sentence structure.

Notes

[ 1 ] I use this word in the sense of identity and understand '$a = b$' to have the sense of '$a$ is the same as $b$' or '$a$ and $b$ coincide'.

[ 2 ] In the case of an actual proper name such as 'Aristotle' opinions as to the sense may differ. It might, for instance, be taken to be the following: the pupil of Plato and teacher of Alexander the Great. Anybody who does this will attach another sense to the sentence 'Aristotle was born in Stagira' than will a man who takes as the sense of the name: the teacher of Alexander the Great who was born in Stagira. So long as the reference remains the same, such variations of sense may be tolerated, although they are to be avoided in the theoretical structure of a demonstrative science and ought not to occur in a perfect language.

[ 3 ] We can include with ideas the direct experiences in which, sense impressions and acts themselves take the place of traces which they have left in the mind. The distinction is unimportant for our purpose, especially since memories of sense-impressions and acts always go along with such impressions and acts themselves to complete the perceptual image. One may on the other hand understand direct experience as including any object, in so far as it is sensibly perceptible or spatial.

[ 4 ] Hence it is inadvisable to use the word 'idea' to designate something so basically different.

[ 5 ] By a thought I understand not the subjective performance of thinking but its objective content, which is capable of being the common property of several thinkers.

[ 6 ] It would be desirable to have a special term for signs having only sense. If we name them, say, representations, the words of the actors on the stage would be representations; indeed the actor himself would be a representation.

[ 7 ] A judgment, for me, is not the mere comprehension of a thought, but the admission of its truth.

[ 8 ] In 'A lied in saying he had seen B', the subordinate clause designates a thought which is said ( 1 ) to have been asserted by A ( 2 ) while A was convinced of its falsity.

( *On Sense and Reference*, A. W. Moore( ed.). Meaning and Reference, Oxford University Press, 23- 42, 1993.)

译文:

# 论涵义和指称*

肖阳,译

　　"同一"①(sameness)观念令人深思。它提出了一些颇不易解答的问题。同一是一种关系吗? 是对象之间的关系呢,还是对象的名称或指号之间的关系? 在我的《概念演算》中,我选择了后一种说法。这样做的理由如下:"a=a"和"a=b"是具有明显不同的认识意义的句子——"a=a"是先验有效的,并且在康德看来是可以称为分析的,而"a=b"形式的句子往往包含了对我们的知识极有价值的扩展,而且这类句子并不总能先验地加以验证。我们发现,每天早晨升起的太阳并非是新的、互不相同的,而是完全同一的;这当然是天文学中最重大的发现之一。即使在今天,对一颗小行星或彗星的确认(鉴别),也并不总是一件无需证明的事。如果我们试图将同一关系看成是"a"和"b"这两个名称所标志的对象之间的关系,那么,在"a=b"为真的情况下,"a=b"和"a=a"似乎也就没有什么不同了。它也只不过表示一个东西与它自身的关系而已,也就是那种存在于每一个东西与它自身之间而非存在于这一个东西与另一个东西之间的关系。人们试图用"a=b"表达的意思似乎是:指号或名称"a"和"b"命名同一个东西,在这种情况下,我们要处理的是那些指号:要对它们之间的关系作出断定。但是这种关系能够成立仅仅因为它们命名或指示了某个东西。这种关系,似乎可以说,是以具有同一个指称的各个指号之间的联系为中介的。可是,这种联系是任意的,你不能够禁止使用一个任意构造的过程或物体作为其他某个东西的指号。因此,像"a=b"这样的句子不再涉及事实的内容,而和我们的命名方式相关;它并不表达真正的知识,但是,在许多情况下却又正是我们想要表达的东西。如果指号"a"和指号"b"仅仅作为物体而相异(这里,通过两者形状上的差异做到这点),而不是通过作为指号这种作用而相异,即不是以其命名方式上的不同而相异,那么,在"a=b"为真时,"a=a"和"a=b"两者的认识意义就会没有什么实质上的差异。差异只产生于下面的情况:指号之间的差异与被命名的对象被给出的方式上的差异是对应的。令 a、b、c 为三角形中连接角与对边中点的直线,则 a 和 b 的交点与 b 和 c 的交点为同一点。这样,我们就有了对于同一个点的不同命名,而且这些名称("a 和 b 的交点","b 和 c 的交点")也表达了这些点被给出的方式。所以,有关句子表达了真正的知识。

　　现在,我们似乎有理由指出:和一个指号(名称,词组,表达式)相联系的,不仅有被命名的对象,它也可以称为指号的指称(nominatum),而且还有这个指号的涵义(sense)、内涵(connotation)、意义(meaning),在其涵义中包含了指号出现的方式和语境。因此,在我们的例子里,"a 和 b 的交点"与"b 和 c 的交点"这两个表达式的指称(nominata)是同一的,而两者的涵义却不同。暮星和晨星的指称虽然是同一个星辰,但这两个名称具有不同的涵义。

　　从上面所阐述的来看,很清楚,我在这里将"指号"或"名称"理解为任何作为专名(proper

---

　　* 英译文由 H.费格尔译自论文"Ueber Sinn und Bedetung"(《论涵义和指称》),载于《哲学和哲学评论》,100,1892 年。所用术语大都是 R.卡尔纳普在《意义和必然性》(芝加哥大学出版社,1947)中所采用的,中译文译自 H.费格尔和 W.塞拉斯编辑的《哲学分析读物》,1949 年。本文标题中的"Sinn"一词,费格尔译为"Sense",而未译为"meaning"。为准确起见,这里也把这个词译为"涵义",而不译为"意义",尽管在弗雷格的著作中,这两个词是通用的。至于"Bedeutung"一词,费格尔译为"Nominatum",有人主张译为"指示",这里仍译为"指称"。

　　① 我用这个词表示"恒等(identity)"的意思,并且将"a=b"理解为"a 与 b 是同一的"或"a 与 b 是完全一致的"。

name)起作用的表达式,专名的指称因而是一个特点的对象(就这个词最广泛的意义而言)。但是,这里,概念和关系都不在考虑之列,这些问题将另文处理。一个单独的对象的名称可以由几个词或各种不同的指号组成。为简便起见,以后任何一个这样的名称我们都要将它看作是一个专名。

任何一个懂得某种语言或全部名称(designation)——专名只是其中的一部分①——的人,都能领会一个专名的涵义。然而,如果存在指称,这也只是以一种极片面的方式阐明指称所在。有关某指称的完整知识要求我们对于任何给出的涵义能够立即说出它是否隶属于此指称,而这是我们永远不能够做到的。

指号,它的涵义和它的指称之间的正常联系是这样的:与某个指号相对应的是特定的涵义,与特定的涵义相对应的是特定的指称,而与一个指称(对象)相对应的可能不是只有一个指号。同一种涵义在不同的语言,甚至在同一种语言中,是由不同的表达式来表述的。这条规律的确也有例外。在完善的指号构型中,当然一定只有一个特点的涵义与每个表达式相对应。但是,从许多方面来看,自然语言都达不到这种要求。我们必须满足于至少在同一语境中同一个词具有相同的涵义。我们也许会同意:如果一个表达式在形式结构上符合语法并且充当专名的角色,那它就具有涵义。但是,至于是否存在与内涵相对应的外延,则还是不确定的。"离地球最远的天体"这些词具有涵义;至于它们是否有指称则很可怀疑。"最弱收敛级数"这个表达式有涵义,但是可以证明,它没有指称,因为对于任何收敛级数,我们总能找到另一个收敛性更弱的级数。因此,对于涵义的把握并不能保证相应的指称的存在。

当我们按通常方式使用语词时,我们谈论的就是它们的指称。但有时我们也需要谈论这些语词本身或它们的涵义。当某人在直接的(通常的)谈话中引用别人的话时,就是在谈论这些词语本身。在这种情况下,他就用自己的语词命名(指示)另一个人的语词,而只有后者的语词才有通常意义下的指称。我们于是有了指号的指号。在书写上,我们利用引号把所谈论的词象(Word-icon)区分出来,引号内的词象因而不能够按通常的方式处理。

如果我们希望谈论表达式"A"的涵义,我们可以通过惯用语"表达式 A 的涵义"很方便地做到这点。在间接谈话中,我们谈到,例如,另外某人的某句话的涵义。从这里,我们清楚地看到,在间接谈话中词语也不具有通常意义下的指称。在这里,它们指示那些通常作为它们的涵义的东西。为了简明地表述这一点,我们说:间接谈话中的词语是被间接地使用的或者它们具有间接的指称。这样,我们区分了一个词语的正常的(customary)指称和间接的(indirect)指称,类似地,也区分了其"正常的"涵义和"间接的"涵义。因此,一个语词的间接指称是它的正常涵义。如果我们希望在任何给出的情况下都能正确地领会指号、涵义和指称之间的联系方式,这样的例外情况必须牢记在心。

指号的指称和涵义都必须和与之相联系的意象(image)区分开来。如果一个指号的指称是感觉的对象,则我关于它的意象是一种内心图像,②这种内心图像来自对于我的内部或外部

---

① 对于"亚里士多德"之类真正的专名,人们对于它们的涵义的理解会出现分歧。可能会出现这样的情况,例如对于专名"亚里士多德"有人会理解为:"柏拉图的学生和亚历山大大帝的老师";另外的人则可理解为"亚历山大大帝的斯塔吉拉老师",对于"亚里士多德生于斯塔吉拉"这个陈述的意义的理解,前者就会和后者不一样。只要指称保持同一,涵义上的这些分歧是可以允许的。但是,在实验科学的系统中应该避免这种情况,而且也不应出现在理想语言中。

② 我们也可以将这种意象与知觉表象联系起来,在知觉表象中,感官印象和活动本身代替了心灵中留下的痕迹。对于我们的目的来说,这种区别并不重要,尤其因为,除了知觉与活动之外,关于知觉与活动的记忆对于直观表象的形成帮助甚大。"知觉表象"也可理解为对象,因为它存在于空间之中,并能为知觉所认识。

的感官印象与活动的记忆。意象往往充满了情感;它的各个部分变化不定。即使对于一个人来说,同一种涵义也并不总是伴随着同一意象。意象是主观的;一个人的意象不是另一个人的意象。所以,和同一个涵义相联系的意象之间也是有各种差异的。画家、骑手、动物学家对于名称"亚历山大大帝的战马"(Bucephalus)可能会有各种各样非常不同的意象。因此,意象在本质上不同于指号的内涵。指号的内涵很可能是许多意象的共同性质,因而并不是个别人心灵中的某一部分或是某个人的一种特殊思维模式;因为,我们不能否认人类拥有代代相传的共同思想宝库。①

因此,尽管没有理由反对在谈话中对意象的涵义不加限制的做法,但为了精确起见,我们必须对于它们是谁的意象和它们是在什么时候产生的意象加以说明。有人可能会说:正如在两个不同的人那里与语词相联系的意象相异一样,相应的涵义在两个人那里也会不同。不过,这种差异仅仅在于联系的方式不同,它并不妨碍两人都能领会相同的涵义,但是他们不能具有同一意象。Si duo idem faciunt,non est idem,(当两个人想象同一个东西时,它们依然有各自的意象。)实际上,有时我们确能探知不同的人的意象的甚至感觉的差异。但是,精确的比较是不可能的,因为这些意象不可能同时出现在一个意识中。

专名的指称就是这个名称所命名的对象本身。我们在那种场合下获得的意象完全是主观的。涵义处于所指的对象和意象之间;诚然,它不再像意象那样是主观的,但它也不是对象本身。下面这个比喻也许有助于说明它们的相互关系:有一个人用望远镜观察月亮,我们把月亮本身比作所指的对象(指称),它是通过它投射到望远镜内物镜上的真实影像和观察者视网膜上的影像而成为观察的对象的。我们把望远镜内物镜上的影像比作涵义,而把视网膜上的影像比作表象(或心理学意义上的意象)。望远镜内物镜上的影像确实是片面的,它取决于观察的地点和角度;但它毕竟是客观的,因为它能够被许多不同的观察者所利用;作些适当的调整,就可以使几个观察者都能利用它,但是,其中每一个人都将仅仅拥有自己的视网膜上的影像。由于眼睛构造上的差异,即使几何形状上的一致也难以达到;而一个真正一致的影像则无论如何是不可能的。通过假设 A 的视网膜影像可以被 B 看见,或者 A 可以从镜子中看到自己的视网膜上的影像,你可以进一步发挥这个比喻。通过这种方式或许你可以表明表象是如何被看成对象的,但是,即使如此,一个(外部的)观察者所看到的,与一个拥有内部意象的人所"看"到的,并不是一码事。不过,我们沿着这条思路已经走得离题太远了。

现在,我们能够清楚地认识到语词表达式和完整语句之间的差异的三个层次。这种差异至多涉及它们的意象,要不就是涵义,但不会涉及指称,或者说,最终也会涉及指称。对于第一层次的差异,我们必须注意,由于意象与语词的关系不确定,一个人也许不能发现存在于另一个人那里的差异。翻译原文时所产生的差异应当不超出第一层次。在这方面可能出现的差异中,我们还要提及诗人在作诗时试图对语词的涵义赋予的各种有声有色的成分。这些有声有色的成分不是客观的。听众和读者不得不根据诗人或演说家的暗示,在理解中加上这些成分。如果人们的意象之间没有某种密切的相似关系,艺术一定是不可能存在的;但是,诗人的意图在多大程度上得到了实现却永远不可能确切得知。

今后,我们将不再谈及意象和画面;讨论它们也仅仅是为了避免将由语词唤起的意象与词的涵义或指称相混淆。

为了便于表达简洁准确,我们作出下列表述:

专名(词,指号,复合指号,表达式)表达它的涵义,并且命名或指示它的指称。我们令指

---

① 由此可见,用一个词"意象"(或"观念")来命名根本不同的东西,是多么不明智。

号表达它的涵义并且命名它的指称。

或许,我们暂时还没有考虑来自观念论和怀疑论方面的异议,那就是:"你已经毫不迟疑地谈论作为对象的月亮,但是,你怎么知道'月亮'这个名称实际上有一个指称呢?你又是怎么知道无论什么名称都有指称呢?"我这样回答:当我们说到"月亮"时,我们的意图并不是谈论月亮的意象,我们也不会满足于它的涵义,相反,在这里,我们预先假定了指称的存在。在句子"月亮比地球小"中,假设我们所涉及的是意象,那么,我们就会失去这个句子的全部意义。假如我们有这样的意图,我们就要使用诸如"我的月亮意象"之类的特殊表达方式。当然,上面的假设可能是错的,而且这种错误以前也时常发生。然而,在这方面我们是否可能总是犯错误的问题,还有待回答;但是,我们总是试图在谈话与思考中证明我们关于指号的指称的有关陈述是正确的,对于这一打算来说,这目前已经足够了,即使我们不得不增加附带条件:假设存在着这样一个指称。

到此为止,我们考虑的仅仅是那些我们称之为专名的表达式、语词和指号的涵义和指称。现在,我们将要研究整个陈述句的涵义和指称。这类语句包含了一个命题( proposition )①。这种语句所表达的思想究竟是语句的涵义,还是语句的指称呢?让我们暂时假定语句有一个指称!如果我们把这个语句中的一个语词换成另一个具有相同指称、但具有不同涵义的语词,那么,这种替换并不会影响语句的指称。但是,我们注意到,在这种情况下语句所表达的思想(命题)发生了变化;例如,"晨星是一个被太阳照耀的天体"和"暮星是一个被太阳照耀的天体"这两个语句所表达的命题是不同的。不知道暮星和晨星是同一个星辰的人,可能认为一个命题为真而另一个为假。因此,命题不可能是语句的指称,相反,它不能不被看做是语句的涵义。那么,语句的指称是什么呢?我们可以提出下面的问题吗:语句作为一个整体或许可以只有涵义而没有指称?无论如何可以预料有这样的语句,就像有一些语句的成分的确有涵义而无指称一样。可以断定:包含了没有指称的专名的语句一定就是这种类型的。"当奥底修斯熟睡的时候,他的船在伊沙卡搁浅了"这个语句显然具有涵义。可是,由于语句中的专名"奥底修斯"是否具有指称值得怀疑,所以,整个句子是否具有指称也有疑问。然而,可以肯定:任何认定这个句子为真或为假的人,都会同意专名"奥底修斯"不仅有涵义而且有指称。因为,很明显,语句中的谓词所表示的属性或者属于或者不属于这个名称的指称。一个不承认指称的人是不会考虑是否把有关属性归属于指称这种问题的。有人可能认为考虑名称的指称没有必要;如果把注意力停留在命题上面,我们可以满足于名称的涵义。如果关心的只是语句的涵义(即命题),那么,由于和语句的涵义相关的只有语句成分的涵义,我们就没有必要关心语句成分的指称。不管"奥底修斯"这个名称有没有指称,那个句子所表达的命题总是保持不变。我们实际上仅仅关心语句成分的指称这个事实表明,我们在通常情况下只承认或要求语句本身的指称。一旦我们得知语句成分没有指称,对语句所表达的命题也就失去了兴趣。因此,除了语句的涵义之外,寻求语句的指称是合理的。但是,为什么我们希望每个专名都既有涵义又有指称呢?为什么仅仅有命题是不充分的呢?回答是这样的:因为我们关心的是真值。不过,情况并不总是如此。例如,听一首史诗的时候,我们被语言的和谐悦耳、语句的涵义以及被唤起的想象和热情强烈地吸引住。至于真理问题,我们就不会考虑艺术欣赏而要探求科学见解。因此一旦把诗看作艺术品,"奥底修斯"有没有指称对于我们就不重要

---

① 我并不认为"命题"指的是思维的主观活动,而应指思维的客观内容,它可以成为许多人的共同财富。

了①。所以,对真理的探求要求我们超出涵义而深入探讨指称。

我们已经认识到,每当语句成分的指称是某种关系重大的东西的时候,我们要寻求的是语句的指称;当且仅当我们寻求真值的时候,正是这种情形。

这样我们不得不将语句的真值当做语句的指称。语句的真值,我指的是语句为真或为假的情况,并不存在其他的真值。为简便起见,我将称一个为真(the True),另一个为假(the False)。因此,对于任何一个陈述句,当我们所关心的是陈述句中语词的指称时,就可以把它看作专名,并且它的指称(如果存在)或者为真或者为假。这两个对象[指真和假,——译者注]为每一个作出判断并且认定任何某种事情为真的人所承认,即使是心照不宣地承认;因而甚至怀疑论者也承认。在现在看来,将真值命名为对象似乎还是一种奇怪的想法或者是纯粹的文字游戏,从中也没有得出任何重要结论。对于我称之为对象的这种东西,只有在将来讨论关系与概念的本质时才能加以讨论。这一点我将留给另一篇文章。但是在这里,有一点或许是清楚的:任何判断②——无论多么明显——总包含了从命题的层次到指称(客观事实)的层次这一步骤。

将命题与真(the True)之间的关系不看作是涵义与指称的关系,而是主词与谓词的关系,这样一种看法颇有吸引力。我们的确可以说:"5 是素数这个命题是真的"。但是进一步仔细考查,我们就会注意到,这个句子并不比简单句"5 是素数"表达了更多的东西。这使得我们清楚了:命题与真的关系决不可和主词与谓词的关系相比。主词和谓词(按照逻辑学的理解)毕竟只是命题的组成部分;在认识意义上它们属于同一层次。将主词和谓词联结起来,我们总是仅仅得到一个命题,在这种做法中我们从未将涵义变作指称或者将命题变作它的真值。我们还停留在同一层次上并未从那里走向另一层次。正如太阳不能是命题的部分,由于真值不是涵义而是对象,它也不能是命题的部分。

如果我们的猜想(即语句的指称是它的真值)是正确的,那么,当语句成分被具有相同指称但是不同涵义的表达式替换时,语句真值应保持不变。实际上,莱布尼茨说过:"Eadem sunt,quae sibi mutuo substitui possunt,salva veritate"(某些语句,虽可转换为其他语形,但仍保留同一真值)如果说任何一个语句都普遍地具有这样一种属性,它与语句成分的指称有关,并且当作出上述那种替换时,这种属性始终保持不变,那么,这种属性除了是语句的真值以外,还能有别的东西吗?

如果语句的真值是它的指称,那么所有真的语句都具有同一指称。同样,所有假的语句也具有相同的指称。这意味着在语句的指称中所有的细节都被抹煞掉了。因此,我们感兴趣的不仅仅是指称,然而仅仅命题也不能给我们知识;只有语句的命题与它的指称即真值合在一起才能够做到这一点。判断,似乎可以看作是从命题走向指称即真值的运动。当然我们并不打算把这种说法当作定义。判断确实是某种独特的事情。有人可能认为判断在于在真值层次上对部分的识别。这种识别通过求助于命题来达到。每个属于一个真值的涵义都以自己的方式对应于这种分析。可是,在这里我是以一种特殊的方式使用"部分"这个词的:我把整体和部分之间的关系从语句转移到语句的指称。通过将自身是语句一部分的语词的指称当作语句指称的一部分,我就做到了这种转换。确实,这种处理事物的方式是会遭到反对的,因为对于指称来说,指称的整体和一部分并不决定它的其他部分,另外,"部分"这个词对于不

---

① 对于只具有涵义的指号,如果能找到一个表达式,那是十分吸引人的。如果我们叫这些指号为"象(icons)",那么舞台上的演员所说的话也就是象;甚至演员自身也是象。

② 判断不仅仅是对于思想或命题的理解,而是对于其真值的承认。

同物体(bodies)具有不同的惯用法。对于上面提出的想法我们必须提出一种新的表述来。

我们现在进一步考察语句的真值是它的指称这个猜想。我们已经知道,当语句中的表达式被一个同义的表达式替换时,语句的指称不变。但是,我们还没有考虑被替换的表达式本身就是语句的情况。如果我们的想法是正确的,那么对于包含另一个语句为其部分的语句来说,当我们将这一部分用另一个具有相同真值的语句替换时,它的真值不变。例外的情况发生在这种时候:在整个句子或其部分这两者中,一个处在直接谈话中,而另一个处在间接谈话中;因为,正如我们已经看到的,在那种情况下语词的指称不是通常的指称。在直接谈话中语句仍指示语句,但在间接谈话中它指示命题。

我们的注意力因此被引向从属句(subordinate sentences)[即从属子句(dependent clauses)]。这些从属子句当然作为语句结构的一部分出现,而语句结构的一部分从逻辑的观点看来似乎也是语句,而且的确像是主要子句。然而我们在这里面临的问题是,语句的指称是它的真值这一点对于从属子句是否也成立。我们已经知道,就间接谈话中的语句而言,情况不是如此。语法家将子句看成是语句构成部分的典型,因此把它们分成了主语子句、关系子句和状语子句。这似乎意谓着子句的指称不是真值而是和名词的或形容词的或副词的指称相类似的东西,简单地说,就是和其涵义不是命题而只是命题的一部分的语句成分的指称相类似的东西。只有彻底的研究才可能弄清楚这个问题。这里我们不准备严格按照语法的线索,而要把逻辑上可以互相比较的类型聚集在一起来进行研究。让我们首先找出这样的例子,在那里,正如我们刚才所猜测的,子句的涵义不是一个自足的命题(self-sufficient proposition)。

以"that"开头的一般子句中,也存在这样的间接引语,我们已经知道其语词具有间接指称,而这种间接指称正好是通常情况下这些语词的涵义。在这种场合下,子句以命题而不是以真值作为它的指称;它的涵义不是命题,而是"……的命题"("the propsition that...")这个词组的涵义,这种涵义不过是那个对应于整个语句结构的命题的一部分。这种情况发生在和"说道"(to say),"听到"(to hear),"认为"(to opine),"认识到"(to be convinced),"推测"(to infer)以及其他类似语词相关的场合。① 在涉及到"得知"(to recognize),"知道"(to know),"相信"(to believe)这样一些语词的时候,情况就不同了,而且要复杂得多,我们在后面再来考虑这个问题。

可以看到,在这些情形中子句是指称确实在于命题,因为命题为真为假对于整个句子的为真是无关紧要的。例如,比较下面两个句子"哥白尼相信行星轨道是圆形的。"和"哥白尼相信太阳运动现象是由地球的真实运动产生的"。在这里,一个子句可以被另一子句所替换而不影响语句的真假。主句和子句合在一起的涵义是一个单独命题;并且整个语句的真假并不意谓着子句为真,也不意谓着子句为假。在这种情形下,不能允许将子句中的一个表达式用另一个具有相同指称的表达式来替换。只有具有相同的间接指称即相同的通常涵义的表达式才能用来作替换。如果有人推断说,语句的指称不是它的真值("因为如果那样,语句就总能为另一个具有相同真值的语句所替换了"),那么他就要证明太多的东西;一个人也可以主张语词"晨星"的指称不是金星,因为他并不总能用"晨星"来替换"金星"。唯一正确的结论是,语句的指称并不总是它的真值,"晨星"并不总是指示"金星";当语词被用于它的间接指称时,情况确实就会这样。这一类的例外事例,在我们处理其指称为命题的子句时已见到了。

---

① 在"A 扯谎说,他见到了 B"这个句子中,子句指示一个被说及的命题,首先,A 断言这个命题是真的,其次,A 认识到它的虚假。

当我们说"这似乎是……"（it seems that…）那么我们的意思是说："对于我这似乎是……"（it seems to me that…）或者"我认为……"（I opine that…）。这仍是同样的情形。下面这类表达式也与此类似："感到高兴"（to be glad），"感到遗憾"（to regret），"赞成"（to approve），"不赞成"（to disapprove），"希望"（to hope），"害怕"（to fear）。当威灵顿在艾南斯高地（La Belle-Alliance）之战快要结束的时候十分高兴普鲁士军队来了，他的喜悦的根据是一种确信。假若实际上他是受骗了，只要他的信念不变，他会同样高兴。即使事实上普鲁士军队已经来了，但在他确信他们的到来之前，他是不会对此感到高兴的。

由于一种确信或信念可以成为一种观点的根据，它也能成为另外一种确信的根据，比如在推理过程中就是这样的。"哥伦布从地球是圆的这一点推断出他向西航行可以到达印度。"在这个句子中，它的构成部分的指称是两个命题：地球是圆的和哥伦布向西航行可以到达印度。这里的问题仅仅是，哥伦布既确信这个命题又确信另一个命题，而一种确信提供了另一种确信的根据。地球是否真是圆的，哥伦布是否真能按他设想的方式到达印度，这些都与我们句子的真假无关。但是，是否用"一颗伴随有直径略大于其直径的四分之一的卫星的行星"来替换"地球"，对于有关句子的真假却是有关的。这里，我们所处理的是语词的间接指称了。

带有"为了"（so that）的目的状语子句同样属于这里的情况；显然，目的是一种命题；所以，以虚拟语气形式表示的语词具有间接指称。

由跟在"命令"（to command），"要求"（to request），"禁止"（to forbid）之后的"that"引出的子句，可能以祈使句形式在间接谈话中出现。祈使句没有指称；它们只有涵义。确实，命令或要求不是命题，但它们与命题同属一种类型。所以跟在命令、要求等等后面的子句具有间接指称。这类语句的指称因而不是真值，而是命令，要求，以及类似的东西。

在由"怀疑是否……"（to donbt if），"不知道什么……"（not to know what）之类引出的独立问句中，我们遇到的是类似情况。容易看出，这里的语词也必须根据它们的间接指称来解释。包含"谁"（who）"什么"（what），"何处"（where），"何时"（when）"怎样"（how），"靠什么"（where by）等副词的疑问子句似乎常常明显地近似于状语子句，在这类状语子句中，语词具有它们的通常指称。这些不同的情况通过动词的语气而在语言学的意义上区分开来。在虚拟语气中我们有一个独立问题和语词的间接指称，因此一个专名一般不能被同一个对象的另一个专名所替代。

在到现在为止考察过的例子中，子句中的语词具有间接指称；这使得下面这一点很容易理解：子句自身的指称是间接的，即子句的指称不是真值，而是命题、命令、要求、问题。这样的子句可以看作名词；甚至可以说，把子句看作命题、命令等等的专名，它在语句结构的语境中发挥专名的作用。

……

（节选自《语言哲学名著选辑》，三联书店，1988）

## 【推荐阅读】

王希杰.论潜词和潜义[J].河南大学学报（哲学社会科学版），1990（2）：96-100.

袁毓林.动词内隐性否定的语义层次和溢出条件[J].中国语文，2012（2）：99-113，191.

# 第四章　语　法

　　语言中的词,是最容易感知到的可分离的语言单位之间进行选择搭配并表达特定意思的方式和规则。这一章我们学习作为语言组织和实用规则的语法。

## 第一节　语法和语法单位

　　"法"就是"法则、规则"。任何事物都有一定之法。语言作为人类最重要的传递信息和交流感情的工具,必须遵循一定的规则。根据语法规则,我们可以说出从未说过的话,理解从未听过的话。平时讲话,我们感觉不到自己在遵循一定的语法规则。但是所有说汉语的人都能判断下面的话是不是可以说。例如:

　　(1)太阳午饭开车门口爬上大树。

　　(2)就好人他从坏路。

　　像例(1)(2)这样只是词语的随意堆砌,我们无从理解其中的意思。外国学生常说些我们可以理解,但总感觉别扭的句子,如:

　　(3)我买了一个大的如意的西瓜。

　　(4)昨天他骂我笨,我不是。

　　(5)这个事情我也以为不是好的。

（6）麻烦我你不要。

所有这些感觉都是汉语的语法在起作用。同样，英语有的句子意思是对的，也可以理解，但说英语的人总感觉别扭。She like me 不对，应该说 She likes me 或 She liked me。用词造句的规则潜藏在每个人的头脑当中，只要一开口，我们就可以判断他说的话是否合适。一般母语者这种关于语言组织规则的语感就是朴素意义上的语法。

语言研究中的语法，是语言学家对某种语言表达规则的归纳、整理，并带有特定的理论色彩。任何语言中的规则，都不是整齐划一的体系，语法学家为了建立自己的语言解释系统，会采取一定的抽象概括层次，去除不规则部分或者对不规则现象进行一定的技术处理。这样做有利于提高语法体系的简洁性，方便语言学习特别是外语学习者掌握，有利于语言的技术处理，如计算机语言理解、机器翻译等。

语法（grammar）也是许多世纪以来学校语言教学的传统内容。直到今天，很多介绍外国语言的基础读本，仍然被称为"语法"，如英语语法、法语语法、德语语法等。这些语法实际上是对一种语言的语音、语义、词汇、句子等各方面的概略介绍，不是语言学意义上的语法。当然，语言体系内的各种规则统称为"语法"也是有道理的。语音有语音组织成词之法、词语也有构造之法，句子语法更是人人皆知。有的语言研究体系直接冠名为"语法"，如乔姆斯基的"转换生成语法"、菲尔默的"格语法"等。他们的研究试图将语言的整个运作机制用统一的解释工具进行说明，范围涉及语言从语音形式的产生、语义分配到句法结构的组织过程。

简而言之，我们头脑中的语言规则是最真实的语法。语言研究中的语法是对真实语法的某种层次的抽象概括。语言研究中的语法很系统，并力图做到完整展现语言规则的真实面貌。传统教学语法和某些语言研究体系语法针对的范围更广，即语言的整个体系都是语法。

表达中的语言是线性存在于时间当中的，语法分析需要把语言切分成一个一个可以识别的片段。我们把这些切分出来的语言片段称为语法单位。有了语法单位，就能够对某种语言的语法关系进行描述和解释，各种语言的语法就能够相互比较。语言研究通过构件和关系两个层次交互作用来说明语言的组织和使用规则。

## 一、语法是语言的组织规则

语法是语言单位之间的关系体系。它涉及语言的语音、词汇、语义等各个方面。所不同的是，语法从关系角度看待语言的形式和意义。也就是说，语法研究考虑由什么样的语音形式、词语构造或者词汇组合，表达什么样的语法意义。cups 是一个英语词，从语音角度看它是/kʌps/，遵循语音组合规则；从词汇角度看，它有其语音形式代表"杯子"这一概念在人们头脑中的反映;从语法角度来看,它是由 cup 和-s 两个语素构成,属于名词类,名词类别决定了它在句子中的使用限制,比如作主语或者宾语。法语 avons 在句子中使用,带有数、人称、时的特点,从词汇角度看它表达"有"的意义,语法则使它只能够搭配第一人称、复数的主语对象,表达现在时时间关系。

语法单位之间的关系,分组合关系和聚合关系两种。聚合关系是语言片段根据共有特征形成某种类别的关系。我们通过聚合关系来确定语法单位。处于可替换位置的语言片段,通常属于同一聚合。词类是最容易理解的语言片段聚合。典型的名词是表示事物名称的词,它们通常出现在主语或者宾语位置。典型的动词表示动作或行为,带有支配对象等。请看下面的例子。

(1) 他　　　昨天　在　商场　里　　买　了　两　件　特别　漂亮　的　衣服。
　　 我　　　上周　跟　店　　里头　卖　过　十　个　特　　有特色的　工艺品。
　　 我们　　下午　从　朋友　处　　拿　来　一　套　格外　好看　的　画儿。
　　 她们　　上次　往　地摊　上　　扔　下　三　张　很　　脏　的　人民币。
　　 ……

同一列的词语大都能构成一类。这样的替换要经过很多组,才能对词类有完整的认识。通过聚合类别,我们还可以区分出语素和句子类型。如:

(2) liked　　　　likes　　　　houses
　　 hated　　　　hates　　　　horses
　　 behaved　　　behaves　　　flowers
　　 rented　　　 rents　　　　pigs
　　 ……

(3) man　　→　　men
　　 woman　→　　women

(4) 我做红烧肉。
　　 他洗碗。
　　 孩子们都想吃饱吃好。
　　 ……

-ed 表示过去时,-s 出现在第三人称单数作主语的句子里表示现在时,-s 附着在名词后面表示复数。通过 a→e 的变化,men、women 都可以表示复数,说明特定语音变化也是复数表达的一种语素。例(4)的三个句子具体意思不同,但都采用"人+干+什么"的模式,语法上可概括为"主谓宾"结构;三个句子都是给出一个信息而非要求别人给予信息,属陈述句句类。

组合关系是指语法单位排列在一起共同出现的相互作用关系。它涉及语法单位的共现类别、共现位置关系等,体现词语之间的制约关系。我们熟悉的汉语、英语特别注重词语配列的顺序。如"我吃饭"这三个词,可以有六种理论上的排列方式。其中"我吃饭"是最常见的方式,另外,"饭我吃""我饭吃"似乎也可以说,不过不那么常用。剩下的"吃我饭""吃饭我""饭吃我"就比较不好接受了。这涉及汉语的词序规则。世界上有的语言采用"我饭吃"①作为最常用的格式,如日语、韩语。还有的语言并不特别看重词语的组合顺序,如拉丁语、《圣经》中用的希伯来语。类似"吃饭我"的排列方式,在世界绝大部分语言中都是不被允许的。其中的奥秘是世界各语言共同遵循的语法普遍规则。

组合关系不仅仅是词类的配列关系,还包括词语配合使用时的表现形式。拉丁语系有很多语言都特别依赖于词的不同形式表达不同的语法关系意义。比如拉丁语、阿拉伯语。

(5)/pater fi:lium amat/ /patrem fi:lius amat/ /pater fi:lio:s amat/
　　　父亲　儿子　爱　　　父亲　儿子　爱　　　父亲　儿子　爱
　　单数主格　单数宾格　　单数宾格　单数主格　　单数主格　复数宾格

(6)/k-t-b/"写"动词不定式

　　/yiktib/ 他写。

　　/tiktib/ 她写。

　　/katab/ 他写。（过去时）

　　/katabit/ 她写。（过去时）

例(5)中三句话分别是"父亲爱儿子""儿子爱父亲""父亲爱儿子们"。词的不同形式能够直接体现句法关系。

## 二、语法单位

为了便于语法描述和解释,我们把语言中的线性成分划分为不同的语法单位。语法单位是语法描写和解释的操作性工具,具有各语言间的可比性。语法单位分语素、词、短语、句子各级。我们集中介绍词、语素、句子这三级语法单位。

(一)传统单位:词

词是传统语法研究中最先注意到的最显著的语法单位。普通人即使没有受过语法训练,也常说自己的语言中"这个词是什么意思""那个词是什么意思"。词出现在词典当中,在话语中具有自然的语音停顿,写出来有相对稳定的形体。特别是在印欧语中,写

---

① 这几种表达形式的常用与否,都是相对表达"我吃饭"这个意义而言的。

出来的词和词之间有空格。词作为语法单位似乎是自然而然、容易区分的。

如果我们考虑世界上所有的语言,包括有文字的和没有文字的、我们熟悉的和不熟悉的,就会发现词是一个需要通过语法分析加以定义的语法单位。比如,汉语书面语没有词与词之间的间隔区分,在计算机处理连续话语时,就有一个分词的必要步骤。"加入班集体"在计算机语义处理时,需要知道是"加入+班集体"还是"加+入班+集体"。

词是语言中能够独立运用的最小的语言单位,它通过移动、替换方法加以确定。"独立运用"是指词具有一定的形式稳定性,可以出现在句中不同的相对位置上,能与其他语言片段分开。我们可以说"the dog bites the cat",也可以说"the cat bites the dog",还可以说"the dog bites a lot""the dog that I bought yesterday bites the cat"。可见"the""dog""cat""bites"可以出现在不同的句法位置,可以被其他成分分开,它们是独立运用的语法单位。"最小"的意思是,词不能被内部拆分且不改变其独立的使用功能。比如"good-hearted"中"good""heart"都可以分开,独立运用,但是"-ed"不能独立使用,且"good"和"heart"的意义组合不等于"good-hearted",所以 good-hearted 是一个词。

研究者曾经提出过界定"词"的多种标准,如在语义上词表示单纯的意义或单一概念。目前主要采取布隆菲尔德提出的"最小自由形式"的形式标准界定词。标准一,词是各种语言单位中最稳定的单位;词的内部构造重新配列的可能性是有限的,而词在句子或者其他语法单位中则具有相对自由度。理论上,一个词可以和其他语言单位构成无限的句子。我们不可能罗列出典型的名词如"太阳""自行车"能够出现的所有句子。标准二,词的相对不可分割性,即词通常不能在中间插入新的成分,如停顿等。一般情况下,我们都说"好"/xɑu/,而不说/xɑ——u/或者/ xɔɑu /。

词的区分对大多数词语是比较容易的,而边缘性的情况并不是没有。通常,词具有特定的语音形式,词和词之间分隔停顿。匈牙利语中大多数语法词的重音都在第一个音节上,日语词末尾不能出现除鼻辅音以外的其他任何辅音。但在法语中,如果句中的词以辅音结尾,其后又跟着一个元音开头的词,那么两词连读。如 mes amis /mɛzami/,il est/ilɛ/,bon air/bɔnɛr/。英语中冠词 the、a 是独立的,但可以弱读依附于名词。在罗马尼亚和斯堪的纳维亚语中,类似的冠词与它修饰的对象组成一个词,如 Norwegian 语 hus/hu:s/ house,huset/hu:sə/ the house;当带有形容词修饰语时,冠词独立出来,如 det store hus/də storə hu:s/。这个类似于英语 the 的成分算不算一个词呢?英语、法语中某些词的弱读形式,如英语 I'll 中的 ll,法语中 je、tu 都不单独出现,它们是不是一个词呢?还有某些机构名称、影剧名称,如"叶问(电影名)""中央直属机关",它们算一个词还是几个词呢?英语中类似的"The Titanic""Anne of Green Gables"用作电影名都是单数,说明它们在语法上看作一个词。

词可以从很多角度进行分类,如区分实词和虚词、语法词和词汇词、封闭类词和非封闭类词等等。

有的语法学家为了把语法单位的"词"与语音学、正字法等的"词"区分开来,提出词位(lexeme)这一概念。词位是从一个词各种形式中抽象出来的单位,它相当于一切语法变化的基底形式,如 make、makes、making、made、maken 中的基本形式 mak/d-与"做"意义结合的抽象单位。我们词典中的词条通常是这样的抽象单位。

(二)分析单位:语素

语素(morphemes)是语法分析的最小单位,是最小的语音语义结合体。词虽然是最基础的语法单位,却不是最小的。我们看到的英语中诸如 loves、goes、sells、hopes 等词,与 love、go、sell、hope 比较之后,能够得到两类语法成分,love-、go-、sell-、hope-和-s、-es。前者表示某种动作,后者表示动作由第三人称单数主语实施。这类成分就是语素。作为词,我们不好区分 loves、goes、sells、hopes 与 love、go、sell、hope 在独立运用上的差别。引入语素概念之后,词的不同形式、词的内部结构等都能够得到更好的说明。

"最小"的意思是,语素是一个语音形式与一个语义结合的最小单位。语素不能够再拆分为更小的可以表达确定意思的语言单位。"玛瑙"是一个语素,分开来的"玛"和"瑙"是两个字代表两个音节,但每个字没有意义。"自由"是一个语素,"自"和"由"有自己的意义,表示"从(借此)",但它们独立开来的意义与"自由"没有任何关联。"heart"不能再分而保持原有的意义联系。分成"he"和"art"虽然分别可以成词,但两者与"heart"没有意义相关性。Element、good、phonology 等可以从语音上分成元音和辅音,但这元音和辅音只是语音单位;没有可以结合的意义,它们就不是语法单位。

语素的确定是通过语言中词的形式比较和分析进行的。例如:

(1) friend-ly　　organiz-ation　　watch-ed　　re-forest

　　man-ly　　classific-ation　　help-ed　　re-flex

　　leisure-ly　　deriv-ation　　consider-ed　　re-generate

　　kind-ly　　form-ation　　fear-ed　　re-gain

　　……

(2) buy　　bought　　bought

　　think　　thought　　thought

　　go　　went　　went

　　sell　　sold　　sold

　　……

语素在话语中出现,会采用不同的形式。我们把同一个语素的不同形式称为语素变体(allomorphs)。受出现环境限制的语素变体,叫环境变体。可以自由出现在各类语境中的变体,叫自由变体。世界多数语言中的多数语素变体都是环境变体,自由变体相对较少。比如英语的名词复数语素-s,跟在不同的名词后面会根据名词末尾音节的发音特征采用不同的语音形式,如 horse-s/-z/、apples/-z/、boxes/-iz/、fox/-iz/、fans/-s/、ships/-s/。一般是元音或浊辅音结尾的名词复数语素采用-z 形式,而清辅音结尾的名词复数采用-s 形式,以-s 结尾的名词为发音方便采用-iz 形式。另外,还有些特殊的复数形式,如 child-children、ox-oxen、foot-feet、sheep-sheep、cattle-cattle 等。英语词内否定语素形式最常见的是 in-,但也根据环境不同有所变化,如 valid-invalid、variable-invariable、reducible-irreducible、regular-irregular、comfortable-uncomfortable、abashed-unabashed、modest-immodest、patient-impatient 等。

语素可以从功能角度进行多种分类。根据语素的构词功能和在句中自由使用的情况,分为自由语素(free)和黏着语素(bound)。自由语素可以独立成词,独立用于组词成句。黏着语素必须和其他或自由或黏着的语素共同作为一个单位出现。如英语 going、doing、making 中 go、do、mak-(make 的语素变体)是自由语素,-ing 是黏着语素。

语素还可以根据其在词中的作用,分为词根语素(roots)和附缀(affixes)。词根语素是词去掉所有附缀后剩下的成分。词根语素表达词汇意义,附缀语素表达类意义。词根语素可能是自由的,也可能是黏着的,根据语言的不同而不同。一种语言的词根语素在数量上是可以变化的,通过吸收外来语、创建新词语而增加,或者由于时代变化而不再使用某些特定时期的语素。附缀都是黏着语素,它们数量有限,可以列举。英语 goodness、reaction、tried、helpful 中 good-、react-、tri-、help-是词根语素,-ness、-tion、-ed、-ful 是附缀语素。同一个词根语素可以带不同的附缀,如 walk、walks、walking、walked。词根语素在附带不同附缀时,其形式可能发生变化,如法语 aller/al-/+/-e/表示 to go,irai/i-/+/-r-/+/-e/表示(I) will go,vont/v-/+/-o/表示(they)go。

自由与黏着,词根语素与附缀的区分采用的是不同的角度,两者没有完全的对应关系。汉语、英语等语言,通常词根语素都是自由的,这并不是说世界所有语言的词根语素都是自由语素。有的语言的词根语素通常是黏着的,拉丁语中/amo:/I love 的动词词根语素是/am-/,/rego:/I rule 中/reg-/等都不能独自构成一个词使用。日语中的动词词根语素必须带着各种附缀出现,不能自由使用,如/kas-/to lend 必须说成/kasu/lend 或者/kasi/lending 或者/kase/lend 等形式。

(三)使用单位:句子

句子是语言中最基本的交际使用单位,是表达思想传递信息的基本形式。句子的主要特点是句子表达的意思是相对完整的。它具有完整的语法结构、特定的语调。句子的语法结构完整,所以无论多长或者多短,只要表达完整意思带有特定语调的语言片段都是句子。最短的句子"Who?""Me.""What?""Looking for Tom."都表达完整的意思,起交际作用。

语感上,句子像词一样是容易判断的语法单位。句子后面跟着一个较长的甚至永久的停顿。句子具有统一的语调模式。在书面语上,句子用句尾的句号、问号、感叹号等标记。不过,这些直觉都很难用确定的形式定义来表述。从语音特征上,句子可以定义为带有完整语调,由停顿结尾的语言片段。但在日常对话中,话语连续性很高,句子本身在结构上省略,句间停顿微弱,我们的句子界限就会变得模糊。也有语法学家从哲学命题的角度看待句子,认为句子表达一个完整的陈述、疑问或者命令。哲学与语言研究有很深的渊源,但哲学命题并不完全等同于陈述句,命题结构也不能够完整地定义句子的范围。语言中有很多命题结构不完整的句子,如省略句。传统的语法研究认为,句子是最大的语法结构单位。它自身具有完整的结构,能够反映语言结构的整体面貌。这样的看法越来越受到语言事实的挑战。我们说的话,做的文章,是一个一个句子简单放置在一起构成的吗?显然不是。外国学生写汉语作文,常有这样的情况。如:

(3)小王星期天起床。小王出门去买菜。小王来了菜市场。菜市场的菜很多。菜都很便宜。他买了两斤肉。这些肉很新鲜。肉二十八块一斤。……

说汉语的人一看这样的作文,就会很头疼。他的句子没问题,意思也连贯,就是觉得不对劲。句子和句子之间应该有照应,有连续。在语法上,我们可以通过省略、回指等方式体现句子的相互关系。像代词"他""我""它"等常需要从其他相关的句子中获得现实解释。句子之上显然还有更大的结构单位。句子是基础性结构模式,可以被反复运用,有机组合,构成更大的语法结构。

句子从功能上可分陈述句、疑问句、感叹句和祈使句等类型。从结构上可分简单句和复合句等。我们熟悉的"主语+谓语"结构就是简单句。但对此结构,研究框架不同,称呼也不一样,如有的称"小句",有的称"子句"。句子在各种语言中的常见表现形式是有差别的。汉语、英语是"名词+动词(短语)"形式的句子最常见。在意大利语、西班牙语中,有时句子形式是一个单独的动词形式。还有的语言中"名词+名词""名词+形容词"的句子形式很常见,如巽他语、马来语、于洛克语。

(4)/manehna prad urit/ he is a soilder

　　/buroŋ itu sakit/ that bird is sick

　　/wok nelet/ this is my sister

再如俄语现在时判断句的例子,如:

(5)Ivan vrač

John doctor-NOM(主格)

John is a doctor.

Мария ребёнок

Mary child-NOM(主格)

Mary is a child.

有意思的是,俄语其他时态①类似的句子需要添加动词。汉语里的形容词判断句也采用"名词+形容词"形式,但对形容词有一定的语法限制。

# 第二节　语法和形态学

语法关系有两类表现手段,一是组词成句的方法,叫句法;一是词的各种语法形式,叫形态。形态学研究词的各种变化形式和词的内部结构。语素是形态学研究最关心的部分。形态学通过词的不同形式来配合和体现不同的语法组合关系。一个词的所有形式构成一个聚合,即词的形态变化。

在不同语言之间,语法单位并不完全对等,中间有各种各样的差异。一种语言中的词,到另一种语言中要用词组或者句子来表达,如爱斯基摩人的语言中对雪区分得很仔细,"细小如沙粒的雪"和"鹅毛大雪"是不同的词,同样的意思,到汉语、英语、德语里要用短语来表达。反过来,"他买鸡蛋"这个句子,在某些语言里,需要词的不同形式参与句法组合,"鸡蛋"需要在词形上标明是单数还是复数,大多数印欧语都是如此;法语、德语中"买"还需要根据第三人称单数主语"他"采用不同的形式。此外,更复杂的情况是某些语言还需要通过动词的不同形式标明是现在、将来、过去或者进行、完成、未完成等情况。有的美洲土著语言中,动词的形式还能体现出句子反映的情况是听说的还是看到的,是第一次转述还是第二次转述。如中部波莫语(北加州印第安人的部落语言):

(1)čʰéemul-ya

rain.fell-VIS

It rained(I saw it). [我看到]下雨了。

(2)čʰéemul-nme

rain.fell-AUD

---

① 其他时态是指非一般现在时,如一般过去时、过去完成时等。

It rained(I heard it).[我听到]下雨了。

也就是说,我们熟悉的组词成句表达意思的方法,在很多语言中是要求词形变化的,词的不同形式和结构是重要的语法关系表达方式。有的语言,语法关系的表达不通过词与词的组合,而相当于直接采用词的不同形式来表达。因此,从世界语言的角度着眼,形态学具有重要的语法研究价值。

## 一、形态与句法

形态与句法在表现语法关系中的作用因语言不同而不同。根据对形态的依赖程度,洪堡特把世界上的语言分为四种基本类型:孤立语(isolating language)、黏着语(agglutinative language)、屈折语(inflected language)、多式综合语(incorporating language)。孤立语是像汉语这样的语言。它们几乎没有什么形态,每个词就只有一个形式,主要通过词序和虚词体现语法关系。苗语、彝语、壮语、缅甸语、越南语等都属于这种情况。所以"他打我"和"我打他"意思完全不同,处于动词前的是施事,动词后的是受事。"我在家看电视"中"家"是地点,汉语用"在"表示。也就是说,孤立语是以句法为主要语法手段的语言。

黏着语将具有一定语法意义的附加成分接合在词根或词干上构成形态变化,然后词与词再进行一定的句法组合。黏着语词的形态变化特点在于由不同的附加成分表达不同的语法意义,各种语法意义的附加成分可以累加,而不是通过词的整体形态变化来表达多种复合的语法意义。芬兰语、斯瓦希里语、土耳其语、匈牙利语、维吾尔语、日语、朝鲜语等都属于这种情况。如斯瓦希里语 watasipokuja "假如他们不来"中 wa-表示第三人称单数,-ta-表示将来时,-si-表示否定,-po-表示假定,-ku-表示动词词性,-ja 是词根"来"。土耳其语 odalarimdan "从我的房间里",oda-房间,-lar-复数,-im-第一人称,-dan 离格。

屈折语采用词的屈折变化形式表达一种或者多种语法意义。印欧语系的法语、拉丁语、俄语、德语等都属于这种情况。如俄语 книга(书)中-a,семья(家庭)中-я 同时代表阴性、单数、主格。拉丁语 incumbat 形式表示"apply+反身+第三人称单数+现在时+虚拟式"的意思。

多式综合语的主要特点是动词上插入各种语法关系成分,构成一个动词就是一个句子的局面。如契努克语 iniǎludam 意为"我来把这个交给她",-d-是词根"给",i-表示过去时,-n-是第一人称单数,-i-相当于代词宾语"这个",-ǎ-相当于"她",-l-表示 ǎ 是间接宾语,-u-表示动作时离开说话的人,-am 表示动作是有明确目的的。美诺米尼语 akuapiinam,意思是"他从水里拿出来",其中 akua-是词根"挪开",-epii-表示"液体",-en-表示"用手",-am 为第三人称施事。Yup'ik Eskimo 是爱斯基摩语的一种,

tuntussuqatarniksaitengqiggtuq 表示"He had not yet said again that he was going to hunt reindeer"。tuntu-表示"驯鹿",-ssur-表示"打猎",-qatar-表示"将来时",-ni-表示"说",-ksaite-表示否定,-ngqiggte-表示再次,-uq 表示第三人称主格未完成时。美洲印第安语和古亚细亚语中有很多这类语言。

需要说明的是,没有任何一种语言单纯属于上述某种形态类别,语言的语法手段总是结合了句法与形态的。并且任何一种语法表现模式都能够达到本社会内部交际的目的,满足社会内部各种交际需要。

在印欧语言研究当中,形态学曾经是语法研究最重要的部分。因为印欧语言的词大部分都具有不同的词形变化,这是词进入句子所必需的。现代英语词的形态不算复杂,与古英语相比更趋向于用句法表现语法关系。英语动词通常有五个不同词形,如 see、sees、saw、seen、seeing;代词最多四个形式,如 I、me、my、mine;名词有单复数和所有格共四个形式,如 desk、desks、desk's、desks';形容词的级有三个形式,如 good、better、best。俄语的形态变化比较复杂,普通名词有单复数区分,单复数又各有六个格,名词又有三种性(阴性、阳性、中性)的变化。形容词有性、数、格,以及长、短尾区分,加起来四十多种形式。理论上,动词各种形式变化加起来,多达一百种。

形态与句法的关系,大致有两种情况。首先,形态与句法存在互补关系。形态变化少的语言,句法规则就比较丰富。所以汉语没有形态变化,汉语的句法规则就不是简单的主谓宾,有很多复杂的句法结构现在还处于研究当中,如把字句、被字句、补语结构的结构限制。形态丰富的语言,如德语、希腊语、拉丁语等,对句法的依赖相对较少,句子有不同语境下的优势语序但总体比较自由,词的形式中包含了丰富的语法信息,语法形式与语法意义的对应关系比较严格。

形态与句法还有相互限制、相互依存同现的关系。词进入句法关系,总要采用一定的形式。人们组词造句的时候,通常是形态和句法的规则都要照顾到。我们学法语知道 être 表示"是",但 je suis、tu es、il est、elle est、nous sommes、vous êtes、ils sont、elles sont 这些组合中,être 的形式都是固定的,改说 je être、tu être、il être 等就不对。俄语中名词、动词、形容词也必须根据它们在句法中的作用采用不同的词形。在上面这些情况中,词形是形态语法所要求的,但不一定是意义上必需的。有时候词的形态变化是意义上必需的,这样我们才能判断词的句法关系,如英语所有格,mothers love 与 mother's love 通过词形区别两个名词的句法关系是主谓还是修饰。

## 二、形态作为语法的表现手段

传统形态学有两个研究领域，一是对词的屈折形式的研究，称为屈折形态学；一是对构词的研究，称为派生形态学。作为语法表现手段的形态，主要有两方面的作用，构形和构词。构形研究着重于词在进入句法组合过程中的词形变化。这种变化不改变词的意义，也不改变词的词性；它的作用是表示词与句子中其他词语的关系，如名词是主动者还是被动者，单数还是复数，动作是刚发生的还是过去的等等。构词研究着重于考察词的内部组成结构，如名词变化为动词，肯定意义变化为否定意义；构词形态会改变词的意义，也可以改变词性。

### （一）构形形态

构形形态是表达词的语法关系而不改变词的意义的形态聚合。构形形态限制和决定着词在句子中的语法功能。构形形态都是屈折形式的。屈折形态的构形形态比构词形态与语法的联系更为密切。法语动词的各种变形变位、冠的数、形容词的性、数，英语名词的数、代词的格、动词第三人称单数形式等等都是构形形态。构形形态的重要特点是每种形态出现的句法关系是固定的，同一个词的不同形态之间是不能换位的。英语说 I work，I am working，I worked。其中 work、working、worked 位置不能替换。法语名词根据阴性或者阳性搭配相应的形容词形态，如 beau cadeau "好礼物"，belle robe"好衣服"。

构形形态在一种语言中的类别数量有限，规律性强。多数名词在英语中都具有复数形式，动词在与第三人称单数搭配时都采用 V-s 类一致形式。由于构形形态的稳定性和句法限定作用，西方语法界常用构形形态作为区别词类的重要根据。

### （二）构词形态

构词形态添加到词根语素上，引起词义或者词性的相关改变，却不能体现词与词的句法关系。也就是说，构词形态只作用于词本身，不直接体现词在组词成句中的作用。当然，改变词性的构词形态会因词性改变造成词的句法作用变化，但这是由句法词类系统决定的，而非构词形态本身决定的。不改变词性的构形形态如英语中-hood 添加到名词 man、nation、boy 等之后，还是构成名词，只是在意义的抽象程度上有差别。英语-ly 添加到某些副词如 quick、hard 等之后，同样构成副词。否定形态如 ir、in、im、un 等也不改变形容词词性。改变词性的构词形态，如 modernize、goodness、imprison、sleepy、renew 当中的-ize、-ness、im-、-y、re-等。

构词形态种类繁多，表现多样。比如同样是名词化的构词形态，有 V-ment、V/Aness、V-ation、V-er、V-ing、A-ty 等形态，根据其中的动词不同而不同，如 government、classification、definition、runner、famer、cooking、beauty 等。动词化的构词形态如 N/A-ify、N/A-ize、notice-notify、organ-organize、domestic-domesticize、pure-purify 等。副词化的形态如 V-y、N-ly、friendly、windy、sunny 等。什么样的词如何构成某种构词形态，有时在同一种语言中还有说话人选择上的差异，比如说英语的人可能会在 comicality 与 comicalness 之间犹豫不决。

构词形态与构形形态也不是完全分离的，某些形态可能处于两者之间。比如英语、拉丁语形容词的比较级、最高级形式。有时候 good、better、best 有句法限定作用。它们在作定语时可以相互替换，如 good condition、better condition、best condition，但在比较句中又带有明显的句法位置限制，如 this is the best condition of all、the condition is better than before。

### (三) 语法范畴

范畴是人头脑中对世界的分类概括。语法范畴指语法关系的各种类聚，如主语、宾语、谓语，名词、动词、形容词等。这里，语法范畴特指词的不同形式体现出来的概括性的语法意义的类。语法研究的注意力常常集中在句子内部不同词类和以此为基础的句子结构上，结构关系构成了语法的核心。实际上，世界上大多数语言在不同程度上都会用特殊的语素形式伴随表达词语之间的句法关系。根据句法关系对词的形态的不同要求，不同的词分成各种不同的词类。

形态方式是语法范畴的主要体现形式，有时形态方式也结合分析性方式使用。如英语现在完成时 have checked 由 have +V-ed（动词形态）构成。分析性方法是指用添加词语的方式表达语法范畴。如汉语"做完"的"完"与表示"进行"的"在看电视"的"在"都不属于形态语法范畴。常见的语法范畴有数、性、格、时、体、态、人称、式等。

**数**，是名词、代词、动词、形容词等表现数量特征的形态范畴。英语名词分单数和复数，复数为有标记-s 类的形式，动词只有第三人称代词单数有 V-s 形式，系词 be 有单复数的屈折形式 is、are。法语的数范畴同样应用于名词和动词，法语冠词 le、les 根据名词单复数选择，形容词也会随着其修饰的名词的数而发生词形变化。如 le cheval royal 和 les chevaux royaux 分别是 the royal horse 的单复数形式。单数和复数区分是数范畴的常见类别，也有的语言在形式上区分单数、双数和复数，古希腊语、梵语、古斯拉夫语，我国的景颇语、佤语都有三类数的形式区别。还有一些语言区分四类数范畴：单数、双数、三数、复数。斐济语的代词就有四种数形式。汉语里没有系统的复数形态。我们用表示数概念的词语标明名词的数，如"一个人""两条黄瓜""三个臭皮匠""很多公园"。有人说"们"是复数形式，其实"们"只能用在很少的表人名词或代词后面，不能算是可以普遍应用于某一词类的数范畴。

数范畴跟日常生活中理解的数量有概念上的联系,表示单一事物的通常标记为单数,多个事物标记为复数。正因为数范畴与数量概念的联系,在一些语言之间,类似的数概念可以相互匹配。如英语的复数在 Norwegian 中表示为/-ər/,在匈牙利语里为/-ok/、/-ek/等,在土耳其语里是/-lar/、/-ler/。但数范畴毕竟是一个语法概念,词语语义与它的关系有很清晰明确的,也有不那么合理的。比如英语中概念类似的 wheat、barley、corn 是单数类,而 oats 却是复数。

**性**,是表现名词、形容词等的性别特征的形态范畴。性在各个语言中的表现各不相同。法语的名词都分阴性和阳性,德语、古希腊语、俄语的名词、形容词区分阴性、中性和阳性。法语名词的性,是语法中规定好的,并由与名词搭配的冠词、形容词变格等体现出来。如阴性冠词 la、une 用于阴性名词之前,la langue(语言)、une langue、la photo(照片)、une photo;阳性冠词 le、un 用于阳性名词之前,le livre(书)、un livre、le frère(兄弟)、un frère。形容词的性与名词的性保持一致,如俄语 красивый дом(美丽的房子,阳性)、красивая комната(美丽的房间,阴性)、красивое окно(美丽的窗子,中性)。

性范畴的语法特征与自然性别有关,但不如数与数量的关系那么密切。语法中只有阴性和阳性,表示人和动物的名词的性一般按自然性别决定,表示事物的名词的性则是纯粹由语法来决定。如在法语中“语言”是阴性的 la langua,而具体的语言如“法语”“英语”“意大利语”都是阳性的 le français、le anglais、le italien。德语中 Mädchen(girl)、Fraülein(young lady)都是中性的,并没有依据自然性别。古希腊语中/téknon/“孩子”,是中性的,无论具体是男还是女。俄语 дом(房子)属阳性,комната(房间)属阴性,окно(窗户)属中性。可见,性与性别是不同领域的不同范畴,这样,不同语言之间的性较难对应。以“太阳”为例,说汉语的人觉得它该是阳性的,其实“太阳”在俄语中是中性的,在德语中是阴性的,在法语中才是阳性的。

**格**,是体现名词、代词等与句法结构中其他词(特别是动词)关系的形态范畴。每种语言对格的表现和分类都不同。俄语名词分主格、属格、与格、宾格、工具格、前置格,也就是说俄语名词单复数分别对应六种形式。如 лётчик(飞行员):

(1) | | 单数 | 复数 |
|---|---|---|
| 主格 | лётчик | лётчики |
| 属格 | лётчика | лётчиков |
| 与格 | лётчику | лётчикам |
| 宾格 | лётчика | лётчиков |
| 工具格 | лётчиком | лётчиками |
| 前置格 | о лётчике | о лётчиках |

土耳其语的六个格,如:

(2)基础格　　　saz　　　　　芦苇(作主语)

　　属格　　　　sazin　　　　芦苇(的)

　　与格　　　　saza　　　　 (给)芦苇

　　宾格　　　　sazi　　　　 芦苇(作宾语)

　　位格　　　　sazda　　　　芦苇(表时间或空间,相当于"在芦苇中")

　　离格　　　　sazdan　　　 芦苇(表示离开,相当于"从芦苇中")

拉丁语也是六个格,古希腊语有五个格,梵语共八个格,芬兰语名词有十五个格,格鲁吉亚语有二十三个格,匈牙利语有二十五个格。拉丁语"女孩,单数"的主格/呼格、受格、属格/与格、夺格分别是 puella、puellam、puellae、puella。英语、法语只有人称代词有主格和宾格的区分,如 I love him/her(我爱他/她),He/She loves me(他/她爱我),je le déteste(我恨他),il me déteste(他恨我)。各种语言名称类似的格的语法意义也不完全相同。

格表示名词、代词与句中其他成分的关系,每个格的具体语法意义不同。一般来说,区分主格和宾格的语言中,主格名词是句中及物动词所表示的动作的实施者,宾格是动作的受影响者,不及物动词通常带主格名词作主语。有的语言表示动作的关涉对象不用宾格,而用与格。如亚瓜语(古巴及委内瑞拉的印第安部落语言)。

(3)sa-díîy nurutí-íva

　　3sg-see alligator-DAT.

与格用于双及物结构,类似于"give the book to the boss"中的"book"采用与格,如冰岛语。西班牙语中,"我喜欢"中的"我"采用与间接宾语一样的与格形式。

(4)Ég　　　　skila-ð-I　　　henni　　　penning-un-um.(冰岛语)

　　1sgNOM returen-PAST-1sg 3FsgDAT money-DEF-DAT①.

　　I returned her the money.

　　me　　　　gusta　　　la　　　yuca(西班牙语)

　　1sg:DAT　　like:3sg ART　manioc

　　I like manioc.

有的语言与格表示领属关系,如澳洲土著语言 Mparntwe Arrernte 的一种特殊的亲属所有格。

---

① NOM,主格。PAST,过去时。1sg,第一人称单数。3Fsg,第三人称阴性单数。DAT,与格。DEF,限定。ART,冠词。

（5）（i）atyenge akngeye

　　1sgDAT father "my father"

　　（ii）Toby-ke alere

　　　　Toby-DAT child "Toby's child"

工具格一般引入行为工具，类似于汉语里说"用锤子"中的"锤子"直接采用工具格表示类似的意思。离格表示动作离开的对象。属格表示领属关系。总之，各个语言中格的数量、名称、表现各不相同。

格范畴与语言外的概念世界关系不如数、性直接。格的语法关系特性非常明显，有了名词、代词不同的格，句中词语的配列就相对自由，词与词的关系非常清晰。

**时**，是动词体现的语法范畴，它常与体、语气结合在一起，指用动词所表示的动作行为发生的时间特征。往往以说话时间为基准，把时分为过去、现在和将来。说话时间以前的情况用过去时，说话当时的情况用现在时，说话时刻以后发生的情况，用将来时。时与时间有一定的关系，但很难简单地说清楚。英语过去时通常表示动作发生在说话时间以前，即过去，如 I hated him，表示我过去恨他（现在可能不恨了），I will buy a new car 是说将来要买车，但还没有买。英语过去时也用在虚拟情态中，如 I wish I knew，希望的是"现在知道"，但也用过去时。英语现在时也可以用于过去，如情景再现性的表述 last night I am running in a park。再如英语将来时有好几种形式，will、to be、be going to、shall等，每一种除表示将来时外，还带有不同的情态意义，to be 有"计划"的意思，shall 有"应当"的含义。汉语中有时间概念，但从动词的形式不能系统地体现这一概念。有研究者把"过"看作汉语过去时标记，这种观点可以探讨。如果只有过去时，没有将来时和现在时，汉语算不算有时范畴呢？

**体**，也是动词体现的语法范畴，它表示由动词代表的活动的时间长短或类型。也就是说，动作有一个从开始到结束的完整过程，动词的体表示动作正处于这个过程的何种阶段。不同语言的体表现形态不同。英语动词分普通体、进行体、完成体。普通体不指明完成或进行，进行体表示动作持续，完成体表示动作已结束持续。如 I sing 为普通体，I am singing 为进行体，I have sung 为完成体。但是英语的体并非完全的形态类别，中间还带有分析形式。英语中像 used to 有人分析为惯常体，即表示"过去常常"。斯拉夫语言分完成体和未完成体，前者表示动作的完成，后者表示动作持续，不指明是否完成。如 on pročital（他读完了），完成体，on čital（他过去常读/当时正在读）。还有些语言分反复体和重复体、起始体或开始体等其他多种体类别。有人把汉语动词重叠看作反复体，把"V-起来"分析为起始体，这些都是值得研究的问题。

**态**，也是动词体现的语法范畴之一，它是动词改变主语和宾语关系，但不改变句子动词与名词的语义关系的方式。"态"主要分主动态和被动态。主动态表示动作是由施动者主动发出的,被动态表示动作是受动者所承受的。这是对同一件事情的不同观察角度。这种不同的角度集中体现为动词的形式变化。如俄语动词 люσлю(爱,主动态)与 люσлюся(爱,被动态)的差别。英语主动态用动词原形 V,被动态用 be V-ed 形式,如 I broke the cup 与 The cup was broken(by me)。汉语里没有态范畴,类似的意思通过词序和介词结构表达,最常见的就是被字句。

动词的时体态范畴结合在一起构成动词的不同类别,如英语的现在完成时、过去进行时、一般现在时、将来完成时等等,这些类别又分主动态和被动态两类。

**式**,又称语态,通过动词的词形变化表示一组对立的句子和对立的语义,如直陈语态、虚拟语态、祈使语态等。在语义上,语态涉及的意义多种多样,但主要是表明说话人对动作行为相关事实内容的态度,如肯定、猜测、推定、含糊等。句法上,不同语言表达范畴"式"的方式不同。英语常用助动词表示,如 may、must、should 等,已经不是纯粹的动词形态的"式"了。例如:

(6) You may go.

You must go.

You should go.

在虚拟式中,英语的动词采用过去时。如 I wish I were you,即事情是不真实的。西班牙语区分相信真实(indicative)的和怀疑(subjunctive)的,比较

(7) Creo que aprende

I believe that learn+3sg+PRES+IND[①]

I believe that he is learning.

Dudo que aprenda

I doubt that learn+3sg+PRES+SUBJ

I doubt that he's learning.

巴布亚语中的 Amele 用过去时和将来时区分"真实"和"非真实",如

(8) ho bu-busal-en                                    age qo-in

pig SIM-run out-3sg+DS+REAL[②]          3pl hit-3pl+REM.PAST

They killed the pig as it ran out.

ho bu-busal-eb                                    age qo-qag-an

pig SIM-run out-3sg+DS+IRR                 3pl hit-3pl-FUT

They will kill the pig as it runs out.

---

① 3sg,第三人称单数。PRES,现在时。IND,真实。SUBJ,怀疑。

② 3pl,第三人称复数。REAL,真实。IRR,非真实。

汉语没有式范畴,通常用副词表示"虚拟""猜测""推定""应当""必须"等意义。

　　**人称**,是动词的语法范畴,表示参与情景的对象的性质和数目。人称主要通过代词和动词形态来体现。一般分三个人称:第一人称,说话者指称自己或包含自己的一群人;第二人称,说话者用来指话语的接收者,即对话的对象;第三人称,说话者指称自己以及受话人以外的其他人或事物。英语代词有三个人称的单复数,通过不同的词表示,只有动词的第三人称单数现在时用 V-s 形态方式表示,动词 be 有少数变位形式 am、are、is。拉丁语、俄语的动词人称变化形态丰富,常与数结合变化,如俄语动词"读"читать 有читаю(第一人称单数)、читатаем(第一人称复数)、читаешь(第二人称单数)、читаете(第二人称复数)、читает(第三人称单数)、читают(第三人称复数)。汉语动词没有人称范畴。

　　语法范畴的数量和类别还有很多,其表现和在各个语言中的作用也不尽相同。但语法范畴用词形来表现,所以我们将它们放到形态一节。一般来说,性、数、格是名词的语法范畴,在有些语言中形容词随名词变化而变化。时、体、态、人称是动词具有的语法范畴。每一种语法范畴都表达共同的意义领域,范畴内部的成员之间是对立互补的关系,范畴中成员所表示的意义取决于它与范畴内其他成员的关系。

# 第三节　词　法

　　词这一级语法单位体现的语法规则,称为词法。词法研究词的构成和变化,主要分三部分:构词法——研究词的内部结构;构形法——研究词在更大的结构当中发挥语法作用所需要的形态变化;词类——研究词的语法类别及其句法作用。

## 一、词根与词缀

　　为了方便对词的内部结构和语法变化形式的分析,我们按照词内成分对词的意义的影响作用,区分词根和词缀。词根(root),是词的基础部分,词的意义主要体现在词根上。词根不能做进一步的分析,不然就会影响到意义的完整性。词缀(affix)是只能黏附在词根上构成新词的成分,它本身不能成词。也就是说,词根是去掉词内所有词缀后剩下的部分。比如,meaninglessness"没有意义(名词)",可以切分成的意义单位有 mean、-ing、-less、-ness。每个单位在这个词中的作用不同。mean"意指、意味,动词",-ing 名词缀,使动词名词化,-less 形容词缀,使名词形容词化并表示相反的意思,-ness 名词缀,使形容词名词化。所以 mean 是词根,其他的都是词缀。词缀又根据它们在词中的添加位置,分前缀、后缀和中缀。前缀就是加在词根前面的词缀,如英语中否定前缀-in、-un、-im;汉语中表排行的"老大""老二"中的"老-",类似英语否定前缀的"非","非主流""非线性""非自愿"等。英语中后缀的例子很多,如表"V 的人"的-er,如 singer、seller、buyer、reader、leader;表"可能性"的-a(i)ble,possible、enable、eatable、workable 等;汉语中外来的后缀"-化",如"现代化""工业化""特殊化""自动化""绿化"等。前缀和后缀在很多语言中都比较常见,而中缀是较为特殊的类别,比较少见。在东南亚语、美洲印第安语、非洲某些语言中,中缀很常见。如前面提到过的阿拉伯语,其常用结构式"CVCVCV",其中辅音 C-C-C 构成词根,不同元音 V 插入词中,表示相关的附加意义。马来语中缀如 patuk(啄)-pelatuk(啄木鸟),-el-就是一个表示动作实施者的中缀。菲律宾语 kayn(堆,未完成体),kinayn(堆,完成体),-in-为中缀。塔加禄语/sulat/(写作,动词),/ sumulat /(作者,名词),/ sinulat /(作品,名词)。

有的研究者区分词缀和词尾,即表达词汇意义的附缀,称为词缀;而表达语法关系意义的附缀,称为词尾。按照这样的区分,英语名词缀-ness、-ation、-ing,动词缀-ify、-ize 等属词缀,而复数-s、-es,第三人称单数-s,动词进行时-ing,动词过去时-ed 等都属于词尾。考虑到每种语言中词的地位和作用不同,影响到附缀的功能多样,我们还是把词法研究中所有附缀统称为词缀。

## 二、构词法

构词法,是最小的语法单位语素构造成词的方法。它由一定的构造成分发挥特定的作用,采用特定的结构,组合成丰富多样的词。根据词中词根与词缀的结构关系,构词法分复合构词法和派生构词法。

(一)复合构词

复合构词,是指词由词根和词根按照一定的组合规则构成。复合法构成的词称为复合词。一般形态较少的语言,采用复合法构词的比较多。如汉语主要采用复合法构词,复合词的组合关系多样。如:

| | | | |
|---|---|---|---|
| 修饰关系 | 雪白 | 黑板 | 大学 |
| 并列关系 | 明亮 | 阐述 | 材料 |

| 补充关系 | 证明 | 说明 | 构成 |
|---|---|---|---|
| 主谓关系 | 司机 | 冬至 | 地震 |
| 支配关系 | 革命 | 告密 | 卖国 |

英语的复合词也比较多,结构关系跟汉语比较接近,如 blackboard、snowwhite、earthquake、superman、honeymoon、horsepower、doorman、classmate、freshman 等等。英语的复合构词非常能产。有时候复合词中词根与词根的关系不是那么明显和直接,我们只能从复合词词根的意义中猜测整词的意思,如 horseman"马+人","骑手";hotfoot,"热+脚","匆忙的、着急的"。

(二)派生构词

派生构词,就是用词根加上词缀的方法构成新的词。派生构词法构成的是派生词。前面已经讲过,派生构词分添加前缀、后缀和中缀的方式。派生构词可以改变原来词根的词性,也可以不改变原来的词性。改变词根词性的词缀,如英语中与名词结合构成形容词和副词的-wise,如 like-wise、clock-wise、length-wise、profit-wise、prestige-wise;类似的还有-ful、-ish,如 wish-ful、wonder-ful、wolf-ish、fool-ish 等。不改变词根词性的词缀如英语 re-、-hood、-ship 等可构成 reprint、resell、resit、childhood、manhood、scholarship 等派生词。

通常,一个派生词缀代表一种意义,但有时同一个派生词缀形式可以表达多种意思。如英语中-ly 有三类派生。第一种是 adj.+ly=adv.,如 main-ly、quick-ly、happi-ly、stupid-ly;第二种是 noun + ly = adj.,如 man-ly、friend-ly、lord-ly、scholar-ly、hour-ly;第三种是 adj.+ly=adj.,如 good-ly、kind-ly 等。

同一个词根可以接受多种派生词缀,构成不同的派生词。如英语 man,可以派生出 manly、mannish、manful、mankind、manless 等;friends 可派生出 friendship、friendly、friendless、friendliness 等;fright 可派生出 frighten、frightening、frightful、frightened 等。多种派生可以叠加到同一个词根上,每一种语言中理论上可以容忍的派生词是没有预定长度的。如 moderization、modern-iz(动词化)、-ation(名词化),再如 frighteningliness 和 redehumidification,前者分析为 fright-en(使动)、-ing(形容词化)、-li(副词化)、-ness(名词化),即"令人害怕的"的名词形式;后者分析为 re(重新做)、-de(去除)、-humid(词根)、-if(动词化)、-cation(名词化),即"再次去除湿气"的名词形式。这两个词的意思通常需要用短语来表达。虽然像 frighteningliness 和 redehumidification 这样的词非常不常见,但我们还是可以根据派生构词规则把它看作一个词并理解它的意思。当然,受到人的记忆和理解方式的限制,词的派生是有实际界限的,这是我们判断 redehumidification 不常见的语感依据。派生构词有时和复合构词在同一个词中运用,如英语 gentlemanfarmer、fridge-freezer 两个词,gentle-man 先复合构词,farm-er 派生构词,然后两者结合成 gentlemanfarmer;

fridge-freezer 是 fridge-freeze 先复合,然后在复合词根上加上名词派生词缀-er。在复杂的词中,需要考虑派生与复合构词的层级和顺序。

除派生构词和复合构词外,还有一些构词方法,如内部屈折、重音位置和声调等。这些方法主要用于改变词性的派生构词。如内部屈折,是指改变词根内部个别发音,以达到构词目的。如 food"食物,名词",通过/fu:d/到/fi:d/的内部屈折,变成动词 feed"喂",full"满的,形容词"变为 fill"填满,动词"。重音方式构词在英语中如重音位置移动(有时候也带有元音屈折变化)export /ˈekspɔ:t/→/ iksˈpɔrt/, convict /ˈkɔnvikt/→/kənˈvikt/。我们可以把名词重音后移看成动词化构词的重音方式,与-ify、-ize 等归为一类;也可以把动词重音前移看作名词化的重音构词方式,与-ment、-tion 等归为一类。从历史的角度来看,每个词的具体情况不同,两种方式都存在。有时候,派生构词与重音方法配合使用。如 energy/ˈenədʒi/与 energetic/enəˈdʒetik/。声调方式构词在汉语中很突出,如"买""卖"就是用声调派生造词而不改变词性,两个词都是表示"商品交易",声调的变化区别"进"和"出"。古汉语中"食"读阳平作名词,表"食物",读去声做动词,表"喂养",与英语 food 类似。

## 三、构形法

构词法构成的是新的词,构形法关注词的不同语法形式的问题。构形法构成的是同一个词位的不同语法表现形式。根据构词还是构形的差别,一个词中构词成分为词干,构形成分就是词尾。词干是词的核心部分,词尾是黏附在词干后面表达语法意义的成分。如英语 pans 中-s,be buying 中-ing,she's 中's,俄语 заводы(工厂,复数)、газеты(报纸,复数)中-ы、стола(桌子,属格)中的-а、столу(桌子、与格)中的-у 等都是词尾。词干有时候就是词根,这时词位由一个词干构成,如 rooms 中 room 既是词根,也是词干。有时候词干由两个以上的词根构成,如 playboys 中的词干 playboy 是词根 play 和 boy 构成的。

由于很多语言中的词与我们通常的概念不同,它们的语法意义也不都是采用附加成分的方法,词尾概念不能适用于所有的情况。词的构形方式很多,包括异根法、交替法、重叠法、重音法、零形式等。异根法是直接改变词根形式,用新的词根加以替代,来表达不同的语法意义。如英语 be 动词的不同人称不同时态形式 am、is、are、was、were;人称代词格的变化 I、me、she、her、he、his、we、us、you、your;比较级 bad、worse、worst 等。

交替法是部分改变词根形式以表达语法意义的方式,也称为内部屈折。如俄语 собрать(采集,完成体)——собирать(采集,未完成体),ходить(走,未完成体)——хаживать(走,完成体)。英语 man—men、woman—women、fly—flew—flown、begin—began—begun、get—got—gotten、sell—sold、leave—left 等。

重叠法是通过词根重叠表达语法意义的方法。如马来语和马来波利尼西亚语中,重叠是构成名词复数的常用形式,如/kapal/(轮船,单数)——/kapal-kapal/(轮船,复数),重叠还可以表示动词的体意义,如俄语动词重叠表"持续"говоришь-говоришь(说着)、работаешь-работаешь(工作着)。汉语中动词重叠也有研究者将其看作体意义,但具体表示"尝试体"还是"短时体"还有一定的争议,如"看看""走走""说说""等等""研究研究"等。形容词重叠可以表示程度性的语法意义,如汉语"高高""红红""大大""矮矮""漂漂亮亮"等,至于具体是否表示程度减轻,还是带有其他的情态意义,还需要进一步研究。印地语也有形容词重叠,表程度加深,如 ламбе(长)、ламбе-ламбе(很长)。

前面构词法讲过,重音移动可以通过改变词性构成新词,改变重音也可以表达一定的语法意义。重音法就是用改变词重音表达词的语法意义的方法。如俄语 ноги/noˈgi/(脚,属格,单数)——ноги/ˈnogi/(脚,主格,复数)、руки/ruˈki/(手,属格,单数)-руки/ˈruki/(手,主格,复数)。

零形式的构形法是指用同一个词形表示不同的语法意义,词根不发生变化。通常,同类词语的语法意义有一种规律性的构形方式。英语大多数名词都有规则的复数词尾-s,而某些名词的复数与单数同形,如 sheep、cattle;英语动词过去时通常采用过去时词尾-ed,而英语有的动词、助动词过去时与现在时同形,如 read、must 等。

我们熟悉的语言中,(词根+词缀)+词尾是最常见的词的结构方式,即词尾位于结构最外层,要么作前缀,要么作后缀。如英语 winn-er-s、modern-iz-ing 中表复数的-s和表进行的-ing 都处于构词词缀之后,即词的最外层。实际上,词缀、词尾与词根的位置关系也会随语言不同而有所变化。如威尔士语的复数词尾就是出现在词中间的。

(2)merch-et-os 小女孩们

　　女孩-复数-小的

　　dyn-ion-ach 弱小的男人们

　　男人-复数-小的

语言在构形上的不同,还表现在形态不丰富的语言,没有成系统的构形法。而特别依赖综合方法表达语法关系意义的语言,很难把整个语言的词的变化形式都归纳为构形法。

## 四、词 类

词类是词的语法归类,也就是按照词在组成句子过程中所起的作用给词分的类。在一种语言中,每一类词出现在特定的句法位置上,具有相似的语法特征(包括形态变化),起着类似的作用(包括组合能力等)。如汉语的名词主要出现在句子的主语、宾语位置,可以受数量短语修饰,不受"很""不"修饰,不能作谓语;汉语的动词主要出现在谓语核心位置,可以受"不""没"修饰,不受"很"修饰,可以加"了"修饰;汉语形容词受"很"修饰,能够修饰名词,能作谓语核心。换句话说,区分了词类,我们就知道每类词大概在句子中应该怎么用,能够根据基本的规则组成句子。同时,我们也能说明短语、句子等的组合规则,得出抽象的句子结构。

词类划分的方法,大致可分为三类:一是形态方法,即同一类词应当具有类似的形态变化。传统的印欧语法,就是以形态来区别词类的。词的形态标志着词的语法意义。通常,名词有性、数、格的形态变化,动词有时、体、人称等变化,形容词随名词有性、数的变化。这样,三大主要词类的界限就清楚了。如英语 cat—cats、dog—dogs、window—windows、bus—buses 与 have—had—having、finish—finished—finishing、listen—listened—listening 以及 cold—colder—coldest、good—better—best、small—smaller—smallest 之间的形态变化规律是显著的,我们很容易将 cat 等归入名词,have 等归入动词,cold 等划为形容词。形态方法对词类的划分比较一致,争议较少。但是形态标准并不能划分出所有词类。一方面,形态是针对特定词类的形式变化,即名词、动词、形容词;即使形态丰富的语言,如俄语、拉丁语,也有相当数量的词没有形态变化。如副词、连词、介词、语气词等,依靠形态标准无法划分词类。另一方面,形态只是部分语言的特征,像汉语、越南语这样缺乏形态的语言,形态方法完全用不上。

第二类方法是采用句法标准划分词类。这是比较公认的适用性更广的划分词类的方法。语言中的词,在组成句子的过程中标志其句法功能,这是词的语法特征的重要体现。反过来讲,句法标准划分的词类,也更有利于说明句子的各种句法结构。按照词的句法标准划分词类,主要考虑词的组合能力和词在句法结构中所起的作用。也就是说,某类词只能和某类词组合,组合顺序如何,组合限制是什么;某类词能够充当哪种句法成分,是作主语还是作宾语,是作定语还是作中心语,能不能被否定词直接否定等等。在英语中,作主语和宾语的通常是名词和代词;出现在表语和定语位置上的,通常是形容词,不受形容词修饰;出现在主语和宾语位置上的是代词;出现在状语位置上的是副词。汉语中,能受数量短语修饰而不受副词修饰的一般是名词,出现在数词之后名词之前的是量词,受程度副词修饰的很可能是形容词,也有可能是心理动词。英语中,常见的句法结构是 NP+VP,就连形容词也必须采用 be+adj.结构。汉语的形容词看起来可以直接构成 NP+adj.句型,这时形容词必须带程度修饰成分才能自由成句。再如英语中 at、from、with、in、on 等,都出现在名词短语之前,与名词共同出现在 often、usually、then 等词出现的位置,它们归入一类,称为介词。a、an、the 都出现在名词或名词短语之前,归入冠词类。

在形态丰富的语言中,句法标准和形态标准通常是一致的,但句法标准适用的范围更广一些。形态标准不能划分词类的情况下,采用句法标准作为补充。当句法标准与形态标准发生矛盾的时候,也通常采用句法标准。如英语动词的不规则变位形式,buy—

bought—bought、sing—sang—sung、think—thought—thought、lead—lead—lead；根据它们在句中与其他规则动词形态 V-ed 一致的位置和组合特征，buy、sing、think、read 都划入动词类；再如英语单音节形容词通常有比较级-er 和最高级-est，如 hot—hotter—hottest、tall—taller—tallest，但多音节形容词则采用添加 more（比较级）和 most（最高级）的形式构成，如more beautiful、most beautiful。根据它们都能作表语、定语的特征，如 This is a tall girl.This is a beautiful girl.The girl is tall.The girl is beautiful.它们都归入形容词类。

　　第三类方法是语义标准，即通过词的意义特征划分词类。词的句法功能和意义之间是有联系的。名词一般表示人或者事物，形容词一般表示某种状态或者性质，动词表示动作行为。这符合我们的语感直觉。但是语义标准只能作为划分词类的辅助标准。因为，语义的定义本身是模糊的、非决定性的。比如"战争""规定"这类复杂事物，可以看作一种动作行为，即动词；也可以看作一种完整的抽象事物，即名词。表现在不同的语言当中，我们所熟悉的"事物"可能是形容词，而我们所熟悉的性状，很可能是动词。如日语中形容词似乎包含类似英语的 to be 形式。

　　（1）/uma　　　wa　　　　haja-i/

　　　　　马　　　主题标记　　快-词尾

　　　　　/uma　　　wa　　　　haja-katta/

　　　　　马　　　主题标记　　快-词尾

　　一般来讲，动词和名词的划分在任何语言中都是存在的，而形容词是否存在会随语言不同而不同。美洲太平洋西部沿岸的努特卡语中所有的词都或者带名词性附缀，或者带动词性附缀，即严格区分动词和名词，没有形容词。语言的词类是根据它们在某种语言中的具体表现来确定的，不能直接套用其他语言已有的词类系统。欧洲语言学家提出的九大词类：名词、动词、代词、形容词、副词、介词、连词、冠词和叹词，是根据他们研究的语言得出来的。汉语中就没有冠词这一词类。

　　总之，我们划分词类采取形态与句法结合的标准，以句法标准为主。语义标准起一定的辅助作用。

　　无论采用何种方法，词类划分都存在一些具体的问题。像汉语的词类灵活性比较高，无法做到"出现在某一固定位置上的词都属于某一词类"，即句法标准不能完全确定词类。同时，汉语又没有形态可利用。举例来说，汉语的名词通常作主宾语，但也直接作定语，如"国家荣誉""类别意义""亲戚关系"；还有的名词可直接作谓语，如"一下子就**晚上**了""他这下**规矩**了"；有的名词直接作状语，如"我**明天**不来了""我们**星期天**加班"。汉语动词的句法功能也很丰富，可以作定语，如"退休工资""处理结果""美白效果"，可以作中心语被形容词修饰，如"详细的规定""残酷的斗争""无尽的忍耐""严肃的批评"等等。有的研究者提出"兼类"概念，处理这种问题。词的兼类，是各语言中都存在的情况。有形态的语言,兼类的词具有多种词类的形态变化,如英语的 work,既有名词复数 works 形式,也有动词过去时 worked,进行时 working 的形式;lock 有名词复数 locks 和动词 locked、locking 等形式,所以 work、lock 兼属于名词和动词。没有词形变化的词,可根据句法功能判定兼类,如英语 home,可以出现在如例(2)的各种位置当中。

(2)The nurse visits patients in their homes.

She is on her way home.

We try to play a big role in the home market.

The torpedo homed in on its target.

home 兼有名词、副词两个词类。同时名词 home 可以用作定语,出现在形容词的定语位置上,偶尔也能活用作动词。兼类的确定并不是随意的,尤其值得注意的是,兼类不能是某一词类中的大部分词;兼类的确定应该有严格的限制,不然,词类划分对句法结构的说明作用就会大受影响。

词类划分是一个层级系统。语言中普遍存在的类和表达意义时最突出的类,是最高的层级。如很多语言区分名词、动词、形容词,有的语言只区分名词和动词,形容词可能属于动词当中的小类。细致地划分层级性的词类,有利于对词的句法功能进行更细致的说明,也能够区分大的词类中典型的和非典型的次类。比如汉语动词根据能否受程度副词修饰,区分出一般动词和心理动词;动词根据能否带受事宾语,区分出及物动词和不及物动词;及物动词又根据能带宾语的数量,分为单及物动词和双及物动词;形容词根据能否受副词修饰,区分出区别词和度量形容词;名词根据能否直接作状语,分时间名词和普通名词等。语言研究的重点之一就是不断细化分类,增强语法描写和说明的精确性。

词类也可以根据性质进行分类和研究。根据词类成员的数量是否有限,词类可分为开放的类和封闭的类。通常,基础词类如名词、动词是开放的类,它们的成员在数量上是无限的,可以随着语言表达的需要而不断创造新的词语。封闭的类中,词类成员是有限的、数量较少的。在不改变特定语言语法结构的情况下,封闭类成员的数量是不变的。代词、介词、连词等一般是封闭的类。根据词类成员是否表示实在的词汇意义,词类还可分为实词和虚词。汉语中名词、动词、形容词等是实词,介词、连词、叹词等是虚词。

# 第四节 句 法

句法,即词以上的语法单位层面的语法,简单地讲,也就是组词成句的规则系统。句法研究一种语言中句内词与词之间的相互关系模式,以及系统地分析和描写这些模式的方法。词与词之间的相互关系,称为句法关系。不同词类的词之间的位置关系,哪些词类必须或者可以一起出现,词以及词组成的结构之间的替换关系等等,都是句法最为关注的内容。

乔姆斯基的转换生成语法就是以句法(syntax)为中心的。他力图用结构替换转写来建构语言生成系统。他的研究是努力对语法规则形式化进行最深入的探索。不过,语言的复杂性,使乔姆斯基对自己的研究体系不断进行修改。传统的结构主义的句法研究主要考虑句法结构、句法关系、句法分析方法和句法结构之间的相互关系等。

## 一、句法关系与句法表现形式

句中词与词(短语)按照一定的模式组合成句法结构。组合之后,结构表达的意义与所有的单个词语相加的意义不同。"好天气"与"好""天气"两个词的词汇意义总和不同,增加了"好"与"天气"的关系意义,"好"修饰"天气"状况。这样,"好天气"与"天气好"的意思就完全不同了。"书买了"和"买书了",所用的词完全一样,只有句法结构不同。两句话看起来意思差不多,仔细分析我们会发现,"书买了"的"书"是限定性的,相当于英语中的 the book,而"买书了"的"书"是非限定的,相当于 a book 或 books。英语 gold 是"黄金、黄金的"的意思,但在 She has a gold heart 中,gold 表示"善良的、美好的",这种意义是由 gold 与 heart 之间的组合关系带来的。I don't think he is right,表面上看,是"我不认为他对",但这句话实际上是"我认为他不对"的一种委婉表达。可见,理解了句法结构的意义,我们才能正确地理解句子意义。我们把这种由句法结构赋予的结构中所有词的意义以外的意义,称为**句法关系意义**。句法关系意义的语言表现形式就是句法形式。

句法关系意义大致表现为五种基本类型:陈述关系、修饰关系、支配关系、补充关系、并列关系。**陈述关系**,指句法结构成分(词及词以上单位)之间相互构成陈述对象与陈述内容的关系。相当于通常所说的"什么+怎么样"的关系。汉语用主谓结构表达陈述关系。也有研究者认为汉语是"话题+说明"的陈述关系,即说话人先提出一个谈论的对象,然后对这一对象的情况进行说明。如:

(1)晚饭/吃馒头。

下午/休息。

桌子/擦了。

星期天/天气好。

苹果/真好吃。

根据信息传递从已知到未知的表达和理解习惯,陈述关系基本采用"陈述对象+陈述内容"的顺序,英语也是如此,包括主谓结构和系表结构。如:

(2)I/ win.

He /liked ice cream.

Today /is Sunday.

The soup /is dilicious.

**修饰关系**,是指结构成分之间构成修饰与被修饰的关系,即一个结构成分限定说明另一个结构成分的性状、范围等特征。修饰关系反映在偏正结构中,如汉语的定中结构和状中结构。

(3)爸爸的/外套

漂亮的/鞋子

立刻/出发

格外/认真

修饰关系两个结构成分的顺序根据语言类型有所不同。通常,(S)OV语言采用"修饰成分+被修饰成分"结构,而(S)VO语言采用"被修饰成分+修饰成分"结构。如日语是SOV语言,其从属句放在被修饰成分之前,私は男を見た"我看见的男人",字面意思为"(那个)我-男人-看见"。汉语的情况比较特殊,它既是(S)VO为主的语言,也采用"修饰成分+被修饰成分"的修饰结构,这样就会出现与此有关的歧义结构。如:

(4)昨天买的/鸡

昨天/买的鸡

同样的意思在英语中就不会有歧义,the chicken we bought yesterday 和 we bought the chicken yesterday 是完全不同的。当然,形态一节中我们讲过,有的语言用名词的格表示修饰关系,如俄语、拉丁语等。这样,修饰项与被修饰项的顺序就显得不是那么绝对。

**支配关系**,是动作行为与动作行为影响制约的对象之间的关系。英语的述宾结构就是典型的支配关系。例如：

(5) take ／a bus

　　break ／a cup

　　run into ／an old friend

　　catch up with／ him

支配关系有 VO 和 OV 两种典型的结构顺序。日语、韩语等是 OV 型。英语、汉语等是 VO 型。支配关系还表现为一些特殊的结构，如汉语的把字句和被字句中，"把"的宾语与动词之间是支配关系，"被"字句的主语与动词之间是支配关系。有一种中动结构，可以从陈述关系和支配关系两个角度来分析。如：

(6) The shoes sells well.

　　鞋子卖得很好。／鞋子很好卖。

"鞋子"当然不能自己卖自己，是人在卖，所以 sell 和 shoe 是一种支配关系。另一方面，"卖得很好"是一种状态，是对鞋子情况的说明，那么 shoe 与 sell(well) 是一种陈述关系。

**补充关系**，是指一个结构成分对另一个结构成分的程度、结果、趋向等进行进一步说明的关系。汉语的述补结构是典型的补充关系。如：

(7) 买／得多

　　拿／出去

　　站／不稳

　　笑／死

英语的补充关系，有时体现在动词短语中，有时是对整个句子的补充。如：

(8) run ／out of the room

　　go ／quickly

　　He hardly catch the bus.

out of the room 补充说明 run 的趋向，quickly 补充说明 go 的状态，hardly 补充说明的是 he catch the bus 这件事。

**并列关系**，是指各个结构成分的作用相当，在语法作用上是平等的。在具有并列关系的句法结构中，结构成分之间的顺序理论上是自由的。如汉语并列结构"苹果、梨和香蕉""上午、下午、晚上"，也可以说成"梨、香蕉和苹果""梨、苹果和香蕉""晚上、下午、上午"。英语中 mothers and fathers、Wednesday and Saturday，也可以说成 fathers and mothers、Saturday and Wednesday。有时候并列成分之间的顺序受到语义、风格、连接成分等的影响，并不是完全自由的，比如"昨天、今天和明天"很少说成"明天、昨天和今天"，"春夏秋冬"可以说"春秋冬夏"，却很少说"春冬夏秋""秋春夏冬"。并列结构的内部关系和排列顺序有专门的研究可参考。

各种基本的句法关系所表达的语法意义复杂多样。我们需要在分清基本结构关系的基础上进一步分析。比如汉语的修饰关系中,定中结构的修饰成分和被修饰成分的关系就很复杂,可以表示领属、范围、性状、来源等等。在具体的语言运用中,五种基本的句法关系会相互配合,形成层级性的丰富的句法结构模式。比如修饰关系构成的结构可以作为并列关系、支配关系或者陈述关系中的一个结构项。像英语 The boy(I met)is your brother 中 I met 与 the boy 是修饰关系,the boy I met 与 is your brother 是陈述关系,而 your 与 brother 是修饰关系,I 与 met 也是陈述关系。

世界上不同的语言,采用不同的方式表达句法关系意义。其中最主要的方法,包括词序、虚词、形态、语调等。**词序**,即词与词组合的线性排列顺序。汉语是非常依赖词序手段的语言。世界上很多语言,都采用以动词为中心,依靠动词支配成分的先后位置区分动作实施者和动作支配对象的手段。比如英语 I love John 和 John love me 不同。日语"田中さんはスタッフガ"(田中先生是公司职员)与"スタッフはは田中氏"(公司职员是田中先生)不同。形态丰富的语言中,有不太依赖词序的语言,如我们前面举过例子的拉丁语。还有一些语言,形态很丰富,同时词序也是固定的。这样的语言能够从形式上细致地表达出不同句法语用的差别。

**虚词**,是表达语法关系意义而不体现现实世界相关概念的词。虚词也是句法关系表达的重要手段。英语中 the、a 区别限定与非限定的语法差别;of、for、since、from、on 等体现句法结构成分间主从、位置等相互关系。虚词一般不充当句子成分,在句法结构中起连接和组织的作用。各种语言对虚词这种句法手段的利用不同,其虚词的种类和数量也不太一样。汉语有连词、助词、语气词等虚词,英语中有冠词、连词、介词等等。每种语言中,名称相近的虚词的句法功能也有差别。

**形态**,也就是用词的不同词形变化,表达不同的句法关系。比如俄语名词的格是一类重要的形态。从俄语名词是主格还是宾格,就知道它和句中动词是陈述关系还是支配关系。如果是属格,就表示名词与相关其他名词具有修饰关系。如果是离格,那么名词相对于动作或者这个句子来说是补充关系。英语虽然形态不丰富,但形态变化也能表达一些句法关系。比如 Please tell him I like her 中,人称的不同能够区分 tell 的支配对象与 like 的支配对象是不同的人。如果是 Please tell him I like him,两个 him 可能是同一个人,也可能不是。汉语类似的句子"告诉他她喜欢他"说出来有歧义,原因就在于这句话用同样的形式表达了不同的结构关系。

**语调**,也是句法关系表达的重要手段,它用说话时语音的规律变化,包括高低、升降、轻重、长短、快慢等表达不同的句法关系。句法关系体现在韵律模式上的例子,如汉语修饰关系的定中结构常与支配关系的动宾结构采用相同的线性序列,但实际说话时两种结构的韵律结构不同。"改进技术"在动宾结构中一般为"轻重"模式,在定中结构中一般为"中轻"模式。英语也有类似方法区分不同的句法关系。语调的句法作用研究日益引起研究者的重视,相关成果日渐丰富。

语言综合运用各种句法手段表达句法关系。没有一种语言是单纯运用某种特定的手段表达句法关系意义的。

词与词组合的句法结构,可根据结构项与整个结构的关系,分为两类:离心结构(exocentric)和向心结构(endocentric)。离心结构中,没有任何一个结构项能够代表整个结构的句法功能。向心结构中,至少有一个结构项与整个结构的句法功能相当。汉语中"美丽的春天""周日的休假""可能回来""基本完成"是向心结构。"春天""休假""回来""完成"作为被修饰成分,就可以表示整个结构的功能。也就是说,将它们放在更大的句法环境中,整个结构关系不变。如:

(9)美丽的春天就要来了。→春天就要来了。

我盼着周日的休假呢。→我盼着休假呢。

妈妈明天可能回来。　→妈妈明天回来。

任务基本完成。　　　→任务完成。

即使去掉修饰成分,例(9)的各个句子还是基本的陈述关系。我们在句法分析中,可以用向心结构的结构中心替代整个结构以达到简化句法结构的目的。反过来,把简单的句法结构扩展为复杂的句法结构,也可以通过单一成分向向心结构扩展的方式来达成。例如:

(10)树绿了。

树都绿了。

山上的树都绿了。

对面山上的树都绿了。

我家对面山上的树都绿了。

我家对面山上的去年种的树都绿了。

我家对面山上的去年种的树都绿了一大半了。

汉语中典型的离心结构是主谓结构,如"我/爱中国"和"他/来了"中"我、他、爱中国、来了"都不能单独代表全句的句法结构。英语中主谓结构、介宾结构、连词小句结构等都是离心结构。如 to me、from England、at the gate、under a tree 中介词 to、from、at、under 不能代表整个结构的功能,因为介词必须和名词、代词配合使用,像 give it to、he come from、she stood at/under 这样的结构是不允许的;名词 England、gate、tree,代词 me 也不能代表整个结构的功能,因为名词代词主要是作主语宾语,或者作定语,不是作状语、补语的,而介词结构的功能主要是状语、补语。英语连词小句结构如 because I know、if you told me 等,是从属于它们所修饰的主句的,单独的连词 because、if 自然不能起到整个结构的句法作用,而 I know、you told me 如果离开了从属连词,原有结构的从属性质就会消失。离心结构在各种语言中都要相对少于向心结构。最基本的句法结构通常是离心结构。如汉语、英语的主谓结构是最常用的句法结构,它们都是离心结构。不过,主谓结构不一定都是离心结构。像意大利语、德语中,动词的变形变位可以包含主语的功能,可以说意大利语等的主谓结构是不太典型的向心结构。

向心结构还可以进一步分为主从结构和并列结构。主从结构的功能相当于结构中一个结构项的功能,而并列结构中任何一个结构项的功能都与整个结构的功能相当。比如英语 good choice、almost win 等结构的功能相当于 choice、win 的功能,它们是主从结构。而英语中 boys and girls;he and me;pen、pencil and ink,tea、cola or water 都是并列结构,结构中除连接成分 and、or 以外的任何一个结构项的功能都与整个结构的整体功能相当。并列结构也是句法扩展的重要方式,如:

(11)I got up.

I got up and dressed myself.

I got up,dressed myself and went to work.

## 二、句法分析方法

**句法分析**,是指采用一定的分析手段对句法结构进行剖析,目的是说明句子的结构类型和成分间的结构关系,以便于理解句义,比较句法结构间的相同点与不同点,总结句法结构规律等。常见的句法分析方法有两种:句子成分分析法和直接成分分析法。

**句子成分分析法**,是以词为中心,分析各个词在句子中的功能的分析方法,又称中心词分析法。根据句子中具有哪些功能性成分,可以确定句子的句型。这是传统的句法分析方法。句子成分分析法区分主语、谓语、宾语、定语、状语、补语六大成分。其中主语、谓语、宾语是基本成分,定语、状语、补语是附加成分。主语通常被定义为"动作的发出者",宾语为"动作的接受者"等等。早期句子成分分析法,用不同的符号表示不同句法成分。主语＿＿,谓语＿＿,宾语〜〜,定语( ),状语〔 〕,补语〈 〉。例如:

(1)我〔在商场〕买了(两斤新鲜的)荔枝。

〔目前〕,(国际金融)危机〔正在〕变得〈越来越严重〉。

这种分析,是线性的多分的方法,会遇到一些难以解决的问题。比如"越来越严重"是"变得"的补语,但"越来越"与"严重"的状中关系就不好标示了。类似的层级性从属结构,都会遇到这样的问题,比如"我知道他来找我"标为"我知道他来找我"第一层结构清楚,但"他来找我"的内部结构就不清楚了。后来,句子成分分析法也引入了直接成分

分析法的层次概念,把主谓作为第一层,动宾作为第二层,偏正作为第三层。复杂的句子再分出更多的次级层次。如:

（2）He opened the red door and went into the room which belongs to his sister.

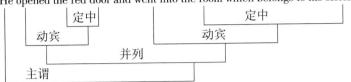

不难看出,例（2）分析的层次还不完全,且"并列"层次不是句子成分分析法本身的结构类型。句子成分分析法,由于主要考虑句中各个词的主次,对于句子层级结构的揭示还是不充分,对于句法关系比较难采用各个层级一致的描述方式。另外,句子成分的认定并不都像典型的主谓宾句那么容易。比如"主语"在各个语言中的地位不同,有形态的语言如拉丁语、俄语等用主格表示主语,没有什么问题。汉语这样的语言,主语是一个有争议的概念,它并不一定是动作的发出者,如"天气很好""钥匙丢了",其中"好"不是"动作","钥匙"不是"丢"的动作发出者,它们是不是主语呢? 如果把动词或者形容词中心语前面的成分看作主语,这也是有问题的。"当天他就把钱给我了"中"当天"不是主语,"他"是主语。"他脾气不好"中"他"和"脾气"哪一个是主语呢? 成分分析法以词为出发点,寻找结构的中心,也会遇到一些问题。比如英语"What he told you is right?"中 what 从句做主语,我们不好分析哪个词是 what he told you 的结构中心。

**直接成分分析法**,是着眼于句法结构层次的二分式的分析方法,又称 IC 分析法（immediate constituent analysis）或层次分析法。直接成分是处于同一层级上的两个[1]直接组合成更高一级句法结构的构成成分。直接成分分析法是由上往下逐级二分,逐层找出该层的直接组成成分的方法。直接成分分析法使句子的结构层次和每个层次上结构项的相互关系清晰明了。例如:

（3）Tom came across his old friend on the way to his office.

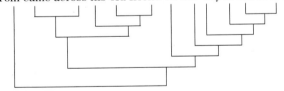

（4）He had been sent outside by his mother.

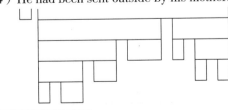

---

[1]　通常为两个,并列结构可以有两个以上直接成分。

例(3)(4)分别是"由小到大"和"由大到小"的结构层次分析。在 Tom came across his old friend on the way to his office 中 Tom 和 came across his old friend on the way to his office 是两个直接成分;came across his old friend on the way to his office 中 came across his old friend 和 on the way to his office 是直接成分,逐级类推,一直分析到词这一级语法单位。直接成分分析法清楚地标明了短语、句子的结构层次,便于对句子进行更深入的理解。某些具有歧义的言语片段,可以通过直接成分分析法区分歧义。如"咬死了主人的狗",有两种层次关系:支配关系"咬死了/主人的狗"和修饰关系"咬死了主人的/狗"。类似的还有英语的 old man and woman,两种层次关系为:old man /and woman 和 old /man and woman,即形容词 old 单独修饰 man 和形容词 old 分别修饰 man 和 woman 两种结构关系。因此,从句法结构上说,这类言语片段不是真正的歧义结构。

直接成分分析法有很多的优势。它能够将层次观念一以贯之地运用到整个句法结构的分析当中,各级语法单位之间的关系清晰明确。但是直接成分分析法也有自身的局限性。首先,直接成分的二分,不能完全离开句子成分的功能。He had been sent outside by his mother 第一层分为 he 和 had been sent outside by his mother 考虑的也是简单成分对复杂成分的替换作用,had been sent outside by his mother 相当于动词 sent。也就是说,这一直接成分中,其他词语都是围绕动词中心的。我们仍然需要根据词在句子中的功能,帮助切分直接成分。后期的直接成分分析法,也引入了主语、谓语、宾语等句子成分概念。其次,直接成分分析法主要是从形式方面出发的,对于隐性的句法关系,缺乏分析能力。比如,英语主动态与被动态表达的两个名词与一个动词的基本句法关系相同,句法结构形式却不同。直接成分分析法无法说明两者之间的相互关系。最后,直接成分分析法在处理一些直接成分并不连续的语言句法分析时,也会遇到一定的问题。如拉丁语中维吉尔的一句诗:

(5)/ultima    cumæi    ve:nit    iam    carminis    aetas/
　　final   of-the-Cumaean   has-come   now   of-the-song   age

英语的意思是 The final age of the Cumaean's song has now come。不过,世界上的语言总是围绕一定的核心组织起来的,与核心直接相关的成分会分布在核心的两边,与核心组成轨层结构。

句子成分分析法和直接成分分析法各有长短,在具体的句法分析中,可以根据实际情况结合使用。

## 第五节 超句法

研究界逐步认识到,把语法研究局限于句子层面以下,并不能揽括语言使用所必需的所有规则。当前,越来越多的研究者把眼光投向比句子更大的语言结构,研究它们的语法规则。我们把比句子大的结构的语法规则,称为超句法。超句法研究的范围很广,且不像句法、词法那样有传统的比较一致的研究范围。超句法涉及句群、篇章、话语等语言片段,在话语分析、篇章语言学、修辞学、文章风格学等研究领域中受到关注。

句群是由两个以上的句子构成的具有一定内在关系的语言片段。句群不是句子的简单堆砌,也不是靠着意义之间的自然关联就能构成的。我们说"他这段英语表达不连贯",意思就是他掌握了英语基本的句法规则,但对如何把句子连成一个语义表达片段的规则还不熟悉;他还没有掌握句群的组织规则。句群的组织规则,包括省略、重复、回指等衔接手段、句群中句与句的连贯规则、句群的组织结构等方面。当前的研究,只对特定的衔接手段,如回指等的某些规则有所了解。比如,代词回指有一定的距离限制,中间能够间隔的同类对象不能太多,回指项与被回指项的出现有一定的顺序等。

*I'm trying to get to sleep but he's at it again, my neighbour, playing the guitar. He actually owns two guitars, a simple acoustic one and an expensive electric one. But he seems to prefer to play the electric one late at night when I'm trying to get to sleep and have to get up at the crack of dawn for work the next day. I don't know what his other neighbour thinks about it, or his wife for that matter. They must be more tolerant than me. The problem is, not only does he play the guitar very loudly, but he also plays it quite badly. I really wish he would take up another hobby altogether, or at least find a quieter musical instrument to play*[①].

代词 he 出现在其具体指称对象 my neighbour 之前,但两者不能隔得太远;代词前指的情况很少,通常是回指。后面几个 he 都是回指 my neighbour,中间没有其他可以指称

---

① 林语堂英语学习网站衔接例文。

的人会影响 he 的回指理解。代词 they 回指 his other neighbours and his wife,因为 they 前面只有这个可用复数第三人称来指称的成分。

实际语用中,句群与复句有时难于区分。复句通常是句法研究的范围。复句由两个以上的基本句法形式组成,具有统一的语调。但在实际话语表述中,完整统一的复句语调难作形式区分,句群与复句的界限就显得不那么分明。我们很难看出"我生病了没去上班单位不会扣我工资"是不同句子组成的句群,还是一个复句。即使使用连词,情况也是一样的,如"他是死脑筋但是人还不错",可以是复句,也可以是转折关系的句群。因此,句群的结构逻辑关系,可借鉴复句的研究成果。

超句规则的研究还很不完善。简单地说,还没有一种语言的句群规则能够保证学习者根据规则就能造出合格的连续表达。我们学习英语,需要专门练习各种衔接与连贯,但老师不能告诉我们关于 it 或者 he 什么时候必须用,什么时候不能用,什么时候可以选择使用的规则。汉语教师也一样,没有办法告诉留学生,说一段话如何做到连贯。我们只能是把学生不连贯的话改过来,有时候甚至不能告诉他们为什么要这样做。

篇章的结构规则是句群规则的扩大,考虑的问题却更多。有的研究者抓住一种篇章类型进行研究,如论辩的内部结构,但也只能做到给出大致的结构框架。对于各种可能的变化类型,可能的结构规则的违背都没有足够的说明。相对而言,日常交际话语的组织规律研究,既简单又复杂。简单的是话语中句子的结构,简单句居多,单个的词也不少;复杂的是话语句子与句子之间的组织关系,为什么对话中多数成分可以省略,如何省略,怎么样的对话才是合适的对话而非一堆词语的堆砌。话语研究的基本单位是话对。话对是相当于"提问—回答""信息—评价""邀请—同意"这样的一对表述。当前话对的研究随着语法功能的研究,日益引起学界关注,并取得了不错的成果,但离完整地说明对话组织的规律还有一段很长的路要走。

超句法与句法的关系非常密切。超句法不仅体现为句子、语段的组织规则,也对超句结构内的句子有句法结构上的限制。比如话题、焦点等概念,虽然指的是句内的某一成分,但这些成分的语法表现是超句环境的要求。再如主动句和被动句,句法关系相似,但只有在特定的语段中,适应语段的协调需要,才能决定采用哪一种句式。基本的句法结构中,我们往往会区分主谓句和非主谓句,完整句和省略句,而在话语中所谓的省略是一种更自然的结构。句群、语段、篇章及话语结构的超句法需要在其组成部分——句子——上得到体现。

超句法研究中尚待开发的领域非常丰富,研究框架、研究手段等都需要进一步深化和发展。

**思考与练习**

1. morphemes 有的研究称为语素,有的称为词素。你觉得哪种称呼好? 说明你的理由。

2.说明下列英语词的构词法,并根据构词法确定它们的词义。

| | | | | |
|---|---|---|---|---|
| Instruction | insubordinate | insulting | decompose | deceitful |
| barefaced | auditorium | anyway | all-out | doorman |
| acknowledge | discharge | disadvantage | exhausted | expressly |
| mythical | quick-tempered | questionable | invalidate | impotent |
| stiff-necked | thoroughbred | thichskinned | underwrite | undeniable |
| whirlpool | worldly | stoppage | resourceful | resolutely |
| assembly | impractical | impurity | godforsaken | faction |
| dwelling | disaffected | backward | catchword | animation |

3.根据形态说明,解释下列句子的意思。

(1) díiga    apé-wi

　　soccer    play+3sg+past-vis(visual)

(2) díiga    apé-yigi̱

　　soccer    play+3sg+past-sec(second information)

(3) ŋindu    bawuŋ-ga    yuwa-dha

　　You+nom middle-loc(location)    lie- imp(imperative)

(4) waŋa:y-ndu-gal        dhagurma-gu yana-y-aga

　　neg(negative)-2nom-pl(plural)    cemetery-dat go-cm(conjugation marker)-irr(irrealis)

(5) waŋa:y-ba:-na        yana-nhi

　　Neg-ass(assertive)-3abs(absolute)  walk-past

(6) ñuka-ta        miku-naya-n-mari

　　I-acc(accusative)    eat-des(desiderative)-3ef.inf(emphatic first-hand information)

(7) wat-h-i

　　Kill-real-1sg+ag(agent)

(8) was-ø-ik

　　Kill-likely-1sg+ag

(9) tola    egite so-ma

　　call    3pl    to-here

（10）umala   kokue-a

　　don't   hit-3sg

4.请举例说明中心词分析法和直接成分分析法的优势和不足。

## 【原典阅读】

# 1.Language

### L.Bloomfield

CHAPTER 11   Sentence-Types

11.1   In any utterance, a linguistic form appears either as a constituent of some larger form, as does *John* in the utterance *John ran-away*, or else as an independent form, not included in any larger (complex) linguistic form, as, for instance, *John* in the exclamation *John*! When a linguistic form occurs as part of a larger form, it is said to be in *included position*; otherwise it is said to be in *absolute position* and to constitute a *sentence*.

A form which in one utterance figures as a sentence, may in another utterance appear in included position. In the exclamation just cited, *John* is a sentence, but in the exclamation *Poor John*! the form *John* is in included position. in this latter exclamation, *poor John* is a sentence, but in the utterance *Poor John ran away*, it is in included position. Or again, in the utterance just cited, *poor John ran away* is a sentence, but in the utterance *When the dog barked*, *poor John ran away*, it is in included position.

An utterance may consist of more than one sentence. This is the case when the utterance contains several linguistic forms which are not by any meaningful, conventional grammatical arrangement(that is, by any construction) united into a larger form, e.g.: *How are you? It's a fine day. Are you going to play tennis this afternoon?* Whatever practical connection there may be between these three forms, there is no grammatical arrangement uniting them into one larger form: the utterance consists of three sentences.

It is evident that the sentences in any utterance are marked off by the mere fact that each sentence is an independent linguistic form, not included by virtue of any grammatical construction in any larger linguistic form. In most, or possibly all languages, however, various taxemes mark off the sentence, and, further, distinguish different types of sentence.

In English and many other languages, sentences are marked off by modulation, the use of secondary phonemes. In English, secondary phonemes of pitch mark the end of sentences, and distinguish three main sentence-types: *John ran away* [.] *John ran away*[?]*Who ran away*[¿].To each of these, further, we may add the distortion of exclamatory sentence-pitch, so that we get in all, six types, as deseribed in §7.6.

This use of secondary phonemes to mark the end of sentences makes possible a construction known as *parataxis*, in which two forms united by no other construction are united by the use of only one sentence-pitch. Thus, if we say *It's ten o'clock* [.] *I have to go home* [.] with the final falling pitch of a statement on *o'clock*, we have spoken two sentences, but if we omit this final-pitch (substituting for it a pause-pitch), the two forms are united, by the construction of parataxis, into a single sentence: *It's ten o'clock* [,] *I have to go home* [.]

Another feature of sentence-modulation in English and many other languages, is the use of a secondary phoneme to mark emphatic parts of a sentence. In English we use highest stress for this ("Now it's *my* turn," § 7.3). The emphatic element in English may be marked also by the use of special constructions (It was *John* who did that) and by word-order (*Away* he ran); in languages where stress is not significant, such methods prevail, as in French *C'est Jean qui l'a fait* [sɛ ʒɑ̃ ki la fɛ] ‘It is *John* who did it’. Some languages use special words before or after an emphatic element, as Tagalog [ikaw ŋar aŋ nagˈsaːbi nijan] ‘you (emphatic particle) the one-who-said that,’ i.e. ‘You yourself said so’; Menomini [ˈjoː hpeh ˈniw, kan ˈwenah ˈwaː pah] ‘Today (emphatic particle), not (emphatic particle) tomorrow.’ Our high stress can even strike forms that are normally unstressed: *of*, *for*, and *by* the people; *im*migration and *e*migration.

11.2　Beside features of modulation, features of selection may serve to mark off different sentence-types. This is the case in some of the examples just given, where a special construction, or the use of a special particle, marks an emphatic element. In English, supplement-questions are distinguished not only by their special pitch-phoneme [¿], but also by a selective taxeme: the form used as a supplement-question either consists of a special type of word or phrase, Which we may call an *interrogative substitute*, or else contains such a word or phrase; *Who? With whom? Who ran away? With whom was he talking?*

Perhaps all languages distinguish two great sentence-types which we may call *full sentences* and *minor sentences*. The difference consists in a taxeme of selection: certain forms are *favorite sentence-forms*; when a favorite sentence-form is used as a sentence, this is a full sentence, and when any other form is used as a sentence, this is a minor sentence. In English we have two favorite sentence-forms. One consists of *actor-action* phrases—phrases whose structure is that of the actor-action construction: *John ran away, Who ran away? Did John run away?* The other consists of a *command*—an infinitive verb with or without modifiers: *Come! Be good!* This second type is always spoken with exclamatory sentence-pitch; the infinitive may be accompanied by the word *you* as an actor: *You be good!* As these examples show, the meaning of the full sentence-type is something like ‘complete and novel utterance’—that is, the speaker implies that what he says is a full-sized occurrence or instruction, and that it somehow alters the hearer's situation, The more deliberate the speech, the more likely are the sentences to be of the full type. The nature of the episememe of full sentences has given rise to much philosophic dispute; to define this (or any other) meaning exactly, lies beyond the domain of linguistics. It is a serious mistake to try to use this meaning (or any meanings), rather than formal features, as a starting-point for linguistic discussion.

Quite a few of the present-day Indo-European languages agree with English in using an actor-action form as a favorite sentence-type. Some, such as the other Germanic languages and French, agree also in that the actor-action form is always a phrase, with the actor and the action as separate words or phrases. In some of these languages, however—for instance, in Italian and Spanish and in the Slavic languages—the actor and the action are bound forms which make up a single word: Italian *canto*[ˈkant-o] 'I sing', *canti*[ˈkant-i] 'thou singest,' *cant-a*[ˈkant-a] 'he(she, it) sings,' and so on. A word which contains a favorite sentence-form of its language is a *sentence-word*.

Some languages have different favorite sentence-types. Russian has an actor-action type of sentence-word finite verbs, like those of Italian: [poˈju] 'I sing,' [poˈjoʃ] 'thou singest,' [poˈjot] 'he(she, it) sings,' and so on. In addition to this, it has another type of full sentence: [iˈvan duˈrak] 'John(is) a fool,' [solˈdatˈxrabr] 'the soldier(is) brave,' [oˈtets ˈdoma] 'Father(is) at home.' In this second type, one component, which is spoken first, is a substantive; the other form is a substantive to which the first is equated, or an adjective (adjectives have a special form for this use), or an adverbial form.

When a language has more than one type of full sentence, these types may agree in showing constructions of two parts. The common name for such bipartite favorite sentence-forms is *predications*. In a predication, the more object-like component is called the *subject*, the other part the *predicate*. Of the two Russian types, the former is called a *narrative* predication, the latter an *equational* predication. For a language like English or Italian, which has only one type of bipartite sentence, these terms are superfluous, but often employed: *John ran* is said to be a predication, in which the actor (*John*) is the subject and the action (*ran*) the predicate.

Latin had the same types of full sentence as Russian, but the narrative type existed in two varieties: one with an actor-action construction: *cantat* 'he (she, it) sings,' *amat* 'he (she, it) loves,' and one with a goal-action construction: *cantātur* 'it is being sung,' *amātur* 'he (she, it) is loved.' The equational type was less common than in Russian: *beātus ille* 'happy (is) he.'

Tagalog has five types of predication, with this common feature: either the subject precedes and a particle [aj] (after vowels, [j]) intervenes, or the reverse order is used without the particle.

There is, first, an equational type: [aŋ ˈbaːta j mabaˈʔit] 'the child is good,' or, with inverse order, [mabaˈʔit aŋ ˈbaːtaʔ] 'good (is) the child.' Then there are four narrative types, in which the predicates are *transient* words, which denote things in four different relations to an action. The four types of transient words are:

actor: [puˈmuːtul] 'one who out'
goal: [piˈnuːtul] 'something cut'
instrument: [ipiˈnuːtul] 'something out with'
place: [pinuˈtuːlan] 'something cut on or from.'

These transient words are by no means confined, like our verbs, to predicative position; they can figure equally well, for instance, in equational sentences, as: [aŋ puˈmuːtul aj si ˈhwan] 'the one who did the cutting was John,' but in the predicate position they produce four types of narrative predication:

actor-action: [sja j puˈmuːtul naŋ ˈkaːhuj] 'he cut some wood'
goal-action: [piˈnuːtul nja aŋ ˈkaːhuj] 'was-cut by-him the wood,' i.e. 'he cut the wood'
instrument-action: [ipiˈnuːtul nja aŋ ˈguːluk] 'was-cut-with by-him the bolo-knife,' i.e. 'he cut with the bolo'
place-action: [pinuˈ tuːlan nja aŋ ˈkaːhuj] 'was-cut-from by-him the wood,' i.e. 'he cut(a

piece) off the wood.'

Georgian distinguishes between an action-type, as [ 'v-ts'er ] 'I-write' and a sensation-type, as [ 'm-e-smi-s ] 'me-sound-is,' i. e. 'I hear.' Such distinctions are never carried out with scientific consistency; Georgian classifies sight in the action-type: [ 'v-naxav ] 'I-see'.

Not all favorite sentence-forms have bipartite structure: the command in English consists of merely an infinitive form( *come*; *be good* ) and only occasionally contains an actor ( *you be good* ).In German, beside a favorite sentence-type of actor-action which closely resembles ours, there is an *impersonal* variety, which differs by not containing any actor: *mir ist kalt* [ mi:r ist 'kalt ] 'to-me is cold,' that is, 'I feel cold;' *hier wird getanzt* [ 'hi:r virt ge'tantst ] 'here gets danced,' that is, 'there is dancing here.' In Russian, there is an impersonal type which differs from the equational predication by the absence of a subject: [ 'nuʒno ] 'it is necessary.'

......

CHAPTER 12　Syntax

12.1　Traditionally, the grammar of most languages is discussed under two heads, *syntax* and *morphology*. The sentence-types, which we surveyed in the last chapter, are placed under the former heading, and so are the types of substitution ( which we shall consider in Chapter 15 ), but grammatical *constructions*, which we shall now examine, are dealt with partly under the heading of morphology. There has been considerable debate as to the usefulness of this division, and as to the scope of the two headings. In languages that have bound forms, the constructions in which bound forms play a part differ radically from the constructions in which all the immediate constituents are free forms. Accordingly, we place the former under the separate heading of morphology. The difficulty is this, that certain formal relations, such as the relation between *he* and *him*, consist in the use of bound forms, while the semantic difference between these forms can be defined in terms of syntactic construction; *he* serves, for instance, as an actor ( *he ran* ) and *him* as an undergoes ( *hit him* ). Nevertheless, the traditional division is justified: it merely happens that in these cases the meanings involved in the morphologic construction are definable in terms of syntax instead of being definable merely in terms of practical life. *Syntactic* constructions, then, are constructions in which none of the immediate constituents is a bound form. Border-line cases between morphology and syntax occur chiefly in the sphere of compound words and phrase-words.

12.2　The free forms ( words and phrases ) of a language appear in larger free forms ( phrases ), arranged by taxemes of modulation, phonetic modification, selection, and order. Any meaningful, recurrent set of such taxemes is a *syntactic construction*. For instance, the English actor-action construction appears in phrases like these:

| | |
|---|---|
| *John ran* | *Bill fell* |
| *John fell* | *Our horses ran away.* |
| *Bill ran* | |

In these examples we see taxemes of selection. The one constituent ( *John*, *Bill*, *our horses* ) is a form of a large class, which we call *nominative expressions*; a form like *ran* or *very good* could not be used in this way. The other constituent( *ran*, *fell*, *ran away* )is a form of another large class. which we call *finite verb expressions*; a form like *John* or *very good* could not be used in this way. Secondly, we see a taxeme of order: the nominative expression *precedes* the finite verb expression. We need not

189

stop here to examine the various other types and sub-types of this construction, which show different or additional taxemes. The meaning of the construction is roughly this, that whatever is named by the substantive expression is an actor that *performs* the action named by the finite verb expression. The two immediate constituents of the English actor- action construction are not interchangeable: we say that the construction has two *positions*, which we may call the positions of *actor* and of *action*. Certain English words and phrases can appear in the actor position, certain others in the action position. The positions in which a form can appear are its *functions* or, collectively, its *function*. All the forms which can fill a given position thereby constitute a *form-class*. Thus, all the English words and phrases which can fill the actor position in the actor-action construction, constitute a great form-class, and we call them nominative expressions; similarly, all the English words and phrases which can fill the action position on the actor-action construction, constitute a second great form-class, and we call them finite verb expressions.

12.3　Since the constituents of phrases are free forms, the speaker may separate them by means of *pauses*. Pauses are mostly non-distinctive; they occur chiefly when the constituents are long phrases; in English they are usually preceded by a pause-pitch.

We have seen( § 11.1) that free forms which are united by no other construction may be united by *parataxis*, the mere absence of a phonetic sentence-final, as in *It's ten o'clock* [ , ] *I have to go home* [.] In ordinary English parataxis a pause-pitch appears between the constituents, but we have also a variety of *close parataxis* without a pause-pitch, as in *please come* or *yes sir*.

A special variety of parataxis is the use of *semi-absolute* forms, which grammatically and in meaning duplicate some part of the form with which they are joined in parataxis, as in *John, he ran away*. In French this type is regularly used in some kinds of questions, as *Jean quand est-il venu?* [ žăkăt ɛt i vny? ] 'John, when did he come?'

*Parenthesis* is a variety of parataxis in which one form interrupts the other; in English the parenthetic form is ordinarily preceded and followed by a pause-pitch: *I saw the boy* [ , ] *I mean Smith's boy* [ , ] *running across the street* [.] In a form like *Won't you please come?* the *please* is a *close* parenthesis, without pause-pitch.

The term *apposition* is used when paratactically joined forms are grammatically, but not in meaning, equivalent, e.g. *John* [ , ] *the poor boy*. When the appositional group appears in included position, one of its members is equivalent to a parenthesis: *John* [ , ] *the poor boy* [ , ] *ran away* [.] In English we have also *close* apposition, without a pause-pitch, as in *King John, John Brown, John the Baptist, Mr. Brown, Mount Everest*.

Often enough non-linguistic factors interfere with construction; what the speaker has said is nevertheless meaningful, provided he has already uttered a free form. In *aposiopesis* the speaker breaks off or is interrupted: *I thought he—*. In *anacolouthon* he starts over again: *It's high time we— oh, well, I guess it won't matter*. When a speaker hesitates, English and some other languages ofter special parenthetic *hesitation-forms*, as [ a ] or [ ɛ ] in *Mr.—ah—Sniffen* or *Mr.—what you may call him—Sniffen* or *that—thingamajig—transmitter*.

12.4　Features of modulation and of phonetic modification play a great part in many syntactic constructions; they are known as *sandhi*.① The form of a word or phrase as it is spoken alone is its *absolute* form; the forms which appear in included positions are its *sandhi-forms*. Thus, in English, the absolute form of the indefinite article is *a*[ 'ej].This form appears in included position only when the article is an emphatic element and the next word begins with a consonant, as in "not *a* house, but *the* house."If the next word begins with a vowel, we have instead a sandhi-form, *an*[ 'ɛn], as in"not *an* uncle, but *her* uncle."

A feature of modulation appears in the fact that when *a*, *an* is not an emphatic element, it is spoken as an unstressed syllable, as in *a house* [ e'haws], *an arm* [ en'ɑrm].In English, a word in absolute form has one high stress ; hence we may say that in a sandhi-form without high stress a word is spoken as if it were part of another word. Various languages use sandhi-forms of this sort; they are known as *atonic* forms. This term is not altogether appropriate, since the peculiarity is not always a lack of stress. In the French phrase *l' homme*[ l ɔm] 'the man,' the article *le* [ lə ]is atonic, because its sandhi-form [ l] could not be spoken alone on account of the phonetic pattern(lack of a vowel). In the Polish phrase [ 'do nuk] 'to the feet,' the preposition *do* 'to' is atonic precisely because it has the stress, for the stress in this language is placed on the next-to-last syllable of each word, and falls on *do* only because this word is treated as part of the following word.

An atonic form which is treated as part of the following word—this is the case in our examples so far—is a *proclitic*. An atonic form which is treated as if it were part of the preceding word is an *enclitic*; thus, in *I saw him*[ aj'sɔ im],the[ aj]is proclitic, but the [ im] enclitic.

The sandhi which substitutes *an* for *a*, and the sandhi by which this and other words are unstressed in phrasal combinations, are examples of *compulsory sandhi*. Other English sandhi habits are *optional*, because paralleled by unaltered variants, which have usually a formal or elevated connotation;for instance, the dropping of [ h] in *him* does not take place in the more elevated variant *I saw him* [ aj'sɔ him]. Beside the sandhi-forms in *did you?* [ 'dijuw?], *won' t you* [ 'wowntʃuw?],*at all* [ e'tɔ:l](in American English with the voiced tongue-flip variant of [ t]), we have the more elegant variants[ 'did juw? 'wownt juw? et 'ɔ:l].

Sandhi-forms may be unpronounceable when taken by themselves; this is the case in a number of English examples:

| ABSOLUTE FORM | SANDHI-FORM |
|---|---|
| *is*[ 'iz] | [ z] John' s ready. |
| | [ s] Dick' s ready. |
| *has*[ 'hɛz] | [ z]*John' s got it.* |
| *am*[ 'ɛm] | [ m] *I' m ready.* |
| *are*[ 'ar] | [ ɛ]*We' re waiting.* |
| *have*[ 'hɛv] | [ v]*I' ve got it.* |
| *had*[ 'hɛd] | [ d]*He' d seen it.* |
| *would*[ 'wud] | [ d]*He' d seen it.* |
| *will*[ 'wil] | [ l]*I' ll go.* |

① This term, like many technical terms of linguistics, comes from the ancient.Hindu grammarians. Literally, it means ' putting together'.

them[ ˈðem ]

not. [ ˈnct ]

and[ ˈɛnd ]

[l] *That' ll do.*

[ əm ] *Watch' em.*

[ nt ] *It isn' t.*

[ nt ] *I won' t.*

[ t ] *I can' t.*

[ n ] *bread and butter.*

The French language has a great deal of sandhi. Thus, the article *la*[ la ] 'the' ( feminine ) loses the [ a ] before a vowel or diphthong: *la femme* [ la fam ] ' the woman,' but *l' encre*[ l ãkr ] ' the ink,' *l' oie*[ l wa ] 'the goose.' The adjective *ce*[ sə ] 'this' ( masculine ) adds [ t ] before the same sounds: *ce couteau* [ sə kuto ] 'this knife,' but *cet homme*[ sət ɔm ] ' this man.' A plural pronoun adds [ z ] before the initial vowel of a verb: *vous faites*[ vu fɛt ] 'you make,' but *vous êtes* [ vuz ɛːt ] 'you are.' A plural noun-modifier behaves similarly: *les femmes*[ le fam ] 'the women,' but *les hommes*[ lez ɔm ] ' the men.' A first-person or second-person verb adds[ z ], a third-person verb [ t ],before certain initial vowels: *va*[ va ] 'go thou,' but *vas-y*[ vaz i ] 'go thou there'; *elle est* [ ɛl ɛ ] 'she is,' but *est-elle?* [ ɛt ɛl? ] 'is she?' A few masculine adjectives add sandhi-consonants before a vowel: *un grand garcon* [ oẽ grã garsõ ] 'a big boy,' but *un grand homme* [ oẽ grãt ɔm ] 'a great man.'

In languages with distinctions of pitch in the word, modifications of pitch may play a part in sandhi. Thus, in Chinese, beside the absolute form [ ˈiˈ ] 'one,' there are the sandhi-forms in [ ˌi⁴ phi² ˈma³ ] 'one horse' and [ i² ko ˈʒən² ] 'one man.'

sandhi-modification of initial phonemes is less common than that of the end of a word; it occurs in the Celtic languages, as, in modern Irish:

| ABSOLUTM FORM | SANDHI-FORM |
|---|---|
| [ ˈboː ] 'cow' | [ an ˈvoː ] 'the cow' |
| | [ ar ˈmoː ] 'our cow' |
| [ ˈuv ] 'egg' | [ an ˈtuv ] 'the egg' |
| | [ na ˈnuv ] 'of the eggs' |
| | [ a ˈhuv ] 'her egg' |
| [ ˈbaːn ] 'white' | [ ˈboːˈvaːn ] 'white cow' |
| [ ˈbog ] 'soft' | [ ˈroːˈvog ] 'very soft' |
| [ ˈbrif ] 'break' | [ do ˈvrif ] 'did break.' |

12.5 Our examples so far illustrate *special* or *irregular* cases of sandhi, peculiar to certain forms and constructions. *General* or *regular* sandhi applies to any and all words in a short ( *close-knit* ) phrase. In some forms of English, such as New England and southern British, words which in absolute position have a final vowel, add [ r ] before an initial vowel: *water* [ ˈwɔtə ]but *the water is* [ ðə ˈwɔtər iz ]; *idea* [ ajˈdijə ] but *the idea is* [ ðij ajˈdijər iz ]. When three consonants come together in French, the word-final adds[ ə ]; thus, *porte* [ pɔrt ] 'carries' and *bien* [ bjẽ ] 'well' appear in the phrase as *porte bien*[ pɔrtə bjẽ ] 'carries well.' A word whose first syllable in absolute form contains [ ə ], either because the word has no other syllabic or because otherwise it would begin with an unpermitted cluster ( §8.6 ), loses this[ ə ] in the phrase whenever no unpermitted group would result: *le*[ lə ] 'the' but *l' homme* [ l ɔm ] 'the man'; *cheval* [ ʃəval ] 'horse,' but *un cheval* [œ̃ ʃval] 'a horse'; *je* [ʒə] 'I,' *ne* [nə] 'not,' *le* [lə] 'it,' *demande* [dəmãd] 'ask,' but *je ne le demande pas* [ʒə n lə dmãd pa] 'I don't ask it' and *si je ne le demande pas* [si ʒ nə l dəmãd pa] 'if I don't ask it.'

In Sanskrit there is a great deal of general sandhi; for instance, final [ah] of the absolute form appears in the following sandhi-variants: absolute [deːˈvah] 'a god,' sandhi-forms: [deːˈvasˈtatra] 'the god there,' [deːˈvaç carati] 'the god wanders,' [deːˈva eːti] 'the god goes,' [deːˈvoː dadaːti] 'the god gives,' and, with change also of a following initial, before [ˈatra] 'here,' [deːˈvoː tra] 'the god here.' Certain words, however, behave differently; thus, [ˈpunah] 'again' gives [ˈpunar dadaːti] 'again he gives' [ˈpunarˈatra] 'again here.' The divergent words may be marked off by some structural feature. Thus, in some Dutch pronunciations the absolute forms *heb* [ˈhep] 'have' and *stop* [stop] 'stop' behave differently in sandhi: *heb ik?* [ˈheb ek?] 'have I?' but *stop ik?* [ˈstop ek?] 'do I stop?' The forms which have the voiced consonant in sandhi have it also whenever it is not at the end of the word, as *hebben* [ˈhebe] 'to have,' in contrast with *stoppen* [ˈstope] 'to stop.' Sandhi-distinctions based on morphologic features like this, may be called *reminiscent sandhi*.

Sandhi may go so far as to restrict the word-final in a phrase beyond the ord restrictions of a language. Thus, the sequence [ta] is permitted medially in Sanskrit, a 'he falls,' but [t] at the end of the word is in close-knit phrases replaced by [d] be absolute [ˈtat] 'that,' but [ˈtad asti] 'that is.'

12.6 Taxemes of selection play a large part in the syntax of most languages; s largely in defining them—in stating, for instance, under what circumstances (witn wnat accompanying forms or, if the accompanying forms are the same, with what difference of meaning) various form-classes (as, say, indicative and subjunctive verbs, or dative and accusative nouns, and so on) appear in syntactic constructions. We have seen that the selective taxemes delimit form-classes. These classes are most numerous in the languages that use most taxemes of selection. The syntactic constructions of a language mark off large classes of free forms, such as, in English, the nominative expression or the finite verb expression. Since different languages have different constructions, their form-classes also are different. We shall see that the great form-classes of a language are most easily described in terms of *word-classes* (such as the traditional "parts of speech"), because the form-class of a phrase is usually determined by one or more of the words which appear in it.

In languages which make a wide use of selective taxemes, the large form-classes are subdivided into smaller ones. For instance, the English actor-action construction, in addition to the general selective taxemes, shows some more specialized taxemes of the same sort. With the nominative expressions *John* or *that horse* we can join the finite verb expression *runs fast*, but not the finite verb expression *run fast*; with the nominative expressions *John and Bill* or *horses* the reverse selection is made. Accordingly, we recognize in each of these two form-classes a division into two sub-classes, which we call *singular* and *plural*, such that a singular nominative expression is joined only with a singular finite verb expression, and a plural nominative expression only with a plural finite verb expression. It would not do to define these sub-classes by meaning—witness cases like *wheat grows* but *oats grow*. Further examination shows us several varieties of selection: (1) many finite verb expressions, such as *can*, *had*, *went*, appear with any actor; (2) many, such as *run*:*runs*, show the twofold selection just described; (3) one, *was*: *were*, shows a twofold selection that does not agree with the preceding; (4) one, finally, *am*:*is*:*are*, shows a threefold selection, with a special form that accompanies the actor *I*, precisely the actor form as to which (2) and (3) disagree:

|   | (1) | (2) | (3) | (4) |
|---|------|------|------|------|
| A | *I can* | *I run* | *I was* | *I am* |
| B | *the boy can* | *the boy runs* | *the boy was* | *the boy is* |
| C | *the boys can* | *the boys run* | *the boys were* | *the boys are* |
|   | A = B = C | A = C | A = B | |

Thus we find among nominative expressions and among finite verb expressions a threefold subdivision, due to taxemes of selection; among nominative expressions sub-class A contains only the form *I*; sub-class B contains those which are joined with finite verb expressions such as *runs*, *was*, *is*, and sub-class C contains those which are joined with finite verb expressions such as *run*, *were*, *are*. In fact, we can base our definition of the three sub-classes on the selection of the three finite verb forms *am*: *is*: *are*. Conversely, we define the sub-classes of finite verb expressions by telling with which nominative expressions (say, *I*: *the boy*: *the boys*) they occur.

The narrower type of selection in cases like this one is in principle no different from the more inclusive type by which our language distinguishes great form-classes like nominative expressions and finite verb expressions, but there are some differences of detail. The narrower type of selection, by which great form-classes are subdivided into selective types, is called *agreement*. In a rough way, without real boundaries, we can distinguish three general types of agreement.

12.7   In our example, the agreement is of the simplest kind, which is usually called *concord* or *congruence*: if the actor is a form of sub-class A, the action must be a form of sub-class A, and so on. Sometimes one of the subdivisions is otherwise also recognized in the structure of the language; thus, in our example, classes B and C of nominative expressions are otherwise also definable in our language; namely, by the use of the modifiers *this*, *that* with class B, but *these*, *those* with class C: we say *this boy*, *this wheat*, but *these boys*, *these oats*. Accordingly, we view the subdivision of nominative expressions into singulars and plurals as more fundamental than that of finite verb expressions, and say that the latter *agree with* or *stand in congruence* with the former. For the same reason, we say that the forms *this*, *that*, *these*, *those* stand in congruence with the accompanying substantive form. Congruence plays a great part in many languages; witness for example the inflection of the adjectives in most Indo-European languages in congruence with various sub-classes (number, gender, case) of the noun: German *der Knabe*, [der 'kna:be] 'the boy,' *ich sehe den Knaben* [ix 'ze:e den 'kna:ben] 'I see the boy,' *die Knaben* [di: 'kna:ben] 'the boys,' where the selection of *der*, *den*, *die* agrees with the sub-classes of the noun (singular and plural, nominative and accusative); in *das Haus* [das 'haws] 'the house,' the form *das*, as opposed to *der*, is selected in agreement with the so-called *gender-classes* into which German nouns are divided. These genders are arbitrary classes, each of which demands different congruence-forms in certain kinds of accompanying words. German has three gender-classes; for each of these I give phrases showing the congruence of the definite article and of the adjective *kalt* 'cold':

"masculine gender": *der Hut* [der 'hu:t] 'the hat,' *kalter Wein* [ˌkalter 'vajn] 'cold wine' "feminine gender": *die Uhr* [ di： 'u：r] 'the clock' *kalte Milch* [ ˌka lte 'milx] 'cold milk'

"neuter gender": *das Haus* [ das 'haws] 'the nouse,' *kaltes Wasser* [ ˌkaltes 'vaser] 'cold water.'

French has two genders, "masculine," *le couteau* [lə kuto] 'the knife,' and "feminine," *la fourchette* [ la furʃɛt] 'the fork.' Some languages of the Bantu family distinguish as many as twenty gender-classes of nouns.

12.8   In other cases the subsidiary taxeme of selection has to do with the syntactic position of the form. For instance, we say I *know* but *watch me*, *beside me*. The choice between the forms *I* ( *he*, *she*, *they*, *we* ) and *me* ( *him*, *her*, *them*, *us* ) depends upon the position of the form: the *I*-class appears in the position of actor, the *me*-class in the position of goal in the action-goal construction ( *watch me* ) and in the position of axis in the relation-axis construction ( *beside me* ). This type of selection is called *government*; the accompanying form ( *know*, *watch*, *beside* ) is said to *govern* ( or to *demand* or to *take* ) the selected form ( *I* or *me* ). Government, like congruence, plays a great part in many languages, including many of the Indo-European family. Thus, in Latin, different verbs govern different case-forms in the substantive goal: *videt bovem* 'the sees the ox,' *nocet bovi* 'he harms the ox,' *utitur bove* 'he uses the ox,' *meminit bovis* 'he remembers the ox.' Similarly, different main clauses may govern different forms of subordinate verbs, as in French *je pense*, *qu'il vient* [ ʒə pãs k i vjɛ̃ ] 'I think he is coming,' but *je ne pense pas qu-il vienne* [ ʒə n pãs pa k i vjɛn] 'I don't think he is coming.'

Identity and non-identity of objects are in many languages distinguished by selective features akin to government. In English we say *he washed him*, when actor and goal are not identical, but *he washed himself* ( a *reflexive* form) when they are the same person. Swedish thus distinguishes between identical and non-identical actor and possessor: *han*, *tog sin*, *hatt* [ han 'to：g si：n 'hat] 'he took his(own) hat' and *han tog hans hatt* [ hans 'hat] 'his (someone else's) hat.' The Algonquian languages use different forms for non- identical animate third persons in a context. In Cree, if we speak of a man and then, secondarily, of another man, we mention the first one as [ 'na：pe：w] 'man,' and the second one, in the so-called *obviative* form, as [ 'na：pe：wa] Thus, the language distinguishes between the following cases, where we designate the principal person as A and the other ( the obviative) as B:

[ 'utinam u'tastutin] 'he ( A) took his ( A's) hat'

[ 'utinam utastu'tinijiw] 'he ( A) took his ( B's) hat'

[ utina'mijiwa u'tastutin] 'the ( B) took his ( A's) hat'

[ utina'mijiwa utastu'tinijiw] 'he ( B) took his ( B's) hat.'

12.9   In the third type of agreement, *cross-reference*, the sub- classes contain an actual mention of the forms with which they are joined. This mention is in the shape of a substitute-form, resembling our pronouns. In non-standard English this occurs in such forms as *John his knife* or *John he ran away*; here the form *his knife* actually mentions a male possessor, who is more explicitly mentioned in the accompanying semi-absolute form *John*; similarly, the *he* in *he ran away* mentions the actor *John*—contrast *Mary her knife* and *Mary she ran away*, In French, cross-reference occurs in the standard language especially in certain types of questions, such as *Jean*, *où est-il?* [ ʒã u ɛt i?] 'John where is he?' that is, 'Where is John?' ( § 12.3). A Latin finite verb, such as *cantat* 'he (she, it) sings,' includes substitutive mention of an actor. It is joined in cross-reference with a substantive expression that makes specific mention of the actor, as in *puella cantat* '(the) girl she-sings.' In many languages verb-forms include substitutive (pronominal) mention of both an actor and an undergoer, as, in Cree ['wa:pame:w] 'he saw him or her'; accordingly, more specific mention of both actor and undergoer is in cross-reference ['wa:pame:w'atimwa a'wa na:pe:w] 'he-saw-him (obviative) a-dog(obviative) that man'; that is 'the man saw a dog.' Similarly, in many languages, a possessed noun includes pronominal mention of a possessor, as, in Cree, ['astutin] 'hat,' but[ni'tastutin] 'my hat,' [ki'tastutin] 'thy hat,' [u'tastutin] 'his, her, its hat'; hence. when the possessor is mentioned in another word or phrase, we have cross-reference, as in['tʃa:n u'tastutin] 'John his-hat,' i.e. 'John's hat.'

......

13.10  Modulation of secondary phonemes often plays a part in morphologic constructions. In English, affixes are normally unstressed, as in *be-wail-ing*, *friend-li-ness* and the like. In our foreign-learned vocabulary, shift of stress to an affix is a taxeme in many secondary derivatives. Thus, some suffixes have *pre-suf-fixal stress*: the accent is on the syllable before the suffix, regardless of the nature of this syllable; thus, *-ity* in *able*: *ability*, *formal*: *formality*, *major*: *majority*; [-jn] in *music*: *musician*, *audit*: *audi-tion*, *educate*: *education*; [-ik] in *demon*: *demonic*, *anarchist*: *an-archistic*, *angel*: *angelic*. In the derivation of some of our foreignlearned nouns and adjectives from verbs, the stress is put on the prefix: from the verb *insert* [in'sə:t] we derive the noun *insert* ['insə:t]; *similarly*, *contract*, *convict*, *convert*, *converse*, *discourse*, *protest*, *project*, *rebel*, *transfer*. In other cases this modulation appears along with a suffix: *conceive*: *concept*, *perceive*: *percept*, *portend*: *portent*; in some, the underlying verb has to be theoretically set up, as in *precept*.

In some languages modulation has greater scope。In Sanskrit, with some suffixes the derivative form keeps the accent of the underlying form:

['ke:ça-] 'hair': ['ke:ça-vant-] 'having long hair'

[pu'tra-] 'son': [pu'tra-vant-] 'having a son.'

Others are accompanied by shift of accent to the first syllable:

['puruʃa-] 'man': ['pa:wruʃ -e:ja-] 'coming from man'

[va'sti-] 'bladder': ['va:st-e:ja-] 'of the bladder.'

Others have presuffixal accent:

['puruʃa-] ' man': [puru'ʃa-ta:-] 'human nature'

[de:'va-] 'god': [de:'va-ta:-] 'divinity.'

Other affixes are themselves accented:

['r ʃi-] 'sage': [a:rʃ -e:'ja-] 'descendant of a sage'

[sa'rama:-] (proper noun): [sa:ram-e:'ja-] 'descended from Sarama.'

Others require an accentuation opposite to that of the underlying word:

['atithi-] 'guest': [a:ti'th-ja-] 'hospitality'

[pali'ta-] 'gray': ['pa:lit-ja-] 'grayness.'

Tagalog uses both stress and vowel-lengthening as auxiliary phonemes; three suffixes of the form [-an] differ in the treatment of these modulations.

Suffix [-an][1] is characterized by presuffixal stress and by long vowel in the first syllable of the underlying form:

　　[ˈiːbig] 'love' :[iːˈbiːgan] 'love-affair'

　　[iˈnum] 'drink' :[iː ˈnuːman] 'drinking-party.'

　　The meaning is 'action (often reciprocal or collective) by more than one actor.'

　　Suffix [-an]² is stressed when the underlying word has stress on the first syllable; otherwise it is treated like[-an]¹:

　　[ˈtuːlug] 'sleep' :[tuluˈgan] 'sleeping-place'

　　[kuˈluŋ] 'enclose' :[kuːˈluːŋan] 'place of imprisonment.'

　　The meaning is 'place of action, usually by more than one actor, or repeated.'

　　Suffix [-an]³ has presuffixal stress when the underlying word is stressed on the first syllable; it is stressed when the underlying word is stressed on the last syllable; there is no vowel-lengthening beyond what is demanded by the phonetic pattern:

　　(a)[ˈsaːgiŋ] 'banana' :[saˈgiːŋan] 'banana-grove'

　　[kuˈluŋ] 'enclose' :[kuluˈŋan] 'cage, crate'

　　(b)[ˈpuːtul] 'cut' :[puˈtuːlan] 'that which may be cut from'

　　[laˈkas] 'strength' :[lakaˈsan] 'that upon which strength may be expended.'

　　The meaning is (a) 'an object which serves as locality of the underlying object, action, etc.,' and (b) 'that which may be acted upon.'

　　In languages with auxiliary phonemes of pitch, these may play a part in morphology. Thus, in Swedish, the suffix -er of agentnouns shows the normal compound word-pitch of polysyllables (§7.7) in the resultant form: the verb-stem [leːs-] 'read' forms *läser* [ˇleːser] 'reader'; but the -er of the present tense demands simple word-pitch in the resultant form: (*han*) *läser* [ˈleːser] '(he) reads.'

　　13.11　In all observation of word-structure it is very important to observe the principle of immediate constituents. In Tagalog, the underlying form [ˈtaːwa] 'a laugh' appears reduplicated in the derivative [taːˈtaːwa] 'one who will laugh'; this form, in turn, underlies a derivative with the infix [-um-], namely [tumaːˈtaːwa] 'one who is laughing.' On the other hand, the form[ˈpiːlit] 'effort' *first* takes the infix [-um-], giving [puˈmiːlit] 'one who compelled,' and is *then* reduplicated, giving [-puːpuˈmiːlit], which underlies [nag-puːpuˈmiːlit] 'one who makes an extreme effort.' Close observation of this principle is all the more necessary because now and then we meet forms which compromise as to immediate constituents. Tagalog has a prefix [paŋ-], as in [aˈtip] 'roofing' :[paŋ-aˈtip] 'that used for roofing; shingle.' The[ŋ] of this prefix and certain initial consonants of an accompanying form are subject to a phonetic modification—we may call it *morphologic sandhi*—by which, for instance, our prefix joins with [ˈpuːtul] 'a cut' in the derivative [pa-ˈmuːtul] 'that used for cutting,' with substitution of [m] for the combination of [-ŋ] plus [p-]. In some forms, however, we find an insonsistency as to the structural order; thus, the form [pa-mu-ˈmuːtul] 'a cutting in quantity' implies, by the actual sequence of the parts, that the reduplication is made "before" the prefix is added, but at the same time implies, by the presence of [m-] for [p-] in both reduplication and main form, that the prefix is added "before" the reduplication is made. A carelessly ordered description would fail to bring out the peculiarity of a form like this.

　　……

197

(*language.* George Allen and Unwin Ltd.1955)

译文:

# 语言论(节选)

## 袁家骅,赵世开,甘世福,等译

第十一章　句子类型

11.1　在任何话语中,一个语言形式总是作为某个较大形式的一个成分出现,如在 John ran away 这个话语里的 John,作为一个不包括在任何较大的(复合的)语言形式中作为独立形式出现,例如,在 John! 这个感叹句里的 John。当一个语言形式作为一个较大的形式的一部分出现时,我们就说它是处于内部位置(included position);否则就说它是处于绝对位置(absolute position),自成一个句子(sentence)。

在一个话语中作为句子出现的形式,在另一个话语中可能处于内部位置。在刚才引用的感叹句里,John 是一个句子,但是在 Poor John! 这个感叹句里,John 这个形式则处于内部位置。在后面这个感叹句里,poor John 是个句子,但是在 Poor John ran away 这个话语里,它却又是处于内部位置上了。再如,在刚才提到的这个话语里,poor John ran away 是个句子,但是在 When the dog barked,poor John ran away(当狗叫的时候,可怜的约翰逃跑了)这个话语里,它又处在内部位置上了。

一个言语片段可以由一个以上的句子组成。这就是说当这个话语片段包含几个语言形式的时候,这些语言形式不是用任何有意义的、习惯的语法配列(即任何结构)组合成为一个较大的形式的,例如 How are you? It's a fine day. Are you going to play tennis this afternoon? (你好吗? 今天天气好。今天下午你去打网球吗?)不管这三个形式之间可能有什么实际的联系,可是没有一种语法配列把它们联成一个较大的形式:因此,这个话语是由三个句子组成的。

可见任何一个句子都是个独立的语言形式,不用任何语法结构包括到任何较大的语言形式里去,单凭这个事实就可以把任何言语里的句子划分出来了。然而,在大多数语言里,或许在所有的语言里,以多种多样的语法单位用来划分句子,并且还能区别不同的句子类型。

在英语以及许多别的语言里,句子是凭藉变调即以次音位的使用来区分。英语里,音调这个次音位标示句子的结尾,并且能区分三种主要的句子类型:John ran away[.]John ran away[?]Who ran away[¿]此外,在这些句型的每一句上,可以加添感叹式的句调的变异,这样我们总起来就有了如 §7.6 中所描写的六种类型。

采用次音位来标志句子结尾的这种方法能使一种结构成为可能,这就是通常所说的罗列结构(parataxis)。在罗列结构里,就是不用别的结构来联结起两个形式,而只用一个句调把它们联结起来。譬如我们说 It's ten o'clock [.]I have to go home[.](十点钟了[。]我该回家了[。]),在 o'clock 上带着一个陈述句的收尾降调,那么我们就连说了两个句子。但是假设我们略过这个收尾的降调(代之以顿调'pause-pitch'),这两个形式就藉着罗列结构而联结成为一个单独的句子了:It's ten o'clock[,]I have to go home[.](十点钟了[,]我该回家了[。])。

在英语以及许多别的语言里,句子的变调的另一特征就是利用一个次音位来标志句子里的着重部分。在英语里,这个特点是利用最强的重音来表示的。("Now its *my* turn","现在这回轮到我了," §7.3)。在英语里,着重部分也可以利用特殊的结构(It was *John* who did that(那是约翰干的事))和词序(*Away* he ran(他逃喽))来标志;在有些语言里,重音没有什么重要性,这样一些方法就占优势了,如法语中 C'est Jean qui l'a fait[s ɛ ʒã ki l a fɛ]'是约翰做了那事'。某些语言用一些特殊的词放在着重部分的前面或后面;如塔加罗语的[ikaw'ŋaʔ aŋ nag'saːbi nijan](你(着重小品词)这一位—他—说了那件事)(即你,你自己这样说过的);美诺米尼语的['joːhpeh 'niw, kan 'wenah 'waːpah]'今天(着重小品词),非(着重小品词)明天'。英语的强重音甚至能加在那些正常不读重音的形式上:*of*,*for*, and *by* the people(民有,民享和民治);*im*migration and *em*igration'移进和移出'。①

11.2　除了语调变化的一些特征以外,选择特征也可以用来区分不同的句子类型。这就是上面刚才举出的一部分例子的情况,即用一种特殊结构,或用一个特殊小品词来标志一个着重成分。在英语里,补充疑问句不仅凭藉特殊的音高音位[¿]而且也凭藉一个选择性语法单位来区别:当作补充疑问句所采用的形式,可由我们称之为疑问代替形式(interrogative substitute)的特殊类型的词或短语构成,或者只用一个这样的词或短语来构成:如 Who?(谁?),With whom?(跟谁?),Who ran away?(谁逃跑了?),With whom was he talking?(他跟谁说话来着?)

也许所有的语言都区分两个大的句子类型,我们可以称之为完整句(full sentences)和小型句(minor sentences)。两者的区别在于语法单位的选择:某些形式是惯用的句子形式(favorite sentence-forms);当一个惯用的句子形式用来作为一个句子时,这就是个完整句,而当任何其他的形式用来作为句子时,这就是小型句。英语里有两种惯用的句子形式。一种是由施事-动作(actor-action)短语组成的,这种短语的构造就是施事-动作结构:John ran away., Who ran away?, Did John run away?。另一种是由命令式(command)组成的——即一个不定式动词带有或者不带有修饰语:Come!(来!),Be good!(乖点!)。第二种类型总是用感叹式的句调讲出来的;不定式动词可以伴有 you 这个词作为施事者:You be good!(你得乖点!)。正如这些例子所表明的,完整句的句子类型仿佛具有'完整而新提出的话语'的意义——也就是说,说话人含意表示他所说的是一件完整的事情或指示,并且多少要改变听话人的情况。言语越是深思熟虑的,句子就越会是完整的类型。完整句的语法元素意义的性质曾经引起许多哲学上的争论;对于这个(或任何别的)意义给以确切的界说是超越语言学的范围的。试图用这个意义(或任何别的意义)而不用形式特征作为语言学讨论的出发点,是一个严重的错误。

现代的印欧系语言中,许多语言在使用施事-动作形式作为一种惯用的句子类型是与英语一致的。有些语言,例如其他的一些日耳曼语言和法语也都符合这样的情况,即施事-动作形式总是一个短语,而把施事者和动作都作为分开来的词或短语。然而,在有些印欧语言——例如意大利语和西班牙语以及斯拉夫诸语言——施事和动作却构成一个单词的粘附形式:意大利语的 canto ['kant-o]'我唱',canti['kant-i]'你唱',canta['kant-a]'他(她,它)唱',等等。一个词含有该语言的一个惯用的句子形式,就是句词(sentence-word)。

有些语言具有不同的惯用的句子类型。俄语,像意大利语一样,具有一种定式动词的句词的施事-动作类型:[po'ju](我唱),[po'joʃ](你唱),[po'jot](他(她,它)唱),等等。除此以外,俄语还具有另一种完整句的类型:[i'van du'rak](伊凡(是个)傻瓜),[sol'dat 'xrabr](这个兵(是)勇敢),[o'tʲets 'doma](父亲(是)在家里)。在这第二种类型里,先讲出来的成分是个名词;另一个形式是跟第一个形式相对等的名词,或是一个形容词(形容词在这种用法上有特殊的形式),或是一个副词性形式。

当一个语言具有不止一种完整句类型时,这些类型都分成两部分的结构。这种由两部分

---

① 指外国侨民迁移进来和本国侨民迁移出去。——译者

构成的惯用句型的普通名称就是谓语型(predications)。在一个谓语型句里,那个比较像事物一类的成分叫作主语,另一成分就叫作谓语。俄语的两种类型中,前者称为叙述式(narrative)谓语型句,后者称为等同式(equational)谓语型句。像英语或意大利语这样的语言,只有一种由两部分构成的句子类型,用这些术语则是多余的,但是往往也把:John ran算是一种谓语型句,其中施事(John)是主语,动作(ran)是谓语。

拉丁语具有跟俄语一样的完整句的类型,但是叙述式类型体现了两种变体:一种是施事-动作结构:cantat'他(她,它)唱',amat'他(她、它)爱'另一种是受事-动作(goal-action)结构:cantātur'它被唱',amātur'他(她,它)被爱'。等同式类型不及俄语里那样普遍:beātus ille'快乐的(是)他'。

塔加洛语有五种谓语式类型的句子,都有一种共同特征:有的是把主语放在前面而以一个小品词[aj](在元音后面则为[j])插在中间,或者是利用颠倒次序而不带小品词。

首先是有一种等同式的类型:[aŋ 'baːta j mabaˈit]'这小孩儿(是)好,再一种是颠倒次序,[mabaˈit aŋˈbaːta?]'好(是)这小孩儿'。然后,还有四种叙述式类型,其中谓语是个暂词(transient words),用来表示跟动作涉及事物的四种不同关系。暂词表示的四种类型是:

施事:[puˈmuːtul]'砍者'

受事:[piˈnuːtul]'被砍的东西'

工具:[ipiˈnuːtul]'用以砍的东西'

地点:[pinuˈtuːlan]'在或从…上面砍'。

这些暂词决不跟我们的动词一样局限于谓语的位置;同样也能出现在例如等同式的句子里:[aŋ puˈmuːtul aj si 'hwan]'过去砍(东西)的那个人是约翰',但是处在谓语的位置上,它们却产生四种类型的叙述式谓语型句:

施事-动作:[sja j puˈmuːtul naŋ'kaːhuj]'他砍了一些木柴'

受事-动作:[piˈnuːtul nja aŋ 'kaːhuj]'被砍了 被他 这木柴',即'他砍了这木柴'

工具-动作:[ipiˈnuːtul nja aŋ gu:luk]'用以砍了的 被他这 波罗刀(bolo-knife)',即'他用这波罗刀砍了'①

地点-动作:[pinuˈtuːlan nja aŋ 'kaːhuj]'从上面被砍了被他 这 木柴',即'他从这木柴上砍下了(一块)'。

乔治亚语(Georgian)把动作类型(action-type)如['v-ts?er]'我-写'跟感觉类型(sensation-type)如['m-e-smi-s]'我-声-音-是'即'我听见'区别开来。这种区别从来就没有科学的一贯性;乔治亚语把视觉归到动作类型里去了:['v-naxav]'我-看见'。

不是所有的惯用的句子形式都具有两部的结构:英语中的命令句仅仅是由一个不定式形式组成的(come;be good),只是偶尔包括施事者在内(You be good)。在德语里,除了一种近似英语施事-动作那种惯用句型以外,还有一种非人称的(impersonal)变体,其区别是不含有任何施事者:mir ist kalt [mi:r ist 'kalt]'对 我 是 冷'即'我觉得冷';hier wird getanzt['hi:r virt ge-'tantst]'这儿跳起舞来了'即'这儿有跳舞'。俄语有一种非人称的类型,它跟等同式谓语型的区别是没有主语:['nuʒno]'有必要'。

……

第十二章 句法

12.1 依照传统的方式,大多数语言的语法都在句法(syntax)和词法(morphology)两个标

---

① 波罗刀源于菲律宾群岛的西班牙语,单刃砍刀。——译者

题下进行讨论。上一章里我们所探讨的句子类型是在前一个标题下进行的,对于(将要在第十五章考虑的)替代类型也是这样,可是对我们现在要考虑的语法结构(constructions),将部分地放在词法的标题之下讨论。关于这种分界的用途以及关于这两个标题的范围,曾经有过很多的争论。在具有粘附形式的那些语言里,粘附形式在结构上起着作用的和在结构上一切直接成分都是自由形式的,两者有根本的区别。因此,我们就把前者单独地放在词法的标题下。困难的地方是:某些形式上的关系,如 he(他——主格)和 him(他——宾格)的关系,包括在粘附形式的用法里,而这些形式的语义上的差别却能依句法结构来规定;例如,he 充当施事者(he ran),him 则充当受事者(hit him)。然而,传统的划分还是有道理的:恰巧在这些例子上,词法结构中所牵涉到的意义是能依据句法来规定的,而不能只依据实际生活来规定。所以,句法结构中没有一个直接成分是粘附形式的结构。介乎词法和句法之间的情形主要出现在复合词和短语词的范围以内。

12.2　一个语言的自由形式(词和短语)在较大的自由形式(短语)里出现,是按变调、变音、选择和语序这些语法单位来安排的。任何有意义的、重复出现的这些成套的语法单位(简称'法位')就是句法结构(syntactic construction)。例如,英语的施事-动作结构在如下的一些短语中出现:

John ran(约翰跑了)　　　　　Bill fell(比尔跌下了)

John fell(约翰跌下了)　　　　Our horses ran away(我们的马儿跑了)

Bill ran(比尔跑了)

在这些例子里我们看见选择法位。其中一个成为(John, Bill, our horses)是一大类的形式,我们管它叫主格词语(nominative expressions);像 ran 或 very good 这一种形式就不能这样使用。另一个成分(ran, fell, ran away)是另外一大类的形式,我们管它叫定式动词词语(finite verb expressions);像 John 或 very good 这一种形式就不能这样使用。其次,我们还看见语序法位:主格词语在定式动词词语的前面。在这儿我们暂且不用去考察这种结构的那些能显示不同的或附加的法位的、多种多样的其他类型和次类型。这个结构的意义大致是这样:任何一个被称为体词词语(substantive expression)的就是一个施事者,他执行被称为定式动词词语的动作。英语施事-动作结构的两个直接成分是不能互换的:我们就说这个结构有两个位置(positions),我们可以称之为施事位置和动作位置。某些英语的词和短语能在施事位置上出现,另外一些能在动作位置上出现。一个形式能出现的一些位置就是它的多种功能(function),或作为总体来说就是它的功能。所有能占据某一特定位置的形式因而就构成一个形类(form-class)。因此,所有英语的词和短语,能在施事-动作结构中占据施事位置的,都构成一个大的形类,我们把它们称为主格词语;同样,所有英语的词和短语,能在施事-动作结构中占据动作位置的,都构成另一个大的形类,我们把它们称为定式动词词语。

12.3　既然短语的各个成分都是自由形式,那末说话人就可以利用停顿(pauses)把它们分开。停顿大都是非区别性的;停顿主要出现在这些成分是较长的一些短语后面;在英语里,停顿以前通常会出现一个停顿音调。

我们在前面(§11.1)曾经看到:不藉别的结构联结起来的自由形式可以利用并列结构(parataxis)——仅仅缺少一个语音性质的句尾——联结起来,例如 It's ten o'clock[,]I have to go home[.](十点钟了[,]我该回家了[.])。在平常的英语并列结构里,一个停顿音调出现于成分与成分之间,但是我们也有另外一种紧接并列结构(close parataxis)不带停顿音调,如 please come(请来吧!)或 yes sir(是啊先生!)。

一种特殊的并列结构就是使用半绝对形式(semi-absolute forms),这种形式在语法上和意义上都是重复跟它联结而成为罗列结构的那个形式的某一部分,如 John,he ran away.。在法语里,这一类型是正规地用于几种问句中,如 Jean quand est-il venu? [ʒã kãt ɛt i vny?]'约翰他什么时候来?'。

插语(parenthesis)是以某一形式打断另一形式的一种罗列结构;在英语里,插语形式的前后通常都有一个停顿音调:I saw the boy[,]I mean Smith's boy[,]running across the street[.](我看见了那个男孩[,],我是说史密斯的男孩[,]跑过街道[.])。在像 Won't you please come?(你愿意来不)? 这一形式中,这个 please(愿意,请,劳驾)是一个紧接插语,不带停顿音调。

同位语这名词是指称那些用罗列结构形式联结起来的形式,它们在语法上,而不是在意义上,是等同的,例如 John[,]the poor boy[,]ran away[.](约翰[,]这可怜的男孩[,]逃跑了[.])。在英语里,我们还有一种紧接同位语,不带停顿音调,如 King John(约翰王)、John Brown(约翰·布朗)、John the Baptist(施洗约翰)、Mr. Brown(布朗先生)、Mount Everest(埃佛勒斯峰)。

有些非语言的因素跟结构相抵触,倒也是常见的;说话人所说的仍然是有意义的,如果他已经讲出来了一个自由形式。在顿绝语(aposiopesis)里,说话人是突然中止或是被打断:I thought he—。(我曾以为他—。)在错格语(anacoluthon)里,说话人是重新开始:It's high time we—oh,well,I guess it,won't matter.(这正是时候我们该—嗳,算啦,我想这没有关系。)当说话人犹豫不决时,英语和某些别的语言提供一些特殊的插语式的犹豫形式(hesitation-form),如在 Mr. —ah—Sniffen(斯—啊—斯尼芬先生)中的[a]或[ɛ],或 Mr. — what you may call him— Sniffen(斯—你怎么称呼他的—斯尼芬先生),或 that —thing—amajig—transmitter'那个—那个什么—发报机'。

12.4  变调和变音的特征在许多句法结构中起很大的作用,就是通常所说的连读变音(sandhj)①。一个词或短语的形式,要是单独讲出来,就是该词或短语的绝对形式(absolute form);出现在内含位置中的形式就是它的连读变音形式(sandhi forms)。这样,在英语里,不定冠词的绝对形式是 a['ej]。这个形式出现在内含位置上时,仅仅是当这个冠词是个着重成分,并且下一个词是以辅音开始的时候,如"not *a* house,but *the* house."(不是一所房子,而是这所房子)。如果下一个词是以元音开始,那末我们就有一个连读变音形式 an['ɛn]取而代之,如"not *an* uncle,but her uncle."(不是一个叔父,而是她的叔父)。

变调特征出现时,如 a,an 不是一个着重成分,而是作为非重读的音节讲出来的,a house [ə'haws](一所房子)、an arm[ən'a:m](一只胳膊),这里便出现了变调特征。在英语里,一个绝对形式的词都有高重音;因此我们可以说,一个连读变音形式词,若没有高重音,讲出来就好像它是另一个词的一部分。各种语言都使用这种连读变音形式;这就是通常所称的非重读(atonic)形式。这个名词不是十分恰当的,因为其特点不一定是缺乏重音。在法语的 l'homme[l ɔm]'这个人'这个短语里,冠词 le[lə]是非重读的,因为它的连读变音形式由于语音模式(缺少一个元音)而不能单独讲出来。在波兰语的['do nuk]'到脚'这个短语里,前置词 do'到'是非重读的,但是它有重音,正因为在这个语言里,重音是放在每个词的倒数第二音节上,而重音落在 do 上仅仅是因为这个词当作下一个词的一部分来对待的。

一个非重读形式当作下面一个词的一部分来对待时——这就是我们上述的一些例子的

---

①  这个术语,跟许多语言学的专门名词一样,来自古印度的语法学家们。照字面讲,它的意义是"放在一起"。——原注

情形——就是前倚音词(proclitic)。一个非重读形式当作好像它是前一个词的一部分来对待的就是后倚音词(enclitic);因此,在 I saw him [aj ˈsɔːim](我瞅见了他)中,这个[aj]是前倚音词,而这个[im]则是后倚音词。

以 an 来代替 a 的这种连读变音以及这个词和其他一些词在短语结合中不读重音的那种连读变音,都是强制性连读变音(compulsory sandhi)的例子。英语别的连读变音习惯却是任意性的(optional),因为通常都有正式的或文雅的意义的不变体可以平行并用;例如,[h]在 him 里丢失了,可是这情况不在比较文雅的不变体 I saw him[aj ˈɔː him](我看见了他)里发生。除了 did you? [ˈdidʒuw?](你那样做了么?)、won't you [ˈwowntʃ uw?]((你)行不行,愿不愿意?)、at all[əˈtɔːl](罢了)(这些是美国英语带有[t]的舌尖浊闪音变体)之外,我们还有比较文雅的变体[ˈdid juw? ˈwownt juw? əˈtɔːl]。

连读变音形式,单独提出来时,也许不能读出音来;许多英语例子就是这样的:

| 绝对形式 | 连读变音形式 |
|---|---|
| is[ˈiz](是) | [z]John's ready.(约翰准备好了。) |
| | [s] Dick's ready.(狄克准备好了。) |
| has[ˈhɛz](已经) | [z] John's got it.(约翰已经得到它了。) |
| am[ˈɛm](是) | [m] I'm ready.(我准备好了。) |
| are[ˈɑː](是) | [ə] We're waiting.(我们正在等待。) |
| have[ˈhɛv](已经) | [v] I've got it.(我已经得到它了。) |
| haa [ˈhɛd](曾经) | [d] He'd seen it.(他曾看见过它。) |
| would[ˈwud](会) | [d] He'd see it.(他会看见它。) |
| will[ˈwil](将,要) | [l]I'll go.(我要走了。) |
| | [l]That'll do.(那就行了。) |
| them[ˈðem](他们) | [əm] Watch'em.(监视他们。) |
| not[ˈnɔt](不) | [nt] It isn't.((这)不是的。) |
| | [nt]I won't.(我不要。) |
| | [t]I can't.(我不能。) |
| and[ˈɛnd](和) | [n] bread and butter.(面包和黄油即黄油面包。) |

法语有很多连读变音。比方,冠词 la[la]'这'(阴性)在元音或复合元音前面就丢掉这个[a]:la femme [la fam]'这女人',但 l'encre[l ã kr]'这墨水'、l'oie[l wa]'这鹅'。形容词 ce[sə]'这个'(阳性)在同样的那些音前面要加[t]:ce couteau[sə kuto]'这把刀',但 cet homme[sɛt ɔm]'这个人'。复数代词在一个动词的起首元音的前面就加[z]:vous faites [vufɛt]'你们做',但 vous êtes[vuz ɛːt](你们是)。复数的名词修饰语也采取同样的方式:les femmes [le fam]'这些女人',但 les hommes[lez ɔm](这些男人)。在某些动词,起首为元音的,第一人称或第二人称动词前加[z],第三人称动词加[t]:va[va]'你去!',但 vas-y [vaz i]'你到那儿去';elle est [ɛl ɛ](她是),但 est-elle? [ɛt ɛl?](是她?)。少数的阳性形容词在元音前面加连读的辅音(sandhi-consonants):un grand garçon [õ grã garsõ],'一个大男孩',但 un grand homme[õ grãt ɔm]'一个大人物'。

在词有声调区别的语言里,变调在连读变音中占有重要地位。比方,在汉语里,除了这个绝对形式[ˈi¹]'一'以外,还有[ˌi⁴ phi² ˈma³]'一匹马'和[i² kə ˈʒən²]'一个人'里的连读变音形式。

词的起首音位发生连读变化(sandhi-modification)不及收尾音位那样普遍;但这出现在凯

尔特(Celtic)诸语言中,如现代爱尔兰语:

| 绝对形式 | 连读变音形式 |
|---|---|
| [ˈboː]'母牛' | [an ˈvoː]'这母牛' |
| | [ar ˈmo]'我们的母牛' |
| [ˈuv]'蛋' | [an ˈtuv]'这蛋' |
| | [na ˈnuv]'这些蛋的' |
| | [a ˈhuv]'她的蛋' |
| [ˈbaːn]'白的' | [ˈboː ˈvaːn]'白的母牛' |
| [ˈbog]'软的' | [ˈroː ˈvog]'很软的' |
| [ˈbriʃ]'打破' | [do ˈvriʃ]'真打破了'。 |

12.5 到目前为止,我们的例子只说明了某些形式和结构的特殊的或不规则的连读变音情形。通常的或规则的连读变音则适用于短的(紧密结合的)短语中所有的任何一个词上。在英语的某些形式,例如新英格兰方言和英国南部方言,处在绝对位置上有词尾元音的词,在一个词首元音前面要加[r]:water[ˈwɔːtə](水),但 the water is[ðə ˈwɔːtər iz](这水是);idea[ajˈdiə](意思),但 the idea is[ðij ajˈdiər iz](这意思是)。在法语里,当三个辅音碰在一起的时候,词尾上就增添[ə];例如 porte[pɔrt]'带'和 bien[bjɛ̃](好)出现在 porte bien[pɔrtə bjɛ̃](带得好)这样的短语里。一个词,处在绝对形式中其第一音节包含有[ə],要是这个词没有其他的成音节的音,在短语里就得丢掉这个[ə],要不的话这个词就得以一个不许可的辅音丛(§8.6)开始,因为一个短语里不会产生一个不许可的辅音丛的:le[lə](这),但 l'homme[l ɔm];cheval[ʃəval](马),但 un cheval[œ̃ʃval]'一匹马';je[ʒə]'我',ne[nə]'不',le[lə]'它',demande[dəmãd]'需求',但 je ne le demande pas[ʒə n lə dmãd pa]'我不需求它'和 si je ne le demande pas[si ʒ nə l dəmãd pa]'如果我不需要它'。

梵语里有很多通常的连读变音;例如,绝对形式的收尾音[ah]出现在下列的连读变音的异体中:绝对形式[deːˈvah](一个神),连读变音形式:[deːˈvas ˈtatra]'这神那儿',[deː ˈvaç carati]。'这神游荡',[deːˈva eːti]'这神走去',[deːˈvoː dadaːti]'这神给与',而且在[ˈatra]'这儿'一词前面还带有一个词首音的变化:[deːˈvoːtra]'这神这儿'。然而,某些词又采取不同的方式;比方,[ˈpunah]'再一次'变成[ˈpunar dadaːti]'再一次是他给',[ˈpunar ˈatra]'又一次在这儿'。这些异形的词可以藉某种结构特征来区别。比方,在荷兰语的某些读音中,绝对形式 heb[ˈhep](有)和 stop[stop](停止)采取不同的连读变音方式:heb ik?[ˈheb ek?](我有么?)但 stop ik?[ˈstop ek?]'我停止么?'。那些在连读变音中有浊辅音的形式者,只要这个辅音不是出现在词的词尾上,就仍然保持浊辅音的性质,如 hebben[ˈhebe]'有——不定式',可与 stoppen[ˈstope]'停止——不定式'对比。像这些以形态特征为根据的连读变音的区别,可以称为追忆性的连读变音(reminiscent sandhi)。

连读变音不仅可以限制短语里的词尾音,甚至超过一个语言对词的中部的一般限制的范围。比方,[ta]这个音序,在梵语的词的当中是许可的,如[ˈpatati]'他跌下',但词的尾巴上的[t],在紧密结合的短语里处在一个元音的前面,就被[d]所代替:绝对形式[ˈtat]'那',但[ˈtad asti]'那是'。

12.6 选择法在大多数语言的句法中占有重要的地位;句法主要在于对这些法位下定义——例如说明在什么环境下(带有些什么伴随形式,或者,假使伴随形式都一样,又带有什么意义上的差别)各种形类(比方说,如直陈式和假定式动词,或与格和宾格名词,等等)出现于不同句法结构中。我们已经看到选择法位给一些形类划出了界限。在使用最多的选择语法单位的语言里,其类别也最繁多。一个语言的句法结构把自由形式分成一些大类,例如英语中的主格词语或定式动词词语。既然不同的语言有不同的结构,那么它们的形类也就各不相同。我们将会看到一个语言的大的形类最容易用词类(word-classes 如传统的所谓词类"parts of speech")来描写,因为一个短语的形类通常是由该短语中出现的一个或多个词来决定的。

在广泛使用选择语法单位的语言里,大的形类可以再分为一些较小的形类。例如,英语的施事-动作结构,除了一般的选择语法单位以外,还可以显示同一类的某些比较特殊化的语法单位。我们能把主格词语 John 或 that horse(那匹马)跟定式动词词语 runs fast(跑得快)连在一起,但不能跟定式动词词语 run fast(复数)连在一起;至于主格词语 John and Bill 或 horses(一些马),我们就得进行相反的选择。因此,我们认为在这两种形类中每类都可以再分成两个次类,我们称之为单数和复数,这样,单数的主格词语就只能跟单数的定式动词词语连在一起,而复数的主格词语就只能跟复数的定式动词词语连在一起。从意义上来为这些次类下定义是行不通的——如 wheat grows(小麦生长)但 oats grow(燕麦生长)这样的例子就是明证。进一步的考察能给我们指出选择的几种花样:(1)有好些定式动词词语,如 can,had,went,能跟任何施事者一道出现;(2)有许多,例如 run:runs,具有刚才所描写的那种双重选择;(3)有一个,即 was:were,具有跟上述情况不一致的双重选择;(4)最后,还有一个,即 am:is:are,具有三重选择,带着一个伴随施事 I(我)的特殊形式,这正是跟(2)和(3)不一致的施事形式:

| | (1) | (2) | (3) | (4) |
|---|---|---|---|---|
| A | I can | I run | l was | I am |
| B | the boy can | the boy runs | the boy was | the boy is |
| C | the boys can | the boys run | the boys were | the boys are |
| | A=B=C | A=C | A=B | |

这样,由于选择语法单位,我们在主格词语和定式动词词语当中就找出一个三重的再分法;在主格词语当中,次类 A 只包含 I 这个形式;次类 B 包含那些跟定式动词词语如 runs、was、is 连在一起的形式,而次类 C 包含那些跟定式动词词语如 run、were、are 连在一起的形式。事实上,我们能依据这三个定式动词形式 am:is:are 的选择来对这三个次类下定义。相反,我们也可以指出这些动词词语跟哪些主格词语(比方说,I:the boy:the boys)出现在一起而对定式动词词语的次类下定义。

像上述这一类情况的较狭小的选择类型,从原则上讲,跟我们语言中用以区分如主格词语和定式动词词语这些大的形类的包罗较广的类型并没有什么不同,然而也有些细微的差别。较狭小的选择类型,即能把大的形类再分为一些选择类型的,叫作一致关系(agreement)。我们大致能区分三种一致关系的普通类型,但并没有真正的分界线。

12.7 在我们上述的例子中,那一致关系是最简单的一种,通常我们叫作谐和关系(concord)或协调关系(congruence):如果施事是次类 A 的一个形式,那么动作就必定是次类 A 的一个形式,以此类推。有时某一种再分法也可在语言的结构中用别的方式认辨出来;比方,在我们的例子中,主格词语的 B 类和 C 类也能在英语中用别的方式来下定义;即在 B 类上使用修饰语 this(这个)、that(那个),而在 C 类上使用 these(这些)、those(那些):我们说 this boy(这男孩)、this wheat(这小麦),但 these boys(这些男孩)、these oats(这些燕麦)。因此,我们认为把主格词语再分为单数和复数两个次类比把定式动词词语这样来分类更为基本,并且后者对前者取得一致的或相互协调的关系。以同样理由,我们说 this、that、these、those 这些形式跟伴随的名词形式是相互协调的。协调关系在许多语言里占有很重要的地位;例如大多数印欧系语言中形容词的屈折变化跟名词的各个次类(数、性、格)相协调的现象就是明证:德语的 der Knabe[der 'knaːbe]'这男孩',ich sehe den Knaben [ix 'zeːe den 'knaːben]'我看见这男孩',die Knaben [diː 'knɑːben]'这些男孩',其中 der、den、die 的选择跟名词的次类(单数和复数,主格和宾格)是一致的;在 das Haus[das 'haws]'这房子'中,选择 das 作为跟 der 相对立的形式,是符合于德语中名词分成的所谓性类(gender-classes)的。这些性别都是任意性的分类,每一类都在某种伴随词中要求不同的协调形式。德语有三个性类;关于每一类,我举些短语例子来说明它跟定冠词和跟形容词 kalt'冷'的协调关系:

"阳性":der Hut[der 'huːt]'这帽子',kalter wein[ˌkalter 'vajn]'冷酒';

"阴性":die Uhr[diː 'uːr]'这种',kalte Milch [ˌkalte'milx]'冷牛奶';

"中性":das Haus [das 'haws]'这房子',kaltes Wasser[ˌkaltes 'vaser]'冷水'。

法语有两个性:"阳性",le couteau[lə kuto]'这刀',和"阴性",la fourchette[la furʃɛt]'这叉'。有些属于班图语系的语言能分出多至二十个的名词性类。

12.8  在另外一些情况下,有一种辅助的选择语法单位,同形式所处的句法位置有关系。譬如,我们说 I know(我知道)但 watch me(注意我),beside me(在我旁边)。在 I(he,she,they,we)和 me (him,her,them,us)两种形式之间进行选择,是依据形式的位置而定的:这个 I 类出现在施事位置上,这个 me 类出现在动作-受事(action-goal)结构(watch me)中的受事位置上和在轴心-关系(relation-axis)结构(beside me)的轴心位置上。这种选择类型就叫做支配关系(government);这就是说伴随形式(know,watch,beside)去支配((govern)或要求(demand)或采纳(take))被选择的形式(I 或 me)。支配关系,跟协调关系一样,在包括印欧语系在内的许多语言中占有很重要的地位。比方,在拉丁语里,不同的动词支配名词受事中的不同的格形式(case-forms):videt bovem'他看见这公牛',nocet bovī'他伤害这公牛',ūtitur bove'他使用这公牛',meminit bovis'他记得这公牛'①。同样,不同的主要分句可以支配从属动词的不同形式,如法语中的 je pense qu'il vient [ʒə pãs k i vjɛ̃]'我相信他正来着呢',但 je ne pense pas qu'il vienne[ʒə n pãs pa k i vjɛn]'我不相信他正来着'。

事物的同一体和非同一体在许多语言里是利用类似支配关系的选择特征来区分的。在英语里,当施事和受事不是同一人时,我们说 he washed him(他给他洗了澡),但当他们是同一个时,我们就说 he washed himself(他自己洗了澡)(一个反身 reflexive 形式)。瑞典语是这样区分同一个和非同一个施事者和所有者的:han tog sin hatt[han 'toːg siːn 'hat]'他拿了他(自己)的帽子'和 han tog hans hatt[hans 'hat]'他拿了他的(另外一个人的)帽子'。阿尔共金诸语言使用不同的形式来表示上下文中非同一的有生性复数第三人称。在克利语里,假使我们谈到一个人,然后附带地又谈到另一个人,那么我们就把头一个说成['naːpeːw]'人',而把第二个用所谓的另指式(obviative)说成['naːpeːwa]。因此这语言可以区分下列一些情形,我们以 A 来表示主要的人称,以 B 来表示其次的(另指式的)人称:

['utinam u'tastutin]'他(A)拿了他的(A 的)帽子'

['utinam utastu'tinijiw]'他(A)拿了他的(B 的)帽子'

[utina'mijiwa u'tastutin]'他(B)拿了他的(A 的)帽子'

[utina'mijiwa utastu'tinijiw]'他(B)拿了他的(B 的)帽子'。

12.9  在一致关系的第三种类型——即互证关系(cross-reference)——中,各种次类包括

---

①  在拉丁语中,bōs"公牛"为阳性名词,属于第三种名词变格:其主格是 bōs,宾格是 bovem,与格是 bovī,离格是 bove,属格是 bovìs,呼格也是 bōs。——译者

连用在一起的诸形式的实际陈述。这种陈述是以一种类似英语代词的替代形式来进行的。在非标准英语里,如在 John his knife(约翰他的刀子)或 John he ran away(约翰他逃跑了)这一类的形式中就出现这种情况;在这儿,his knife 这形式事实上已说明了一个男性的所有者,在 John 这个伴随着的半绝对形式中叙述得更为明确;同样,在 he ran away 中的 he 是叙述 John 这个施事者——可跟 Mary her knife(玛丽她的刀子)和 Mary she ran away(玛丽她逃跑了)作对比。在法语里,互证关系出现在标准语中,特别是在某些类型的问句里,例如 Jean où est-il?[ʒãu ɛt i?]'约翰他在哪儿?'即'约翰在哪儿?'(§12.3)。一个拉丁语的定式动词如 cantat'他(她,它)唱'本身就包含施事者的代词形式。在互证关系中它是跟一个明确提到施事者的名词词语连在一起,如 puella cantat'(这)女孩她-唱'。在许多语言里,动词形式本身就包含施事者和受事者两方面的代词(代名词)形式,例如,克利语['waɪ pameːw]'他看见了他或'她';因此,在互证关系中就对施事者和受事者两方面都叙述得更加明确:['waɪpameːw 'atimwa a'wa naɪpeːw]'他-看见了-他(除外式)一只-狗(除外式)那个男人',即'这男人看见了一只狗'。同样,在许多语言里,表示所有物的名词本身就包含所有者的代词形式,例如,在克利语里,['astutin](帽子),但[ni'tastutin](我的帽子),[ki'tastutin](你的帽子),[u'tastutin]'他的,她的,它的帽子';因此,当所有者在另一词或短语中被提到的时候,我们就有互证关系,如['tʃɑːn u'tastutin]'约翰　他的-帽子',即'约翰的帽子'。

……

13.10　次音位的变化往往在形态结构上占有重要地位。英语里,词缀正常是不读重音的,如 be-wail-ing,friend-li-ness,等等。在英语外来雅词的重音向词缀上转移,在许多次要派生词中是一个法位。比方,有些后缀带有位于后缀前的重音(pre-suffixal stress):重音是在后缀的前一音节上,不管这个音节的性质是什么;如,-ity 在 able(能):ability(能力),formal(正式的):formality(正式),major(主要的):majority(占多数)中;[-jn]在 music(音乐):musician(音乐家),audit(查账):audition(听觉),educate(教育):education(教育)之中;[-ik]在 demon(恶鬼):demonic(恶鬼似的),anarchist(无政府主义者):anarchistic(无政府的),angel(天仙):angelic(天仙般的)之中。在有些由外来语动词转为名词和形容词的派生结构中,重音落在前缀上:从动词 insert [in'səːt](插入)派生出名词 insert ['insəːt];同样,还有 contract(紧缩),convict(证明有罪),convert(转变),converse(交谈),discourse(谈话),protest(抗议),project(设计),rebel(反叛),transfer(移交)。在另外一些例子上,这种变化跟后缀一道出现:conceive(构思):concept(观念),perceive(观看):percept(知觉),portend(预示):portent(预兆);在有些例子上,基础动词不得不从理论上建立起来,如 precept(告诫)。

在有些语言中,变调具有较大的范围。在梵语中,带有后缀的派生形式保留基础形式的重音:

['keːça-](头发):['keːça-vant-](有长头发)

[pu'tra-](儿子):[pu'tra-vant-](有一个儿子)。

另外也有重音转移到第一音节上去的情形:

['puruʃa-](男人):['paːwruʃ-eːja-](来自男人)

[va'sti-](气泡):['vaːst-eːja-](气泡的)。

另外一些有位于后缀前的重音:

['puruʃa-](男人):[puru'ʃa-taː-](人性)

[deː'va-](神):[deː'va-taː-](神性)。

另外有些后缀本身有重音:

［ˈrʃi-］'哲人'：［aːrʃ-eːˈja］'一个哲人的后代'

［saˈramaː-］（专有名词）：［saːram-eːˈja-］'从 Sarama 传下来的'。

另外一些派生形式需要有跟基础词的重音转到对立方面：

［ˈatithi-］（客人）：［aːtiˈth-ja-］（好客，款待）（名词）

［paliˈta-］（灰色的）：［ˈpaːlit-ja-］（灰色）。

塔加洛语利用重音和元音延长两者作为辅助音位；［-an］这个形式的三种后缀在变调（modulations）①的处理上有所不同。

后缀［-an］¹ 的特点是表现重音在后缀前一位，也表现在基础形式的第一音节为长元音：

［ˈiːbig］（爱）：［iːˈbiːgan］（爱情）

［iˈnum］（饮）：［iː ˈnuːman］（酒会）。

意义是'由一个以上的施事者所进行的（往往是相互的或集体的）行为'。

后缀［-an］² 是有重音的，如果基础词的重音是在第一音节上；否则跟［-an］¹ 一样处理：

［ˈtuːlug］'睡'：［tuluˈgan］'睡的地方"

［kuˈluŋ］'围绕'：［kuː ˈluːŋan］'监禁的地方'。

这儿意义是"经常由一个以上的施事者所进行的行为或重复的行为的地点"。

后缀［-an］³ 具有位于后缀前的重音，如果基础词的重音是落在第一音节上的；这个后缀是读重音的，如果基础词的重音落在最后音节上；超越了语音模式所要求的范围就没有元音延长的现象：

（a）［ˈsaːgiŋ］'香蕉'：［saˈgiːŋan］'香蕉丛林'

［kuˈluŋ］'围绕'：［kuluˈŋan］'笼子，篓子'

（b）［ˈpuːtul］（砍）：［puˈtuːlan］'可以从上面砍下的东西'

［laˈkas］（力量）：［lakaˈsan］'力量可以消耗在上面的东西'。

这儿意义是(a)'一个物体可以当作基础物体，行为等等的地点用'，(b)'可以在上面进行某种行为的东西'。

在带有音高作为辅助音位的语言里，这种辅助音位可以在词法上起作用。比方，在瑞典语里，施事名词的后缀-er 可以显示合成形式中多音节（§7.7）的正规的复合词调（compound wordpitch）：由动词词干［leːs-］'读'形成的 läser［ˇleːser］'读者'；但是现在时的-er 只要求在合成形式中具有单纯词调（simple wordpitch）：(han) läser［ˈleːser］(他)'读'。

13.11　对词的结构进行一切观察时，非常重要的是要遵守直接成分的原则。在塔加洛语里，基础形式［ˈtaːwa］'一笑'重叠时变成派生词［taˈtaːwa］'将要笑的人'中；这个形式又可以作为一个带有中缀［-um-］的派生词的基础，即［tumaˈtaːwa］（正在笑的人）。另一方面，［ˈpiːlit］（努力）这个形式首先插入一个中缀［-um-］，产生［puˈmiːlit］（曾强迫行动的人），然后加以重叠，产生［-puːpuˈmiːlit］作为［nag-puːpuˈmiːlit］（尽极大努力的人）的基础。密切注意遵守这个原则更有必要的是，因为我们时常遇见一些形式在直接成分上彼此迁就。塔加洛语有一个前缀［paŋ-］，如［aˈtip］'盖屋顶'：［paŋ-aˈtip］'盖屋顶用的东西，盖屋板'。这个前缀的［ŋ］和一个伴随形式的某些词首辅音易于发生一种语音变化——我们可以管它叫形态连读变音（morphologic sandhi）——譬如，由于这种语音变化，我们的前缀跟［ˈpuːtul］'切一片，砍一

----

① modulations 不但指音高和音重的变化，这儿涉及 Tagalog 语，也用来指音长的变化。可见，modulations 这一个词可指音重、音高、音长三者之中任何一种或两种变化，或泛指三种变化。这儿指的是音重和音长两种的变化。参看上文 §13.4 脚注。——译者

下'连在一起,就产生派生词[pa-'muːtul]'砍或切东西用的工具',其中[m]代替了[-ŋ]加[p-]的结合体。然而,在有些形式上,我们发觉结构次序上不一致的情况;比方,[pa-mu-'muːtul](成批或大量地砍切)这个形式,根据组成部分的实际序列来看,意味着在前缀加上去'以前'就进行了重叠,但是就重叠和主要形式中都是[m]代替了[p]的出现情况来看,它同时也意味着在进行重叠'以前',前缀就已经加上去了。安排得不细心的描写一定不能成功地把上面这一形式的特点显示出来。

(节选自《语言论》,商务印书馆,1980)

## 2. Parts of Speech
### C.F. Hockett

**26.2　The Tripartite Plan.** The most revealing way to view a part-of-speech system is as a few large stem classes, the stems in which resemble each other in basic ways, divided into successively smaller classes on the basis of additional criteria. No matter what criteria are chosen as basic, it almost always turns out that the assignment of a few stems must be changed when further criteria are considered. If we treat Latin in this hierarchical manner, the result is as follows:

Stems inflected for case (*nouns* in a broad sense):

Stems belonging to a gender or indifferent to gender (*substantives*, or nouns in a narrower sense, and *pronouns*): *puer* 'boy' (masculine): *puella* 'girl' (feminine), *cīvis* 'citizen' (indifferently masculine or feminine), *ebur* 'ivory' (neuter). Certain stems, such as that of *ego* 'I' (indifferent to gender), show special features which lead to their segregation as pronouns.

Stems inflected for gender (*adjectives*):

Stems having an adverbial form (*descriptive adjectives*): *clārus* 'clear' (adverbial form *clārē* 'clearly').

Stems having no adverbial form (*pronominal adjectives*): hic 'this,' *tōtus* 'all.'

Stems having inflected forms which show person and number of a subject (*verbs*):

Stems inflected for voice: *amāre* 'to love' (passive voice *amārī* 'to be loved').

Stems not inflected for voice:

Always active in form: *facere* 'to make, do.'

Always passive in form: *sequī* 'to follow.'

Uninflected stems (*particles*): *in* 'in, into,' *postquam* 'after.' Syntactical criteria establish various subclasses, suggested by the traditional terms *prepositions*, *adverbs*, *conjunctions*, *interjections*.

All parts of the above classification could be carried further by specifying additional criteria. A few stems which show no inflection show syntactical behavior so nounlike that we class them as nouns rather than as particles: *nihil* 'nothing,' *quattuor* 'four.'

The main advantage of hierarchical presentation is that it brings out facts which tend to be concealed by a mere listing of eight or ten smaller stem-classes all on a par. Thus it is a fact that

Latin substantives and adjectives resemble each other more in their behavior than either resemble verbs or particles.

A second advantage is that it usually provides for the assignment of stems with peculiarly limited paradigms or syntactical uses. We shall see a demonstration of this in § 26.5 below.

A third advantage is that the hierarchical procedure renders easier the comparison of the part of speech systems of different languages. Setting all subclasses aside, the basic scheme of Latin is tripartite: nouns (in the broadest sense), verbs, and particles. This is the most widespread basic scheme in the languages of the world.

Differences within the basic scheme appear, however, with the very first subclassification. In Latin, and in many of its kindred languages in the Indo-European family, stems with "descriptive" or "adjectival" meanings ('red', 'big,' 'little,' and so on) belong to the same fundamental class with names of objects ('boy,' 'table,' 'sky'). In Georgian, which is not Indo-European, and in Armenian, which is, such words do not even form a separate subclass from other nouns: for 'red' one uses cither a noun meaning 'red thing' or, more rarely, a noun meaning 'redness.' In Japanese, some words with what to us are descriptive meanings are nouns, while others are verbs. By far the commonest situation, however, is for all such words to be verbs. In Menomini, /mɛhko • n/ 'he is red' belongs to the same subclass of verbs as / pa • pɛhcen/ 'he falls,' while/mɛhki • w/ 'it is red', together with/pa • pɛhnɛn/'it falls,' belong to a different subclass of verbs. Chinese *húng* 'red,' *dà* 'big,' *syǎu* 'small,' and the like form a separate subclass of verbs, but with the same basic syntax as words like *lái* 'come,' *chī* 'eat,' and *yàu* 'want, want to.'

As a further illustration of how details vary, we shall survey the subclassification of nouns in Menomini and Chinese, which differ in this respect as much from each other as either does from Latin.

(1) Menomini mouns fall into two principal subtypes: nouns proper and pronouns. The segregation of pronouns is much as in Latin. Nouns proper are further classed as *independent* or *dependent*, and as *animate* or *inanimate*.

Independent nouns are inflected for *possession*: /neto • s/ 'my canoe,'/oto • s/ 'his cance,' and so on; but also have *unpossessed* forms: /o • s/ canoe.' Dependent nouns have only possessed forms: /ne • k/ 'my dwelling,' /ke • k/ 'thy dwelling,' /ke • kowaw/ 'your dwelling,' and so on. In the main, dependent nouns refer to body parts, types of kin, and a few items of intimate possession.

Animate and inanimate are gender classes, comparable in grammatical function to those of Latin. Animate nouns include all those that refer to people, animals, and spirits; some body parts but not others; some plants and plant products but not others; and a few objects that neither we nor the Menomini think of as alive, such as 'kettle,' 'doll,' 'high bluff along a river.' All other nouns are inanimate. Animate nouns form the plural with one suffix (/enɛ-niw/ 'man,'/enɛ • niwak/'men'), inanimates with another (/we • kewam/ 'house,'/we • kewaman / 'houses'). Animates have an inflected form which inanimates lack: one which shows the subsidiary importance in the context of that named by the noun (/enɛ • niwan/ 'the other man or men'). As objects of verbs and as subjects of intransitive verbs, animates and inanimates require different verbs.

Little of this is reminiscent of Latin. A sharper difference is the total absence in Menomini of anything like the Latin inflectional category of case.

(2) Chinese nouns are all uninflected. They fall into five main classes: *demonstratives*, *numerals*, *measures*, nouns proper or *substantives*, and (*personal*) *pronouns*. The first four are differentiated by their relative positions in a nest of attributive constructions involving one of each: *jèi sān jāng jwōdz* 'this three flat-thing table' = 'these three tables.' The first IC cut in this four-word phrase is before the last word, *jwōdz* 'table,' a substantive. The next one breaks the first word, *jèi* 'this,' a demonstrative, from the middle two. The third one separates *sān* 'three,' a numeral, and *jāng* 'flat-thing,' a measure. In briefer forms, such as *jèi jāng jwōdz* 'this table' or *sān jāng jwōdz* 'three tables' (or even merely *jwōdz* 'table, tables'), the words of course retain the part-of-speech affiliation determined by their position in the longer phrase. The pronouns (e.g.*wǒ* 'I') do not occur in this nest of attributive constructions.

Measures and substantives cannot be distinguished in terms of meaning, but only in terms of syntax. Measures occur directly after numerals, while substantives do not. To count something named by a measure, one merely prefixes the number to it: *sān gwó* 'three countries,' *sān tyān* 'three days.' To count something named by a substantive, one must insert an appropriate measure between the numeral and the substantive: *sānge gwójyā* 'three fatherlands,' *sānge lǐbài* 'three weeks.' In both of these, the measure *ge* carries virtually no meaning, but simply fills the measure position, which is necessarily occupied by some form. In other cases the choice of measure is semantically relevant: *sān kwài chyán* 'three hunk money' = 'three dollars,' but *sān fēn chyán* 'three division money' = 'three cents'; *yíge syānsheng* 'a gentleman' but *yí wèi syānsheng* 'an honorable gentleman.'

26.3 Bipartite Systems. At least one language, Nootka, is known to have a bipartite system. One significance of this system is that it disproves any assumption that the contrast between noun and verb is universal on the level of parts of speech.

Nootka stems are either *inflected* or *uninflected*: these are the two major parts of speech. Inflected stems all have the same potential range of inflectional possibilities, whether from their meanings we should expect them to be nouns or verbs or something else. Some of the inflected forms are nounlike in their syntax, while others are verblike. Thus consider the four stems /wala·k-/ 'go,' /qo·ʔas-/ 'man, person.'/ʔi·ḥ-/ 'large,' and / ʔatḥija-/ 'at night.' With no overt inflectional affix these all have nounlike syntactical uses and can be translated 'a going, a trip,' 'a man, a person,' 'a lage thing,' and 'the night time.' With inflectional affix /-ma/, all four have an implicit third person singular subject, are used syntactically in verblike ways, and can' be translated 'he goes,' he is a man,' 'he is large,' and 'he does it at night.'

26.4. Multipartite Systems. A number of languages, including English, have more than three basic parts of speech. English is not like Latin because many English stems are used in ways that parallel two or more of the Latin parts of speech: *fancy in a strange fancy* (noun, like a Latin substantive), in *fancy dresses* (adjective), and in *They fancy themselves dancers* (verb). Equally, English is not like Nootka, because by no means all stems have strch a wide range of use: *strength* is used only as a noun, *icy* only as an adjective, and *describe* only as a verb.

Setting aside the particles of all three languages, we can compare the remaining stocks of stems to three athletic squads, coached in different ways to play much the same game. Several skills are required for the game. The Latin coach trains specialists. The Nootka coach tries to make an all-' round player or triple-threat man of every member of the squad. The English coach combines these techniques, producing some specialists but also good mumbers of double-threat and triple-threat men. In a pinch, a specialist may be thrown into a game to do something for which he is not well equipped ( *son in That nice young man really sonned the old lady* ) , on the analogy of *That nice old lady really mothered the young man* ) , but this is very different from the genuine versatility of *fancy or faint*.

A player is a stem. A skill is a pattern of use in inflection or syntax or both. The set of players on a single squad who all have the same range of skills, wide or narrow, is a part of speech.

The terms "noun," "adjective," and "verb,", when English is discussed, refer to skills rather than to the players that have the skills.

Thus the pattern of use indicated by the word "noun" involves most or all of the following: Inflection for plural ( *boy*:*boys* ) ,though this is not inevitable—*music* follows the rest of the pattern but is rarely pluralized. Use as head in nests of attributive constructions, often with initial *a* or *an*, *the*, *this* or *these*, *that* or *those*, or unstressed *some*(/səm/) : *a boy*, *an elephant*, *the boy*, *this boy*, *these boys*, *that boy*, *those boys*, *some boys* , *some milk*. The resulting endocentric phrase, or sometimes the bare word, occurs typically as a subject ( *The boy is here* ) , as an object of a verb ( *We saw the boys* ) , as an object of a preposition ( *Look at the boys* ) ,and as a nominal predicate attribute ( *My chidren are boys* ).

English stems which follow the noun pattern of usage just described,but do not also follow the adjective pattern or the verb pattern yet to be described, belong to a part of speech we shall call *class N*. Examples are *strength*, *food*, *action*, *day*, *friend*, *art*, *danger*, *music*, *boy*, *elephant*.

The adjective pattern of use turns mainly on inflection for degree ( *pretty* : *prettier* : *prettiest* ) or on participation in equivalent inflectional phrases ( *beautiful* : *more beautiful* : *most beautiful* ) ; and on inflection with-*ly* for adverbial use ( *prettily*, *beautifully* ) ; without-*ly*, the whole words are used as or in adjectival predicate attributes: *She is pretty*, *Jane is more beautiful than Mary*. English stems which follow the adjective pattern but not also the noun or verb pattern belong to a part of speech we shall call *class A*. Examples are *long*, *false*, *likely*, *certain*, *icy*, *sleepy*, *short*, *soft*, *civil*, *beautiful*.

Both stems of class N and those of class A ( as well as those of some of the classes yet to be described ) are often used as preposed attributes to a noun head: *action program*, *long program*; *art student*, *sleepy student*. This usage is followed by such a wide variety of stems, differing from each other so greatly as to their other uses, that it does not help us in determining the part-of-speech affiliation of stems.

However, there are many stems which follow both the noun and the adjective patterns, though not the verb pattern described below. These stems belong to *class NA*. Examples are *American*, *sweet*, *savage*, *private*, *human*,*male*, *white*, *red*, *innocent*; thus, *a good American*, *He is an American*, *They are Americans* ( all noun pattern ) , but *He is American*, *They are American*, *John is more American than his sister* ( all adjective pattern ). In *American life* we see a class NA stem functioning in a way typical also of both class N stems and class A stems. This function does not fall within either the noun pattern or the adjective pattern.

The verb pattern in general involves inflection. *Be* has eight inflected forms: *be*, *am*, *are*, *is*, *was*, *were*, *been*, *being*. Many have five: *sing*, *sings*, *sang*, *sung*, *singing*. Most have only four phonemically different ones: *describe*, *describes*, *described*, *describing*. A few have only two: *can*, *could*. And the syntactical use of *must*, *ought* classes them with verbs despite the absence of inflection. Syntactically, the typical uses are as verb in an objective construction (*saw John*), as verb in an intransitive predicate (*I see*, *John was singing loudly*), and as connector in a connective construction in an equational predicate (*They seem tired*). Stems which show this pattern of usage but not the noun nor adjective pattern belong to *class V*: *describe*, *admit*, *punish*, *bury*, *strengthen*, *falsify*, *penetrate*, *collaborate*, *denazify*. Class V stems do not often occur as preposed attributes to nouns, but in their inflected forms with-*ed* or-*ing* they do: *an admitted fault*, *a penetrating remerk*.

Stems which show both the noun pattern and the verb pattern belong to *class NV*: *walk*, *love*, *cure*, *change*, *air*, *eys*, *nose*, *beard*, *elbow*, *finger*, *cut*, *build*.

Stems showing both adjective and verb patterns belong to *class AV*: *clean dry*, *thin*, *slow*, *clear*, *busy*, *idle*, *true*.

Finally, stems showing all three patterns belong to *class NAV*: *fancy*, *faint*, *black*, *yellow*, *blue*, *brown*, *gray*, *damp*.

Use as preposed attribute to a noun is not the only function which is indecisive for part-of-speech affiliation. There is an affix-*ed*, much like the verb inflectional affix-*ed*, which occurs in expressions like *a blooded hound*, *a fluted column*, *a windowed house*, *a gifted student*, though it is more typically added to phrases, as in *a full-bodied flavor*, *a many-windowed house*, *a four-footed animal*. This is not the same as the verb inflectional affix, and the mere occurrence of a stem with this affix does not place the stem in class V, AV, NV, or NAV rather than in one of the other classes.

English stems which do not belong to one of the seven major classes described above(N, A, V, NA, NV, AV, and NAV) belong to an eighth class of *particles*, with many subclasses, differentiated by syntax. Even a few of the particles are versatile enough to play subsidiary roles as noun, adjective, or verb: thus *up* and *down* are particles in *He went up*, *He walked down* (adverbs), *He went up the street*, *He fell down the hill*(prepositions); but verbs in *He upped the price*, *He downed the medicine* and nouns in *We all have our ups and downs*. The seven major classes are all quite large; the class of particles is redatively smalier and its subclasses smaller still. Words like *he*, *she*, *it*, *this*, *that*, *every*, *each* belong marginally to one or another of the majon classes, but show special features of behavior (inflectional or syntactical on both) which set them off from the other major-class stems ( §30.3)

(*A Course in Modern linguistics*. New York: Macmillan Publishing co., Inc. 1958)

译文:

# 词 类

索振宇,叶蜚声,译

26.1

　　词类是词干的形类,属于同一词类的词干在屈折上,句法上,或者在屈折和句法两方面有同样的表现。一种语言的词类系统就是根据屈折上和句法上表现的异同对全部词干作出的分类。因为每个完整的词,按照定义,只包含一词干,所以词类系统也能说成是词的分类:一个词的词类就是它的词干的词类。

两种语言词类系统完全相同的情况是少见的,但是好多语言词类系统的基本格局相同,差别只在细节方面。少数几种语言则偏离较大。下面描写最常见的基本格局,然后举两个偏离较大的例子:努特卡语和英语。

26.2　三分格局

考察词类系统的最有揭示能力的方法是先根据词干在基本方面的异同分出少数几个大类,然后根据附加的标准层层分出小类。不管所选的基本标准是什么,当考虑深一层的标准时差不多总有少数词干的归属必须改变。如果我们用这种层级方式处理拉丁语,其结果如下:

词干有格屈折的是广义的名词:

词干专属于一种性或不计较性的是体词或狭义的名词和代名词:puer(男孩)——阳性,buella(女孩)——阴性,cīvīs(公民)——不计较是阳性还是阴性,ebur(象牙)——中性。有些词干如 ego(我)——不计较性,表现出一些特征,使它们从名词分出来而成为代名词。

词干有性屈折的是形容词:

词干有副词形式的是描写性形容词:

clārus(清楚的)(副词形式是 clārē[清楚地])。

词干无副词形式的是代词性形容词:

hic(这),tōtus(所有的)。

词干有表示主语的人称和数的屈折形式的是动词:

词干有态屈折的:amāre(爱)(被动态 amārī[被爱])。

词干无态屈折的:

始终是主动态形式:facere(做)。

始终是被动态形式:sequī(跟随)。

词干不屈折的是虚词:in(在……里),postquam(在……之后)。按句法标准定出不同的小类,传统术语提到的有:

介词,副词,连词,感叹词。

上述分类的各个部分都能通过指明附加标准而进一步细分。有少数几个词干,没有屈折变化,句法表现很像名词,我们把它们归到名词一类而不划为虚词:nihil(虚无),quattuor(四)。

这种分层级描写的主要优点,是能揭示出被一下子平行列出八个或十个较小的词干类所易于隐蔽的事实。例如拉丁语体词和形容词的各种表现的彼此相似的地方就多于和动词或虚词相似的地方。

第二个优点是它通常能解决屈折变化非常特殊,或者句法用途特别受限的词干的归类问题。例见§26.5。

第三个优点是这种分层级的做法易于对不同语言的词类系统进行比较。把小类全撇在一边,拉丁语的基本系统是三分格局:名词(广义的),动词,虚词。这是世界语言最普遍的基本系统。

可是一开始细分,基本系统内部就会出现差异。在拉丁语和印欧语系中与拉丁语同源的许多语言里,具有"描写"或"形容"意义的词干("红","大","小",等等)是和物体的名称

("孩子","桌子","天空")属于同一个基本类。在非印欧语系的格鲁吉亚语和印欧语系的亚美尼亚语里,这些词甚至在小类上也跟其他名词不分,例如"红"可以用作名词,"表示红色的东西",也可以(比较少见)用作名词,表示"红的属性"。在日语里,有些在我们看来具有描写意义的词是名词,有些词是动词,可是最常见的情况是它们都属于动词。在梅诺米尼语里,/mɛhko·n/(他是红的)和/pa·pɛhcen/(他跌倒)属于动词的同一个小类,而/mehki·w/(它是红的)和/pa·pɛhnɛn/(它跌倒)则属于动词的另一小类。汉语的"红","大","小",等等属于动词里面单独的一个小类,但它们的基本句法功能跟"来","吃","要",等等相同。

为了进一步说明细节上的千差万别,让我们概述一下梅诺米尼语和汉语名词的小类,它们彼此的差别固然很大,各自与拉丁语的差别也同样可观。

(1)梅诺米尼语的名词分为两大类:名词本身和代名词。代名词的分出,很像拉丁语。名词本身又分为独立名词和从属名词,有生名词和无生名词。

独立名词有表示领属的屈折形式:/neto·s/(我的独木舟),/oto·s/(他的独木舟),等等;也有非领属的形式:/o·s/(独木舟)。从属名词只有领属形式:/ne·k/(我的住所),/ke·k/(你的住所),/ke·kowaw/(你们的住所),等等。大体上,从属名词涉及身体的各部分,亲属关系的类型和少数几种关系密切的领有物。

有生和无生是性的类,在语法功能上跟拉丁语的性相似。有生名词所指的事物包括:人,动物,精灵;身体的某些部分(而不是全体);某些植物和植物产品(而不是所有的);以及不论梅诺米尼人还是我们都不认为有生命的少数几样东西,像"(烧水)壶","洋娃娃","陡峭的河岸"。有生名词之外的其他名词都是无生名词。两类名词形成复数所加的后缀不同:有生名词如/enɛ·niw/(男人),/enɛ·niwak/(男人们);无生名词如/we·kewam/(房子),/we·kewaman/(许多房子)。有生名词有一个屈折形式是无生名词所没有的,它用来表示名词提到的事物在行文中居于次要地位,例如/enɛ·niwan/(其他的男人或男人们)。作动词的宾语或不及物动词的主语时,有生名词和无生名词要求的动词不同。

上面这些特点跟拉丁语很少有相似之处。更明显的差别是:梅诺米尼语中完全没有拉丁语那样的格的屈折范畴。

(2)汉语的名词完全无屈折。名词分为五大类:指示词,数词,量词,名词本身或体词,(人称)代名词。其中前四类可以从它们在"这三张桌子"这个多重修饰型结构中所占的相对位置区别开来,每个位置一类。这个四词短语第一次直接成分切分是在"桌子"的前面,"桌子"是体词。接着切分"这三张":切出的第一个词"这"是指示词。再接着切分"三张":"三"是数词,"张"是量词。如果把形式缩短成"这张桌子",或者"三张桌子",或者光杆的"桌子",这些词当然仍保持按那个比较长的短语中的位置定出的词性。代名词(例如"我")在这个多重的修饰型结构中没有出现。

量词和体词不能从意义上去区别,只能从句法上去区别。量词直接出现在数词之后,体词不是这样。计点用量词指称的事物,只要在事物名称前面加上数词即可:"三国","三天"。计点用体词指称的事物,则必须在数词和体词之间插入一个适当的量词:"三个国家","三个礼拜"。在这两个例子中,量词"个"实际上没有什么意义,只是填补量词的位置,因为这个位置必须得由某个形式占着。在另外的情况下,量词的选择跟语义有关系:"三块钱"和"三分钱";"一个先生"和"一位先生"。

26.3　二分格局

我们至少知道有一种语言——努特卡语是二分格局。这种格局有一个重要的意义,它驳斥了在词类的平面上名词和动词的对立是普遍的这一设想。

努特卡语的词干分为屈折的和不屈折的两类:这就是两种主要的词类。屈折词干都有同样潜在范围的屈折可能性,不管从意义上看我们以为它们应该是名词,动词,或者别的什么。有些屈折形式在句法上类似名词,另一些则类似动词。例如考察下列四个词干:/waɫa・k-/(去),/qo・ˀas-/(男人),/ˀi・h-/(大),/ˀathija-/(在夜间)。不带明显的屈折词缀,它们都有类似名词的句法功能,可以译为"一次行程","一个男人","一件大东西","夜间"。带屈折词缀/-ma/,四个词干都暗含第三人称单数主语,都有类似动词的句法功能,可以译为"他去","他是男人","他是大个子","他在夜间干"。

26.4 多分格局

许多语言,包括英语,它们的基本词类都在三种以上。英语和拉丁语不同,因为英语的许多词干的用法相当于拉丁语的两个或两个以上词类。例如:在 a strange fancy(奇妙的幻想)中的 fancy(幻想)是名词(像拉丁语的体词),在 fancy dresses([化装舞会上的]奇特的服饰)中的 fancy(奇特的)是形容词,而在 They fancy themselves dancers(他们想象自己是舞蹈演员)中的 fancy(想象)是动词。同样,英语和努特卡语也不同。因为英语中并不是所有的词干都有那么宽的使用范围,strength(力量)只用作名词,icy(冰冷的)只用作形容词,而 describe(描写)只用作动词。

把英语,拉丁语和努特卡语这三种语言的虚词撇在一边,我们把剩下的全部词干比作三个运动队,各队接受训练的办法不同,任务是参加同样的比赛。比赛要求几种技能。拉丁队的教练培训专门选手。努特卡队的教练要把每个运动员都培训成全能的或者三用的选手。英国队的教练则把两种办法结合起来,既培训一些专门选手,也培训相当数量的两用或三用选手。在紧要关头,一个专门选手可能投入他并不在行的一场比赛,例如按照 That nice old lady really mothered the young man(那位好心肠的老太太真是母亲般地照管这年轻人)类推出来的 That nice young man really sonned the old lady(那位好心肠的年轻人真像儿子一样地孝顺这老太太)中的 son,但是这跟 fancy 或 faint 的名副其实的多面性是很不一样的。

一个运动员就是一个词干。一种技能就是屈折中或句法中,或者屈折和句法中的一种用法类型。一队里面技能范围(不论宽窄)相同的一组运动员就是一个词类。

就英语来说,"名词","形容词","动词"等术语是指技能而不是指具有这些技能的运动员。

例如"名词"这个词所指的用法类型包括下列各项:有表示复数的屈折(boy:boys),不过也不一定,例如 music 这个词,用法全都一样,但很少变成复数。作多重修饰型结构的中心语,结构的开头常常有 a 或 an,the,this 或 these,that 或 those,或非重读的 some(/səm/):a boy,an elephant,the boy,this boy,these boys,that boy,those boys,some boys,some milk。结果形成的向心短语,或者有时是光杆词,在句子中典型地出现为主语(The boy is here),动词的宾语(we saw the boys),介词的宾语(look at the boys)和名词性表述成分(My children are boys)。

英语里,符合上面描写的名词的用法类型,而不同时也符合将在下面介绍的形容词或动词的用法类型的词干属于一个词类,我们称之为 N 类。例如:strength,foot,action,day,friend,art,danger,music,boy,elephant。

形容词类型的用法主要是有表示级的屈折(pretty:prettier:prettiest)或者参与表示级的屈折短语(beautifull:more beautiful:most beautiful);加 ly 用作副词(prettily,beautifully);无-ly,整个词用作或者用于形容词性的表述成分:she is pretty(她是漂亮的),Jane is more beautiful than

Mary(珍尼比玛丽更漂亮)。英语里,符合形容词类型,而不同时符合名词或动词类型的词干,属于一个词类,我们称之为 A 类。例如:long,false,likely,certain,icy,sleepy,short,soft,civil,beautiful。

N 类词干和 A 类词干(此外还有尚未描写的一些类的词干)常常作名词中心语的前置修饰语:action program(行动纲领),long program(长长的节目单),art student(学美术的学生),sleetpy student(懒散的学生)。有这种用法的词干范围很广,彼此在其他用法上的差别很大,所以这种用法无助于确定词干的类别。

可是有许多词干既符合名词类型又符合形容词类型,但不符合下面介绍的动词类型。这些词干属于 NA 类。例如:American, sweet,savage,private,human,male,white,red,innocent。以 American 为例:a good American(一个好的美国人),He is an American(他是美国人),They are Americans(他们是美国人),这些例句中的 American 全是名词类型。在 He is American(他是美国派头),They are American(他们是美国派头),John is more American than his sister(约翰比他的姐姐更加美国派),这些例句中的 American 全是形容词类型。在 American life(美国人的生活,美国式的生活)中,American 是个 NA 类的词干,兼有 N 类词干和 A 类词干的典型功能。这样的功能在名词类型或形容词类型内是没有的。

一般说来,动词类型包含屈折。Be 有八种屈折形式:be,am,are,is,was,were,been,being。许多动词有五种屈折形式,如:sing,sings,sang,sung,singing。多数动词只有四种音位上不同的形式,describe, describes, described, describing。少数动词只有两种不同形式,如:can,could。must,ought 虽然没有屈折,但句法用途把它们归入动词类型。在句法上,动词的典型的用途是在动宾结构中作动词(saw John[见到约翰]),在不及物谓语中作动词(I see[我看见],John was singing loudly[约翰大声地歌唱]),在等式谓语的系连结构中作连接成分(They seem tired [他们好像累了])。符合这种用法的类型,但不符合名词或形容词类型的词干属于 V 类:describe,admit, punish, bury, strengthen, falsify, penetrate, collaborate, denazify。V 类词干常常不作为名词的前置修饰语出现,但带有-ed 或-ing 的屈折形式则可以:an admitted fault(公认的错误),a penetrating remark (透辟的评论)。

兼有名词类型和动词类型的词干属于 NV 类:walk,love,cure,change,air,eye,nose,beard,elbow,finger, cut, build。

兼有形容词类型和动词类型的词干属于 AV 类:clean,dry,thin,slow,clear,busy,idle,true。

最后,兼有名词,形容词和动词三种类型的词干属于 NAV 类:fancy,faint,black,yellow,blue,brown,gray,damp。

不能确定词性的功能,并不限于作名词的前置修饰语一种。有一种词缀-ed,很像动词的屈折词缀-ed,出现在例如 a blooded hound(尝过猎物血的猎狗),a fluted column(有槽的柱子),a windowed house(装上窗户的房子),a gifted student(有天赋的学生)之类的说法中,但更加典型的是加在短语上:a full-bodied flavor(醇纯的香味),a many-windowed house(多窗的房子),a four-footed animal(四脚动物)。这个词缀跟动词的屈折词缀-ed 不是一回事,只凭和它一起出现,无法把词干归入 V 类,AV 类,NV 类,或者 NAV 类,也无法归入其他的类。

英语的词干中凡不属于上述七大类(N,A,V,NA,NV,AV,NAV)之一的,都属于第八类:虚词。虚词又按句法分为许多小类。有少数虚词用途广泛,甚至能起到作名词、形容词或动词的次要作用。例如 up 和 down,在 He went up(他上去),He walked down(他走下来)中是虚词(副词);在 He went up the street(他沿街走去),He fell down the hill(他跌下山来)中是虚词

（介词）；但在 He upped the price（他抬高物价），He downed the medicine（他服下药）中则是动词；在 we all have our ups and downs（我们各有顺利和倒霉的经历）中又是名词。七个大类的范围都相当大；虚词类相对地小些，它下面的小类更小些。像 he，she，it，this，that，every，each 这些词只是擦边地属于某个大类，它们在屈折上或句法上，或者在屈折和句法上的表现又有自己的特征，使自己有别于其他大类的词干。

（节选自《现代语言学教程》，北京大学出版社，2002）

# 第五章　文　字

　　文字是语言的载体,是在语言产生之后随着社会生活的需要而产生的一种标记语言的符号系统。文字突破了时空的限制,使得不同时期、不同地域的语言能以符号的形式记录下来,它是语言的"留声机""复印机",文字的发明和创造是人类文明和进步的重要坐标。

## 第一节　文字的起源

　　人类自开始以来并没有文字,什么时候开始发明了文字,并没有确切的记载。只是在不同的国度有着不同的传说,但可以肯定的是,人类的文字是与人类的文明同步发展而来的,这里的"文明"涉及社会生活的方方面面,它使得文字成为语言交际的一种必要辅助工具。

　　最开始的文字并不像我们今天所看到的文字那样,更无所谓系统和成型。我们的祖先在劳动生产生活中逐渐认识到需要对自己所拥有的东西进行记录,例如,今天出门打猎又猎获了一只野猪,如何记录这只新捕获的野猪? 某处是猎物常出没的地方,需要给予标记以帮助记忆,等等。于是人们就开始选择以何种方式进行记录,不同肤色的先民们不无例外地都采用过实物记事。所谓实物记事是一种借助生活实物,例如绳索、木头等物品,对生活中的某些事件、物件的数量等信息进行记录和表达的方式。

　　无论是印第安人的求援标记,还是萨科人和福克斯人的"弥甘"以及阿尔衮琴人的"穴标",都是一种原始的实物记事,是我们今天的路标、方向标、暗号等非语言符号的原始形式。从民俗学、人类学、考古学等的发现来看,原始的结绳记事方法在不同的肤色、不同的民族、不同的地域中都存在过,有的甚至还一直被保留到了今天。美洲的印第安部落现在还在使用的一种"奇普(khipu)"结绳的方法就是来自原始的结绳记事。根据相关的研究,这是一种计数方法,当时的人们使用植物纤维或者动物的毛制成绳结。1982年联合国教科文组织《信史》第 4 期中登载有乔治·艾弗拉哈(摩洛哥学者)所写的《结绳记事》一文,其研究表明"以绳子为计算单位,上面可根据需要打结,最多打九个,打在两根相邻绳子上的结表示十位数,打在三根绳子上的结表示百位数,以此类推"。后来的研究者还认为这是一种类似计算机语言的二进制码,这样的三维立体绳结除了记数之外还记录了当时的社会生活事件。在我国的古文献中,例如《周易·系辞下》中,也表述了我们的先民结绳的现象,"上古结绳而治,后世圣人易之以书契。百官以治,万民以察。"郑玄《周易注》说:"结绳为约。事大,大结其绳;事小,小结其绳。"李鼎祚《周易集解》引《九家易》中也说道:"古者无文字,其有约誓之事,事大,大其绳,事小,小其绳。结之多少,随物众寡。各执以相考,亦足以相治也。"东汉时期的许慎在其《说文解字·叙》中这样记述:"神农氏结绳为治而统其事。"尽管缺乏具体的结绳方法以及相关信息的详细记述,但这些记录都给我们陈述了一个事实,即原始的人们用结绳的方式进行过相关的记录。结绳记事在某种意义上更多是帮助记忆的存储,甚至包括绳结使用不同的颜色代表不同的含义,以及绳结的缠绕方式也是通过提示作用来记录某些事件。

　　讯木是另外一种实物记事的方法。在已经发现的物件中,它是一种辅助记忆、传达信息的方式,在我国古代就已经有文献记载,例如《北史·魏本纪》中所说的:"射猎魏业,淳朴为俗,简易为化,不为文字,刻木结绳而已。"在木片、竹片等上面刻画花纹符号以记录数字、事件等,也可以插入各种东西,有的类似后来的信约。我国一些少数民族仍然保留了这种表达方式,例如(图 1)傈僳族人的一封写给当地政府领导的信中就使用了长短不同的"｜""○"以及"×"这样的契刻符号,表达的含义是在月圆之时约见三位政府官员并分别赠送大小不等的礼品各一件。而我国的半坡遗址中所发现的陶符也是契刻符号,

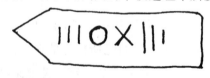

图 1

（选自李家瑞《云南几个民族记事和表意的方法》,《文物》1962,第 1 期）

而且其中的一些符号据裘锡圭先生的研究来看,很可能已经比较固定地用来表示某些意义了,但这些符号本身并不是文字。

图画记事是另外一种重要的记事方法,相比实物记事它更加形象具体,人们在解读上更加容易。比较典型的案例是印第安人奥基布娃(Ojibuwa)部落的一封女子写给情人的信件,这是写在赤杨树皮上的一封信,信中的内容就是一幅图画。从世人的解读来看,以男女双方的图腾符号作为男女的代指符号,左上角是女方的图腾“熊”,左下角为男方的图腾“泥鳅”,图中的“人”字形的线条代表男女约会的路线,而图的中部上方是“十”字,表示天主教徒,再加上两个帐篷图标,表示这是天主教徒聚居处,而帐篷中有个站立的人形,表明女方在此等候男方,整幅图的右边还以三个圆形标识湖泽,以定位帐篷的位置。这封信的解读很直接,表明了女方对男方的到来的殷切之情。类似的图画记事又如1849年北美奥杰布华人的一封保护渔业权的请愿书。这封请愿书上是生活在湖中的七种动物,同时是七个部落的图腾,动物的心、眼分别由线牵引着指向同一个方向,而线的另一头连着苏必略湖。

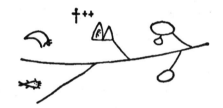

图2 印第安人奥基布娃部落女子的情书　图3 北美奥杰布华人渔业权请愿书

无论是实物还是图画,都和后来真正意义上的文字有着本质的区别,真正的文字具有可说可读性,并且具有广泛的社会性、继承性和相对的稳定性。实物记事和文字的起源并没有直接的关系,而图画记事却是文字的雏形。当一幅图画进一步被简单化、抽象化和符号化,从而使图画符号同它所记录的语言之间建立起紧密的联系,即以一个图形符号记录语言中的一个结构单位,这样才产生了真正的文字。

# 第二节　文字的类型

## 一、几种分类

从不同的角度分析可以得出不同的文字类型,最为常见的类型是"表音文字""表意文字"和"意音文字"。这是从文字的字符同语音、语义之间的关系的角度所作的划分,而按照文字的字符与语言中的何种语言单位相联系来划分又可以分为"词语文字""语素文字""音节文字"和"音位文字"(辅音音位文字和全音位文字)。此外,还有从发生学的角度所做的划分,可以分为"自源文字"和"他源文字"。

第一种分类实际上是对人类文字所做的一个最为通用的分类,世界上的文字大体都可以纳入这种分类中的某一类,即"表音文字""表意文字"或"意音文字"。我们知道语言是一个分层的装置,而表音文字和表意文字实质分别对应于这个装置的下层和上层,具体而言是下层的一套音位和上层的音义结合的符号和符号的序列,包括语素、词和句子。

我们通常所说到的"表意文字"指的是通过符号的组合来表达词或语素的意义,而符号不表音或与声音没有直接的关系。汉字就是典型的表意文字,又称为"表词文字""词语文字"。它是从最初的记事图画、符号演变而成为相对简化的图形符号,并和语言中的词有了固定的对应关系。迄今为止,我国最早的成系统的文字体系是甲骨文,甲骨文的字形所体现的就是记事图画、符号经过演变而形成的结果。事实上,我们所熟悉的美索不达米亚的苏美尔楔形文字、古埃及的圣书文字以及中美洲的玛雅文字,这些古代文字同我国古代的文字一样都是表词文字、词语文字。

表 1　甲骨文

注:选自徐中舒《甲骨文字典》

表 2　楔形文字的演变

| 意义 | 早期图形字 | 楔形文字中的象形字 | 早期巴比伦文字 | 亚述文字 |
|---|---|---|---|---|
| 日 | | | | |
| 鸟 | | | | |
| 公牛 | | | | |
| 鱼 | | | | |
| 站、往 | | | | |
| 谷 | | | | |

注:选自令狐若明《世界上古史》、崔连仲《世界史古代史》

　　在这些古老的文字中可以看到一个共同的特点,即使用表形、表音、表意三种方法。表形法即直接描绘词语所代表的事物,以甲骨文中的文字来看,上面表 1 中所列举的文字都是对相应事物直接的刻画,"目"是眼睛的样子,包括眼球和眼睑;"鱼"是一条完整的鱼的样子,有鱼的头、身、尾,甚至包括鱼鳍和鱼鳞;"雨"是天空降雨滴落的样子。而表意法是以间接的方式进行描绘表意,例如甲骨文中表示"上""下"含义的字分别为"⌒"

223

"⌒",是在一长弧线的上下分别添加一个短横符号加以指事;"刃"的甲骨文写作"◁",是在"刀"的表形符号即表示刀刃的位置上增加一个短横,指事这是刀刃的意思;而表示"女子生育孩子"这个意思则要通过图形符号间接来表示,甲骨文的"⺋"这个字符就表示了这个概念;而上下台阶的意思则通过"⻖(陟)""⻖(降)"这样的形象符号进行会意表达,"陟"的甲骨文是通过上下两只脚趾朝上的脚攀爬右边的高处,来会意登高;而"降"的上下两只脚,脚趾朝下,表示脚从高处向低处走,来会意下降。表音法是在表形法和表意法无法充分使用的情况下,对语言中的一些现象通过音借的形式来表示。在殷墟甲骨卜辞中我们发现存在大量的借音字,无论是国名、地名还是人名、水名等,都在极大程度上反映了这种语言现象。而我们语言中也有一些典型的例子,古汉语中的一些虚词是无法用图形符号来直接描绘的,因此只能采用借音的方式。甲骨文"⋈"字,是簸箕的象形,是"箕"字的初文,它和语言中作代词、语气词等用的语言单位具有相同的读音。而人们无法对这种虚词进行描绘,于是就将语言中已经存在的有相同读音的字借用过来,作为这个语言单位的符号,因此这时的这个符号"⋈"就纯粹是一个表示读音的表音符号,而与这个符号原本所具有的簸箕意义毫无干涉。再比如甲骨文的"⻳"字,是禽鸟的象形,汉字中从"隹"的字大凡都与鸟禽相关,这个字在甲骨卜辞中被音借作为虚词,表示后来的"维""唯""惟"。汉字中有一种造字方式是形声字,是由表示声音的声符和表示意义的形符结合而成的字,例如"鸡"繁体作"雞",在甲骨文中写作"⻳",其中的"奚"是声符,而"隹"则表示飞禽类含义。"凤"字在甲骨文中有两种表现形式,一种是单纯的象形字,即凤鸟的样子,另一种形式是增加了"凡"字符作为音符,即"⻳",而"凤"为形符表示凤鸟这个含义。"星"的甲骨文写作"⋇",其中的"生"作为声符,而"晶"作为形符表示天上星体。从上面这些分析,我们不难看出,"表形""表意"和"表声"这三种方法,相对于我们的古文字而言,实际上和"六书"具有一致性,其中的表形法本质而言是象形的造字方法,许慎在《说文解字·叙》中对这六种方法(象形、指事、会意、形声、假借、转注,后人称前四者为"造字法",后二者为"用字法")给予了详细的解释,可参见后面的原典阅读,此不赘述。"表意法"又和指事、会意具有一定的对应性,而"表声法"又和形声、假借以及转注具有相关性。

在其他的几种古文字中也同样存在这三种方法,尤其是表形法,埃及象形文字中有和甲骨文相似的文字,例如太阳是一个大圆圈中间有一个小圆圈。古埃及文字中"⻳(猫头鹰)""⇔(嘴)""〰〰〰(水)"等都是描摹实物的图形符号。从表 2 中也可以看到楔形文字中的象形字,也是通过对实物的描绘来表达意义。而在古埃及圣书体文字和苏美尔楔形文字中也通过间接的图示来表达某些词语的意义,例如苏美尔语言中表示"生育"的字是通过一只鸟和一个卵来会意。古埃及圣书体文字在结构性质上是表意同时表音,700 个左右的表意符号中就有 100 个同时表音,表音符号中有单辅音 24 个,其余为复辅音。在这种语言中也存在音借现象,一些抽象的意义在没法形象化的时候,往往还是需要借用已有的读音相同的字符来表示。不难看出,埃及文字中的类似汉字中的"声符"的这部分实际上是从单一的表意文字转化而来的。不同的词可以使用相同的表音符号即辅音拼写,即使用相同的象形文字,要区别意义还需要另外增加定义符,定义符可以起到区别同音字的作用,类似一个形声字中的形符或者意符,这样的定义符在苏美尔楔形文字中也存在。从表 2 中所展示的楔形文字的演变来看,这种文字符号除了有定义符的存在之外,主要包括表意符号和表音符号两种,而到亚述文字的后期已经逐渐演变为音节文字了。

表 3 埃及圣书体中的表音符号

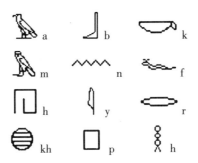

从这三种古老的文字的发展演变来看,表意文字阶段是人类文字发展的必经阶段。这三种古老的文字虽然命名为表意文字,是从文字的大的发展历程来归类的,实际上这些文字中也有表音的符号,汉字也被认为是"意音文字"就是这个道理。这个说法更多的理由在于汉字中有大量的形声字存在,这些字既有表音的部件,也有表意的部件。文字只是语言的一种载体,在文字产生之前语言就已经存在了。而语言符号是所指(概念)和能指(音响形象)的结合体。因此,这三种文字的每一个字符实际都是音义的结合体。从这个意义上来说,这三种古老的文字都可以认为是意音文字。古埃及人已经有了表音的字母,只是当时的人们还没有意识去整理归纳并用于实际的语言中,这些事实都说明了文字发展的总趋势在于使用的经济和便捷。而标音符号的存在正是这三种古老文字符合文字发展演变规律的特征性体现。同时,我们也可以看到,世界上的语言不可能纯粹地属于某种文字类型,要么有所交叉,要么有所侧重。但文字的发展走向总是遵循着表意文字(表词文字)→表音文字(音节文字→音位文字)这个规律,而音位文字被认为是最科学、经济的文字方式。在这个进化过程中,有的语言文字死亡了,例如古埃及文字、苏美尔楔形文字;有的在死亡的文字或者现存的文字的基础上另辟蹊径重新改造,将文字向前推进,例如波斯文字、日文、韩文;有的则始终停滞在某个阶段缓慢行进,例如汉字。

所谓"表音文字"又称为"音符文字",是通过一套符号来拼写语言中的词语、句子,并记录语言的声音。以记录的语言单位的不同可以分为"音节文字"和"音位文字"。"音节文字"是指一个文字符号表示一个音节,音节也是最小的书写单位。最典型的语言代表是日语中的假名(假名是对汉字的偏旁加以改造而形成的书写符号,包括片假名和平假名,草书体的叫平假名,楷书体的叫片假名),每一个假名代表一个确定的音节,不同的音节用不同的假名表示。日语的五十音图中除去三个重复的字和音之外,一共有四十七个字和四十四个音节。

表4　五十音图

| 段<br>行 | あ段 | | | い段 | | | う段 | | | え段 | | | お段 | | |
|---|---|---|---|---|---|---|---|---|---|---|---|---|---|---|---|
| | 平 | 片 | 音 | 平 | 片 | 音 | 平 | 片 | 音 | 平 | 片 | 音 | 平 | 片 | 音 |
| あ行 | あ | ア | a | い | イ | i | う | ウ | u | え | エ | e | お | オ | o |
| か行 | か | カ | ka | き | キ | ki | く | ク | ku | け | ケ | ke | こ | コ | ko |
| さ行 | さ | サ | sa | し | シ | shi | す | ス | su | せ | セ | se | そ | ソ | so |
| た行 | た | タ | ta | ち | チ | chi/ti | つ | ツ | tsu/tu | て | テ | te | と | ト | to |
| な行 | な | ナ | na | に | ニ | ni | ぬ | ヌ | nu | ね | ネ | ne | の | ノ | no |
| は行 | は | ハ | ha | ひ | ヒ | hi | ふ | フ | fu/hu | へ | ヘ | he | ほ | ホ | ho |
| ま行 | ま | マ | ma | み | ミ | mi | む | ム | mu | め | メ | me | も | モ | mo |
| や行 | や | ヤ | ya | (い | イ) | i | ゆ | ユ | yu | (え | エ) | e | よ | ヨ | yo |
| ら行 | ら | ラ | ra | り | リ | ri | る | ル | ru | れ | レ | re | ろ | ロ | ro |
| わ行 | わ | ワ | wa | (い | イ) | i | (う | ウ) | u | (え | エ) | e | (お | オ) | o |

书写符号如果表示音节,就可以使用较少的文字符号来记录语言,真正意义上的音节文字除了上面说到的日语中的假名之外,还有亚述-巴比伦文字、塞浦路斯文字、埃塞俄比亚文字等。

"音位文字"又叫"拼音文字""音素文字",是指文字符号以字母的形式表现出来。人类最早的拼音文字是居住在美索不达米亚和埃及之间的闪米特人(即腓尼基人)创造的,这种文字所创造的字母是我们今天所使用的字母的雏形。闪米特人是一个从商的民族,他们没有自己的文字,只好借用古埃及文字和苏美尔楔形文字。但这种借用的主要目的是用来记账,而古埃及文字和苏美尔楔形文字的繁杂并不能满足他们的需求。于是在经商过程中开始对古埃及文字进行整理改造,最终摆脱了古埃及文字中的冗杂的意符、定义符等的束缚,将图形符号简化,形成了以记音为主,便于书写记忆和识别的22个辅音文字符号(实际每个辅音都隐含一个元音a),即腓尼基字母。

目前世界上绝大多数语言都采用字母的方式进行记录,它包括元音和辅音,以辅音音位的方式表现的称为辅音音位文字,以元音音位同辅音音位相结合的方式表现的称为全音位文字。从音位本身的特点来看,"音位文字"所涉及的字母数量相对较少,对于学习和记忆都有帮助。无论是希腊字母、拉丁字母、斯拉夫字母,还是阿拉伯字母都是从古代的腓尼基字母发展演变而来的,而英语、俄语、德语、法语等使用了这些字母,是音位文字,严格说是全音位文字。阿拉伯文字体系被认为是一种辅音音位文字,阿拉伯文字字符表示该语言中的辅音音位,而没有元音的字符。

最后要提到的是从发生学的角度分析的文字类型,包括自源文字和他源文字(或借源文字)两种类型。自源文字是指本民族人民自己创制的文字,是一种本土生长发展的文字。例如我们前面所提到的世界上的古老的文字:古埃及圣书体、我国的甲骨文、古楔形文字,这些表词文字都属于自源文字。他源文字是指一个民族通过借用、模仿改造其他民族已有的文字来创制的文字。这种类型的文字很多,前面所说到的大多数的表音文字都是他源文字,无论是借用表音文字的表音符号而形成的腓尼基字母,还是由它所分化出来的各种字母文字都是他源文字。

## 二、字母的产生和发展

作为拼音文字始祖的腓尼基文字,由于其字母的简便,而且只有辅音字母,因此很快就向周边流传,所到之处便结合当地语言特点改造成当地字母。腓尼基字母的传播大致分为东西两向,向东传播形成阿拉米字母系统,向西传播形成迦南字母系统、希腊拉丁字母系统。

表5 腓尼基字母

西传的迦南字母现在已经不为人用,成为化石古文字。大约在公元前11世纪,希腊人借用腓尼基字母,对这些字母加以整改形成了形体更加简明、匀称,便于书写的24个希腊字母,最重要的是增加了元音字母,使希腊字符能够完整地记录音位,成为全音位文字。

表6 希腊字母表

| α | β | γ | δ | ε | ζ | η | θ | ι | κ | λ | μ | ν | ξ | ο | π | ρ | σ | τ | υ | φ | χ | ψ | ω |
|---|---|---|---|---|---|---|---|---|---|---|---|---|---|---|---|---|---|---|---|---|---|---|---|
| A | B | Γ | Δ | E | Z | H | Θ | I | K | Λ | M | N | Ξ | O | Π | P | Σ | T | Y | Φ | X | Ψ | Ω |

公元前7世纪,罗马人从厄特鲁斯根字母(采自希腊字母)中选取了其中的21个字母,发展成为拉丁字母,即罗马字母。从形体来看,罗马字母简便易于书写,字体匀称美观,后来又增加了"I""U""W""Z""Y"这五个字母,最终形成了今天完整的26个字母,

并成为世界上最通行的字母。世界上很多国家都使用了拉丁字母,包括西欧、美洲、澳洲和非洲的大部分民族,东欧(波兰、捷克斯洛伐克、匈牙利、立陶宛、罗马尼亚、爱沙尼亚、阿尔巴尼亚等)以及亚洲的一些地区(印度尼西亚、马来西亚、菲律宾、越南、土耳其等)。新中国成立之初所指定的汉语拼音方案也使用了拉丁字母,甚至我国某些少数民族也是以此作为基础创造了自己的文字。

表7 罗马字母表

| a | b | c | d | e | f | g | h | i | j | k | l | m | n | o | p | q | r | s | t | u | v | w | x | y | z |
|---|---|---|---|---|---|---|---|---|---|---|---|---|---|---|---|---|---|---|---|---|---|---|---|---|---|
| A | B | C | D | E | F | G | H | I | J | K | L | M | N | O | P | Q | R | S | T | U | V | W | X | Y | Z |

公元前9世纪,基督教拜占庭教会正教传教士基立尔根据希腊字母并结合斯拉夫语言的语音创制了43个字母,因此又被称作"基立尔字母"。十月革命之前一直是东欧信奉正教的各斯拉夫民族所使用的字母,在革命之后它被扩大传播,成为苏联境内外大多数民族所使用的字母,例如俄罗斯、保加利亚、蒙古、南斯拉夫等。基立尔还创制了一种叫"格拉戈尔"的字母,这种字母也是以希腊字母为母本,一共40个字母,形体多体现为方形、三角形和圆形等几何图,在书写上不如基立尔字母便捷,但字母的名称和排列顺序与基立尔相同,基立尔字母书写上的简便使得它最终取代了格拉戈尔字母。现代所使用的基立尔字母,都是经历了多次修改,一些不必要的字母最终被去除了,因此现在的俄语和乌克兰语有33个字母,而保加利亚和塞尔维亚语只有30个字母。

表8 俄文字母表

| а | б | в | г | д | е | ё | ж | з | и | й | к | л | м | н | о |
|---|---|---|---|---|---|---|---|---|---|---|---|---|---|---|---|
| А | Б | В | Г | Д | Е | Ё | Ж | З | И | Й | К | Л | М | Н | О |
| п | р | с | т | у | ф | х | ц | ч | ш | щ | ъ | ы | ь | э | ю | я |
| П | Р | С | Т | У | Ф | Х | Ц | Ч | Ш | Щ | Ъ | Ы | Ь | Э | Ю | Я |

腓尼基字母东传的支系形成了阿拉米字母系统,阿拉米字母大约形成于公元前8世纪,在随后的几个世纪中它一直在所传区域占据主导地位。这些区域曾经一度是楔形文字盛行的地方,直到波斯帝国的瓦解,它开始分化派生出不同的支系,例如希伯来人以阿拉米字母为基础,形成了希伯来方块字,另外还有古波斯字母、叙利亚字母、那巴特字母、印地文字母等,从印度字母又演变出了藏文、缅甸文、傣文等字母,而蒙古文、满文等则是从叙利亚字母演变而来的。那巴特人曾经居住在阿拉伯地区,他们用阿拉米字母来记录自己的语言,后来形成了阿拉伯字母。阿拉伯字母的流传很广泛,遍及欧亚非三洲,例如埃及、伊拉克、约旦、也门、阿富汗等国家都使用阿拉伯字母书写自己的语言。阿拉伯字母是仅次于拉丁字母的最广泛通用的字母。这种字母共有28个,这28个字母只表示辅音,后来用其中的三个字母alif(ا)、waw(و)、ya(ﻱ)来兼表长元音a、i、u,有的元音通过加

诸如点或横这样的附加符号来表示,如此一来,辅音字母也被迫使用附加符号来进行区别,因此,就形成了阿拉伯字母的一种特殊现象,即一个字母在行文中的形式会因为独立使用或在词首、尾部、中部而有所不同,使得阿拉伯文字书写出来的效果显得有点斑驳凌乱。

表9　阿拉伯母表

| alif | | | | ba | | | | ha | | | | sin | | | | waw | | | |
|---|---|---|---|---|---|---|---|---|---|---|---|---|---|---|---|---|---|---|---|
| 独用 | 词首 | 中间 | 尾部 | 独用 | 词首 | 中间 | 尾部 | 独用 | 词首 | 中间 | 尾部 | 独用 | 词首 | 中间 | 尾部 | 独用 | 词首 | 中间 | 尾部 |
| ا | ا | ا | ا | ب | بـ | ـبـ | ـب | ح | حـ | ـحـ | ـح | س | سـ | ـسـ | ـس | ي | وـ | ـوـ | ـو |

古印度早期的文字有两种,一种是佉卢文(Kharoshthi),来源于阿拉米字母系统,另外一种被称为"婆罗米字母(Brahmi)",有的学者认为这种字母也属于阿拉米字母体系统,它的书写形式与阿拉米相同,而早期的字母与阿拉米字母也有很大的相同、相似性,但元音不完善。这种字母形成之后的两千年间不断分化改造,到公元前四五世纪的笈多王朝时期出现了笈多文字,从而分化出悉达字母,而这种字母则演变成了天成体字母——一种曾经被用来拼写过梵语的字母。现在的印地文字母、藏文字母等都和天体字母有渊源。

# 第三节　文字的应用

清代学者陈澧在其《东塾读书记》卷十一中这样论述道:"声不能传于异时,于是乎之为文字。文字者,所以为意与声之迹也。"这段话说明了语言和文字的关系,并且说明了语言和文字谁是第一性,谁是第二性。世界上的文字无论数量有多少,使用有多广泛,也仅仅是作为语言的一个载体和工具。正如亚里士多德在《解释篇》中所说的:"口语是心灵的经验的符号,而文字则是口语的符号。"语言是先于文字而产生的,而文字是在有声语言产生之后随着人们社会生活需求才逐渐产生的。

文字既然是作为社会的需求而产生,必然有其重要的使用功能。从文字产生的缘由上我们不难看出。在人类社会早期,人与人、人与社会的交流来往是通过口耳相传的形式进行的。而这种方式有其利也有其弊,弊就在于声音是转瞬即逝的物质,而且人的听觉和记忆功能也并非一直处于最佳状态。当人听觉下降时,也可能因为声音产生的环境不适,比如环境嘈杂或者远距离交谈,甚至是陈澧所谓的"传于异地,留于异时",例如唐朝人说的话,宋朝的人是无法听见的,于是口耳相传有时达不到接受有效声讯的目的;另外从科学的角度来看,人脑的记忆功能会随着年龄的增长而逐渐衰退,因此常常有忘记、记不清楚的时候。而文字的出现就弥补了语言交流上的这些弊端,成为记录语言和书写语言的符号系统。世界上的任何一种文字都是适应了它所记录的语言的结构和语音等特点的产物。

文字给人类带来的巨大方便表现在很多方面,有历史的层面,也有现实的层面。历史的层面是我们今天能通晓我们祖先的各种精神财富,继承并开创更好的思想成果和发明。我们能借这些以文字书写的纸质文献了解当时的社会、生活、政治、经济、文化等方方面面的情况,以史为鉴,古为今用。现实的层面,文字的功用越来越显著,世界的大融合、国际化、语言的沟通往来显得尤为重要,而文字在这当中成为不可或缺的重要工具。除了原本应有的文字记录之外,越来越多的思想交流都开始以文字来记载并加以传播。当下的互联网络对于文字的依赖程度远远超越了非网络的时代,人们书信来往、聊天、写博客、记录和发布新闻、打广告等等,无不与文字打交道。

计算语言学作为语言学和计算机相结合的交叉学科,在语言学研究中越来越受到重视。文字对于计算机的开发是基础性的工作,如何能将文字在计算机中输出,这里就涉及文字与代码的转化问题。中英文信息处理中的文字的编码最终以 Unicode 的统一编码进行处理,汉字的编码问题一直都是计算语言学专家们所关注的。汉字有自身的特点,汉字中除了常用字还有非常用字,这些非常用字是一些出现在古籍文献中的偏僻字。对于语言研究的人们来说,这是非常重要的,而汉字又存在一音多形的情况,同一个汉字也可能存在不同的写法,如何能实现这些汉字的准确输出,涉及字和码的关系问题,而一字多码即重码问题也是重要的问题。针对不同语言文字的输入法已经开发并得以广泛应用,因此能很快利用不同文字的输入法输出不同语言的文字来。就汉字的输入法来看,比较常用的有拼音输入法、五笔输入法、语音输入法,都是结合汉字自身特点而开发的,例如对声韵调、笔画笔顺偏旁部件所进行的分析。汉字的繁体-简体转化的问题也得到了很好的处理,不仅有专门的软件,而且在输入法中也实现了繁体输入与简体输入的切换。

在信息化的社会中,资讯每天都如潮水一样涌来,如何在海量的资讯中迅速获取有效的资源,除了要有敏锐的头脑和眼光之外,还需要资讯本身具有独特性。在视听广告中对于文字的利用和处理成为广告行业的一个重要技术。谐音作为一种重要的文字应用方式,在越来越多的翻译名、广告中出现了,例如"Goldlion"的翻译采用了"金利来"这三个汉字,有财源不断的含义在里面;"胃,你好吗?"(斯达舒广告语),"胃"与"喂"音同相谐,又妙用了日常生活的招呼语。像这样的例子不胜枚举,既能吸引人们的视听,又能让人们长久不忘。大量的艺术字展示在生活中,装点着环境同时又吸引着人们的眼球,而且电脑中的字库也有不同的风格形式。英文字符有不同的体例,例如 Times New Roman。宋体、楷体、隶书、行书、魏碑体、琥珀体、姚体、彩云体、小篆等等,这些形体实际上源自我们古人所创造的书法体例,古奥的甲骨文、金文已经不再只是博物馆的陈列品和专家的研究对象,在日常的生活中,我们可以看到甲骨文、金文作为装饰体出现在家居物品、广告字幕上。篆书、隶书、草书、行书作为书法艺术也深得人们的喜爱,尤其是草书,更多的是一种欣赏作品,由于它的笔画随意张狂,是书写者性情张扬的一种方式,而不便于作为语言信息交流的文字。

文字既要应用,同时也要进行必要的规范,文字的规范是对文字的形、音、义、书写、印刷等进行合理而有效的规范,使得文字的应用更加符合文字发展规律,符合社会生活的实际需要。自文字产生以来,文字的规范行为基本是以官方的形式进行,无论是字母文字还是表词文字,都在不断地进行规范整理,其中最常见的是异体字的规范整理,异体字是音义相同而书写形式不同的字。这种字在字母文字和表词文字中都普遍存在,是文字发展过程中必然会产生的一种现象。例如英语中的 colour 与 color、older 与 elder 等等,而汉语中的这种情况就更多了,历朝历代都有对文字进行规范而形成的字书,例如《说文解字》《玉篇》《字汇》《康熙字典》,在新中国成立之后也进行了异体字的整理,制定了相关的《异体字表》,例如 1955 年发布了《第一批异体字整理表》,1956 年拟定了《第二批异体字整理表草案(初稿)》,1959 年拟定了《异体字整理表(初稿)》,1964 年拟定了《异体字整理总表》第一、二、三批字组,1965 年拟定出第四、五批字组,1986 年重新发布了《异体字整理总表》。文字还有简化的问题,世界上各种文字在发展过程中总的趋势是趋于简化,字母文字从产生之初到现在的形态已经经历了不断地整理和简化,表词文字也是如此。以汉字为例,汉字的简化问题不是一个近现代才存在的问题,而是在整个汉字的发展过程中一直进行着,汉字的形体经历了甲骨文—金文—篆书—隶书—楷书—草书—行书的演变。每一种形体内部都存在字体的繁简形式,同一个字既有繁复的写法,也有简单的写法。近代一些仁人志士提倡简化汉字,1935 年钱玄同完成了《简体字谱》,同年国民政府发布了《第一批简体字表》。新中国成立之后,于 1956 年公布了《汉字简化方案》,1962 年发布了《简化字总表》,1977 年公布了《第二次简化方案(草案)》,1986 年重新发布《简化字总表》。到目前为止,除港澳台等地区还在使用繁体字外,汉字简化字已经在全球通行,甚至东南亚一带的国家也采用简化汉字。关于文字的规范和整理方面还涉及字音、字义等多方面,不同的民族国家对本民族的文字的读音都会根据自身的语言发展等特点加以统一和调整。英语虽为世界通用语之一,但它会与当地的语言习惯相结合,而形成具有国家特色的口音,例如英式英语和美式英语。由于文字涉及多音多义、一音多义等问题,在文字应用时这些都是需要注意和规范的。

# 第四节 书面语

口语同书面语是相对而出的概念。前面我们提到过,人类在创造出图画、文字之前,是通过口耳相传来进行社会生产活动交流的,语音形态成为语言的表现方式,即口语成为语言的重要载体,所形成的是一种听说符号系统。自从文字被创造出来之后,人们的社会交流活动开始有了文字的记录,而这种记录是以文字符号进行书写的,从而形成一种视觉符号系统。书面语是在口语的基础上产生的,是对口语的进一步加工整理而形成的,而文字是体现书面语的物质形式,因此,口语是第一性的,书面语是第二性的。简单地说,书面语是用来看的,口语是用来说和听的,前者是书面上使用的以文字作为载体的词汇、语法系统,后者是口头上使用的一套相应于书面语的系统。严格地说,书面语是在口语的基础上经过加工整理规范的语言形式,不是所有语言都有书面语,但所有的语言都有口语。因此,书面语和口语是因语言交际环境和场合的不同而形成的同一种语言的不同变体。

口语的表达往往会有很多综合因素的参与。首先是听觉,听和说是不可或缺的,在说的同时人耳也在听,听到之后通过大脑神经的传输就会马上作出说的回应。说话是在一定的语境中进行的,可以带有一定的语气语调甚至口头禅,也会伴有一定的肢体表情的运动。这些肢体语言一方面会强调口语的内容,另一方面也可以省略需要用口语说出来的内容,比如有些动作是显而易见的,沮丧的面容代表悲伤、情绪低落,摆手表示不同意,等等。在口语表达中随意性很强,说话的方式不拘一格,如果在说话进行当中,另有人参与进来,很大可能不会马上明白双方交流的目的所在。在说话过程中,谈话者可以重复表达自己的观点,听话者也可以重复问对方某个没有听清楚或听明白的问题。因此,作为口语来说,它所具有的特点也就很明显了,口语表达可以达到生动活泼、感染力强的效果,口语省略句多、完整句子少,而短句、断句多,可以随意停顿,任意插入其他话题,连贯性不强,可以重复、修改、强调。而书面语则是以文字形式书写在介质上,可以记录下谈话人的谈话内容,也可以记录下书写人想要表达的内容。书写者可以单独进行书写记录,不需要交际双方同时出现,对语言的表述方式可以进行规范化,例如语法结构,可以对表达的词句进行思考斟酌,推敲修正,使表达连贯而清晰明确,因此长句、完整句比较多,也可以选择不同的文体风格。在没有录音设备的时代,文字成为突破时空界限的有效的保存信息的重要物质材料。书面语相对于口语来说,能更好地避免因为口语而产生的一些歧义现象,例如汉语中有很多同音字词,在口语表达中会因为音同而产生歧义。

从口语的特点可以看出,它比书面语更灵活,是一个开放系统,而书面语是一个相对保守的系统。又因为口语是第一性的,因此口语的发展演变必然会带动书面语的发展演变。通常而论,口语和书面语在一般情况下基本的语言成分是一致的,因此书面语和口语的一致性比较强(这一点尤其体现在拼音文字语言中),但有时候这种一致性也会出现失衡,例如我国古代的文言文是书面语,起初是和口语较接近的,但口语的流动性很强,于是口语发展迅速,以至于书面语和口语脱离了。后来产生了白话文书面语这种形式,即白话文,清末兴起了"白话文运动"以推动白话这种新的书面语取代文言文,直到新中国成立后才彻底取代了文言文,从此白话文真正成为汉民族的书面语。同理,这种"言、文"失衡现象还出现在拉丁语与口语的脱节上。

口语和书面语虽然是两个不同的系统,但是它们却是相辅相成、互相影响、相得益彰的。作为第一性的口语会不断涌现出新词新语现象,也会从书面语中借鉴吸收词句,从而使口语变得更加规范化,而书面语同时也会受到口语的影响,不断吸收口语中的新词新语,从而完善自己。

我们常常还会听到"文学语言"的说法,但不能狭义地理解为"文学作品的语言"。"文学语言"是书面语言的一种高级形式,有学者称之为"标准语",它是指经过专家学者等的加工整理和语音、词汇、语法以及文字等各方面规范化之后的书面语。它包括报纸杂志、学术论著、自然社会科学报告以及文学作品、剧本等所用的书面语言。此外,还包括广播影视戏剧作品中的人物对白、台词等。文学语言既然是书面语的一种高级形式,必然也具有书面语的所有特点,但和书面语比较而言更加严密规范,它能为民族共同语提供规范参照标准,促进民族共同语的发展,促进地域、民族间的交流。

文学语言包括视觉系统语言和听说系统语言,以书面形式表现的是视觉系统语言,以口头形式表现的是听说系统语言。演员在戏中说出来的话只是将书面形式转化为口语形式表现出来,而这些话来自剧本,是经过加工整理规范了的书面语言、文学语言。演讲者在台上说的话,是经过事前的纸稿准备,熟记在心中或者按照纸稿念读,也是一种文学语言。值得注意的是书面语是可以通过口头形式表达的。

文学语言同样是以口语作为基础,口语的发展演变会影响文学语言,为文学语言提供基本的语言素材,而文学语言对口语和书面语也有规范、引导作用。文学语言的使用范围会受到一定的时代和社会的约束限制,当文学语言被一定的阶级政权掌握,就成为服务于他们的语言。真正的文学语言是同人民大众的口语相结合,服务于全民社会,是一种民族共同语的规范化形式。日本、朝鲜等周边曾经没有文字的国家就借用过我国古代的文学语言。

# 第五节 文字的创造与变革

## 一、文字的创造

关于文字的创造，我们可以分两个方面来看，一是历史上各种文字的创造过程；二是在现代社会中为没有文字的语言创造文字。历史上的文字的创造在前面的内容中大致提到了，这里再做些简要的梳理。

从历史层面看，世界上最古老的三种文字都产生在大河流域。大约在公元前 3200 年，两河流域（幼发拉底河和底格里斯河一带）产生了古苏美尔文字；在公元前 4000 年尼罗河下游的三角洲地区产生了古埃及文字，最晚产生的文字是中国殷商时期的甲骨文，大约在公元前 1300 多年。但据文献考古资料来看，在夏代已经有文字的产生，因此中国最早的古文字的产生应该再往前推。这三种文字在创造的时候所使用的工具是不同的，早期的楔形文字是图形符号，这一点可以参看前面的表 2，后来由于压写的不便，图形符号的线条开始逐渐变换为钉子头形状的笔画。苏美尔的楔形文字以小木棍和泥板为写字的材质，用木棍的一头在泥板上压出钉子头形状的笔画，从而构架起文字。从开始的从上往下的书写方向变为后来的从左到右的书写方向，文字也随之旋转了一个直角，变成横卧式。埃及的圣书体刻写在石碑、墙体上，文字流畅，书写方式多样，由左到右、由右到左、由上到下、由两侧向中间，如果说圣书体是正体字，那么与之相应的还有僧侣体，后来还有大众体，僧侣体和大众体相当于俗体字，字形符号化，书写方式从右到左。中国的甲骨文是用器具契刻在龟甲兽骨上的文字，为了契刻的方便，往往采取先直笔后横笔的刻法，由上向下书写，卜辞的行款通常是左边行刻往右读，右边行刻往左读。字母文字的创制可参见第二节内容，此从略。

从现实层面来看，世界上有相当数量的语言是没有文字的，我国一些少数民族就是如此，因此通过借用等方式可以为这些没有文字的语言创制出自己的文字。20 世纪 50

年代以来,我国语言学家在少数民族聚居的地方,例如云南、贵州、广西、宁夏等地,进行广泛的调查,了解少数民族语言的特点,包括语音、词汇、语法,结合其分布情况,为纳西族、傈僳族、景颇族、傣族、白族、苗族、彝族、布依族、哈尼族、侗族、壮族、佤族、黎族、土家族等少数民族创制了自己的文字,并有效地开展双语教学,帮助当地少数民族群众学习和掌握新创的民族文字。文字的创制要遵循自愿必要的原则,文字是语言的载体,以文字的方式进行交流可以避免因口语而产生的误解,而对于一些人口多的民族来说,文字的创制更加有必要,有利于社会文化生活的交流,能将少数民族语言以文字的形式加以保留,也为以后的语言研究提供了依据。从创制的文字来看,除了本身就借用其他民族文字的以外,应该顺应文字发展的规律,尽可能地以方便简洁的字母进行设计,既方便本民族的语言交流,也方便了与其他民族的语言交流。

## 二、文字的变革

文字具有相对的稳定性和独立性,受诸多条件的约束,包括社会的分化和统一、方言的分歧、文化历史传统甚至书写的工具和材料等,文字的书写形式一旦形成之后就不会轻易地发生改变。我们常常会发现一些有趣的现象,《诗经》原本是押韵的诗歌,为何到了今天的人来读却不再押韵了呢,而文字依然是文字,也是古今通用的,其中的原因就在于文字的语音在漫长的社会历史发展长河中不断地发生着变化,以至于古音非今音。为此人们还总结了语音的变化规律,例如"古无轻唇音""古无舌上音""娘日归泥""照系二等归精系""喻三归匣""喻四归定"等来重新拟定上古某个字的真实读音。这种书写形式和语音不一致,在英语中也可以见到,英语的"light""right""sight",实际的发音应该为[lait][rait][sait],其中的"-gh-"是不发音的,这同样是因为语音在历史发展中发生了变化。英语的这些书写形式从15世纪以来就没有发生变化,但在那个时候"gh"是要发作舌根擦音的,但在英语语音的发展中,这个音逐渐消失了,只是在书写形式中依然还保留着"-gh-"。针对英语中的这种情况,对学习和使用造成了一定的困难,于是有人提出了改革拼写法的倡议。而对于表意形态的汉字而言,和拼音文字相比显得更难学习、记忆和书写,为此也有人讨论汉字转变为拼音文字的问题。

我国的汉字改革早在辛亥革命前后就已经被提出了,当时的人们积极地创制各种拼音方案,其中的"注音字母"试图改变汉字反切注音形态,而赵元任先生等人制定的"国语罗马字",是第一次用拉丁字母拼写汉字。新中国成立之后,颁布了《汉语拼音方案(草案)》并推行汉语拼音方案,这个方案采用拉丁字母,是一套合理的汉字注音工具。汉字之所以长期处于意音文字阶段,和汉语自身的特点分不开,至少到现阶段,汉字的这种"形-音-义"三位一体的状态是和汉语的特征相适应的。尽管如此,前面所提到的日语的片假名、朝鲜的谚文以及越南的喃字却都是借用汉字的形体、偏旁部首笔画来创造出了自己的表音文字,可见,汉字对其他民族的拼音文字的创制起过作用。

## 思考与练习

一、名词解释

1.文字

2.实物记事

3.表意文字

4.表音文字

5.自源文字

6.他源文字

7.六书

二、填空

1.按照文字的字符与语言中的何种语言单位相联系来划分文字,可以分为(　　　)、(　　　　　)、(　　　　)、(　　　　　)。

2.文字发展走向总要遵循的规律是(　　　　　　　　　　　　　)。

3.腓尼基字母的传播大致分为东西两向系统,向东(　　　　　),向西(　　　　　)。

三、简答题

1.图画记事和文字有何关系?

2.简述表音文字和表意文字的区别和联系,并举例说明。

3.简述字母的产生和发展,并举例说明。

4.谈谈社会生活中所存在的文字应用,并举例说明。

5.什么是口语,什么是书面语,二者有何区别和联系,它们同文学语言有何关系?

6.谈谈你对汉字拼音化问题的看法。

# 【原典阅读】

## 1.说文解字·第十五（叙）

### 许 慎

古者庖羲氏之王天下也，仰则观象于天，俯则观法于地，视鸟兽之文与地之宜，近取诸身，远取诸物，于是始作《易》八卦，以垂宪象。及神农氏结绳为治而统其事，庶业其繁，饰伪萌生。黄帝史官仓颉，见鸟兽蹄迒之迹，知分理之可相别异也，初造书契。百工以乂，万品以察，盖取诸夬。"夬，扬于王庭"，言文者宣教明化于王者朝庭，君子所以施禄及下，居德则忌也。

仓颉之初作书也，盖依类象形，故谓之文；其后形声相益，即谓之字。文者，物象之本；字者，言孳乳而浸多也。箸于竹帛谓之书。书者，如也。以迄五帝三王之世，改易殊体，封于泰山者，七十有二代，靡有同焉。

《周礼》：八岁入小学，保氏教国子，先以六书。一曰指事。指事者，视而可识，察而见意，上、下是也。二曰象形。象形者，画成其物，随体诘诎，日、月是也。三曰形声。形声者，以事为名，取譬相成，江、河是也。四曰会意。会意者，比类合谊，以见指撝，武、信是也。五曰转注。转注者，建类一首，同意相受，考、老是也。六曰假借。假借者，本无其事，依声讬事，令、长是也。

及宣王太史籀，著大篆十五篇，与古文或异。至孔子书六经，左丘明述《春秋传》，皆以古文，厥意可得而说。

其后诸侯力政，不统于王。恶礼乐之害己，而皆去其典籍，分为七国，田畴异亩，车涂异轨，律令异法，衣冠异制，言语异声，文字异形。

秦始皇帝初兼天下，丞相李斯乃奏同之，罢其不与秦文合者。斯作《仓颉篇》，中车府令赵高作《爰历篇》，太史令胡毋敬作《博学篇》。皆取史籀大篆，或颇省改，所谓小篆也。

是时，秦烧灭经书，涤除旧典。大发吏卒，兴戍役。官狱职务繁，初有隶书，以趣约易，而古文由此绝矣。自尔秦书有八体：一曰大篆，二曰小篆，三曰刻符，四曰虫书，五曰摹印，六曰署书，七曰殳书，八曰隶书。

汉兴，有草书。尉律：学僮十七以上始试。讽籀书九千字，乃得为史。又以八体试之。郡移太史并课。最者以为尚书史。书或不正，辄举劾之。今虽有尉律，不课，小学不修，莫达其说久矣。

孝宣皇帝时，召通《仓颉》读者，张敞从受之。凉州刺史杜业，沛人爰礼，讲学大夫秦近，亦能言之。孝平皇帝时，征礼等百余人，令说文字未央廷中，以礼为小学元士。黄门侍郎扬雄，采以作《训纂篇》。凡《仓颉》以下十四篇，凡五千三百四十字，群书所载，略存之矣。

及亡新居摄，使大司空甄丰等校文书之部。自以为应制作，颇改定古文。时有六书：一曰古文，孔子壁中书也。二曰奇字，即古文而异也。三曰篆书，即小篆。秦始皇帝使下杜人程邈所作也。四曰左书，即秦隶书。五曰缪篆，所以摹印也。六曰鸟虫书，所以书幡信也。

壁中书者,鲁恭王坏孔子宅,而得《礼记》《尚书》《春秋》《论语》《孝经》。又北平侯张苍献《春秋左氏传》。郡国亦往往于山川得鼎彝,其铭即前代之古文,皆自相似。虽叵复见远流,其详可得略说也。

而世人大共非訾,以为好奇者也,故诡更正文,乡壁虚造不可知之书,变乱常行,以耀于世。诸生竞逐说字解经谊,称秦之隶书为仓颉时书,云:"父子相传,何得改易。"乃猥曰:"马头人为长,人持十为斗,虫者,屈中也。"廷尉说律,至以字断法:"苛人受钱,苛之字止句也。"若此者甚众,皆不合孔氏古文,谬于《史籀》。

俗儒鄙夫,翫其所习,蔽所希闻。不见通学,未尝覩字例之条。怪旧执而善野言,以其所知为祕妙,究洞圣人之微恉。又见《仓颉篇》中"幼子承诏",因曰:"古帝之所作也,其辞有神僊之术焉。"其迷误不谕,岂不悖哉!

《书》曰:"予欲观古人之象。"言必遵修旧文而不穿凿。孔子曰:"吾犹及史之阙文,今亡矣夫。"盖非其不知而不问。人用己私,是非无正,巧说邪辞,使天下学者疑。

盖文字者,经艺之本,王政之始。前人所以垂后,后人所以识古。故曰:"本立而道生。""知天下之至啧而不可乱也。"

今叙篆文,合以古籀,博采通人,至于小大,信而有证。稽譔其说,将以理群类,解谬误,晓学者,达神恉。分别部居,不相杂厕也。万物咸覩,靡不兼载。厥谊不昭,爰明以喻。其称《易》孟氏、《书》孔氏、《诗》毛氏、《礼》周官、《春秋》左氏、《论语》《孝经》,皆古文也。其于所不知,盖阙如也。

……

此十四篇,五百四十部,九千三百五十三文,重一千一百六十三,解说凡十三万三千四百四十一字。其建首也,立一为耑。方以类聚,物以群分。同牵属条,共理相贯。杂而不越,据形系联。引而申之,以究万原。毕终于亥,知化穷冥。

于时大汉,圣德熙明,承天稽唐,敷崇殷中。遐迩被泽,渥衍沛滂。广业甄微,学士知方。探啧索隐,厥谊可传。

粤在永元,困顿之年。孟陬之月,朔日甲申。曾曾小子,祖自炎神。缙云相黄,共承高辛。太岳佐夏,吕叔作藩。俾侯于许,世祚遗灵。自彼徂召,宅此汝濒。窃卬景行,敢涉圣门,其弘如何,节彼南山。欲罢不能,既竭愚才。惜道之味,闻疑载疑。演赞其志,次列微辞。知此者稀,傥昭所尤,庶有达者,理而董之。

(选自清·段玉裁《说文解字注》,上海古籍出版社,1981)

# 2.Representation of a Language by Writing

## Saussure

§ 1. *Why it is necessary to study this topic*

The actual object we are concerned to study, then, is the social product stored in the brain, the language itself .But this product differs from one linguistic community to another. What we find are languages. The linguist must endeavour to become acquainted with as many languages as possible, in order to be able to discover their universal features by studying and comparing them.

Languages are mostly known to us only through writing. Even in the case of our native language, the written form constantly intrudes. In the case of languages spoken in remote parts, it is even more necessary to have recourse to written evidence. The same is true for obvious reasons in the case of languages now dead. In order to have direct evidence available, it would have been necessary to have compiled throughout history collections of the kind currently being compiled in Vienna and in Paris, comprising recordings of spoken samples of all languages. Even then writing is necessary when it comes to publishing the texts thus recorded.

Thus although writing is in itself not part of the internal system of the language, it is impossible to ignore this way in which the language is constantly represented. We must be aware of its utility, its defects and its dangers.

§ 2. *The prestige of writing: reasons for its ascendancy over the spoken word*

A language and its written form constitute two separate systems of signs. The sole reason for the existence of the latter is to represent the former. The object of study in linguistics is not a combination of the written word and the spoken word. The spoken word alone constitutes that object. But the written word is so intimately connected with the spoken word it represents that it manages to usurp the principal role. As much or even more importance is given to this representation of the vocal sign as to the vocal sign itself. It is rather as if people believed that in order to find out what a person looks like it is better to study his photograph than his face.

This misconception has a long history, and current views about languages are tainted with it. For instance, it is commonly held that a language alters more rapidly when it has no written form. This is quite false. In certain circumstances, writing may well retard changes in a language. But, on the other hand, linguistic stability is in no way undermined by the absence of a written form. The Lithuanian which is still spoken today in Eastern Prussia and part of Russia is attested in written documents only since 1540; but at that late period it presents on the whole as accurate a picture of Proto-Indo-European as Latin of the third century B. C. That in itself suffices to show the extent to which a language is independent of writing.

Certain very subtle linguistic features can long survive without the assistance of written notation. Throughout the Old High German period, we find the written forms *tōten*, *fuolen* and *stōzen*, but at the end of the twelfth century appear the spellings *töten*, *füelen*, whereas *stōzen* persists. What is the origin of this difference? Wherever it occurred, there had been a *y* in the following syllable: Proto-Germanic had *daupyan*, *fōlyan*, but *stautan*. On the eve of the literary period, about 800, this *y* weakened and vanished from writing for three hundred years. However, it had left a slight trace in pronunciation, with the result that about 1180, as noted above, it reappears miraculously in the form of an 'umlaut'! This nuance of pronunciation had been faithfully transmitted without any support in writing.

A language, then, has an oral tradition independent of writing, and much more stable; but the prestige of the written form prevents us from seeing this. The first linguists were misled in this way, as the humanists had been before them. Even Bopp does not distinguish clearly between letters and sounds. Reading Bopp, we might think that a language is inseparable from its alphabet. His immediate successors fell into the same trap. The spelling *th* for the fricative *þ* misled Grimm into believing not only that this was a double consonant, but also that it was an aspirate stop. Hence the place he assigns to it in his Law of Consonantal Mutation or 'Lautverschiebung'. Even nowadays educated people confuse the language with its spelling; Gaston Deschamps said of Berthelot 'that he had saved the French language from ruin' because he had opposed spelling reforms.①

But what explains the prestige of writing?

1. The written form of a word strikes us as a permanent, solid object and hence more fitting than its sound to act as a linguistic unit persisting through time. Although the connexion between word and written form is superficial and establishes a purely artificial unit, it is none the less much easier to grasp than the natural and only authentic connexion, which links word and sound.

2. For most people, visual impressions are clearer and more lasting than auditory impressions. So for preference people cling to the former. The written image in the end takes over from the sound.

3. A literary language enhances even more the unwarranted importance accorded to writing. A literary language has its dictionaries and its grammars. It is taught at school from books and through books. It is a language which appears to be governed by a code, and this code is itself a written rule, itself conforming to strict norms—those of orthography. That is what confers on writing its primordial importance. In the end, the fact that we learn to speak before learning to write is forgotten, and the natural relation between the two is reversed.

4. Finally, when there is any discrepancy between a language and its spelling, the conflict is always difficult to resolve for anyone other than a linguist. Since the linguist's voice often goes unheeded, the written form almost inevitably emerges victorious, because any solution based on writing is an easier solution. In this way, writing assumes an authority to which it has no right.

§ 3. *Systems of writing*

There are only two systems of writing:

1. The ideographic system, in which a word is represented by some uniquely distinctive sign which has nothing to do with the sounds involved. This sign represents the entire word as a whole, and hence represents indirectly the idea expressed. The classic example of this system is Chinese.

2. The system often called 'phonetic', intended to represent the sequence of sounds as they occur in the word. Some phonetic writing systems are syllabic. Others are alphabetic, that is to say based upon the irreducible elements of speech.

Ideographic writing systems easily develop into mixed systems. Certain ideograms lose their original significance, and eventually come to represent isolated sounds.

The written word, as mentioned above, tends to become a substitute in our mind for the spoken word. That applies to both systems of writing, but the tendency is stronger in the case of ideographic writing. For a Chinese, the ideogram and the spoken word are of equal validity as signs for an idea. He treats writing as a second language, and when in conversation two words are identically pronounced, he sometimes refers to the written form in order to explain which he means. But this substitution, because it is a total substitution, does not give rise to the same objectionable consequences as in our Western systems of writing. Chinese words from different dialects which correspond to the same idea are represented by the same written sign.

Our survey here will be restricted to the phonetic system of writing, and in particular to the

---

① The reforms in question were proposed just a few years before Saussure's lectures were given. The issue was a topical one. (Translator's note)

system in use today, of which the prototype is the Greek alphabet.

At the time when an alphabet of this kind becomes established, it will represent the contemporary language in a more or less rational fashion, unless it is an alphabet which has been borrowed from elsewhere and is already marred by inconsistencies. As regards its logic, the Greek alphabet is particularly remarkable, as will be seen on p. [64]. But harmony between spelling and pronunciation does not last. Why not is what we must now examine.

§ 4. *Causes of inconsistency between spelling and pronunciation*

There are many causes of inconsistency: we shall be concerned here only with the most important ones.

In the first place, a language is in a constant process of evolution, whereas writing tends to remain fixed. It follows that eventually spelling no longer corresponds to the sounds it should represent. A spelling which is appropriate at one time may be absurd a century later. For a while spelling is altered in order to reflect changes in pronunciation; but then the attempt is abandoned. This is what happened in French to *oi*.[①]

|   | *period* | *pronounced* | *written* |
|---|---|---|---|
| 1 | 11th c. | *rei*, *lei* | *rei*, *lei* |
| 2 | 13th c. | *roi*, *loi* | *roi*, *loi* |
| 3 | 14th c. | *roè*, *loè* | *roi*, *loi* |
| 4 | 19th c. | *rwa*, *lwa* | *roi*, *loi* |

In this case, spelling followed pronunciation as far as stage 2, the history of orthography keeping in step with the history of the language. But from the fourteenth century onwards, the written form remained stationary while the language continued its evolution. From that point, there has been an increasingly serious disparity between the language and its spelling, Eventually, the association of incompatible written and spoken forms had repercussions on the written system itself: the digraph *oi* acquired a phonetic value ([wa]) unrelated to those of its constituent letters.

Such examples could be cited *ad infinitum*. Why is it that in French we write *mais* and *fait*, but pronounce these words *mè* and *fè*? Why does the letter *c* in French often have the value of *s*? In both cases, French has kept spellings which no longer have any rationale.

Similar changes are going on all the time. At present our palatal *l* is changing to *y*: although we still go on writing *éveiller* and *mouiller*, we pronounce these words *éveyer* and *mouyer* (just like *essuyer* and *nettoyer*).

Another cause of discrepancy between spelling and pronunciation is the borrowing of an alphabet by one people from another. It often happens that the resources of the graphic system are poorly adapted to its new function, and it is necessary to have recourse to various expedients. Two letters, for example, will be used to designate a single sound. This is what happened in the case of *þ* (a voiceless dental fricative) in the Germanic languages. The Latin alphabet having no character to represent it, it was rendered by *th*. The Merovingian king Chilperic tried to add a special letter to the Latin alphabet to denote this sound, but the attempt did not succeed, and *th* became accepted. English in the Middle Ages had both a close *e* (for example, in *sed* 'seed') and an open *e* (for

---

① The examples in the table are the French words for 'king' (*roi*) and 'law', (*loi*). (Translator's note)

example, in *led* 'to lead' ): but since the alphabet did not have distinct signs for these two sounds, recourse was had to writing *seed* and *lead*. In French, to represent the consonant *š*, the digraph *ch* was used. And so on.

Etymological preoccupations also intrude. They were particularly noticeable at certain periods, such as the Renaissance. It is not infrequently the case that a spelling is introduced through mistaken etymologising: *d* was thus introduced in the French word *poids* ( 'weight' ), as if it came from Latin *pondus*, when in fact it comes from *pensum*. But it makes little difference whether the etymology is correct or not. It is the principal of etymological spelling itself which is mistaken.

In other cases, the reason for a discrepancy is obscure. Some bizarre spellings have not even an etymological pretext. Why in German did they write *thun* instead of *tun*? It is said that the *h* represents the aspiration following the consonant: but in that case an *h* should have been written wherever the same aspiration occurred, and yet there are very many words ( *Tugend*, *Tisch*, etc.) which have never been soelt this wav.

§ 5. *Consequences of this inconsistency*

An exhaustive list of the inconsistencies found in writing systems cannot be given here. One of the most unfortunate is having a variety of characters for the same sound. In French, for *ž* we have: *j*, *g*, *ge* ( *joli*, *geler*, *geai* ). For *z* we have both *z* and *s*. For *s* we have *c*, *ç* and *t* ( *nation* ), *ss* ( *chasser* ), *sc* ( *acquiescer* ), *sç* ( *acquiesçant* ), and *x* ( *dix* ). For *k* we have *c*, *qu*, *k*, *ch*, *cc*, *cqu* ( *acquérir* ). On the other hand, different sounds are sometimes represented by the same sign: we have *t* representing *t* or *s*, *g* representing *g* or *ž*, and so on.

Then there are 'indirect' spellings. In German, although there are no double consonants in *Zettel*, *Teller*, etc., the words are spelt with *tt*, *ll*, simply in order to indicate that the preceding vowel is short and open. An aberration of the same kind is seen in English, which adds a silent final *e* in order to lengthen the preceding vowel, as in *made* ( pronounced *mēd* ) as distinct from *mad* ( *mād* ). This *e* gives the misleading appearance of indicating a second syllable in monosyllabic words.

Irrational spellings such as these do indeed correspond to something in the language itself: but others reflect nothing at all. French at present has no double consonants except in the future tense forms *mourrai*, *courrai*: none the less, French orthography abounds in illegitimate double consonants ( *bourru*, *sottise*, *souffrir*, etc.).

It also happens sometimes that spelling fluctuates before becoming fixed, and different spellings appear, representing attempts made at earlier periods to spell certain sounds. Thus in forms like *ertha*, *erdha*, *erda*, or *thrī*, *dhrī*, *drī*, which appear in Old High German, *th*, *dh*, and *d* evidently represent the same sound: but from the spelling it is impossible to tell what that sound is. Hence we have the additional complication that when a certain form has more than one spelling, it is not always possible to tell whether in fact there were two pronunciations. Documents in neighbouring dialects spell the same word *asca* and *ascha*: if the pronunciation was identical, this is a case of fluctuating orthography: but if not, the difference is phonetic and dialectal, as in the Greek forms *paízō*, *paízdō*, *paíddō*. In other cases the problem arises with a chronological succession of spellings. In English, we find at first *hwat*, *hweel*, etc. , but later *what*, *wheel*, etc., and it is unclear whether this is merely a change in spelling or a change in pronunciation.

The obvious result of all this is that writing obscures our view of the language. Writing is not a garment, but a disguise. This is demonstrated by the spelling of the French word *oiseau*, where not one of the sounds of the spoken word (*wazo*) is represented by its appropriate sign and the spelling completely obscures the linguistic facts.

Another result is that the more inadequately writing represents what it ought to represent, the stronger is the tendency to give it priority over the spoken language. Grammarians are desperately eager to draw our attention to the written form. Psychologically, this is quite understandable, but the consequences are unfortunate. The use acquired by the words 'pronounce' and 'pronunciation' confirms this abuse and reverses the true relationship obtaining between writing and the language. Thus when people say that a certain letter should be pronounced in this way or that, it is the visual image which is mistaken for the model. If *oi* can be pronounced *wa*, then it seems that *oi* must exist in its own right. Whereas the fact of the matter is that it is *wa* which is written *oi*. To explain this strange case, our attention is drawn to the fact that this is an exception to the usual pronunciation of *o* and *i*. But this explanation merely compounds the mistake, implying as it does that the language itself is subordinate to its spelling. The case is presented as contravening the spelling system, as if the orthographic sign were basic.

These misconceptions extend even to rules of grammar: for example, the rule concerning *h* in French. French has words with an unaspirated initial vowel, but which are nevertheless spelt with an initial *h*, because of the corresponding Latin form, e. g. *homme* 'man' (in former times *ome*), corresponding to Latin *homo*. But there are also French words of Germanic origin, in which the *h* was actually pronounced: *hache* ('axe'), *hareng* ('herring'), *honte* ('shame'), etc. As long as the *h* was pronounced, these words conformed to the laws governing initial consonants. You said *deu haches* ('two axes'), *le hareng* ('the herring'), whereas in accordance with the law for words beginning with a vowel you said *deu-z-hommes* ('two men'), *l' omme* ('the man'). At that period, the rule which said 'no liaison or elision before aspirate *h*' was correct. But nowadays this formulation is meaningless. For aspirate *h* no longer exists, unless we apply the term to something which is not a sound at all, but before which there is neither liaison nor elision. It is a vicious circle: the aspirate *h* in question is an orthographic ghost.

The pronunciation of a word is determined not by its spelling but by its history. Its spoken form at any given time represents one stage in a phonetic evolution from which it cannot escape. This evolution is governed by strict laws. Each stage may be ascertained by referring back to the preceding stage. The only factor to consider, although it is most frequently forgotten, is the etymological derivation of the word.

The name of the town of Auch is *oš* in phonetic transcription. It is the only case in French orthography where *ch* represents *š* at the end of a word. It is no explanation to say: *ch* in final position is pronounced *š* only in this word. The only relevant question is how the Latin *Auscii* developed into *oš*: the spelling is of no importance.

Should the second vowel of the French noun *gageure* ('wager') be pronounced *ö* or *ü*? Some say *gažör*, since *heure* ('hour') is pronounced *ör*. Others say it should be pronounced *gažür*, since *ge* stands for *ž*, as in *geôle* ('jail'). The dispute is vacuous. The real question is etymological. For the noun *gageure* was formed from the verb *gager* ('to bet'), just like the noun *tournure* ('turn') from the verb *tourner* ('to turn'). Both are examples of the same type of derivation. The only defensible pronunciation is *gažür*. The pronunciation *gažör* is simply the result of ambiguous spelling.

But the tyranny of the written form extends further yet. Its influence on the linguistic community may be strong enough to affect and modify the language itself. That happens only in highly literate communities, where written documents are of considerable importance. In these cases, the written form may give rise to erroneous pronunciations. The phenomenon is strictly pathological. It occurs frequently in French. The family name *Lefèvre* (from Latin *faber*) had two spellings: the popular, straightforward spelling was *Lefèvre*, while the learned etymological spelling was *Lefèbvre*. Owing to the confusion of *v* and *u* in medieval writing. *Lefèbvre* was read as *Lefèbure*, thus introducing a *b* which never really existed in the word, as well as a *u* coming from an ambiguous letter. But now this form of the name is actually pronounced.

Probably such misunderstandings will become more and more frequent. More and more dead letters will be resuscitated in pronunciation. In Paris, one already hears *sept femmes* ('seven women') with the *t* pronounced. Darmesteter foresees the day when even the two final letters of *vingt* ('twenty') will be pronounced: a genuine orthographic monstrosity.

These phonetic distortions do indeed belong to the language but they are not the result of its natural evolution. They are due to an external factor. Linguistics should keep them under observation in a special compartment: they are cases of abnormal development.

(*Course in General Linguistics*. London: G. Duckworth. 1983)

译文:

# 文字表现语言

高名凯,译

1.研究这个题目的必要性

我们研究的具体对象是储存在每个人脑子里的社会产物,即语言。但这种产物是随语言集体而不同的:我们有许多语言。语言学家必须认识尽可能多的语言,对它们进行观察和比较,从其中抽取出具有普遍性的东西。

我们一般只通过文字来认识语言。研究母语也常要利用文献。如果那是一种远离我们的语言,还要求助于书写的证据,对于那些已经不存在的语言更是这样。要使任何场合都能利用直接的文献,我们必须像当前在维也纳和巴黎所做的那样①,随时收集各种语言的留声机录音的样本。可是这样记录下来的原件要为他人所认识,还须求助于文字。

因此,文字本身虽然与内部系统无关,我们也不能不重视这种经常用来表现语言的手段;我们必须认识它的效用、缺点和危险。

2.文字的威望:文字凌驾于口语形式的原因

语言和文字是两种不同的符号系统,后者唯一的存在理由是在于表现前者。语言学的对象不是书写的词和口说的词的结合,而是由后者单独构成的。但是书写的词常跟它所表现的

---

① 维也纳和巴黎是当时世界上两个最早和规模最大的实验语音学研究中心,各藏有很丰富的用留声机记录的各种语言的音档。——校注

口说的词紧密地混在一起,结果篡夺了主要的作用;人们终于把声音符号的代表看得和这符号本身一样重要或比它更加重要。这好像人们相信,要认识一个人,与其看他的面貌,不如看他的照片。

这种错觉是任何时候都存在的,目前有人兜售的关于语言的见解也沾上了它的污点。例如人们普遍相信,要是没有文字,语言会变化得更快:这是极其错误的。诚然,在某些情况下,文字可能延缓语言的变化,但是,反过来,没有文字,决不会损害语言的保存的。立陶宛语今天在东普鲁士和俄国还有一部分人说①,它是从 1540 年起才有书面文献的;但是就在这很晚的时期,它的面貌总的说来却跟公元前三世纪的拉丁语一样忠实地反映出印欧语的情况②。只这一点已足以表明语言是怎样离开文字而独立的。

有些很细微的语言事实是不依赖任何符号记录的帮助而被保存下来的。在整个古高德语时期,人们写的是 töten“杀死”,fuolen“充满”和 stōzen“冲撞”,到十二世纪末出现了 töten、füelen 的写法,但 stōzen 却没有改变。这种差别是从哪里来的呢? 原来凡是发生这种差别的地方,后一个音节都有一个 y:原始日耳曼语有 \*daupyan,\*fōlyan,但是 \*stautan。在文学语言初期,大约是公元 800 年左右,这个 y 已逐渐弱化,以致在以后三个世纪,在文字上都没有保存它的任何迹象,但在发音上却留下了很轻微的痕迹。到 1180 年左右,正如我们上面已经看到的,它竟又神奇地以“变音”(Umlaut)的形式出现了! 由此可见,即使没有文字的帮助,这个发音上的细微色彩也很准确地留传了下来。

所以语言有一种不依赖于文字的口耳相传的传统,这种传统并且是很稳固的,不过书写形式的威望使我们看不见罢了。早期的语言学家,也像他们以前的人文主义者一样,在这一点上上了当。连葆朴本人也没有把字母和语音很清楚地区分开来;读他的著作会使人相信,语言和它的字母是分不开的③。他的直接继承者也堕入了这一陷阱。擦音 þ 的写法 th 曾使格里木相信,这不仅是一个复合音,而且是一个送气塞音;他在他的辅音演变规律或“Lautverschiebung”中就是这样派定它的地位的④。直到今天,还有些开明人士把语言和它的正字法混为一谈。加斯东·德商(Gaston Deschamps)不是说过,贝尔特洛(Berthelot)因为反对正字法改革,“曾使法语免于沦亡”吗⑤?

但是文字何以会有这种威望呢?

(1)首先,词的书写形象使人突出地感到它是永恒的和稳固的,比语音更适宜于经久地构成语言的统一性。书写的纽带尽管是表面的,而且造成了一种完全虚假的统一性,但是比起自然的唯一真正的纽带,即声音的纽带来,更易于为人所掌握。

(2)在大多数人的脑子里,视觉印象比音响印象更为明晰和持久,因此他们更重视前者。结果,书写形象就专横起来,贬低了语音的价值。

(3)文学语言更增强了文字不应该有的重要性。它有自己的词典,自己的语法。人们在学校里是按照书本和通过书本来进行教学的。语言显然要受法规的支配,而这法规本身就是

---

① 立陶宛语现在是苏联立陶宛共和国的正式语言、在波兰也有少数立陶宛人使用这种语言。——校注

② 立陶宛语在语言、词的结构、名词变格和声调方面都很接近古印欧语。——校注

③ 葆朴的《比较语法》一书第一篇有一章叫做《文字系统和语音系统》,从字母和语音方面论述印欧系各种语言。他所建立的“语音定律”有时称语音,有时称字母,所以德·索绪尔在这里说他没有把字母和语音分得很清楚,读了会使人相信,语音和字母是分不开的。——校注

④ 格里木在他的《德语史》中认为日耳曼语的语音演变规律是由清塞音变为送气音,送气音变为浊塞音,浊塞音变为清塞音,其中所谓送气音就包含着写成 th 的 þ[θ]这个擦音。——校注

⑤ 法语的正字法十分复杂,但不规则,过去已经有许多自由主义者认为是法国的一种“民族灾难”,要求加以改革,但也遭到了不少人的反对,贝尔特洛就是其中反对最有力的一个。——校注

一种要人严格遵守的成文的规则:正字法。因此,文字就成了头等重要的。到头来,人们终于忘记了一个人学习说话是在学习书写之前的,而它们之间的自然关系就被颠倒过来了。

(4)最后,当语言和正字法发生龃龉的时候,除语言学家以外,任何人都很难解决争端。但是因为语言学家对这一点没有发言权,结果差不多总是书写形式占了上风,因为由它提出的任何办法都比较容易解决。于是文字就从这位元首那里僭夺了它无权取得的重要地位。

3.文字的体系

只有两种文字的体系:

(1)表意体系。一个词只用一个符号表示,而这个符号却与词赖以构成的声音无关。这个符号和整个词发生关系,因此也就间接地和它所表达的观念发生关系。这种体系的典范例子就是汉字。

(2)通常所说的"表音"体系。它的目的是要把词中一连串连续的声音模写出来。表音文字有时是音节的,有时是字母的,即以言语中不能再缩减的要素为基础的。

此外,表意文字很容易变成混合的:某些表意字失去了它们原有的价值,终于变成了表示孤立的声音的符号。

我们说过,书写的词在我们的心目中有代替口说的词的倾向,对这两种文字的体系来说,情况都是这样,但是在头一种体系里,这倾向更为强烈。对汉人来说,表意字和口说的词都是观念的符号;在他们看来,文字就是第二语言。在谈话中,如果有两个口说的词发音相同,他们有时就求助于书写的词来说明他们的思想。但是这种代替因为可能是绝对的,所以不像在我们的文字里那样引起令人烦恼的后果。汉语各种方言表示同一观念的词都可以用相同的书写符号。

我们的研究将只限于表音体系,特别是只限于今天使用的以希腊字母为原始型的体系①。只要不是借来的、已经沾上了自相矛盾的污点的字母,起初的字母总是相当合理地反映着语言。从逻辑方面看,我们在后面将可以看到,希腊字母是特别值得注意的。但是这种写法和发音间的和谐不能持久。为什么呢? 这是我们要考察的。

4.写法和发音发生龃龉的原因

原因很多,我们只谈其中一些最重要的。

首先,语言是不断发展的,而文字却有停滞不前的倾向,后来写法终于变成了不符合于它所应该表现的东西。在某一时期合理的记音,过了一个世纪就成了不合理的了。有时人们要改变书写符号来适应发音上的变化,过后却又把它放弃了。例如法语的 oi 是这样的:

| | 发音 | 写法 |
|---|---|---|
| 十一世纪…… | 1.rei,lei | rei,lei |
| 十三世纪…… | 2.roi,loi | roi,loi |
| 十四世纪…… | 3.roè,loè | roi,loi |
| 十五世纪…… | 4.rwa,lwa | roi,loi② |

由此可见,直到第二个时期,人们还注意到发音上的变化,书写史上的阶段与语言史上的阶段相当。但是从十四世纪起文字已经固定下来,而语言还继续发展,从那以后,语言和正字

---

① 希腊字母源出于腓尼基,大约公元前七世纪由希腊传到埃特鲁利亚,再由埃特鲁利亚传到罗马,演变成为今天的拉丁字母。另一方面,由希腊字母变成基利耳字母,再由基利耳字母变成今天的斯拉夫字母。德·索绪尔在这里谈的主要是拉丁字母。——校注

② 法语的 roi"国王"来自拉丁语的 regem,loi"法律"来自拉丁语的 legem,现在的写法反映着十三世纪的发音;十四世纪以后,发音变了,而写法并没有跟着改变。——校注

法之间的龃龉就越来越严重。最后,由于人们不断弥合二者的不和而对文字体系本身产生了反作用,于是书写形式 oi 就获得了与它所由构成的要素无关的价值。

这样的例子不胜枚举,例如人们为什么把我们的发音 mè 和 fè 写成 mais"但是"和 fait"事实"呢①? 法语的 c 为什么往往有 s 的价值呢②? 这是因为我们保存了一些已经没有存在理由的写法。

这个原因在任何时候都会起作用:法语的腭化 l 现在已经变成 y;我们说 éveyer,mouyer,就像说 essuyer"揩",nettoyer"清楚"一样,但是还继续写成 éveiller"唤醒",mouiller"浸湿"③。

写法和发音发生龃龉的另一个原因:当一个民族向另一个民族借用它的字母的时候,这一书写体系的资源往往不能适应它的新任务,于是不得已而求助于一些随机应变的办法;例如用两个字母表示一个声音。日耳曼语的 þ(清齿擦音)就是这样:拉丁字母中没有任何符号表示这个音,于是就用 th 来表示。梅洛温吉王希尔贝里克(Chilpéric)曾试图在拉丁字母之外添上一个特别符号来表示这个音,但没有成功,结果用了 th④。中世纪的英语有一个闭 e(例如 sed"种子")和一个开 e(例如 led"引导"),字母表里没有不同的符号表示这两个音,于是想出了 seed 和 lead 的写法。法语求助于双符音 ch 来表示嘘音 š⑤,如此等等。

此外还有词源上的偏见:这在某些时期,例如文艺复兴时期很盛行。人们往往甚至把一个错误的词源强加到写法身上,例如法语的 poids"重量"添上了 d,好像它是来自拉丁语的 pondus 似的,实际上,它是从 pensum 变来的。但这个原则应用得是否正确还是小事,实际上词源文字的原则本身就是错误的。

有些地方找不出原因,某些怪现象甚至不能以词源为理由而加以原谅。德语以前为什么用 thun 来代替 tun"做"呢? 有人说,h 表示辅音后面的送气。但是,这样一来,凡有送气的地方都应该写出这个 h,可是有许多词(如 Tugend"道德",Tisch"桌子"等等)却从来没有这样写过。

5.写法和发音发生龃龉的后果

要把文字中各种自相矛盾的现象加以分类,将会花费太长的时间。其中最不幸的一种就是用许多符号表示同一个音。例如法语表示 ž⑥ 的有 j,g,ge(joli"美丽的",geler"结冰",geai"松鸦");表示 z 的有 z 和 s;表示 s 的有 c,ç,t(nation"国家、民族"),ss(chasser"打猎"),sc(acquiescer"默认"),sç(acquiesçant"默认的"),x(dix"十");表示 k 的有 c,qu,k,ch,cc,cqu(acquérir"得到")。相反,也有用同一个符号表示几个音值的,例如用 t 表示 t 或 s,用 g 表示 g 或 ž 等。

此外还有所谓"间接写法"。德语的 Zettel"纸条",Teller"盘子"等等虽然没有任何复辅音,可是要写成 tt、ll,唯一的目的是要指出前面的元音是短而开的元音。英语要添上一个词末的哑 e 来表示前面的元音念长音,也出于同一类的胡乱处理;试比较 made("做",念 mēd)和 mad("疯狂",念 măd)。这个 e 实际上只跟一个音节有关,但看起来却好像造成了第二个

---

① 法语的 mais"但是"来自拉丁语的 magis"更大",fait"事实"来自拉丁语的 facfum"事实",其中元音在十一世纪变成了[ɛi],十二世纪以后变成了[ɛ](德·索绪尔在这里标成 è),但是写法没有改变。——校注

② 法语的 c,古拉丁语念[k],自八世纪下半叶起在 i,e 之前变成了 s,所以现在法语的 c 有两种发音:在 a,o,u 之前念[k],i,e 之前念[s]。——校注

③ 法语的腭化 l 在古代念[ʎ],自十六世纪起变成了[j](德·索绪尔在这里标成 y)。——校注

④ 见格利戈里·图尔斯基的《法兰克史》。这种办法在古日耳曼语里是很普遍的。——校注

⑤ 用国际音标应为[ʃ]。——校注

⑥ 用国际音标应为[ʒ]。——校注

音节。

这些不合理的写法在语言里还算有一些东西和它们相当,另外有一些却简直是毫无意义。现代法语除古代的将来时 mourrai"我将死",courrai"我将跑"以外,没有任何复辅音;但是法语的正字法却有许许多多不合法的复辅音(bourru"抑郁",sottise"愚蠢",souffrir"受苦"等)。

有时,文字还没有固定,正在探索规则,犹豫不决,因此而有反映过去时代为了表示声音所尝试作出的举棋不定的拼写法。例如古高德语的 ertha,erdha,erda"土地"或 thrī,dhrī,drī"三",其中的 th、dh、d 都表示同一个声音要素。但是哪一个呢?从文字上无法知道。结果造成了复杂的情况:遇到表示同一形式的两种写法,常不能决定那是否真是两种发音。在相邻方言的文献里,同一个词有的写作 asca,有的写作 ascha"灰";如果发音相同,那就是一种举棋不定的拼写法;否则,那就好像希腊语的 paízō、paízdō、paíddō"我玩耍"等形式①一样,是音位上的和方言上的差别。问题还可能涉及两个连续的时代;在英语里,我们首先见到 hwat,hweel 等,然后见到 what"什么",wheel"车轮"等②,那究竟是写法上的变化呢?还是语音上的变化呢?

这一切的明显的结果是:文字遮掩住了语言的面貌,文字不是一件衣服,而是一种假装。我们从法语 oiseau"鸟"这个词的正字法上可以很清楚地看到这一点;在这里,口说的词(wazo)中没有一个音是用它固有的符号表示的,这可连那语言的一点儿影子也没有了。

另一个结果是:文字越是不表示它所应该表现的语言,人们把它当做基础的倾向就越是增强;语法学家老是要大家注意书写的形式。从心理方面说,这是很容易解释的,但会引起一些令人烦恼的后果。人们使用"念"和"念法"这些字眼,就是把这种滥用奉为神圣不可侵犯,而且把文字和语言间的真正的和合理的关系给弄颠倒了。我们说某个字母应该怎么怎么念,那就是把声音的书写形象当作声音本身。要使 oi 能念成 wa,它本身必须独立存在。那实际上是 wa 写成了 oi。为了解释这种怪现象,人们还说,在这种情况下,那是 o 和 i 的一种例外的发音。这又是一种错误的说法,因为它意味着语言依附于书写的形式。这无异是说,人们可以容许有某种违反文字的东西,好像书写符号就是规范。

这种虚构甚至可以表现在语法规则方面,例如法语的 h。法语有些词的开头元音不带送气,但是为了纪念它们的拉丁语形式,却添上了一个 h:例如 homme("人",从前是 ome),因为拉丁语的形式是 homo。但是另外有些来自日耳曼语的词,其中的 h 确实是发音的,如 hache"大斧",hareng"鲞鱼",honte"耻辱"等。当送气继续存在的时候,这些词都服从有关开头辅音的规律。那时人们说 deu haches"两把大斧",le hareng"鲞鱼",同时按照以元音开头的词的规律,又说 deu-z-hommes"两个人",l'omme"人"。在那时期,"送气的 h 之前不能有连续和省音"这条规则是正确的。但是到现在,这个公式已经失去意义;送气的 h 已不再存在,这个名称不再指音,只不过表示在它的前面不能有连读或省音而已。于是这就成了一种循环论,h只不过是一种来自文字的虚构的东西。

决定一个词的发音的,不是它的正字法,而是它的历史。它在某一时期的形式代表着它必须经历的发展中的一个时期,而词的发展要受一些确切的规律支配。每一阶段都可能决定

---

① 希腊语这个词的三个形式,paizo 是根据伊奥尼亚·阿狄克方言的发音,paizdō 是根据埃奥利亚方言的发音,paiddō 是根据多利亚方言的发音,都是"我玩耍"的意思。——校注

② 古英语诗法规定,hw 和 h 可以互押关韵。自十六世纪起,英语的 hwat,hweel 变成了 what,wheel,但是根据一般古英语语法学家的研究,那时实际上的发音并没有改变,可见那只是一种写法上的变化,而不是语音上的变化。可是现代英语的标准语把 wh 念[w],那就已经是语音上的变化了。——校注

于前一阶段。唯一要考虑的,也是人们最容易忘记的,是词的祖先,它的词源。

　　奥施(Auch)城的名称用语音转写是 oš。这是法语正字法的 ch 在词末表示 š 音的唯一例子。说词末的 ch 只有在这个词里念 š,不是解释。唯一的问题是要知道拉丁语的 Auscii 在变化中怎样会变成 oš;正字法是不重要的。

　　法语的 gageure"赌注"应该念成带有一个 ö 还是 ü 呢①? 有些人回答:应该念成 gažör,因为 heure"小时"念 ör。另一些人说:不,应该念成 gažür,因为 ge,在比方 geôle"监牢"这个词里,等于 ž。这种争论真是枉费心机! 真正的问题在于词源:gageure 是由 gager"赌"构成的,正如 tournure"风度"是由 tourner"旋转"构成的一样;它们都属于同一类型的派生法:gažür 是唯一正确的,gažör 只是由于文字上的暧昧不明而引起的发音。

　　但是字母的暴虐还不仅止于此:它会欺骗大众,影响语言,使它发生变化。这只发生在文学语言里,书面文献在这里起着很大的作用。视觉形象有时会造成很恶劣的发音。这真是一种病理学的事实,我们在法语里往往可以看到。例如 Lefèvre( 来自拉丁语的 faber)这个姓有两种写法:一种是通俗简单的 Lefèvre,一种是文绉绉的,讲究词源的 Lefebvre。由于在古文里 v 和 u 不分,Lefèbvre 曾被念成 Lefébure,其中的 b 从来没有在这个词里真正存在过,u 也是来路不明,而现在人们可真照着这个形式念了。

　　这类畸形现象将来也许会出现得更加频繁;把那些没有用的字母念出来的情况会越来越多。现在在巴黎已经有人把 sept femmes"七个女人"中的 t 念出来②;达尔姆斯特忒( Darmesteter)预见到有朝一日人们甚至将会把 vingt"二十"这个词的最后两个字母念出来③,那可真是正字法上的怪现象呢!

　　这些语音上的畸形现象当然是属于语言的,但并不是它的自然作用的结果,而是由一个与语言无关的因素造成的。语言学应该有一个专门部分研究它们:这些都是畸形学的病例④。

(选自《普通语言学教程》,商务印书馆,2009)

## 【推荐阅读】

B.A.伊斯特林.文字的历史[M].左少兴,译.北京:中国国际广播出版社,2018.
裘锡圭.文字学概要(修订本) [M].北京:商务印书馆,2013.

---

①　用国际音标应为[œ]和[y]。——校注
②　法语的 sept"t"单用时念[sɛt],后面跟着一个辅音时念[sɛ],把 sept femmes"七个女人"中的 t 念出来,本来是不合规范的。可是后来在巴黎已经有人把这个 t 念出来。——校注
③　达尔姆斯特忒(1846—1888),法国语言学家。索绪尔在这里所说的这一段话,见于他所著的《法语历史语法教程》一书。法语的 vingt(二十)念[vɛ̃],但是因为在写法上最后有 gt 这两个字母,他预料有一天将会有人把它念成[vɛ̃gt]。——校注
④　瑞士语言学家席业隆(Gilliéron)曾著《语言的病理学和治疗法》一书,里面谈到许多语言中的畸形现象和补救方法。德·索绪尔在这里采用了好些这本书里的术语。——校注

# 第六章 语言的发展

## 第一节 语言发展的原因和特点

### 一、语言发展的原因

语言是人类社会最重要的交际工具,社会的需要是它产生、存在和发展的基本条件。语言是一种社会现象,它是为了社会的需要而产生的。语言产生以后,作为社会的交际工具,它也只存在于社会对它的使用之中,一旦退出社会的交际活动,没有人使用了,它就会成为死的语言。比如,在我国历史上存亡时间大约与宋代平行的西夏政权,其主体民族党项族所操的西夏语,随着党项族历经元、明两代被其他民族同化几乎无人使用,最终走向了消亡。如果死语言又没有文字保存它的遗迹,它就会消失得无影无踪。比如我国古代的鲜卑人所说的鲜卑语,随着鲜卑人同汉族的融合而消失,由于没有文字记录,今天人们已经无法知晓它到底是一种什么样的语言了。因此,脱离了社会,也就没有语言的产生和存在。同样地,语言依存于社会而发展。

社会的进步会推动着语言发展。随着社会的发展,新事物、新概念不断涌现,人们的思维也愈来愈缜密复杂,这些都会向语言提出新的要求,推动语言不断地充实词语的数量,提高词义的概括程度,完善语法形式,以适应社会发展的需要。从现代汉语和古代汉语的比较中我们可以发现,虽然由于古代许多事物的消失,一些古词也随之消亡了,但随着更多新事物的出现,大量的新词不断出现。比如新的通信方式出现后,出现了"手机""短信""电子邮件"等词语。此外,组词造句的格式也多样化了。比如,助动词构成的句式,现在一个句子里既可以让不同的助动词带上相同的动词性成分,如"我们不能这样做,也不愿这样做",也可以让不同的助动词共同带一个动词性成分,如"我们不能,也不愿这样做",而这后一种句式在古代汉语中是没有的。

社会间的接触也会推动语言的发展。随着社会的发展,不同社会,包括不同的国家、民族之间免不了要相互接触、相互影响。在彼此接触的过程中,离不开语言的使用,因此,社会的接触必然会带来语言的接触,引起不同语言之间的相互影响,从而引起语言的变化,推动语言的发展。比如,改革开放之后,由于我国对外交流的不断深化,汉语从其他语言特别是英语中吸收了大量的新词,如"克隆""迷你""迪斯科""高尔夫"等。从另一方面来说,英语也向汉语借了不少词,如 Kungfu(功夫)、Taikonaut(中国太空人,中国宇航员)等,这些词的语音形式最大限度地保留了汉语普通话的音节结构。不仅如此,在语言接触的过程中,还可能出现结构规则的借用。比如我国的纳西语的动宾结构原本只有"宾+动"的语序,在汉语的影响下,现在也出现了"动+宾"的语序。

社会的交际间接地决定着一种语言发展的方式。社会因素推动着语言的发展,但是语言如何发展,则是由语言系统内部的各种因素的相互关系决定的。语言是用来表达思想、交流信息的符号系统,社会交际要求它必须能够利用自身的形式手段把不同的意义区别开来,达到表意的明确性,保持不同语言形式之间的有效区别。为了适应这一要求,语言系统的各个组成部分以及每一个组成部分内部的各个成分分工合作,构成一个严密的系统,共同担负区别意义的职责,使语言能够发挥交际工具的作用。如果语言中的某个因素因某种原因发生了变化,使原有的分工遭到破坏,影响了表意的明确性,语言中的其他有关部分就会相应地发生变化,以重新调整它们之间的分工,恢复不同语言形式之间的有效区别,消除表意不清的现象。例如,古藏语是没有声调的,在发展过程中由于浊音清化、前缀辅音的脱落和韵尾辅音的简化,语言中的同音现象大量增加,使本来互有区别的词不再有多大的区别了,于是声调作为新的区别意义的手段就产生了。这样,无声调的古藏语就发展为今天有声调的藏语拉萨方言、康方言了。可见,语言内部各要素的相互影响制约着一种语言演变发展的具体方式,但是,在这种制约的背后仍然是社会的交际在起作用。

总之,语言依存于社会,各种社会因素促使着语言的发展。

## 二、语言发展的特点

语言是人类社会最重要的交际工具,人类在绝大多数时候都离不开语言,这就决定了语言的发展不能太迅猛,只能渐进式地发展;另一方面,语言系统内部的各个组成部分的发展速度又是不平衡的。因此,渐变性和不平衡性是语言发展的两大特点。

语言发展的"渐变性"是说语言的发展演变是逐步进行的。这是因为语言是全社会成员一刻也离不开的交际工具,语言的这一根本属性决定了它必须是稳固的,不能以突变的方式演变和发展。社会中的每个成员都需要学会和掌握语言这个交际工具,只有这样,他才能够参与各种社会活动。如果语言不稳固,一下子变得面目全非,今天掌握的词语和用法,明天就不能用了,必须重新学新的,那么人们就永远也不可能掌握语言这个交际工具。在日常生活中,人们要依靠语言来互相沟通和交往;在社会生产中,人们要依靠语言来进行协作和管理。如果语言不稳固,一下子就改变了面貌,就会导致语言使用的中断。人们的日常生活和社会生产就会随之陷入混乱。因此,作为社会的交际工具,语言必须是稳固的。但是,另一方面,随着社会的发展,日益增长的交际需要又不断地促使语言发生变化。稳固和变化这两个对立的要求都是语言作为交际工具的性质决定的。所以,语言的演变只能在不切断社会交流的情况下采取渐变的方式,不能以突变的方式来进行。

语言发展的另一个特点是不平衡性。"不平衡性"指的是语言的语音、词汇、语法各要素的发展有快有慢;甚至在各要素内部,同样的语言现象由于所处的条件不同,其发展也有快有慢;以及在不同的地域之间,语言发展演变的速度和方向也是不一致的。

在语言的三要素语音、词汇和语法中,与社会发展联系最密切、最直接的是词汇,所以,词汇对社会发展的反映最灵敏,变化也最快。相比而言,语音和语法就稳定得多。三者的变化速度显示出不平衡性。社会生活中新事物的产生,旧事物的消亡,人们观念的改变,随时都会在语言的词汇中得到反映,表现为旧词的消亡、新词的产生和词义的发展。比如,第二次世界大战以后,世界政治格局发生了很大的变化,这些变化给英语增添了不少新词,如 cold war(冷战)、arm race(军备竞赛)、sit-in(静坐示威)等;随着经济全球一体化的形成,英语中出现了 World Trade Organization(世界贸易组织)、Organization of Petrol Exporting Countries(石油输出国)等;随着科技的迅猛发展,各种高科技产品不断问世,大量科技词汇不断涌现,如 Internet(因特网)、E-mail(电子邮件)、clone(克隆)等。新事物的产生、人们观念的改变还在词义的发展上体现了出来。比如英语词 brain 原义主要为"头脑",由于一些新事物的出现,它已发展出新义,与一些名词、动词一起构成许多具有新义的词语,如 brain box(电脑,电子计算机)、brainchild(脑力劳动成果)、brain drain

（人才外流）、brain gain（人才流入）、brainstorm（群策群力;献计献策）、brain trust（智囊团）、brain truster（智囊;顾问）、brainwash（对……实行洗脑;强制灌输）、brainwork（脑力劳动）、brainworker（脑力劳动者）等。

　　语言中成千上万的词都是通过有限的语音形式表达出来的。在一种语言里,几十个音位的排列组合完全能够满足语言表达的需要。即使词汇发生急剧的演变,新词产生,旧词消亡,也不会很快给语音系统带来明显的影响。因为新产生的词只能使用已有的语音形式,否则就不会被社会接受;旧词虽然消失了,但是它的语音形式还保留在其他词语里。比如,我们曾经把火柴称为"洋火",现在几乎已经没有人说了,但是这个词所使用的音位和音位组合形式并没有随着这个词的逐渐消失而消失,像"海洋、火花"等词语就是由这些音位组合而成的。可见,语言中的词汇即使迅速发展,也不会立即引起语音系统的演变。所以,语言中的语音系统是比较稳定的,它的演变速度是缓慢的。

　　语法是组织语言材料的结构规则,每项规则都支配着整类的语言成分。新词的产生和旧词的消失一般不会引起语言成分类型格局的变动,因而也就不会立即引起语法规则的改变。比如,汉语里的心理活动动词和形容词一般都能受程度副词修饰,如"很轻视""特别尊敬""很轻盈""特别恭敬"。但是心理活动动词能带宾语,如"轻视他""尊敬老师",而形容词一般不带宾语,如不能说"轻盈他""恭敬长辈"。汉语中心理活动动词和形容词的这个区别不会因为新词的产生和旧词的消失而改变,汉语中的上述语法规则也不会随着词汇的发展而在短期内发生变化。所以,语法发展速度也是缓慢的。

　　不仅语音、词汇、语法各要素的发展速度不平衡,就是在同一要素内部,其各组成部分的发展也是不平衡的。比如,词汇的变化虽然比较快速,但主要是其中的一般词汇变化比较快,其中的基本词汇却是不容易起变化的。一方面是因为它们所反映的都是交际中最常用的基本概念,另一方面是因为它们还是构造新词的主要材料,是词汇发展的基础。一般词汇对社会发展变化的灵敏反应和基本词汇的相对稳固性是语言发展的渐变性和不平衡性的一种表现。又如,古英语名词、代词和形容词都有主格、宾格、属格（又称所有格）、与格和工具格五种。发展到现代英语,代词还保留三种格:主格、宾格和属格;名词只剩下两种格:通格和属格（如 Tom 和 Tom's）;而形容词则没有格的变化了。这是语言发展的不平衡性在语法系统内部的具体表现。

　　另一方面,在不同的地域内,同一语言现象的发展速度也可能是不平衡的。比如,古汉语的入声声调在今天的北方方言区中已经基本消失了,但在吴方言、粤方言等南方的方言区中还存在。这种语言发展演变在地域上的不平衡性是一种语言分化出不同的地域方言或亲属语言的重要原因之一。

　　语言发展的渐变性和不平衡性这两个特点,使作为交际工具的语言既能随时满足新的交际要求,又能维持稳固的基础,保证交际的顺利进行。

# 第二节　语言的分化和统一

## 一、语言随着社会的分化而分化

社会的分化有两种基本类型:一是社会分化为不同的地域,即一个统一的社会在其发展过程中,在地域上逐渐分化为若干个相对独立或完全独立的部分;二是社会分化为不同的社群,就是在一个统一的社会内部,因阶级、阶层、职业、年龄、性别、文化程度、宗教等社会特征的不同而形成不同的社会集团(又叫"社群")。在社会分化和语言的发展演变这两个因素的共同作用下,一种统一的语言会随着社会的分化而分化:社会分化为不同的地域会导致语言的地域分化,在一种语言内部形成不同的"地域方言",在一定的社会政治历史条件下还可能使一种语言的方言不断扩大自己的特点,成为不同的"亲属语言";社会分化为不同的社群会导致语言的社群分化,在一种语言或方言内部形成不同的"社会方言"。

### (一)地域方言

同一国家因山水阻隔而分化为不同的地域,即会发生社会的不完全地域分化,同一语言会随之慢慢地分化为不同的地域方言。地域方言是同一种语言由于语音、词汇和语法等方面的差异而在不同的地区形成的地域分支或变体。人们通常所说的"方言"一般指的就是这种地域方言。

"方言"是一个总的概念,往下还可以分出各种"次方言",再往下又可分出各种"土语"。比如汉语的北方方言分布的地域很广,包括长江以北各省,长江以南、镇江以上、九江以下沿江地带,以及云贵川等地,约占全国汉语地区的四分之三。在这样一个广阔的地域内,不同地区的人所说的话并不完全一样,因此在北方方言的内部,又可以分出"华北方言""西北方言""西南方言"和"江淮方言"四个次方言。"西北方言"内部又可以分出"金城话""银吴话""河西话""塔密话"四个土语群。

那么,划分方言的标准是什么呢? 听得懂、听不懂不能作为划分方言的标准。比如说俄语、乌克兰语、白俄罗斯语、波兰语、捷克语、塞尔维亚语的人彼此间就能听懂对方所说的话，但他们说的却是不同的语言。地处汉语各方言之间的差别比上述各语言的差别大得多，说这些方言的人相互间很难听懂，甚至根本听不懂对方说的话，但他们说的却是同一种语言的不同的方言。划分方言，要同时考虑三方面的因素：统一的社会，语言对外的差异性和对内的共同性。方言是统一社会里的方言，像前面所举的俄语、乌克兰语、白俄罗斯语、波兰语、捷克语、塞尔维亚语等，虽然能够相互交流，但是不是存在于统一的社会里，所以它们是独立的语言，而不是分散于各地的方言。统一的社会是划分方言的前提，在这个前提下，方言之间一定要有差别，否则就谈不上方言。因为差异性能够充分显示出方言的个性，对于这一方言系统以外的其他方言具有"排他性"。像吴方言和赣方言之间的一个明显的差别表现在古全浊声母字今天读音很不相同，再加上其他一些差别，所以把它们划分为两个不同的方言。古全浊声母字在今天的吴语中仍然读浊音，比如"稻"和"技"都是全浊声母字，在上海里分别读[dɔ²]和[dzi²]，与清声母字"到"和"寄"的读音[tɔ²]和[tɕi²]是不同的。而古全浊声母字在今天的赣语中读塞音、塞擦音时读为送气清音。今读送气清塞音的古全浊声母字如"头"和"大"，南昌话读[t'ɛu]和[t'ai]，今读送气清塞擦音的古全浊声母字如"茶"和"坐"，南昌话读[ts'a]和[ts'o]。不过究竟要有多大的差别才算是不同的方言，这却没有统一的标准，而要以不同语言的具体情况而定。比如英语和俄语内部都可以分出不同的方言，但这些方言之间的差别要比汉语方言之间的差别小得多。另外，在统一的社会的前提下划分方言，还要考虑语言对内的共同性，因为共同性能够充分显示出方言的共性，对于这一方言系统以内的诸次方言、土语群和方言点具有"一致性"。比如吴语下面分为太湖片（又叫北吴语片）、台州片、温州片、婺州片和丽衢片几个次方言，是因为它们之间有差异性，但是它们之间也有共性，其中一个较大的共性是古全浊声母字在今天仍然读浊音，所以把它们视为是同一方言。同样地，究竟要有多少共性就可看作是同一方言，这也没有统一的标准，也要以不同语言的具体情况而定。

一般来说，方言之间的差别主要表现在语音上，所以在划分方言的时候，通常把语音上的差别作为主要的依据。现代汉语一般分为七大方言：北方方言、吴方言、湘方言、赣方言、客家方言、粤方言和闽方言，这些方言主要就是根据不同的语音特点来确定的。比如，在声母方面，吴方言和部分湘方言中有浊塞音、浊塞擦音，其他方言一般只有清塞音和清塞擦音。在韵母方面，北方方言和吴方言都没有以辅音[-m][-p][-t][-k]收尾的韵母，但粤方言和客家方言里却有这类韵母。在声调方面，北方方言的代表北京话只有四个声调，没有入声，而吴方言、粤方言、客家方言、闽南方言、闽北方言等其他方言的声调则大都在六个或六个以上，并且都有入声。

方言间在词汇和词义上也有一些差异。这首先表现在同样的事物、动作等在不同的方言里可能有不同的说法。比如,同一种植物,北京话叫"白薯",呼和浩特、洛阳等地称"红薯",成都称"红苕",贵阳叫"番薯",上海叫"山芋";又如,普通话中作动词用的"下",粤方言多用"落",如"落车"(下车)、"落水"(下雨)、"落课"(下课)、"落手"(下手)等。其次,相同的词语在不同的方言里可能指称不同。比如,"蚕豆"这个词在绍兴、宁波话里指的是别处的"豌豆";"手"这个词在闽方言里可以兼指"手臂"。

方言间在语法上的差别相对来说比语音、词汇上的差别小一些。不过,方言之间的语法差别会表现在语法的各个方面,而且差别是各式各样的。现代汉语各方言里的名词都可以跟量词结合,但哪些名词能跟哪些量词结合在一起,不同的方言却可能有不同的特点。比如,北京话说"一棵树",广州话说"一坡树",厦门话说"一丛树",成都话说"一窝树"。在语序上,不同的方言也可能各有一些自己的特点。比如,北京话说"先走",广州话说"走先";北京话说"给我一块钱",成都话说"给块钱我"。

尽管方言之间存在着这样或那样的差别,但是由于不同的方言都是从同一种语言里分化出来的,因此不论它们之间的差别有多大,也总会有一些明显的共同点。在分歧的语音现象之间,往往存在着有规则的对应关系。例如,比较现代汉语的上海话和北京话的双唇塞音,我们就会发现,上海话有三个双唇塞音[p,p',b],北京话有两个双唇塞音[p,p'],它们之间有对应关系:上海话以[p,p']为声母的北京话也以[p,p']为声母,如"碑、臂、比"和"怕、派、炮"等;上海话以[b]为声母的字,在北京话里可能是[p],也可能是[p'],条件是仄声字是[p],如"别、拔、避"(在上海都是仄声);平声字是[p'],如"皮、爬、盆"(在上海都是平声)。这种方言之间所具有的、有规律的而非个别的语音之间互相对应的关系叫作"语音对应关系"。由于这种对应关系不只存在于个别的词语当中,而是涉及成批的词语,因此不可能是偶然的,而只能用不同的方言具有共同的历史来源来解释。

各方言中的词汇之间也有共同之处,这表现在各方言的构词语素一般都相同,只为一种方言所特有的构词语素是比较少的。下面试以北京话、成都话和上海话的某些有关人体部分的词作比较:

| 北京 | 成都 | 上海 |
|---|---|---|
| 头,脑袋,脑袋瓜 | 脑壳 | 头发 |
| 头发 | 头发 | 头发 |
| 脸 | 脸 | 面孔 |
| 眉毛 | 眉毛 | 眉毛 |
| 眼珠 | 眼仁珠珠 | 眼乌珠 |
| 嘴 | 嘴巴 | 嘴巴 |
| 嘴唇 | 嘴皮 | 嘴唇皮 |

以上三种方言有关的词有的完全相同；有的虽然不是完全相同，但有一个共同的构词语素；完全不同的很少。这些词所用的构词语素差不多都是三种方言所共有的。当然，如果多比较一些词，或是比较广州话和北京话，就会发现更多的差别，但是无论如何共同点仍然不少。

至于个别方言的语法，它们之间的相同点一般要比不同点多。

由于不同的方言都是从同一种语言里分化出来的，是古代同一种语言在不同地域发展不平衡产生的，所以它们有分歧，也有共性，我们正可以根据某种语言的方言之间的分歧和共性来推断该语言在古代的状况。

(二) 亲属语言

一个社会、一个民族或一种文化凭着语言等手段得以凝聚和整合，在一定的政治历史条件下，一个社会在地域上相对独立的部分进一步分化，走向完全独立，分裂成几个各自完全独立的社会，原来相对独立的地域所使用的方言可能会逐渐转变为各自独立的语言。比如，拉丁语随着古罗马帝国的解体，它的各个方言就逐步转变为后来的法语、意大利语、西班牙语、葡萄牙语、罗马尼亚语等独立的语言。这种从同一种语言中分化出来的使用于不同社会的各种语言，被称作"亲属语言"。

亲属语言有共同的来源，它们之间具有的这种历史同源关系被称作"亲属关系"。比如汉语和藏语就是有共同来源的语言，它们都来自原始汉藏语，因此它们之间有亲属关系，是亲属语言。当然，所谓"亲属语言""亲属关系"只不过是对语言间历史同源关系一种比喻的说法，和生物学上所说的"亲属"是不同的。

亲属语言既然有共同的历史来源，是同一种语言分化发展而来的，它们之间在语音上会存在着有规律的对应关系，在基本词汇和语法结构方面也会保留某些共同的成分。就这一点来说，亲属语言与方言并没有本质的不同。下面的例子就体现出几种亲属语言语音上的对应关系：

|  | 英语 | 德语 | 荷兰语 | 丹麦语 | 瑞典语 |
|---|---|---|---|---|---|
| 田鼠 | maws | maws | møɥs | muːʔs | muːs |
| 虱子 | laws | laws | løɥs | luːʔs | luːs |
| 出去 | awt | aws | øɥt | uːʔð | uːt |
| 棕色 | brawn | brawn | brøɥn | bruːʔn | bruːn |

（引自布龙菲尔德《语言论》）

我们从上面的例子中可以看出，英语和德语的[aw]、荷兰语的[øɥ]、丹麦语的[uːʔ]和瑞典语的[uː]互相对应。这种出现在成批词语中的语音对应现象是它们同出一源而又有规律地各自发展的结果，因而语音对应现象也就成为语言间亲属关系的重要标志。

又如，汉语和藏语是亲属语言，藏语的基本词[sum]和汉语的基本词"三"[san]不仅语音相近，而且意思相同，也是"三"的意思，它们是原始汉藏语的同一个基本词的历史变化的产物。又如，汉语的"其"（[tɕ'i]＜[g*ji]）和藏语表示领属关系的语法成分[g'i][g'ji][i][ji]是同源成分，它们都是原始汉藏语的同一个语法成分的历史变化的产物。

了解了语言之间的亲属关系，我们便可以根据语言的历史来源或语言的亲属关系对世界上的语言进行分类，把有亲属关系的语言归在一起，这种分类叫作语言的"谱系分类"。凡有亲属关系的语言组成一个语系。同一语系中的语言还可以根据它们亲属关系的亲疏远近依次分为语族、语支、语群等。同一个语群或语支中的语言的亲属关系最接近，不同语支乃至不同语族之间的语言，其亲属关系就比较疏远。语系、语族、语支、语群这种谱系分类的层级体系，反映了原始基础语随着社会的分化而不断分化的历史过程和结果。例如，原始印欧语先是分化出印度—伊朗语族、斯拉夫语族、日耳曼语族、拉丁语族等，其中日耳曼语族又分化出东部、西部、北部三个语支，而西部语支又进一步分化出英语、德语、荷兰语等语言，北部语支则进一步分化出丹麦语、瑞典语、挪威语、冰岛语等语言。

世界上的各种语言按其亲属关系大致可分为汉藏语系、印欧语系、乌拉尔语系、阿尔泰语系、闪含语系、高加索语系、达罗毗荼语系、马来-波利尼西亚语系、南亚语系等九大语系以及其他一些语群和语言。汉藏语系和印欧语系是世界上使用人数最多的两个语系。

（三）社会方言

稍加留意，我们会发现不同年龄、性别、职业、阶级、阶层、文化程度、宗教信仰的人群所说的话有一定的差异，语言学上把这些不同的人群称为"言语社团（speech community）"，他们所说的话被称作"社会方言"。社会方言指的是同一种语言或地域方言在不同的言语社团中表现出来的各种变体。比如网民这个言语社团在网络聊天室和论坛上进行交流时所创制和使用的所谓"网络语言"就是一种社会方言。社会方言没有自己独立的结构系统，它所用的材料和结构规则基本上都是全民语言或当地方言所共同具有的，多数情况下是所使用的词语有某些值得注意的、不同于其他社群的特点而已，因而它们之间的差异一般并不会妨碍人们之间的言语交际。

社会方言是社会分化为不同的社群导致语言的社群分化而形成的。究竟哪些社会因素会导致社会分化为不同的社群，从而使语言内部产生各种分歧形成社会方言，目前语言学界还难以提供出一份详尽完备的清单，不过不少语言中的事实已经证明，年龄、性别、职业、阶级、阶层、文化程度、宗教信仰、政治分化等社会因素都有可能对语言产生影响。比如医生之间谈医学和教师之间谈教学所说的话是有差异的，这些差异与职业这一社会因素有关；知识分子和工人的话有一些差别，这些差别与文化程度这一社会因素有关。

　　不同的宗教信仰有可能形成不同的社群,如果相互之间的交往不那么频繁,就有可能形成因宗教因素而产生的社会方言。在一般情况下,由宗教信仰而形成的语言特点只限于一些宗教用语。但是也有极端的情况:因宗教信仰不同而形成的社会方言最终成为两种不同的语言。在第二次世界大战以前,在英属印度境内的主要语言是印地语,由于使用印地语的人有的信印度教,有的信伊斯兰教,信印度教的用印度文字来书写印地语,信伊斯兰教的用阿拉伯字母来书写印地语,并把这种语言改称为乌尔都语。这样,两种具有浓厚宗教色彩的社会方言就形成了。随着印度和巴基斯坦成为两个独立的国家,这两种不同的社会方言也就进一步成为两种不同的语言。

　　政治分化也是社会方言形成的因素。中国海峡两岸的汉语有比较明显的差异,主要就是政治分化造成的。1927年第一次国共合作的破裂及随后国共两党语言取向的显著不同铸就了日后两岸语言差异的基础。国民党的文告语言近乎文言文,共产党的则是地道的白话文。共产党有意遵循"五四"倡导的"白话文",朝"话"的方向发展,而国民党则更乐意采用"文言"色彩浓郁些的书面语,朝"文"的方向发展。国统区不但没有废掉"五四"所不提倡的半文半白的语言,反而使之成为国统区汉语书面语的典型特征,"国语"和半文半白的书面语在文坛占主导地位。共产党以"五四"式白话文为基点,发挥瞿秋白等人所提倡的"大众语"风格,逐渐过渡到后来革命根据地式的语言,最后发展为现在的普通话及更口语化的大陆书面语。

　　当社会上出现了由于各种原因而形成的秘密团体之后,就有可能产生秘密语言,又叫作"隐语"。隐语是一种特殊的社会方言。其他社会方言没有排他性,不排斥其他社群的成员了解和运用,因而其中的有些词语也可以被其他言语社团或者全民语言所吸收,比如麻将用语"翻番"被经济领域吸收,"清一色"已成为日常的交际用语。但隐语则有明显的排他性,它总是故意让局外人听不懂,目的是不让他人了解秘密团体成员之间的谈话内容。黑社会使用的隐语通常被称作"黑话",比如从前广东的盗贼集团内部把"刀"叫作"利",抢人财产叫作"做生意",绑架人叫作"吊参",做贼叫作"当太公"等;当今香港的黑社会把金镯子叫作"黄圈",吸鸦片叫作"摆横",警察叫作"花腰",女人叫作"吉佬",外国人叫作"灰斗",打架叫作"开片",等等。

　　社会方言是因为社会成员集聚为不同的言语社团而产生的,因而一个人如果交叉地生活在几个言语社团中,他就能同时掌握几种社会方言。一个人掌握的社会方言数量的多少,取决于他的社会活动的广度和深度。一般来说,一个人的社会活动越狭窄,他所处的语言环境就越单纯,他所掌握的社会方言的数量也就越少;反之,他所掌握的社会方言就越多。

## 二、语言随着社会的统一而统一

随着社会的发展,原来一个地方割据的、不太统一的社会可以完全统一起来;原来几个独立的社会也可以统一为一个社会。在社会统一的时候,统一是语言发展的总倾向。这是由于语言是人类社会最重要的交际工具,社会统一时经济、政治、文化要求这个工具为整个社会的统一更好地服务。于是,在这种社会要求的推动下,语言就会随着社会的统一而逐步走向统一。语言的统一有两种情况,一是一种语言逐步消除方言分歧而走向统一;二是多种语言统一为一种语言。

(一)一种语言逐步消除方言分歧而走向统一

在存在方言分歧的社会里,不同地区之间的人们为了交际的方便,往往会选择一种方言作为各方言区之间的交际工具,我们可以把这种语言形式叫作"通用语"。我国古代所谓的"雅言""通语""四方之语"以及后来的"官话",都是当时的人们给这种通用语起的名称。但是,在经济上自给自足的、分散的、没有形成统一市场的封建社会里,各地区之间的相互往来不很普遍,频率也比较低,通用语的使用者就可能只局限于一些官员、商人和读书人,人数势必不多。这样,通用语也就难以对广大民众所使用的方言产生大的影响,对消除方言分歧也不会起多大的作用。

在社会打破地域隔阂走向统一的时候,地域方言赖以形成和存在的基础会逐步瓦解,这时会出现一种新的语言形式——共同语。在多数情况下,共同语就是过去的通用语。但是,由于所处的社会历史条件以及在语言统一过程中所起的作用等方面的不同,它们的地位也有所不同,性质也不一样。对方言来说,共同语是一种高级形式,它能够影响方言的发展,引导方言向自己靠拢,并准备最后取代方言。

一种语言的共同语是在某一个方言的基础上形成的。这种作为共同语基础的方言叫作"基础方言"。所谓作为共同语的基础,指的是共同语的语音、词汇和语法系统是来自基础方言的。在一种语言的各个方言中,哪一种方言成为基础方言,不是人为规定的,而是由客观的社会政治、经济、文化等方面的条件决定的。

现代汉民族共同语,即普通话,以北方方言为基础方言,这主要是由政治上的原因决定的,当然也还有文化上的原因。北方方言的代表点北京,是辽、金、元、明、清的都城,近千年来一直是一个政治中心;以北京话为代表的北方方言,几百年来被用作中央政府实施国家管理的工具,被称作"官话",在全国各地的方言中影响最大。加之近千年来,许多重要的文学作品,如宋人话本、元曲和明清小说等,大多是用北方方言或以北方方言为基础写成的;而且,使用北方方言的人也最多。这些因素使北方方言在汉语众多方言中地位最为重要,影响也最大,因而它就成为现代汉民族共同语的基础方言,北京语音就成为共同语的标准音。

包括伦敦方言在内的南部方言成为英吉利共同语的基础方言,则主要是经济上的原因。英国产业革命后,南部的经济发展迅速,特别是首都伦敦成为工业的中心,需要大量的劳动力,各地居民纷纷迁入,同原来的居民杂居在一起,使英吉利民族共同语在包括伦敦方言在内的南方方言的基础上,吸收其他方言的一些成分而发展起来。

托斯卡纳方言成为意大利共同语的基础方言主要是文化的原因。在意大利统一之前,著名的文豪如但丁、彼特拉克、薄伽丘等人已用这种方言写下了许多脍炙人口的作品,随着这些作品的流传,托斯卡纳方言也在整个意大利半岛产生了很大的影响,确立了它在各方言中的特殊地位,成为共同语的基础方言,而该方言区的首府佛罗伦萨的语音就成为意大利民族共同语的标准音。

从共同语的形成到普及有一个过程,共同语的形成并不意味着全体社会成员都已经掌握了这种语言形式,也不意味着方言分歧已经消失。比如汉民族共同语——普通话至今也还没有普及到全体汉民族成员,在方言区内部,方言仍然是人们使用的主要语言形式,很多人还只会听而不会说普通话,少数边远地区甚至还有人听不懂普通话。共同语的普及过程,实际上也就是逐渐缩小方言差异,使语言趋于统一的过程。在这个过程中,共同语可以在两个方面对方言产生强烈的影响。一是引导方言的发展方向,吸引方言向自己靠拢。自 20 世纪 50 年代普通话推广工作展开以来,汉语各方言都出现了明显的向普通话靠拢的趋势。比如,四川话与齐撮口呼相拼的舌根音声母,除了"街""减"等口语中的常用字的声母,受普通话读音的影响,其余的字的声母与普通话趋同,读作舌面音,比如"(房)间""嵌""限"等字的声母即是如此。又如,即使在方言特色非常明显的粤方言区,我们都可以听到某些字句带有普通话的语音影响。二是共同语会逐步扩大自己的使用范围,方言的使用范围则将随之缩小。比如,在各方言区的中小学里,过去有不少教师使用当地方言进行教学,现在随着普通话的日益普及,使用普通话进行教学的教师越来越多。共同语的形成和发展虽然可以使方言分歧逐渐缩小,但语言的统一通常是一个长期的过程,不是一朝一夕就可以完成的。对一个地域广阔、人口众多、方言分歧严重、社会经济又欠发达的社会来说尤其如此。所以对我国来说,推广普通话,缩小方言差别,将是一个长期任务。

在共同语形成的过程中,人们会根据语言的实际情况为共同语制定一套规范,也就是共同语在语音、词汇和语法方面的明确标准,这套标准可以告诉人们什么样的话才是共同语。比如汉民族共同语——普通话的标准是"以北京语音为标准音,以北方方言为基础方言,以典范的现代白话文著作为语法规范",只有符合这些标准的话才算是普通话。如果一个民族共同语有了这样明确的规范,就可以叫作"民族标准语"(简称"标准语")。普通话就是汉民族标准语。

以上说的共同语是就一个社会(如一个民族)内部的语言形式而言的,在一个多民族的国家里,为了维系整个国家内部各民族之间的联系,还需要有共同的交际工具,这一共同的交际工具通常被称作"国家共同语"(简称"国语")或"国家通用语言"。2000 年 10 月 31 日,我国第九届全国人民代表大会常务委员会第十八次会议通过、2001 年 1 月 1 日起施行的《中华人民共和国国家通用语言文字法》,以法律形式明确规定,普通话是我国的国家通用语言。

因为国家通用语言是国家通过一定的程序确定下来的,所以有的人又把它称为"官方语言"。有些国家法定的国家通用语言不止一种,比如,加拿大的国家通用语有英语和法语两种,但以英语为主。新加坡宪法规定了四种官方语言,即马来语、华语(汉语)、泰米尔语和英语,但是另一方面却又规定马来语是新加坡国语,主要用来唱国歌;英语是新加坡行政、教育和贸易用语,也是各民族间交际的共同语。总的来看,这些国家虽然有多种国家通用语言,但往往是以一种语言为主。

一个国家采用一种还是多种国家通用语言,采用哪种或哪几种语言作为国家通用语言,这是由各国的语言规划决定的。一个国家在选择国家通用语言时,往往会充分考虑本国和本国各民族的长远利益,选用国内多数人使用的语言,或是国内经济文化发展水平较高,因而较有影响的民族的语言。

(二)多种语言统一为一种语言

多种语言统一为一种语言,是随着不同民族的接触和融合,通过语言转用的方式而产生的一种语言现象。语言转用指的是一个或几个民族放弃自己的语言而选用另一个民族的语言作为交际工具的现象。有人称这种现象为"语言融合"或"语言替换"。

语言融合是在一定的社会条件下发生的。首先,民族融合是语言融合的前提条件。民族融合有时是借助军事和政治上的征服进行的,在这种民族融合的过程中,征服者往往会强迫被征服民族放弃本民族的语言而改用征服者的语言。例如,大约公元前 500 年,凯尔特人从欧洲大陆侵入并占领了不列颠岛后,就迫使当地的伊比利亚人放弃自己的语言而使用凯尔特语。约到公元 449 年,北欧的盎格鲁、萨克逊、朱特三个日耳曼部族侵入不列颠居岛,又使用强制手段迫使当地民族放弃凯尔特语而改用盎格鲁-萨克逊语,即古英语。民族融合也可以不依靠强制手段而自愿融合。伴随民族的自愿融合,语言融合也可以自然发生。例如,我国的北魏时期,鲜卑族和汉族处于民族融合的关系之中,鲜卑族的统治者顺应社会经济和文化发展的需要,提倡鲜卑人学习并使用汉语,结果汉语取代了鲜卑语,成为鲜卑族和汉族共同的交际工具。其次,各族人民必须杂居在同一地区,在一个较长的时期内保持密切的联系,才有语言融合的可能性。例如,鲜卑族在中原建立政权之后,杂居在数量占优势的汉族人民中间,加之鲜卑族统治者实行有利于民族融合的政策,汉语最终取代了鲜卑语。后来的契丹、女真等民族在入主中原后也与汉族人民杂居,逐步与汉族融合,他们的语言也随之逐步与汉语融合。与之不同的是,蒙古族在建立元朝政权之后,仍然保持相对聚居的局面,蒙古族统治者又采取了一些防止与汉族融合的措施,加上元朝的统治时间不太长,蒙古族和蒙古语基本上没有与汉族和汉语融合。与之形成对照的是,元朝灭亡后,驻守云南的蒙古族官兵留在当地定居,与数量占优势的彝族人民杂居在一起,并同彝族女子通婚,这就促使他们放弃了本民族语言而使用彝语了。

在民族融合过程中,哪一种语言能够替代其他语言而成为全社会的交际工具,主要取决于哪一种语言的使用者占有经济、文化发展水平和人口数量优势这样的社会因素,而语言使用者在政治上的统治地位并不是决定因素。自魏晋以来,匈奴、鲜卑、羯、氐、羌、契丹、女真等民族都曾把汉族置于自己的统治之下,但是他们最后都放弃了自己的语言,转而使用汉语,这主要在于汉族人口众多,文化发展水平比较高,经济比较发达。

语言融合的过程大体上是一个从单语到双语,再由双语到新的单语的过程,一般要经历相当长的时间才能完成。这一过程大致是:开始的时候,一个民族在使用本族语的同时,出于社会交往的需要,逐渐学会另一民族的语言而形成双语现象,而后新学会的语言在交际中所起的作用越来越重要,使用的范围不断扩大,本民族语言则随之退居次要地位,使用范围逐渐萎缩,直至最后完全停止使用,至此语言融合过程完成。我们常常可以看到一些散居在主体民族之中的少数民族家庭,一家三代,第一代既使用本民族的语言,又会说主体民族的语言,但前一种语言通常只在家庭内使用,在公共场合则使用后一种语言;第二代只能听懂而不会说本民族的语言,到了第三代,就只会主体民族的语言了。这种一个家庭内部由双语到单语的变化,可以看作是语言融合的缩影。语言融合必然要经历一个双语阶段,没有这个阶段,语言融合就不可能实现,因为只有双语这种形式才能保证在从使用本民族语言向使用另一种语言的过渡中,不会造成语言使用的中断。在我国,那些基本放弃本民族语言而转用汉语的少数民族,如土家族、畲族、仡佬族、满族等,在转用汉语的过程中,毫无例外地都曾经历过一个双语程度很高的阶段。语言融合虽然必须经过一个双语阶段,但双语现象并非都会导致语言融合。一个民族兼用其他民族语言的双语现象可能长期、稳定地存在下去,因为语言融合的发生还要受到民族文化、民族心理、聚居程度、历史传统等因素的影响。例如,我国的白族早在隋唐时期就已有不少人兼用汉语,但至今仍处于比较稳定的双语阶段。

语言融合的过程,是一个两种语言密切接触的过程,在这个过程中必然产生语言间的相互影响,即使是被替代的语言,也会在胜利的语言中留下自己的痕迹。例如"邋遢"、"哈尔滨"、"齐齐哈尔"("哈尔"是"江"的意思)等,就是满语遗留在汉语中的一些成分。

又如,挪威人、丹麦人和诺曼底-法兰西人入侵英吉利之后,最后放弃了自己的语言而说英语,但英语也从这些语言中吸收了很多东西。例如,现代英语中的 they、them 和 their 等来自斯堪的纳维亚诸语言, 而 state、government、count、people、army、court、glory、fine、literature、art 等词以及-ment、-able、-tion 和-ess 等构词后缀则是法语遗留在英语中的成分。总之,在语言融合的漫长过程中,双语现象时期语言之间会相互影响。随着一种语言的消亡,这种痕迹就成为两种语言融合的历史见证。

# 第三节　语言接触与语言的发展

## 一、语言因社会的接触而接触

语言因为使用语言的人的接触而发生接触。因为贸易往来、人口迁徙、战争征服、海外殖民、文化交流等,历史上原本没有接触的社会由此发生人员接触,各个社会人员所使用的语言也就随之有了接触。发生接触的人可能使用的是同一种语言的不同方言,也可能使用的是不同的语言。语言学上所说的"语言接触",指的是不同民族或者不同社群由于社会生活中的相互接触而引起的语言接触关系。因此,语言接触可以说是一种社会语言学的状况。

从接触的途径方面看,语言接触可以分为直接接触和间接接触两种类型。直接接触是在人和人面对面的接触中通过口语交际实现的,间接接触主要是人通过文本与另一种语言、另一个人群的接触,所以发生接触的双方语言在时间和空间上是分离的。由于空间距离的阻隔,书面文本是间接接触的主要媒介,在现代社会里,间接语言接触也可以通过广播、电视、网络等非书面媒介发生。

接触的结果会出现语言借用、语言并存、语言转用和语言混合等情形。语言借用,指的是一种语言把别的语言的成分并入自己的语言系统的现象。语言并存,指的是某一言语社团使用两种或两种以上语言的一种社会现象。比如,我国北方地区的蒙古族和朝鲜族人口中,很多人都能够自由使用本民族语和汉语;居住在新疆伊犁地区的锡伯族中有会母语和汉语并通晓维吾尔语的人。语言转用,指的是一个或几个民族放弃自己的语言而选用另一个民族的语言作为交际工具的现象。比如,公元前 1000 年左右,欧洲莱茵河、塞纳河、卢瓦尔河流域和多瑙河上游居住着讲凯尔特语的凯尔特人,可从公元 4 世纪开始,这些地方的凯尔特人受到罗马人和日耳曼人的攻击,他们大部分的居住地并入罗马版图,接受了罗马文化,转用了拉丁语,今天的法语就是从那里的拉丁语演变而来的。语言混合,指的是在不同的语言频繁接触的地区,来源于不同语言的成分可能混合在一起,产生一种新的交际工具的现象。比如,鸦片战争之后到新中国成立之前在上海的来华商人、买办使用的洋泾浜英语,殖民地国家或地区使用的以英语、法语等语言为基础而形成的克里奥尔语等都是语言的混合形式,只是洋泾浜英语是特定人群在特殊的交际场合使用的交际工具,而克里奥尔语是某个社会群体把它当作母语来使用的混合语。

## 二、语言接触与语言的发展

语言并存、语言转用和语言混合三种语言接触结果中都有语言借用的影子。因为在语言并存的双语社团的两种语言的接触中,两种语言常常会彼此借用对方的语言成分;语言转用虽然是一种语言取代其他语言成为不同民族共同的交际工具,但是作为不同民族共同的交际工具的语言多多少少都借用了被替代语言的成分,比如现代汉语中的地名"哈尔滨""齐齐哈尔"等就是直接借用的满语的表达,其中"哈尔"是满语"江"的意思;而语言混合产生的新的语言形式本身就是采用了接触双方语言的成分混合而成的交际工具。所以,毋宁说语言并存、语言转用和语言混合是语言接触对社会语言生活的影响,语言借用则是语言接触对语言系统本身的影响。这样的话,语言借用多多少少会影响到作为借用方的语言的发展。接触语言学中把借用了其他语言的成分的语言称作接受语(recipient language),输出了语言成分的语言称作来源语(source language)。

如果两个社会的接触程度不深,即地域上不相邻且只有一般性的物质交换或文化交流,语言的借用一般只限于向对方语言借用自己语言中所没有的事物或观念的名称,即"不成系统的词汇借用"。但如果接触双方在地域上相邻且长期接触,还可能出现语音和语法方面的借用。这些借用对接受语的发展造成的影响表现在,因为借用来源语的词语而丰富了接受语的词汇系统,因为吸收来源语的语音成分而改变了接受语的语音系统的格局,因为借用来源语的语法规则而充实了接受语表达方式的多样性。

### (一)词语借用与接收语词汇系统的发展

从别的语言中借用来的词语叫借词,典型的狭义的借词又叫"外来词",指的是音和义都借自外语的词。比如,汉语在和英语的接触中,增加了从英语那里借入的"拷贝""雷达""克隆"等词语。而英语在和法语的接触中,增加了源于法语的 arms(武器、武装)、art

（艺术）、chic（别致、潇洒）等词语。借词和意译词、仿译词都不同,意译词是用本族语言的构词材料和规则构成的词,只是意义是从外语里移植进来的。就词形而言,意译词有两种,一种是接受语固有的词,比如,"解脱"是一个汉语固有词,义为"解除、解开",佛经翻译中,用这个词去意译梵语词 vimukti,获得了佛教词义"摆脱(痛苦或灾难)"。另一种意译词是用接受语的构词材料和规则构造新词,比如"提琴(violin)""墨水(ink)""水泥(cement)"等词语都是用汉语的构词语素和规则意译英语中相应的词产生的新词。仿译词则是用本族语的语素逐个对译外语原词的语素造成的词,这种词不仅把外语词的词义翻译过来,而且保持了外语词的内部构造方式。比如,"黑板"是对 blackboard 的仿译,"篮球"是对 basketball 的仿译,"机关枪"是对 machine gun 的仿译。

词语的借用,可以扩充接受语的词汇系统。以汉语为例,上古汉语以单音词为主,汉字在甲骨文中的数量约为 3500 个,到了《说文解字》中增加到 9353 个,到了南朝顾野王的《玉篇》,增加到 16917 个,明代梅膺祚的《字汇》共收字 33179 个,清代张玉书等编的《康熙字典》则共收字 47035 个。尽管其中有很多异体重文,但单音节的汉字一般等于词,加之一词多义,上面一个个增加的数字无疑反映了汉语在发展过程中词汇量的增加。汉语词汇之所以丰富,一方面与汉民族悠久的文明史有关,但另一方面也与汉民族在与其他民族的接触过程中吸收其他民族的语言成分有很大的关系。纵观汉语词汇史,至鸦片战争之前,汉语共有三次较大规模地吸收外来词:(1)公元前 3 世纪至五胡乱华以前,主要吸收了匈奴和西域的词语,比如,"骆驼"就是从匈奴语借用的,"狻猊""石榴""菠萝"是从西域借用的词。(2)东汉末到隋唐时期,主要从梵语系统借用了大量的佛教词语。(3)从唐代末期至 19 世纪鸦片战争之前,其间,自明末起,开始从西方接受新词。这三次大规模的外来词的吸收,极大地丰富了汉语词汇系统,不仅充实了汉语包括哲学、民俗、文学及日常用语等领域的常用词汇,而且"魔""塔""佛"等词语的吸收也扩大了汉语的基本词汇。

其实,词语的借用,除了可以扩充接受语的词汇系统以外,还可以加速接受语某种词语节律模式的发展,促进词汇体系格局的形成。比如,双音节化是汉语词语发展的大趋势。上古汉语中的词语以单音节为主,到了汉魏六朝时期,双音节词明显增加,其间,因佛经翻译产生的大批佛教词语大大加速了汉语双音节化的进程。而始于 16 世纪末的耶稣会士的西书翻译,尤其是进入 19 世纪以后,新教传教士主导的宗教或者世俗书籍的翻译以及汉外辞典的编纂,都催生了大量的双音节词;19 世纪末 20 世纪初,在汉译日本书的影响下,双音节词数量再次空前增长,最终奠定了现代汉语词汇体系以双音节词为主的基本格局。

（二）语言接触与接受语其他语言要素的发展

自 20 世纪 50 年代以来,我国语言学界一般认为语言是由语音、词汇和语法三大要素组成的。随着科学的发展和语言学家们认知的深化,语言学理论也取得了长足的发展。近年来,语言学界普遍认为语言是由语音、词汇、语义和语法四大要素组成的,且这一认识也基本上是我国语言学界的共识。

在语言接触中,不仅有词语的借用,语音、语义和语法都可能发生借用,且影响接受语的发展。

语音方面的借用包括音位的借用和音位组合形式的借用,其结果是接受语会增加相应的音位和音位组合。比如,非洲南部的祖鲁语从克瓦桑语群借入了吸气音;我国的回辉话在汉语影响下产生了声调范畴,前者属于音质音位的增加,后者属于非音质音位的增加。我国裕固语在和汉语的接触过程中,增加了从汉语借入的新的音位组合形式——16 个复元音:［ai］［au］［ei］［ie］［uo］［ye］［ian］［iən］［uai］［əu］［ia］［io］［ua］［uə］［ue］［ya］。其中后面 7 个复元音不仅用于汉语借词,而且还用于本族语言的词语。

在语言接触中,语义借用是很常见的。词语借用,必然伴随着语义的借用,除此之外,意译和仿译也是接受语增加新词义的途径。由于意译是利用接受语已有词语或者在接受语构词材料和规则基础上构造新词去翻译来源语相应的词语,所以意译的结果要么是为接受语固有词增加外来词义,要么是以新造意译词为载体引进新词义,前者如“因缘”,在汉语里本是“机会”的意思［《史记·田叔列传》:（任安）求事为小吏,未有因缘也。］,佛经翻译用为梵语词 hetupratyaya 的意译,指“得以形成事物、引起认识和造就业报等现象所依赖的原因和条件”。后者如“电话”和“银行”等,都是用汉语的构词材料和规则构成新词意译英语词 telephone 和 bank。而“马力”和“蜜月”则分别是对英语词 horsepower 和 honeymoon 的仿译,不仅使汉语增加了新词,而且增加了新义。接受语借用来源语的词义,填补了自己语言系统的表义空白。

语法方面的借用包括词缀的借用、虚词的借用和语法规则的借用。例如,英语从拉丁语借用了后缀-ive、-ish、-ous 等,而伴随 algebra（代数学）、alcohl（酒精）、alkali（强碱）等外来词的借用,从阿拉伯语借用了前缀 al-。我国的侗族语吸收了汉语的结构助词“的”以及介词“比”“连”“为”等。我国有些少数民族语言在大量借用汉语词语的基础上,还吸收了汉语的一些语法结构规则。比如,纳西语的动宾结构原来只有“宾+动”的语序,如“补天”要说“mɯ³³（天）iə²¹（补）”,“关闭天缝”要说“mɯ³³（天）khu⁵⁵（缝）tər⁵⁵（关闭）”。但由于汉语的影响,现在纳西语里也有了“动+宾”的语序了。汉语主从复句的语序,从上古到五四前,一直是从句位于主句之前,但近代与印欧语系语言,尤其是与英语的接触中,受英语主从复句的语序规则的影响,在很多情况下,从句的位置不再固定在主句之前,而是可前可后了。

# 第四节　语言系统的发展

语言的发展首先表现在语音、语汇、语法等语言系统内部的各个组成部分上。只是它们的发展变化通常比较缓慢,所以人们不易觉察。

## 一、语音的发展

### (一)语音发展的规律性

随着时间的推移,语音在发生着变化。在读古诗的时候我们常常会遇到按诗律本该押韵的字不押韵的情况,这就是语音变化造成的。

语音的变化不是杂乱无章的,而是遵循着一定的规律,因为语音变化往往不是一个音的孤立的变化,而是一种发音习惯的改变。一种发音习惯支配着一个系列音位的语音表现,它的改变自然会影响这一个系列的音位的变化。例如汉语从中古到近代这段历史时期,北方地区的双唇浊声母音位/b/清化为/p/,说明辅音发音时的声带颤动这一发音习惯发生了变化,这一习惯变化影响所及,所有的浊辅音都清化为相应的清辅音。由于一系列的音位的变化隐含着一个共同的发音习惯的改变,因此我们只要抓住这种发音习惯的变化,就可以在纷乱的变化中整理出语音演变的规律,将之总结概括为一定的音变规律。比如,"古无轻唇音""古无舌上音"和格里姆定律就分别是关于汉语和印欧语系音变规则的精辟概括。

语音演变有很强的规律性。这种演变的规律性有几个明显的特点。第一个是条件性。语音变化有一定的条件限制。比如汉语中古"见/k/""精/ts/"两组声母在近代腭化为/tɕ/组声母,其条件是它们要处在齐、撮二呼之前。凡符合条件的一律都变,没有例外。如果出现例外,也可以找出产生例外的原因。比如"精"组的"卡"字在北京话中有两读,一读 qiǎ(如"卡住"的"卡"),符合汉语"精"组声母的腭化规律,可是另一读 kǎ(如

"卡车"的"卡")却是一个例外读音。其原因涉及语音演变规律的第二个特点,时间性。语音演变规律只在一段时期内起作用,过了这一时期,即使处于同样的条件下也不会遵循原来的规律发生语音变化。在北京话中,"卡车"的"卡"读 kǎ,不按腭化演变规律读 qiǎ,其原因是"精"组腭化在 18 世纪之前已经完成,"卡车"一词来自粤语对英语 car 的翻译,当它被北方话吸收时,北方汉语"精"组声母的腭化已经完成了,此处的"卡"的读音就不再遵循腭化演变的规律,而按其方言音读了。第三,地区性。语音演变只在一定的地域中进行,越出一定的地域,某一演变规律就不会起作用。比如,浊音清化的规律在北方话系统中普遍起作用,而在吴语区和湘语区则仍然保留原来的浊音,并没有发生清化的现象。又如,第二次世界大战之后,词语中的 r 在美国英语中要发音,而在英国英语中仍然和第二次世界大战前一样不发音,这也是语音具有地域性的表现。

（二）音位系统的发展

个别的语音演变可能引起语言中音位系统的发展。音位系统的发展主要包含以下内容:

1.音位的合并。比如由于浊音清化的结果,中古汉语的一系列浊音音质音位到了现代汉语普通话里都并入相应的清音音质音位,音位的数目减少了。以中古/＊d/音质音位的归并为例:

| 例字 | 中古汉语的声母 | 现代汉语普通话声母 |
|---|---|---|
| 斗 | ＊t | t |
| 偷 | ＊t' | t' |
| 豆 | ＊d(仄声) | t |
| 头 | ＊d(平声) | t' |

中古汉语三个舌尖中音音位在现代汉语普通话中合并成了/t,t'/两个音位。

2.音位的分化。例如,上古汉语无轻唇音"非[pf]、敷[pf']、奉[bv]、微[ɱ]",只有重唇音"帮[p]、滂[p']、并[b]、明[m]",到了中古,从重唇音中分化出了轻唇音。

音位的合并和分化有时是交错进行的。例如上面举过的汉语浊音清化的例子,从/＊t,＊t',＊d/三个音位演变为/t,t'/两个音位来说,是音位的合并;但从/＊d/演变为/t,t'/的过程来说,又是音位的分化。

非音质音位在历史发展中也会发生合并和分化。例如中古汉语有平、上、去、入四个调位,到了现代汉语普通话就变为另外四个调位:阴平、阳平、上声和去声。其间的分合情况是:中古的平声清声母和浊声母分化为现代汉语普通话的阴平和阳平;上声清声母和次浊声母合并为上声;上声全浊声母和去声合并为去声;入声分化为阴平、阳平、上声和去声。也可以说平声清声母和部分入声合并为阴平;平声浊声母和部分入声合并为阳平;上声清声母、上声次浊声母和部分入声合并为上声;上声全浊声母、去声和部分入声合并为去声。

3.音位关系的改变。音位的分合必然使音位间的对立关系发生变化。例如中古汉语/＊p,＊p',＊b/、/＊t,＊t',＊d/、/＊k,＊k',＊g/三组塞音音位中各有清浊的对立,在清塞音音位之间又有送气与不送气的对立。到了现代汉语普通话,/＊b,＊d,＊g/的消失引起清浊对立的消失,以上三组音位只剩下/p,p'//t,t'//k,k'/送气与不送气的对立。除了对立关系外,音位间的组合规则(包括音节结构)也会在语音的发展中起变化。例如在古汉语里,舌尖齿龈音音位/＊ts,＊ts',＊s/和舌根音音位/＊k,＊k',＊x/都能出现在音位/＊i/或/＊j/之前,如"酒"［＊tsju］、"心"［＊sjm］、"饥"［＊ki］、"欺"［＊k'i］,现代汉语普通话却没有这种组合。

## 二、语法的发展

在语言系统的各个组成部分中,语法具有很大的稳固性。不过,在表达的要求、语音的演变和语法的类推等各种因素的影响下,语法还是在逐渐地发展演变。语法的发展包括语法的组合规则和聚合规则的演变。而组合规则和聚合规则互有联系,所以一类的演变可能会引起另一类的演变。

(一)组合规则的发展

组合规则的发展主要表现为词序的改变。

印欧语最早的词序,从古印度的文献《梨俱吠陀》中可以看出,宾语在动词的前面。"宾-动"的次序是当初句法的主要特点。随着语言的发展,印欧系语言大多由"宾-动"型变成"动-宾"型。

汉语是不依赖严格意义的形态变化的语言,词序在表示语法关系和语法意义方面占有特殊的地位。从文献材料来看,先秦的古代汉语发展到现代汉语,词序总的来说变化不是很大,不过还是有一些变化。比如,先秦汉语中,疑问代词作宾语或人称代词在否定句中作宾语,应该放在动词之前。例如,"臣实不才,又谁敢怨?"(《左传·成公三年》),"梁客辛垣衍安在?"(《战国策·赵策》);"我无尔诈,尔无我虞"(《左传·宣公十五年》)"我胜若,若不吾胜"(《庄子·齐物论》);等等。自汉魏以后,特别是南北朝以后,代词宾语的位置逐步移到动词后面。

又如,先秦文献中,处所介词词组基本位于所修饰的中心成分之后,例如,"子击磬于卫"(《论语·宪问》),"逢蒙学射于羿"(《孟子·离娄下》);而在现代汉语中,这种介词词组很少位于所修饰的中心成分之后了。

270

五四以后,汉语由于受到西方语言的影响,有了一些新兴的词序。例如汉语中的主从复合句一般都是从句在前,主句在后,而在英语等西方语言里,从句前置、后置均可。五四以后,汉语中的从句也出现了后置的情况。例如,"所以什么谎都可以说,只要说得好听;做贼,赌钱,都可以做,只要做得好看。"(丁西林《一只马蜂》)五四以后,汉语文学语言还吸收了西方语言叙述对话的一种结构形式,就是在复合句的中间用"某某说"之类的语句隔开。例如,"完了?"赵太爷不觉失声地说,"哪里会完得这样快呢?"(鲁迅《阿Q正传》)

（二）聚合规则的发展

语法聚合规则的发展主要表现为形态的改变,语法范畴的消长和词类的发展。

聚合规则在发展中最引人注目的是形态的改变。比如现代英语名词的单、复数多半是用加或不加词尾"s"("es")来表示的:

| 单数 | bird | field | son | book |
| 复数 | birds | fields | sons | books |

可是,在历史上,名词单、复数的形式可能与现在很不相同。例如在古代英语中,上面所举的四个词的形式是:

| 单数 | bridd | feld | sunu | bōc |
| 复数 | briddas | felda | suna | bēc |

可见,这些词的单复数形式在英语的发展过程中都起了变化。

形态的改变还会引起语法范畴的消长。据拟测,原始印欧语名词有三个性、三个数、八个格的变化,因而有性、数、格的语法范畴。这些形态变化在现代法语里已经发生了很大的变化,名词性的范畴只剩下阴阳性;数的范畴只剩下单复数的对立,双数已经消失;格范畴则已经消失。

语法聚合规则的发展还表现在词类的发展上。在各种语言中,有不少虚词是实词虚化而来的。比如古代汉语中的动词"在""把""被""向"等,在历史发展过程中,逐渐虚化为介词。又如,英语完成时态的语法标记 have 是从表示"拥有、持有、据有某物"之义的实义动词虚化而来的。

语法中的聚合规则和组合规则有密切的联系,一方面的变化往往引起另一方面的变化。例如拉丁语有丰富的形态变化,词与词的关系可以通过词形变化表现出来,词序不占重要位置。比如"父亲爱儿子"这样一句话可以有各种词序(pater,父亲,主格;filium,儿子,宾格;amat,爱)

Pater amat filium. / Pater filium amat. / Filium amat pater. / Filium pater amat. / Amat pater filium. / Amat filium pater.

由于音变的结果,拉丁语中原来表示格的变化的词尾在法语里由弱化而脱落,原来由聚合规则表示的词与词之间的语法关系改由词序、虚词等组合手段来表示。上面这句话的意思在现代法语中的词序只有一种:

Le père aime le fils.

这是聚合规则的变化引起组合规则变化的一个典型例子。

## 三、词汇的发展

简单地说,词汇就是词语的总汇。词汇发展的一般趋势体现为一些词语产生、一些词语消失和词语的替换。

词汇随着社会的发展而发展。社会发展,新事物不断涌现,词汇中随之会不断出现新词语。比如,自20世纪90年代中后期以来,网络逐渐进入中国寻常百姓的生活,随之产生了许多与网络有关的词语,如"网民""上网""网管""网聊""博客""播客"等。社会发展,一些事物随之消亡,又会使一些词语消失,如汉语中"太子""天子""宰相""丞相"等词语都随着旧事物的消失而在人们的日常生活中不用了。社会发展,人们的观念也在发生变化,对于某些事物的称谓可能会更换一种说法,使得词汇中的一些词语被替换。例如1949年之前通行的含有等级观念的"戏子""车夫""司令官"等词语后来被"演员(艺人)""司机""司令员"等词语取代。

语言系统内部的原因也会引起词汇的发展。语言是人类最重要的交际工具。人们在运用语言表达思想、进行交际的时候,用词总是力求经济、准确,避免可能的混淆。语言中的同音词过多会给交际带来麻烦。为了使语言能有效地表达思想,避免同音混淆带来的歧义,汉语在发展过程中产生了大量的复音词;原来词汇中的主要成员单音词有的消失了,有的成了构词语素,如"鲤鱼""桃子""杏树""美丽""增高"等词语中的"鲤""桃""杏""美""丽""增"等曾经都是能够独立使用的词语,现在都成了构词语素。词汇中单音词为主变为复音词为主的过程,也是复音词替换单音词的过程。

词汇在发展过程中,一些词语产生,一些词语消失,一些词语被替换,其结果是导致词语数量的增减,也可能导致词汇系统面貌的改变。例如汉语词汇系统由单音词为主变为复音词为主,就是词汇系统面貌的改变。

## 四、词义的发展

(一)词义发展的表现

词义的发展是指词在它所处的语义场中的地位发生了变化。讨论词义的发展,要以义位为单位,而不能笼统地以一个词为单位,就像我们前面讨论语音的发展是以音位为单位一样。词义的发展表现在词的义位数量的增减和原有义位的变化两个方面。例如,"快"在古代有一个义位"愉快",现代仍然保留了这个义位,同时又产生了一个新的义位"迅速",这是义位数量的增加。"慢"在古代有两个义位:"怠慢"和"缓慢",到现代"怠慢"这一义位基本消失,只保留"缓慢"这一义位,这是义位的减少。又如,"子"在上古有"子女"和"男子的美称"两个义位,在历史发展过程中,"男子的美称"义基本消失,但另外又产生了两个新的义位"种子"(如"子实")和"幼小的"(如"子猪""子鸡"),也就是说,"子"的义位的数量既有减少也有增加。

原有义位的变化表现在义位的扩大、缩小或转移三个方面。

一个义位在历史发展过程中减少了限定性义素,这个义位由下位义变成上位义,这就是词义的扩大。例如,"唱"在古代指领唱,现代指一切歌唱,它的义素变化是:

唱(古):[带头]+[唱]→唱(今):[唱]。

在发展过程中,"唱"减少了曾有的限定性义素"带头",所以它的词义扩大了。又如,法语的 arriver 原来仅指经由水路的"靠岸"的意思,现在泛指"到达",不管是经由水路、陆路还是航空路线的到达,限定义素减少了,属于词义的扩大。

一个义位在历史发展过程中增加了限定性义素,这个义位由上位义变成下位义,这就是词义的缩小。例如,"谷(穀)",古代指百谷,就是粮食作物的总称,现在北方指小米,南方指稻谷。其义素变化为:

谷(古):粮食作物→谷(今):一种粮食作物(北方指小米,南方指稻谷)。

又如英语的 deer 最初是"动物"的意思,现在只指"鹿"这种动物,其意义也由上位义变成了下位义,也属于词义的缩小。

转移是一个义位某一限定义素保留,其他义素特别是中心义素变化而引起的词义变化。其结果是使得这个义位由一个语义场转入到另一个语义场。如"兵",古代指兵器,和"甲""革""乘"等处于同一语义场,其义素为[作战用的]+[器械],中心义素是[器械]。现代指士兵,和"工""农""学""商"等处于同一语义场,其义素为[持兵器的]+[人],中心义素是[人]。比较古代的"兵"和现代的"兵",它们有共同的义素(前者的义素全部包含在后者之中),但是古代的"兵"发展到现代,其中心义素和所处的语义场都变

273

了,所以从古代到现代,"兵"的词义发生了转移。

词义扩大或缩小后,一般是新义代替了旧义,即随着新义的产生,旧义就消失了。而转移则不同。转移有两种情况:一是新义产生后旧义消失,如上面举的"兵"就属这种情况;一是新义产生后旧义依然存在,如"子"从"子女"义引申出"种子"(如"子实")义就属这种情况。原有义位的转移可能导致一个词义位数量的增加或减少。可见原有义位的变化与义位数量的增减是有关系的。

(二)词义发展的原因

义位数量的增减和原有义位的扩大、缩小或转移是词义发展的结果。那么促使词义发展的原因是什么呢?

现实现象的变化会引起词义的变化。例如,"钟"是古代的一种乐器,与"磬""埙""簧"等乐器处于同一语义场,自从西方的时钟传入我国以后,"钟"则用来指报时的时钟,与"表"同属于计时器语义场。"钟"词义的变化是由现实现象的变化引起的。

人们对现实想象认识的发展也会引起词义的变化。比如一个词义位数量的增加,往往是人们对现实想象认识的发展引起的,如前面所举的"子"增加的"种子"和"幼小的"两个义位就因人们对"子女"不同角度的认识而产生的(人的"子女"是"子",植物的"子女"也可以是"子";"子女"在父母眼中总是"幼小的")。

词义之间的相互影响也会引起词义的变化。例如,"快"有"迅速"的意思,后来产生出"(刀、斧、剪等)锋利"的意思,于是"快"的反义词"慢"在北方话的一些地区中也逐渐产生出和"锋利"对立的"钝"的意思,出现了"刀慢"之类的说法。又如,佛教传入中国后,因僧人多穿黑衣,"黑"有了"僧人"的意思,在它的影响下,其反义词"白"增加了一个义位"俗徒"。词义之间相互影响引起词义变化,其背后的机制则是人们的类推,比如,刀锋利既然可以说成"刀快",通过类推,刀钝就可以说成"刀慢","慢"于是发展出"(刀)钝"的意义。

(三)词义发展的途径

以上所说的几种因素都会引起词义的发展,词义发展变化的途径最主要的是引申。引申是基于联想作用而产生的一种词义发展。从甲义引申出乙义,两个意义之间必然有某种联系,或者说意义有相关的部分。正是这种联系或相关,使人们产生联想,联想出来的意义如果被经常使用,它就会固定下来,成为一个从甲乙中引申出来的乙义。

引申的方式有隐喻和换喻两种。隐喻是因为相似而产生的联想。比如英语的 green(绿色),可指水果未成熟,因为一般而言绿色的水果还未成熟,而无经验的人在某一点上就像绿色的水果还未成熟,二者之间的这一个相似性,使得 green 引申出了"(人)无经验"(如 a green hand,生手)的意思。

换喻是因为相关而产生的联想。两类现象之间如果存在着某种相关关系,这种相关在人们心目中经常出现而固定化,因而可用指称甲类现象的词去指称乙类现象。比如,"帆"本是船的一部分,后来发展出"船"(孤帆远影碧空尽)的意思,就是通过换喻的方式引申出来的。

## 思考与练习

简答题

1.语言发展的原因是什么?

2.语言发展有什么样的特点?

3.举例分析语言发展的不平衡性。

4.地域方言形成的原因。

5.举例说明地域方言之间的差别。

6.举例说明社会方言产生的原因。

7.简要说明语言统一的两种情况。

8.简要说明语言系统发展的概况。

## 【原典阅读】

# 1. Diachronic Linguistics
## Saussure

CHAPTER I　General Observations

Diachronic linguistics studies the relations which hold not between the coexisting terms of a linguistic state, but between successive terms substituted one for another over a period of time.

Absolute stability in a language is never found. All parts of the language are subject to change, and any period of time will see evolution of greater or smaller extent. It may vary in rapidity or intensity. But the principle admits no exceptions. The linguistic river never stops flowing. Whether its course is smooth or uneven is a consideration of secondary importance.

It is true that this uninterrupted evolution is often hidden from us by the attention paid to the corresponding literary language. A literary language is superimposed upon the vernacular, which is the natural form a language takes, and it is subject to different conditions of existence. Once a literary language is established, it usually remains fairly stable, and tends to perpetuate itself unaltered. Its dependence on writing gives it special guarantees of conservation. Hence this is not the place to look if we wish to see how variable natural languages are when free from literary regimentation.

Historical phonetics, and historical phonetics in its entirety, is the first object of study in diachronic linguistics. Sound change cannot be reconciled with the notion of a linguistic state. Comparing sounds or groups of sounds with what they were at an earlier period means establishing a diachronic succession. The earlier period may be remote or recent; but as soon as two periods merge, then we are no longer dealing with historical phonetics. We are dealing with the sounds of a single linguistic state, and that is the province of descriptive phonetics.

The diachronic character of historical phonetics is in complete conformity with the principle that nothing in historical phonetics is significant or grammatical, in the broad sense of the term. For establishing the history of the pronunciation of a word, its meaning is irrelevant. One need consider only the material envelope of the word. One can segment it into phonetic parts without inquiring whether these parts have any meaning. One can ask, for example, what happened in Attic Greek to the group *-ewo-*, which has no meaning. If the evolution of a language were nothing more than the evolution of its sounds, the contrast between what belongs to the two branches of linguistics would be immediately conspicuous. One would see clearly that diachronic is to be equated with non-grammatical, and synchronic with grammatical.

But what apart from sounds changes over time? Words change their meanings. Grammatical categories change. Some of the latter disappear along with the forms which served to express them (e. g. the dual in Latin). But if all the various associative and syntagmatic facts have their histories, how can any absolute distinction between diachrony and synchrony be maintained? It becomes very difficult once one goes beyond pure historical phonetics.

Let us note, however, that many changes classed as grammatical changes turn out to be sound changes. In German, the creation of noun plurals of the type *Hand* ('hand') vs. *Hände* ('hands'), and their substitution for plurals of the type *hant* vs. *hanti*, is to be explained entirely by sound change. The same is true of German compounds of the type *Springbrunnen* ('fountain', i. e. 'spring-well'), *Reitschule* ('riding-school'), etc. In Old High German, the first element of these compounds was not a verb but a noun: *beta-hūs* meant 'prayer house'. But when the final vowel fell (*beta→bet-*, etc.), it became linked semantically with the verb 'to pray' (*beten*) and *Bethaus* came to mean 'house for praying'.

Something similar happened to the compounds formed in early Germanic with the word *lich* 'external appearance' (e.g. *mannolīch* 'having the appearance of a man', *redolīch* 'having the appearance of reason'). Today, German has a great number of adjectives in which *-lich* has become a suffix (*verziehlich* 'pardonable', *glaublich* 'credible'), rather like the French suffix *-able* (*pardonnable* 'pardonable', *croyable* 'credible'). At the same time, the interpretation of the first element in these German words has changed, being no longer looked upon as a noun but as a verb root. This is because in a number of cases the fall of the final vowel of this first element (e.g. *redo→ red-*) caused it to be assimilated to a verb root (the *red-*of *reden* 'to speak').

Thus in *glaublich*, *glaub-* is connected with *glauben* ('to believe') rather than *Glaube* ('belief'). Similarly, in spite of the difference in the stems, *sichtlich* ('visibly') is connected with *sehen* ('to see') and no longer with *Sicht* ('sight').

In all these cases and many comparable ones, the distinction between the two orders remains clear. But it is necessary to bear it in mind. Otherwise, one may loosely claim to be doing historical grammar when in fact one is doing two things: first, studying a sound change (which falls in the diachronic domain), and then examining its consequences (which falls in the synchronic domain).

But this does not resolve all the problems one encounters. The evolution of any grammatical feature, associative group, or syntagmatic type is not comparable to that of a sound. For it is not a single thing. It splits up into a number of separate things, of which only some belong to historical phonetics. In the birth of a new syntagmatic type, such as the French future tense *prendrai* ('I will take') from *prendre+ai* ('to take' +'I have'), at least two factors must be distinguished. One is psychological—the synthesis of two conceptual elements. The other is phonetic and depends on the first—the reduction from two stresses, one on *prendre* and one on *ai*, to a single stress giving *prendrai*.

The flexional system of Germanic strong verbs, represented in modern German by *geben* ('to give'), with past tense *gab* ('gave'), past participle *gegeben* ('given'), etc. (cf. Greek *leípō*, *élipon.*, *léloipa*, etc.), is mainly based upon the umlaut affecting stem vowels. The alternations, which were originally fairly straightforward, are clearly the result of a purely phonetic change. For these oppositions to acquire such functional importance, the early flexional system had to undergo simplification by a variety of processes. They included the disappearance of many varieties of present tense forms, together with the different shades of meaning associated with them, the disappearance of the imperfect, the future, the aorist, the reduplicated perfect, and so on. There was nothing essentially phonetic about these changes. But they reduced verb flexion to a very small set of forms. The stem alternations thus acquired a significant value of great importance. We can say that the opposition *e* vs. *a* is more significant for German *geben* vs. *gab* than is the opposition *e* vs. *o* for Greek *leípō* vs. *léloipa*, because of the absence of reduplication in the German perfect.

Although sound change often intervenes in some way or other in linguistic evolution, it does not explain everything, When the phonetic factor has been given its due, there still remains a residue which appears to justify the notion that there is a 'history of grammar'. That is where the real difficulty lies. The distinction—which must be upheld—between diachronic and synchronic calls for detailed explanatioris which cannot be given here.[1]

In what follows, we shall examine in turn sound change, alternation, and analogy. Finally, we shall deal briefly with popular etymology and agglutination.

---

[1] To this didactic, external reason another must perhaps be added. Saussure never lectured on the linguistics of speech. It will be recalled that in his view linguistic innovations always begin with various isolated occurrences. One might suppose that Saussure refused to recognise these as grammatical facts, since an isolated occurrence is necessarily divorced from the language and its system, which depends entirely on a whole set of communal habits. As long as facts belong to speech, they are merely special, occasional instances of the use of an established system. Only when an innovation, by frequent repetition, becomes fixed in the memory and thus enters the system does it have the effect of disturbing the equilibrium of values, and the language is *ipso facto* changed immediately. The remarks on p. [36] and p. [121] concerning phonetic evolution could also be applied to grammatical evolution: its development lies outside the system. For one never sees the system itself evolving. It is merely found to be different at different stages. This attempted explanation is no more than a suggestion we should like to out forward (Editorial note).

## CHAPTER II  Sound Changes

### § 1. *Their absolute regularity*

Sound change, as we have seen affects not words, but sounds. A given speech sound alters, and this is an isolated occurrence, like all diachronic events. But the consequence is that all the words in which the sound in question occurs alter in an identical way. In this sense, phonetic changes are absolutely regular.

In German, $\bar{\imath}$ became *ei*, and then *ai*: thus *wīn*, *trīben*, *līhen*, *zīt*, became *Wein*, *treiben*, *leihen*, Zeit. German $\bar{u}$ became *au*: so *hūs*, *zūn*, *rūch* became *Haus*, *Zaun*, *Rauch*. German $\bar{u}$ became *eu*: so *hūsir* became *Häuser*, etc. On the other hand, the German diphthong *ie* became $\bar{\imath}$, although it continues to be written *ie*, as in *biegen*, *lieb*, *Tier*. In a parallel way, *uo* became $\bar{u}$: so *muot* became *Mut*, etc. German *z* became *s* (written *ss*): so *wazer* became *Wasser*, *fliezen* became *fliessen*, etc. German *h* between vowels fell: so *līhen* became *leien* (still written *leihen*), and *sehen* became *seen* (still written *sehen*), German *w* became labiodental *v* (still written *w*): so *wazer* became *vasr* (written *Wasser*).

In French, palatal *l'* became a yod ($y$): so *piller*, *bouillir* are now pronounced *piye*, *buyir*, etc.

In Latin, intervocalic *s* became *r*: \**genesis* became *generis*, \**asēna* became *arēna*, etc.

Any phonetic change, seen in correct perspective, confirms the perfect regularity of these developments.

### § 2. *Conditioning of sound changes*

The foregoing examples show that sound changes, far from being quite general, are usually restricted by specific conditions. In other words, it is not the sound type itself which alters, but the sound as it occurs in certain conditions determined by environment, stress, etc. Thus s became *r* in Latin only between vowels and in one or two other positions: otherwise it remained (cf. *est*, *senex*, *equos*).

Unconditioned changes are extremely rare. When they do occur, they often appear to be unconditioned because the conditioning factor is obscure, or else very general. Thus in German $\bar{\imath}$ became *ei*, then *ai*, but only in stressed syllables. Proto-Indo-European $k_1$ becomes *h* in Germanic (cf. Proto-Indo-European $k_1$*olsum*, Latin *collum*, German *Hals*); but the change does not take place after s (cf. Greek *skótos*, Gothic *skadus* 'shadow').

The distinction between conditioned and unconditioned changes rests in any case on taking a superficial view of the phenomena involved. It is more rational to speak, as is increasingly done, of *spontaneous* and *combinative* changes. Sound changes are spontaneous when produced by some internal cause, and combinative when the result of the presence of one or more other sounds. The change of Proto-Indo-European *o* to *a* in Germanic (e.g. Gothic *skadus*, German *Hals*) is a spontaneous change. The consonantal mutations, or *Lautverschiebungen*, of Germanic are typical of spontaneous change. Thus Proto-Indo-European $k_1$ becomes *h* in Proto-Germanic (cf. Latin *collum*, Gothic *hals*). Proto-Germanic *t*, kept in English, becomes *z* (pronounced *ts*) in High German (cf. Gothic *taihun*, English *ten*, German *zehn*). The change of Latin *ct* and *pt* to *tt* in Italian, on the other hand, (Latin *factum*→Italian *fatto*, Latin *captīvum*→Italian *cattivo*) is a combinative change, since the first consonant was assimilated to the second. The German umlaut is also due to an external cause, the presence of $i$ in the following syllable: thus while *gast* remains unchanged, *gasti* becomes *gesti*, then *Gäste*.

In neither type of case, it should be noted, does it make any difference what the result is. Nor is it even important whether a change takes place or not. If we compare Gothic *fisks* with Latin *piscis*, and Gothic *skadus* with Greek *skótos*, it will be observed that in the first case the $i$ remains, whereas in the second case there has been a change of $o$ to $a$. So in one instance a sound has stayed unchanged, while in the other a sound has altered. But the crucial point is that both developments are spontaneous.

If a sound change is combinative, it is always conditioned. But if it is spontaneous, it is not necessarily unconditioned, because it may be conditioned negatively by the absence of certain factors relevant to change. Proto-Indo-European $k_2$ spontaneously becomes $qu$ in Latin (e. g. *quattuor*, *inquilīna*), but not when followed, for example, by $o$ or $u$ (cf. *cottīdie*, *colō*, *secundus*, etc.). Likewise, the survival of Proto-Indo-European $i$ in Gothic *fisks*, etc. is governed by a condition: it must not be followed by $r$ or $h$, in which case it becomes $e$ (written $ai$): e.g. *wair* = Latin *Uir maihstus* = German *Mist*.

......

§ 4. *Causes of sound change*

Investigating the causes of sound change is one of the most difficult tasks in linguistics. Various explanations have been proposed. None is entirely satisfactory.

Ⅰ. It is said that racial predispositions determine the direction of sound changes. There is a question of comparative anthropology involved. But does the vocal apparatus vary from one race to another? No. Hardly more than from one individual to another. A negro brought to France at birth speaks French as well as any Frenchman. Further more, to speak of 'the Italian vocal apparatus' or to say 'the German mouth does not allow this' is to risk presenting as a permanent characteristic what is merely a historical fact. It is a mistake comparable to formulating a sound change in the present tense. To claim that the Ionian vocal apparatus rejects long $\bar{a}$ and changes it to $\bar{e}$ is quite as erroneous as saying that $\bar{a}$ 'becomes' $\bar{e}$ in Ionic.

The Ionian vocal apparatus had not the slightest reluctance to pronounce $\bar{a}$, for that vowel is indeed found in certain cases. Thus there is no question of any physiological incapacity, but simply of a change of articulatory habits. Similarly Latin, which had not kept intervocalic s ( *genesis→ generis*), reintroduced it a little later ( *rīssus-rīsus*).These changes do not point to any permanent disposition of the Latin vocal apparatus.

It is indeed possible to recognise a general tendency in phonetic changes at a given period in a given community. The reduction of diphthongs to monophthongs in modern French manifests the same general tendency. But one could find similar general movements in political history, without being led on that account to question their purely historical nature or to suspect the operation of some underlying racial factor.

Ⅱ. Phonetic change has often been regarded as an adaptation to geographical and climatic conditions. In Europe, certain languages of the north are full of consonants, while certain languages of the south make a more liberal use of vowels, and thus strike the ear as harmonious. Climate and living conditions may well have some effect upon a language. But the problem becomes complicated as soon as one looks at the details. For example, although Scandinavian languages may be overburdened with consonants, the languages of the Laps and the Finns are more vocalic even than Italian. It must also be noted that the accumulation of consonants in modern German is, in most cases, a quite recent development due to the fall of post-tonic vowels; that some dialects of southern France are less reluctant to accept consonant groups than northern French; that Serbian has as many as the Russian of Moscow; and so on.

Ⅲ. Appeal has been made to the law of least effort. This is held to explain the replacement of a double articulation by a single articulation, or a difficult one by an easier one. The idea, whatever may be said of it, is worth considering. It may to some extent throw light on the cause of sound change, or at least indicate where to look for it.

The law of least effort appears to explain a certain number of cases: changes from stop to fricative (e.g. $b \to v$ in Latin *habēre* → French *avoir*); the fall of enormous numbers of final syllables in many languages; assimilation (e.g. $ly \to ll$ in \**alyos* → Greek *állos*, $tn \to nn$ in \**atnos* → Latin *annus*); monophthongization of diphthongs, which is simply one type of assimilation (e.g. $ai \to ę$ in French *maizōn* → *męzō*, 'house'); and others.

The difficulty is that one can cite just as many cases where exactly the opposite happens. With monophthongisation one can contrast for instance the change of German $ī$, $ū$ and $ü$ to *ei*, *au* and *eu*. If it is held that the Slavic shortening of $ā$, $ē$ to $ă$, $ĕ$ is due to economy of effort, it must be supposed that the opposite phenomenon in German (*făter* → *Vāter*, *gĕben* → *gēben*) is due to increase of effort. If voiced sounds are held to be easier to pronounce than voiceless sounds (e.g. $p \to b$ in Latin *opera* → Provençal *obra*), the opposite must require greater effort; and yet Spanish changed $ž$ to $\chi$ (*hiχo* 'son', written *hijo*) and Germanic changed $b$, $d$, $g$, to $p$, $t$, $k$. If loss of aspiration (as in Proto-Indo-European \**bherō* → Germanic *beran*) is considered a diminution of effort, what is one to say of German, which puts it in where it used not to be (*Tanne*, *Pute*, etc. pronounced *Thanne*, *Phute*)?

These observations are not intended to provide a refutation of the explanation proposed. The fact is, however, that it is scarcely possible to determine for every language what is easier or more difficult to pronounce. If it is true that shortening demands less effort as regards duration, it is equally true that careless pronunciation favours lengthening, and a short sound requires more careful attention. So by assuming different tendencies to be operative it is possible to explain quite opposite facts as being alike. Likewise, if we take $k$ changing to $tš$, as in Latin *cēdere* → Italian *cedere*, and consider only the initial and final stages of the process, it looks like a case of increased effort. But it might look different if we were to reconstruct the chain of events. Thus $k$ becomes palatal $k'$ by assimilation to the following vowel, and then $k'$ moves to $ky$. This does not make the pronunciation any more difficult, as two elements run together in $k'$ have now been clearly differentiated. Next, from $ky$ we move in stages to $ty$, $t'$ and $tš$: each stage involves progressively less effort.

There is a vast field of study here. In order to be exhaustive, it should take into account at the same time both physiological considerations (questions of articulation) and also psychological considerations (questions of attention).

Ⅳ. An explanation favoured for some years now attributes changes in pronunciation to our phonetic education in infancy. The seeds of change lie in the many hesitations, trials and corrections the infant has to make in order to manage to pronounce what he hears around him. Certain inaccuracies which go uncorrected supposedly survive in the pronunciation of the individual and become established in that generation growing up. Children often pronounce *t* instead of *k*, but there is no corresponding sound change in the evolution of languages. That is not the case, however, with other mispronunciations. For example, many Parisian children say *fl'eur*, *bl'anc* with a palatal *l'*; and this is analogous to the process by which in Italian *florem* became *fl'ore* and then *fiore*.

Observations of this nature cannot be ignored: but they leave the problem unsolved. For it is difficult to see why one generation settles for preserving certain inaccuracies and not others, since all of them are just as natural. The selection of certain mispronunciations appears to be purely arbitrary, and one can see no reason for it. Furthermore, one is led to ask why the mispronunciation survived on one particular occasion but not on another occasion.

A similar question could, moreover, be asked in respect of all the preceding causes, if they are admitted as valid. Climatic influences, racial predispositions, and a tendency to less effort are permanent or long-standing factors. Why should they act intermittently, affecting now one point and now another in the sound system? Any historical event must have a determining factor: but in these cases we are not told what triggered a change for which the general cause had long existed. This is the most difficult point to clear up.

V. Sometimes the causes of sound changes are sought in the general state of a nation at a given period. Languages go through periods of relatively greater upheaval at certain times. It is claimed that these periods correspond to periods of historical upheaval, and so a connexion is established between political instability and linguistic instability. The next step is to apply these conclusions about the language in general to sound changes in particular. It is observed, for example, that the most radical changes in Latin in the course of its development into the Romance languages coincide with the very disturbed period of the barbarian invasions. If we do not wish to be led astray in these matters, two distinctions must be kept clearly in mind.

(a) Political stability does not influence the language in the same way as instability. There is no *quid pro quo*. When political stability slows down linguistic evolution, that is the action of a positive factor, albeit an external one. Political instability, with the opposite effect, can act only negatively. Linguistic immobility, the relative stabilisation of a language, may be the result of factors external to it (the influence of a court, of education, of an academy, of writing, etc.) which in turn are actively favoured by social and political stability. On the other hand, if some external upheaval in the life of the nation sets off linguistic evolution, that means that the language simply regains its freedom to follow a normal course of change. The immobility of Latin during the Classical period was due to external factors, and cannot be compared with the changes it later underwent, since these occurred of their own accord in the absence of certain external conditions.

(b) Sound changes only are under consideration here, and not linguistic change in general. It is understandable that grammatical change should be affected by these factors, since grammar involves thought in some way, and thus is more sensitive to the repercussions of external upheavals, which have a direct effect upon the mind. But nothing warrants accepting the idea that the turbulent periods in a nation's history correspond to the precipitation of evolution in the sound system.

In any case, it is impossible to find any period, even when the language is superficially stable, which is free from sound change altogether.

VI. Appeal has also been made to the hypothesis of an 'earlier linguistic substratum'. On this hypothesis, certain changes are due to an indigenous population absorbed by newcomers. Thus the difference between Provencal and French is held to be explained by reference to a different proportion of the indigenous Celtic population in the two areas of Gaul. A similar theory has been applied to the different dialects of Italian, which are attributed to Ligurian. Etruscan. etc. influences, according to the region in question. It must first of all be pointed out that this hypothesis appeals to circumstances which occur only rarely. Furthermore, the hypothesis stands in need of clarification. Does it claim that in adopting the new language the earlier population introduced something of their own habits of pronunciation? That is acceptable, and quite natural. But if this is another appeal to imponderable racial factors, it takes us back to the obscurities already mentioned above.

VII. Finally, there is an explanation—which scarcely merits the name—which likens sound changes to changes in fashion. But no one has accounted for changes in fashion: all we know is that they are based on laws of imitation, in which psychologists take a great interest. However, even if this explanation does not solve the problem it has the advantage of making that problem part of a much bigger problem. It treats the principle underlying sound changes as purely psychological. The difficulty is, however, to identify the starting point of the imitative process. That is what is obscure, both in the case of sound change and of changes of fashion.

......

CHAPTER III   Grammatical Consequences of Phonetic Evolution

§ 1. *Breaking grammatical links*

One consequence of sound change is to break the grammatical link connecting two or more terms. Thus it comes about that one word is no longer felt to be derived from another. For example:

( Latin )    *mansiō—*mansiōnāticus*  }
( French )    *maison* || *ménage*      } 'house—household'

Formerly, linguistic awareness recognized in *mansiōnāticus* a derivative from *mansiō*. Then phonetic vicissitudes separated them. Similarly:

( Latin )           *vervēx—vervēcārius*   }
( Vulgar Latin )    *berbīx—berbīcārius*   } 'sheep-shepherd'
( French )          *brebis* || *berger*   }

This separation naturally has an effect upon the value of the terms: hence in some local patois French *berger* becomes specialised to mean 'oxherd'.

Similar cases are:

( Latin )    *Grātiānopolis—grātiānopolitānus*   } 'Grenoble—of Grenoble'
( French )   *Grenoble* || *Grésivaudan*         }
( Latin )    *decem—undecim*                      } 'ten-eleven'
( French )        *dix* || *onze*                 }

Another is that of Gothic *bītan* ('to bite')—*bitum* ('we have bitten')—*bitr* ('biting, bitter'), which, as a result of the change *t* →*ts* (*z*) and the conservation of the group *tr*, became in West Germanic *bīʒan*, *biʒum* || *bitr*.

Sound change also breaks the usual links between inflected forms of the same word. Thus Latin *comes—comitem* becomes in Old French *cuens* ‖ *comte*; *barō—barōnem→ber* ‖ *baron*; *presbiter—presbiterum→prestre* ‖ *provoire*.

In other cases, a flexional ending may split in two. Proto-Indo-Euro-pean marked all accusative singulars with a final *-m*,[1] e.g. $ek_1wom$, $owim$, $podm$, $māterm$. In Latin, this state of affairs underwent no important change. But in Greek, the very different treatment of nasal sonants and adsonants created two separate series of forms: *híppon*, *ó(w)in* ‖ *póda*, *mǎtera*. The Greek accusative plural shows a similar development: *híppous* ‖ *pódas*.

### § 2. *Obliteration of word-composition*

Another grammatical effect of sound change is that distinct parts of a word, which contributed to fixing its value, may cease to be analysable: the word becomes an indivisible whole. Examples are: French *ennemi* ('enemy') from Latin *in-imīcus* (cf. *amīcus* 'friend'); Latin *perdere* ('to lose') from *per-dare* (cf. *dare* 'to give'); Latin *amiciō* ('I cover') from $ambjaciō$ (cf. *jaciō* 'I throw'); German *Drittel* ('third') from *drit-teil* (cf. *teil* 'part').

It is clear that these cases resemble those of the preceding paragraph. If *ennemi* is unanalysable, that means it is no longer possible to connect it with another form in the way that *in-imīcus* is connected with *amīcus*. The formula

(Latin) 　　　　　*amīcus — inimīcus*

(French) 　　　　　*ami* ‖ *ennemi*

is entirely comparable to

(Latin) 　　　　　*mansiō —mansiōnāticus*

(French) 　　　　　*maison* ‖ *ménage*

The same applies to *decem—undecim*: *dix* ‖ *onze*.

The Classical Latin simple forms of the demonstrative *hunc*, *hanc*, *hāc*, etc., ('this') go back to *hon-ce*, *han-ce*, *hā-ce* etc., as is shown by forms on old inscriptions. These are the result of agglutination of a pronoun and the particle *-ce*. Originally, *hon-ce* etc. could be related to *ec-ce* ('behold'); but with the eventual fall of final *-e* this became impossible. In other words, the constituent elements of *hunc*, *hanc*, *hāc*, etc. were no longer distinguishable.

Sound change begins by making word analysis difficult, before making it altogether impossible. Noun flexion in Proto-Indo-European provides an example.

The Proto-Indo-European declension once had the following pattern: nominative singular $pod-s$ ('foot'), accusative $pod-m$, dative $pod-ai$, locative $pod-i$, nominative plural $pod-es$, accusative $pod-ns$, etc. The declension of $ek_1wos$ ('horse') was exactly parallel at first: $ek_1wo-s$, $ek_1wo-m$, $ek_1wo-ai$, $ek_1wo-i$, $ek_1wo-es$, $ek_1wo-ns$, etc. At that stage, the stem $ek_1wo-$ could be identified as easily as the stem $pod-$. But later vocalic contractions altered this: dative $ek_1wōi$, locative $ek_1woi$, nominative plural $ek_1wōs$. From this point on, the identity of the stem $ek_1wo-$ was compromised, and analysis could be misled. Later still, new developments such as the differentiation of accusatives obliterated the last traces of the original state of affairs. Xenophon's contemporaries probably thought the stem of the word for 'horse' was *hipp-*, and the endings were vocalic: *hipp-os*, etc. Hence the types $ek_1wo-s$ and $pod-s$ were now entirely separate. In the domain of flexion, as everywhere else, whatever interferes with analysis contributes to a loosening of grammatical connexions.

### § 3. *There are no phonetic doublets*

In both types of case examined in §§ 1 and 2, evolution separates entirely two forms which were once grammatically united. This phenomenon might lead to a serious error of interpretation.

When we realise the relative identity of Late Latin *barō* : *barōnem* as compared with the disparity between Old French *ber* and *baron*, are we not tempted to say that one and the same primitive unit (*bar-*) has developed divergently and produced two forms? No. For the same element cannot simultaneously undergo two different changes in the same place. That would be contradictory to the very definition of sound change. In itself, the evolution of sounds is incapable of creating two forms in place of one.

Certain objections may be raised to this thesis. They can be illustrated by the following examples.

Latin *collocāre* ('to place'), it may be urged, gave in French both *coucher* ('to lay down') and *colloquer* ('to collocate'). No. *Collocare* gave only *coucher*. *Colloquer* is only a learned borrowing of the Latin word. Cf. *rançon* and *rédemption*.

But did not Latin *cathedra* ('chair') give the two forms *chaire* ('throne') and *chaise* ('chair'), both of them authentically French? The fact is that *chaise* in French is a dialect form. In Parisian pronunciation, intervocalic *r* became *z* : *père* ('father') and *mère* ('mother') became *pèse*, *mèse*. But literary French retained only two examples of this local pronunciation : they are *chaise* and *bésicles* ('goggles'), the latter a doublet of *béricles*, derived from *béryl* ('beryl'). The case is exactly comparable to that of the Picard form *rescapé* ('survivor'), which has recently passed into general French usage and thus belatedly finds itself contrasting with the corresponding French form *réchappé* ('survivor'). French also has side by side *cavalier* ('rider') and *chevalier* ('knight'), as well as *cavalcade* ('cavalcade') and *chevauchée* ('ride'); but *cavalier* and *cavalcade* come from Italian. (In the final analysis, these cases are parallel to Latin *calidum* ('hot') giving *chaud* ('hot') in French, but *caldo* ('hot') in Italian.) All these are instances of borrowing.

It may perhaps be claimed that the Latin pronoun *mē* ('me') is represented in French by two forms, *me* and *moi* (cf. *it me voit* 'he sees me' vs, *c'est moi qu'il voit* 'It's me he sees'). The answer is that it was the Latin unstressed *mē* which became French *me*, whereas the stressed form *mē* became *moi*. Now presence or absence of stress depends not on the phonetic laws which changed *mē* into both *me* and *moi*, but upon the role of the word in the phrase. The duality is a grammatical one. In German, similarly, *ur-* remained as *ur-* when stressed, but changed to *er-* in a protonic syllable (cf. *úrlaub* 'leave' vs. *erlaúben* 'allow'). But this variation of stress is itself bound up with the types of word-composition in which *ur-* played a part, and hence with conditions of a grammatical, synchronic nature. Finally, to revert to our first example, the differences of form and accent seen in the pair *bárō* : *barónem* are clearly earlier than the sound change in question.

The fact is that one never finds examples of phonetic doublets. Phonetic evolution increases already existing differences, nothing more. Wherever these differences are not due to external causes, as in the case of borrowed words, they are based on grammatical and synchronic dualities which have nothing whatever to do with sound change.

### § 4. *Alternation*

In two words like French *maison* ('house') and *ménage* ('household'), one finds little temptation to inquire into the difference between the two forms, either because the contrasting elements *-ezō* and *-en-* do not easily lend themselves to comparison, or because no other pair of French words shows a parallel opposition. But often it happens that two neighbouring terms differ only in respect of one or two elements easily picked out, and that the same difference recurs regularly in a series of parallel pairs of forms. This is a case of the most widespread and common grammatical feature in which sound change plays a part: it is termed *alternation*.

In French every Latin *ō* in an open syllable became *eu* when stressed, or *ou* if protonic. Hence French pairs like *pouvons* ('(we) can') vs. *peuvent* ('(they) can'), *œuvre* ('work') vs. *ouvrier* ('workman'), *nouveau* ('new') vs. *neuf* ('new'). In these pairs, one detects without difficulty an element of differentiation and regular variation. In Latin, rhotacisation brings about alternations between *gerō* ('I carry') and *gestus* ('carried'), *oneris* ('of a burden') and *onus* ('burden'), *maeror* ('sorrow') and *maestus* ('sorrowful'), etc. In Germanic the varying treatment of *s* according to where the stress falls produces in Middle High German *ferliesen* ('to lose') vs. *ferloren* ('lost'), *kiesen* ('to choose') vs. *gekoren* ('chosen'), *friesen* ('to freeze') vs. *gefroren* ('frozen'), etc. The fall of Proto-Indo-European *e* is reflected in modern German in such oppositions as *beissen* ('to bite') vs. *biss* ('bit'), *leiden* ('to suffer') vs. *litt* ('suffered'), *reiten* ('to ride') vs. *ritt* ('rode'), etc.

In all these examples, it is the stem of the word which is affected. But it goes without saying that any part of a word may show oppositions of the same kind. Nothing is commoner, for example, than a prefix appearing in different forms depending on the nature of the first sound of the stem: e.g. Greek *apo-dídōmi* ('give back') vs. *apérchomai* ('go away'), French *ẽ* in *inconnu* ('unknown') vs. *in-* in *inutile* ('useless'). The Proto-Indo-European alternation *e : o*, which must ultimately be phonetic in origin, is found in a great number of suffixal elements in Greek: e.g. nominative *híppos* ('horse') vs. vocative *híppe*, *phér-o-men* ('we carry') vs. *phér-e-te* ('you carry'), nominative *gén-os* ('race') vs. genitive *gén-e-os* (for *\*gén-es-os*). Old French has a special development of Latin stressed *a* after palatals, which results in the alternation *i : ie* in a number of endings: e.g. *chant-er* ('to sing'), *chant-é* ('sung'), *chant-ez* ('(you) sing') vs. *jug-ier* ('to judge'), *jug-ié* ('judged'), *jug-iez* ('(you) judge').

Alternation may thus be defined as: *a correspondence between two sounds or groups of sounds, changing regularly as between two coexisting series of forms*.

Just as sound change alone does not explain doublets, so it is easily seen that sound change is neither the sole nor the most important cause of alternation. When it is said that the Latin root *nov-* became through sound change both *neuv-* and *nouv-* in French (*neuve* 'new' from Latin *novam*, and *nouveau* 'new' from Latin *novellus*), that amounts to inventing an imaginary unit and overlooking a synchronic duality already in existence. Latin *nov-* in *nov-am*, was already in a different position in the word from *nov-* in *novellus*. That difference was both grammatical in nature (cf. *barō : barōnem*) and also prior to any French phonetic development; and it was that difference which lay at the origin of the French alternation and made it possible. This was not a case of sound change splitting up an original unit, but of sound change making an already established opposition of coexisting terms more obvious by distinguishing the sounds. It is an error many linguists make: to suppose that alternation is a phonetic phenomenon, simply because sounds are the vehicle for it, and changes in sounds lie at its origins. But in fact, whether one looks at the starting point or the conclusion of the process, alternation belongs invariably to grammar and to synchrony.

......

§ 6. *Alternation and grammatical link*

We have seen how phonetic evolution, by changing the forms of words, has the effect of severing the grammatical links uniting them. But that applies only to isolated pairs such as French *maison* ('house') vs. *ménage* ('household'), German *Teil* ('part') vs. *Drittel* ('third'). As soon as alternation appears, this is no longer so.

It is evident in the first place that any more or less regular sound contrast between two elements tends to establish a link between them. In German *Wetter* ('weather') is instinctively connected with *wittern* ('to smell') because there is a familiar alternation of *e* and *i*. Even more so, when speakers feel that a sound contrast is governed by a general law this habitual correlation compels attention and contributes to strengthening the grammatical link rather than loosening it. Thus it is that the German *Ablaut* ('vowel gradation') reinforces a perception of the unity of the stem through its vocalic variations.

The same applies to alternations which are not significant, but are bound up with purely phonetic conditions. The French prefix *re-* (as in *reprendre* 'to retake', *regagner* 'to regain', *retoucher* 'to retouch') is reduced to *r-* before a vowel (e.g. *rouvrir* 'to reopen', *racheter* 'to buy back'). Likewise the French prefix *in-*, very much alive in spite of its learned origin, appears in two different forms under the same conditions as *re-*: as *ē-in inconnu* ('unknown'), *indigne* ('unworthy'), *invertébré* ('invertebrate') etc., but as *in-* in *inavouable* ('unavowable'), *inutile* ('useless'), *inesthétique* ('unaesthetic'), etc. This difference in no way disrupts the conceptual unity, because meaning and function are conceived as identical, and because the language has decided which form to use in which case.

......

CHAPTER IV  Analogy

§ 1. *Definition and examples*

Sound change, it is clear from the preceding chapter, is a source of linguistic disturbance. Wherever it does not give rise to alternations, it contributes towards loosening the grammatical connexions which link words together. It increases the sum total of linguistic forms to no purpose. The linguistic mechanism becomes obscure and complicated inasmuch as irregularities produced by sound change take precedence over forms grouped under general types; in other words, inasmuch as what is absolutely arbitrary takes precedence over what is only relatively arbitrary.

Fortunately, the effect of these changes is counterbalanced by analogy. Analogy is responsible for all the normal modifications of the external aspect of words which are not due to sound change.

Analogy presupposes a model, and regular imitation of a model. *An analogical form is a form made in the image of one or more other forms according to a fixed rule.*

The Latin nominative singular *honor* ('honour') is analogical. Originally it was *honōs*, with an accusative *honōsem*. Then, following the rhotacisation of *s*, it was *honōs*, with an accusative *honōrem*. Thus the stem then took two different forms. This duality was reduced by creating a new nominative *honor*, on the model of *ōrātor: ōrātōrem*. The process will be examined in detail below. In essence, it involves a computation of the missing fourth term in the proportion:

$$\bar{o}r\bar{a}t\bar{o}rem : \bar{o}r\bar{a}tor = hon\bar{o}rem : x.$$

Here the solution is: $x$ = honor.

It can thus be seen that, in order to counterbalance the diversifying effect of sound change (*honōs : honōrem*), analogy has once more brought the forms together and re-established regularity (*honor: honōrem*).

In French, the forms of the verb *prouver* ('to prove') for a long period included *preuve* ('(he) proves'), *prouvons* ('(we) prove'), and *preuvent* ('(they) prove'). Today *preuve* and *preuvent* have been replaced by *prouve* and *prouvent*, forms which cannot be explained by sound change, Whereas *aime* ('(he) loves') can be traced back phonetically to Latin *amat*, *aimons* ('(we) love') is an analogical replacement of Old French *amons*. Similarly *aimable* ('kind') is an analogical replacement of *amable*. In Greek, intervocalic *s* fell, with the result that *-eso-* became -*eo-* (e.g. *géneos* for *\*genesos*). However, this intervocalic *s* is found in the future and aorist forms of all verbs with vowel stems, e.g. *lū̆ sō* ('I shall loose'), *élūsa* ('I loosed'). Here the analogy of other forms like *túpsō* and *étupsa*, where the *s* did not fall, preserved the *s* in the future and aorist. In German, while *Gast* ('guest'): *Gäste* ('guests'), *Balg* ('skin'): *Bälge* ('skins') are phonetically regular plurals, *Kranz* ('wreath'): *Kränze* ('wreaths') is analogical, replacing *kranz: kranza*. So too is *Hals* ('neck') : *Hälse* ('necks'), where the plural was formerly *halsa*.

Analogy works in favour of regularity and tends to unify formational and flexional processes. But it is sometimes capricious. In German, beside *Kranz: Kränze* etc. one finds also *Tag* ('day'): *Tage* ('days'), *Salz* ('salt'): *Salze* ('salts'), etc. which for one reason or another have resisted analogy. So it is impossible to say in advance how far imitation of a model will extend, or which patterns are destined to provoke it. It is not always the more numerous forms which set analogy working. In Greek, the perfect of *pheúgō* ('flee') has active forms *pépheuga*, *pépheugas*, *pepheúgamen*, etc., but all the middle voice flexions lack the *a*: *péphugmai*, *pephúgmetha*, etc. The language of Homer shows that this *a* was originally missing from the plural and the dual of the active voice (cf. Homeric Greek *ídmen*, *éïkton*, etc.). The analogy began just with the active first person singular and was extended to almost the whole of the perfect indicative paradigm. The case is also remarkable because here analogy attaches to the stem an element (-*a*-) which is flexional in origin (hence *pepheúga-men*); whereas the opposite development—a stem element becoming attached to a suffix—is, as will be seen, much more frequent.

Often two or three isolated words are enough to create a general form—an ending, for instance. In Old High German, weak verbs of the type *habēn*, *lobōn*, etc. have an -*m* in the first person singular of the present: *habēm*, *lobōm*. This -*m* originates with a few verbs, *bim*, *stām*, *gēm*, *tuom*, which are like the Greek verbs in -*mi*. These few alone imposed their -*m* on the whole class of weak verbs. In this case it should be noted that analogy did not regularise any phonetic diversity, but generalized a morphological formation.

§ 2. *Analogies are not changes*

The early linguists failed to understand the nature of analogical phenomena, which they described as 'false analogy'. They thought that by inventing the nominative form *honor* to replace *honōs*, Latin had made a 'mistake'. In their view, anything which departed from an established

287

order was an irregularity, a violation of an ideal form. Their illusion, very characteristic of the period, was that the original state of the language represented something superior, a state of perfection. They did not even inquire whether that earlier state had not been preceded by a still earlier one. Any liberty taken with it was an anomaly. The Neogrammarians were the first scholars to assign analogy to its rightful place, by showing that it is, along with sound change, the main factor in the evolution of languages, and the process by which they pass from one state of organisation to another.

But what is the nature of analogical phenomena? Are they, as is commonly believed, changes?

Every analogy is a drama involving three characters. They are: (ⅰ) the legitimate heir to the succession (e.g. Latin *honōs*), (ⅱ) the rival (*honor*), (ⅲ) a collective character, made up of the forms which sponsored this rival (*honōrem*, *ōrātor*, *ōrātōrem*, etc.). *Honor* is often regarded as a modification or 'metaplasm' of *honōs*, from which it derives most of its substance. But the one form which plays no part at all in the genesis of *honor* is *honōs* itself!

The phenomenon can be represented as follows:

| TRANSMITTED FORMS | | NEW FORM |
|---|---|---|
| *honōs* (which plays no active role) ] | *honōrem ōrātor*, *ōrātōrem*, etc. (sponsoring group) } | →*honor* |

It is clear that this is a case of 'paraplasm', of the installation of a rival alongside the traditional form—in short, of creation. Whereas sound change introduces nothing new without eliminating what formerly existed (as with *honōrem* replacing *honōsem*), an analogical form does not necessarily eliminate its rival. *Honor* and *honōs* coexisted for a time and were interchangeable. However, since a language dislikes maintaining two signals for a single idea, it usually turns out that the primitive, less regular form falls into disuse and disappears. It is this outcome which makes it look as if a change of form has taken place: once the analogical process is completed, the old state of affairs (*honōs* : *honōrem*) and the new (*honor* : *honōrem*) appear to be opposed in the same way as would have resulted from sound change. But at the stage when *honor* first appears nothing is changed, because *honor* does not replace anything. Nor is the disappearance of *honōs* a change either, since it is quite independent of the appearance of *honor*. Wherever we can follow the course of linguistic events in detail, we find that analogical innovation and elimination of the old form are two separate events. Nowhere does one discover a change in process.

Analogy has nothing to do with replacing one form by another: often, indeed, it produces forms which replace nothing. In German, one can form a diminutive from any noun with a concrete meaning by adding the diminutive suffix *-chen*. But if a form *Elefantchen* ('little elephant') gained acceptance in the language, it would supplant nothing already in existence. Similarly in French on the model of *pension* : *pensionnaire* ('pension : pensioner'), *réaction* : *réactionnaire* ('reaction : reactionary'), etc. someone could invent *interventionnaire* meaning 'in favour of intervention', or *répressionnaire* meaning 'in favour of repression'. The process is clearly the same as that involved in the genesis of *honor*. Both fit the same formula:

$$réaction : réactionnaire = répression : x$$
$$x = répressionnaire.$$

In neither case is there the least pretext for speaking of a 'change'. The word *répressionnaire* replaces nothing. Another example of this kind would be the following. For the plural of the French adjective *final* ('final'), one hears the analogical form *finaux*, which is said to be more regular than *finals*. Now suppose someone invented the adjective *firmamental* ('of the firmament') and gave it a plural *firmamentaux*. Would one say that *finaux* is an example of change, but *firmamentaux* an example of creation? Both cases involve creation. On the model of *mur*: *emmurer* ('wall : immure'), there were formed *tour* : *entourer* ('circuit: surround') and *jour*: *ajourer* ('daylight: perforate (as in fretwork)'). These derivatives, being relatively recent, strike us as creations. But if I discover that French of an earlier period also had the verbs *entorner* and *ajorner*, based on the same nouns *torn* and *jorn* ( = modern French *tour* and *jour*), should I now change my mind and declare that *entourer* and *ajourer* are modifications of the earlier forms? The illusion of analogical 'change' comes from a relation established with the term which has been ousted by the new one. But this is a mistake, because these so-called 'changes' (like *honor*) are the same as what we call 'creations' (like *répressionnaire*).

### § 3. *Analogy as the creative principle in languages*

If, having demonstrated what analogy is not, we now study it from a positive point of view, it becomes immediately apparent that its principle is simply identical with that of linguistic creation in general. What is this principle?

Analogy is a psychological phenomenon. But that alone does not suffice to distinguish it from sound change, which may also be considered as such. One must take a step further, and say that analogy is a grammatical phenomenon. It presupposes awareness and grasp of relations between forms. Where sound is concerned, ideas count for nothing; whereas they necessarily intervene in the case of analogy.

In the change of intervocalic *s* to *r* in Latin, as in *honōsem*→*honōrem*, no part is played by comparison with other forms, nor by the meaning of the word. It is the corpse of the form *honōsem* which survives as *honōrem*. On the contrary, to account for the appearance of *honor* beside *honōs* we have to appeal to other forms, as indicated in the formula of the four-term proportion:

$$\bar{o}r\bar{a}torem : \bar{o}r\bar{a}tor = hon\bar{o}rem : x.$$
$$x = honor.$$

This combination would have no rationale if the mind did not associate the forms involved on the basis of their meanings.

So in analogy, everything is grammatical. But to this it must immediately be added that the creation which results can only belong at first to speech. It is the work of a single speaker. This is the sphere, on the fringe of the language, where the phenomenon must first be located. None the less, two things must be distinguished: (1) grasping the relation which connects the sponsoring forms, and (2) the result suggested by this comparison, i.e. the form improvised by the speaker to express his thought. The latter alone belongs to speech.

Analogy teaches us once again, then, to distinguish between the language itself and speech. It shows us how speech depends on the language, and allows us to put our finger on the operational linguistic mechanism, as earlier described. Any creation has to be preceded by an unconscious comparison of materials deposited in the store held by the language, where the sponsoring forms are

289

arranged by syntagmatic and associative relations.

So one whole part of the phenomenon has already been completed before the new form becomes visible. The continual activity of language in analysing the units already provided contains in itself not only all possibilities of speaking in conformity with usage, but also all possibilities of analogical formation. Thus it is a mistake to suppose that the generative process occurs only at the moment when the new creation emerges: its elements are already given. Any word I improvise, like *in-décor-able* ('un-decorat-able') already exists potentially in the language. Its elements are all to be found already in syntagmas like *décor-er* ('to decorate'), *décor-ation* ('decor-ation'), *pardonn-able* ('pardon-able'), *mani-able* ('manage-able'), *in-connu* ('un-known'), *in-sensé* ('in-sane'), etc. Its actualisation in speech is an insignificant fact in comparison with the possibility of forming it.

To summarise, analogy in itself is simply one aspect of the phenomenon of interpretation, a manifestation of the general activity which analyses units in order then to make use of them. That is why we say that analogy is entirely grammatical and synchronic.

This characteristic of analogy prompts two observations which support our views on absolute and relative arbitrariness.

1. One could classify words according to their relative capacity for giving rise to others, depending on the extent to which they are themselves analysable. A simple word is, by definition, unproductive: e.g. *magasin* ('shop'), *arbre* ('tree'), *racine* ('root'). The word *magasinier* ('store-keeper') was not engendered by *magasin*: it was formed on the model of *prisonnier : prison* ('prisoner : prison'), etc. Similarly *emmagasiner* ('to store') owes its existence to the analogy of *emmailloter : maillot* ('to swaddle : swaddling clothes'), *encadrer : cadre* ('to frame: frame'), *encapuchonner : capuchon* ('to hood : hood'), etc.

So in every language there are productive words and sterile words. But the proportions vary. What this comes down to is the distinction previously drawn between 'lexicological' and 'grammatical' languages. In Chinese, the majority of words are unsegmentable; whereas in artificial languages they are nearly all segmentable. An Esperantist is fully at liberty to construct new words on any given root.

2. We have already noted that any analogical creation can be represented as an operation like the computation of the fourth term of a proportion. Very often this formula is used to explain the phenomenon itself, whereas we have sought its rationale in the analysis and reconstruction of elements supplied by the language.

There is a conflict between these two conceptions. If the proportion is a sufficient explanation, what purpose is served by the hypothesis which appeals to analysis of the elements? To form *indécorable*, there is no need to extract its elements (*in-décor-able*): it suffices to take the whole and place it in the equation:

$$pardonner : impardonnable, \text{ etc.} = décorer : x.$$
$$x = indécorable.$$

In that way there is no need to credit the speaker with a complicated operation too much like the conscious analysis of the grammarian. In a case like *Krantz : Kräntze*, based on *Gast : Gäste*, decomposition seems less plausible than the proportion, since in the model the stem is *Gast*-in one case and *Gäst*- in the other; it looks as though a phonetic feature of *Gäste* has simply been replicated on *Kranze*.

Which of these theories corresponds to the reality? Let us note first of all that the case of *Kranz* does not necessarily preclude analysis. We have seen alternation operative in roots and prefixes, and a feeling for alternation may exist alongside a positive analysis.

These two conflicting conceptions are reflected in two different grammatical doctrines. Our European grammars operate with the proportion. They explain the formation of a preterite in German, for example, on the basis of complete words: the pupil is told to form the preterite of, say, *lachen* ('to laugh') on the model of *setzen : setzte* ('to sit : sat'). A Hindu grammar, on the contrary, would devote one chapter to the study of the roots (*setz-*, *lach-*, *etc.*), and a different chapter to the endings of the preterite (*-te*, etc.). It would give the elements resulting from the analysis, and one would then have to recombine them to form whole words. In any Sanskrit dictionary, the verbs are arranged in an order determined by their root.

Depending on the predominant tendency in each linguistic group, the grammatical theorists will incline to the one or the other of these methods.

Early Latin seems to favour the analytic procedure. Here is a clear demonstration of the fact. The vowel length of *a* is not the same in *făctus* ('made') and *āctus* ('done'), although it is in *făciō* ('I make') and *ăgō* ('I do'). One must suppose that *āctus* goes back to *ăgtos* and attribute the lengthened vowel to the voiced consonant which follows. This hypothesis is fully confirmed by the Romance languages. The opposition *spĕciō : spĕctus* ('I see : seen') vs. *tĕgō : tēctus* ('I cover : covered') is reflected in French *dépit* ('spite' : Latin *despĕctus*) vs. *toit* ('roof' : Latin *tēctum*). Cf. also Latin *confĭciō : confĕctus* ('I complete : completed') vs. *rĕgō : rēctus* ('I. rule : ruled') : whereas *confĕctus* gives French *confit*, *dīrēctus* gives French *droit*. But *agtos*, *tegtos*, *regtos* were not inherited from. Proto-Indo-European, where the corresponding forms were certainly *ăktos*, *tĕktos*, etc. It was prehistoric Latin which introduced *agtos*, *tegtos*, *regtos*, in spite of the difficulty of pronouncing a voiced consonant immediately before a voiceless one. This could only have been done if there was a strong consciousness of the stem units *ag-*, *teg-*, etc. Early Latin thus possessed a high degree of awareness of the constituent parts of a word (stems, suffixes, etc.) and of their fitting together. It is probale that in our modern languages it is not felt so acutely. But German probably has it more than French.

(*Course in General Linguistics*. London: G. Duckworth, 1983)

译文: # 历时语言学

高名凯，译

第一章　概述

历时语言学研究的已不是语言状态中各项共存要素间的关系，而是在时间上彼此代替的各项相连续的要素间的关系。

事实上，绝对的不变性是不存在的；语言的任何部分都会发生变化。每个时期都相应地有或大或小的演化。这种演化在速度上和强度上可能有所不同，但是无损于原则本身。语言的长河川流不息,是缓流还是急流,那是次要的考虑。

的确,对于文学语言的注意,往往会把我们的眼睛蒙住,看不见这种不断的演化。我们在下面将可以看到,文学语言是凌驾于流俗语言即自然语言之上的,而且要服从于另外的一些生存条件。它一经形成,一般就相当稳定,而且有保持不变的倾向。对文字的依靠使它的保存有了特殊的保证。所以它不能向我们表明,自然语言摆脱了一切文学的统制会改变到什么程度。

语音学,而且整个语音学,是历时语言学的头一个对象。事实上,语音演化是跟状态的概念不相容的;把音位或音位的组合同以前的情况相比就等于是建立历时态。以前的时代可能远些,也可能近些;但是如果两个时代混而不分,语音学就插不上手,这时只有语言状态的声音描写,那是音位学所要做的。

语音学的历时特性很符合一条原则,即语音学上的一切,就广义来说,没有什么是表示意义的或语法的。研究一个词的声音历史,可以不管它的意义,只考虑它的物质外壳,把它切成音段,而不过问这些音段是否有意义。例如我们可以探索阿狄克希腊语的-ewo-这个音组变成了什么音,而这个音组是没有意义的。要是把语言的演化归结为声音的演化,那么语言学两个部分固有对象的对立就立即明若观火。我们将可以很清楚地看到,历时的就等于非语法的,正如共时的等于语法的一样。

但是随着时间起变化的只有声音吗? 词的意义改变着;语法范畴演变着,其中有些随着表达它们的形式一起消失了(例如拉丁语的双数)。如果联想共时态和句段共时态的一切事实都各有它们的历史,那么历时态和共时态的绝对区别又怎能得以维持呢? 只要我们离开了纯粹语音学的范围,这就会变得非常困难。

但是我们要注意,许多我们认为是语法的变化实际上都是语音的变化。像德语以 Hand∶Hände "手" 代替 hant∶hanti 这样一种语法类型的创造,就完全可以用语音事实来加以解释。像 Springbrunnen "喷泉",Reitschule "骑术学校" 之类的复合词也是以语音事实为基础的。在古高德语里,它们的头一个要素不是动词,而是名词。Beta-hūs 是 "祈祷室" 的意思,但是由于结尾元音在语音上的脱落(beta- → bet- 等等),它跟动词(beten "祈祷" 等等)建立了语义上的接触,而 Bethaus 终于变成了 "祈祷用的房子" 的意思了。

在古日耳曼语用 līch "外貌" 这个词构成的复合词中(试比较 mannolīch "有男子汉的外貌的",redolīch "有理性的外貌的" 等等),也曾发生过完全同样的变化。现在,在许多形容词里(试比较 verzeihlich "可原谅的",glaublich "可信的" 等等),-lich 已经变成后缀,可以跟法语 pardonn-able "可原谅的" croy-able "可信的" 等等的后缀相比。同时,人们对于这些词的头一个要素的解释也发生变化:不再把它看作名词,而看作动词词根。那是因为在许多情况下,头一个要素由于结尾元音的脱落(例如 redo- → red-)而变得跟动词词根(red-来自 reden)一样了。

因此,在 glaublich "可信的" 一词里,glaub-与其说是跟 Glaube "信仰" 接近,不如说是跟 glauben "相信" 接近。尽管词根不同,sichtlich "可见的" 也只是跟 sehen "见" 相关联,而不再跟 Sicht "光景" 相关联。

在所有这些和其他许多类似的例子里,历时态和共时态的区别仍然是很明显的。我们必须记住这种区别,这样,当我们实际上在历时的领域内研究语音变化,继而在共时的领域内考究语音变化所产生的后果时,才不致轻率地断言是在研究历史语法。

但是这种限制不能解决一切困难。任何语法事实的演化,无论是联想的聚合还是句段的类型,都不能跟声音的演化相提并论。它不是简单的,它可以分解成许多特殊的事实,其中只有一部分跟语音有关。在一个句段类型的产生中,如法语的将来时 prendre ai 变成了 prendrai

"我将拿",我们至少可以分辨出两个事实:一个是心理的,即两个概念要素的综合①;另一个是语音的,它并且取决于前一个事实,即组合中的两个重音缩减为一个重音(préndre aí→prendraí)。

日耳曼语强式动词的屈折变化(如现代德语的 geben"给",gab,gegeben 等等,试比较希腊语的 leípo"我留下",élipon,léloipa 等等),大部分以词根的元音交替为基础。这个交替系统最初是相当简单的,无疑是纯粹的语音事实的结果。但是要使这些对立在功能上变得这样重要,那原始的屈折变化系统必须通过一系列不同的过程进行简化:现在时的多种变异及其所附的意义色彩的消失,未完成过去时、将来时和不定过去时的消失,全过去时重叠式的消除等等。这些在本质上同语音毫无关系的变化把动词的屈折变化缩减为一小组形式,使词根的元音交替在里面获得了头等重要的表示意义的价值。例如我们可以断言,geben:gab 中 e:a 的对立比希腊语 leípō:léloipa 中 e:o 的对立更具有表意价值,因为德语的全过去时没有基本音节的重叠。

所以语音学虽然经常从某一方面介入演化,却不能说明它的全部。一旦把语音学的因素除去,就会剩下似乎证明"语法史"的概念有其正当理由的残余,这是真正的困难所在。历时态和共时态的区别——我们应该保持这种区别——需要详密的解释,而这是本教程的范围所容纳不了的②。

我们在下面将依次研究语音变化、语音交替和类比事实,最后简单地谈谈流俗词源和黏合。

### 第二章　语音变化

#### §1.语音变化的绝对规律性

我们在前面已经看到,语音变化不影响到词,而只影响到音。发生变化的是音位。正如一切历时的事件一样,这是一个孤立的事件,但是它的后果会使凡含有这个音位的词都同样改变了样子。正是在这个意义上,语音变化是绝对有规律的。

在德语里,所有的 ī 都变成了 ei,然后变成 ai:wīn,trīben,līhen,zīt 变成了 Wein"酒",treiben"赶",leihen"借",Zeit"时间"。所有的 ū 都变成了 au:hūs,zūn,rūch→Haus"房子",Zaun"篱笆",Rauch"烟"。同样,ū 变成了 eu:hūsir→Häuser"房子(复数)"等等。相反,复合元音 ie 变成了 ī,仍写作 ie:试比较 biegen"折",lieb"亲爱的",Tier"兽类";此外,所有的 uo 都变成了 ū:muot→Mut"勇敢"等等。所有的 z 都变成了 s(写作 ss):wazer→Wasser"水",fliezen→fliessen"流"等等。两个元音间的 h 都消失了:līhen,sehen→leien,seen(写作 leihen

---

①　法语的将来时 prendrai"我将拿"来自 prendre+ai,prendre(不定式)是"拿"的意思,ai 是"我有"的意思,本来是两个概念要素,可是在 prendrai 中已经综合成为一个概念了。——校注

②　除了这个数学上的和外部的理由之外,也许还可以加上另外一个理由:费·德·索绪尔在他的讲授中从来没有讲过言语的语言学。前面说过,一种新的用法总是从一系列个人的事实开始的。我们可以认为作者不承认这些个人事实具有语法事实的性质,因为一个孤立的行为必然跟语言及其只决定于全部集体习惯的系统无关。只要这些事实属于言语,它们就只是一些利用已有系统的特殊而完全偶然的方式。一个创新,只有当它被反复使用,铭刻在人们的记忆里,并且进入了系统的时候,才能发生转移价值平衡的效果,而语言也就因此而自发地起了变化。我们在前面所说的关于语音演化的话也可以适用于语法的演化:它的转变是在系统之外的,因为演化中的系统是永远看不见的;我们只是不时感到它不是原来的面目。这一试作的解释只是我们的一种简单的提示。——原编者注

"借",sehen"见"）。所有的 w 都变成了唇齿音 v(写作 w)：wazer→wasr（Wasser"水"）①。

在法语里,所有腭化的 l 都变成了 y：piller"抢劫",bouillir "沸腾"念成 piye,buyir 等等②。

在拉丁语里,两个元音间的 s 在另一个时代变成了 r：*genesis,*asēna→generis"产生",arēna"决斗场"等等③。

任何语音变化,从它的真实情况看,都可以证明这些演变是完全有规律的。

§2.语音变化的条件

上面所举的例子已可以表明,语音现象并不永远都是绝对的,它们往往同一定的条件联系着。换句话说,发生变化的不是音种,而是在某些环境、重音等等条件下出现的音位。例如拉丁语的 s 只在两个元音间和某些其他位置上变成了 r,而在别处却保持着不变(试比较 est "他是",senex"老人",equos"马")。

绝对的变化是极其罕见的。它们往往是由于条件具有隐蔽的或过于一般的性质,才看来好像是绝对的。例如德语的 i 变成了 ei,ai,但只是在重读音节④。印欧语的 $k_1$⑤ 变成了日耳曼语的 h(试比较印欧语的 $k_1$olsom,拉丁语的 collum,德语的 Hals"脖子"),但是在 s 的后面却不发生变化(试比较希腊语的 skótos 和峨特语的 skadus"阴影")。

此外,把变化分为绝对的变化和条件的变化,那是以一种对事物的肤浅的看法为基础的,比较合理的是像越来越多的人那样,称为自发的语音现象和结合的语音现象。由内在的原因产生的是自发的变化,由一个或几个别的音位引起的是结合的变化。例如由印欧语的 o 变为日耳曼语的 a(试比较峨特语的 skadus"阴影",德语的 Hals"脖子"等等)⑥就是一个自发的事实。日耳曼语的辅音演变或"Lautverschiebungen"也属自发变化的类型：例如印欧语的 $k_1$ 变成了原始日耳曼语的 h(试比较拉丁语的 collum"脖子"和峨特语的 hals"脖子")。英语还保存着原始日耳曼语的 t,但是在高德语里已变成了 z(念作 ts),试比较峨特语的 taihun"十",英语

---

① 古代德语的长元音 i,ū,ṻ 于十四世纪至十六世纪之间复合元音化,变成了 ei(其后念成 ai),au,äu(其后念成 eu),如 wīn→wein(念 wain)。hūs→Haus,hūsir→Häuser(念 heuzər)。同时,复合元音 ie,uo,单元音化,变成了 ī ū,如 tier→tir(仍写作 Tier),muot→mūt。z 变成了 s(写作 ss),如 wazer→wasser。两个元音间的 h 脱落了,如 sehen→seen(仍写作 sehen)。w 变成了 v,但写法不变,如 wazer→vasr(写作 Wasser)。所有这些把中古德语和现代德语区别开来。——校注

② 古代法语颚化的 l 于十七世纪开始变为 y,十八世纪初有些语法学家曾讥为"巴黎小资产阶级的发音",直到十八世纪三十年代才逐渐固定了下来,但写法不变。——校注

③ 古拉丁语的 s 在两个元音间变成了 r,如*arbosen→arboren"树"。这一点,古罗马语法学家瓦罗(Varro)在《论拉丁语》(De lingua latina)一书中已经指出。——校注

④ 德语有一部分后缀,虽然是非重读音节,也由 ī 变成了 ei 和 ai,如 Fräulein "姑娘"的-lein 在中古德语是-lin,后变为-lein,念成-lain。——校注

⑤ 印欧语的 k 分两种：一种是颚音,标作 $k_1$；一种是舌根音,标作 $k_2$。$k_1$ 在 satəm 语言中变成了 s,如梵语的 çatam"一百",阿维斯塔语的 satəm"一百",立陶宛语的 šiṁtas"一百",古斯拉夫语的 съто；在 centum 语言中变成了 k,如希腊语的 ε-κατόν"一百",拉丁语的 centum"一百",威尔士语的 cant"一百"等等。日耳曼语属 centum 语言,但这个 $k_1$,却变成了 h,如峨特语的 hund"一百",德语的 hundert"一百",英语的 hundred"一百"。这里所举的例子也属这一类型。——校注

⑥ 峨特语 skadus"阴影"源出于印欧语的 skótos,德语的 Hals "脖子"源出于印欧语的 $k_1$olson,其中由印欧语的 o 变成日耳曼语的 a 都是自发的语音变化。——校注

的 ten"十"，德语的 zehn"十"①。相反，由拉丁语的 ct,pt 变为意大利语的 tt(试比较 factum→fatto"事实"，captīvum→cattivo"俘虏")却是一个结合的事实，因为前一个要素为后一个要素所同化。德语的"变音"也是由外在的原因引起的，即下一个音节有一个 i：gast 不发生变化，而 gasti 却变成了 gesti,Gäste"客人们"②。

必须指出，不论哪种情况，结果不是问题所在，有没有变化也并不重要。例如我们试把峨特语的 fisks"鱼"和拉丁语的 piscis"鱼"，峨特语的 skadus"脖子"和希腊语的 skótos"脖子"比较，就可以看到，在前一个例子里，i 保持着不变，而在后一个例子里，o 却变成了 a。这两个音，头一个不变，后一个却起了变化；但主要的是，它们都是独自行动的。

结合的语音事实总是有条件的；自发的事实却不一定是绝对的，它可能是消极地因为缺乏某些变化的因素而引起。例如印欧语的 $k_2$ 自发地变成了拉丁语的 qu(试比较 quattuor"四"，inquilīna"外来的"等等)，但是它的后面不能跟着比如 o 或 u(试比较 cottīdie"每天"，colō"我种田"，secundus"第二"等等)。同样，印欧语的 i 在峨特语的 fisks"鱼"等词中保持不变，也有一个条件，即后面不能跟着 r 或 h，否则就变成了 e，写作 ai(试比较 wair＝拉丁语的 vir"男人"，maihstus＝德语的 Mist"屎")。

……

§4.语音变化的原因

这些原因的探讨是语言学中最困难的问题之一。曾有人提出过好几种解释，没有一种是能够完全说明问题的。

Ⅰ.有人说，人种有一些素质预先划定了语音变化的方向③。这里提出了一个有关比较人类学的问题：发音器官是否会随人种而不同呢？ 不，并不比个人间的差异大多少。一个出生后就移居法国的黑人说的法语跟法国本地人所说的一样漂亮。此外，如果我们使用像"意大利人的发音器官"或者"日耳曼人的嘴不容许这么说"之类的说法，就会有危险把纯粹历史的事实变为永恒的特质。这种错误无异于用现在时表述语音现象。硬说伊奥尼亚人的发音器官不适宜于发长 ā，所以把它变成 ē，这跟说伊奥尼亚方言的 ā"变成"④ē 是一样错误的。

伊奥尼亚人的发音器官对于发 ā 音并没有什么嫌忌，因为在某些情况下，它也容许发这个音。所以这并不是什么人类学上的无能的问题，而是发音习惯改变的问题。同样，拉丁语一度不保留两个元音间的 s(*genesis→generis"产生")，可是稍后又重新把它引了进来(试比较 *rissus→rīsus"笑")；这些变化并不表明拉丁人的发音器官有什么永恒的素质。

诚然，一个民族在一个时代的语音现象有个一般的方向。现代法语复合元音的单元音化就是同一倾向的表现⑤。但是我们在政治史上也可以找到类似的一般潮流，却从不怀疑它们

---

① 辅音演变规律或 Lautverschiebung 是德国语言学家格里木(J. Grimm)于十九世纪初发现的，又称"格里木定律"，内分第一次辅音演变规律和第二次辅音演变规律两部分(参看岑麒祥《语言学史概要》，第 111 页)。第一次辅音演变规律把印欧语系日耳曼族语言和其他族语区别开来，第二次辅音演变规律把日耳曼族的高德语和其他语言区别开来。——校注

② 拉丁语的 ct,pt 变成了意大利语的 tt，这在语音学上是一种逆同化。德语的"变音"(Umlaut)，如 gasti 的 a 因受 i 的影响变成了 e，也是一种逆同化。在语音学上，凡音的同化都属结合的变化。——校注

③ 当时持这种观点的有洛兹(Lotze)、麦克尔(Merkel)、谢勒(Scherer)、奥斯特霍夫(Osthoff)诸人，他们都强调不同种族的发音器官具有特殊的生理结构。法国实验语音学创始人卢斯洛(Rousselot)在所著《土语研究》一书中也认为语音变化决定于神经中枢系统的特点。德·索绪尔在这里批评了他们的这种观点。——校注

④ "变成"在这里用的是现在时(devient)，不是指已成事实的"变成了"(est devenu)。——校注

⑤ 这是指的古代法语从十二世纪至十六世纪这段时间内复合元音的单元音化，如 fait"事实"念[fɛ]，tout"完全"念[tu]，haut"高"念[o]等等。这些词的复合元音虽然起了变化，但写法还是一样。——校注

的纯历史的特征,也没有看到有什么人种的直接影响。

Ⅱ.往往有人把语音变化看作对土壤和气候情况的适应①。某些北方的语言堆积着许多辅音,某些南方的语言更广泛地利用元音,因此它们的声音很和谐。气候和人们的生活条件可能对语言有影响,但是仔细研究起来,问题却很复杂:例如斯堪的纳维亚的语言充满着辅音,而毗邻的拉普人和芬兰人的语言,元音却比意大利语还要多。我们还可以注意到,现代德语辅音的堆积,在许多情况下都是晚近由于重音后元音的脱落而产生的;法国南部的某些方言没有北部的法语那么厌恶辅音群,而塞尔维亚语和莫斯科的俄语却有一样多的辅音群,如此等等。

Ⅲ.有人援引省力律来加以解释,那就是用一次发音来代替两次发音,或者用比较方便的发音来代替困难的发音。这一观念,不管怎么说,很值得考察。它在某种程度上可以说明现象的原因,或者至少指出应该往哪个方向去探讨这种原因。

省力律似乎可以解释某些情况:例如由塞音变擦音(拉丁语 habēre→法语 avoir"有"),许多语言中大量结尾音节的脱落,同化现象(例如 ly→ll,*alyos→希腊语 állos"别的";tn→nn,*atnos→拉丁语 annus"年"),复合元音单元音化其实只是同化的一个变种(例如 ai→ẹ,法语 maizōn→mẹzõ"房子")等等。

不过,我们也可以举出一样多的恰恰相反的情况。例如,同单元音化相对,我们可以举出德语的 ī、ū、ṻ 变成了 ei,au,eu。如果说斯拉夫语的 ā、ē 变成短音 ǎ、ě 是省力的结果,那么德语的相反的现象(fǎter→vāter"父亲",gěben→gēben"给")就应该认为是费力的结果了。如果认为发浊音比清音容易(试比较 pera→普罗旺斯语 obra"工作"),那么相反的就应该更加费劲,可是西班牙语的 ž 却变成了 x(试比较 hixo "儿子",写作 hijo),日耳曼语的 b,d,g 变成了 p,t,k。如果我们把送气的消失(试比较印欧语 *bherō→日耳曼语 beran)看作力量的减省,那么德语在原来没有送气的地方加上了送气(Tanne"罗汉松",Pute"火鸡"等等念成 Thanne,Phute),又该怎么说呢?

这些评论并不是想要反驳大家提出的解决办法。事实上,我们很难为每种语言规定什么音比较易发,什么音比较难发。如果就音长来说,短音化符合省力的原则,这固然是对的,那么,漫不经心的发音常落在长音上面,而短音却要求更多的注意,这同样也有道理。因此,假设有不同的素质,我们就可以从相同的观点举出两个相反的事实。同样,由 k 变为 tš(试比较拉丁语 cēdere→意大利语 cedere"退让"),假如只考虑变化的两头,似乎是力量的增强;但是如果把演变的链条构拟出来,也许会得出不同的印象:k 由于与后面的元音发生同化变成了颚化的 k'。然后由 k'变成 ky,纠缠在 k'音中的两个要素明显地起了分化,发音并不变得更加困难,然后由 ky 陆续变为 ty,tx',tš,处处都显得用力更小。

这里有一个广泛的研究要进行,这个研究要做得完备,必须既考虑到生理观点(发音问题),又考虑到心理观点(注意力问题)。

Ⅳ.近年来有一个盛行一时的解释,把发音的变化归因于幼年时所受的语音教育②。儿童要经过多次的摸索、尝试和纠正之后,才能发出他从周围的人所听到的声音;这里就是语音变化的萌芽。某些未经纠正的不正确的发音在个人方面获得胜利,在成长的一代中固定了下来。我们的孩子往往把发 k 发成 t,我们的语言在它们的历史上并没有表现出相应的语音变

---

① 当时持这种观点的主要有梅耶尔(H. Meyer)、施里能(Schrijnen)等人,而冯德(Wundt)和鄂尔特尔(Oertel)却是反对这一观点的。——校注

② 特别参看布雷默(Bremer)的《德语语音学》,鄂尔特尔(Oertel)的《语音研究讲话》,他们都主张一种所谓"世代理论"。——校注

化;但是另外有些变形却不是这样。例如在巴黎,有许多孩子用颚化的 l 发 fl'eur"花",bl'anc"白",意大利语的 florem 就是经过同样的过程变为 fl'ore,然后变为 fiore"花"的。

这些验证很值得注意,但是还解决不了问题。事实上,我们看不出为什么某一代人同意保存某些不正确的发音而排除另外一些不正确的发音,尽管它们都同样自然。实际上,他们对于不正确的发音的选择显然是纯粹任意的,我们看不出其中有什么道理。此外,为什么某种现象这一次行得通,而在另一次却行不通呢?

这种看法也适用于上面提到的一切原因,如果我们承认这些原因能起作用的话。气候的影响、民族的素质、省力的倾向都是永恒的或持久的原因;它们为什么总是交替地起作用,有时影响到音位系统的这一点,有时影响到音位系统的那一点呢? 历史事件应该有一个决定的原因,但是没有人能说出在每种情况下,如果变化的一般原因久已存在,那么,它是由什么发动的呢? 这就是最难解释的一点。

Ⅴ.有时候,人们想从民族在某一时期的一般状况去找一种决定的原因①。语言所经历的各个时代,有些是多事之秋,于是有人企图把语言跟外部历史的动荡时期拉上关系,从而找出政治上的不稳定和语言的不稳定之间的联系;他们相信这样一来就可以把一般关于语言的结论应用于语音变化。例如,大家看到,拉丁语变为罗曼族诸语言的过程中,最严重的动荡就发生在非常混乱的入侵时代。为了避免误入歧途,我们应该紧握住以下两种区别:

(a)政治上的稳定和不稳定影响语言的方式是不同的,这里面没有任何相互关系。当政治的平衡延缓语言发展的时候,那是一种积极的,虽然是外部的原因,而具有相反效果的政治不稳定只能消极地起作用。一种语言的不变性,相对稳固性,可能来自语言外部的事实(宫廷、学校、科学院、文字等等的影响),这些事实又会因社会和政治上的平衡而获得积极的维护。相反,如果民族的状况中猝然发生某种外部骚动,加速了语言的发展,那只是因为语言恢复了它的自由状态,继续它的合乎规律的进程。拉丁语在古典时代的稳固不变是由于一些外部事实的结果,不能跟它后来遭受的变化相比,因为这些变化是由于缺少某些外部条件而自发发生的。

(b)这里讨论的只是语音现象,不是语言的各种变更。我们要知道,语法变化正是这种原因产生的;语法事实总在某一方面跟思想有关联,而且比较容易受到外部骚动的反响,这些骚动对于人们的心理有更直接的反应。但是谁也无法承认,一种语言声音的急速发展会跟民族历史的动荡时代相符。

此外,我们举不出任何时代,哪怕是当语言处在一种人为的不变状态的时代,语音是不发生变化的。

Ⅵ.也有人援用"先居民族的语言底层"的假设,认为有些变化是由于新来的民族并吞当地居民所产生的结果②。例如 oc 语和 oïl 语③的差别就跟克勒特语土著成分在高卢两部分的不同比例相应。这一理论也曾被用来解释意大利语方言的分歧,把它们归结为各地区分别受过里古利亚语、埃特鲁斯克语等等的影响。但是这一假设首先必然以很少见的情况为依据。其次还要明确:那是不是说,以前的居民在采用新语言的时候,曾引进了自己的某些语音习惯

---

① 特别参看施密德(J. Schmidt)的《印度日耳曼元音系统的历史》和《响音理论》,浮士勒(K. Vossler)在《语言中的精神和文化》一书中也持这一主张。——校注

② "底层理论"最先是由意大利语言学家阿斯戈里(Ascoli)提出用来解释罗曼族诸语言间的差别的,其后许多语言学家如保罗、舒哈尔德和梅耶等都曾广泛加以利用。——校注

③ oc 语指法国南部的方言,oïl 语指法国北部的方言,以罗亚尔河为分界线。oc 和 oïl 都是"是"的意思;oc 语把"是"说成 oc,oïl 语把"是"说成 oïl,因以得名。——校注

呢？这是可以接受的,而且是相当自然的。但是假如再求助于种族等等无法估量的因素,那就会重新陷入上面所指出的漆黑一团。

Ⅶ.最后一个解释——不大值得叫做解释——把语音变化和风尚的变化看作一样东西①。但是风尚的变化是什么,谁也没有解释过。大家只知道这种变化要取决于模仿规律,那是许多心理学家所研究的。可是这种解释尽管解决不了问题,却有一个好处,就是把这问题带进了另一个更广泛的问题:语音变化的原则纯粹是心理的。不过,模仿的出发点在哪里,这对于语音变化和风尚的变化来说都是一个谜。

……

第三章　语音演化在语法上的后果

§1.语法联系的破裂

语音现象的头一个后果是割断了两个或几个要素间的语法联系,因此人们有时会感到某个词不是从另一个词派生出来的。例如:

$$mansiō——{}^*mansiōnāticus$$

$$maison“家” \parallel ménage“家务”$$

人们的语言意识从前把 ${}^*$mansiōnāticus 看作 mansiō 的派生词,后来,语音的变化把它们分开了。同样:

$$(vervēx—vervēcārius)$$

$$民间拉丁语 berbīx—berbicārius$$

$$brebis“母羊” \parallel berger“牧童”$$

这种分隔对于意义自然有所反应,因此,在有些地方土语里,berger 已专指“看牛的人”。又如:

$$Grātiānopolis—grātiānopolitānus \qquad decem—undecim$$

$$Grenoble(地名) \parallel Grésivaudan“格雷西佛丹” \qquad dix“十” \parallel onze“十一”$$

类似的情况还有峨特语的 bītan“咬”—bitum“我们已经咬”—bitr“刺痛的,痛苦的”。一方面由于 t→ts(z)变化的结果,另一方面由于保存着 tr 这个音组,西部日耳曼语把它变成了 bīzan,bizum $\parallel$ bitr。

语音演化还割断了同一个词两个屈折形式间的正常关系。例如 comes“伯爵(主格)”—comiten“伯爵(宾格)”变成了古法语的 cuens $\parallel$ comte,barō“男爵(主格)”—barōnem“男爵(宾格)”→ber $\parallel$ baron,presbiter“祭司(主格)”—presbiterum“祭司(宾格)”→prestre $\parallel$ provoire。

在别的地方,一个词尾分成了两个。印欧语的任何单数宾格都有同一个词尾-m②(${}^*$ek₁wom“马”, ${}^*$owim“酒”, ${}^*$podm“脚”, ${}^*$māterm“母亲”等等)。拉丁语在这一方面没有根本的变化;但是在希腊语里,由于鼻响音和鼻辅响音的变化极不相同,因此造成了两套不同的形式:híppon, ó(w)in∶póda, mā́tera③。复数宾格的情况也十分相似(试比较 híppous 和

---

① 这是指的弗里德利希·缪勒(Friedrich Müller)所主张的语音风尚理论。德·索绪尔在这里顺带批评了塔尔德(Tarde)及其拥护者叶斯泊森(O. Jespersen)的模仿理论。——校注

② 或者-n? 试比较第 126 页附注。——原编者注

③ 德·索绪尔在这里根据勃鲁格曼于 1876 年在《希腊语和拉丁语语法研究》第九期发表的《印度日耳曼基础语的鼻响音》一文和他自己于 1879 年发表的《论印欧语元音的原始系统》中关于响音的理论,从希腊语 a 和拉丁语 em 的对应关系确定印欧基础语的鼻响音和鼻辅响音,认为它们在拉丁语里没有根本变化,但是在希腊语里却变成了两套不同的形式。——校注

pódas）。

§2.词的复合结构的消失

语音变化在语法上的另一个后果是使过去有助于确定一个词的意义的不同部分变得不能分析：整个词变成了分不开的整体。例如法语的 ennemi "敌人"（试比较拉丁语的 in-imīcus—amīcus "朋友"），拉丁语的 perdere "损失"（试比较更古的 per-dare—dare "给"），amiciō "我包上"（代替 *ambjaciō—jaciō "抛掷"），德语的 Drittel "三分之一"（代替 drit-teil—teil "部分"）。

我们还看到，这种情况可以归结为前一节的情况：例如，ennemi 是不能分析的，那等于说我们不能像 in-imīcus 那样把它跟单纯词 amicus 比较：

$$amīcus—inimīcus$$
$$ami "朋友" \parallel ennemi "敌人"$$

这个公式和

$$mansiō—mansiōnāticus$$
$$maison "家" \parallel ménage "家务"$$

完全一样。又试比较：decem—undecim：dix "十" ‖ onze "十一"。

古典拉丁语的单纯形式 hunc "此（阳性、单数、宾格）"，hanc "此（阴性、单数、宾格）"，hāc "此（阴性、单数、离格）"等等，可以追溯到碑铭所表明的形式，hon-ce，han-ce，hā-ce，乃是代词和虚词-ce 黏合的结果[1]。从前，hon-ce 等等可以同 ec-ce "由此"比较，后来由于-e 的脱落，这已成为不可能，那等于说，我们再也辨不出 hunc，hanc，hāc 等等的要素了。

语音演化在使分析成为完全不可能之前，是从扰乱分析开始的。印欧语的名词屈折变化可以提供一个这样的例子。

印欧语的名词变格是：单数主格 *pod-s，宾格 *pod-m，与格 *pod-ai，方位格 *pod-i，复数主格 *pod-es，宾格 *pod-ns 等等。起初，*ek₁ wos 的屈折变化也完全一样：*ek₁ wos，*ek₁ wo-m，*ek₁ wo-ai，*ek₁ wo-i，*ek₁ wo-es，*ek₁ wo-ns 等等。在那个时代，*ek₁ wo-同 *pod-一样，很容易分出。但是后来元音的缩减改变了这种状态：与格 *ek₁ wōi，方位格 *ek₁ woi，复数主格 *ek₁ wōs。从此，词干 *ek₁ wo-的明晰性受到了损害，分析时不好捉摸。其后又发生了新的变化，例如宾格的分化，把原始状态的最后一点痕迹全给抹掉了。色诺芬同时代的人[2]或许已有一种印象，认为词干是 hipp-，词尾是元音性的（hipp-os 等等），其后，*ek₁ wo-s 和 *pod-s 两种类型就截然分开了。在屈折变化的领域内，如在其他地方一样，扰乱分析就会促使语法联系的松弛。

§3.没有语音上的同源对似词

在第一、第二节所考察的两种情况里，语音演化把两项起初在语法上有联系的要素彻底地分开了。这种现象很可能引起解释上的严重错误。

当我们看到中古拉丁语的 barō：barōnem 有相对的同一性，而古法语的 ber：baron 却截然不同的时候，我们能不能说那是同一个原始单位（bar-）朝着两个不同的方向发展，产生了两个形式呢？不能。因为同一个要素不可能同时在同一个地方发生两种不同的变化；这是违反

---

① 古典拉丁语 hǐc（阳性、单数），haec（阴性、单数），hǒc（中性、单数）是近指代词，有"此"的意思。这里所说 hunc 是 hǐc 的宾格，hanc 是 haec 的宾格，hāc 是 haec 的离格，其中的-c 都是由-ce 变来的，-ce 原来是一个虚词。——校注

② 色诺芬（Xénophon），雅典史学家和将军，约生于公元前434年，死于公元前355年。色诺芬的同时代人即指公元前五世纪至公元前四世纪的希腊人。——校注

语音变化的定义的。语音演化本身不能创造两个形式来代替一个形式。

人们对我们的主张可能提出异议,我们假定这些异议以下列举例的方式提出:

有人说,拉丁语的 collocāre 变成了法语的 coucher"躺下"和 colloquer"安置"。不对。collocāre 只变成了 coucher;colloquer 只是借用这拉丁词的雅词(试比较 rançon"赎"和 rédemption"赎罪"等等)。

但是 cathedra 不是变成了 chaire"讲座"和 chaise"椅子"这两个真正的法语的词吗? 实际上,chaise 是一个方言的形式。巴黎土话把两个元音间的 r 变成了 z,例如把 père"父亲",mère"母亲"说成 pèse, mèse。法兰西文学语言只保存了这种地区发音的两个样品:chaise 和 bésicles(béricles 的同源对似词,来自 béryl①)。这种情况恰好可以同毕卡迪方言的 rescapé"脱险者"相比,它刚进入共同法语,一下子就同 réchappé"幸免于难的人"对立而并存。现代法语有 cavalier"骑兵"又有 chevalier"骑士",有 cavalcade"骑马队"又有 chevauchée"骑马行列",那是因为 cavalier 和 cavalcade 是从意大利语借来的。这归根到底跟拉丁语的 calidum"热"变成法语的 chaud 和意大利语的 caldo 是一样的。所有这些例子都涉及借词的问题。

如果有人问,拉丁语的代词 mē"我"在法语里怎么变成了 me 和 moi 两个形式(试比较 il me voit"他看见我"和 c'est moi qu'il voit"他看见的是我"),那么,我们可以回答:变成 me 的是拉丁语的非重读的 mē;重读的 mē 变成了 moi。然而是否出现重音并不取决于使 mē 变成 me 和 moi 的语音规律,而是取决于这个词在句子中的作用;这是语法上的二重性。同样,德语的 *ur- 在重读音节仍然是 ur-,而在重音之前却变成了 er-(试比较 úrlaub"休假":erláuben"允许");但是重音的这种作用本身是跟含有 ur- 的结构类型相关联的,因此也是跟语法条件和共时条件有关的。最后,回到我们在开头所举的例子,bárō:barṓnem 这两个词在形式上和重音上的差别显然在语音变化之前就已经存在了。

事实上,我们不管在什么地方都看不到语音上的同源对似词。语音演化只是加强了在它之前早已存在的差别。这些差别只要不是由于外部原因例如借词引起的,就一定会有语法上的和共时的二重性,而这是跟语音现象绝对没有关系的。

§4. 交替

在像 maison:ménage 这样的两个词里,或者由于其中表示差别的要素(-ezṓ 和 -en-)不好比较,或者由于没有别的成对的词具有相同的对立,人们往往不耐烦去探究它们何以会有差别。但是有时两个相邻要素间的差别只在于一个很容易挑出的成分,而且这个差别在一系列平行的成对的词里有规律地反复出现,那就是语音变化在里面起作用的最广泛的、最平常的语法事实:我们管它叫交替。

在法语里,所有拉丁语开音节的 ŏ 在重读音节里都变成了 eu,在重音之前都变成了 ou;因此而有像 pouvons"我们能够":peuvent"他们能够",œuvre"作品":ouvrier"工人",nouveau"新":neuf"新"等等这样的成对的词,我们可以毫不费力地从中挑出一个表示差别的、有规律地起变化的要素来。在拉丁语里,r 音化使 gerō"我引带"和 gestus"被引带",oneris"负担(属格)"和 onus"负担(主格)",maeror"悲伤"和 maestus"悲伤的"等等互相交替。在日耳曼语里,由于 s 随着重音的位置而有不同的变化,所以中古高德语有 ferliesen"遗失":ferloren"遗失(过去分词)",kiesen"选择":gekoren"选择(过去分词)",friesen"冷冻":gefroren"冷冻(过去

---

① Bésicles 是一种旧式的大型眼镜,跟 bérides 是同源对似词,来自一种绿柱石 béryl,因为这种眼镜就是用 béryl 制成的,加上后缀 -cle 表示"小"的意思。十五世纪至十七世纪这个期间,巴黎人习惯于把两个元音间的 r 念成 s[z],于是 béricles 变成了 bésicles。十七世纪后,巴黎人的这种特殊发音虽已消失,但是 bésicles 这个词却被保存了下来。——校注

分词)"等等。现代德语 beissen"咬":biss"咬（过去时）",leiden"遭受":litt"遭受（过去时）",reiten"骑":ritt"骑（过去时）"等等的对立可以反映出印欧语 e 的脱落。

在所有这些例子里,受影响的都是词根要素;但是,不消说,词的任何部分都可以有类似的对立。最普通的,像前缀可以随词干开头部分的性质而有不同的形式(试比较希腊语的 apo-dídōmi"偿还":ap-érchomai"离开",法语的 inconnu"不认识的":inutile"无用的")。印欧语 e：o 的交替,最后分析起来,应该是由于语音的原因;这种交替,我们在许多后缀要素里都可以找到[希腊语的 híppos"马":híppe"马（呼格）",phér-o-men"我们携带":phér-e-te"你们携带",gén-os"宗族":gén-e-os"出生"代替了 *gén-es-os 等等]。在古法语里,拉丁语重读的 a 在颚音后有特殊的变化;因此在许多词尾里都有 e：ie 的交替[试比较 chant-er"唱":jug-ier"判断",chant-é"喝（过去分词）":jug-ié"判断（过去分词）",chant-ez"你们唱":jug-iez"你们判断"等等]。

因此,我们可以给交替下个定义:在两系列共存的形式间有规则地互换的两个音或音组的对应。

正如语音现象不能单独解释同源对似词一样,我们可以很容易看到,它同样既不是交替的唯一原因,也不是主要原因。有人说拉丁语的 nov-由于语音变化变成了 neuv-和 nouv-(法语的 neuve"新"和 nouveau"新"),那是一个捏造的虚幻的统一性,而且不知道在它之前早已存在着一种共时的二重性。nov-在 nov-us 和 nov-ellus 里的位置不同①是语音变化之前就存在的,同时显然是属于语法方面的(试比较 barō：barōnem)。正是这种共时的二重性引起一切的语音交替,并使它们成为可能。语音现象没有破坏统一性,它只是由于抛弃了一些声音而使各项共存要素间的对立显得更为明显。只是因为声音构成了交替的材料,以及声音的更迭在交替的产生中起作用,而认为交替属于语音方面,这是不对的。不少语言学家有这错误看法。事实上,交替无论从它的起点或终点看,都总是属于语法的和共时态的。

§5. 交替的规律

交替能否归结为规律,这些规律又是什么性质的呢?

试举现代德语里常见的 e：i 交替②为例。如果乱七八糟地把所有的例子都列举出来[geben"给":gibt"他给",Feld"田地":Gefilde"原野",Wetter"气候":wittern"嗅",helfen"帮助（动词）":Hilfe"帮助（名词）",sehen"看见":Sicht"景象"等等],我们将无法定出任何一般的原则。但是如果我们从这一大堆杂乱无章的例子中抽出 geben gibt 这成对的词来同 schelten"叱骂":schilt"他叱骂",helfen"帮助":hilft"他帮助",nehmen"拿":nimmt"他拿"相对比,就可以看到,这种交替是跟时制、人称等等的区别一致的。在 lang"长":Länge"长度",stark"强":Stärke"强度",hart"硬":Härte"硬度"等等里,同样的 a：e 对立③都跟用形容词构成名词有关;在 Hand"手":Hände"手（复数）",Gast"客人":Gäste"客人（复数）",等等里都跟复数的构成有关。诸如此类的许多常见的情况,日耳曼语语言学家叫做"转音"④。[又参看 finden"寻找":fand"寻找（过去时）",或 finden：Fund"发现",binden"捆绑":band"捆绑（过去时）",或

---

① nov- 在 nov-us 里是重读音节,到法语变成了 neuv-;在 nov-ellus 里是非重读音节,到法语变成了 nouv-。——校注

② 这是由于 e 为后一个音节的元音 i 所同化的结果,可是这最后的 i 在现代德语里已经消失了。这种现象在德语语言学里叫做"断韵"（Brechung）。——校注

③ 这是指的 a 因为后一个音节的 i 所同化而变成了 ä[ɛ],i 接着变成了 e,如 lang：Länge,Hand：Hände 等等。这种现象,德国语言学家叫做"变音"（Umlaut）。——校注

④ "转音"（Ablaut）即与语法上的对立符合的词根元音变化,如 finden：fand,finden：Fund 等等。——校注

binden:Bund"联盟",schiessen"射击":schoss"射击(过去时)":Schuss"发射",flessen"流":floss"流(过去时)":Fluss"河流"等等]。转音,或者与语法上的对立相合的词根元音变化,是交替的主要例子,但是没有任何特殊的特征使它区别于一般现象。

由此可见,交替通常有规则地分布在几项要素之间,而且同功能上、范畴上或限定上的重要的对立相吻合。我们可以谈到交替的语法规律,但这些规律只是它们所由产生的语音事实的偶然结果。语音事实在两系列具有意义对立的要素间创造了一种有规则的语音对立,人们的心理就紧握住这种物质上的差别,使它具有意义,担负起概念上的差别。同一切共时规律一样,交替规律也只是简单的配置原则,没有命令的力量。人们常随便说,Nacht"夜"的 a 变成了复数 Nächte 的 ä,这是非常错误的;它会给人一种错觉,以为由一个要素过渡到另一个要素曾发生某种受命令性原则支配的变化。这其实只是一种由语音演化的结果造成的形式上的对立。诚然,我们下面将要讨论的类比可以造成一些新的具有相同的语音差别的成对的词[试比较仿照 Gast"客人":Gäste"客人(复数)"造成的 Kranz"花冠":Kränze"花冠(复数)"等等];交替规律似乎可以当作向惯用法发号施令直至使它改变的规则来应用。但是我们不要忘记,在语言里,这些转换(permutation)是要受相反的类比影响摆布的,这已足以表明这类规则总是不牢靠的,而且完全符合共时规律的定义。

引起交替的语音条件,有时可能还更明显。例如我们在前面所引的那些成对的词在古高德语里具有 geban:gibit,feld:gafildi 等形式。在那个时代,如果词干后面跟着一个 i,那么它本身就带有 i,而不是 e,可是在其他情况下都带有 e。拉丁语 faciō"我做":conficiō"我完成",amīcus"朋友":inimīcus"敌人",facilis"容易":difficilis"困难"等等的交替也跟某一语音条件有关联,说话者会把这条件说成:faciō,amīcus 等等这类词里的 a,如果在同族的词里处于内部的音节,那么跟 i 相交替。

但是这些声音上的对立恰恰向人们提示了适用于任何语法规律的同样的看法:它们是共时的。忘记了这一点,就会犯前面指出的解释上的错误。面对着像 faciō:conficiō 这样的成对的词,我们必须提防不要把这些共存的要素间的关系同历时事实中前后连续的要素(confaciō→conficiō)间的关系混为一谈。如果有人混为一谈,那是因为语音分化的原因在这两个词里还可以看得出来;但是它的效能已成过去,而且对说话者来说,只有一个简单的共时的对立。

所有这一切可以证实我们上面所说的交替具有严格的语法特性。人们曾用"转换"(permutation)这个术语来表示交替,那是很贴切的,但是最好还是避开不用,因为人们往往把它用于语音变化,而且会在只涉及状态的例子里唤起一种运动的错误观念。

§6.交替和语法联系

我们在上面已经看到,语音演化改变词的形式,其效果会怎样割断词与词之间可能存在的语法联系。但这只有对 maison:ménage,Teil:Drittel 等等孤立的、成对的词是这样。至于说到交替,情况就不同了。

首先,很明显,两个要素的任何稍有点规则的语音对立都有在它们之间建立一个联系的倾向。Wetter"天气"在本能上就跟 wittern 有关,因为人们已习惯于看到 e 与 i 交替。何况说话者一旦感到有某种一般规律支配着语音对立,这惯常的对应就必然会引起他们的注意,有助于加强而不是削弱语法联系。例如德语的"转音"就是这样透过元音的变化加强人们对于词根单位的认识的。

对于那些不表示意义但是跟某种纯语音的条件有联系的交替来说,情况也是这样。法语的前缀 re-(reprendre"取回",regagner"恢复",retoucher"校订"等等)在元音之前缩减为 r-

（rouvrir"再开"，racheter"买回"等等）。同样，前缀 in-虽然来自文言，但是还很有生命力，它在相同的情况下有两个不同的形式：ē-(inconnu"不认识的"，indigne"不配"，invertébré"无脊椎的"等等）和 in-(inavouable"不能承认的"，inutile"无用的"，inesthétique"非美学的"等等）。这种差别丝毫没有破坏概念的统一性，因为大家体会到它们的意义和功能都是相同的，并且语言已经确定了在什么情况下要用这个形式或那个形式。

### 第四章　类比

#### §1.定义和举例

由上面所说可以看到，语音现象是一个扰乱的因素。无论什么地方，语音现象不造成交替，就削弱词与词之间的语法联系。形式的总数陡然增加了，可是语言的机构反而模糊起来，复杂起来，以至语音变化产生的不规则形式压倒了一般类型的形式，换句话说，绝对任意性压倒了相对任意性。

幸而类比抵消了这些变化的后果。词的外表上的正常变化，凡不属于语音性质的，都是由类比引起的[1]。

类比必须有一个模型和对它的有规则的模仿。类比形式就是以一个或几个其他形式为模型，按照一定规则构成的形式。

例如拉丁语的主格 honor"荣幸"就是一个类比形式。人们起初说 honōs"荣幸"：honōsem"荣幸（宾格）"，后来由于 s 的 r 音化变成了 honōs：honōrem。此后，词干就有了双重的形式。接着，这双重的形式为 honor 这个新的形式所勾销；honor 是仿照 ōrātor"演说家"：ōrātōrem"演说家（宾格）"等等的模型造成的。模仿的程序我们下面再来研究，现在把它归结为以下一个四项比例式[2]：

$$\bar{o}r\bar{a}t\bar{o}rem : \bar{o}r\bar{a}tor = hon\bar{o}rem : x$$

$$x = honor$$

由此可见，为了抵消语音变化造成分歧的效能（honōs：honōrem），类比又重新把这两个形式统一起来，再次使它们成为有规则的（honor：honōrem）。

法国人有一个很长的时期说：il preuve"他证明"，nous prouvons"我们证明"，ils preuvent"他们证明"，现在却说 il prouve，ils prouvent，这些形式在语音上是无法解释的。il aime"他爱"来自拉丁语的 amat，而 nous aimons"我们爱"却是代替 amons 的类比形式；同样，aimable"可爱的"本来也应该是 amable。希腊语的 s 在两个元音间已经消失：-eso-变成了 -eo-(试比较 géneos 代替了 *genesos）。可是我们在元音式动词的将来时和不定过去时里仍能找到这种元音间的 s：lūsō"我将解开"，élūsa"我解开了"等等。这是因为类比了 túpsō"我将敲打"，étupsa"我敲打了"型的形式，其中的 s 没有脱落，还保存着用 s 表示将来时和不定过去时的陈迹。在德语里，Gast"客人"：Gäste"客人（复数）"，Balg"兽皮"：Bälge"兽皮（复数）"等等是语音上的，而 Kranz"花冠"：Kränze"花冠（复数）"（更早是 kranz：kranza），Hals"脖子"：Hälse"脖子（复数）"（更早是 hals：halsa）等等却是模仿的结果。

类比作用有利于规则性，倾向于划一构词和屈折的程序，但有时也反复无常。例如德语

---

① 德·索绪尔在这里把类比看作语言形式划一的原则，是跟新语法学派的观点完全一致的。类比作用是新语法学派语言学理论中一个很重要的原则，这学派的每一个成员都曾采用它来解释语言变化的现象。保罗在《语言史原理》第十章里曾特别加以详细的讨论。法国亨利(Henri)也曾出版《类比》一书专门阐述它的意义和作用。——校注

② 采用四项比例式来解释借助类比构成新词的方式，是新语法学派所惯用的方法。这方法经保罗推广后在语言学中曾获得了普遍的应用，所以又称"保罗比例式"。——校注

除了 Kranz"花冠":Kränze"花冠（复数）"等等之外，还有 Tag"日子":Tage"日子（复数）",Salz"盐":Salze"盐（复数）"等等由于某种原因抗拒了类比作用的形式。所以我们不能预言一个模型的模仿会扩展到什么地步，或者什么样的类型会引起大家模仿。例如发动类比的不一定都是最多数的形式。希腊语的全过去时，除主动态的 pépheuga"我逃跑了"、pépheugas"你逃跑了"、pepheúgamen"我们逃跑了"等等以外，一切中动态的屈折变化都没有 a，如 pépugmai"我自己逃跑了"。pephúgmetha"我们自己逃跑了"等等，而且荷马的语言表明，这个 a 在古代主动态的复数和双数里都是没有的（试比较荷马的 ídmen"我们知道了"，éïkton"但愿你们知道了"等等）。类比只是以主动态单数第一人称做出发点的，然后扩展到直陈式全过去时的几乎整个范例①。这种情况很值得注意，因为在这里，类比把一个本来是屈折变化的要素-a-归属于词干，因而有 pepheúga-men。相反的情况——把词干要素归属于后缀——我们在后面将可以看到，更为常见得多。

两三个孤立的词往往就足以造成一个一般的形式，比方说一种词尾。在古高德语里，像 habēn"有"，lobōn"夸奖"等等这样的弱式动词的第一人称单数现在时有一个-m，如 habēm，lobōm。这个-m 可以一直追溯到类似希腊语以-mi 结尾的一些动词：bim"是"，stām"站立"，gēm"去"，tuom"做"，正是它们把这个词尾强加于整个弱式的屈折变化。应该指出，在这里，类比并没有抹掉语音上的分歧，而是把一个构词的方式推广了。

§2. 类比现象不是变化

早期的语言学家没有了解类比现象的性质，把它叫做"错误的类比"②。他们认为拉丁语发明 honor 的时候是把 honōs 那个原型"弄错"了。在他们看来，一切偏离规例的现象都是不规则的，都是对理想形式的违反。由于那个时代特有的一种错觉，他们把语言的原有状态看作某种优越的、尽善尽美的东西，甚至不屑查问一下在这状态之前是否还有其他状态，因此稍有不合就认为是变则。新语法学派指出，类比同语音变化一样，都是语言演化的重要因素，语言从一种组织状态过渡到另一种状态所经由的程序，从而确定了类比的适当地位。

但类比现象的性质是怎样的呢？它们真像一般人所相信的那样是变化吗？

任何类比事实都是由三种角色合演的一出戏，即（1）传统的、合法的继承人（例如 honōs）；（2）竞争者（honor）；（3）由创造这竞争者的各种形式（honōrem ōrātor，ōrātōrem 等等）组成的集体角色。人们常愿意把 honor 看作 honōs 的一种变化，一种"后生质"，仿佛它的大部分实质都是从 honōs 抽取出来的。可是在 honor 的产生中，唯一不算数的形式恰恰是 honōs！

我们可以把类比现象绘成下图：

传统形式　　　　　　　　　　　　　新形式

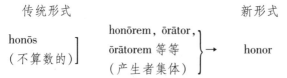

honōs
（不算数的）　honōrem，ōrātor，ōrātorem 等等（产生者集体）　⟶　honor

我们可以看到，这是一种"旁生质"，把竞争者安顿在传统形式旁边，毕竟是一种创造。语音变化引入新的，必须把旧的取消（honōrem 代替了 honōsem），而类比形式却不一定非使它的双重形式消失不可。Honor 和 honōs 曾同时共存了一个时期，而且是可以互相代用的。可是由于语言不喜欢保持两个能指来表示同一个观念，那比较不规则的原始形式往往就因为没有

① 德·索绪尔在这里完全同意了勃鲁格曼的观点。后者认为类比的出发点是一个最常用的形式，然后扩展到整个词形变化范例，见他在《形态学研究》创刊号上发表的《动词后缀 a》一文。——校注

② "错误的类比"这个术语是古尔替乌斯在他跟新语法学派的论战中提出来的，德·索绪尔在这里站在新语法学派的立场批评了他的这种观点。——校注

人使用而消失了。正是这种结果使人以为那是一种变化：类比的效能一经完成，那旧状态（honōs∶honōrem）和新状态（honor∶honōrem）的对立看来似乎跟语音演化所造成的对立没有区别。然而在 honor 产生的时候，什么也没有改变，因为它并不代替任何东西；honōs 的消失也并不是变化，因为这种现象不依存于前者。只要我们能跟踪语言事件的进程，就到处可以看到类比创新和旧形式的消失是不同的两回事，哪里都找不到变化。

类比的特点很少是用一个形式代替另一个形式，因此我们往往看到它产生一些并不代替任何东西的形式。德语可以从任何带有具体意义的名词派生出以-chen 结尾的指小词；如果有一个形式 Elephantchen"小象"被引进那语言里，它并不代替任何前已存在的形式。同样，在法语里，人们可以按照 pension"寄宿舍"∶pensionnaire"寄宿生"，réaction"反动"∶réactionnaire"反动派"等等的模型创造出 interventionnaire 或 répressionnaire 来表示"干涉派"、"镇压派"。这个程序显然跟刚才产生 honor 的一样：二者都可以列成同一个公式：

$$réaction ∶ réactionnaire = répression ∶ x$$
$$x = répressionnaire.$$

不论哪种情况，都没有一点可以谈到变化的借口；répressionnaire 并不代替任何东西。再举一个例子：一方面，我们可以听见人家按类比把大家认为更有规则的 finals"最后的（复数）"说成 finaux；另一方面，可能有人造出 firmamental"天空的"这个形容词，并把它的复数说成 firmamentaux。我们可以说 finaux 是变化而 firmamentaux 是创造吗？这两种情况都是创造。曾有人按照 mur"墙"∶emmurer"围以墙"的模型造出了 tour"周围"∶entourer"围绕"和 jour"光线"∶ajourer"透孔"（如 un travail ajouré"网眼织品"）；这些晚近出现的派生词，我们觉得似乎都是创造。但是如果我注意到人们在前一个时代已经在 torn 和 jorn 的基础上构成了 entorner 和 ajorner，我是否要改变意见，宣称 entourer 和 ajourer 是由这些更古的词变来的呢？可见，关于类比"变化"的错觉来自人们要在新要素和它所篡夺的旧要素之间建立一种关系。但这是一种错误，因为所谓变化的构成（如∶honor）跟我们所称的创造的构成（如 répressionnaire）是性质相同的。

§3.类比是语言创造的原则

指出了类比不是什么之后，如果我们从正面去进行研究，那么马上可以看到它的原则简直跟一般语言创造的原则没有什么分别。什么原则呢？

类比是属于心理方面的，但是这不足以把它跟语音现象区别开来，因为语音现象也可以看作属于心理方面的。我们还要进一步说类比是语法方面的：要我们意识和理解到各形式间的关系。观念在语音现象里没有什么作用，但是类比却必须有观念参与其事。

在拉丁语的两个元音间的 s 变为 r 的过程中（试比较 honōsem→honōrem），我们看不到它跟其他形式的比较，也看不到词的意义参与其间：那是 honōsem 这个形式的尸体变成了 honōrem。相反，为了理解怎样在 honōs 面前出现 honor，却必须求助于其他形式，如下面的四项比例式所表明的：

$$ōrātōrem ∶ ōrātor = honōrem ∶ x$$
$$x = honor$$

要是人们不在心中把组成这结合的各个形式按照它们的意义联结起来，那么这结合就绝不会出现。

因此，在类比中，一切都是语法的；但是我们要马上补充一句：作为类比结果的创造，首先只能是属于言语的；它是孤立的说话者的偶然产物。我们首先应该在这个范围内和语言的边缘寻找这种现象。但是必须区别开两样东西：（1）对各个能产形式间相互关系的理解；（2）比较所提示的结果，即说话者为了表达思想临时构成的形式。只有这个结果是属于言语的。

所以类比再一次教导我们要把语言和言语分开。它向我们表明，后者要依存于前者，而且指出了我们在前面所描绘的语言机构的作用。在任何创造之前都应该对语言的宝库中所储存的材料作一番不自觉的比较，在这宝库中，各个能产的形式是按照它们的句段关系和联想关系排列好了的。

所以类比现象一大部分是新形式出现之前就已经完成了的。连续不断的言语活动把提供给它的各个单位加以分解，它本身不仅含有按照习惯说话的一切可能性，而且含有类比构成的一切可能性。所以，认为只有在创造出现的瞬间才发生生产的过程，那是错误的；要素是现成的。临时构成的词，例如 in-décor-able "不可装饰的"，早已潜存于语言之中，它的全部要素都可以在比如 décor-er "装饰（动词）"，décor-ation "装饰（名词）"；pardonn-able "可以原谅的"，mani-able "易于管理的"：in-connu "不认识的"，in-sensé "没有理智的"等句段中找到。它在言语中的实现，跟构成它的可能性比较起来是微不足道的。

总之，类比就其本身来说，只是解释现象的一个方面，是识别单位以便随后加以利用的一般活动的一种表现。因此，我们说，它完全是语法的和共时的。

类比的这种性质有两点可以证实我们关于绝对任意性和相对任意性的看法：

（1）词由于本身可分解的程度不同，产生其他词的相对能力也不一样。我们可以把各个词按照这相对的能力加以分类。单纯词，按定义说，是非能产的（试比较 magasin "商店"，arbre "树"，racine "根"等等）。magasinier "店员"不是由 magasin 产生的，而是按照 prisonnier "监犯"：prison "监狱"等等的模型构成的。同样，emmagasiner "入栈"是按 emmailloter "裹以褓褓"，encadrer "镶以框架"，encapuchonner "戴上风帽"等等的类比构成的，其中就包含着 maillot "褓褓"、cadre "框架"、capuchon "风帽"等等。

所以每种语言都有能产的词和非能产的词，但是二者的比例不同。总括起来，又使我们回到在前面所作出的"词汇的"语言和"语法的"语言的区别。汉语的大多数的词都是不能分解的；相反，人造语言的词差不多都是可以分析的。世界语者有充分的自由根据某一词根构成新词①。

（2）我们在前面已经指出，任何类比创造都可以描绘成类似四项比例式的运算。人们往往用这个公式来解释现象本身，而我们却在分析和重建语言所提供的要素中探索了它的存在理由。

这两个概念是互相冲突的。如果四项比例式的解释是充分的，何苦还要进行要素分析呢？为了构成 indécorable，我们没有必要抽出它的各个要素（in-décor-able），只消把它整个放进方程里就够了，例如：

$$pardonner：inpardonnable\ 等等 = décorer：x$$
$$x = indécorable.$$

这样，我们就不必假定说话者方面要进行一种极像语法学家的有意识的分析那样的复杂的运算。在按照 Gast：Gäste 的模型构成 Kranz：Kränze 这一例子里，分解似乎没有四项比例式那么接近真实；因为那模型的词干有时是 Gast-，有时是 Gäst-；人们只消把 Gäste 的语音特点移到 Kranze 上面去就行了。

这些理论中哪一个是符合实际的呢？首先我们要注意，Kranz 并不一定要排除分析。我

---

① 例如 patr-o 是"父亲"的意思，patr-in-o 是"母亲"的意思，bo-patr-o 是"岳父"的意思，bo-patr-in-o 是"岳母"的意思，如此等等。——校注

们已经看到词根和前缀中的交替,交替的感觉是大可以跟积极的分析同时并存的。

这两个相反的概念反映在两种不同的语法理论里。我们欧洲的语法是运用四项比例的;例如它们从整个词出发来解释德语过去时的构成。人们对学生说:按照 setzen"安放":setzte"安放(过去时)"的模型构成 lachen"笑"等等的过去时。相反,印度的语法却在某一章研究词根(setz-,lach-等等),另一章研究词尾(-te 等等);它只举出一个个经过分析所得到的要素,人们必须把它们重新构成整个的词。在任何梵语词典里,动词都是按照词根所指示的顺序排列的①。

语法理论家将按照每一语群中占优势的趋势,倾向于采用这种或那种方法。

古拉丁语似乎有利于采用分析的方法。这里有一个明显的证据。fǎctus"事实"和 āctus"动作"的音长是不同的,尽管也有 fǎciō"我做"和 ǎgō"我行动"。我们假定 āctus 是由 *ǎgtos 变来的,而其中元音之所以延长是由于后面有一个浊音。这个假设在罗曼族语言中得到了充分的证实。法语 dépit"怨恨"( = despěctus)和 toit"屋顶"( = tēctum)反映出 spěciō"我看":spěctus"景象"与 těgō"我盖":tēctus"屋顶"的对立:试比较 confǐciō"我完成":confěctus"渍物"(法语 confit)与 rěgō"我校正":rēctus"正确"(dīrēctus→法语 droit"直的")的对立。但是 *agtos, *tegtos, *regtos 并不是从印欧语继承下来的,印欧语一定是说 *ǎktos, *těktos 等等。那是史前拉丁语把它们引进来的,尽管在清音之前发出浊音很困难。这要对 ag-,teg-等词根单位有很强烈的意识才能做到。可见古拉丁语对词的各种零件(词干、后缀等等)及其安排有高度的感觉。也许我们的现代语言已没有这样敏锐的感觉了,但是德语的感觉要比法语的敏锐。

(节选自《普通语言学教程》,商务印书馆,2017)

# 2.Mixture of Varieties

## Hudson

### 2.5.1　Code-switching

We have been concerned so far in this chapter with the status of ' varieties ' in the language system—to what extent is our collection of linguistic items compartmentalised into separate varieties, each with its own social links, and to what extent are social links restricted to these large-scale varieties, rather than the individual linguistic items? The effect of the earlier discussion was to give varieties a relatively unimportant role in the language system, though we did not deny their existence altogether. We now turn to a different kind of question about varieties: even when we can recognise varieties as clearly distinct languages (for example, English versus Spanish), to what extent do their speakers keep them separate? This divides into two separate questions: do they keep them separate in speech? and do they keep them separate as language systems? The first two sections are concerned with the first question: are languages always kept separate in speech? Here too we find that the variety-based view is far too rigid to do justice to human linguistic behaviour.

---

① 这就是巴尼尼语法体系来说的。按照这个体系,先要把每个词的词根分析出来,然后按一定顺序排列成词典。这跟西方语文的词典名词用单数主格的形式,动词用不定式的形式按字母的顺序排列截然不同。——校注

We start with CODE-SWITCHING, which is the inevitable consequence of bilingualism ( or. more generally, multilingualism ). ( For a brief but very helpful survey see McCormick 1994a. Romaine 1989 is a good book-length discussion of this and other conscquences of bilingualism.) Anyonc who speaks more than one language chooses between them according to circumstances. The first consideration, of course, is which language will be comprehensible to the person addressed : generally speaking, speakers choose a language which the other person can understand ( though interesting exceptions arise for example in religious ceremonies ). But what about members of a community where everybody speaks the same range of languages? In community multilingualism the different languages are always used in different circumstances, and the choice is always controlled by social rules. Typically one language is reserved exclusively for use at home and another is used in the wider community ( for example, when shopping ); for example, according to Denison ( 1971 ), everyone in the village of Sauris, in northern Italy, spoke German within the family, Saurian ( a dialect of Italian) informally within the village, and standard Italian to outsiders and in more formal village settings ( school, church, work ). Because of this linguistic division of labour, each individual could expect to switch codes ( i.e. languages) several times in the course of a day. ( The term ' code-switching' is preferred to 'language-switching' in order to accommodate other kinds of variety : dialects and registers. )

More precisely, this kind of code-switching is called SITUATIONAL code-switching because the switches between languages always coincide with changes from one external situation ( for example, talking to members of the family) to another ( for example, talking to the neighbours). The choice of language is controlled by rules, which members of the community learn from their experience, so these rules are part of their total linguistic knowledge. Now a very obvious question arises : why should a whole community bother to learn three different languages, when just one language would do? If everyone in Sauris knows standard Italian, why don't they stick to this all the time and let the local German and Italian dialects disappear? No doubt Saurians themselves have a clear answer : standard Italian would just feel wrong at home. The rules link the languages to different communities ( home, Sauris, Italy), so each language also symbolises that community. Speaking standard Italian at home would be like wearing a suit, and speaking German in the village would be like wearing beach-clothes in church. In short, each language has a social function which no other language could fulfil. These social functions are more or less arbitrary results of history, but they are no less real for that. The same seems to be typical of bilingual communities in general. The main reason for preserving the languages is because of the social distinctions that they symbolise. ( We saw another example of the same pattern in the discussion of the Indian village Kupwar, where three languages are used in order to maintain the caste system see 2.3.4. )

Given this heavy symbolic load that languages bear, it is entirely to be expected that bilingual speakers will use their choice of language in order to define the situation, rather than letting the situation define the choice of languages. In clear cases, we can tell what situation we are in just by looking around us; for example, if we are in a lecture-room full of people, or having breakfast with our family, classifying the situation is easy, and if language choice varies with the situation it is clearly the situation that decides the language, not the other way round. But in some cases the situation is less clear, either because it is ambiguous or because the speaker decides to ignore the observable external situation and focus instead on less observable characteristics of the people concerned. Such cases, where it is the choice of language that determines the situation, are called METAPHORICAL CODE-SWITCHING (Blom and Gumperz 1971).

An example which is quoted by Jan-Petter Blom and John Gumperz arose out of their research in a town in northern Norway, Hemnesberget, where there is a diglossic situation, with one of the two standard Norwegian languages (Bokmål) as the High variety and a local dialect, Ranamal, as the Low one.

> In the course of a morning spent at the community administration office, we noticed that clerks used both standard and dialect phrases, depending on whether they were talking about official affairs or not. Likewise, when residents step up to a clerk's desk, greeting and inquiries about family affairs tend to be exchanged in the dialect, while the business part of the transaction is carried on in the standard. (Blom and Gumperz 1971:425)

Examples like this show that speakers are able to manipulate the norms governing the use of varieties in just the same way as they can manipulate those governing the meanings of words by using them metaphorically. This is something everyone knows from everyday experience, but it is worth explicit reference in a book on sociolinguistic theory because it helps to avoid the trap of seeing speakers as sociolinguistic robots able to talk only within the constraints laid down by the norms of their society.

### 2.5.2 Code-mixing

In code-switching the point at which the languages change corresponds to a point where the situation changes, either on its own or precisely because the language changes. There ate other cases, however, where a fluent bilingual talking to another fluent bilingual changes language without any change at all in the situation. This kind of alternation is called CODE-MIXING (or CONVERSATIONAL CODE-SWITCHING, a rather unhelpful name). The purpose of code-mixing seems to be to symbolise a somewhat ambiguous situation for which neither language on its own would be quite right. To get the right effect the speakers balance the two languages against each other as a kind of linguistic cocktail—a few words of one language, then a few words of the other, then back to the first for a few more words and so on. The changes generally take place more or less randomly as far as subject-matter is concerned, but they seem to be limited by the sentence-structure, as we shall see.

The following is an extract from the speech of a Puerto-Rican speaker living in New York, quoted by William Labov (1971). The stretches in Spanish are translated in brackets.

> Por eso cada [therefore each...], you know it's nothing to be proud of, porque yo no estoy [because I'm not] proud of it, as a matter of fact I hate it, pero viene Vierney Sabado yo estoy, tu me ve hacia mi, sola [but come(?) Friday and Saturday I am, you see me, you look at me, alone] with a, aqui solita, a veces que Frankie me deja [here alone, sometimes Frankie leaves me], you know a stick or something...

Examples like these are interesting since they show that the syntactic categories used in classifying linguistic items may be independent of their social descriptions. For instance, in the above extract the Spanish verb *estoy* 'am' needs to be followed by an adjective, but in this case it is an English adjective (*proud*). This supports the view that at least some syntactic (and other) categories used in analysing language are universal rather than tied to particular languages.

An even clearer example of conversational code-switching within a single sentence is quoted by Gillian Sank off, from a speech by an entrepreneur in a village in New Guinea (Sank off 1972;45). Here the languages concerned are a language called Buang and Neo-Melanesian Pidgin, or Tok Pisin (to which we shall return in 2.5.3). In Buang, negation is marked by using *su* before the predicate (i.e. the verb and its objects), and *re* after it; but in one sentence(which is too long to quote here) the predicate was mostly in English, but was enclosed within the Buang *su...re* construction. Again we may conclude that items from languages even as different as Buang and Neo-Melanesian Pidgin are classified, by speakers as well as by linguists, in terms of a common set of syntactic categories (in this case something like the category'predicate').

An important question about code-mixing is what syntactic constraints apply to it, and attempts to answer this question have constituted one of the main points of contact over the last few years between sociolinguistics and non-social linguistics. There is no doubt that there are syntactic constraints; people who belong to code-mixing communities can judge whether particular constructed code-mixed examples are permitted or not, and these judgments are on the whole born out by studies of texts. For example, both Spanish and English have a word which is used just before an infinitive (*to* in English, *a* in Spanish), and language-change is possible after either—*to* can be followed by a Spanish infinitive, and *a* by an English one. But what is apparently not possible is for a Spanish verb which is normally followed by *a* to be followed by *to* instead (Blake 1987) This example is typical and could be multiplied from the growing literature.

The reason why code-mixing has interested non-social linguists is that these restrictions call for an explanation. Are they peculiarities of each language pair involved in mixing, or are there more general patterns that apply to all code-mixing—and if there are, what are they and why do they exist? The research is still in its inlancy and the results are quite inconclusive, but it is hard to avoid the conclusion that constraints vary from community to community (see, for example, Clyne 1987, Choi 1991) in spite of the enthusiastic attempts to provide universal explanations (see, for example, di Sciullo et al.. 1986, Belazi et al..1994).

2.5.3　Borrowing

Another way in which different languages may become mixed up with each other is through the process of BORROWING (Heath 1994). At this point, however, we are shifting our view from speech to language-systems. Whereas code-switching and code-mixing involved mixing languages in speech, borrowing involves mixing the systems themselves, because an item is 'borrowed' from one language to become part of the other language. Everyday examples abound—words for foods, plants, institutions, music and so on, which most people can recognise as borrowings(or LOAN-WORDS), and for which they can even name the source language. For most English speakers the following would probably be included:*karaoke* (Japanese), *paella* (Spanish), *schnapps*(German),*eisteddfod* (Welsh), *sputnik*(Russian) and *fait accompli* (French).

Examples like these are relevant to sociolinguistics because of their 'doubleallegiance':we treat them as ordinary English words, used in ordinary English sentences, but at the same time we know that they are modelled on words in other languages, which gives them a more or less foreign 'flavour'. We can make this rather vague description more precise by building on the discussion of code-switching and code-mixing, where we agreed that each language has a distinctive symbolic value for people who use it regularly because of its links to particular kinds of people or kinds of situation. The same can be true, to a more limited extent, of languages that we do not use regularly, and which we may hardly know at all—languages that we associate with holidays, particular kinds of culture and so on. One reason for using a word from such a language is to pretend, just for a moment, to be a native speaker with whatever social characteristics we associate with the stereotype. Another reason, of course, is that there is simply no other available word, in which case the link to the country may be irrelevant, or at least unintended. (In some countries all loan-words are frowned upon because of their foreign associations, so steps have to be taken to invent native words with the same meaning.)

It is important to distinguish examples like these from the enormous number of words which are borrowings only in the historical sense, and which ordinary people no longer associate with any other language. Such words account for more than half of the vocabulary of English, which has borrowed a great deal from Latin, Greek and French. Words like *money*, *car*, *church* and *letter* can all be traced to borrowings from these languages, but none of us are aware of this and use them just like any other English word, without any trace of foreign associations. However it is also important to recognise that borrowings can keep their foreign associations for a very long time, whether or not we recognise them as loans. It is very easy to show this in English, where so-called 'Latinate' vocabulary is quite distinct in spelling, in morphology and in register. For example, in 2.4.1 we contrasted *get* and *obtain* as informal and formal; what we did not mention is that *obtain* was once a borrowing from Latin, whereas *get* is not.(Actually, *get* was also borrowed, but it was borrowed from Old Norse.) At the time of the borrowing Latin was the language of scholarship, the law and so on—in fact, it was the High language in a diglossic situation, with English as the Low (and French in between as the language of the Court). This being so, *obtain* had the prestige of Latin when it was borrowed— and it still has, many centuries later, even though most people do not know its origin. The same is true of most Latinate vocabulary in modern English. In sum we certainly cannot call these words 'borrowings', in the strict sense of words that ordinary users know to be borrowed, but we can at least explain the 'High' status which sets them off from the historically non-Latinate vocabulary as a relic of the mediaeval diglossia in which Latin was High.

It may be helpful to diagram these distinctions. Figure 2.4 shows the knowledge-structure for someone who knows *fait accompli*, uses it as an ordinary English word(-pair)(for example, *It's a fait accompli*), but recognises it as a French loan (for example, by using a semi-French pronunciation). The arrow pointing from the French *fait accompli* to the English one shows that the person concerned knows the historical connection between the two.

Now contrast this with Figure 2.5, for the difference between *get* and *abtain*. Here we assume that the person concerned may or may not know that *obtain* has a link to Latin(hence the question mark), but the social category to which it is linked is the same as it would have been with that link. The link to a specific Latin word is no longer known.

One curious and importance consequence of borrowing is that (once again) the boundaries between languages come into question. We have assumed so far that a loan word is definitely part of the borrowing language, but this is in fact a matter of degree. It is common for items to be *assimilated* in some degree to the items already in the borrowing variety, with foreign sounds being replaced by

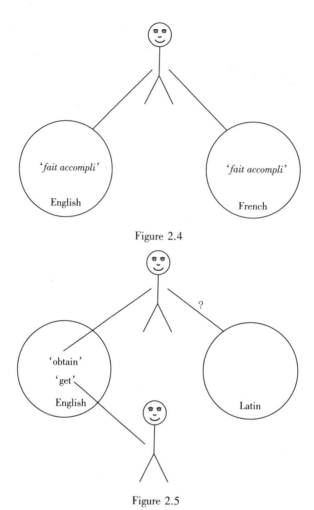

Figure 2.4

Figure 2.5

native sounds and so on. For instance, the word *restaurant* lost its uvular *r* when it was borrowed from French into English, so that it would occur with a uvular *r* in an English sentence only as an example of codeswitching. On the other hand, assimilation need not be total, and in *restaurant* many English speakers still have a nasal vowel at the end, which would not have been there had the word not been borrowed from French. Words like this make it very hard to draw the neat line round 'English' which is required by and description of 'the English phoneme system', since the English system gets mixed up with systems from other languages. On the other hand, this partial assimilation of borrowed words is an extremely common phenomenon both in English and in other languages. (Consider, in British English, the velar fricative at the end of *loch* and the voiceless lateral fricatives in *Llangollen*, both of which are very unusual in English words.)

The completely unassimilated loan-word is at one end of a scale which has at the other end items bearing no formal resemblance to the foreign words on which they are based. Such items are called LOAN TRANSLATIONS (or 'calques'). For example, the English *superman* is a loan translation of the German *Übermensch*, and the expression *I've told him I don't know how many times* is a direct translation of the French *Je le lui ai dit je ne sais pas combien defois* (Bloomfield 1933:457). What these examples illustrate is that borrowing may involve the levels of syntax and semantics without

312

involving pronunciation at all, which brings us back to the question of areal features, discussed in 2.3.4, where we saw that it is common for features of syntax to be borrowed from one language into neighbouring ones, via people who are bilingual in both. We now have three mechanisms which may help to explain how this happens. First, there is a tendency to eliminate alternatives in syntax (see 2.3.4). Then there is the existence of specific loan-translatons like those just quoted, which may then act as models from which regular 'native' constructons can be developed. And third, there is code-mixing (2.5.2), which encourages the languages concerned to become more similar in their syntax so that items from each may be more easily substituted for one another within the same sentence; if both languages put the object on the same side of the verb, for example, code-mixing is easier than if one puts it before and the other after.

The question is, whether there are any aspects of language which *cannot* be borrowed from one language into another. The answer appears to be that there are not (Bynon 1977:255). Even the inflectional morphology of a language may be borrowed, as witness a Tanzanian language called Mbugu which appears to have borrowed a Bantu inflectional system from one or more Bantu neighbours, although other aspects of its grammar are non-Bantu (Goodman 1971). Its non-Bantu features now include the personal pronouns and the numbers from one to six, which would normally be considered to be such 'basic' vocabulary as to be immune from borrowing (Bynon 1977:253). In such cases there are of course problems for the family tree model, since it ought to be possible to fit the language into just one tree, whereas some features suggest that it ought to be in the Bantu tree, and others, like those mentioned above, indicate that it belongs in some other tree (possibly the tree for 'Cushitic' langnages). How should one resolve the conflict? Can any general princlps be applied in balancing the evidence of inflectional morphology against that of basic vocabulary? (It should be noted, incidentally, that the inflectional morphology is matched by Bantu-type rules of concord, which are presumably part of syntax.) One wonders whether there is *any* kind of external reality against which an answer to questions such as these might be measured.

Assuming that there are no parts of language which cannot be borrowed, it is still possible to ask questions which may distinguish one part from another. For example, are there any restrictions on the circumstances under which different parts of language may be borrowed? We might suspect, for instance, that some kinds of item will be borrowed only under conditions of widespread bilingualism, while others may occur where only a few members of a society are bilingual in the relevant languages. Aspects of the first type would count as least, and the second type as most, subject to borrowing, so we could set up a scale of accessibility to borrowing, on which inflectional morphology, and 'basic vocabulary' such as small numbers, would presumably be at the 'least accessible' end, and vocabulary for artefacts (like *aeroplane* or *hamburger*) at the other. A word for the number 'one', for instance, will be borrowed only when almost everyone speaks both the 'borrowing' and the 'source' languages, whereas a word for 'aeroplane' could easily be borrowed when nobody is fully proficient in the two languages, but one or two people are familiar enough with the source language to know the word for 'aeroplane'. However, the truth may turn out to be much more complex than is suggested by this hypothesis, which is in any case by no means simple as far as the organisation of linguistic items into separate levels, such as syntax, vocabulary and phonology, is concerned, since different vocabulary items are put at opposite ends of the scale. Thus borrowing is a phenomenon which may throw light on the internal organisation of language, and certainly on the relations of language to society, once the right research has been done.

### 2.5.4    Pidgins

There is yet another way, apart from code-switching and borrowing, in which varieties may get mixed up with each other, namely by the process of creating a new variety out of two (or more) existing ones. This process of 'variety-synthesis' may take a number of different forms, including for instance the creation of artificial auxiliary languages like Esperanto and Basic English (for which see Crystal 1987: 352-5). However, by far the most important manifestation is the process of pidginisation, whereby PIDGINLANGUAGES, or PIDGINS, are created. These are varieties created for very practical and immediate purposes of communication between people who otherwise would have no common language whatsoever, and learned by one person from another within the communities concerned as the accepted way of communicating with members of the other community. (An excellent brief survey of the issues discussed here and in 2.5.5 is Aitchison 1994; for a scholarly survey in two volumes, see Holm 1988, 1989.)

Since the reason for wanting to communicate with members of the other communities is often trade, a pidgin may be what is called a TRADE LANGUAGE, but not all pidgins are restricted to being used as trade languages, nor are all trade languages pidgins. Instead, the ordinary language of some community in the area may be used by all the other communities as a trade language. It will be recalled from 1.2.2 that in the north-west Amazon area, Tukano is the language of one of the twenty-odd tribes but is also used as a trade language by all the others. Similarly, English and French are widely used as trade languages in many parts of Africa. In contrast with languages like this, a pidgin is a variety specially created for the purpose of communicating with some *other* group, and not used by *any* community for communication among themselves.

There are a large number of pidgin languages, spread through all the continents including Europe, where migrant workers in countries like Germany have developed pidgin varieties based on the local national language. Each pidgin is of course specially constructed to suit the needs of its users, which means that it has to have the terminology and constructions needed in whatever kinds of contact normally arise between the communities, but need not go beyond these demands to anticipate the odd occasion on which other kinds of situation arise. If the contacts concerned are restricted to the buying and selling of cattle, then only linguistic items to do with this are needed, so there will be no way of talking about the quality of vegetables, or the emotions, or any of the many other things about which one can talk in any normal language.

Another requirement of a pidgin is that it should be as simple to learn as possible, especially for those who benefit *least* from learning it, and the consequence of this is that the vocabulary is generally based on the vocabulary of the dominant group. For instance, a group of migrant workers from Turkey living in Germany will not benefit much from a pidgin whose vocabulary is based on Turkish, since few Germans would be willing to make the effort to learn it, consequently they take their vocabulary from German. Similarly, in a colonial situation where representatives of a foreign colonial power need to communicate with the local population in matters of trade or administration, and if it is in the interests of the local population to communicate, then the pidgin which develops will be based on the vocabulary of the colonial power force, the very large number of pidgins spread round the globe based on English, French, Portuguese and Dutch.

However, although the vocabulary of a pidgin may be based mainly on that of one of the communities concerned, the 'dominant' variety, the pidgin is still a compromise between this and the subordinate varieties, in that its syntax and phonology may be similar to the latter, making the pidgin easier for the other communities to learn than the dominant language in its ordinary form. As for morphology, this is left out altogether, which again makes for ease of learning. To the extent that differences of tense, number, case and so on are indicated at all, they are marked by the addition of separate words. Indeed, one of the most characteristic features of pidgins is the lack of morphology, and if some variety is found to contain morphology, especially inflectional morphology, most specialists in this field would be reluctant to treat it as a pidgin( which does not of course mean that every language without inflectional morphology must be a pidgin).

The best way to illustrate these characteristics of pidgins is by discussing a sentence from Tok Pisin, the English-based pidgin spoken in Papua New Guinea( Todd 1994:3178,4622).

Bai em i no lukim mi. 'He will not see me.'

The English origins of the vocabulary are not immediately obvious in the official spelling, which reflects the words' current pronunciation rather than their origins, so the following notes may be helpful.

| | |
|---|---|
| Bai | From *by and by*, an adverb used instead of the auxiliary verb *will* to indicate future time. |
| em | From *him*, meaning 'he'. |
| i | From *he*, but obligatorily added to a verb whose subject is third person( like the English suffix -*s*). |
| no | From *no* or *not*, used instead of the verb *doesn't*. |
| luk- | From *look*, but means 'see'. |
| -im | From *him*, but added obligatorily whenever the verb has an object, in addition to this object. |
| mi | From *me*. |

The example shows how different the syntax is from English, but how rigidly rule-governed it is, in particular by the rules which require the redundant *i* before the verb and -*im* added to it-a far cry from the idea of a makeshift attempt at speaking English. Another point which emerges clearly is the question of classification: is this a variety of English? Such cases highlight the general problem of deciding where the boundaries of languages lie.

Let us return to the more general question of the relation between pidgins and the societies which create them. As we have seen, pidgins are sometimes developed as trade languages, which we may take in a fairly broad sense as varieties used only for trade and administration. This is how Neo-Melanesian Pidgin or Tok Pisin ( i.e., 'pidgin talk'-see 2.5.1) developed during the present century for communication between the English-speaking administrators of Papua New Guinea and the local population, who themselves speak a large number of mutually incomprehensible languages ( one of which is Buang, which was involved in code-mixing with Tok Pisin in the example quoted in 2.5.2).

However, not all pidgins have arisen as trade languages, as Tok Pisin did. Another situation in which pidgins are needed is when people from different language backgrounds are thrown together and have to communicate with each other, and with a dominant group, in order to survive. This is the situation in which most Africans taken as slaves to the New World found themselves, since the slavers would break up tribal groups to minimise the risk of rebellion. Thus the only way in which the slaves could communicate either with each other or with their masters was through a pidgin which they generally learned from the slavers, based on the latter's language. Since most slaves had little opportunity to learn the ordinary language of their masters, this pidgin, remained the only means of communication for most slaves for the rest of their lives. This had two consequences. One was that pidgins became very closely associated with slaves, and acquired a poor reputation as a result (and the slaves also got the reputation of being stupid since they could not speak a 'proper' language!). The other consequence was that pidgins were used in an increasingly wide range of situations, and so gradually acquired the status of creole languages(see 2.5.5).

It may be helpful to bring together some characteristics of pidgins which distinguish them from other types of variety and variety-mixture.

(1) A pidgin based on language X is not just an example of 'bad X', as one might describe the unsuccessful attempt of an individual foreigner to learn X. A pidgin is itself a language, with a community of speakers who pass it on from one generation to the next, and consequently with its own history. Indeed, it has even been suggested that many pidgins have a common origin in the Portuguese-based pidgin which developed in the Far East and West Africa during the sixteenth century, under the influence of Portuguese sailors, and that this Portuguese-based pidgin might in turn have had its roots in the 'Lingua Franca' developed in the Mediterranean as early as the Crusades. This suggestion represents one of a number of attempts to explain the existence of a fairly large mumber of similar features which have been found in pidgins from many different parts of the world (Todd 1994).

(2) A pidgin is not simply the result of heavy borrowing from one variety into another, since there is no pre-existing variety into which items may be borrowed. An 'X-based pidgin' is not a variety of X which has borrowed a lot of syntactic constructions and phonological features from other varieties, since there may well be no model in these other varieties for any of the changes, such as the loss of inflections to which we referred above. Nor is it a variety of some other language which has borrowed a lot of vocabulary from X, since the syntax, phonology and morphology need not be the same as those of any of the other varieties involved. In any case, it is not clear which community would be the borrowers, since the pidgin is developed jointly by both sides of the communication gap, each trying to help bridge the gap. Of course, there is an interesting problem in relation to borrowing, since we *can* talk of borrowing into a preestablished pidgin, just as we can in connection with any other kind of variety, whereas we cannot invoke borrowing as a process in the establishment of the pidgin in the first place. The problem is that this implies too clear a distinction between the periods before and after the establishment of the pidgin.

(3) A pidgin, unlike ordinary languages, has no native speakers, which is a consequence of the fact that it is used only for communication between members of *different* communities. On the other hand, this distinction is not clear-cut since there are situations, such as those of slavery, where a community can come into existence with a pidgin as its only common variety, although all the members of the community learned it as a second language. The lack of a clearly defined group of

native speakers has the effect of putting most pidgins near the 'diffuse' end of the scale contrasting 'focussing' and 'diffusion' (1.3.1), in contrast with highly focussed standard languages such as French, and this is another reason why pidgins are of such considerable interest to sociolinguists.

## 2.5.5　Creoles

A pidgin which has acquired native speakers is called a CREOLE LANGUAGE, or CREOLE, and the process whereby a pidgin turns into a creole is called 'creolisation'. It is easy to see how pidgins acquire native speakers, namely by being spoken by couples who have children and rear them together. This happened on a large scale among the African slaves taken to the New World, and is happening on a somewhat smaller scale in urban communities in places like Papua New Guinea.

From a social point of view, creoles are of more interest than pidgins. Most creole languages are spoken by the descendants of African slaves and are of great interest, both to their speakers and to others, as one of the main sources of information on their origins, and as a symbol of their identity. A similar interest is shown by people who speak varieties whose origins are in a creole, but which have since been 'decreolised', i.e. moved towards the dominant variety at the expense of most distinctive characteristics of the creole. It is possible that the English of black people in the United States is such a variety, and because of this creoles and decreolised languages are of particular interest to many American linguists (see 1.3.2, 5.4.2 and, a good survey, Fasold 1990). Another reason for the interest in creoles is that there are minority groups, such as West Indian immigrants in Britain, whose members speak some form of creole. If their creole is one based on the majority language of the country into which they have immigrated—for example, an English-based creole in the case of immigrants to Britain—then serious educational problems may arise if neither teachers nor taught can be sure if this creole is a different language from the majority one or a dialect of it. If the former, it may be appropriate to use second-language teaching methods to teach the majority language, but this is by no means an appropriate method if it is a dialect. Consequently research is needed in order to establish the extent of the difference between the creole and the majority language. Similar problems arise in countries where the majority language is itself a creole, if the language expected by the education system is the standard version of the language on which the creole is based, as in many Caribbean countries. The problem is not helped, of course, by the fact that the difference between 'same' and 'different' is rather meaningless when applied to language varieties, as we argued in 2.2, so it may be that a more realistic model of language might help to solve some of these problems.

From the point of view of what they tell us about language, however, creoles are of less immediate interest, since they are just ordinary languages like any others, except in their origins. There are just two qualifications to be made to this claim, both of which are matters of language change: creoles, unlike ordinary language, arise through a process called (naturally enough) creolisation, and they are likely to gradually lose their identity by decreolisation (Aitchison 1994: 3184- 6). It is only in between these two stages that they are ordinary languages.

Taking DECREOLISATION first, this is what happens when a creole is spoken in a country where other people speak the creole's lexical source-language (for example, English). Since the latter has so much more prestige than the creole, creole speakers tend to shift towards it, producing a range of intermediate varieties. Sociolinguists call the creole the BASILECT and the prestige language the ACROLECT, with the intermediate varieties lumped together as MESOLECTS. This range of varieties spanning the gap between basilect and acroliect is called a ' POST-CREOLE CONTINUUM '.

This term reflects an interesting factual claim about the relationships among the mesolects. Like the acrolect and basilect, each mesolect is a vast collection of items which could (in principle at least) constitute the entire language of a group of speakers. The basilect is likely to be as different from the acrolect as Tok Pisin is from English, so it is easy to see that thousands of items must vary and that, linguistically speaking, most of them are quite independent of one another: the way in which future time is expressed has nothing to do with the form of the pronoun *I* or *me*, and so on through the grammar and vocabulary. Each mesolect represents one combination of basilect and acrolect items, so it is easy to imagine a rather chaotic scene in which different mesolects combine items in completely different ways. The claim that lies behind the term ' continuum ', however, is that the relations are actually much more orderly, and there is at least a strong tendency for mesolects to line up along a single scale from most basilectal to most acrolectal.

For example, here is a series of alternative ways of saying 'I came and carried it away' that are allowed by the post-creole continuum of Nigeria (Todd 1994:3181):

(1) A bin kam, kariam go.

(2) A kom, kariam go.

(3) A korn, kariam awe.

(4) A kem and kari it awe.

If these examples are typical, then there are at least four degrees of ' height ' from the lowest basilect (1) to the highest mesolect (4). Each of the linguistic items concerned can be given all index to show the range of heights that it covers:

| | | | | | |
|---|---|---|---|---|---|
| bin kam | (1) | kariam | (1-3) | go | (1-2) |
| kom | (2-3) | kari it | (4) | awe | (3-4) |
| kem | (4) | | | | |

Each mesolect represents a consistent selection on this scale, in which all the items are allowed to have the same relative height. If this is so, then no mesolect allows *bin kam* (1) and also *awe* (3-4), nor is there one which combines either *bin kam* or *kom* as well as *kari it*.

Post-creole continuums have been reported from several countries, perhaps the best documented being the one in Guyana (Bickerton 1975). They are clearly of great interest socially, if we can take them as evidence for a general tendency for such communities to create single-scale social ranking systems, although a more chaotic pattern is so easy to imagine. However, what makes post-creole continuums particularly interesting for a sociolinguist is the clear evidence they give for the independent social classification of single linguistic items. The scale of ' height ' in the last paragraph applies to individual items, with each item assigned a particular range on the scale. Notions like ' dialect ' are of no help at all in this kind of situation, and what is actually needed is a way of giving detailed social information about individual items. This conclusion should come as no surprise after the discussion above about the centrality of individual linguistic items.

We turn now to the other peculiarity of creoles, the process of CREOLISATION. As we noted at the beginning of this section, a creole is a pidgin that has native speakers. As it stands, this is simply a fact about how we use the words *pidgin* and *creole*, and it is a matter of fact whether having native speakers entails any other differences between creoles and their pidgin sources. Tok Pisin has just recently gone through this process of 'acquiring native speakers' (a nice reversal of the usual process whereby native speakers acquire a language!). Imagine a couple in New Guinea who speak Tok Pisin to each other for lack of any other common language, but who each have some other language as their native language. They have a baby, who starts to speak Tok Pisin. (As we saw in the north-west Amazon, it is possible for a child's first language to be a language which is not the mother's native language.) The essential difference between the baby and the parents is that the baby is learning Tok Pisin as its first language, whereas when they learned it they already knew another language. The question is whether this difference necessarily affects the outcome of the learning process. In other words, will the Tok Pisin which the child eventually speaks as an adult be different in essential ways from the Tok Pisin spoken by its parents?

The answer to this question is the subject of an intense debate not only among creole specialists but also among non-social linguists. On the one hand, are the linguists who, following Noam Chomsky (1986), believe that every child is genetically prepared ('programmed') to learn a human language like English or Japanese; in other words, that our ability to learn language is innate. When children are born into a family where the only language they hear is a mere pidgin, their genes push them to up-grade it to a full language by enriching it with relative clauses and other complexities not needed in a mere pidgin. The main proponent of this view is Derek Bickerton (1981, 1988), who calls the genetic predisposition to learn a full language the 'bioprogram'. On the other side of the debate are the majority of sociolinguists and creolists, who are less impressed by Chomsky's arguments for an innate language faculty. They question Bickerton's factual claims about differences between creoles and pidgins, and also his claims about similarities between creolisation and the processes of ordinary first-language acquisition (Aitcheson 1994:3185). In any case the kinds of feature which Bickerton assumes to be innate seem very different from those which Chomsky has argued for, so the two views conflict rather than support one another. (For a helpful review of this debate, see Romaine 1988.)

A somewhat different view is that pidgins can become richer to the extant of being similar to ordinary languages without the intervention of infant language-learners. On this view, the only difference between a creole and an enriched pidgin is that the former has native speakers and the latter does not. We have seen that some pidgins are already sufficiently developed to be used as standard languages, as in the case of Tok Pisin. One particularly interesting piece of research has been done on Tok Pisin in this connection, by Gillian Sank off and Penelope Brown (1976), who studied the recent history of relative clauses in Tok Pisin and showed how a consistent marker of relative clauses was gradually developed out of the word *ia* (based ultimately on the English here), which is now put both before and after many relative clauses.

> Na pik *ia* ol ikilim bipo *ia* bai ikamap olsem draipela ston.
> (Now pig here past kill people here future become huge stone)
> 'And this pig which they had killed before would turn into a huge stone.'
> (Sankoff and Brown 1976:632)

This construction may illustrate the influence of the syntax of the local languages on that of the pidgin, since Buang, for instance, has a word which is used both as a demonstrative and as a marker of relative clauses in the same way as *ia*. What is particularly interesting about this research is that speakers of a pidgin continue to develop it, using whatever resources are available, in a process that does not depend on creolisation. Indeed, Sankoff and Brown have evidence that it had started at least ten years before there were any significant numbers of native speakers of Tok Pisin. Again, there is no research evidence of changes that have happened during creolisation which cannot be matched by changes to a pidgin without native speakers.

The conclusion to which this discussion seems to lead is that there is no clear difference between pidgins and creoles, apart from the fact that creoles have native speakers and pidgins do not. No other differences between pidgins and creoles seem necessarily to follow from this one. Since we have also claimed that creoles are just ordinary languages (with some reservations about creole continua) and that pidgins are rather peculiar, it follows that the distinction between the 'normal' and the 'peculiar' (as represented by early stages of pidginisation) is unclear, and is in fact a continuum rather than a qualitative difference. Moreover, it is clear that there is no moment in time at which a particular pidgin suddenly comes into existence, but rather a process of variety-creation called pidginisation, by which a pidgin is gradually built up out of nothing. We might well ask whether this process is essentially different from what happens in everyday interaction between people who think they speak the same language, but who are in fact constantly accommodating their speech and language to each other's needs. (Compare the suggestion by Robert Le Page (1977b) that 'every speech act is ... the reflex of an "instant pidgin" related to the linguistic competence of more than one person'.) For instance a parallel may be drawn between the New Guinea natives learning an approximation to English vocabulary from each other and the local English speakers, on the one hand, and students of linguistics learning an approximation to the vocabulary of their teachers from each other and from their teachers, on the other. In both cases it is clear who has to do the bulk of the learning, though the dominant group may sometimes use the forms which they know the subordinate group use, in order to make things easier for them. In both cases what develops is a variety of language which is passed on from one person to another, developed out of countless encounters between teachers and students and between students themselves. The reader of this book may be amused at the idea of being a speaker of 'pidgin linguistics', but the suggestion is intended to be taken quite seriously.

(*Sociolinguistics*. Combridge university Press, 1980)

译文:

# 变体的混合

卢德平, 译

一、代码转换

为了有助于本节的讨论,我们将使用"变体"这一术语,去指传统上当作某种语言、方言或语域的那种东西。然而,仍有更多理由表明,不可把这一概念慎重其事地当作社会语言学的一个组成部分,因为所谓变体,甚至在同一言语片段之中,都会令人绝望地混合在一起。这一情况最明显和最流行的例子就是所谓**代码转换**,这里,单独一个说话人在不同时间使用不同的变体。这当然就是"语域"存在的自动结局,因为同一说话人在不同场合必然使用不同语域

（关于特殊社区之中代码转换现象的明确叙述，请参看 Denison, 1971; Parkin, 1977）。如果这就是代码转换之中所包括的全部内容，那么这一概念就不会对我们业已知道的东西有所补充。不过，意犹未尽。

首先，存在着所谓**隐喻性代码转换**（Blom & Gumperz, 1971），这里，通常只用于某种情景之中的某一变体被用于不同种类的状况之中，因为有关话题乃是通常出现在第一类情景之中的那一种。让-裴特·布隆姆和约翰·甘姆勃兹援引的一条例子，取自他们对挪威北部的赫姆尼斯伯格镇的研究，在那里，存在着一种双言情景；两种标准挪威语之一（包克马尔语）用做高等变体，而地方方言惹那马尔语则作为低等变体。

在社区行政办公室一上午的时间进程里，我们注意到，职员们使用标准语和方言两方面的词语，这取决于他们是否谈到公务。同样，当居民走近职员的办公桌时，打招呼和对家务事的询问倾向于用方言交流，而商谈的事务部分则用标准语进行（Blom & Gumperz, 1971:425）。

像这样的例子表明，说话者能够驾驭支配变体应用的法则，就像能通过隐喻性地使用它们，去驾驭制约词汇意义的法则一样。此乃个人由其日常经验出发知道的东西，不过，在一本论述社会语言学理论的著作之中，这一点值得明确提及，因为它有助于避免把说话人看作种种社会语言学自动机这一圈套，也就是说，他们只能在社会法则奠定的限制条件之内说话。

使得代码转换更为有趣的另一件事情在于，说话人可以在单独一条句子之内转换代码（即变体），乃至可以数次如此。约翰·甘姆勃兹（1976）建议对这种类型采用术语**会话代码转换**，以便把它和情景代码转换区别开来（事实上，他在上述强调的更广泛意义上称之为"双言现象"），这里，每一转换点都对应于有关情景的某种变化。在会话性代码转换的情景中，并不存在这样的变化，在也许会导致隐喻性代码转换的话题里面也没有任何变化。换句话说，人们得到印象认为，有关目的只不过是按某种特定的，可以说大体上同等的比例，去产生两种变体的若干例子。这一平衡可以通过用一种变体表达某一句子，用另一变体表达下一句子，如此等等来实现，但就两种变体用于单个句子的不同部位而论，也同样是可能的。看起来，会话性代码转换在某些社会之中得到容许，而在另一些社会不然；除非在和容许的某一社区的哥们儿说话，否则，这就不是操双语的个别人所干的事情。

会话性代码转换最明确的例子，自然属于有关变体迥然不同下的情形，正如当它们是不同语言时所表现的那样。下面一段文字摘自住在纽约的一名波多黎各人所说的话，曾被威廉·拉波夫引用过（1971）。西班牙语片段转译在括号中。

por eso cada[因而每一……]，你知道它不是可以引以为自豪的术语，porque yo no estoy[因为我不是]对此引为自豪，事实上，我恨它，pero viene Vierne y Sabado yo estoy, tu me ve hacia mi, sola[不过，我是星期五和星期六来(?)，你看我，端详我，自个儿]with a, aqui solita, a veces que Frankie me deja[这里怪孤单的，有时候弗兰基撇开我]，你晓得根棍子或什么的……

像这样的例子饶有趣味，因为它们表明，用来对语言学项目进行分类的有关句法范畴独立于其社会描述。例如，在上述摘录之中，西班牙语动词 estoy "是"后面跟着一个形容词，不过，在这种场合系一英语形容词（proud[自豪]）。这就支持了以下观点，即用于语言分析的某些句法（以及其他）范畴，至少是普遍的，而非和特殊语言联系在一起。

有关单个句子之内会话代码转换的一条更明确的例子，是由吉连·珊柯夫从新几内亚一所村庄的中间商口语里援引而来（Sankoff, 1972:45）。这里有关语言是一门叫做布昂语和新马来尼西亚洋泾浜语，或托克·皮辛语的语言（我们拟在第一章，第四节，第三小节重温这一点）。在布昂语里面，否定是通过在谓语前面使用 su（即动词与其宾语），以及在谓语之后使用 re 标志的，不过，在一条句子之内（这条句子引用起来太长了），谓语大多用英语表示，但包孕在布昂语 su……re 结构之中。再者,我们可以断定,甚至取自像布昂语和新马来尼西亚洋泾浜语这样迥然不同语言的项目,既是由语言学家,也是由若干使用者,根据一组共同的句法范畴(在这种情况下像范畴"谓语"之类的东西)来分类的。在容许会话代码转换的某一社区之中,一项值得研究的课题就在于,关于转换可以发生在什么地方,是否有任何限制——例如,它会发生在名词短语的中间吗? 不管这样的限制最终是否归因于社会规范或人类大脑的局限性,有关结果肯定都是有意思的。

二、借用

不同变体彼此可能会变得混而不分的另一条方式,乃是通过借用这一途径(一篇优秀的简短概要是 Burling,1970:第 12 章,更长一点的系 Bynon,1977:第 6 章)。当某一项目被接受过来之际,把锁、树干和桶从某一变体借用到另一变体,其意义为何是显而易见的,例如,当法语一碟菜的名称,像勃艮第牛肉(boeuf bourguignon)被借用作某种英语说法,同时完全带着法语发音时(带小舌音 r,等等),情况就是这样。明白该项目是外语成分的英语使用者,仅仅是通过改变其自"法语"到"英语"(或者更可能是自"由法国人所用"至"为我所用")的社会描述,来对这一项目重新进行分类的。与代码转换相对照,当如此一种项目被用于英语句子,如让我们吃点勃艮第牛肉时,这事实上并不包括任何有关变体的变化,因为就说话人而论,勃艮第牛肉现在成了英语的一部分。另一方面,如果说话人曾经说过让我们来点勃艮第牛肉(Let's have du boeuf bourguignon),那么他可能一直就在进行代码转换;因为单词 du"一点"是法语,而不是英语,并且常常只和一个法语名词一道出现,所以我们可以相当可靠地推知,让我们来点面包(Let's have du bread)永远不会出现,除非面包(bread)已经从英语借用到法语里来,并因而可以算作一个法语词。像 du 之类的词,自然远不如勃艮第牛肉之类的词有可能作为单个项目被借用,这只是因为不可能有必要将它们搁在借用来的变体之中。

对有些项目来讲,在某种程度上同化到业已出现于借用变体之中的项目上去,是习以为常的,与此同时,异邦语音亦为土著语音所代替,如此等等。例如,餐馆(restaurant)一词从法语借到英语时失去其小舌音 r,以致仅仅是作为代码转换的一条例子,会带着小舌音 r 出现于英语句子之中。另一方面,同化不必一刀切,在餐馆一词里,许多英语使用者就仍然在词尾带有一个鼻化元音,而要是该词不是借自法语,这东西就不会在那里出现。像这样的词使得围绕"英语"划一条简洁的线索,并对"英语音位系统"进行描述,变得颇为困难,因为英语系统和其他语言的系统由此混淆起来。另一方面,这在英语和其他一些语言里,又是一种极其常见的现象(请考虑在英国英语之中出现于 loch[湖]词尾的软腭擦音,以及出现于 Llangollen[地名]①一词之中的清边擦音,其中每一个都可以出现于一条转换性英语常用句子之中)。

完全未被同化的借词出现于尺规一端,而在另一端,有些项目则与它们所依据的外语词汇没有任何形式上的相似之处。这样的项目被称做**移译词**(或"仿借词")。英语 superman(超人)就是德语 Übermensh 的移译词,而 I've told him I don't know how many times(不晓得告诉过他多少遍我不知道)则是法语 Je le lui ai dit je ne sais pas combien de fois 的直译形式(Bloomfield,l933:457)。这些例子所阐明的问题在于,借用可以包括句法和语义方面,而根本不包括发音;这一点又把我们带回到第一章,第二节,第四小节讨论的有关地域特征的问题上去了,在那里,我们看到,句法特征由一门语言借用到若干邻近语言,同时经由谙于两类语言的人们;这一点尤其常见。我们现在有三种机制可供解释这一点是如何发生的。首先,有一种趋势是,排除句法中的可选性成分(参见第一章,第二节,第四小节)。其次,存在着像方才

---

① 威尔士东北部一小镇,以举办一年一度的国际威尔士音乐比赛节而著名。——译注

引用过的特殊移译现象,它们可以由此充当常规"土著"结构赖以发展而成的模式。第三,存在着会话代码转换(第一章,第四节,第一小节),它促使有关语言在句法上变得更相似,以致在同一条句子之内,每一语言的项目彼此可以更容易被替代。如果两种语言比如都把宾语放在动词的同一边,那么,代码转换较之其中一种把它放在前面,而另一种把它放在后面,要容易一些。

问题在于,是否有什么语言成分不能从一门语言借用到另一门语言。答案好像不然(Bynon,1977:255)。甚至一门语言的屈折形态都可以借用,正如叫做姆布固语的一门坦桑尼亚语所明证,它似乎是从一种或一种以上的班图语邻里借用了某种屈折系统,尽管其语法的别的方面不属于班图语。它的非班图语特征时下包括人称代词和从1到6的数词,它们通常被看作是如此"基本"的词汇,以致免于借用(Bynon,1977:253)。在此类情况下,自然还存在着有关谱系树模式方面的问题,因为理应有可能将语言放进一棵树里面,不过,有些特征暗示,它应当置于班图语树之中,而另一些,正如上文所提到的那些情况,表明它属于其他某棵树(可能是"库什特"诸语树)。应当怎样解决这一冲突呢?有什么普遍原则,能用来将屈折形态学的例证和基本词汇的证据平衡起来么?(应该连带注意到,屈折形态学是由班图类型的一致规则匹配的,它大概是句法的一部分)。人们搞不清楚,是否存在着任何种类的外部现实性,而有关此类问题的回答可以针对这一点加以衡量。

假定说任何区域均可借用,那么我们将对某一区域和另一区域借以分别开来的语言提些问题。例如,关于语言的不同侧面赖以借用的环境,有什么限制吗?比方说,我们不妨猜测,某些种类的项目只在广泛流行的双语制条件之下借用,而另一些则可以出现于只有少数几个社会成员谙于两类语言的地方。第一种类型的若干方面常常算做最少屈于借用,第二种类型则算做最多屈于借用,因此,我们可以建立一根借用可及性尺规,在它上面,屈折形态以及少量数词之类的"基本词汇"大概处于"最少可及"端,而表示人工制品的词汇(像飞机或汉堡牛排)则位于另一端。例如,表示数量"__"。的词,只有当几乎每个人既说"借用"语言,也说"源"语言时,才会借用,然而,表示"飞机"的词在无人精于两门语言的时候,亦可轻而易举借用过来,不过,要有一两个人对源语言熟悉到足以知道表示"飞机"的那一词。不管怎么说,真相也许最终比这一假设所提示的要复杂得多;就语言学项目被组织成不同平面,诸如句法、词汇和音系而论,后者在任何情况下亦绝非易事,因为不同的词汇项目被搁在尺规的对立两端。这样,借用就成了一种可以阐明语言内部组织的现象,并且一旦正确的研究付诸实施,确实就照亮了语言和社会的关系。

三、洋泾浜语

除了代码转换和借用之外,还有一种方法可使变体相互混合起来,即通过从两个(或更多)既存变体之中创造一种新变体的过程。这一"变体—综合"过程也许具有一些不同形式,例如包括有关世界语和基本英语之类人工辅助语言的创制(关于这一点,请看 Bolinger,1975:580)。然而,最重要的表现形式乃是洋泾浜化过程,洋泾浜语言或洋泾浜语由此创造而来。这些是为非常实用和直接的人际交流目的创造的变体,否则这些人无论怎么说都不会有任何共同语可言,并且,是由某人在有关社区之中,作为和另一社区的成员交流的公认方式,从另一人那里学来的(有关此处和第一章,第四节,第四小节所讨论问题的精彩概述是 DeCamp,1977)。

鉴于要求和其他社区的成员进行交流的原因常常系贸易,所以洋泾浜语可以是所谓**贸易语言**,但不是所有洋泾浜语仅限于用做贸易语言,也并非所有贸易语言都是洋泾浜语。换句话说,在有关地域,某一社区的语言可以由其他所有社区用作一种贸易语言。记忆犹新的是,在亚马逊西北部地区，土卡诺语是二十几个部落里面某一部落使用的语言，但亦被所有其他部落用做一种贸易语言。与这样的语言相对照，洋泾浜语就是为了和其他某个集团进行交际而特意创造的变体，并不由任何社区用于自己内部的交流。

术语"洋泾浜"被许多人（尽管不是全部）认为来自英语 business（商业）一词，正如在中国发展起来的洋泾浜英语所显示的（也即后者被称做"商业英语"，发成"洋泾浜英语"；参看DeCamp，1971a）。有大量洋泾浜语穿过包括欧洲在内的所有大陆扩展开去，那里，像德国这种国家的移民工人已经根据地方民族语发展出一些洋泾浜变体。每种洋泾浜语自然都是特意构造起来，以便适应其使用者的要求，这意味着，它不得不拥有社区之间通常产生的无论何种接触都需要的术语和结构，不过，没有必要越出这些要求，去预示其他类型的状况所由产生的离奇环境。如果有关接触限于耕牛的买卖，那么，只有与此相关的语言学项目才是必要的，因此，无法谈及蔬菜质量、感情，或其他许多东西，而对此，任何正常语言都能用来谈论。

洋泾浜语的另一前提是，应该学起来尽可能简单，对学会它获益很少的人来说尤其如此；由此形成的结果在于，有关词汇一般依据主导集团的词汇。比方说，居住在德国的一组土耳其移民工人，不会从某种以土耳其语为词汇基础的洋泾浜语里面获益太多，因为只有极少数德国人愿意花气力学会它，由此，他们从德国人那里接受其词汇。同理，在殖民局面之中，外国殖民力量的代理人需要在贸易或行政事务方面与当地人进行交流，并且这种交流有利于当地人的利益，那么，由此形成的洋泾浜语将根据殖民力量的词汇——因此有很大数量的洋泾浜语蔓延全球，它们是以法语、葡萄牙语和荷兰语为基础的。

不管怎么说，尽管洋泾浜语词汇也许主要依据有关社区之一的情形，即"主导"变体，但是洋泾浜语仍然系这一变体和附属变体之间的某种折中现象，这就是说，其句法和音系可能更像后者，同时对其他有关社区而言，又使得洋泾浜语的掌握，较之以正常形式出现的主导语言，要容易一些。就形态学而论，这一点被全盘忽略了，这又有利于学习之便。就时、数、格等方面的差异确实被指明这一程度而言，它们是通过添加不同小品词标志的。诚如其然，洋泾浜语最鲜明的特征之一就是缺乏形态，并且要是某一变体被发现包括形态，尤其包括屈折形态的话，那么这一领域的大多数专家就不会心甘情愿将它看成一种洋泾浜语（这自然不等于说，每一不带屈折形态的语言都必须是一种洋泾浜语）。

屈折形态在洋泾浜语里的欠缺本身就是有意思的，这特别是由于，如同在主导语言缺乏屈折形态的地方一样（例如英语），在有关语言都拥有丰富屈折形态的地方，这正是接触局面的一种特征。这也许触及到人类语言的某种普遍特征：屈折形态在某种意义上乃是表达语义和句法分工的一种非自然机制。因而，甚至当某种语言拥有根据屈折进行分工这一便捷方法时（例如，英语以规则复数-s作词尾），它也从未在基于那门语言的洋泾浜语之中用作有关分工的标志，而总是为不同词所替代。关于屈折形态，如果确有什么东西根本上就困难，或在交流中是无效的话，那么它在有些语言之中流行如此之广就奇怪了，并且有许多语言在其屈折形式方面承受住如此之多的复杂性和不规则性，而这并不有益于任何人，就更为奇怪了。在绪论，第二节，第一小节，我曾指出，隐藏在维持和发展屈折不规则特性背后的策动力，乃是驱使个人与之一致的压力。情况也可能是，存在着某种发自社会的类似压力，它大体上解释了屈折形态无论是在规则还是在不规则两方面的发展和持续，并能防止被排除出去，正如单独一条标准就可有效和便当时所表现的那样。

换句话说，如果某一变体是你的本土语言，那么你会用它将自己和有关社区同一起来，后者乃是通过与有关法则，降至发音的最小细节，同时包括与屈折形态方面的东西相协调来使用它的。对形态学进行简化或调整正是某人自己系门外汉的标志。但如果有关变体是一种洋泾浜语,那么就没有任何人把它作为某种集体认同方式加以应用,因而,也就没有压力去维持发音的无效方面。这一建议当然完全是推测性的,不过,屈折形态在洋泾浜语里的欠缺需要一点解释,这至少是一种值得加以探讨的可能性。从上面的讨论不难看出,为什么语言学家对洋泾浜语给予了那么多的注意力,正如关于语言倘不用作社会认同符号时发发生的现象所证实的。

让我们重温一下,关于洋泾浜语与创造它们的社会之间的关系这一更为普遍的问题。正如我们已看到的,洋泾浜语有时是作为贸易语言发展而成的,我们可以在某种非常宽泛的意义上,把它们看作是只用于贸易和行政方面的一些变体。在这些条件下发展起来的洋泾浜语之一例乃是新马来尼西亚语,或托克·皮辛语,即"洋泾浜言谈"(参见第一章,第四节,第一小节)。这是用于新几内亚以及附近岛屿的一种依据于英语的洋泾浜语,它是本世纪期间为操英语的行政官员和当地人之间进行交际而发展起来的,后者本身也讲大量相互无法理解的语言(其中之一就是布昂语)。下列取自托克·皮辛语的句子(引自 Bolinger,1975:356)阐明了它和英语之间的关系。括号中的词语展示了前面托克·皮辛语的英语来源。

Bimeby[by and by] leg belong you he-all-right gain[again].

"你的腿会康复"

sick he-down-im[him]me.

"我病了"

me like-im saucepan belong cook-im bread.

"我要只平锅做面包"

就像其他一些洋泾浜语那样,托克·皮辛语已经如此有效地发展起来,并在那么多的局面之中,作为交际媒介逐渐为人们所接受,以致在新几内亚已经被认为是一种民族语(Hall,1972)(正如我们在第一章,第四节,第四小节将会看到的,它近来又变成了一种克里奥尔语)。

然而,并不是所有洋泾浜语都像托克·皮辛语那样,作为贸易语言出现。洋泾浜需要的另一种状况在于:正值来自不同语言背景的人们被撮合到一起,并且不得不在相互之间,以及和主导集团,发生交流,以便幸存。这就是被作为奴隶贩运到新大陆的绝大多数非洲人发现自己所面临的局面,因为奴隶贩子会解散部落集团,以期将叛乱危险减小到最低限度。因此,奴隶无论相互之间,抑或与其主人所能进行的交流,都是从奴隶贩子那儿学来,并依据后者语言中的某种洋泾浜语加以习得的。因为大多数奴隶都绝少有机会学习其主人的日常语言,因而,这种洋泾浜语对大多数奴隶而言,就成为其余生的唯一交际手段。这一点有两条结局。一种是洋泾浜语变得与奴隶联系极紧,结果就得了一种坏名声(而奴隶们也给弄成一种蠢名声,因为他们不能说一种"适时"语言)。另一条结果是,洋泾浜语被用于范围日渐广泛的局面之中,因而慢慢获得了克里奥尔语言的地位(参见第一章,第四节,第四小节)。

把洋泾浜语的若干特征归纳起来也许是有益的,这些特征将它们与其他类型的变体和变体-混合区分开来。

(1)依据于变体 X 的洋泾浜语并不就是"劣质 X"之一例,正如人们不妨描述一下个别外国人学习 X 的不成功尝试所表现的那样。洋泾浜语本身就是一种变体,与此相应,某一社区的使用者将它一代代传递下去,因而就拥有其自己的历史。确实,甚至已有人指出,许多洋泾浜语都共同起源于以葡萄牙为基础的洋泾浜语,它是 16 世纪期间,在葡萄牙航海者的影响下,于远东和西非发展起来的,而且,这种以葡萄牙语为基础的洋泾浜语,也许肇始于早在十字军东征就已在地中海地区发展起来的那种"通用语"。这一建议代表了下述试图解释大量类似特征之存在的尝试,而这些特征是在世界许多不同地区的洋泾浜语之中发现的(有关这些问题的精彩概述,请参看 DeCamp,1971a;1977)。

(2)洋泾浜语并不仅仅是从一种变体严重借用到另一变体的结果,因为没有任何预先存在的变体可供这些项目借用进来。"以 X 为基础的洋泾浜语"不属于从其他变体之中借用了大量句法结构和音系特征的 X 的某一变体,因为就词形的任何变化,尤其是就我们上文所提到的屈折形式的失落而论,在这些变体之中不会有任何模式可言。它也不是已经从 X 借用了大量词汇的某种别的语言的变体,因为句法、音系和形态没有必要和其他任何有关变体的情况一样。无论怎么说,哪一社区会是借用者,并不明确,因为洋泾浜语是由交际豁口的两个侧面衔接而成,其中每一面都竭力有助于沟通这一豁口。自然,有一条与借用联系在一起的有趣问题,因为我们可以谈及借用到某一既定洋泾浜语这一点,就像我们和其他任何种类的变体联系起来那样;但首先,我们不能把借用作为确定洋泾浜语的一种手段而乞灵于它。问题就是,这一点意味着,在洋泾浜语确立之前和确立之后的有关阶段之间,某种差异太明显了。问题大概在于过分强调"变体"概念这一结果,对此,我们已经发现有理由予以怀疑。

(3)洋泾浜语,和日常语言不一样,没有土著使用者,它是只用于"不同"社区成员之间的交际这一事实所导致的结果,在这里,没有任何常用变体可以充当一条纽带。另一方面,这一区别也并非泾渭分明,因为不存在像奴隶制之类的局面,这里,某一社区可以将洋泾浜语作为其唯一的共同变体与之共存下去,尽管该社区的所有成员都把它作为一种第二语言加以学习。确凿分明,土著使用者集团的缺乏,具有把大多数洋泾浜语置于"集约"和"扩散"这一对比分明之尺规里"扩散"一端的效用(绪论,第二节,第一小节),这种情况和法语之类高度集约的标准语言形成对比,而这就是何以洋泾浜语之于社会语言学家有着如此浓厚兴趣的另一原因。然而,正如我们已经注意到的,有几种洋泾浜语时下用作标准语,这大概意味着,它们已经沿着这一尺规迈向"集约"'一端——值得对语言和社会之间关系感兴趣的人加以研究的另一现象。

四、克里奥尔语

已经拥有土著使用者的洋泾浜语被称做**克里奥尔语言**或**克里奥尔语**,而洋泾浜语借以变为克里奥尔语的过程则称做"克里奥尔化"。不难看出,洋泾浜语是怎样获得土著使用者的,也即通过由一起养育孩子的一对对夫妇讲用而实现。这一点大规模发生在带到新大陆的非洲奴隶之中,并且正以稍小规模发生于像新几内亚之类地方的城镇社区之中。

从社会角度看,克里奥尔语出于三种原因较之洋泾浜语更为有趣。首先,克里奥尔语的使用者比洋泾浜语更多,有一种估计是,克里奥尔语使用者介于 1000 万到 1700 万之间,与此相比较,正常使用洋泾浜语的人在 600 万到 1200 万之间(DeCamp,1977)。其次,绝大多数克里奥尔语是由非洲奴隶的后裔使用的,并且,对其使用者和其他人而言,作为关于其发祥地的信息来源之一,以及作为其认同的一种象征,趣味十足。类似的兴趣也由使用若干变体的人们表现出来;这些变体源自克里奥尔语,但此后被"非克里奥尔化"了,也即以牺牲克里奥尔语的绝大多数鲜明特征为代价,而迈向有关主导变体。看起来有可能,美国的黑人英语也是这样一种变体,并且由于这一点,一些克里奥尔语之于许多美国语言学家,有着特殊兴趣(参见绪论,第三节,第二小节;第四章,第三节,第二小节,以及沃尔夫兰的精彩概述)。

第三,存在着像英国的西印度移民之类的少数派集团,其成员讲某种形式的克里奥尔语。如果其克里奥尔语系依据于他们所移居的有关国家的主要语言——例如,在迁至英国的移民实例下,以英语为基础的克里奥尔语——那么,倘既没有教师,也没有教学法可供保证这一克里奥尔语究竟是有别于主要语言者,抑或属于它的一种方言,就会引起严重的教育问题。如果是前一种情况,那么采用外语教学法来教授主要语言也许是妥当的,但如果系一种方言,这绝不是妥当的方法。因此,研究是必要的,目的是确定在克里奥尔语和主要语言之间差异所及的范围。类似的问题也在主要语言本身就是一种克里奥尔语的国家出现,倘若教育系统期望的语言系克里奥尔语所依据语言的标准样式的话,那么就如此;这种现象正如许多加勒比国家所表现的那样。这一问题自然得不到下列事实帮助:"同一"和"分歧"之间的区别,在用于语言变体时,是相当无意义的,正如我们在第一章,第一节所争辩的那样;因此,情况也许是,某种更实际的语言模式可能有助于解决若干此类问题(有关更深入的讨论,例如,请参看Le·Page,1968b)。

　　然而,从它们向我们透示的有关语言的情况看来,克里奥尔语绝少有直接兴趣,因为它们除了在来源上以外,乃是像任何其他语言一样的日常语言(Sankoff,1977)。对这一主张大概可以施加一条限制,也就是,在克里奥尔语和作为主导语言所代表的有关变体之间,也许存在着某种颇为特殊的联系,而其先辈洋泾浜语乃是建立在主导语言的基础之上,倘若这两种现象在同一国家并存,正如它们常常表现的那种情况的话。面临这一情况的国家其中之一是圭亚那,其克里奥尔语已由德里克·比克尔顿特意进行了研究(Derek Bickerton,1971;1973;1935)。根据美国克里奥尔语研究的奠基者之一,威廉·斯提瓦特(William Stewart)使用的术语,比克尔顿称纯粹的克里奥尔语为"低言"(BASILECT)(就像在massive[众多]之中,发音带短a),称标准英语的地方形式为"高言"(ACROLECT)(希腊语akro-"最高级",正如在Acropolis卫城]和acrobat[杂技演员]之中的情况)。他拟设了一种连续体,来把低言和高言,经由一连串中言,联系起来,这种中言乃是想通过更接近于高言,从而去"改进"其语言的使用者所能通行的唯一途径;同时,他还提供了非常有说服力的研究证据,从而表明,在他所研究的大量样例中,至少绝大多数使用者都可以置于这一连续体(有关进一步讨论,请参看第四章,第四节,第二小节)。他还指出,高言和低言之间在句法和语义方面,尤其是在对时间和时态关系的处理上存在着大量差异。例如,在低言里,动词的相同形式是用以指说话时发生的事情,正如与先前,甚至过去提到的其他一些事情发生于同一时间的某些情况一样;然而在高言,即标准英语里面,动词的不同形式常常用于这两种情况之中(试比较"我发现了我的错误"与"找了一小时之后我才发现到我的错误")(Bickerton,1975:46)。

　　与人们预料的没有克里奥尔语的地方相比较,此种"克里奥尔语连续体"存在着两个特点。第一,在并存于有关社区的变体中间,与人们在由方言构成的某一社区之中预料的情况相比,存在着更为深刻的差异;并且,由于第一章,第二节,第四小节所讨论的原因尤其在句法方面,存在着比人们常常希望的更多变异。被发现的差异,事实上更像双言条件下所能预料的情况,尽管克里奥尔语连续体自然不是一种双言实例;这是因为高言和低言二者都由不同集团在内部使用。高言和低言之间存在着这些巨大差异的原因在于,它们事实上不是首先通过正常的扩散过程分开的,这些促成了方言差异,而毋宁是借助洋泾浜化的过程实现的,这自动导致了洋泾浜语和主导语言之间的剧烈分歧。

　　克里奥尔语连续体的另一特点是,只有一根变体链钭低言和高言联系起来,同时只允许说话人有一条语言学维度,借此,他们参照社会的其余部分立足于其上。比克尔顿所描绘的画面事实上有点更为复杂,因为个别使用者可以使用这一连续体上一定的变体,而不是限于单个情形(Bickerton,,1975:203);但仍然只有一条语言学维度,可供使用者在特定场合立足于其上。这一情况和大量独立维度构成了鲜明对比,此乃某一变体的若干项目通常提供给使用者以定位自己的东西。关于这一点的理由,准有可能又潜伏在克里奥尔语发展史之中,但要确切理解这一理由为何,可谓困难(关于某条提议,请参看Bickerton,1975:17、178)。

　　除了关于其连续体的这一颇为重要的限制外,克里奥尔语乃是一些日常语言,而对我们一般去理解语言并不增加什么特殊的名堂。这一主张在应用于克里奥尔语时,确实是正确无误和毋庸争论的,像这样的克里奥尔语已经存在数代之久。大多数克里奥尔语已经归入这一范畴,因为它们肇端于奴隶贸易,并且在那些日子里已经开始作为克里奥尔语存在着。其中有许多甚至可以通过书面文献回溯几个世纪之远(关于这一情况的例子,涉及到尼加拉瓜依据于英语的克里奥尔语,请看 Holm,1978)。不过,洋泾浜语和克里奥尔语之间的差异,远不及从它们的定义之中可以推断的清楚,并且,克里奥尔语的早期阶段也许和洋泾浜语一样,之于语言学理论同样引起人的兴趣。

记忆犹新的是,克里奥尔语"早期阶段"发生在获取到土著使用者的时候,因此就不再是一种洋泾浜语了;当两类虚拟的变化可以预料时亦然。首先,存在着归因于作为第一语言而不是作为第二语言加以学习的有关变体的变化。就儿童在遗传上只预备学习"日常"语言这一范围而言,并且就洋泾浜语不具备此类语言的有关属性而论,当儿童努力学习洋泾浜语时,我们也许有希望看到一些变化,因为他们需要在不同于日常语言的地方,对其作出调整,以便使之可学。(儿童在遗传上只预备学日常语言这一观点,特别和诺姆·乔姆斯基有关;例如,参见 Chomsky,1965:47;1968)。不管怎么说,目前并无证据表明,这样的变化实际发生了。

另一种虚构的变化归因于,语言现在被更广泛地应用于家庭这一事实,因为它谈论的是这样一种贸易语言所无需涉及的东西。但显而易见,这类变化只不过是表明洋泾浜语的某种连续,因而对克里奥尔化过程而言;就不是独一无二的了。父母必须在子女生下来之前,就发展出某种用洋泾浜语相互谈论家务事的方法,而且我们已经看到,某些洋泾浜语已经充分发展起来,以致用作标准语,正如托克·皮辛语的情况。在这方面,关于托克·皮辛语的一项特别有趣的研究已由吉连·珊柯夫和裴尼罗普·布朗作出(Penelope Brown)(1967),他们研究了托克·皮辛语关系从句近几年的历史;并指出,关系从句的一种恒贯标志就是从单词 ia(最终依据英语 here[这里])渐渐发展而成;它既位于许多关系从句之前,也位于其后。

Na pik ia ol ikilim bipo ia bai ikamap olsem draipela ston.

(Now pig here past kill people here future become huge ston)

"还有,他们以前曾经杀死的这头猪会变成一块大石头。"(Sankoff & Brown,1976:632)

这一结构也许会阐明地方语言句法对洋泾浜语句法的影响,因为布昂语例如就拥有一个既用作指示词,也用作关系从句标志的单词,所采用形式和 ia 没有二致。关于这一研究特别有趣的一点在于,洋泾浜语使用者在继续发展之,并在不取决于克里奥尔化的某一过程之中,对任何可行的素材都加以使用。诚如其然,珊柯夫和布朗有证据表明,在存在数量可观的托克·皮辛语土著使用者之前,至少已有十年之久。再者,没有任何研究证据表明,发生于克里奥尔化过程之中的若干变化不能由若干无土著使用者时指向洋泾浜语的变化所匹配。

这一讨论所导致的结果是,克里奥尔语有土著使用者,而洋泾浜语则没有,在洋泾浜语和克里奥尔语之间并不存在任何明显的分歧。洋泾浜语和克里奥尔语之间也没有任何其他差异必然来自这一分歧。鉴于我们已经断言克里奥尔语就是日常语言(关于克里奥尔语连续体有些保留),并且还宣布,洋泾浜语是相当特殊的,由此,"通常"和"特殊"之间的差异(正如洋泾浜化的若干早期过程所代表的)就不清楚,而且事实上更是一种连续体而非定性差异。进而言之,没有任何特殊的洋泾浜语突然诞生,而只是称做洋泾浜化的一种变体创造过程,借此,洋泾浜语渐渐从无到有建构而成。我们也许会问,这一过程是否根本不同于日常人际影响之中发生的东西,而这些人认为他们讲同一种语言;但事实上,人们是根据彼此的需要时常调节其言语和语言的(试比较 Robert·Le·Page 的建议(1977b):"每一言语行为乃是……与不止一个人的语言能力相联系的'瞬时洋泾浜语'的反映)。例如。一方面,在彼此互学英语词汇之近似现象的新几内亚土著人和当地英语使用者之间，可以勾划出一根平行线；另一方面，在彼此互学与从教师那儿学习有关其导师词汇之近似值这两类语言学学子之间，也可以划一根平行线。在这两种情况下，何人得进行大量学习，显而易见，尽管主导集团有时候可以使用他们知道属于附属集团采用的有关形式，从而让事情对他们来讲容易一些。在这两种情况下，由此形成的乃是从一个人过渡到另一个人的某种语言变体，它是从老师和学生之间，以及学生本人之间的无数次晤面发展而来的。本书的读者也许对他自己作为一个"洋泾浜语言学"使用者这一看法有兴趣，但这一建议要非常慎重地加以对待。

（节选自《社会语言学》，华夏出版社，1989）

# 第七章 当代语言学流派及理论概述

"理论"一词广泛应用于各种学科中,其含义非常丰富,在不同场合往往所指各异。严格来说,"理论"通常包含某一特定学科的基本原理、概念和目标。某一种理论限定与之相关的现象,并对该理论在系统描述与分析中使用的概念作出定义。语言学理论同样如此:一方面,它关注各种语言现象;另一方面,从各种无穷无尽的语料中抽象出语言学术语,并用抽象出来的语法规则来描述语言现象。不同的语言学家对语言现象的限定也不同,有的人认为和语言学相关的现象应该是科学有效的,因此如体会、判断、喜好等过于个性化的现象不应该在语言学讨论的范围之内。另一些人则认为这些个人现象是最真实可靠的,恰恰是语言学研究最有价值的材料。不同的倾向使语言学理论朝多元方向发展。

## 第一节 索绪尔与日内瓦学派

瑞士语言学家索绪尔(1857—1913)是语言学史上一位重量级的人物。1907 年至 1911 年间,他在日内瓦大学讲授普通语言学课程,向学生传授了其语言学理论中的精华部分。他本人尚未来得及将这些内容整理成书便与世长辞了,所幸他的同事和学生意识到这些理论的重要性。他的学生查尔斯·巴利(Charles Bally)和阿尔伯特·薛施霭(Albert Sechehaye)等人搜集整理了索绪尔的讲稿和学生的课堂笔记,编成《普通语言学教程》(*Cours de linguistique générale*)一书,于 1916 年首次出版。该书汇集了索绪尔语言学理论的精华,日后不仅对语言学的发展至关重要,还深刻影响到人类学、心理学、社会学、文学批评等学术领域。乔纳森·卡勒(Johnathan Culler)曾说:"费迪南·德·索绪尔是现代语言学之父,他使系统的语言研究得到新的发展,让 20 世纪语言学研究成果成为可能。仅凭此一点我们就可以称他为一位现代大师。"①

索绪尔认为,语言是一个由符号组织起来的系统,语言符号包括表达形式和内容两个方面,是声音形象与语义的结合体。为了区分语言符号的两个方面,索绪尔提出能指(signifiant)与所指(signifié)的概念。作为现代语言学的奠基人,索绪尔最先提出语言学有历时研究和共时研究。在历史语言学占统治地位的形势下,索绪尔的划分使语言学的研究中心逐渐从语言的历史演变转移到对语言共时系统的描写,让语言系统本身成为语言学研究的重要组成部分。此外,索绪尔特别区分了语言(langue)和言语(parole)、形式(form)和实体(substance)、表达(expression)和内容(content)、组合(syntagmatique,或译句段关系)与聚合(associatif,或译联想关系)等概念。他的这些基本思想对语言学界产生了深远的影响。

索绪尔的弟子巴利、薛施霭等人受导师的影响,把研究重点集中在语言的静态方面,几乎不再考虑语言中的历史因素。他们对语言的心理成分和社会成分十分关注,在语言文学领域取得了不小的成就。

从索绪尔开始,语言学研究的主要对象从语言的历史演变逐步转移到语言系统本身的结构成分及其相互关系,索绪尔也因此被看作欧洲结构主义的开创者。因为索绪尔任教于日内瓦大学,他的学术思想主要是在日内瓦授课期间形成的,所以有人称索绪尔及其弟子和追随者为日内瓦学派。

# 第二节　布拉格学派

1926 年 10 月,布拉格语言学会召开第一次会议,标志着布拉格学派的形成,创建人为第一次大会的主席马泰休斯(Vilem Mathesius),包括雅各布森(Roman Jakobson)、特鲁

---

① 　J.卡勒.索绪尔[M].张景智,译.北京:中国社会科学出版社,1989:1.

贝茨柯依（Nikolai Trubetzkoy）、卡尔采夫斯基（Sergei Karcevskiy）、穆卡若夫斯基（Jan Mukařovský）等。第一次会议的重要议程之一是召集学者撰写论文，为1929年在布拉格召开的第一次国际斯拉夫学者代表大会（the First International Congress of Slavists）作准备。在大会上，该学会学者递交了《论纲》，强调语言是一种功能体系，全面阐述了学会的语言学观点。后来学会出版了八卷《布拉格语言学会论丛》（*Travaux de Cercle Linguistique de Prague*），自1935年起还创办了期刊《词与语文》，让布拉格学派的声明传播于世。1939年3月德军占领捷克，学会成员流散，活动一度中断，至1948年方恢复，但到20世纪50年代初组织终于解散。后来，特伦卡（Bohumil Trnka）、瓦赫克（Josef Vachek）等人以及一些年轻的捷克学者继承布拉格学派的传统，在捷克斯洛伐克科学院继续从事语言学研究工作。

布拉格学派的鼎盛时期是20世纪20年代末和20世纪30年代。当时学会同各国语言学界建立了广泛的联系，进行过许多学术交流活动。有些语言学家虽非学会成员，但因观点不同程度地接近布拉格学派，也对功能语言学的发展作出了贡献，如法国的马丁内（André Martinet）和班维尼斯特（Émile Benveniste）、挪威的萨默费特（Alf Sommerfelt）、荷兰的格罗特（Albert Willem de Groot）等。

布拉格学派受索绪尔影响，把语言看成功能上相互关联的系统，是为一定目的服务的表达手段，因此要以功能的观点加以研究。为了强调自己的特点，该学派曾明确表示应该把自己称为功能语言学派。布拉格学派的研究重点是音系学。特鲁贝茨柯依和雅各布森等人根据索绪尔关于音位值对立关系的理论，提出了音系特征（phonological feature）的概念。特鲁贝茨柯依在代表作《音位学原理》（*Principles of Phonology*）中阐明了音位的性质，将音位体系定义为能用以区别词汇意义和语法意义的音位对立体的综合。特鲁贝茨柯依指出，音位是语言中最小的语音单位，在语言系统中起主导作用的并非语音本身，而是能区分意义的对立差异。特鲁贝茨柯依从语言系统的角度，对音位进行了详尽的分类，包括偶项对立（Bilateral Opposition）、多变对立（Multilateral Opposition）、正负性对立（Privative Opposition）、成比性对立（Proportional Opposition）、可中和对立（Neutralizable Opposition）、孤立对立（isolated opposition）等。此后，雅各布森又通过实验和对历时音位学的研究，对布拉格语言学会早期的音位理论进行了某些补充和发展。

# 第三节　哥本哈根学派

哥本哈根学派又称丹麦学派,与布拉格学派、美国描写语言学派并称为结构主义语言学三大流派。1931 年,丹麦哥本哈根大学的语言学教授叶尔姆斯列夫(Louis Hjelmslev,1899—1965)与语言学家布伦达尔(Viggo Brødal,1887—1942)等人仿照布拉格语言学会,共同创立了哥本哈根语言学会。其中叶尔姆斯列夫的研究方法更接近形式主义,吸引了乌尔达勒(1907—1957,Hans Jørgen Uldall)、若根森(Eli Fischer Jørgensen)等一批追随者。叶尔姆斯列夫等人试图建立一个高度抽象的形式系统,并用精确的术语来描述语言系统各个部分及其相互关系。他的主要理论观点在《语言理论导论》(*Prolegomena to a Theory of Language*)和《语言理论简论》(*Résumé of a Theory of Language*)中表现得最为集中,此外还有《格的范畴》(*La catégorie des cas*)等著作。哥本哈根语言学会为北欧的一小批语言学家提供了讨论语言学问题的平台,最初他们主要研究语言学和音位学的问题,后来逐渐发展出一套新的语言学理论,并称之为"语符理论"(Glossematics)。因此,也有人把哥本哈根学派称为"语符学派"。学会成员出版了《哥本哈根语言学会丛刊》(*Travaux du Cercle Linguistique de Copenhague*)和《语言学学报》(*Acta Linguistica*,后改名为 *Acta Linguistica Hafniensia*)等刊物。一直担任学会主席的叶尔姆斯列夫于 1965 年去世,语符理论尚有待发展。1989 年,哥本哈根学派的一些成员受认知语言学和西蒙·C.迪克(Simon C. Dik)的功能主义理论启发,创立了"丹麦功能语法学派",综合了叶尔姆斯列夫、布伦达尔以及迪德瑞森(Paul Diderichsen)、叶斯伯森(Otto Jespersen)等人的理论,并吸收了现代功能语言学的研究方法。语言学家哈德(Harder)的著作《丹麦功能语法》(*Danish Functional Grammar*)为重要代表作之一。

哥本哈根学派内部成员的观点并不统一,因此该学派并不像布拉格学派那么有凝聚力。叶尔姆斯列夫是学派中最重要的代表人物,他关于语符学的理论对整个学派影响深远。叶尔姆斯列夫继承了索绪尔把语言系统的形式和实体严格区分的思想,从索绪尔的"语言是形式,而不是实质"出发,把语言分成"内容"和"表达"两个平面,又将之推广到形式和实体两个方面,得到内容实体(content substance)、内容形式(content form)、表达形式(expression form)、表达实体(expression substance)四个平面。内容实体是客观世界中的万事万物,表达实体则指我们在客观世界所见闻的各种文字、图形、声音等。语言学的主要研究对象是形式,包括内容形式和表达形式。他分析了这两个平面的所有成分,将其中最基本的成分称作"语符(glosseme)"。"表达形式"的基本成分是音位或音位特征;"内容形式"的基本成分是语义特征。如"姐姐"这个词的语义特征包括"动物""人""女性""亲属"等,其表达形式则为其发音,特别是与其他词语相区别的音位特征。

叶尔姆斯列夫等人对实体过分排斥,使语言研究难以立足。其理论过于抽象,用语生僻,又很少真正用于语言的具体分析,因而对语言学的影响远不如布拉格学派和美国描写语言学派,甚至被人讥为纸上谈兵。不过,哥本哈根学派将索绪尔相关观点进一步发挥,把语言划分为更为细致的四个平面,确实为语言系统的精确描写提供了严密的方法,这对后人有不少启发。

# 第四节　美国的结构主义学派

美国的语言学研究并不像欧洲那样有着结构主义的传统,但是在 20 世纪初期,美国的语言学研究发生了一些实质性的变化。美国土著语言繁多,当时本土不少印第安语言面临消亡的绝境,亟需有人对这些语言进行整理和记录。因此,美国语言学研究当时在理论上没有太大的发展,在语言描写方面却论争四起。最早进行这些语言研究工作的主要是一些传教士和人类学家,其中人类学家兼语言学家博厄斯(Franz Boas,1858—1942)的工作特别突出。博厄斯当年在墨西哥以北地区进行考察,并撰写了《美洲印第安语言手册》(*Handbook of American Indian Languages*)一书,其中序言和部分章节对语言描写的基本方法和初步理论进行了详细的介绍。他指出,人类语言丰富多样,对语言事实的描写必须客观;对每种语言都应该有相应的、特定的语法研究范畴;描写不同结构的语言,应该创立新的概念和方法。博厄斯训练了大量语言研究工作者,几十年来不少美国知名语言学家直接或间接受到他的教诲。

另一位重要代表人物萨丕尔(Edward Sapir,1884—1939)于 1900 年和博厄斯相遇。受博厄斯影响,他开始采用新的方法考察印第安语言,尽量客观地通过当地母语者来记录和描写语言,而不是像传统方法那样,将印欧语法强加于所有其他语言。萨丕尔的代表作是《语言论》(*Language*，1921)。他认为语言是"纯粹人为的，非本能的，凭借自觉地制造出来的符号系统来传达观念、情绪和欲望的方法"。该书涉及语言成分、语音、语法程序、语法概念、语言结构的类型、语言的历史演变、语言之间的交互影响、语言和种族、文化、文学的关系等内容，把语言研究同人类心理、社会和文化联系在一起。后来的美国结构主义者致力于对语言结构作形式描写，传统主要就来自博厄斯和萨丕尔两人。由于他们在长期的语言调查实践中主张对语言现象客观描写，因此也被称为"美国描写语言学派(American descriptivists)"。

从整个学派的发展史来看，布龙菲尔德(Leonard Bloomfield，1887—1949)堪称该学派的核心人物。布龙菲尔德1914年出版的《语言研究导论》(*Introduction to the Study of Language*)借助心理学来阐释语言。1933年，他的代表作《语言论》(*Language*)出版，对美国结构主义语言学派的研究进行了概述，确定了该学派语言研究的基本原则和描写方法。布龙菲尔德的研究非常强调语言学的科学基础和语料分析形式的操作程序。在历史语言学方面他接受了欧洲新语法学派的传统，但在对语言结构的共时描写方面则对博厄斯和萨丕尔有所继承和发展。在分析语言结构时，他主张以可以观摩到的语言素材为依据，反对用非语言因素(特别是心理因素)作为标准，并强调形式的分析和归类。布龙菲尔德的语言理论名噪一时，以至于20世纪30—40年代的美国结构主义被称为"布龙菲尔德时期"。他对结构主义语言学的影响一直延续到20世纪50年代和60年代，此后乔姆斯基的"生成语法"逐渐发展崛起。

同欧洲的结构主义学派相比，美国学派完全排斥一切与语义和功能相关的因素，只关注"表达形式"这个平面。该学派探索出一套严格的语言描写方法，认为语法范畴的定义和划分不是依据语义，而是从分布出发；结构分析有特定的程式，各成分相互联系。他们首先对语音记录进行层层切分，以能否相互替代为标准来确定各种语言成分出现的位置，然后以这种分布状态为基础对语言成分进行分类。由于美国结构主义学派研究方法的这种特点，有人又称之为分布学派(Distributionalists)或分类学派(Taxonomists)。

# 第五节　伦敦学派

伦敦学派也是现代语言学重要学派之一,创始人为弗斯(John Rupert Firth, 1890—1960)。1944 年,弗斯获得伦敦大学普通语言学教席,这是英国第一个普通语言学教席,标志着语言学在英国逐渐成为一门独立的学科。弗斯自 20 世纪 30 年代起,在伦敦大学东方和非洲研究院语音学系任教,因此以他为主要代表的这一语言学流派常被称为"伦敦学派"。弗斯之前,斯威特(Harry Sweet, 1845—1912)和琼斯(David Jones, 1881—1967)特别强调语音的训练,他们要求学生能非常精确地感受、描述和重复语音的细小差异,比美国的行为主义语言学家们的要求更为苛刻,而弗斯的研究中正需要这种超强的语言能力。此外,弗斯还受到人类学家马林诺夫斯基(Bronislow Malinowski,1884—1942)的影响。作为伦敦大学的教师,弗斯培养或影响了一批重要的语言学家,其中包括韩礼德(Michael A. K. Halliday)等人。

马林诺夫斯基自 1927 年起开始在伦敦经济学院(London School of Economics)任教。作为一名人类学教授,他对新几内亚东岸的特洛布里安群岛(Trobriand Island)土著文化进行研究,提出特有的语言观。基于对土著语言的研究,他发现话语意义和情景总是紧密相连。他提出,语言是一种行为模式,话语的意义不是来自组成话语的语词,而是源于话语发生的情景语境(context of situation)。马林诺夫斯基将情景语境分为三类:①言语与身体行为相关的情景;②叙述情景;③言语用来填补交谈空白的情景,也就是应酬语。

弗斯吸收了马林诺夫斯基的一些观点,认为语言是人类社会生成的形式,而不仅是一大堆约定俗成的符号和标记。对他而言,意义就是用途,是任一平面上的成分和该成分在此平面上的语境之间的关系。任何句子的意义都包括以下五个部分:①每个因素和其语音环境之间的关系;②句中每一词项和其他词项之间的关系;③每个词的形态关系;④该例句的句型;⑤该句与其所处情景语境之间的关系。和马林诺夫斯基一样,弗斯最关注的是情景语境。他认为情景语境不仅包括言语发生时人们行为活动的语境,还包括整个言语的文化背景和说话人的个人历史。弗斯提出"典型情景语境(typical context of situation)"的概念,认为社会环境决定说话者扮演的社会角色,尽管句子变化无穷,人们在社会生活中所扮演的角色是有限的,典型情景语境也是有限的。因此,谈话其实就像某种规定好的仪式,一旦有人开始对你说话,你的角色基本上就确定了。由此,语义学就是对适合的典型情景语境中的话语进行分类。

此外,弗斯对韵律学也作出了重要贡献。他最早在《声音和韵律》(*Sounds and Prosodies*)中提出关于音系的相关理论。他反对当时重要音系学家如特鲁贝茨柯依和布龙菲尔德等人所做的纯粹的语音分析,认为音位学和音系学完全不同。人的话语是连续的语流,要想分析语言,仅靠单纯的语音描写或音位描写都是不够的,因此应当将抽象的音系学和具体的语音描述相结合。弗斯描述了韵律的组成成分,包括重读、鼻化、音长、送气等特征。

韩礼德是伦敦学派的另一位重要成员。他曾在北京大学师从罗常培学习汉语,后又在岭南大学得到王力的教诲,于 1955 年完成博士论文,先后在英国牛津大学、爱丁堡大学、伦敦大学等处任教。受到弗斯、叶尔姆斯列夫及布拉格学派的影响,韩礼德进一步发展了系统语法理论,并对语法的功能范畴进行了特别的研究。韩礼德的系统语法和其他流派的理论相比有几个特点:①非常重视从社会学的层面来研究语言;②把语言看作一种行为的形式,而不是认知的形式,区别了潜在语言行为(linguistic behaviour potential)和实际语言行为(actual linguistic behaviour);③以渐变的方式描述了语言的各个方面(如用不符合语法-不常见-比较不常见-比较常见-符合语法等一系列术语来连续地描述语言现象);④中心范畴为系统范畴,语言是"系统的系统"。

韩礼德认为,语言系统由多个系统组成,总的来说,系统又分为链系统(Chain system)和选择系统(Choice system)。链系统是横向的,反映的是句法关系,如句子成分的排列,主要涉及语法的表层平面,包括句子结构、语言单位等。选择系统是纵向的,和语义层面相关。比如说,英语中的数系统包括单数和复数两种选择;德语中性别系统有阴性、阳性、中性三种;法语词汇的性别系统则只有阴性、阳性两种;再比如英语中时态有过去时、现在时、将来时三种等。每一系统中的项目总是相互排斥的,选择其一则不可选其二;系统是有限的,系统中每一项目的含义取决于同一系统中其他项目的含义。

韩礼德一直从系统和功能的角度来研究语言,他认为语言的社会需求决定其结构,学习语言就是学习如何表达意思的过程。对儿童来说,语言是用来达到某种意图的工具,有着若干种功能。随着儿童的成长,其语言也会因功能的不同而发生变化,总的来说其功能可归结为三大类:达意功能(ideational)、人际功能(interpersonal)、语篇功能(textural)。达意功能用来传递新信息,人际功能包括表达社会或个人关系的语言的使用,这两者都与人类的经验相关;语篇功能则指语言的连贯机制,使话语成为连贯、统一的文本,能够表达真实的信息,而不是随便凑在一起的句子。三种功能共同作用,形成完整的语言系统。

# 第六节 转换-生成语法理论

1957 年,乔姆斯基(Avram Noam Chomsky, 1928— )的《句法结构》(*Syntactic Structures*)一书出版,首次推出转换-生成语法(Transformational-generative linguistics, TG)的概念,在语言学界掀起一场重大革命。

乔姆斯基发现儿童学习母语时速度快,效果好,通常在五岁左右就能熟练使用母语,这在其他领域的学习中是不可思议的。孩子一开始接触的往往是些不规范的语句,简化的词汇等,但通过有限的语言输入,孩子却能逐渐掌握完美的语言体系,制造出无限多的句子来。儿童在有限的时间内接触有限的语言事实,却能学会完整的语法体系,他们学会的不是单独的句子,而是一整套规则。因此,乔姆斯基认为,儿童可能天生就具有学习语言的先天条件,其实质是一种人脑具有的与语言知识相关的特定状态,一种使婴儿能学会人类任何语言的物理及相应的心理机制。婴儿生来就具有"语言获得装置"(language acquisition device, LAD),这种装置包括三个因素:假设机制(hypothesis-making device)、语言共通性(linguistic universal)和评估程序(evaluation procedure)。所谓的语言共通性,就是指所有人类语言共有的特点,这些语言的共同特点构成所谓的普遍语法(universal grammar)。

转换-生成语法的发展主要经历了几个阶段。第一阶段从 20 世纪 50 年代到 1965 年,着重研究形式语言理论的基本原理,乔姆斯基的两本代表作——《语言理论的逻辑结构》(*The Logical Structure of Linguistic Theory*,1955)和《句法结构》(1957)在此时期出版。乔姆斯基认为语法是一系列语言生成的规则,规则先于结构。句子根据规则被划分为名词性短语和动词性短语等,短语又根据规则进一步被分割。这一阶段被看作"第一语言模式时期"(the period of the first linguistic model)。对乔姆斯基而言,第一种规则是短语结构规则(PS rules, Phrase Structure rules)。这套规则与传统的直接成分分析法有相似之处,但其中的划分线不能相交,因此凡是不连续的成分都不适应此规则。我们以下图为例:

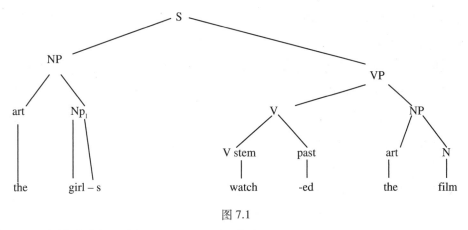

图 7.1

图 7.1 常被称为标记树（labelled trees），其中，

S（句子）→ NP（名词性短语）+ VP（动词性短语）

VP（动词性短语）→V（动词）+ NP（名词短语）

NP（名词性短语）→art（冠词）+ Ns（名词单数形式）或 Npl（名词复数形式）

V（动词）→V stem（动词词根）+过去式

其他类型的结构也可能出现在标记树中，比如从句或并列句可以作为子句（S1、S2……）镶嵌在母句中，然后再依照以上规则划分。但是，用短语结构规则显然不足以描述所有的句子，这也是直接成分分析法面临的最大问题。因此，乔姆斯基提出"转换规则（transformational rules）"。转换规则不是用来分割句子，而是用来解决句子结构的变化或重组的，包括句子成分顺序的变化，句子成分的增减等。有了转换规则，句子的主动与被动、肯定与否定、陈述句、祈使句、问句等特殊现象都能被描述，转换规则在必要时重组句子成分的顺序，形成新的分析标记树。在转换规则的帮助下，一些可能产生歧义的句子就能得到更好的解释。比如英语中"flying planes"既可以指正在飞行的飞机，又可以指驾驶飞机的行为；汉语中的"印染手帕"既可以指用印染的方式制造的手帕，也可以指"用印染的方式制造手帕的过程"，用转换法则就能更好地描述这类短语。再比如，"the book was written by the famous writer"和"the book was written in 1985"中，第一句介词 by 后面的 the famous writer 是写书的施动者，后一句施动者被省略，介词 in 后面是时间状语。光用传统的直接分析法或者单凭短语结构规则都无法表明二者的区别，转换规则的应用基本解决了这一问题。此外，乔姆斯基还提出了音系规则（P rules，Phonological rules），这种规则主要负责将前两种规则产生的结构符号化，转化为真正的话语。对乔姆斯基而言，语法系统中的规则像用数学公式一样，不断生成句子，不同的规则生成不同句子。

1965 年，乔姆斯基撰写《句法理论要略》（*Aspects of the Theory of Syntax*，1965）一书，在原有的理论基础上做了一些重要的改变。首先，乔姆斯基为了使规则体系更完善，重新引入了语义学的观点；其次，提出了语言深层结构（deep structure）和表层结构（surface structure)的概念;最后,减少了转换规则,从而丰富了基本短语结构或深层结构的内容。乔姆斯基逐渐意识到句子的语义解析可以与深层结构联系到一起,而语音解析则可以与表层结构联系在一起;句子结构的转换受深层结构的控制。否定、被动、问句,甚至从属关系、并列关系等原归于转换规则的内容,现在和名词的数、性、动词的及物、不及物等属性一起,都被看成深层结构的基本元素。与表层结构相比,不同语言的深层结构更为相近;深层结构的句法特征和一些语义特征被看作是人类语言所共有的特点,不同语言之间的语法差异正是表层结构的差异所致。该理论被称作标准理论(Standard theory),深层结构、表层结构与语法的关系可表现为图 7.2①。

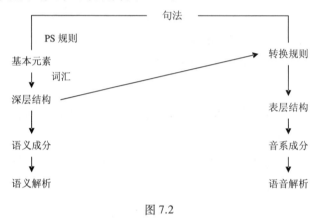

图 7.2

从 1965 年到 1970 年,研究的焦点主要在语义问题,主要研究趋势即减少转换规则,增加基本元素的内容。这一阶段研究又被称作"标准理论时期(the period of Standard Theory)"。此后,语言学家对标准理论进行了一些修正,认为表层结构对语义解析也有作用,进入生成语法的"标准理论扩展时期(the period of Extended Standard Theory)",着重研究语言的普遍规律和普遍语法。

1981 年,乔姆斯基在《关于管辖与约束的讲话》(*Lectures on Government and Binding*)中提出了句法研究的主要理论——管辖与约束理论,标志着生成语法正式进入第四阶段——"管约时期(GB period)"。转换-生成语法诞生之初,主要是为了让人们更好地理解语言和语法,这些语法是人类孩提时期习得的规则,并以某种方式体现在说话者的大脑中,因此特别重视对各种语言成分的详细分析。近年来,学者将更多兴趣放在普遍语法(universal grammar)上。布龙菲尔德曾指出,要想得出所谓的"普遍"语法,就必须对大量的语言进行归纳,这在短时期内是无法完成的。乔姆斯基及其追随者却认为在对一些语言进行研究后,可以得出一定的推论,除非有证据证明推论错误。他们削弱普遍语法在具体语言中应用,在普遍语法的基础上推出"核心"语法,基本能广泛适用于所有语言,

① 罗宾斯.普通语言学概论[M].北京:外语教学与研究出版社,2000:289.

但在特定的条件下,可能在某些语言中得不到表现。比如在英语中 Who do you think the name is the writer of the book？ 让人摸不着头脑,而问句 Who do you think is the writer of the book？ 是规范的句子,哪怕被说成 Do you think who is the writer of the book？ 的不规范形式,人们也能够理解。事实上其他语言中的句序可能不同,如汉语中我们就会问:"你认为谁是这本书的作者?"与之对应的英语正是"You think who is the writer of the book？"这些细节的不同并没有阻挡语言学家发展普遍语法的决心。他们正是基于此种情况提出核心普遍语法(universal core grammar)的概念。核心普遍语法包括若干组成部分,管辖和约束即其中重要的两点。

转换-生成语法理论经历若干阶段,普遍语法仍处于假设阶段,并未被完全证实,但是该理论在一定程度上使我们摆脱了行为主义语言学的束缚,指出了人们习得语言的心理机制和先天条件等问题,在当代语言学界影响深远。直到现在,转换-生成语法相关理论仍是语言学界关心的重要问题。

# 第七节　认知语言学

认知语言学作为语言学的一门分支学科,它以第 2 代认知科学和体验哲学为理论背景,在反对主流语言学转换生成语法的基础上诞生,在 20 世纪 80 年代后期至 90 年代开始成型。

认知语言学涉及人工智能、语言学、心理学、系统论等多种学科,它针对生成语言学天赋观,提出:人的语言知识来自对语言的运用(即基于运用的模型),语言的创建、学习及运用,基本上都必须能够透过人类的认知而加以解释,因为认知能力是人类知识的根本。

此外,认知语言学还提出了一系列反对生成语言理论的观点,包括:认为人的语言能力并不是一种独立的能力,而跟人的一般认知能力紧密相关;认为句法作为语言结构的一部分并不是自足的,句法跟语言的词汇部分、语义部分是密不可分的,后者甚至更重要;认为语义不仅仅是客观的真值条件,而是主观和客观的结合,研究语义总要涉及人的主观看法或心理因素;认为语言中的各种单位范畴,和人所建立的大多数范畴一样,都是非离散性的,边界是不明确的;在承认人类认知共通性的同时,充分注意不同民族的认知特点对语言表达的影响。

认知语言学的创立者普遍被认为是乔治·雷可夫(George Lakoff)、马克·约翰逊(Mark Johnson)及朗奴·兰盖克(Ronald Langacker)。其中,乔治·雷可夫和马克·约翰逊主要研究语言中的隐喻及其与人类认知的关系;而朗奴·兰盖克的专长在于认知语法。

认知语言学不是一种单一的语言理论,而是一个开放的理论体系,代表着一种研究范式,是多种从认知角度研究语言的理论的统称,其特点是把人们的日常经验看成是语言使用的基础,着重阐释语言和一般认知能力之间密不可分的联系。这些语言理论虽不相同,但对语言所持的基本假设都大同小异,都不同程度地坚持体验哲学观,认可人的语言知识来自对语言的运用。各个理论流派只是讨论和关注的具体语言现象有所差别。认知语言学主要理论流派有:雷可夫、泰尔米(Talmy)等人的"认知语义学(Cognitive Semantics)";兰盖克(Langacker)的"认知语法(Cognitive Grammar)";菲尔莫尔(Fillmore)、戈德伯格(Goldberg)等人的"构式语法(Construction Grammar)";以及 S.兰姆(S. Lamb)的"神经认知语言学(Neurocognitive Linguistics)"等。

虽然认知语言学各个流派的理论存在着各自的研究视角,但是他们都坚持着一些相同的基本概念和原则,包括:

(1)概念语义。坚持意义等同于概念化(即心理经验的各种结构或过程,而不是可能世界中的真值条件),一个表达式的意义就是在说话人或听话人的大脑里激活的概念,更为具体地说,意义存在于人类对世界的解释中,它具有主观性,体现了以人类为宇宙中心的思想,反映了主导的文化内涵、具体文化的交往方式以及世界的特征等。这一原则表明,意义的描写涉及词与大脑的关系,而不是词与世界之间的直接关系。

(2)百科语义。认为词及更大的语言单位是进入无限知识网络的入口。对一个语言表达式的意义要进行全面的解释,通常需要考虑意象(视觉的和非视觉的)、隐喻、心理模型以及对世界的朴素理解等。因此,一个词的意义单靠孤立的词典似的定义一般来说是不能解决问题的,必须依赖百科知识方可达到目的。

(3)典型范畴。范畴并不是由标准属性模型定义的,也不是由必要和充分特征定义的;相反,范畴是围绕典型、家族成员相似性,范畴中各成员之间的主观关系组织起来的。

(4)语法性判断。语法性判断涉及范畴化。一个话语的语法性或可接受性并不是二分的(即要么可接受,要么不可接受),而是渐进的。因此,语法性判断是渐进的,并且同语境、语义以及语法规则密切相关。认知语言学家并不像生成语法学家那样,要把语法写成是一部生成一种语言中所有并且是唯一合乎语法的句子那样的语法体系,因为语法性判断具有渐进性、可变性以及语境的依赖性,要实现生成语法学家所期望的目标显然十分艰难。

（5）语言与其他认知。认知语言学之所以为认知语言学是因为它要在一般的认知中寻找语言现象的类似物。认知语言学家积极吸收心理学关于人类范畴化、注意以及记忆等的研究成果来丰富自己的理论从而使认知语言学更加具有活力。由此可见语言与其他认知机制具有密切的关系。

（6）句法的非自主性。句法是约定俗成的模式，声音（或符号）通过这种模式传达意义，因此，句法并不需要自己特殊的元素（primitives）和理论结构。约定俗成的符号模式是说话人通过实际话语获得的，而要获得语法知识只有通过这样的符号模式才能实现。

认知范式中虽有不同的理论方法，但以上六条基本概念和原则足以把这些理论方法紧密联系起来。它们界定了认知语言学的内涵和范围，并使认知语言学与其他认知学科区别开来。

目前认知语言学家根据研究视角和研究内容的不同，将认知语言学划分成了不同的研究分支领域，如埃文斯（Evans）等人将认知语言学划分为认知语义学和认知语法两大分支；福康涅（Fauconnier）将认知语言学划分为了认知语义学、认知语法、隐喻研究及心理空间与概念整合四个分支；而 Dirven 则将认知语言学分为了五个分支：基于格式塔心理学的研究（包括认知语义学、认知语法、构式语法）、基于现象学的研究（包括原型理论、词汇网络理论、概念隐喻、体验现实主义、概念转喻）、认知语篇研究（包括心理空间与概念整合理论、认知诗学、衔接的认知语篇研究）、认知社会语言学（包括认知词汇变化研究、认知意识形态研究、文化认知模型研究）、认知心理语言学（包括意向图示的心理真实性、隐喻性语言理解、基于使用的语言习得模式、词汇网络的发展）。

# 第八节　其他学派及理论

尽管乔姆斯基及其追随者是语言学界当之无愧的领军人物，却不能独占沙场。事实上，不同的理论在语言学研究领域里各占一席之地，或对立，或关联，呈现出当今语言学研究理论纷呈、流派林立的局面。这些理论从各自的角度出发来研究语言，为语言研究开辟新的领域。对于我们语言学习者来说，了解各种不同语言学流派及理论可以拓宽视野，十分必要。由于理论数量纷杂，此处仅选择一些较有影响的理论进行简要介绍，以供参考。

## 一、广义短语结构语法

1985 年,英国的伽兹达(Gerald Gazdar)、萨格(Ivan Sag)、克莱恩(Ewan Klein)和美国的普勒姆(Geoffrey Pullum)出版了一系列著作,共同创立了广义短语结构语法(Generalized phrase structure grammar, GPSG)理论。该流派的研究目的与乔姆斯基的生成语法大同小异,是通过建立对个别语言明晰完整的描写结构来考察自然语言。他们通过严格的规则来具体表现语法规范句子的树形结构,不用转换规则,也不考虑深层结构和表层结构的差异,并拒绝任何心理学角度的语法研究方式。取代转换规则的是一套更为丰富的基本概念。广义短语结构语法对早期的短语结构规则作了改进,其句法范畴根据句法特征和语义特征来分类,如动词可以分为及物、不及物,可省略宾语的及物、双及物等类型。规则有两种:直接支配规则(immediate dominance rules)和线性优先规则(rules of linear precedence)。前者由各语法项的特征来决定,后者则描述前一规则的产物的正常词序。例如句子"他送李红一枝玫瑰"用直接支配规则来描述则为:

S(句子) → NP(名词性短语),VP(动词性短语)

VP →V(动词),NP$_1$(名词性短语 1),NP$_2$(名词性短语 2)(其中动词为双及物动词)

而用线性优先规则来描述则为:

NP < VP

V < NP$_1$< NP$_2$, < 反映线性序列

该流派提出元规则(metarules)的概念。所谓元规则,即生成规则的规则,句法的生成即由元规则和特征系统完成。广义短语结构语法形式严格,充满了烦琐的标记和公式,较适于计算机演算,受到计算语言学家的重视。但是该理论的可行性最终还需在自然语言的应用中得到证实。除了以上提到的伽兹达等人的著作外,还有不少学者将此理论对英语之外的语言进行应用,特别是日语的研究较为突出。

## 二、关系语法

关系语法(Relational grammar)形成于 20 世纪 70 年代,由帕尔穆特(David Permutter)和波斯塔尔(Paul Postal)等建立起的一种句法理论。这一理论以语法关系为基本概念,研究语法关系在关系网络不同层次中的转化,并在此基础上描述句法结构。这种理论从某种程度上来说,是转换-生成语法的一种替代理论,是针对普遍语法中被动化问题研究产生的。当时转换-生成语法对这些问题没有做出普遍性的解释,因此不少学者被关系语法所吸引。但是,很快人们发现关系语法中的理论对许多语法现象无法做出合理解释,

这一理论到 20 世纪 80 年代后影响甚微。

在关系语法中,语法关系是有限的,包括主语、直接宾语、间接宾语等,因此每个语法项在句子结构不同层级中总是处于多重关系之中,各种语法关系共同组成语言的关系网络。不论这些语法关系在特定语言中有何不同,它们都是跨语言的原始因素。也就是说,它们是所有语言中都可能发现的关系。和转换语法不同的是,转换的基础不是句子成分之间的顺序关系,而是关系范畴之间的句法关系。比如说主动与被动的转化可能涉及主语变为施事短语、直接宾语或间接宾语变为主语等过程,这些变化可能表现为句序的变化(如英语),也可能表现为词的形态变化(如拉丁语)。关系语法描述句子不用直接成分树形图,而常以用数字标明论元(arguments)和谓词(predicates)成分的方式来描述。简单的例子如下:

| 1 | P | 3 | 2 |
|---|---|---|---|
| Jack | gave | Rose | a kiss. |

其中 1 标记着主语,2 标记着直接宾语,3 标记着间接宾语,P 指谓语。

## 三、词汇-功能语法

词汇-功能语法(Lexical-functional grammar,LFG)是在转换-生成语法标准化理论的基础上演化而来的。前面提到的广义短语结构语法将语法理论与计算机编程联系在一起,认为对心理关联的探索在目前的语言研究中还为时过早,而词汇-功能语法则认为语法结构中的"心理事实"是非常重要的。该理论的支持者摈弃了乔姆斯基对说者-听者语言能力(competence)的绝对理想化,而更关注实际说话者在与语言能力相关的范围内所作出的实际语言表现(performance),其目的和涉及心理过程及话语阐释的实验结果相一致。

在词汇-功能语法中,主、谓、宾等概念也被看成普遍的原始理论因素。句法特征和语义特征有着重要意义。句法由两种平行的结构组成,即成分结构和功能结构。成分结构和早期转换-生成语法中的重写规则(rewriting rules)有些类似,表达句子的排列,决定句子的语音表达等信息;在此基础上再加入同一句子的功能结构,代表句子的语义,表达句子中各语义成分之间的关系,使语义阐释成为可能。霍洛克斯(Horrocks)有一个例子如图 7.3①:

---

① G. C. Horrocks, *Generative Grammar*[M]. London: Longman Publishing Group, 1987:246-247.

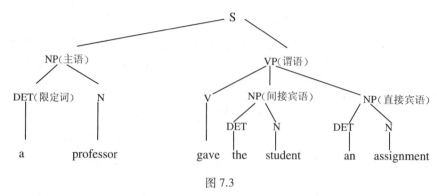

图 7.3

图 7.3 中,句子成分一一列出,此外,句子的功能结构也作了标记,如 a professor 是主语,gave 是谓语等。值得注意的是,这两种结构看起来和乔姆斯基的深层结构与表层结构有相似之处,但是并不相同。词汇-功能语法并不打算借助结构的转换来描述句法,而是以成分结构和功能结构中都用到的语法功能作为中介,将句法范畴与语义功能联系在一起。词汇-功能语法也几经发展,后来在迪克(Simon Dik)的《功能语法》(*Functional grammaar*)和佛雷(Foley)及瓦林(Van Valin)共撰的《功能句法和普遍语法》(*Functional Syntax and Universal Grammar*)中均有新的阐述。

## 四、依存语法

前面讨论的大多数理论中对句法的分析都在句子成分之间进行。我们知道,句子的成分是句法结构的基本单位,通常由不止一个词构成,因此我们常用短语来表示。但是,也有一些语言学家倾向于用词之间的关系来分析句法,并把这种词与词之间的关系称作依存关系,这种语法常被称为"依存语法(Dependency grammars)"。

依存语法由来已久,古印度语法家就采用类似的方法来分析语法。1959 年,法国语言学家吕西安·泰尼埃(Lucien Tesnière)出版了《结构句法要义》(*Éléments de syntaxe structurale*)一书,在传统理论的基础上发展了依存理论,并有多种语料对句法结构形式进行了复杂的描述。依存语法与短语结构语法最不同之处就在于用词而非短语作为分割的单位。句子结构由支配成分词头(head)和其附属词(dependents)之间的关系来决定,不一定要靠特别的词序来决定,对于那些没有固定词序的语言来说特别适用。因此,尽管该理论在英语界影响不大,在描述捷克语、土耳其语等非固定词序语言时却较有用。比如一个简单的含有动词的句子中,动词就是主要的支配成分,不依存于其他词,但是这个动词的附属词却有可能成为其他词的支配成分。我们来看一个例子:

再如古汉语中"某贻余核舟一",用简单的英语词对应用依存语法来表现如下:

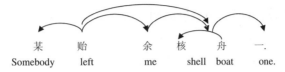

此句英文的正常语序应为:Somebody left me one shell boat. 箭头的方向将会发生一点变化。在更复杂的句子中,箭头可能会出现交叉的情形。

在依存语法的基础上,学者们又发展出几何句法、扩展的依存语法、混合依存语法等理论。如混合依存语法中分析的单位不仅包括传统的单词,有时也包括短语。总的来说,依存语法对句法的描述不如树形图、成分分析等方法彻底,但是在某些方面给其他语法理论提出了一些问题,因此也值得我们了解。

## 五、法位学

法位学(Tagmemics)由美国语言学家派克(Kenneth L. Pike)创立。由于该学派的研究以密歇根大学为中心,因此常被称作美国描写语言学的密歇根学派。派克受到布龙菲尔德的行为主义语言观影响,将语言作为人类行为进行分析,并从音位、音素出发开始自己的研究。其代表作包括 1947 年的《音位学》(*Phonemics: a technique for reducing languages to writing*)和 1967 年的《语言与人类行为结构通论》(*Language in Relation to a Unified Theory of the Structure of Human Behavior*)等。该学派的大多数学者致力于语言的实地调查分析,常常活跃于传教活动。事实上,这批学者的研究最初就是为圣经翻译和教会工作服务。他们每年开设"暑期语言研究班",在调查中美和南美地区的语言研究中取得了不少成绩。

法位学的核心概念即法位(tagmeme)。法位这个词在布龙菲尔德的《语言论》中已经出现,但意义有所不同。所谓法位,是指句法或形态学结构中的某个位置以及占据这个位置的某个语言成分,它把传统的主、谓、宾、补、施事、受事等语法概念和处于这些句法位置上的名词、动词、代词、形容词、副词等联系起来。比如在简单句"我爱中国"中,我们可以说有三个词法位:主语位置的代词、谓语位置的及物动词和宾语位置的专有名词。总的来说,每个法位包含四种信息:①在结构中所处的位置,如主、谓、宾、短语中的中心语、修饰语等;②处在该位置的语言成分所属语类,如名、动、代、名词短语、动词短语等;③该法位在结构中的功能,如施事、受事、时间、方位等;④各法位之间的相应关系,如主、谓等在性、数、人称上的一致等。句子中可能有不同的法位层级,包含长短不一的法位,如句子、从句、短语、词等可以一级级分下去。通常在直接成分分析法中,句子总是先被分为名词性成分和动词性成分,初始的短语结构规则总是 S→ NP + VP,而法位句法中,法位可以有多个。法位学将语音和音素的区别延伸到语法和语义层面,正如音位变体(allophone)和语素变体(allomorph)一样,同一法位上某个位置与占据该位置的词类之间的关系被看作是没有语法差别的,被称作同位法子变体(allotagmas)。

派克还提出"主位(emic)"与"客位(etic)"的概念。这组概念源自语言学术语phonemic(音位的)和 phonetic(语音的),前者指从说话者的角度来描述语言行为,因此对某种语言的主位描述直接来源于母语者。后者指从观察者的角度来描述语言行为,因此"客位"描述在文化上显得更为客观。派克认为这组描述语言的概念适用于任何人类行为的描述,事实上,这组概念后来在人类学及其他行为科学和社会科学中得到广泛应用。

## 六、层次语法

层次语法(Stratificational linguistics)在 20 世纪 50 年代到 60 年代由美国语言学家兰姆(Sydney M. Lamb)提出。20 世纪 50 年代末期,兰姆提出语言模型由音素(phoneme)、语素(morpheme)、形态音素(morphophoneme)三个层次构成,为其后来的层次语法奠定了基础。兰姆深受哥本哈根学派代表人物叶尔姆斯列夫影响,认为语言是一个关系系统。这个关系系统并非显而易见的,语言学家的任务就是通过分析构建描述语言结构的关系系统,而语言描述的目的就是发现语言结构的关系特点。

兰姆指出,语言分析可以看作一个简化和归纳的过程。正如数学公式 abc+abd+abe+abf 可以简化为 ab(c+d+e+f)一样,语言学家在分析语言时也可采取类似的方法。层次语法就是在这种简化与归纳的原则上发展出来的。

层次语法中有两类基本的语言关系:组合关系(tactics)和表现关系(representation 或 realization)。前者指同一层次中各个单位可能的排列组合,后者指相邻层次间各单位的关系。

组合关系可用简单的例子来说明,如"红花、绿草、大树、小房子"这组词的修饰部分与被修饰部分可以形成不同的组合,可表现为

| 红 | 花 | 红花 | 红草 | 红树 | 红房子 |
| 绿 | 草 | 绿花 | 绿草 | 绿树 | 绿房子 |
| 大 | 树 | 大花 | 大草 | 大树 | 大房子 |
| 小 | 房子 | 小花 | 小草 | 小树 | 小房子 |

或简单表现为(红,绿,大,小)(花,草,树,房子)。

表现关系分析可以从横向组合(horizontal grouping)、横向分裂(horizontal splitting)、

纵向组合(vertical grouping)、纵向分裂(vertical splitting)四类入手。例如法语中的 au 实际结构可分裂为 à le,这就是一种横向分裂。而英语中过去式、过去分词与表现形式-ed、-en 等就是上下两层之间的纵向关系了。层次语法中,一个意义概念和其音响形象之间并无直接联系,语言结构体系由不同层次组成,其中最重要的层次从上至下分别为语义层(sememic)、词汇层(lexemic)、语素层(morphemic)和音素层(phonemic),每一层又可再分。层次语法试图用点和线将各种语言关系层层编织起来,将语义和语音联系在一起。通过层次语法的分析,读者能够从上至下或从下至上剥析语言的结构。

和其他理论相比,层次语法与心理学的关系也很紧密。许多语言学都试图从语言现象的客观分析中抽象出语法规律,兰姆却希望能了解人脑中的语言体系,因此他又把自己的理论称作“认知层次理论(Cognitive Stratificational Theory)”,后来又发展为“神经认知语言学(Neurocognitive Linguistics)”。

由于兰姆已不再继续研究层次语法,这一理论现在趋于沉寂。

## 七、韵律语法学

韵律语法学(Prosodic Grammar)是从韵律的角度研究人类语言语法的一个新学科,是当代语言学(也常称作现代语言学)的产物,是当代形式句法学的一个分支。在现代汉语语法研究中,学者们很早就关注到韵律与词法、句法的关系,但立足现代汉语的语言事实,冯胜利是明确提出“韵律语法”这一新概念并提出一套完整的韵律语法学理论的。

韵律语法学的发展可以分为以下几个阶段。第一阶段是理论初创阶段,以 Feng 和冯胜利为代表,从韵律和词法的关系以及韵律和句法演变的关系入手,探讨韵律与词法、句法的互动问题。

第二阶段是基础构架阶段,冯胜利提出了“韵律词、自然音步”等基础概念以及核心重音与动词短语互动的机制。

第三阶段为领域拓新阶段,进入 21 世纪,越来越多的学者从不同的方面探索韵律和语法的关系。首先,对汉语材料的进一步深入挖掘,涉及嵌偶词、介词的长度与分布、三音节形式、副词与动词的关系、被动句复制代词、非典型疑问句等研究。其次,韵律语法由普通话向汉语方言、少数民族语言、古代汉语等领域拓展。最后,韵律语法由语言学向语体学、文学等领域拓展。

第四阶段是体系建构阶段,建立了韵律语法的整体框架。冯胜利提出了韵律-句法层级对应模式(Prosody-Syntax Co-hierarchy Model),这种模式及围绕该模式建立的相关概念体系、建构的单位层级,使韵律语法学越来越成熟。

韵律语法学在借鉴生成语言学、形式节律音系学等国外语言学前沿理论上,立足汉语语言事实建立的理论体系,同时推动了国际学界的相关研究。首先,大量汉语韵律语法的研究成果发表在国际刊物上或是专著被翻译为外文,国际韵律语法年会已先后召开了 7 届。其次,汉语韵律语法学的研究也和国际语言学界的前沿研究始终保持互动,既吸收了欧美学界的前沿成果,也反过来影响了国际语言学界对韵律和语法关系的研究。

在韵律语法学的发展过程中,汉语节律音系学的理论研究也在同步进行,并与汉语韵律语法学彼此互动。

以上介绍的流派及理论远不是当今世界语言学研究的全貌,但可以为普通学习者提供管窥之见。事实上,还有不少理论值得我们了解,比如同样形成于 20 世纪 60 年代末的格语法(Case Grammar)以及稍晚一点的生成语义学(Generative Semantics)、蒙塔格语法(Montague Grammar)等,都受到了一定的关注。

## 思考与练习

一、名词解释

结构主义语言学

系统功能语法

二、简答

1.简述索绪尔在现代语言学中的地位。

2.哥本哈根学派、布拉格学派与美国描写语言学派并称为结构主义语言学三大流派,三者主要共同点是什么? 又有何差异?

3.乔姆斯基的转换-生成语法从产生至今分别经历了怎样的变化?

## 【原典阅读】

## General Principles

### Saussure

CHAPTER I  Nature of the Linguistic Sign

§ 1. *Sign*, *signified*, *signifier*

For some people a language, reduced to its essentials, is a nomenclature: a list of terms corresponding to a list of things. For example, Latin would be represented as:

：ARBOR

 ：EQUOS

etc.　　　　etc.

This conception is open to a number of objections. It assumes that ideas already exist independently of words ( see below ). It does not clarify whether the name is a vocal or a psychological entity, for *ARBOR* might stand for either. Furthermore, it leads one to assume that the link between a name and a thing is something quite unproblematic, which is far from being the case. None the less, this naive view contains one element of truth, which is that linguistic units are dual in nature, comprising two elements.

As has already been noted in connexion with the speech circuit, the two elements involved in the linguistic sign are both psychological and are connected in the brain by an associative link.[①] This is a point of major importance.

A linguistic sign is not a link between a thing and a name, but between a concept and a sound pattern.[②] The sound pattern is not actually a sound; for a sound is something physical. A sound pattern is the hearer's psychological impression of a sound, as given to him by the evidence of his senses. This sound pattern may be called a 'material' element only in that it is the representation of our sensory impressions. The sound pattern may thus be distinguished from the other element associated with it in a linguistic sign. This other element is generally of a more abstract kind: the concept.

The psychological nature of our sound patterns becomes clear when we consider our own linguistic activity. Without moving either lips or tongue, we can talk to ourselves or recite silently a piece of verse. We grasp lthe words of a language as sound patterns. That is why it is best to avoid referring to them as composed of 'speech sounds'. Such a term, implying the activity of the vocal apparatus, is appropriate to the spoken word, to the actualisation of the sound pattern in discourse. Speaking of the *sounds* and *syllables* of a word need not give rise to any misunderstanding,[③] provided

---

① This associative link is to be distinguished from the associative relations which link one sign with another. ( Translator's note)

② Saussure's term 'sound pattern' may appear too narrow. For in addition to the representation of what a word sounds like, the speaker must also have a representation of how it is articulated, the muscular pattern of the act of phonation. But for Saussure a language is essentially something acquired by the individual from the outside world. Saussure's 'sound pattern' is above all the natural representation of the word form as an abstract linguistic item, independently of any actualisation in speech. Hence the articulatory aspect of the word may be taken for granted, or relegated to a position of secondary importance in relation to its sound pattern. ( Editorial note)

③ None the less, as various passages in the *Cours* bear witness, it would have been in the interests of clarity to introduce a terminological distinction and keep to it. ( Translator's note)

one always bears in mind that this refers to the sound pattern.

The linguistic sign is, then, a two-sided psychological entity, which may be represented by the following diagram.

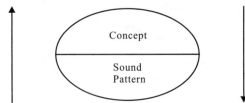

These two elements are intimately linked and each triggers the other. Whether we are seeking the meaning of the Latin word *arbor* or the word by which Latin designates the concept 'tree', it is clear that only the connexions institutionalised in the language appear to us as relevant. Any other connexions there may be we set on one side.

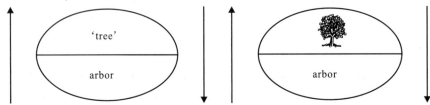

This definition raises an important question of terminology. In our terminology a *sign* is the combination of a concept and a sound pattern. But in current usage the term *sign* generally refers to the sound pattern alone, e.g. the word form *arbor*. It is forgotten that if *arbor* is called a sign, it is only because it carries with it the concept 'tree', so that the sensory part of the term implies reference to the whole.

The ambiguity would be removed if the three notions in question were designated by terms which are related but contrast. We propose to keep the term *sign* to designate the whole, but to replace *concept* and *sound pattern* respectively by *signification* and *signal*. The latter terms have the advantage of indicating the distinction which separates each from the other and both from the whole of which they are part. We retain the term *sign*, because current usage suggests no alternative by which it might be replaced.

The linguistic sign thus defined has two fundamental characteristics, In specifying them, we shall lay down the principles governing all studies in this domain.

§ 2. *First principle: the sign is arbitrary*

The link between signal and signification is arbitrary. Since we are treating a sign as the combination in which a signal is associated with a signification, we can express this more simply as: *the linguistic sign is arbitrary*.

There is no internal connexion, for example, between the idea 'sister' and the French sequence of sounds *s-ö-r* which acts as its signal. The same idea might as well be representee by any other sequence of sounds. This is demonstrated by differences between languages, and even by the existence of different languages. The signification 'ox' has as its signal *b-ö-f* on one side of the frontier,[①] but *o-k-s* ( *Ochs* ) on the other side.

No one disputes the fact that linguistic signs are arbitrary. But it is often easier to discover a truth than to assign it to its correct place. The principle stated above is the organising principle for the whole of linguistics, considered as a science of language structure. The consequences which flow from this principle are innumerable. It is true that they do not all appear at first sight equally evident. One discovers them after many circuitous deviations, and so realises the fundamental importance of the principle.

It may be noted in passing that when semiology is established one of the questions that must be asked is whether modes of expression which rely upon signs that are entirely natural ( mime, for example) fall within the province of semiology. If they do, the main object of study in semiology will none the less be the class of systems based upon the arbitrary nature of the sign. For any means of expression accepted in a society rests in principle upon a collective habit, or on convention, which comes to the same thing. Signs of politeness, for instance, although often endowed with a certain natural expressiveness ( prostrating oneself nine times on the ground is the way to greet an emperor in China) are none the less fixed by rule. It is this rule which renders them obligatory, not their intrinsic value. We may therefore say that signs which are entirely arbitrary convey better than others the ideal semiological process. That is why the most complex and the most widespread of all systems of expression, which is the one we find in human languages, is also the most characteristic of all. In this sense, linguistics serves as a model for the whole of semiology, even though languages represent only one type of semiological system.

The word *symbol* is sometimes used to designate the linguistic sign, or more exactly that part of the linguistic sign which we are calling the signal. This use of the word *symbol* is awkward, for reasons connected with our first principle. For it is characteristic of symbols that they are never entirely arbitrary. They are not empty configurations. They show at least a vestige of natural connexion between the signal and its signification. For instance, our symbol of justice, the scales, could hardly be replaced by a chariot.

The word *arbitrary* also calls for comment. It must not be taken to imply that a signal depends on the free choice of the speaker.( We shall see later than the individual has no power to alter a sign in any respect once it has become established in a linguistic community.) The term implies simply that the signal is *unmotivated*: that is to say arbitrary in relation to its signification, with which it has no natural connexion in reality.

In conclusion, two objections may be mentioned which might be brought against the principle that linguistic signs are arbitrary.

1. *Onomatopoeic* words might be held to show that a choice of signal is not always arbitrary. But such words are never organic elements of a linguistic system. Moreover, they are far fewer than is generally believed. French words like *fouet* ( 'whip' ) or *glas* ( 'knell' ) may strike the ear as having a certain suggestive sonority. But to see that this is in no way intrinsic to the words themselves, it suffices to look at their Latin origins. *Fouet* comes from Latin *fāgus* ( 'beech tree' ) and *glas* from Latin *classicum* ( 'trumpet call' ). The suggestive quality of the modern pronunciation

---

① The frontier between France and Germany.( Translator's note )

of these words is a fortuitous result of phonetic evolution.

As for genuine onomatopoeia (e. g. French *glou-glou* ('gurgle'), *tictac* 'ticking (of a clock)'), not only is it rare but its use is already to a certain extent arbitrary. For onomatopoeia is only the approximate imitation, already partly conventionalised, of certain sounds. This is evident if we compare a French dog's *ouaoua* and a German dog's *wauwau*. In any case, once introduced into the language, onomatopoeic words are subjected to the same phonetic and morphological evolution as other words. The French word *pigeon* ('pigeon') comes from Vulgar Latin *pīpiō*, itself of onomatopoeic origin, which clearly proves that onomatopoeic words themselves may lose their original character and take on that of the linguistic sign in general, which is unmotivated.

2. Similar considerations apply to *exclamations*. These are not unlike onomatopoeic words, and they do not undermine the validity of our thesis. People are tempted to regard exclamations as spontaneous expressions called forth, as it were, by nature. But in most cases it is difficult to accept that there is a necessary link between the exclamatory signal and its signification. Again, it suffices to compare two languages in this respect to see how much exclamations vary. For example, the French exclamation *aïe*! corresponds to the German *au !* Moreover, it is known that many exclamations were originalty meaningful words (e.g. *diable !* 'devil', *mordieu*! 'God's death').

In short, onomatopoeic and exclamatory words are rather marginal phenomena, and their symbolic origin is to some extent disputable.

§ 3. *Second principle*: *linear character of the signal*

The linguistic signal, being auditory in nature, has a temporal aspect, and hence certain temporal characteristics: (a) *it occupies a certain temporal space*, and (b) *this space is measured in just one dimension*: it is a line.

This principle is obvious, but it seems never to be stated, doubtless because it is considered too elementary. However, it is a fundamental principle and its consequences are incalculable. Its importance equals that of the first law. The whole mechanism of linguistic structure depends upon it. Unlike visual signals (e.g. ships' flags) which can exploit more than one dimension simultaneously, auditory signals have available to them only the linearity of time. The elements of such signals are presented one after another: they form a chain. This feature appears immediately when they are represented in writing, and a spatial line of graphic signs is substituted for a succession of sounds in time.

In certain cases, this may not be easy to appreciate. For example, if I stress a certain syllable, it may seem that I am presenting a number of significant features simultaneously. But that is an illusion. The syllable and its accentuation constitute a single act of phonation. There is no duality within this act, although there are various contrasts with what precedes and follows.

CHAPTER II   Invariability and Variability of the Sign

§ 1. *Invariability*

The signal, in relation to the idea it represents, may seem to be freely chosen. However, from the point of view of the linguistic community, the signal is imposed rather than freely chosen. Speakers are not consulted about its choice. Once the language has selected a signal, it cannot be freely replaced by any other. There appears to be something rather contradictory about this. It is a kind of linguistic Hobson's choice. What can be chosen is already determined in advance. No individual is able, even if he wished, to modify in any way a choice already established in the language. Nor can the linguistic community exercise its authority to change even a single word.① The community, as much as the individual, is bound to its language.

A language cannot therefore be treated simply as a form of contract, and the linguistic sign is a particularly interesting phenomenon to study for this reason. For if we wish to demonstrate that the rules a community accepts are imposed upon it, and not freely agreed to, it is a language which offers the most striking proof.

Let us now examine how the linguistic sign eludes the control of our will. We shall then be able to see the important consequences which follow from this fact.

At any given period, however far back in time we go, a language is always an inheritance form the past. The initial assignment of names to things, establishing a contract between concepts and sound patterns, is an act we can conceive in the imagination, but no one has ever observed it taking place. The idea that it might have happened is suggested to us by our keen awareness of the arbitrary nature of the linguistic sign.

In fact, no society has ever known its language to be anything other than something inherited from previous generations, which it has no choice but to accept. That is why the question of the origins of language does not have the importance generally attributed to it. It is not even a relevant question as far as linguistics is concerned. The sole object of study in linguistics is the normal, regular existence of a language already established. Any given linguistic state is always the product of historical factors, and these are the factors which explain why the linguistic sign is invariable, that is to say why it is immune from arbitrary alteration.②

But to say that a language is an inheritance from the past explains nothing unless we take the question further. Is it not possible from time to time to change established laws which have been handed down from the past?

This question leads us to consider a language in its social context and to pursue our enquiry in the same terms as for any other social institution. How are social institutions handed down from generation to generation? This is the more general question which subsumes the question of invariability. It is first necessary to realise the different degrees of freedom enjoyed by other institutions. Each of them, it will be seen, achieves a different balance between the tradition handed down and society's freedom of action. The next question will be to discover why, in any given case, factors of one kind are more powerful or less powerful than factors of the other kind. Finally, reverting to linguistic matters in particular, it may then be asked why historical transmission is the overriding factor, to the point of excluding the possibility of any general or sudden linguistic change.

The answer to this question must take many considerations into account. It is relevant to point

---

① This is not a denial of the possibility of linguistic legislation, nor even of its potential effectiveness. What Saussure denies is that the collective ratification required is a matter for collective decision. It may be illegal for trade purposes to call Spanish sparkling wine 'champagne'; but that will be merely one external factor bearing on speech (*parole*), which may or may not ultimately affect the word *champagne* as a linguistic sign. (Translator's note)

② For Saussure's generation, questions of language planning had not acquired the importance they have today. Although criticism of commonly accepted linguistic forms of expression has a long history in the Western tradition, only small minorities of thinkers, teachers and writers had ever concerned themselves with such matters. (Translator's note) out, for example, that linguistic changes do not correspond to generations of speakers. There is no vertical structure of layers one above the other like drawers in a piece of furniture; people of all ages intermingle and communicate with one another. The continuous efforts required in order to learn one's native language point to the impossibility of any radical change. In addition, people use their language without conscious reflexion, being largely unaware of the laws which govern it. If they are not aware of these laws, how can they act to change them? In any case, linguistic facts are rarely the object of criticism, every society being usually content with the language it has inherited.

These considerations are important, but they are not directly to the point. Priority must be given to the following, which are more essential, more immediately relevant, and underlie all the rest.

1. *The arbitrary nature of the linguistic sign.* The arbitrary nature of the linguistic sign was adduced above as a reason for conceding the theoretical possibility of linguistic change. But more detailed consideration reveals that this very same factor tends to protect a language against any attempt to change it. It means that there is no issue for the community of language users to discuss, even were they sufficiently aware to do so. For in order to discuss an issue, there must be some reasonable basis for discussion. One can, for example, argue about whether monogamy is better than polygamy, and adduce reasons for and against. One could likewise discuss the pros and cons of a system of symbols, because a symbol has a rational connexion with what it symbolizes. But for a language, as a system of arbitrary signs, any such basis is lacking, and consequently there is no firm ground for discussion. No reason can be given for preferring *soeur* to *sister*, *Ochs* to *boeuf*, etc.①

2. *The great number of signs necessary to constitute a language.* The implications of this fact are considerable. A system of writing, comprising between 20 and 40 letters, might conceivably be replaced in its entirety by an alternative system. The same would be true of a language if it comprised only a limited number of elements. But the inventory of signs in any language is countless.

3. *The complex character of the system.* A language constitutes a system. In this respect, it is not entirely arbitrary, for the system has a certain rationality. But precisely for this reason, the community is unable to change it at will. For the linguistic system is a complex mechanism. Its workings cannot be grasped without reflexion. Even speakers who use it daily may be quite ignorant in this regard. Any such change would require the intervention of specialists, grammarians, logicians, and others. But history shows that interference by experts is of no avail in linguistic matters.

4. *Collective inertia resists all linguistic innovations.* We come now to a consideration which takes precedence over all others. At any time a language belongs to all its users. It is a facility unrestrictedly available throughout a whole community. It is something all make use of every day. In this respect it is quite unlike other social institutions. Legal procedures, religious rites, ships' flags, etc. are systems used only by a certain number of individuals acting together and for a limited time. A language, on the contrary, is something in which everyone participates all the time, and that is why it is constantly open to the influence of all. This key fact is by itself sufficient to explain why a

---

① Saussure's general point here is confirmed by the fact that current debates about for instance, whether 'sexist' terms (such as *chairman*) should be replaced by unbiassed terms (e.g. *chairperson*) arise only when a reason *can* be given for preferring one to the other. But in such cases the reason given is usually social or political, rather than linguistic. (Translator's note)

linguistic revolution is impossible. Of all social institutions, a language affords the least scope for such enterprise. It is part and parcel of the life of the whole community, and the community's natural inertia exercises a conservative influence upon it.

None the less, to say that a language is a product of social forces does not automatically explain why it comes to be constrained in the way it is. Bearing in mind that a language is always an inheritance from the past, one must add that the social forces in question act over a period of time. If stability is a characteristic of languages, it is not only because languages are anchored in the community. They are also anchored in time. The two facts are inseparable. Continuity with the past constantly restricts freedom of choice. If the Frenchman of today uses words like *homme* ('man') and *chien* ('dog'), it is because these words were used by his forefathers. Ultimately there is a connexion between these two opposing factors: the arbitrary convention which allows free choice, and the passage of time, which fixes that choice. It is because the linguistic sign is arbitrary that it knows no other law than that of tradition, and because it is founded upon tradition that it can be arbitrary.[①]

§ 2. *Variability*

The passage of time, which ensures the continuity of a language, also has another effect, which appears to work in the opposite direction. It allows linguistic signs to be changed with some rapidity. Hence variability and invariability are both, in a certain sense, characteristic of the linguistic sign.[②]

In the final analysis, these two characteristics are intimately connected. The sign is subject to change because it continues through time. But what predominates in any change is the survival of earlier material. Infidelity to the past is only relative. That is how it comes about that the principle of change is based upon the principle of continuity.

Change through time takes various forms, each of which would supply the subject matter for an important chapter of linguistics. Without going into detail here, it is important to bring out the following points.

First of all, let there be no misunderstanding about the sense in which we are speaking of change. It must not be thought that we are referring particularly to phonetic changes affecting the signal, or to changes of meaning affecting the concept signified. Either view would be inadequate. Whatever the factors involved in change, whether they act in isolation or in combination, they always result in *a shift in the relationship between signal and signification.*

---

① The epigrammatic concision of this summary of the connexion between the nature of the linguistic sign and its socio-historical role epitomises Saussure's brilliance as a linguistic theorist. It was not until half a century after his death that detailed socio-linguistic investigations began to provide in abundance the kind of evidence which would corroborate the connexion Saussure here postulates. What is ironical is that the evidence in question was often interpreted as throwing doubt upon the validity or adequacy of a Saussurean approach to the study of language. What is perhaps even more ironical is that the Saussurean implications of a reciprocal limitation between choice and tradition remained largely unexplored as a result. (Translator's note)

② It would be a mistake to criticise Saussure for being illogical or paradoxical in assigning two contradictory characteristics to the linguistic sign. The striking contrast between these terms is intended simply to emphasise the fact that a language changes even though its speakers are incapable of changing it. One might also say that it is impervious to interference although open to development. (Editorial note)

As examples, one might cite the following. The Latin word *necāre* meaning 'to kill' became in French *noyer* meaning 'to drown'. Here the sound pattern and the concept have both changed. It is pointless to separate one aspect of the change from the other. Tt suffices to note as a single fact that the connexion between sound and idea has changed. The original relationship no longer holds. If instead of comparing Latin *necāre* with French *noyer*, one contrasts it with Vulgar Latin *necare* of the fourth or fifth century, meaning 'to drown', the case is somewhat different. But even here, although the signal has undergone no appreciable change, there is a shift in the relationship between the idea and the sign.[①]

The Old German word *dritteil* meaning 'a third' became in modern German *Drittel*. In this case, although the concept has remained the same, the relationship has changed in two ways. The signal has altered not only phonetically but also grammatically. We no longer recognise it as a combination including the unit *Teil* meaning 'part': Instead, it has become a single unanalysable word. That counts too as a change in relationship.

In Anglo-Saxon, the preliterary form *fōt* meaning 'foot' remained as *fōt* (modern English *foot*), while its plural *\*fōti*, meaning 'feet', became *fēt* (modern English *feet*). Whatever changes may have been involved here, one thing is certain: a shift in the relationship occurred. New correlations between phonic substance and idea emerged.

A language is a system which is intrinsically defenceless against the factors which constantly tend to shift relationships between signal and signification. This is one of the consequences of the arbitrary nature of the linguistic sign.

Other human institutions—customs, laws, etc. —are all based in varying degrees on natural connexions between things. They exhibit a necessary conformity between ends and means. Even the fashion which determines the way we dress is not entirely arbitrary. It cannot depart beyond a certain point from requirements dictated by the human body. A language, on tile contrary, is in no way limited in its choice of means. For there is nothing at all to prevent the association of any idea whatsoever with any sequence of sounds whatsoever.

In order to emphasise that a language is nothing other than a social institution, Whitney quite rightly insisted upon the arbitrary character of linguistic signs. In so doing, he pointed linguistics in the right direction. But he did not go far enough. For he failed to see that this arbitrary character fundamentally distinguishes languages from all other institutions. This can be seen in the way in which a language evolves. The process is highly complex. A language is situated socially and chronologically by reference to a certain community and a certain period of time. No one can alter it in any particular. On the other hand, the fact that its signs are arbitrary implies theoretically a freedom to establish any connexion whatsoever between sounds and ideas. The result is that each of the two elements joined together in the linguistic sign retains its own independence to an unparalleled extent. Consequently a language alters, or rather evolves, under the influence of all factors which may affect either sounds or meanings. Evolution is inevitable: there is no known example of a language immune from it. After a certain time, changes can always be seen to have taken place.

This principle must even apply to artificial languages. Anyone who invents an artificial language

---

① In the interests of terminological consistency, the term *sign* should here be replaced by *signal*. (Translator's note)

retains control of it only as long as it is not in use. But as soon as it fulfils its purpose and becomes the property of the community, it is no longer under control. Esperanto is a case in point. If it succeeds as a language, can it possibly escape the same fate? Once launched, the language will in all probability begin to lead a semiological life of its own. Its transmission will follow laws which have nothing in common with those of deliberate creation, and it will then be impossible to turn the clock back. Anyone who thinks he can construct a language not subject to change, which posterity must accept as it is, would be like a hen hatching a duck's egg. The language he created would be subject to the same forces of change as any other language, regardless of its creator's wishes.

The continuity of signs through time, involving as it does their alteration in time. is a principle of general semiology. This principle is confirmed by systems of writing, by deaf-and-dumb languages, and so on.

But on what is the necessity for change based? We may perhaps be criticised for not being as explicit upon this point as upon the principle of invariability. The reason is that we have not gone into the different factors involved in change. A great variety of such factors must be taken into account in order to determine to what extent change is a necessity.

The causes of linguistic continuity are in principle available to observation. The same is not true of the causes of change through time. That is why in the first instance it would be misleading to attempt to identify them precisely. It is more prudent to speak in general terms of shifts in relations. For time changes everything. There is no reason why languages should be exempt from this universal law.

The argument advanced so far, based on the principles established in the introduction, may be summarised as follows.

1.Avoiding the sterility of merely verbal definitions, we began by distinguishing, within the global phenomenon of *language*, between *linguistic structure* and *speech*. Linguistic structure we take to be language minus speech. It is the whole set of linguistic habits which enables the speaker to understand and to make himself understood.

2.But this definition fails to relate linguistic structure to social reality. It is a definition which misrepresents what a language is, because it takes into account only how the individual is affected. But in order to have a language, there must be a *community of speakers*. Contrary to what might appear to be the case, a language never exists even for a moment except as a social fact, for it is a semiological phenomenon. Its social nature is one of its internal characteristics. A full definition must recognise two inseparable things, as shown in the following diagram:

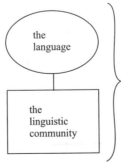

But even then there is something missing. The language thus represented is a viable system, but not a living one. It is a social reality, but not a historical fact.

3.Since the linguistic sign is arbitrary, a language as so far defined would appear to be an adaptable system, which can be organised in any way one likes, and is based solely upon a principle of rationality. Its social nature, as such, is not incompatible with this view. Social psychology, doubtless, must operate on more than a purely logical basis: account must be taken of everything which might affect the operation of reason in practical relations between one individual and another. But that is not the objection to regarding a language as a mere convention, which can be modified to suit the interests of those involved. There is something else. We must consider what is brought about by the passage of time, as well as what is brought about by the forces of social integration. Without taking into account the contribution of time, our grasp of linguistic reality remains incomplete.

If a language were considered in a chronological perspective, but ignoring the social dimension (as in the case of a hypothetical individual living in isolation for hundreds of years), there might perhaps be no change to observe. Time would leave no mark upon the language. On the other hand, if one looked at the community of speakers without taking the passage of time into account, one would not see the effect of social fotces acting upon the language. In order to come to terms with reality, therefore, one must supplement our first diagram by some indication of the passage of time:

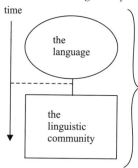

When this is taken into account, the language is no longer free from constraints, because the passage of time allows social forces to be brought to bear upon it. One is left with a principle of continuity which precludes freedom of choice. At the same time, continuity necessarily implies change. Relations will alter in some respect or other.

(*Course in General Linguistics.* London: G. Duckworth, 1983)

译文：

# 一般原则

高名凯,译

第一章　语言符号的性质

§1. 符号、所指、能指

在有些人看来,语言,归结到它的基本原则,不外是一种分类命名集,即一份跟同样多的事物相当的名词术语表。例如:

这种观念有好些方面要受到批评。它假定有现成的、先于词而存在的概念。它没有告诉我们名称按本质来说是声音的还是心理的，因为 arbor"树"可以从这一方面考虑，也可以从那一方面考虑。最后，它会使人想到名称和事物的联系是一种非常简单的作业，而事实上决不是这样。但是这种天真的看法却可以使我们接近真理，它向我们表明语言单位是一种由两项要素联合构成的双重的东西。

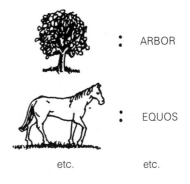

我们在前面谈论言语循环时已经看到，语言符号所包含的两项要素都是心理的，而且由联想的纽带连接在我们的脑子里。我们要强调这一点。

语言符号连结的不是事物和名称，而是概念和音响形象①。后者不是物质的声音，纯粹物理的东西，而是这声音的心理印迹，我们的感觉给我们证明的声音表象。它是属于感觉的，我们有时把它叫做"物质的"，那只是在这个意义上说的，而且是跟联想的另一个要素，一般更抽象的概念相对立而言的。

我们试观察一下自己的言语活动，就可以清楚地看到音响形象的心理性质：我们不动嘴唇，也不动舌头，就能自言自语，或在心时默念一首诗。那是因为语言中的词对我们来说都是一些音响形象，我们必须避免说到构成词的"音位"。"音位"这个术语含有声音动作的观念，只适用于口说的词，适用于内部形象在话语中的实现。我们说到一个词的声音和音节的时候，只要记住那是指的音响形象，就可以避免这种误会。

因此语言符号是一种两面的心理实体，我们可以用图表示如下：

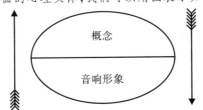

这两个要素是紧密相连而且彼此呼应的。很明显，我们无论是要找出拉丁语 arbor 这个词的意义，还是拉丁语用来表示"树"这个概念的词，都会觉得只有那语言所认定的连接才是符合实际的，并把我们所能想象的其他任何连接都抛在一边。

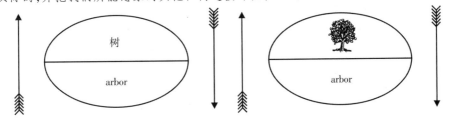

这个定义提出了一个有关术语的重要问题。我们把概念和音响形象的结合叫做符号，

---

①　音响形象这个术语看来也许过于狭隘，因为一个词除了它的声音表象以外，还有它的发音表象，发音行为的肌动形象。但是在德·索绪尔看来，语言主要是一个贮藏所，一种从外面接受过来的东西。音响形象作为在一切言语实现之外的潜在的语言事实，就是词的最好不过的自然表象。所以动觉方面可以是不言而喻的，或者无论如何跟音响形象比较起来只占从属的地位。——原编者注

但是在日常使用上,这个术语一般只指音响形象,例如指词(arbor 等等)。人们容易忘记,arbor 之所以被称为符号,只是因为它带有"树"的概念,结果让感觉部分的观念包含了整体观念。

如果我们用一些彼此呼应同时又互相对立的名称来表示这三个概念,那么歧义就可以消除。我们建议保留用符号这个词表示整体,用所指和能指分别代替概念和音响形象。后两个术语的好处是既能表明它们彼此间的对立,又能表明它们和它们所从属的整体间的对立。至于符号,如果我们认为可以满意,那是因为我们不知道该用什么去代替,日常用语没有提出任何别的术语。

这样确定的语言符号有两个头等重要的特征。我们在陈述这些特征的时候将同时提出整个这类研究的基本原则。

§2.第一个原则:符号的任意性

能指和所指的联系是任意的,或者,因为我们所说的符号是指能指和所指相联结所产生的整体,我们可以更简单地说:语言符号是任意的。

例如"姊妹"的观念在法语里同用来做它的能指的 s-ö-r(soeur)这串声音没有任何内在的关系;它也可以用任何别的声音来表示。语言间的差别和不同语言的存在就是证明:"牛"这个所指的能指在国界的一边是 b-ö-f(bœuf),另一边却是 o-k-s(Ochs)①。

符号的任意性原则没有人反对。但是发现真理往往比为这真理派定一个适当的地位来得容易。上面所说的这个原则支配着整个语言的语言学,它的后果是不胜枚举的。诚然,这些后果不是一下子就能看得同样清楚的;人们经过许多周折才发现它们,同时也发现了这个原则是头等重要的。

顺便指出:等到符号学将来建立起来的时候,它将会提出这样一个问题:那些以完全自然的符号为基础的表达方式——例如哑剧——是否属于它管辖范围②。假定它接纳这些自然的符号,它的主要对象仍然是以符号任意性为基础的全体系统。事实上,一个社会所接受的任何表达手段,原则上都是以集体习惯,或者同样可以说,以约定俗成为基础的。例如那些往往带有某种自然表情的礼节符号(试想一想汉人从前用三跪九叩拜见他们的皇帝)也仍然是依照一种规矩给定下来的。强制使用礼节符号的正是这种规矩,而不是符号的内在价值。所以我们可以说,完全任意的符号比其他符号更能实现符号方式的理想;这就是为什么语言这种最复杂、最广泛的表达系统,同时也是最富有特点的表达系统。正是在这个意义上,语言学可以成为整个符号学中的典范,尽管语言也不过是一种特殊的系统。

曾有人用象征一词来指语言符号,或者更确切地说,来指我们叫做能指的东西③。我们不便接受这个词,恰恰就是由于我们的第一个原则。象征的特点是:它永远不是完全任意的;它不是空洞的;它在能指和所指之间有一点自然联系的根基。象征法律的天平就不能随便用什么东西,例如用一辆车,来代替。

任意性这个词还要加上一个注解。它不应该使人想起能指完全取决于说话者的自由选择(我们在下面将可以看到,一个符号在语言集体中确立后,个人是不能对它有任何改变的)。我们的意思是说,它是不可论证的,即对现实中跟它没有任何自然联系的所指来说是任意的。

---

① 法语管"牛"叫 bœuf[bœf],德语管"牛"叫 Ochs[ɔks]。——校注

② 这里暗指冯德(Wundt)认为语言的声音表情动作出于自然的哑剧运动,参看他所著的《民族心理学》第一编《语言》。——校注

③ 这里特别指德国哲学家卡西勒尔(Cassirer)在《象征形式的哲学》中的观点。他把象征也看作一种符号,忽视了符号的特征。德·索绪尔认为象征和符号有明显的差别。——校注

最后,我们想指出,对这第一个原则的建立可有两种反对意见:

(1)人们可能以拟声词为依据认为能指的选择并不都是任意的。但拟声词从来不是语言系统的有机成分,而且它们的数量比人们所设想的少得多。有些词,例如法语的 fouet"鞭子"或 glas"丧钟"可能以一种富有暗示的音响刺激某些人的耳朵;但是如果我们追溯到它们的拉丁语形式(fouet 来自 fāgus"山毛榉",glas 来自 classicum"一种喇叭的声音")[①],就足以看出它们原来并没有这种特征。它们当前的声音性质,或者毋宁说,人们赋予它们的性质,其实是语音演变的一种偶然的结果。

至于真正的拟声词(像 glou-glou"火鸡的叫声或液体由瓶口流出的声音",tic-tac"嘀嗒"等等),不仅为数甚少,而且它们的选择在某种程度上已经就是任意的,因为它们只是某些声音的近似的、而且有一半已经是约定俗成的模仿(试比较法语的 ouaoua 和德语的 wauwau"汪汪"(狗吠声)。此外,它们一旦被引进语言,就或多或少要卷入其他的词所经受的语音演变,形态演变等等的旋涡(试比较 pigeon"鸽子",来自民间拉丁语的 pipiō,后者是由一个拟声词派生的):这显然可以证明,它们已经丧失了它们原有的某些特性,披上了一般语言符号的不可论证的特征。

(2)感叹词很接近于拟声词,也会引起同样的反对意见,但是对于我们的论断并不更为危险。有人想把感叹词看作据说是出乎自然的对现实的自发表达。但是对其中的大多数来说,我们可以否认在所指和能指之间有必然的联系。在这一方面,我们试把两种语言比较一下,就足以看到这些表达是多么彼此不同(例如德语的 au!"唉!"和法语的 aïe! 相当)。此外,我们知道,有许多感叹词起初都是一些有确定意义的词(试比较法语的 diable! (鬼 =)"见鬼!"mordieu!"天哪"! =mort Dieu"上帝的死",等等)。

总而言之,拟声词和感叹词都是次要的,认为它们源出于象征,有一部分是可以争论的。

## §3.第二个原则:能指的线条特征

能指属听觉性质,只在时间上展开,而且具有借自时间的特征:(a)它体现一个长度,(b)这长度只能在一个向度上测定:它是一条线。

这个原则是显而易见的,但似乎常为人所忽略,无疑是因为大家觉得太简单了。然而这是一个基本原则,它的后果是数之不尽的;它的重要性与第一条规律不相上下。语言的整个机构都取决于它。它跟视觉的能指(航海信号等等)相反:视觉的能指可以在几个向度上同时迸发,而听觉的能指却只有时间上的一条线;它的要素相继出现,构成一个链条。我们只要用文字把它们表示出来,用书写符号的空间线条代替时间上的前后相继,这个特征就马上可以看到。

在某些情况下,这表现得不很清楚。例如我用重音发出一个音节,那似乎是把不止一个有意义的要素结集在同一点上。但这只是一种错觉。音节和它的重音只构成一个发音行为,在这行为内部并没有什么二重性,而只有和相邻要素的各种对立。

## 第二章　符号的不变性和可变性

### §1.不变性

能指对它所表示的观念来说,看来是自由选择的,相反,对使用它的语言社会来说,却不是自由的,而是强制的。语言并不同社会大众商量,它所选择的能指不能用另外一个来代替。

---

[①] 现代法语的 fouet"鞭子"是古代法语 fou 的指小词,后者来自拉丁语的 fāgus"山毛榉":glas"丧钟"来自民间拉丁语的 classum,古典拉丁语的 classicum"一种喇叭的声音",c 在 l 之前变成了浊音。——校注

这一事实似乎包含着一种矛盾,我们可以通俗地叫做"强制的牌"①。人们对语言说:"您选择罢!"但是随即加上一句:"您必须选择这个符号,不能选择别的。"已经选定的东西,不但个人即使想改变也不能丝毫有所改变,就是大众也不能对任何一个词行使它的主权;不管语言是什么样子,大众都得同它捆绑在一起。

因此语言不能同单纯的契约相提并论;正是在这一方面,语言符号研究起来特别有趣;因为如果我们想要证明一个集体所承认的法律是人们必须服从的东西,而不是一种可以随便同意或不同意的规则,那么语言就是最明显的证据。

所以首先让我们来看看语言符号怎样不受意志的管束,然后引出这种现象所产生的严重后果。

在任何时代,哪怕追溯到最古的时代,语言看来都是前一时代的遗产。人们什么时候把名称分派给事物,就在概念和音响形象之间订立了一种契约——这种行为是可以设想的,但是从来没有得到证实。我们对符号的任意性有一种非常敏锐的感觉,这使我们想到事情可能是这样。

事实上任何社会,现在或过去,都只知道语言是从前代继承来的产物而照样加以接受。因此,语言起源的问题并不像人们一般认为的那么重要。它甚至不是一个值得提出的问题②。语言学的唯一的真正的对象是一种已经构成的语言的正常的、有规律的生命。一定的语言状态始终是历史因素的产物。正是这些因素可以解释符号为什么是不变的,即拒绝一切任意的代替。

但是仅仅说语言是一种遗产,如果不更进一步进行考察,那么问题也解释不了。我们不是随时可以改变一些现存的和继承下来的法律吗?

这种反驳使我们不能不把语言放到它的社会环境里去考察,并像对待其他社会制度一样去提出问题。其他社会制度是怎样流传下来的呢?这是一个包含着不变性问题的更一般的问题。我们首先必须评定其他制度所享受的或大或小的自由;可以看到,对其中任何一种来说,在强制的传统和社会的自由行动之间各有一种不同的平衡。其次,我们要探究,在某类制度里,为什么头一类因素会比另一类因素强些或弱些。最后再回到语言,我们不禁要问为什么累代相传的历史因素完全支配着语言,排除任何一般的和突如其来的变化。

为了回答这个问题,我们可以提出许多论据。比方说语言的变化同世代的交替没有联系③,因为世代并不像家具的抽屉那样一层叠着一层,而是互相混杂,互相渗透,而且每一世代都包含着各种年龄的人。我们也可以考虑一下一个人学会自己的母语需要花多大的力气,从而断定全面的变化是不可能的。此外,我们还可以再加上一句:语言的实践不需要深思熟虑,说话者在很大程度上并不意识到语言的规律,他们既不知道,又怎能改变呢?即使意识到,我们也不应该忘记,语言事实差不多不致引起批评,因为任何民族一般都满意于它所接受的语言。

这些考虑很重要,但不切题。我们在下面将提出一些更主要、更直接的考虑,其他一切考虑都取决于它们:

---

① "强制的牌(la carte forcée)"是变戏法的人使用的一种障眼术:他在洗牌的时候私下把一张牌夹在一副纸牌里让人家挑选,但是说,"你必须选择这张牌,不能选择别的。"——校注

② 语言起源的问题是十八世纪欧洲各派学者最喜欢讨论的问题,从十九世纪起,许多语言学家由于一种实证主义精神的激发,往往拒绝讨论这个问题,尤以法国语言学家表现得最为突出。德·索绪尔正是在这种精神的影响下提出这个问题的。——校注

③ 十九世纪八十年代,欧洲有些语言学家如洛伊德(Lloyd)和皮平(Pipping)等认为语音的自发变化是由儿童和成年人发同一个音有差别引起的。德·索绪尔在这里不同意他们的这种"世代理论"。——校注

(1) 符号的任意性。在上面,符号的任意性使我们不能不承认语言的变化在理论上是可能的;深入一步,我们却可以看到,符号的任意性本身实际上使语言避开一切旨在使它发生变化的尝试。大众即使比实际上更加自觉,也不知道怎样去讨论。因为要讨论一件事情,必须以合理的规范为基础。例如我们可以辩论一夫一妻制的婚姻形式是否比一夫多妻制的形式更为合理,并提出赞成这种或那种形式的理由。我们也可以讨论象征系统,因为象征同它所指的事物之间有一种合理的关系。但是对语言——任意的符号系统——来说,却缺少这种基础,因此也就没有任何进行讨论的牢固的基地。为什么要用 sœur 而不用 sister,用 Ochs 而不用 bœuf① 等等,那是没有什么道理可说的。

(2) 构成任何语言都必须有大量的符号。这一事实的涉及面很宽。一个文字体系只有二十至四十个字母,必要时可以用另一个体系来代替。如果语言只有为数有限的要素,情况也是这样;但语言的符号却是数不胜数的。

(3) 系统的性质太复杂。一种语言就构成一个系统。我们将可以看到,在这一方面,语言不是完全任意的,而且里面有相对的道理,同时,也正是在这一点上表现出大众不能改变语言。因为这个系统是一种很复杂的机构,人们要经过深切思考才能掌握,甚至每天使用语言的人对它也很茫然。人们要经过专家、语法学家、逻辑学家等等的参与才能对某一变化有所理解;但是经验表明,直到现在,这种性质的参与并没有获得成功。

(4) 集体惰性对一切语言创新的抗拒。这点超出了其他的任何考虑。语言无论什么时候都是每个人的事情;它流行于大众之中,为大众所运用,所有的人整天都在使用着它。在这一点上,我们没法把它跟其他制度作任何比较。法典的条款,宗教的仪式,以及航海信号等等,在一定的时间内,每次只跟一定数目的人打交道,相反,语言却是每个人每时都在里面参与其事的,因此它不停地受到大伙儿的影响。这一首要事实已足以说明要对它进行革命是不可能的。在一切社会制度中,语言是最不适宜于创制的。它同社会大众的生活结成一体,而后者在本质上是惰性的,看来首先就是一种保守的因素。

然而,说语言是社会力量的产物还不足以使人看清它不是自由的。回想语言始终是前一时代的遗产,我们还得补充一句:这些社会力量是因时间而起作用的。语言之所以有稳固的性质,不仅是因为它被绑在集体的镇石上,而且因为它是处在时间之中。这两件事是分不开的。无论什么时候,跟过去有连带关系就会对选择的自由有所妨碍。我们现在说 homme“人”和 chien“狗”,因为在我们之前人们就已经说 homme 和 chien。这并不妨碍在整个现象中两个互相抵触的因素之间有一种联系:一个是使选择得以自由的任意的约定俗成,另一个是使选择成为固定的时间。因为符号是任意的,所以它除了传统的规律之外不知道有别的规律;因为它是建立在传统的基础上的,所以它可能是任意的。

§2.可变性

时间保证语言的连续性,同时又有一个从表面看来好像是跟前一个相矛盾的效果,就是使语言符号或快或慢发生变化的效果;因此,在某种意义上,我们可以同时说到符号的不变性和可变性②。

最后分析起来,这两件事是有连带关系的:符号正因为是连续的,所以总是处在变化的状

---

① Sœur 是法语的词,sister 是英语的词,都是“姊妹”的意思;Ochs 是德语的词,bœuf 是法语的词,都是“牛”的意思。——校注

② 责备德·索绪尔认为语言有两种互相矛盾的性质不合逻辑或似是而非,那是错误的。他只是想用两个引人注目的术语的对立着重表明这真理:语言发生变化,但是说话者不能使它发生变化。我们也可以说,语言是不可触动的,但不是不能改变的。——原编者注

态中。在整个变化中,总是旧有材料的保持占优势;对过去不忠实只是相对的。所以,变化的原则是建立在连续性原则的基础上的。

时间上的变化有各种不同的形式,每一种变化都可以写成语言学中很重要的一章。我们不作详细讨论,这里只说明其中几点重要的。

首先,我们不要误解这里所说的变化这个词的意义。它可能使人认为,那是特别指能指所受到的语音变化,或者所指的概念在意义上的变化。这种看法是不充分的。不管变化的因素是什么,孤立的还是结合的,结果都会导致所指和能指关系的转移。

试举几个例子。拉丁语的 necāre 原是"杀死"的意思,在法语变成了 noyer"溺死",它的意义是大家所知道的。音响形象和概念都起了变化。但是我们无须把这现象的两个部分区别开来,只从总的方面看到观念和符号的联系已经松懈,它们的关系有了转移也就够了①。如果我们不把古典拉丁语的 necāre 跟法语的 noyer 比较,而把它跟四世纪或五世纪民间拉丁语带有"溺死"意义的 necare 对比,那么,情况就有点不同。可是就在这里,尽管能指方面没有什么显著的变化,但观念和符号的关系已有了转移②。

古代德语的 dritteil"三分之一"变成了现代德语的 Drittel。在这里,虽然概念还是一样,关系却起了两种变化:能指不只在它的物质方面有了改变,而且在它的语法形式方面也起了变化;它已不再含有 Teil"部分"的观念,变成了一个单纯词。不管是哪种变化,都是一种关系的转移。

在盎格鲁·撒克逊语里,文学语言以前的形式 fōt"脚"还是 fōt(现代英语 foot),而它的复数 *fōti 变成了 fēt(现代英语 feet)。不管那是什么样的变化,有一件事是确定的:关系有了转移。语言材料和观念之间出现了另一种对应。

语言根本无力抵抗那些随时促使所指和能指的关系发生转移的因素。这就是符号任意性的后果之一。

别的人文制度——习惯、法律等等——在不同的程度上都是以事物的自然关系为基础的;它们在所采用的手段和所追求的目的之间有一种必不可少的适应。甚至服装的时式也不是完全任意的:人们不能过分离开身材所规定的条件。相反,语言在选择它的手段方面却不受任何的限制,因为我们看不出有什么东西会妨碍我们把任何一个观念和任何一连串声音联结起来。

为了使人感到语言是一种纯粹的制度,辉特尼曾很正确地强调符号有任意的性质,从而把语言学置于它的真正的轴线上③。但是他没有贯彻到底,没有看到这种任意的性质把语言同其他一切制度从根本上分开。关于这点,我们试看看语言怎么发展就能一目了然。情况是最复杂不过的:一方面,语言处在大众之中,同时又处在时间之中,谁也不能对它有任何的改变;另一方面,语言符号的任意性在理论上又使人们在声音材料和观念之间有建立任何关系的自由。结果是,结合在符号中的这两个要素以绝无仅有的程度各自保持着自己的生命,而语言也就在一切可能达到它的声音或意义的动原的影响下变化着,或者毋宁说,发展着。这种发展是逃避不了的;我们找不到任何语言抗拒发展的例子。过了一定时间,我们常可以看到它已有了明显的转移。

---

① 在十九世纪末和二十世纪初,许多语言学家和心理学家,如德国的保罗和冯德,常把语言变化分为语音变化和意义变化两部分,并把它们对立起来。德·索绪尔在这里认为应该把两部分结合起来,考虑它们之间的关系。——校注

② 德·索绪尔在这期讲课里(1911 年 5 月至 7 月),常把"观念"和"符号"以及"所指"和"能指"这些术语交替运用,不加区别。——校注

③ 辉特尼的这一观点,见于他所著的《语言的生命和成长》。——校注

　　情况确实如此,这个原则甚至在人造语方面也可以得到验证。人造语只要还没有流行开,创制者还能把它控制在手里;但是一旦它要完成它的使命,成为每个人的东西,那就没法控制了。世界语就是一种这样的尝试①;假如它获得成功,它能逃避这种注定的规律吗? 过了头一段时期,这种语言很可能进入它的符号的生命,按照一些与经过深思熟虑创制出来的规律毫无共同之处的规律流传下去,再也拉不回来。想要制成一种不变的语言,让后代照原样接受过去的人,好像孵鸭蛋的母鸡一样:他所创制的语言,不管他愿意不愿意,终将被那席卷一切语言的潮流冲走。

　　符号在时间上的连续性与在时间上的变化相连,这就是普通符号学的一个原则;我们在文字的体系,聋哑人的言语活动等等中都可以得到验证。

　　但是变化的必然性是以什么为基础的呢? 人们也许会责备我们在这一点上没有说得像不变性的原则那么清楚。这是因为我们没有把变化的各种因素区别开来;只有考察了多种多样的因素,才能知道它们在什么程度上是必然的。

　　连续性的原因是观察者先验地看得到的,而语言随着时间起变化的原因却不是这样。我们不如暂时放弃对它作出确切的论述,而只限于一般地谈谈关系的转移。时间可以改变一切,我们没有理由认为语言会逃脱这一普遍的规律。

　　我们现在参照绪论中所确立的原则,把上面陈述的各个要点总括一下。

　　(1)我们避免下徒劳无益的词的定义,首先在言语活动所代表的整个现象中分出两个因素:语言和言语。在我们看来,语言就是言语活动减去言语。它是使一个人能够了解和被人了解的全部语言习惯。

　　(2)但是这个定义还是把语言留在它的社会现实性之外,使语言成了一种非现实的东西,因为它只包括现实性的一个方面,即个人的方面。要有语言,必须有说话的大众。在任何时候,同表面看来相反,语言都不能离开社会事实而存在,因为它是一种符号现象。它的社会性质就是它的内在的特性之一。要给语言下一个完备的定义,必须正视两样分不开的东西,如右图所示:

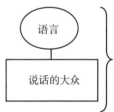

　　但是到了这一步,语言只是能活的东西,还不是活着的东西;我们只考虑了社会的现实性,而没有考虑历史事实。

　　(3)语言符号既然是任意的,这样下定义的语言看来就好像是一个单纯取决于理性原则的,自然而可以随意组织的系统。语言的社会性质,就其本身来说,并不与这种看法正面抵触。诚然,集体心理并不依靠纯粹逻辑的材料进行活动,我们必须考虑到人与人的实际关系中使理性屈服的一切因素。然而我们之所以不能把语言看作一种简单的、可以由当事人随意改变的规约,并不是因为这一点,而是同社会力量的作用结合在一起的时间的作用。离开了时间,语言现实性就不完备,任何结论都无法作出。

　　要是单从时间方面考虑语言,没有说话的大众——假设有一个人孤零零地活上几个世纪——那么我们也许看不到有什么变化;时间会对它不起作用。反过来,要是只考虑说话的

---

　　① 世界语(Esperanto)是波兰眼科医生柴门霍夫(Zamenhof)于1887年创制的一种人造语,只有二十八个字母,十六条语法规则,词根百分之七十五出自拉丁语,其余的出自日耳曼语和斯拉夫语,简单易学。这种语言自问世后曾引起许多语言学家的讨论。新语法学派奥斯特霍夫和勃鲁格曼于1876年曾撰《人造世界语批判》一书,对一般人造语持极端怀疑的态度。德·索绪尔在这里对世界语的评价,大致采取了其中的观点。但是拥护世界语的人,如波兰的博杜恩·德·库尔特内和法国的梅耶等,却认为这种人造语只是一种国际辅助语,不能代替自然语言,不必考虑它会发生什么样的变化。——校注

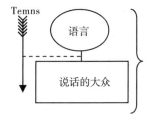

大众,没有时间,我们就将看不见社会力量对语言发生作用的效果。所以,要符合实际,我们必须在上图中添上一个标明时间进程的符号:(见右图)

这样一来,语言就不是自由的了,因为时间将使对语言起作用的社会力量可能发挥效力,而我们就达到了那把自由取消的连续性原则。但连续性必然隐含着变化,隐含着关系的不同程度的转移。

(节选自《普通语言学教程》,商务印书馆,2017)

## 【推荐阅读】

Noam Chomsky. Linguistics Then and Now: Some Personal Reflections [J]. Annual Review of Linguistics. 2021,7(1):1-12.

George Lakoff, Mark Johnson. Metaphors We Live by [M]. Chicago and London: University of Chicago Press, 1980

# 第八章 语言学和其他学科的关系

语言学是一门多边缘、多层次的立体性学科。它和文学、哲学、人类学、社会学、心理学等社会科学以及计算机等自然科学都有着紧密的联系。随着人类进入信息时代,语言学在整个信息处理技术上占有重要地位。语言学问题已成为当代哲学、心理学、数学、信息论、控制论、计算机科学不可缺少的研究课题,语言学的进展已成为心理学、人工智能、编译理论等取得突破的关键。

## 第一节 语言学和文学

语言学和文学作为独立的学科门类虽然研究对象和研究方法各异,两者之间却存在着千丝万缕的联系。

这一点首先可以从语言学发展的历史线条里追溯得到。无论是在西方还是东方,现代普通语言学在成为一门独立学科以前都曾经历过语文学的发展阶段,那时候还不存在现代意义上的语言学,对语言发生兴趣并对之进行研究的主要是哲学家、经学家或其他什么"家",研究的对象是记载典籍的书面语,任务主要是解释典籍的确切含义。这里的典籍里有很大一部分亦同是文学典籍,如中国的《诗经》、印度的《吠陀》、希伯来文化的《圣经》、希腊文化中的史诗等。这样的学问在古代中国被称为小学,在大多数欧洲语言里代表这一领域的是语文学,英文为 philology,法语和德语为 *philologie*。德语里的 *philologie* 就专指通过文学典籍对古代文化和文明的研究。这一术语的使用,很大程度上承认了作为科学的语言学与文学等人文研究之间的联系。

文学典籍虽然曾经是语文学的研究对象,为现代普通语言学的研究提供了素材,但长期以来西方教育对文学的偏向导致语言研究长期处于被统治的地位。在西方,从文艺复兴开始,直到近半个世纪以来自然科学在教育体系中崛起,语言的研究和教学都是出于对文学的考虑,拉丁语和古希腊语作为保存西方古代文学的主要文字在语言教学中长期占主导地位。在文学的统辖内即使存在部分语言研究,也仅限于文字。很多没有文字记载的民间故事、诗歌、民谣、叙事诗、神话等长期被排斥在文学范畴之外,当然就更谈不上语言研究了。

文学的统治地位以及对口头文学的忽视使语言研究的对象长久以来局限于书面语和文字,语法规则和语法体系主要以文学作品为蓝本提取,句子结构和词形的种类也就局限于书面语,方言和语音的研究一直未受重视。而一种语言的书面文字所代表的仅仅是众多方言中占主导地位的一种,很多被视为正统的方言里往往保留了一种语言过去的语法语音现象,如许多英语北方方言里就保存着第二人称代词所对应的动词词形曲折变化,学者也发现苏格兰方言还保存着元音后/r/,汉语的吴粤方言里存在许多入声字。这些已经消失在现行书面语里的语言现象也因为对方言口语的忽视而流落在语言研究的外围。

不过,中国文人历来十分关注语音。早在南北朝开始,学士骚人就开始关注音韵问题。首先是周隅对汉语语音的天然音调进行规范,沈约又将这些研究成果运用到诗歌创作中去,提出"四声八病"之说,开永明体之先,令声韵之道大行。"声病"之兴,固然在某种程度上束缚了当时的文章体格,对后来律诗发展的影响却也不可低估。后隋朝陆法言、颜之推、魏渊等人共商音韵,促成《切韵》一书,以成诗文楷式。此后历代均有韵书相传。这些韵书的出发点主要是教人辨音用韵,作文吟诗,同时也助人了解诗文,欣赏作品,可以说主要是为文学创作和文学鉴赏服务的。但是流传至今,记录了不同时期的汉语语音系统,对于探索汉语语音发展的历史和规律等都颇有帮助。尽管这些韵书尚无现代语言学的理论高度和系统性,仍可看作汉语语言学研究的重要文献,也从另一方面反映了语言学和文学之间密不可分的关系。

语言学,作为对语言进行科学研究的独立学科,其研究对象理所当然应当覆盖语言的各个方面。不论史前史后,文学作为呈现于所有文化中的语言运用的一种形式,包含了很多语言的独特用法,并形成了各种文体,是特定语言以及人类语言功能运用研究中非常重要而有价值的语言材料。

在所有文学种类里,无论是作者的写作技巧还是文学作品本身都在一定程度上取决于语言材料的独特应用,即特定语言的语音、语法、词汇构成或方言的穿插(如果作品中存在大量方言并构成某种语言风格)。一部文学作品的文学特性中语言要素的重要性因作品种类而异。欧洲文学中诗歌和演讲散文就比叙事散文和记史散文更依赖于语言本身;在诗歌里面,抒情诗对语言本身的依赖性又比叙事诗和戏剧作品中的诗歌更强。相对于语言外的因素,文学作品的文学特质在多大程度上取决于语言材料本身,从作品的翻译难度中可窥见一二。在所有文学作品中,语言层面对于作品都具有美学利用价值,但是在部分几乎无法翻译的作品里,如中国的唐诗,语言形式本身就是作品特定体裁及美学价值的重要成分。因为不同的语言具有不同的表音表意特征,一旦作品形式所依赖的语言特征改变,作品本身的体式也就难以保存。在拉丁文学古典时期,拉丁文诗人继承了希腊诗歌中的格律(metre),在用拉丁语进行诗歌创作时必须遵守希腊语的某些创作规则。即使是拉丁文学最伟大的挽歌作者奥维德(Ovid)的挽歌对句,也不得不严格遵守诗歌中长短音节的排位顺序。尽管拉丁语和希腊文在用韵上有相似之处,用拉丁语取代希腊语创作诗歌时要保存希腊语诗歌神韵和精髓还是颇有难度。这也说明拉丁诗人作为希腊诗歌的继承者,把希腊语的语言特征视为足以影响诗歌艺术性的最为重要的因素。

不同语言统辖下相关文体的差异很多都可以从语言的差异中找到原因。拉丁语、希腊语、英语和法语虽同属印欧语系,表现韵律的方式却不尽相同。相对法语诗歌,英语诗歌整体来说更少押韵,希腊罗马文学古典时期的诗歌也基本不押韵。这是因为英语的韵律通过重读音节和非重读音节的相间来体现,而古希腊语和拉丁语诗歌的韵律不重押韵,重长短音,主要通过长音节和短音节的相间来表现诗歌的节奏和韵律。法语的韵则是以音节为单位,诗歌中重读长短音的区别相比英语和拉丁语而言不是很明显。分析语言的重读和音节长短等特征本是语言学家的任务,随着这种对语言音节构词规律、语法和搭配模型的分析、比较和多角度的考察,很多文学家们不知不觉也卷入对文学艺术中语言成分的思考中。

任何伟大艺术家的直觉都需借助媒介来表达,不论这种媒介是青铜、大理石、颜料、音乐还是语言。语言作为文学的媒介其本身的特质对文学作品创作者有一定的强制力,而文学的创作才能很大一部分在于抓住语言本身内在的特性并以此为手段将作品构筑其间。文学家本身不必是语言学家,不需要详细研究自己语言的结构。语言学家的任务则在于运用语言学的独特研究方法,分析语言的形式和结构,明晰其特征,并揭示出语言特征对文学特质的相关性和重要性。文学作品与语言的相关性是可供语言学和文学共同研究的领域。在这过程中,语言学家运用语言学的研究方法深入特定的语言材料可以进一步加深人们对不同文体的认识,也使文学艺术家对语言的运用得到更清晰的阐释。虽然这方面的研究尚未完全,但从语言学和文学的渊源和内在联系中可以看到合作的必要性和可能性。

# 第二节　语言学和哲学

　　语言和哲学的联系也由来已久。在中国古代的哲学典籍中,不乏关于语言的讨论。有学者认为,中国古代哲学一开始就采取蔑视和放弃语言的态度,具有明显的反语言学倾向。[①] 比如老子说"道可道,非常道;名可名,非常名"(《道德经》第一章),庄子说"言者所以在意,得意而忘言"(《庄子·外物》)都表现出对语言可靠性的质疑。实际上,换个角度来看,中国哲学非但不排斥语言问题,反而高度重视语言问题。从先秦的"名实之辨",到孔子"正名",甚至到老庄对语言的怀疑,都表现了对语言问题的高度重视。

　　在西方,语言研究尤其是语义和语法问题的研究,早在古希腊时期就已经和哲学研究结缘。有文字记载的语言研究最早可以追溯到两千多年前的古希腊。古代希腊语言学可以分为雅典时期和希腊化时期。在雅典时期,最早接触语言问题的正是一些哲学家,当时有关语言的讨论正是在哲学的研究范围内展开,属于哲学的一个分支。大约在公元前 5 世纪,希腊人就对语言问题进行过两场有名的大论战。

　　第一场论战在"自然发生派"和"约定俗成派"之间展开,公元前 4 世纪柏拉图的《对话录》中可以找到这场论战的记录。论战的焦点集中在语言的形式与意义之间的关系上。"自然发生派"认为,名称反映事物的本质,事物的本质决定了名称的原始正确性。他们以语言中的象声词为依据,得出语言是自然发生的结论。"约定俗成派"则认为,名称在本质上是根据习惯约定而成的,和事物的性质没有什么必然联系。语言中的象声词是极少数,即使没有它们也不会影响语言交际。由此,他们认为语言是约定俗成的产物。这场论战持续良久而没有什么结果,但它促进了对词源的研究,在哲学这个总框架中开创了研究语法的先河。柏拉图在"自然发生派"和"约定俗成派"的论战中持中立态度。他认为,有些词直接反映了事物的本质;但有许多词,其语音形式与意义之间究竟有些什么联系是无法判断的。他在分析单词与意义的关系时,把词分为主词和述词两大类,是西方语言学史上第一个对词进行分类的学者。

---

　　① 邓晓芒.论中国哲学中的反语言学倾向[J].中州学刊,1992(2):42-47.

第二场论战发生在"类推派（analogist）"与"变则派（anomalist）"间，争论的焦点集中在语法结构是否规则这一问题上。"类推派"认为世界上的一切事物都要受法则支配，语言也不例外。它虽然有不规则的现象，但总体来说还是规则的。"变则派"则认为，语言是自然发生的，不规则的，并以语言中许多不规则现象作为立论的依据。

由于这两场论战所涉及的语言仅仅是希腊语，而希腊语既有规则的成分，也有不规则的因素，所以论战的双方谁也说服不了谁。双方观点后来分别得到亚里士多德和斯多葛学派的捍卫。亚里士多德是坚定的"约定俗成论"者。他在柏拉图的词类两分法的基础上认为那些既不属于主词又不属于述词的词自成一类（大约相当于我们今天所说的连词）。他还注意到名词有格的变化、动词有时态变化等这样一些结构上的特征，并第一次给词下了定义。后来的"变则派"斯多葛学派在亚里士多德的词类三分的基础上，进一步把词分为冠词、名词、动词和连词，又把名词分为专有名词和普通名词。他们还对动词的时态和名词的格等问题进行了细致的研究，认为名词有主格、宾格、与格、所有格和呼格之分。

在这场论战中，希腊语法得到了整理并初具体系，这些后来又为拉丁语法学家继承并应用到拉丁语研究中，可以说这场希腊哲学家之间的论战为整个欧洲的传统语法理论和语言教学打下了坚实的基础，具有重大历史意义。

西方哲学在其产生发展的两千多年间经历了三个阶段：古代本体论、近代认识论和现代语言哲学，实现了两大转向：近代的"认识论转向"和现代的"语言学转向"。"语言学转向"被西方大多数哲学家看作是 20 世纪最有意义的哲学事件，构成了现当代哲学的总体特征。

两千多年来，自然科学取得了扎扎实实的进步，而哲学似乎在原地循环，哲学的"落后"和科学的进步形成鲜明的对照。分析哲学家认为造成这种情况的主要原因是：哲学的理论不能像科学理论一样被检验；哲学的语言不能像科学语言一样被大家都理解；哲学的方法玄虚混乱，不像科学方法那样确实可靠。因此，要推动哲学的发展，就必须改变原来的那种哲学与科学之间的关系，哲学不再是科学的红衣主教，而应为科学服务。哲学家不应去创造一套凌驾于科学之上的体系，而应把自己的研究范围限于对已经提出的理论进行逻辑分析，剔除那些因语言误用而产生的无意义的伪命题，找出符合所代表的事实又具有最好最简明逻辑形式的命题，同时研究语言的特性进而研制一种科学的语言作为哲学表达的工具。当然，哲学的发展与科学的进步不能简单类比，但分析哲学家的观点反映了现代哲学研究与语言的密切关系。

随着欧美分析哲学的兴起，语言已经成为 20 世纪哲学研究的中心。正如吉伯特·赖尔（Gilbert Ryle）所说，20 世纪的哲学研究很大程度上来说都和意义的语言学概念相关。英美分析哲学的代表人物路德维希·维特根斯坦（Ludwig Wittgenstein，1889—

1951)也在他的哲学著作《逻辑哲学论》(*Tractatus Logico-Philosophicus*)中写道:"哲学的大多数问题和设想都因我们对自身语言逻辑的不了解而产生……所有的哲学问题都是'关于语言的批判'……"20世纪以来,西方哲学的语言转向大大促进了语言学和哲学间的理论渗透。逻辑经验主义、日常语言哲学等各大哲学学派纷纷开始关注语言科学,试图从哲学和逻辑的角度来挖掘语言学中对解决哲学困境有帮助的研究成果。逻辑实用主义代表奎因(Quine,1908—2000)是把语言学相关理论应用到哲学问题上的第一人。在《语言学中的意义问题》(*The Problem of Meaning in Linguistics*)一书和《经验论的两个教条》(*Two Dogmas of Empiricism*)等论文中,他都阐述了自己对当前语言学研究的一些见解,并将语言学理论应用到哲学研究中。

真正让哲学家们确定语言学和哲学相关性的是乔姆斯基的语言学研究成果对哲学界的巨大影响。1957年,乔姆斯基的《句法结构》出版,转换语法蜚声哲学界,使语言理论得以多层面地展示句子结构,也使一些表层语法结构相似句的深层逻辑差别得以显现。转换语法的层次性又恰好与分析哲学家们对句子表层句法结构和深层逻辑结构的区分不谋而合。此外,乔姆斯基生成语法中强调普遍语法的先天性,认为语法是内化于说话人语言机制中的语言知识——即乔姆斯基常用术语 language competence,人们通过语言环境中足量输入的刺激逐渐获取先天内化的语言能力。这一理论再现了理性主义有关内在知识的天赋观念,引起了哲学界的关注及讨论。乔姆斯基的《语言学的解释模型》(*Explanatory Models in Linguistics*)出版四年后,在美国哲学协会举行的一次研讨会上,乔姆斯基和一群哲学家对语言天赋论展开了讨论。此后的许多例子也表明,不少语言学问题都能在哲学家那里找到共鸣,许多哲学家在语言学研究中也颇有造诣。

自乔姆斯基的生成语法以后,又有很多新的语言学理论涌现,对这一领域不熟悉的哲学家想要将语言学的理论应用于哲学研究并非易事,况且哲学和语言学关注语言的焦点并不相同。语言学家关心的是特定语言里句子的形式结构,而哲学家关注的是哲学命题的逻辑结构和指称的多样可能性,无关乎任何特定语言的语法细节,除非这些细节关乎哲学语言使用的差异。但是任何哲学命题都只能在特定语言特定句法结构允许范围内得到表达,即便是数理逻辑中那些极度抽象的公式化命题,它们所指称的仍然是某种自然语言里合乎语法规则的语句。既然哲学想要前行离不开语言学的陪伴,便有学者倡导建立一门与数学哲学、物理哲学平行的哲学分支学科——语言哲学,时刻关注语言学的最新发展动态,将新出现的语言理论分门别类,以一种让哲学家更易接受的方式将可供选择的语言理论与相关的哲学问题相连接。建立语言哲学不仅是哲学现状的需要,其本身也具有很高的理论价值。

# 第三节　语言学和人类学

从语源学上讲,人类学是研究人的科学,起源于地理大发现时代欧美学者对现代西方技术文明之外的社会的研究。目前人类学的研究领域已经扩展到现代社会内部,试图概括人类行为的普遍性问题,并对社会和文化现象进行整体性的描述。人类学大致可分为研究形态、遗传、生理等人体特征的人体人类学和以风俗、文化史、语言等文化为研究对象的文化人类学,以及专门研究史前时期的人体和文化的史前人类学。

语言学和人类学的交迭首先得从语言和文化的关系说起。许多语言学家对二者的相互关系有过精彩论述。如萨丕尔在他的《语言论》中对语言、人类思维和民族文化的亲密关系有过明确阐述,他把语言成分看作“概念”的符号,认为语言模式决定思维模式,还将语言和思维的关系比作数学符号和推理,认为没有语言,思维就如同没有数学符号的推理难以进行。在对语言本质的界定上,萨丕尔否认语言是一种本能行为,认为“语言只是声音符号的习惯系统”,突出了语言的文化功能,认为语言的内容和文化有着密切的关系,语言的词汇多多少少忠实地反映出它所服务的文化。萨丕尔的学生沃尔夫发展了萨丕尔的观点,除了坚持语言影响说话人的思想和行为外,还试图解释不同语言语法体系和语言使用的差别如何影响语言使用者对宇宙的看法。他们的观点浓缩为萨丕尔-沃尔夫假说(Sapir-Whorf Hypothesis)。

语言作为人类特有的符号系统以及最重要的交际工具,其本身属于文化范畴,也就自然在文化人类学的研究范围之内。文化人类学家想要研究人类文化必然要涉及各民族语言,因为很多反映民族生活方式的有意义的细节就潜藏在某些词句里,通过特定情境中的语义分析可以看到特定民族宗教、伦理道德、亲属关系、社会等级等各方面文化生活的特点。文化人类学又十分关注那些远离先进技术文明没有文字的原始部落,因此语言描写方法是不可或缺的。人类学的研究途径除了观察还有问询,不了解部落的语言就很难清楚描绘部落的文化生活。因此很多欧美著名人类学家诸如洪堡特、萨丕尔、马林诺夫斯基等同时也是出色的语言学家。美国结构语言学的先驱博厄斯懂得多种印第安方言,于 1911 年组织出版了最早的《美洲印第安语言手册》(*A Handbook of American Indian Language*),他为该书所写的序言一直被列为语言学的经典著作。博厄斯在研究过程中发现,每一种语言都有自己的一套语音、形态、词汇和语法结构特点,一种语言只能根据其特定的结构来描写,他的这一主张被称为"描写语言学"理论,在当时具有划时代的意义。这种语言描写方法对于研究无文字民族的语言尤其有效,可使研究人员跳过当地的语料提供者(informant),不受其政治、宗教、经济、亲属关系及其他社会习惯等造成的负面影响,从而避免了信息的"二次加工(secondary rationalizations)"。就此博厄斯被认为是把语言学引入正式人类学研究的第一人。

追溯人类学和语言学的发展史,可以发现二者的相互影响从未间断过。19 世纪,人类学与历史比较语言学联系紧密。洪堡特等历史比较语言学家在那时就已经开始研究印第安语、卡维语等部落语言,并对民族语言和民族精神的相互关系做了许多富有创见性的探讨。进入 20 世纪,人类学又与结构主义语言学结盟,美国描写语言学作为结构语言学中发展最完善的一个学派就是在对美洲印第安语的调查和研究基础上逐步形成和发展起来的。象征人类学和认知人类学在研究方法上深受索绪尔结构主义语言学理论的影响,认知语言学中所用到的特征分析(feature analysis)正源于结构主义语言学中的成分分析(componential analysis),认知人类学者利用这个方法成功地分析了许多"史前族群"的亲属称谓体系。雅各布逊的音位理论更是对法国人类学家列维-斯特劳斯(Claude Levi-Strauss)的结构人类学产生了重要影响。1945 年,列维-斯特劳斯在他的《语言学和人类学中的结构分析》中首次提出把音位学中的结构分析法运用到人类学研究中去。20 世纪 50 年代后期,转换生成语言学同样对结构人类学构成了巨大影响力。列维-斯特劳斯认为,乔姆斯基关于表层结构和深层结构的理论具有普遍意义。他把社会文化视为一种深层结构体系,把个别的习俗、神话等表层文化材料看作"语言"元素,认为人类心灵的无意识结构通过各种文化形式表现出来,其典型研究方法是在文化材料中寻求结构性二元对立,推导转换生成的形式,从而挖掘出人类意识不到的文化深层结构。

从语言学和人类学的亲缘关系来看,出现语言人类学(linguistic anthropology)这样的交叉学科几乎是必然的。由于世界各国的学科渊源不尽相同,语言人类学的学科界定以及学科归属不尽相同。现在学术界一般认为,语言人类学是人类学研究语言与文化关系的一个学科,旨在通过语言的研究或借助语言学的研究成果达到深化认识人类文化的目的,有时也可称作人类语言学。

作为一门学科,语言人类学是在美国建立和发展起来的。美国著名的人类学家 L.H.摩尔根(L. H. Morgan,1818—1881)在深入调查研究易洛魁印第安人的基础上,于 1851 年出版了《易洛魁联盟》一书,追溯了易洛魁人数百年的历史,详细地记录了他们的生活环境、经济活动、习俗、宗教和语言。1871 年,他又发表了《人类家族的血亲和姻亲制度》,从语言学的角度讨论了印第安人的奇特亲属称谓和族源问题,开始了对人类早期社会组织原则及其普遍发展规律的探索。20 世纪 20 年代至 30 年代,人类学家在对印第安人的土著文化进行深入研究时,发现印第安人的语言不同于印欧语系诸语言,在描写印第安语的过程中开创了美国描写语言学派。20世纪中叶以来,语言人类学作为一门学科日臻完善。这一阶段出现了大量的语言人类学成果,尤以菲力普森(Robert Philipson)、萨斯曼(Zdenek Salzmann)等人为代表。菲力普森从语言人类学视角对英语进行了个案研究,指出由于文化上的不平衡,英语的支配地位造成了英语帝国主义,实际上是间接反映了一种盎格鲁文化中心观。萨斯曼同样从语言人类学的视角对语言、文化和社会的相互关系进行了论述,指出不同的语言结构与其所反映的思维方式具有协同性;同时还对当今的语言人类学"实用性"展开了论述,在一定程度上推动了语言人类学学科理论与方法的发展。[①]

# 第四节 语言学和心理学

心理学是研究人和动物心理现象发生、发展和活动规律的一门科学。早期心理学脱胎于哲学,欧洲传统中很多有关人类心理的问题都被放置在哲学的框架内讨论。直到19世纪中叶,德国哲学家、教育学家赫尔巴特才首次提出心理学是一门科学。冯特等现代意义上的心理学家认为心理学与自然科学一样,都是关于经验的科学,言语仅仅被视作发音动作,一种向他人传达意志的便捷方式。行为主义则把心理学的研究对象确定为可以外部观察的行为,坚持以客观的实验方法来研究人的行为;而精神分析则认为心理学的研究对象是无意识现象,特别是潜意识现象。20世纪60年代以前,传统心理学探究的两大主题是"心理"与"行为",尽管语言是人类表达心理与行为的重要媒介,然而注重实证量化研究的经典心理学却并不关注生活世界的日常语言。哲学的束缚和现实主题导致了语言在传统心理学研究中的缺席。

语言进入心理学的研究视野与20世纪哲学的语言学转向有关。20世纪60年代,哲学解释学提出了一种新颖的看法:人创造了语言,但却从属于语言;人创造的不是一种工具,而是人自己的存在方式。从这个角度看,就不是人在使用语言,而是语言构成人的存在。海德格尔所说的"语言是存在的家园",伽达默尔所说的"能理解的存在就是语言"

---

① 谭志满.语言人类学及其在中国的发展[J].广西民族研究,2006(3):55-59.

等,都是对这种观点的不同形式的表达。哲学从认识论到语言学的转向成为反思科学主义心理学的一次契机,使语言本身的理性知识被提升到心理学基本问题的地位。自此,话语分析、话语形态、话语结构以及表达方式成为心理学研究的新视角。现代心理学理论所运用的解释与结构的分析方法突出了语言在我们认知过程中所具有的不容忽视的重要作用,指出我们的感觉和理解过程,无不渗透着语言的影响。

从心理学理论的发展史来看,将"语言"问题带入心理学的尝试则要归功于现象学心理学。在胡塞尔的现象学的影响下,不少心理学家致力于建构旨在揭示日常生活世界的心理学理论。现象学心理学关注主体间性,强调理解他人行动之时要强调言说者的姿态、声音、字面意义和意图。

20 世纪 50 年代,语言学转向这一知识潮流以及语言学与心理学之间的内部联系催生了心理语言学(Psycholinguistics)这一交叉学科。50 年代初,美国举行了几次关于心理学和语言学的跨学科讨论会,促使心理学家和语言学家相互熟悉对方的理论、概念和方法。1954 年,奥斯古德和西比奥克合编了《心理语言学——理论和研究问题概述》,一般认为这是心理语言学的开端。此后,心理语言学的研究蓬勃发展,吸引了许多学者的注意,心理语言学这一术语也被广泛使用。

心理语言学是研究语言活动中的心理过程的学科,它涉及人类个体如何掌握和运用语言系统,如何在实际交往中使语言系统发挥作用,以及为掌握和运用这个系统应具有什么知识和能力。虽然心理语言学所研究的"客体"是语言,但研究的实质不仅仅是心理学所关心的心理机制或语言学所关注的语言本身的结构特性的描写和建构,而是语言使用者的心理机制的运作过程和运作规律以及包括哲学在内的一切同语言相关的思维现象。

心理语言学受现代语言学理论的影响很大。从心理语言学的发展过程来看,乔姆斯基的转换生成语法理论是造成心理语言学的研究方向从行为主义转向认知心理学的主要因素。在 20 世纪 50 年代,心理语言学主要受以华生 (J. B. Watson) 和斯金纳(B.F. Skinner)为代表的行为主义理论及结构主义语言学理论的影响,当时的心理语言学家用行为主义的观点来解释心理语言现象。他们认为言语行为和人的其他一切行为一样,也是出于对刺激的反应,借强化而获得。这样,心理语言学的理论基本上是行为主义学习理论在言语活动中的具体表现。这个研究方向的代表人物是奥斯古德,他虽然不像斯金纳那样把意义排斥在语言现象之外,引用了中介过程来说明语言的意义,但他仍坚持认为行为主义的学习理论可以解释言语行为。

20 世纪 60 年代,在乔姆斯基的转换生成语法产生和盛行之后,心理学界对行为主义语言学习理论的抨击增多,认为行为主义不能解释言语活动中的许多现象。以米勒为代表的心理学家把生成转换语法运用到心理语言的研究中,认为人们掌握的不是语言的个别成分,而是一套规则系统,因此,言语活动不是对刺激的反应,而是由规则产生和控制的行为。他们还认为心理语言学研究的重点不是人类各种语言的不同结构,而是存在于各种语言底层的普遍规则,研究这些普遍规则如何转化为某一种特殊的语言。这种研究方向在 20 世纪 60 年代后已成为心理语言学研究中的主要倾向。近年来,心理学家还用一些新的语言模式来研究心理语言问题,不过它们仍属于认知心理学的研究方向。

　　心理语言学研究成果的大量涌现始于 20 世纪 80 年代初期。从目前已出版的作品来看,仅在 1975—1997 年间,已问世的有关心理语言学研究的专著和论文就多达 600 多种。心理语言学的研究在美国开展得比较广泛。苏联、英国、法国、德国、荷兰等欧洲国家也都有心理学家从事这方面的工作,其特点是力图把心理语言学的研究与本国的心理学传统结合起来。但是纵观美、德、俄、中等国心理语言学的研究现状,大都仍是基于美国心理语言学家以英语为客体所做的研究,超出美国心理语言学研究框架的很少。特别是在"心智本质"和"语言理解"关系的深层研究方面,还有待更深入的探索。

# 第五节　语言学和社会学

　　社会学起源于 19 世纪末期,是一门利用经验考察与批判分析来研究人类社会结构与活动的学科。19 世纪 30 年代,法国社会学、哲学家孔德(Auguste Comte)在《实证哲学教程》第四卷中第一次提出了社会学这个新名词以及建立这门新学科的大体设想,后经卡尔·马克思、斯宾塞、迪尔凯姆、马克斯·韦伯等学者的不断发展,逐渐形成一门有独立理论、研究方法和范式的社会科学。社会学的研究对象范围十分广泛,与历史、政治、经济、社会结构、人口变动、民族、城市、乡村、社区、婚姻、家庭与性、信仰与宗教、现代化等领域都有交叉,小到几个人面对面的日常活动,大到全球化的社会趋势无不囊括其中。

　　社会学是以直面经验事实的面目出现的,而经验事实是人们通过日常交往行动展开的,借助语言沟通的交往行动是社会事实的基本内容。因此,当孔德和迪尔凯姆为社会学规定了直接面对经验事实来研究社会现象这个任务时,就已内在地注定了社会学回避不了语言学问题。

　　在社会学领域里,首先把语言问题作为社会学研究对象的是米德(Mead),而米德所开展的社会学的语言学研究受到了詹姆斯(James)和杜威(John Dewey)等人实用主义理论的影响。按照实用主义的经验一元论原则,不仅理性根据、情感意志、价值要求和感性活动等属于经验过程不可缺失的要素,人际交往和语言沟通等因素也囊括其中,因为这些在经验过程中都是同时存在的。在米德之后,符号互动论、人际交换论、结构功能论、社会冲突论等社会学理论都在不同程度上论述了语言问题。

语言问题真正成为社会学主要研究对象始于 20 世纪 60 年代以后。在利科的阐释学社会学、哈贝马斯的交往社会学、布迪厄的反观社会学、福柯和利奥塔德等人的后结构主义社会学中,能够清楚地看到语言学问题已经成为当代社会学主流的研究对象。利科从文字文本的阐释转向对行动文本的阐释,把阐释学的语言学研究同社会学的社会行动研究直接统一起来。受阐释学影响,哈贝马斯把自己的理论视野集中在以语言沟通为主要内容的交往行动上,建立了别开生面的交往社会学。以福柯、利奥塔德等人为代表的法国后结构主义社会学,在 20 世纪 60 年代以来也开始了语言学转向。

这期间,第一个通过语言学研究使社会学发生革命的是后结构主义社会学代表福柯。福柯的语言学研究,不注重语言的语义学和心理学分析,而是把语言看作人们的基本生命形式,试图通过语言来解释人们生存的困境,进而把握人类基本生存方式的历时性研究。福柯也像结构主义语言学家那样注重语言的结构分析,但并非认可语言结构分析,而是要摧毁日常语言中的结构。他在语言学研究中提出要打破中心,不给任何中心以特权,这里的中心是指"人类中心主义"和"逻各斯中心主义"。他认为,人本主义者过度强调人的主体地位,科学主义者则过度强调语言的结构规则和外界事物的逻辑规律,二者实质是在主客观的二元对立下思考问题和回答问题,这种传统的思维方式不仅不能真实地解释现实生活,而且作为千年不变的思维模式禁锢着人们的社会行动,引起社会生活各种层面的普遍异化。所以社会学理论的根本任务在于摧毁结构和拆除中心,而不是再揭示出什么新结构,确立何种新中心①。

20 世纪 60 年代,随着日常生活语言成为社会学的主要研究对象,语言学把社会学引入了一个交往对话沟通的世界。与此同时,社会语言学(Sociolinguistics)作为一门边缘学科也在美国兴起,其主要代表人物有 W.布莱特(W. Bright,1966)、J.费希曼(J. Fishman,1972)、D.海姆斯(D. Hymes,1974),每个人对这门新兴学科的研究范畴界定和研究视角都不相同。布莱特认为社会语言学主要研究语言变异,研究内容涉及说话者和听话者的社会身份、会话场景、社会方言的历时与共时研究、平民语言学、语言变异程度、社会语言学应用等七个方面。费希曼将社会语言学二分为宏观和微观:微观社会语言学以语言为出发点,研究社会方言和语言变异,考察社会因素对语言结构的影响;宏观社会语言学则以社会为出发点,研究语言在社区组织中的功能。海姆斯则特别强调社会语言

① 刘少杰.社会学的语言学转向[J].社会学研究,1999(4):89-97.

学目标的广泛性和跨学科性。

随着 20 世纪 60 年代以后语言学家对语言异质性认识的加深,社会语言学又发展出交际民族志学、跨文化交际、交际社会语言学、语言社会化和语言习得、会话分析、语言变异研究等学派。

作为一门新兴交叉学科,社会语言学覆盖了大量有关语言和社会的问题,各个学派从不同的研究视角对其做出了多层面的阐发,但是作为一门学科它仍然缺乏较为固定的内涵和稳定的外延。

# 第六节 语言学和语言教学

语言学和语言教学的对象都是语言,但语言学家研究语言的目的和语言教师教学的目的很不相同。教师最关心的可能不是语言的描写与分析,而是如何有效地让学生掌握一门语言。并非每一位语言教师都接受过语言学的训练,但掌握一定的语言学知识对语言教学必然有帮助。事实上,语言学的知识可以很好地应用在语言教学中,同时语言教学中获得的经验和数据又反过来为纯粹的语言研究提供更多依据。

一名教师组织课堂的方法反映了他自己对语言的观点,而教课的内容和顺序则反映了他对这门语言的基本判断。有的教师可能更加强调语法、词汇知识,有的教师可能强调句型结构和情景会话,有的教师可能注重句型在交际中的功能,有的教师可能认为发音的正确性胜过书写的正确性,还有的教师可能更注重表达的流畅性和会话的结构。不管教师的教学方法为何,在方法的背后都直接或间接地潜藏着教师的语言观。也就是说,语言教学法实际上总是和语言学理论相适应。一般而言,语法研究理论主张在教学中采用语法翻译法;结构主义者多采用视听法,注重句型操练;而社会语言学主张使用交际法培养学生的目的语交际能力。

## 一、语法翻译法

语法翻译法(The grammar-translation method)又称"传统法"或"古典法",可以说是迄今为止最广为人知、使用最为广泛的语言教学法,也是最古老的外语教学法。早在中世纪的欧洲,语法翻译法就被用于教授希腊语、拉丁语等"死语言"。到了 18 世纪末,欧洲的学校虽然开设了现代外语课,但仍然沿用语法翻译法,其代表人物是奥伦多夫( H.G. Ollendoff )。后来语法翻译法被用来学习现代外语,并逐步演变成一种科学的外语教学法体系。本世纪初,这种教学法在许多国家的外语教学中占主导地位。我国解放初期的外语教学,特别是俄语教学,大都采用这种方法。

语法翻译法的目的是让学生能够阅读外语资料和文献,一般首先让学生学习目的语的词汇发音和书写方法,然后进行系统的语法教学,采用演绎法讲解语法规则,大量举例,同时利用翻译的手段让学生学习和掌握语法规则。并随后运用这些语法规则进行句子和语篇翻译。它特别强调短语、句型结构的正确表达,也特别强调语法规则及其特例,重视语言对比,在教学实践中把翻译既当成教学目的,又当成教学手段。因为语法翻译法的重点在书面语,并不注重发展学生口语表达的流畅性与自发性,所以它着力培养学生的读写能力,并要求学生掌握大量的词汇。由于语法翻译法的重点在语法方面,这使学生往往只注重语言知识的学习,忽视了语言应用能力的掌握,不一定能自如地使用目的语。此外,语法翻译法采用母语与目的语互译的方法进行教学,容易使学习者过分依赖母语,影响学习效果。

## 二、直接法

直接法( The direct method )是 19 世纪下半叶始于西欧的外语教学改革运动的产物。当时的许多学者和语言教师对传统的语法翻译法提出批评,认为儿童习得母语时不断听说,是习得语言的自然途径,而翻译反而是一种不自然、不必要的障碍。语法翻译法会让学生对翻译产生依赖,一旦他们需要用目的语表达观点时,他们只会在头脑中用母语思考再翻译成目的语,这不利于训练学生直接使用目的语思维的能力。由于语音学的兴起,当时的研究者们越来越重视口语,越来越多的教师指出,交际的真正手段是"说"而非"写"。

直接法的主要特点是在教学中仅仅使用目的语,并主张采用口语材料作为教学内容,要求学生们在课堂上模仿教师,通过这样的方式来熟悉并掌握目的语的相关知识。在直接法教学中教师尽量不用学生的母语,常常借用图片、手势以及其他一些生动手段来辅助教学。接受直接法的学生可能有更好的口头表达能力,但是由于学生练习的重点为会话,而大部分会话都具有一定的标准模式,因此容易造成学生的机械模仿。另外,由于强调口语能力,学生的读写能力则相对较为薄弱,表达精确度也难以保证。

许多教师目前仍在使用直接法教学,通常是在一些正规学校或者强化性的教学课程中使用。虽然这种方法有一定缺陷,几乎所有的语言教学都借鉴了直接法的一些特点,例如用图片或其他形象的辅助手段等。

## 三、听说法

听说法（The audio-lingual method）产生于 20 世纪 40 年代的美国，在 20 世纪五六十年代得到了广泛的发展，是结构语言学理论和斯金纳（S.B. Skinner）的心理学理论完美结合的产物。受到美国结构主义语言学和行为心理学的影响，听说法采纳了直接法的许多原则和过程，强调语言的形式（即结构）甚于意义。它主张通过句型操练加强对语言结构（特定的刺激与应答）的记忆，因而听与说就成了这一教学法的重点。此外，听说法还尤为强调听和说的顺序，它主张，听先于说，说先于读，读先于写。教师通常鼓励学生对特定的"语言刺激"养成良好的习惯，使之能正确应答，尤其注意学生表达上的错误并给以纠正，因为多次的错误会发展为习惯，最终难以纠正。这种"刺激—应答（stimulus-response）"和不断巩固正确表达法的学习模式被称为"条件作用（conditioning）"。

许多语言教师至今仍不时使用听说法的某些技巧，如句型操练。不过，践行听说法仍有一定困难。句型的操练往往脱离语境，因此容易走向机械的无意义的重复。即使学生能够迅速对句型作出反应，也并不代表他们一定了解句子的含义，更不能保证他们在交际中顺利使用这一表达。另外，"刺激—应答"的观点也多为今天的学者所诟病。语言的学习相当复杂，它要求学习者在有限的语言环境中分析和概括语言规则，远不能止步于养成一系列"习惯"。同时，大部分学者也不认同听说法将母语学习和第二语言学习混为一谈的观点。

## 四、情境法

情境法（Situational language teaching）兴起于 20 世纪 30 年代至 60 年代，由英国应用语言学家帕尔默（Harold Palmer）和霍恩斯比（A.S. Hornsby）等人发展而来。情境法的支持者认为"口语"是语言的基础，其中语言的机构（句型）更是会话能力的基础。但是，词汇和文法必须在合适的情境中予以介绍，才能使学生获得在相应情境中作出合理反应的习惯。教师总是鼓励学生通过情境来归纳和理解正确的表达方式。情境法的主要目的是培养学生听、说、读、写的实际能力，而"说"是一切外语能力的基础，所以口语表达是教学的重点。情境法特别强调所谓"PPP"，即呈述（presentation）、练习（practice）和产出（production）。由于课程内容针对词汇和句型来设计，课本中并没有相应的情境，教师上课时必须准备教案，且通常有课程进度表，通过教学活动将情境演示给学生。

情境法如今已不再风行，但其中的一些教学理念仍然为语言教师所用，特别是在第二语言教学中,仍有一定影响,比如该法强调口语练习、语法练习和句型练习的观点仍然得到不少人的支持。到 20 世纪 60 年代,情境法的一些缺点逐渐显现出来,语言学家在此基础上进行修正。

## 五、功能法

20 世纪 70 年代,由结构和情境出发的教学方法受到了很大的挑战,于是功能法(Functional language teaching)应运而生。功能法主张教学时要阐释语言形式所承担的语用功能,教学目的不是要告诉学生语言是什么,而是让他们掌握语言的功用,提高交际能力。功能法对抽象语法知识的教学总是与其特定的语用功能紧密联系,强调在功能的基础上循序渐进地安排教学活动。例如"提出帮助(offering)"这一主题,教学的内容会涉及从"正式用法""礼貌用法"到"非正式用法"的一系列语言形式,可以从"Would you like something to drink?""Have a drink?"到"Drink?"。功能性的语言教学强调语言的功用,因此教学的基本单元是短小的交流(exchanges)。语法知识的讲授也与它们的具体功能紧密结合。这样的教学方法强调了以交际的主题、听说双方间的关系及各自的角色来进行恰当的会话,并同时注意发展学生会话的流畅性。

功能法的理论基础源自语义学和对言语行为(speech acts)的研究。人们早就注意到语言的功能性,发现人们说话不仅仅是为了说,还为了达成某件事情。韩礼德的系统功能语言学(Systemic Functional Linguistics)加深了"语言具有功能性"这一观点的影响。这些观点在语言教学中得到反映,表现为根据不同的主题和会话双方的关系,安排不同的语言形式及其功能。

功能法也存在一定问题。它没能指出语言功能的定义和种类,也没有具有说服力的教学进度安排。语言还有许多非功能性的用法,太过强调语言的功能性会削弱语言的其他方面。同时,语言的形式和功能之间并没有必然的联系,同一种功能可以由不同的语言形式来表达,反之亦然。如果完全以功能为纲安排教学,有可能同视听法一样会造成语法知识的混乱和复杂。此外,功能法强调会话的流畅性和语用的恰当性,却常常忽略语言表达的精确性,这也是它的一大缺陷。

## 六、交际法

近年来,语言学家和语言教师都越来越重视语言在交际中的运用,而不是仅仅将语言看作一个抽象的系统。教师们更愿意从功能出发来组织语言教学,这也表明了目前越来越注重语言交际性的趋势。不过,以功能出发组织教学并不是说教学完全以会话为内容,也不一定要在教学中强调会话。因为以功能为纲并不意味着在教学上采用"交际法(Communicative language teaching)",甚至在不注重交际的情况下完全可以进行功能性的语言教学。

交际法并不像听说法等教学法一样具有单一、鲜明的理论立场,它更多的是站在一个折中的角度,博采众长,倡导教与学不仅要为交际服务,并且要以交际为手段,也就是说教与学本身就是一个交际的过程。交际法背后的语言学理论与功能法类似,如语义学、言语行为理论、社会语言学、心理语言学等。此外,交际法也吸取话语分析(discourse analysis)理论、语篇衔接、连贯的观点等。简言之,任何通过交际展开的语言研究在理论方向上都与交际法相一致。交际法旨在帮助学习者获得交际的能力,在传统语言教学法的基础上进行了一系列改革,比如要求教师角色、学生角色、教材内容、教学技巧、教学态度等方面的改变,一切都是为了提高学生的主动性,使学生在交际中掌握语言的应用。

## 七、其他语言教学法

此外,还有很多语言教学法,它们建立在其他语言学研究理论之上,或是以人类学习模式而不是语言性质为出发点。例如,美国加州圣约瑟大学心理学教授詹姆士·阿歇尔(James Asher)于 20 世纪 60 年代提出的全身反应法(Total physical response),倡导把语言和行为联系在一起。20 世纪 60 至 70 年代,美国教育家加特格诺(Caleb Gattegno)设计的沉默法(The silent way)主张外语教师在课堂上应该尽量沉默,而让学生尽量多开口。保加利亚精神病疗法心理学家 G.罗扎诺夫(G.Lozanov)于 20 世纪 60 年代中期创立的暗示法(Suggestopedia)通常采用会话、情景、翻译等多种手段展示和操练语言,尤其强调通过音乐、视觉图像和游戏等轻松的活动创造一个尽量舒适有效的学习环境。而由美国应用语言学家克拉申(Stephen D. Krashen)和西班牙语教师泰勒(Tracy D.Terrel)于 1983 年提出的自然教学法(The natural approach)则通过在第二语言习得的研究中借助自然主义的原则,强调自然地发展学生的交际能力。又如任务法(Task-based language teaching),让学生用地道的目的语来完成一系列任务,从而培养学生在特定语境中运用语言的能力。近年来,美国学者吴伟克(Galal Walker)等人又提出体演文化教学法(Performed Culture Approach),主张语言即文化,语言即行为,学习语言就是学习目的文化及演练目的文化。体演文化教学法强调教师的引导性及学生的主体性,教师只作为引导者和管理者出现在课堂中,在教学过程中教师通过积极引导,为学生提供汉语学习的文化氛围,学生则在表演中真实地体验语言的功能、用法及使用语境。

诸多语言教学法在语言教学实践中大显身手,特别是在外语教学中非常有意义。在我国,随着国家经济、文化实力的不断增强,对外汉语教学蓬勃发展,该学科也日益成熟。

对外汉语教学学科主要研究作为第二语言的汉语学习和教学,包括贯穿于对外汉语教学过程中的教材编写、课堂设计、语言测试等。如何更好地运用语言学知识和语言教学方法来扩大对外汉语教学的影响,使更多的海外学习者掌握汉语,了解中华文化,是当今对外汉语教学面临的重大新课题。

# 第七节　语言学和神经科学

21世纪被称为脑科学的世纪。人类对脑科学的发展给予厚望,希望脑科学的研究能够解密人类各种高级认知功能的神经基础。语言作为人脑的重要功能之一,是脑科学研究的重要内容。

早在19世纪,M.戴克斯(M.Dax)、P.布洛卡(P. Broca)、C.韦尼克(C.Wernicke)等人就开始研究言语障碍与脑区之间的关系,20世纪开始,神经科学家进一步引进语言学概念,对言语活动进行语言学分析。但是,以往对人脑运作机制的研究是非常间接的,只能把大脑当成一个黑匣子,然后通过设计行为学实验推断大脑的功能。即便如此,研究者设计巧妙的控制实验获得了很多关于大脑语言功能的重要成果。比如,Hardyck等人在1977年就发现,将文字分别呈现在左右视野时,右视野中的文字比左视野中的更容易识别,因此推断右视野对文字的加工有优势。有趣的是,后来Tzeng等学者的汉字实验结果正好相反,呈左视野优势,说明汉语作为现存的主要语言中唯一的语标文字语言(logographic language),脑机制可能与拼音文字语言有所不同。

随着科学技术的进步,多种脑科学研究实验技术被发明,从而使无损伤地直接观测记录人脑的运行机制成为可能。这些实验技术主要包括脑电图、脑磁图、近红外光谱仪、正电子发射计算机断层扫描、功能性磁共振成像等。另外,随着临床医学的发展,神经外科的开颅手术越来越多。开颅手术过程中通过直接颅内记录(direct intra-cranial record)大脑活动也成为神经科学家探索大脑功能的重要技术手段之一。

大脑的语言功能像人类的意识、记忆、情绪、决策等高级功能一样,神经基础极其复杂深奥。利用现代脑科学实验技术研究大脑的语言功能已有几十年历史,重要的研究成果简要列举如下:

言语感知方面,研究发现元音、辅音、音节、词形、词义、声调等在大脑中有长期记忆,这些记忆在言语感知过程中迅速自动激活(约 150 毫秒),无需意识参与。这一过程是人类能够非常迅速并且十分轻松地理解言语的重要基础。这些构成言语的基本单元的长时程记忆主要存在于左脑颞上回和左脑额叶下回附近。但是,词义的记忆可能弥散分布于大脑皮层,并且有趣的是,Pulvermuller 和 Fadiga 发现,与动作相关的词义可能存在于运动皮层,与颜色、形状相关的词义可能存在于视觉皮层。此外,音位的长期记忆大约是在出生后 6 至 12 个月形成,成年之后学习第二语言也会在大脑中逐渐形成第二语言中音位的长期记忆。特别的是,词形和词义的长时程记忆十分容易形成。Shtyrov 等人进一步研究发现只需要被动地听(即无需注意力参与)一个新词几分钟时间即可在大脑中产生该新词的长期记忆,这是人类在日常生活中能够不断学习大量新的词汇的神经基础。

文字阅读方面,最重要的研究发现之一是位于左脑梭状回的视觉词形区(visual word form area)。该区域的大脑皮层对文字有强烈的反应,被认为是负责加工文字的脑区。视觉词形区的一个重要功能是筛选符合正字法(orthographic)的文字进行进一步加工。相对于不符合正字法的文字(如英语辅音组合"bjdpms")或者其他非文字(如字符组合" * &^＄％"),视觉词形区对符合正字法的文字(如英语假词"paind")有更强的反应,并且反应时间非常迅速(100~200 毫秒)。但是目前的研究尚未明确发现视觉词形区能够区分真词和符合正字法的假词。大脑对视觉词的加工时间进程和空间脑区,目前还存在很大争议。有研究者认为对视觉词的加工和听觉词一样非常迅速(约 150 毫秒),另一些研究者则认为视觉词的加工发生在 300 毫秒之后。除了通过真词假词的对比研究词的视觉加工过程,将高频词与低频词诱发的大脑反应进行对比也可以推断词的加工的时间进程和空间脑区。最新的颅内记录通过比较真词和假词,以及比较高频词和低频词,发现视觉词的加工可能最早(约 250 毫秒)发生在左脑梭状回中部。

无论是听觉词还是视觉词,激活的词义信息都要整合到上下文的语境中。Kutas 等人发在实验中构建包含语义冲突的句子,如"他在热面包上涂上了袜子",然后记录大脑的反应,结果发现在约 400 毫秒的时候大脑对语义冲突的关键词"袜子"有一个非常强的反应,这一事件相关电位(event-related potential)被称为 N400。后续研究发现无论关键词在句子中出现的位置,无论听觉词还是视觉词甚至是非词,只要包含语义冲突都会诱发 N400,并且其强度和完形概率(cloze probability)相关。N400 也可以被常识的冲突诱发,比如"荷兰的火车是白色的"(现实中荷兰的火车都是黄色的)。关于 N400 的研究表明,句子的语义整合是一个复杂的多成分的过程,涉及众多脑区的参与。

语法是一门语言的重要构成。大脑对语法加工的神经机制同样也是大脑语言功能的重要组成。语法的研究与语义整合的研究类似,通常也是构建包含语法冲突的句子,然后观察记录大脑对这个句子的反应。比如"裁缝把裁了"句中的"裁"即是诱发语法冲突的关键词。研究发现语法冲突会在 100 至 200 毫秒左右诱发出一个非常快的大脑反应,称为 ELAN(Early Left Anterior Negativity),以及一个约 600 毫秒的晚期反应 P600。Batterink 和 Neville 等研究者发现,与语义冲突诱发的 N400 成分不同的是,语法冲突在没有注意力参与的情况下也能诱发 ELAN 和 P600,这意味着语法的加工类似于词的加工,是基于自动的、内隐的神经机制。

除以上简要列举的研究成果之外,言语产出、第二语言习得、手语、语言功能障碍(包括失读症、失语症以及语言发育障碍)等也是人脑语言功能研究的重要方面。这些研究形成了一门新的学科"神经语言学(Neurolinguistics)"。这门学科基于现代脑科学技术,正在蓬勃发展,不断涌现新的重要成果,体现在每年有大量的研究论文发表在高水平国际学术期刊上。神经语言学是当前语言学相关领域产出成果最多的学科。21 世纪如果能像人类期望的那样成为脑科学的世纪,人类对于自身语言功能的理解也将迎来一个全新的局面,比如,有可能通过神经语言学的研究解释各种语言学现象,验证语言学理论,让人工智能拥有语言功能等等。值得一提的是,汉语相对于世界上其他的拼音文字语言非常不同,研究发现汉语相关的神经机制很大程度上也不同于其他语言。因此,基于其他语言的神经语言学研究成果往往不能直接套用于汉语,所以十分需要中国的学者为汉语的相关研究做出贡献。

## 思考与练习

一、名词解释

1.语文学

2.语言学转向

3.应用语言学

二、简答题

1.你认为庄子所说的"言者所以在意,得意而忘言"表现了怎样的语言观? 和西方传统的语言观有何不同?

2.举例说明语言与其他学科之间的交叉影响。

3.根据自己教外语或学外语的经验,以一种语言教学法为主要教学方式设计一堂语言课,并举例说明具体的教学和学习法。

4.根据自己的经验,你认为学习外语最难培养的是什么能力? 最重要的是什么能力? 为什么? 你认为应该怎样培养这些能力?

## 【原典阅读】

# 1.Nature and Constitution of Language

## Wilhelm von Humboldt

Since the diversity of languages rests on their form, and the latter is most intimately connected with the mental aptitudes of nations and the power that suffuses them at the moment of creation or new conception, it now becomes necessary to develop this notion in greater detail.

In pondering on language in general, and analysing the individual tongues that are clearly distinct from one another, two principles come to light: the *sound-form* and the *use* made of it to designate objects and connect thoughts. The latter is based on the requirements that *thinking* imposes on language, from which the *general laws* of language arise; and this part, in its original tendency, is therefore the same in all human beings, as such, until we come to the individuality of their mental endowments or subsequent developments. The sound-form, on the other hand, is the truly constitutive and guiding principle of the diversity of languages, both in itself, and in the assisting or obstructing power it presents to the inner tendency of the language. As an element of the whole human organism, closely related to the inner mental power, it is, of course, equally precisely connected with the collective outlook of the nation; but the nature and basis of this tie are veiled in a darkness that scarcely permits of any clarification. Now from these two principles, together with the inwardness of their mutual interpenetration, there proceeds the *individual form* of each language, and they constitute the points that linguistic analysis must examine and try to present in connection. The most indispensable thing here is for the undertaking to be based on a correct and proper view of language, the depth of its origin and the breadth of its scope; and hence we must first of all take time to examine these latter.

I take the *practice of language* here in its widest extent, not merely in its relation to speech and the stock of its verbal elements, which are its direct product, but also in its connection with the capacity for thought and feeling. We are to consider the whole route whereby, proceeding from the mind, it reacts back upon the mind.

Language is the formative organ of *thought. Intellectual activity*, entirely mental, entirely internal, and to some extent passing without trace, becomes, through *sound*, externalized in speech and perceptible to the senses. Thought and language are therefore one and inseparable from each other. But the former is also intrinsically bound to the necessity of entering into a *union* with the verbal sound; thought cannot otherwise achieve clarity, nor the representation become a concept. The inseparable bonding of *thought*, *vocal apparatus* and *hearing* to language is unalterably rooted in the original constitution of human nature, which cannot be further explained. The concordance of sound and thought is nevertheless plain to see. Just as thought, like a lightning-flash or concussion, collects the whole power of representation into a single point, and shuts out everything else, so sound rings out with abrupt sharpness and unity. Just as thought seizes the whole mind, so sound has predominantly a penetrating power that sets every nerve atingle. This power that distinguishes it from all other sense-impressions is evidently due to the fact ( which is not always so with the other senses, or is so differently), that the ear receives the impression of a movement, and in the echoing sound of the voice the impression, even, of a veritable action; and this action proceeds here from within a living creature, a thinking creature if the sound is articulated, and a feeling one if it is not. Just as thought at its most human is a yearning from darkness into light, from confinement into the infinite, so sound streams outward from the heart's depths, and finds a medium wonderfully suited to it in the air, the most refined and easily moveable of all elements, whose seeming incorporeality is also a sensuous counterpart to the mind. The cutting sharpness of the vocal sound is indispensable to the understanding in apprehending objects. Both things in external nature, and the activity excited within, press in upon man all at once with a host of characteristics. But he strives to compare, separate and combine, and in his higher purposes to fashion an ever more embracing unity. So he also insists upon apprehending objects in a determinate unity, and demands the unity of sound to deputize in place of it. But sound suppresses none of the other impressions which objects are capable of producing upon outer or inner sense; instead, it becomes the bearer of them, and in its individual composition, connected with that of the object—and this precisely according to the way that the speaker's individual sensibility grasps the latter—it appends a new designating impression. At the same time the incisiveness of sound permits an incalculable number of modifications which are yet precisely distinctive when presented, and do not mingle in combination, a thing not found to the same degree in any other sensory effect. Since intellectual effort does not just occupy the understanding, but arouses the whole man, this too is chiefly promoted by the sound of the voice. For as living sound it comes forth from the breast like breathing life itself, is the accompaniment, even without language, to pain and joy, aversion and desire, and thus breathes the life it flows from into the mind that receives it, just as language itself always reproduces, along with the object presented, the feeling evoked by it, and within itself couples, in ever-repeated acts, the world and man, or, to put it otherwise, the spontaneously active and the receptive sides of his nature. And suited, finally, to vocalization is the upright posture of man, denied to animals; man is thereby summoned, as it were, to his feet. For speech does not aim at hollow extinction in the ground, but demands to pour freely from the lips towards the person addressed, to be accompanied by facial expression and demeanour and by gestures of the hand, and thereby to surround itself at once with everything that proclaims man human.

After this preliminary view of the aptitude of sound to the operations of the mind, we can now go more accurately into the connection of *thought* and language. Subjective activity fashions an *object* in thought. For no class of ideas can be regarded as a purely receptive contemplation of a thing already present. The activity of the senses must combine synthetically with the inner action of the mind, and from this combination the idea is ejected, becomes an object *vis-à-vis* the subjective power, and, perceived anew as such, returns back into the latter. But *language* is indispensable for this. For in that the mental striving breaks out through the lips in language, the product of that striving returns back to the speaker's ear. Thus the idea becomes transformed into real objectivity, without being deprived of subjectivity on that account. Only language can do this; and without this transformation, occurring constantly with the help of language even in silence, into an objectivity that returns to the subject, the act of concept-formation, and with it all true thinking, is impossible. So quite regardless of communication between man and man, speech is a necessary condition for the thinking of the individual in solitary seclusion. In appearance, however, language develops only *socially*, and man understands himself only once he has tested the intelligibility of his words by trial upon others. For objectivity is heightened if the self-coined word is echoed from a stranger's mouth. But nothing is robbed from subjectivity, for man always feels himself one with his fellow-man; indeed it is strengthened, since the representation transformed into language is no longer the exclusive possession of a single subject. In passing over to others, it joins the common stock of the entire human race, of which each individual possesses a modification containing the requirements for completion by others. The greater and more active the social collaboration on a language, the more it gains, under otherwise similar circumstances. What language makes necessary in the simple act of thought-creation is also incessantly repeated in the mental life of man; social communication through language provides him with conviction and stimulus. The power of thinking needs something that is like it and yet different from it. By the like it is kindled, and by the different it obtains a touchstone of the essentiality of its inner creations. Although the cognitive basis of truth, of the unconditionally fixed, can lie for man only within himself, the struggle of his mental effort towards it is always surrounded by the risk of deception. With a clear and immediate sense only of his mutable limitedness, he is bound to regard truth as something lying outside him; and one of the most powerful means of approaching it, of measuring his distance away from it, is social communication with others. All speaking, from the simplest kind onwards, is an attachment of what is individually felt to the common nature of mankind.

Nor is it otherwise with *understanding*. There can be nothing present in the soul, save by one's own activity, and understanding and speaking are but different effects of this power of speech. Conversing together is never comparable with a transfer of material. In the understander, as in the speaker, the same thing must be evolved from the inner power of each; and what the former receives is merely the harmoniously attuning stimulus. Hence it is also very natural for man to re-utter at once what he has just understood. In this way language resides in every human being in its whole range, which means, however nothing else but that everyone possesses an urge governed by a specifically modified, limiting and confining power, to bring forth gradually the whole of language from within himself, or when brought forth to understand it, as outer or inner occasion may determine.

But understanding could not, as we have just found, be based upon inner spontaneity, and communal speech would have to be something other than mere mutual arousal of the hearer's speech-capacity, did not the diversity of individuals harbour the unity of human nature, fragmented only into separate individualities. The comprehension of *words* is a thing entirely different from the understanding of *unarticulated sounds*, and involves much more than the mere mutual evocation of the sound and the object indicated. The *word*, to be sure, can also be taken as an indivisible whole, just as even in writing we recognize the meaning of a word-group, without yet being certain of its alphabetic composition; and it may be possible that the child's mind proceeds thus in the first beginnings of understanding. But just as not merely the animal's sensory capacity, but the human power of speech is excited (and it is far more probable that even in the child there is no moment when this would not be the case, however feebly), so the *word*, too, is perceived as articulated. But now what *articulation* adds to the mere evocation of its meaning (which naturally also occurs more perfectly thereby), is that it presents the word directly through its form as part of an infinite whole, a language. For even in single words, it is by means of this that we are given the possibility of constructing, from the elements of the language, a really indeterminate number of other words according to specific feelings and rules, and thereby to establish among all words an affinity corresponding to the affinity of concepts. The soul, however, would get no intimation at all of this artificial mechanism, would no more apprehend articulation than the blind do colours, if it did not harbour a power of rendering this possibility actual. For language cannot indeed be regarded as a material that sits there, surveyable in its totality, or communicable little by little, but must be seen as something that eternally produces itself, where the laws of production are determined, but the scope and even to some extent the nature of the product remain totally unspecified. The *speech-learning* of children is not an assignment of words, to be deposited in memory and rebabbled by rote through the lips, but a growth in linguistic capacity with age and practice. What is heard does more than merely convey information to oneself; it readies the mind also to understand more easily what has not yet been heard; it makes clear what was long ago heard, but then half understood, or not at all, in that a similarity to the new perception suddenly brings light to the power that has since become sharpened; and it enhances the urge and capacity to absorb from what is heard ever more, and more swiftly, into the memory, and to let ever less of it rattle by as mere noise. The advances thus accelerate in a constantly increasing ratio, since the growth of power and the acquisition of material mutually strengthen and enlarge each other. That in children there is not a mechanical learning of language, but a development of linguistic power, is also proved by the fact that, since the major abilities of man are alloted a certain period of life for their development, all children, under the most diverse conditions, speak and understand at about the same age, varying only within a brief time-span. But how could the hearer gain mastery over the spoken word, solely through the growth of that power of his own, developing in isolation within him, if there were not in both speaker and hearer the same essence, merely segregated individually and appropriately to each, so that a signal so fine, yet created from the very deepest and most intrinsic nature of that essence, as is the articulate sound, is enough to stir both parties, by its transmission, in a matching way?

One might wish to object to the foregoing that the children of any people, when displaced to an alien community before learning to speak, develop their linguistic abilities in the latter's tongue. This undeniable fact, we might say, is a clear proof that language is merely an echoing of what is heard, and depends entirely on social circumstances, without regard for any unity or diversity of the essence. In cases of this kind, however, it has hardly been possible to observe with sufficient accuracy how laboriously the native pattern has had to be overcome, or how perhaps in the finest nuances it has still kept its ground unvanquished. But even without paying attention to this, the phenomenon in question is sufficiently explained by the fact that man is everywhere one with man, and development of the ability to use language can therefore go on with the aid of every given individual. It occurs no less, on that account, from within one's own self; only because it always needs an outer stimulus as well, must it prove analogous to what it actually experiences, and can do so in virtue of the congruence of all human tongues. But the power of descent upon these can be seen, nonetheless, with sufficient clarity, in their distribution by nations. It is also readily intelligible in itself, since descent has so predominantly powerful an effect on the whole individuality, and the particular language at any time is again most intimately connected with this. If language, by its origin from the depths of man's nature, did not also enter into true and authentic combination with physical descent, why otherwise, for both cultured and uncultured alike, would the native tongue possess a strength and intimacy so much greater than any foreign one, that after long abstention it greets the ear with a sort of sudden magic, and awakens longing when far from home? This obviously does not depend upon its mental content, the thought or emotion expressed, but rather on the very thing that is least explicable and · most individual, its sound; it is as if we were perceiving, in the native tongue, a portion of ourselves.

The picture of language as designating merely *objects*, already perceived in themselves, is also disconfirmed by examination of what language engenders as its product. By means of such a picture we would never, in fact, exhaust the deep and full content of language. Just as no concept is possible without language, so also there can be no object for the mind, since it is only through the concept, of course, that anything external acquires full being for consciousness. But the whole mode of *perceiving* things *subjectively* necessarily passes over into cultivation and the use of language. For the *word* arises from this very perceiving; it is a copy, not of the object in itself, but of the image thereof produced in consciousness. Since all objective perception is inevitably tinged with *subjectivity*, we may consider every human individual, even apart from language, as a unique aspect of the world-view. But he becomes still more of one through language, since as we shall see later, by an added meaning of its own the word constitutes itself an object for the mind, and superimposes a new character. Via the latter, *qua* character of a speech-sound, a pervasive analogy necessarily prevails in the same language; and since a like subjectivity also affects language in the same notion, there resides in every language a characteristic *world-view*. As the individual sound stands between man and the object, so the entire language steps in between him and the nature that operates, both inwardly and outwardly, upon him. He surrounds himself with a world of sounds, so as to take up and process within himself the world of objects. These expressions in no way outstrip the measure of the simple truth. Man lives primarily with objects, indeed, since feeling and acting in him depend on his presentations, he actually does so exclusively, as language presents them to him. By the same act whereby he spins language out of himself, he spins himself into it, and every language draws about the people that possesses it a circle whence it is possible to exit only by stepping over at once into the circle of another one. To learn a *foreign language* should therefore be to acquire a new standpoint in the world-view hitherto possessed, and in fact to a certain extent is so, since every language contains the whole conceptual fabric and mode of presentation of a portion of mankind. But because we always carry over, more or less, our own world-view, and even our own language-view, this outcome is not purely and completely experienced.

Even the *beginnings of language* should not be thought restricted to so meagre a stock of words as is commonly supposed when, instead of seeking its inception in the original summons to free human *sociality*, we attribute it primarily to the need for mutual *assistance*, and project mankind into an imagined state of nature. Both are among the most erroneous views that can be taken about language. Man is not so needy, and to render assistance, unarticulated sounds would have sufficed. Even in its beginnings, language is human throughout, and is extended unthinkingly to all objects of casual sense perception and inner concern. Even the languages of so-called *savages*, who would have, after all, to come closer to such a state of nature, exhibit, in fact, a wealth and multiplicity of expressions that everywhere exceeds what is required. Words well up freely from the breast, without necessity or intent, and there may well have been no wandering horde in any desert that did not already have its own songs. For man, as a species, is a singing creature, though the notes, in his case, are also coupled with thought.

But language does not merely implant an indefinable multitude of *material elements* out of nature into the soul; it also supplies the latter with that which confronts us from the totality as *form*. Nature unfolds before us a many-hued and, by all sensory impressions, a diverse manifold, suffused with a luminous clarity. Our subsequent reflection discovers therein a *regularity* congenial to our mental form. Aside, from the bodily existence of things, their outlines are clothed, like a magic intended for man alone, with external beauty, in which regularity and sensory material enter an alliance that still remains inexplicable to us, in that we are seized and carried away by it. All this we find again in analogous harmonies within language, and language is able to depict it. For in passing, by means of it, into a world of sounds, we do not abandon the world that really surrounds us. The regularity of language's own structure is akin to that of nature; and in thereby arousing man in the activity of his highest and most human powers, it also brings him closer, as such, to an understanding of the formal impress of nature, since, the latter, too, can after all be regarded simply as a development of mental powers. Through the rhythmical and musical form whose linkages are peculiar to sound, language enhances the impression of beauty in nature, transposing it into another sphere, but acts, even independently of this, through the mere cadence of speech upon the temper of the soul.

What is *uttered* at any time differs from *language*, as the body of its products; and before leaving the present section, we must take time to examine this difference more closely. A language, in its whole compass, contains everything that it has transformed into sounds. But just as the matter of thinking, and the infinity of its combinations, can never be exhausted, so it is equally impossible to do this with the mass of what calls for designation and connection in language. In addition to its already formed elements, language also consists, before all else, of methods for carrying forward the work of the mind, to which it prescribes the path and the form. The elements, once firmly fashioned, constitute, indeed, a relatively dead mass, but one which bears within itself the living seed of a never-ending determinability. At every single point and period, therefore, language, like nature itself, appears to man—in contrast to all else that he has already known and thought of—as an inexhaustible storehouse, in which the mind can always discover something new to it, and feeling perceive what it has not yet felt in this way. In every treatment of language by a genuinely new and great talent, this phenomenon is evinced in reality; and in order to encourage him in the constant labour of his intellectual struggle, and progressive unfolding of his mental life, man does in fact require that, beyond the field of past achievements, a vista should remain open to him into an infinite mass that still waits to be gradually unravelled. But language contains at the same time, in two directions, a dark unrevealed depth. For rearwards, even, it flows out from an unknown wealth that is still to a certain extent discernible, but then closes off, leaving only a sense of its unfathomability. For us, who receive light from a brief past only, language shares this *infinitude*, without beginning or end, with the whole existence of mankind. But in it we gain a clearer and more vivid sense of how even the distant past is still linked with the feeling of today; for language has traversed through the experience of earlier generations and preserved a breath of this; and these generations have a national and family kinship to us in these same sounds of the mother-tongue, which serve to express our own feelings as well.

This partly *fixed* and partly *fluid* content of language engenders a special relationship between it and the *speaking generation*. There is generated within it a stock of words and a system of rules whereby it grows, in the course of millennia, into an independent force. As we noted above, the thought once embodied in language becomes an object for the soul, and to that extent exerts thereon an effect that is alien to it. But we have primarily considered the object as having arisen from the subject, the effect as having proceeded from that upon which it reacts. We now encounter the opposite view, whereby language is truly an alien object, and its effect has in fact proceeded from something other than what it works on. For language must necessarily be a joint possession (pp.56,57), and is in truth the property of the whole human species. Now since, in writing, it also keeps slumbering thoughts ready for arousal to the mind, it comes to enjoy a peculiar existence, which in every case, admittedly, can only hold good in the current act of thinking, but in its totality is independent of this. The two opposing views here stated, that language belongs to or is foreign to the soul, depends or does not depend upon it, are in actuality combined there and constitute the peculiarity of its nature. Nor must this conflict be resolved by making language in part something alien and independent, and in part neither one nor the other. Language is objectively active and independent, precisely in so far as it is subjectively passive and dependent. For nowhere, not even in writing, does it have a permanent abode; its ' dead ' part must always be regenerated in thinking, come to lire in speech and understanding, and hence must pass over entirely into the subject. But this act of regeneration consists, precisely, in likewise making an object of it; it thereby undergoes on each occasion the full impact of the individual, but this impact is already in itself governed by what language is doing and has done. The true solution of this opposition lies in the *unity* of *human nature*. In what stems from that, in what is truly one with myself, the concepts of subject and object, of dependence and independence, are each merged into the other. Language belongs to me, because I bring it forth as I do; and since the ground of this lies at once in the speaking and having-spoken of every generation of men, so far as speech-communication may have prevailed unbroken among them, it is language itself which restrains me when I speak. But that in it which limits and determines me has arrived there from a human nature intimately allied to my own, and its alien element is therefore alien only for my transitory individual nature, not for my original and true one.

When we think how the current *generation* of a people is governed by all that their *language* has undergone, through all the preceding centuries, and how only the power of the single generation impinges thereon—and this not even purely, since those coming up and those departing live mingled side by side—it then becomes evident how small, in fact, is the *power* of *the individual* compared to the might of language. Only through the latter's uncommon plasticity, the possibility of assimilating its forms in very different ways without damage to general understanding, and through the dominion exercised by every living mind over its dead heritage, is the balance somewhat restored. Yet it is always language in which every individual feels most vividly that he is nothing but an outflow of the whole of mankind. For while each reacts individually and incessantly upon it, every generation nevertheless produces a change in it, which only too often escapes notice. For the change does not always reside in the words and forms themselves, but at times only in their differently modified usage; and where writing and literature are lacking, the latter is harder to perceive. The reaction of the individual upon language becomes more apparent if we consider, as we must not omit to do if our concepts are to be sharply defined, that the *individuality* of a language (as the term is commonly understood) is only comparatively such, whereas true individuality resides only in the *speaker* at any given time. Only in the individual does language receive its ultimate determinacy. Nobody means by a word precisely and exactly what his neighbour does, and the difference, be it ever so small, vibrates, like a ripple in water, throughout the entire language. Thus all understanding is always at the same time a not—understanding, all concurrence in thought and feeling at the same time a divergence. The manner in which language is modified in every individual discloses, in contrast to its previously expounded *power*, a dominion of man over it. Its power may be regarded (if we wish to apply the term to mental forces) as a physiological efficacy; the dominion emanating from man is a purely dynamical one. In the influence exerted on him lies the *regularity* of language and its forms; in his own reaction, a principle of *freedom*. For a thing may spring up in man, for which no understanding can discover the reason in previous circumstances; and we should misconceive the nature of language, and violate, indeed, the historical truth of its emergence and change, if we sought to exclude from it the possibility of such inexplicable phenomena. But though freedom in itself may be indeterminable and inexplicable, its bounds can perhaps be discovered, within a certain sphere reserved to it alone; and linguistic research must recognize and respect the phenomenon of freedom, but also be equally careful in tracing its limits.

(*On Language*: *On the Diversity of Human Language Construction and its Influence on the Mental Development of the Human Species.* 世界图书出版公司, 2008)

译文:

# 语言的一般性质和特点

姚小平, 译

13

　　由于语言的差别取决于其形式, 而形式与民族的精神禀赋, 与那种在创造或改造之际渗入它之中的精神力量关系极为密切, 所以, 有必要进一步阐述这些概念, 至少要更详细地考察语言的某些主要方面。为此, 我将选择一些最能说明问题的方面, 它们会十分明确地告诉我们, 内在的力量怎样对语言产生影响, 而语言又怎样反过来影响了这一力量。

　　在对语言作一般的思考和对相互明显有别的具体语言进行分析时, 我们会遇到两个重要的因素: 其一是语音形式; 其二是语音形式的运用, 即用于表达事物的名称和联系思想。语音形式的运用取决于思维对语言提出的要求, 由此而形成了语言的一般规律; 这些规律就其初始的活动而言, 对所有的人来说是共同的, 虽然人们的精神禀性或者其日后的发展各有特点。至于语音形式, 则与此相反。不论就语音形式本身来看, 还是从把它跟内在语言倾向对立起来、起着促进或抑制作用的精神力量来看, 语音形式都是构成和主导着语言差异的真正原因。作为与内在精神力量密切相关的人类有机整体的组成部分, 语音形式自然也同民族的全部精神禀赋相关联, 但这种联系的实质和原因业已湮灭在几乎不可能探明的黑暗之中。在上述两个因素及其相互渗透的基础之上,便形成了每一语言的个别形式。语言分析的目的就在于研究和描述这两个因素之间的关系。最要紧的是,需要树立起一种有关语言和语言深远的源流、广泛的作用范围的正确观点,在这种观点的基础上进行我们的研究。关于这个问题我们还将继续讨论。

**14**

在此,我从最广的角度来讨论语言的运作(Verfahren),即不仅要涉及语言跟言语、跟作为其直接产品的全部词汇要素有关的方面,而且也要探讨语言与思维—感知能力的关系。语言如何从精神出发,再反作用于精神,这是我要考察的全部过程。

语言是构成思想的器官(das bildende Organ des Gedankens)。智力活动完全是精神的和内在的,一定程度上会不留痕迹地逝去,这种活动通过声音而在言语中得到外部表现,并为感官知觉到。因此,智力活动与语言是一个不可分割的整体。但智力活动本身也有必要与语音建立联系,否则思维就无法明确化,表象就不能上升为概念。思想、发音器官、听觉同语言之间密不可分的联系,无疑出自无法进一步加以解释的人类本性的原始安排。同时,语音与思想的吻合也十分明白易见。思想可比作一道闪电或一声霹雳,它在爆发的瞬间将全部的想象力集于一点,排斥所有其余的对象;同样,语音作为一个统一体,也以断续、明确的形式发出。正如思想控制着整个心灵,语音首先具备一种能够渗透和震撼所有神经的力量。语音的这个特点使它有别于所有其他的感觉印象,这种特点显然跟下述事实有关:听觉(它往往或始终不同于其他感官)获得了一种运动的印象,即通过发出的声音接收到一种实际行为,而这一行为是从一个有生命体的内心深底生成的;进一步看,感觉的生物能发出非分节音,思维的生物则还能发出分节音。正如最合乎人性的思维在黑暗中渴慕着光明,于囹圄中向往着无限的自由一样,声音从胸腔的深底向外冲出,在空气这种最精微、最易于流动的元素中觅得一种极其合适的媒质,而这一媒质表面上看并不具备实体性,这使得它在感觉上也与精神一致。语音切分的明确性对于理解事物的知性是不可或缺的。无论外部自然的事物,还是内在心灵的活动,都以大量的特征对人产生着影响,而人则努力进行比较、区分、联系,他的更远大的目标是力求达到日益丰富的统一性。因此,他也要把事物理解为确定的统一体,并要求用一个语音的统一体来代表统一的事物。语音并不排斥事物加于外部感觉和内部意识之上的任何其他印象,而是成为它们的载体;讲话者怎样凭个人感觉把握事物,语音也就怎样以其独特的、与事物属性相关联的性质表达一个特殊的新印象。同时,语音的清晰性这一特点允许它拥有大量变体(Modificationen),这些变体的数量难以确定,但相互间明确区别开来,不会发生混淆。显然,任何其他感觉渠道都不可能达到如此丰富的变异程度。人的智力活动不仅促使头脑思考,而且还促使人的全身活跃,因此,语音对智力活动起着特别重要的推动作用。发音器官发出的声音恰似有生命体的呼气,从人的胸中流出,即使在未使用语言的情况下,声音也可以传达痛苦、欢乐、厌恶和渴望,这意味着,声音源出于生命,并且也把生命注入了接收声音的感官;就像语言本身一样,语音不仅指称事物,而且复现了事物所引起的感觉,通过不断重复的行为把世界与人统一起来,也就是说,语音把人的独立自主性与被动接受性联系了起来。最后,人所独有而不为动物所具的直立行走姿势,也与语音相适应。这种姿势似乎是由语音导致的。因为,言语不应被压抑在地面上,它期待着自由地从一个人的嘴中发出,传递给另一个人,它伴随有面部表情和手势,换言之,言语与使人成其为人的一切有关。

关于语音对精神运动的适宜性,我们暂时讲到这里。现在,我们可以更详细地来讨论思维与语言的内在联系。主观的活动在思维中构成一个客体。事实上,没有任何一类表象能够被认为是对某个现存事物所作的单纯接受性的观察。感官的活动必须与精神的内部行为综合起来,从这种联系之中便产生了表象;表象成为对立于主观力量的客体,而它作为客体又被重新知觉到,从而回到主观力量上来。对于这个过程,语言的参与是必不可缺的。因为,精神努力要借助语言经由嘴唇而开辟通向外部的道路,同时这一努力的结果又折回讲话者自己的耳朵。这就是说,表象获得了真实的客观性,却并不因此而失去主观性。这一过程唯有借助语言才能完成。语言始终参与了表象的转化,即使在沉默不语的情况下,表象也会借助语言而获得客观性,然后再回到主体上来。没有这种过程,就不可能构成概念,不可能有真正意义的思维。所以,即使不考虑人与人之间交际的需要,讲话也是个人在与世隔绝的寂寞中进行思维的一个必要条件。然而,从表现形式看,语言只能在社会中发展,一个人只有在别人身上试验过他的词语的可理解性,才能够达到自我理解。当一个自己生造的词从别人嘴里说出来时,词的客观性便得到了提高;而它的主观性也丝毫未损,因为人与人的感觉始终是统一的。不仅如此,由于转变为语言的表象不再仅仅属于一个主体,主观性甚至可以说得到了加强。获得了语言表达的观念为他人所接受,于是便成了整个人类共有的财富,而每一个人都拥有这种观念的变体之一,在他人的观念变体的影响下,这种个人的观念变体会朝着完善化的目标发展。在相同的条件下,集体对一种语言的影响越强烈、越广泛,该语言所获得的东西也就越多。在形成思想的简单行为中,语言是不可或缺的,在人的精神生活中,自始至终也同样需要语言;通过语言进行的社会交往,使人赢得了从事活动的信心和热情。思维的力量需要有某种既与之类似又与之有别的对象;通过与之类似的对象,思维的力量受到了激励,而通过与之有别的对象,思维的力量得以验证自身内在创造的实质。尽管认识永恒真理的基础在于人的内心之中,但人求索真理的精神努力始终有误入歧途的危险。人会清楚地意识到自己的易变性和局限性,他不得不把真理看作某种外在于他的存在,而使他能够衡测他与真理的距离并接近真理的最强有力的手段,便是他同其他个人的社会交往。所有的讲话行为,包括最简单的讲话,都是个人的认识与人类共同本性的结合。

理解也同样如此。理解在心灵中只能借助人本身的活动进行,其实,理解和讲话只不过是同一种语言力量的不同作用。相互间的交谈绝不等于相互之间传递同一种语言材料。理解者必须像讲话者一样,借助自己的内在力量重新把握同一些语言材料;他所知觉到的,只是能够引发相同感受的刺激。由于这个缘故,人会很自然地把刚刚听懂的话马上重新说出来。语言便是以这样的方式整个地存在于每一个人的身上,这就是说,在每个人身上都表现出一种受到某一确定的力量调节、推动或约束的倾向:在外部和内部因素的诱导下,个人逐渐从自身中产生出整个语言,并使其语言为他人所理解。

人类本性是统一的,它只是显示为分离存在的个性。假如在具体个人的差异中并不存在统一的人类本性,那么,理解就不可能像我们上面指出的那样依赖于独立自主的内在力量,共同的言语交往也无法通过唤起听话者的语言能力来进行。对词的理解完全不同于对非分节音的理解,区别在于,前一种理解远不限于仅仅指出声音和所指事物的相互联系。当然,词也可以被当作不能分割的整体,好比我们在读文字作品时,虽说还不清楚词的字母组成关系,却已经能理解一个词组的意思了;也许,儿童的心智在理解力发展的最初阶段就是这样起作用的。但是,如果参与理解活动的不仅有动物式的感觉能力,而且也包括人的语言能力(在儿童身上很可能就已如此,尽管其语言能力还很弱小),那么词就会被知觉为分节的单位。由于具有分节性,词不仅在听者身上唤起相应的意义(分节性显然能使这一过程更加完善),而且作为一个无限的整体——即一种语言——的一部分直接呈现在听者的面前。事实上,分节性使得人们有可能根据一定的感觉和规则,利用一些具体的词的要素构成数量不定的其他的词,从而在所有的词中间建立起一种与概念上的类似性相吻合的类似关系。另一方面,在我们的心灵中必定存在着一种将上述可能性付诸实现的力量,否则,我们甚至不可能猜度到这种人为的构造方式,也不可能意识到分节性的存在,就像盲人分辨不出颜色一样。因为,语言不应被视为一种整体上可以一览无遗的或者可以拆散开来逐渐传递的质料,而应被看作是一种永不停顿地自我创造的质料;创造的规律是确定的,但产品的范围以及一定程度上创造的方式却完全是非确定的。儿童学讲话,并不是接受词语、嵌入记忆和用嘴唇咿呀模仿的过程,而是语言能力随时间和练习的增长。听到的话不只是告诉我们些什么,而且还有助于心灵更容易理解过去从未听到过的东西;听到的话会使很久以前听到过,但当时似懂非懂或者完全未懂的内容变得清楚明白,因为,经过长期磨砺的精神力量会突然悟识到,很久以前听到的话与刚刚听到的话有相似之处;此外,听到的话还促使听者把词语越来越多、越来越快地转入记忆,同时越来越少地把它们当作空无内容的声音放过去。所以,这样的进步与学习单词不同。学习单词只是通过加强记忆力的训练,以平均的速度增长;而我们在此所说的进步,则是一种始终在自我提高的发展,因为语言能力的提高和语言材料的累积是相互促进的。儿童并不是机械地学习语言,而是发展起语言能力,这就证明了一个事实:由于人最主要的各种能力是在一生的某个确定时期内发展起来的,所以,处在极不同条件下的所有儿童差不多都在同一伸缩性很小的年龄期学会讲话和理解。假如说话人和听话人不具备一种适合于双方,但以个人形式分隔存在的人类共同本质,那么听话人仅仅依靠他自身孤立地发展起来的能力,何以能够驾驭说出来的话? 分节音是一种微妙的符号,它正是由人类共同本质最深刻、最实在的特性造就的,借助于这种符号,听说双方才能够以协调一致的方式进行交往。

有人可能会对这种看法提出异议,指出:任何一个民族的儿童如果在开始学讲话前被置于另一个民族的环境之中,都将发展起该民族的语言能力。人们会说,这一无可辩驳的事实清楚地证明,语言只不过是对听到的话语所作的重复;语言只依赖于社会交往,而与人类本质的统一性和不同表现形式无关。但持这种观点的人恐怕未能足够细心地注意到,要战胜本族语的型式(die Stammanlage)①有多么困难。或许,在最细微的色彩方面,这种型式终于未被克服而保留了下来。然而,即使不考虑这一点,儿童能获得任一语言的能力这种现象也足以说明,人与人到处是同一的,因此,语言能力在任何个人身上都可以生长起来。而另一方面,语言能力同样可以说是从个人内部发展起来的,只是由于自始至终需要外部刺激,语言能力的发展才必须适应于外部环境的影响,并且在跟人类所有语言的一致关系上都保持着这种适应性。当然,语言受到民族起源的制约,这一点相当明显地反映在语言按民族来划分这个事实上。这种制约是不言而喻的,因为民族起源极其强烈地影响着个性,而每一具体语言则极为紧密地与个性联系在一起。语言产生自人类本质的深底,同时,语言与人的民族起源也建立起了真正的、实质性的联系。假如不是这样,那么,为什么母语无论对于文明人还是对于野蛮人都具有一种远胜过异族语言的强大力量和内在价值? 为什么母语能够用一种突如其来的魅力愉悦回归家园者的耳朵,而当他身处远离家园的异邦时,会撩动他的恋乡之情? 在这种场合,起决定作用的因素并不是语言的精神方面或语言所表达的思想、情感,而恰恰是语言最不可解释、最具个性的方面,即其语音。每当我们听到母语的声音时,就好像感觉到了我们自身的部分存在。

当我们分析通过语言创造出来的东西时,同样不能证实这样一种看法,即语言似乎仅仅表示已被知觉到的对象。根据这种看法,事实上是不可能穷尽语言深刻和全面的内容的。没有语言,就不会有任何概念,同样,没有语言,我们的心灵就不会有任何对象。因为对心灵来

---

① 参考英译:the native pattern,俄译:врожденные задатки。——译者

说,每一个外在的对象唯有借助概念才会获得完整的存在。而另一方面,对事物的全部主观知觉都必然在语言的构造和运用上得到体现。要知道,词正是从这种知觉行为中产生的。词不是事物本身的模印,而是事物在心灵中造成的图像的反映。任何客观的知觉都不可避免地混杂有主观成分,所以,撇开语言不谈,我们也可以把每个有个性的人看作世界观的一个独特的出发点。但个人更多的是通过语言而形成世界观,因为正如我们下面还要讲到的那样,词会借助自身附带的意义而重新成为心灵的客观对象,从而带来一种新的特性。在同一语言中,这种特性和语音特性一样,必然受到广泛的类推原则的制约;而由于在同一个民族中,影响着语言的是同一类型的主观性,可见,每一语言都包含着一种独特的世界观。正如个别的音处在事物和人之间,整个语言也处在人与那一从内部和外部向人施加影响的自然之间。人用语音的世界把自己包围起来,以便接受和处理事物的世界。我们的这些表达绝没有超出简单真理的范围。人同事物生活在一起,他主要按照语言传递事物的方式生活,而因为人的感知和行为受制于他自己的表象,我们甚至可以说,他完全是按照语言的引导在生活。人从自身中造出语言,而通过同一种行为,他也把自己束缚在语言之中;每一种语言都在它所隶属的民族周围设下一道樊篱,一个人只有跨过另一种语言的樊篱进入其内,才有可能摆脱母语樊篱的约束。所以,我们或许可以说,学会一种外语就意味着在业已形成的世界观的领域里赢得一个新的立足点。在某种程度上说,这确是事实,因为每一种语言都包含着属于某个人类群体的概念和想象方式的完整体系。掌握外语的成就之所以没有被清楚地意识到,完全是因为人们或多或少总是把自己原有的世界观,甚至原有的语言观(Sprachansicht),带进一种陌生的语言。

即使是语言的初始时期,也不像通常认为的那样,只有寥寥可数的一些词。人们习惯上不是到人类自由的群体交往这一原初的使命中去寻找语言的起源,却以为语言的发生主要是由于人与人需要相互提供帮助,结果是把人类置于一种假想的自然状态之中。这样的观点是极其错误的。人绝不会贫困到如此地步,为了相互提供帮助,人也只需要有不分节的声音就足够了。语言从一开始就纯属人类所有,它任意地扩展开来,接触到偶然的感性知觉和内心思考的一切对象。所谓的野蛮人可能比较接近这样一种自然状态,但他们的语言恰恰处处显示了大量超出需要、丰富多样的表达。语词并不是迫于需要和出于一定目的而萌生,而是自由自在地、自动地从胸中涌出的;任何荒原上的游牧人群,恐怕都有自己的歌曲,因为人作为动物的一类,乃是会歌唱的生物,所不同的是他把曲调同思想联系了起来。

语言不仅仅从自然界中提取出数量不定的物质要素植入我们的心灵,而且也把作为一个整体呈现出来的形式赋予了这些要素。大自然无比清晰地向我们展示了一个纷繁综杂、形态万千、富有一切感性特征的现象世界,我们则通过思考,从中发现一种与我们的精神形式相适应的规律。同时,事物的外在之美脱离了其物质实存,如同只对人起作用的魔法一般附着在事物的轮廓上,而正是在这一外在的美里面,我们所发现的规律与感性材料结合了起来;虽然我们受到这种结合的影响和牵制,却无法对之作出解释。在语言中,我们可以看到与以上所述相类似的一切,语言能够反映出这一切。因为,当我们随语言而进入一个声音的世界时,我们并未弃周围的现实世界于不顾;语言结构的规律与自然界的规律相似,语言通过其结构激发人的最高级、最合乎人性的(menschlichste)力量投入活动,从而帮助了人深入认识自然界的形式特征。其实,这类形式特征本身就反映了精神力量不可解释的发展。语音组合具有独特的节律和音乐形式,借助于这种形式,语言把人带入了另一个领域,强化了人对自然中的美的印象,但语言并不依赖于这些印象,它只是通过语声的抑扬顿挫对内心情绪产生影响。

语言不同于每次所讲的话,它是讲话产品的总和。我们在结束本节以前,还要进一步详细讨论这一差别。一种语言的整个范围,包括通过该语言而转化为声音的一切。思维的材料以及思维的联系是永无穷尽的,语言中大量的名称和关系也同样难以穷尽。除了已经形成的要素外,语言最主要的部分也是由方法(Methoden)构成的,这些方法为精神劳动规定下了继续发展的道路和形式。要素的形式一经确定,要素本身在某种意义上说就成了死的物质,然而,这一物质含有生动的、永远无法限定的胚胎。所以,在每个具体的时刻或历史时期,语言正像自然界本身一样,对人来说显得跟他已知的和所想到的一切相反,是一个取之不尽的宝库。精神始终能够不断地从这个宝库中发掘出未知的东西,感觉也始终能够以新的方式从中知觉到以前从未体验过的对象。这个事实反映在真正新型的、伟大的天才人物对语言的每一项处理之中;在永无止境的智力追求和不断扩充的精神生活中,人必须时刻保持不衰的热情,因此,人不能满足于已获成功的领域,他还必须看到一个无限广阔的、逐渐明朗开来的前景。但语言同时在两个方向上包含着模糊不清、未被揭启的深底。因为往回看,语言也是从不为我们所知的财富发展而来,这一财富只能在一定范围内为我们认识到,其余的部分则锁闭起来,只给我们留下了深不可测的印象。语言的这种起始上和终结上的无穷尽性,与人类的整个存在一样,能够被解释清楚的只是一段短短的过去史。然而,人们在语言中可以更明确、更生动地感觉和猜测到,遥远的过去仍与现在的感情相维系,因为语言深深地渗透着历代先人的经验感受,保留着先人的气息。这些先辈与我们的民族联系和亲缘关系,体现在同一种母语的同一些语音上,我们自己就是用这种母语来表达感情。

语言的这种半稳固、半流动的性质,导致了语言和讲话的一代人之间的独特关系。语言累积起词汇,确立起一个规则系统,借助这一切,语言历经千万年而成长为一种独立自主的力量。前面我们曾讲到,语言所吸收的思想转化为心灵的客观对象,在此意义上说,思想是从外部对心灵产生着影响。但在这种场合,我们主要把客体看作是主体的产物,认为客体产生的影响导源于其反作用所施及的主体本身。现在我们则要来讨论另一种相反的观点,根据这一观点,语言的的确确是一个外在的客体,它所产生的影响来自与这种影响施及的对象不同的另一个源泉。事实上,语言必然既属主体,又属客体,它是整个人类的财产。甚至在文字作品中,语言也保存着能够由精神唤醒的潜在思想,所以,语言本身便构成了一种独特的实存,这一实存虽然始终只能在每一次具体的思维行为中得到实现,但整体上并不依赖于思维。这里提出的两种对立的观点,即语言有异于、独立于心灵和语言隶属于、依赖于心灵,实际上可以统一起来,说明语言的本质特性。语言所包含的这种矛盾,我们不应当这样来理解:似乎语言部分是外在和独立的,而部分则并不如此。事实是,语言客观地、独立自主地发挥作用,另一方面它恰恰在同一程度上受到主观的影响和制约。因为,语言在任何场合,哪怕是在文字作品里,都不会停滞不动,那些仿佛僵死的语言成分始终必须在思维中得到重新创造,生动地转变为言语或理解,并最终全部转入主体;而正是通过这同一种创造行为,语言成了客体:语言每次都以这样的方式经受着个人的全部影响,但这种影响却受到语言本身正在造就和业已造就的东西的束缚。上述矛盾对立的真正答案在于人类本性的统一之中。主体与客体、依赖性与独立性的概念,在与自我原本一致的人类本性中相互转化。语言属于我,因为我以我的方式生成语言;另一方面,由于语言的基础同时存在于历代人们的讲话行为和所讲的话之中,它可以一代一代不间断地传递下去,所以,语言本身又对我起着限制作用。然而,语言中限制、确定着我的东西,出自与我有着内在联系的人类本性,因此,语言中的异物只是有异于我瞬时的个人本性,而非有异于我原初的真正本性。

一个民族的语言多少世纪来所经验的一切,对该民族的每一代人起着强有力的影响,而接触这种影响的只不过是单独一代人的力量,更何况这种力量从来就不是纯一的,因为正在成长中的一代人和正在消逝的一代人总是交混生活在一起。如果考虑到这些,就可以看出,面对语言的威力(Macht),个人的力量实在是微不足道的。只有依靠语言的极大可塑性(Bildsamkeit),依靠以许多不同方式把握语言的形式但又无损于一般理解的可能性,以及依靠生动的精神力量对僵死的传统质料所施予的强力(Gewalt),个人才能保持他与语言的平衡关系。语言始终能使一个人清楚地意识到,他仅仅是整个人类的一分子。但由于每一个人都单独地、连续地反作用于语言,每一代人于是都会在语言中引起一些变化。不过,这些变化常常不为人们所注意,因为它们并不总是发生在词和词的形式上,有时起变化的只是词及其形式的不同用法;后一类变化在缺乏文字和文献的场合更难以察觉。一种语言的个性(按照通常对这个词的理解)只是比较起来才可以说是个性,真正的个性则仅仅包含在每次讲话的具体个人之中。这个事实,在给有关概念下准确的定义时是不可忽略的,我们可以从中更明了地看出具体个人对语言的反作用。只有在个人身上,语言才获得了最终的规定性。运用词语时,每个人都跟别人想得不一样,一个极其微小的个人差异会像一圈波纹那样在整个语言中散播开来。所以,任何理解同时始终又是不理解,思想和情感上的所有一致同时也是一种离异。语言在每一个人身上产生的变异,体现了人对语言所施的强力,这种强力同上面讲到过的语言对人的威力刚好相反。语言的威力(如果用这个表达指精神力量的话)可以被视为一种生理学的作用(ein physiologisches Wirken),而人对语言的强力则是一种纯动态的作用(ein rein dynamisches Wirken)。语言及其形式的规律性,决定着语言对人的影响,而决定着人对语言的反作用的是一种自由性原则。因为,在人身上可以萌现某种新生的东西,其原因任何知性在先前的状态中都无法找到;否认有发生这种不可解释的现象的可能,就意味着忽略了语言的本性,并且恰恰歪曲了语言产生和变化的历史事实。另一方面,虽然自由性本身是无法确定、不可解释的,但在它所独享的一定活动范围内,我们也许有可能发现它的界限。语言研究者必须承认和尊重这种自由性原则的作用,同时也要细致地探索其界限。

(节选自《论人类语言结构的差异及其对人类精神发展的影响》,商务印书馆,2017)

# 2.庄子(选段)

## 庄 子

夫言非吹也,言者有言。其所言者特未定也。果有言邪?其未尝有言邪?其以为异于鷇音,亦有辩乎?其无辩乎?道恶乎隐而有真伪?言恶乎隐而有是非?道恶乎往而不存?言恶乎存而不可?道隐于小成,言隐于荣华。故有儒墨之是非,以是其所非而非其所是。欲是其所非而非其所是,则莫若以明。……

故曰:莫若以明。

以指喻指之非指,不若以非指喻指之非指也;以马喻马之非马,不若以非马喻马之非马也。天地一指也,万物一马也。(庄子·齐物论第二)

世之所贵道者,书也。书不过语,语有贵也。语之所贵者,意也,意有所随;意之所随者,不可以言传也;而世因贵言传书。世虽贵之,犹不足贵也,为其贵非其贵也。故视而可见者,形与色也;听而可闻者,名与声也。悲夫!世人以形色名声为足以得彼之情。夫形色名声,果不足以得彼之情,则知者不言,言者不知,而世岂识之哉!(庄子·天道第十三)

荃者所以在鱼,得鱼而忘荃;蹄者所以在兔,得兔而忘蹄;言者所以在意,得意而忘言。吾安得夫忘言之人而与之言哉!(庄子·杂篇·外物第二十六)

（节选自《庄子浅注》,中华书局,2000）

## 【推荐阅读】

Culler, Jonathan. Literary theory: a Very Short Introduction [M]. New York: Oxford University Press, 1997.

# 参考文献

[1] 弗兰兹·博厄斯.原始人的心智[M].项龙,王星,译.北京:国际文化出版公司,1989.

[2] 布龙菲尔德.语言论[M].袁家骅,赵世开,甘世福,译.北京:商务印书馆,1980.

[3] 曹础基.庄子浅注[M].北京:中华书局,1982.

[4] 岑运强.语言学概论[M].北京:中国人民大学出版社,2004.

[5] 陈平.现代语言学研究:理论·方法与事实[M].重庆:重庆出版社,1991.

[6] 许慎.说文解字注[M].段玉裁,注.上海:上海古籍出版社,1981.

[7] 冯胜利,施春宏.韵律语法学的构建历程、理论架构与学理意义[J].语言科学,2021,20(1):38-59.

[8] 高更生.现行汉字规范问题[M].北京:商务印书馆,2002.

[9] 高名凯,石安石.语言学概论[M].北京:中华书局,1987.

[10] A.J.格雷马斯.结构语义学[M].吴泓缈,译.北京:生活·读书·新知三联书店,1999.

[11] 葛本仪.语言学概论[M].2版.济南:山东大学出版社,1999.

[12] 郭熙.中国社会语言学[M].南京:南京大学出版社,1999.

[13] R.A.郝德森.社会语言学[M].卢德平,译.北京:华夏出版社,1989.

[14] 威廉·冯·洪堡特.论人类语言结构的差异及其对人类精神发展的影响[M].北京:商务印书馆,2002.

[15] 胡明扬.语言学概论[M].北京:语文出版社,2000.

[16] 胡壮麟,刘润清,李延福.语言学教程[M].北京:北京大学出版社,2001.

[17] 霍凯特.现代语言学教程[M].索振羽,叶蜚声,译.北京:北京大学出版社,2002.

[18] 贾彦德.汉语语义学[M].2版.北京:北京大学出版社,1999.

[19] 蒋绍愚.古汉语词汇纲要[M].北京:北京大学出版社,1989.

[20] 杰弗里·N.利奇.语义学[M].李瑞华,等,译.上海:上海外语教育出版社,1987.

[21] 林惠祥.文化人类学[M].北京:商务印书馆,2011.

[22] 林焘.语音探索集稿[M].北京:北京语言学院出版社,1990.

[23] 刘富华,孙炜.语言学通论[M].北京:北京语言大学出版社,2009.

[24] 陆俭明.近百年现代汉语语法研究评说[J].东北师大学报(哲学社会科学版),2019(6):1-14.

[25] 陆俭明.韵律语法研究小议[J].韵律语法研究,2020(1):1-15.

[26] 罗常培,王均.普通语音学纲要[M].北京:商务印书馆,1981.

[27] 诺姆·乔姆斯基.乔姆斯基语言学文集[M].宁春岩,等,译注.长沙:湖南教育出版社,2006.

[28] 裘锡圭.文字学概要(修订本)[M].北京:商务印书馆,2013.

[29] 爱德华·萨丕尔.语言论[M].陆卓元,译.北京:商务印书馆,2002.

[30] 费尔迪南·德·索绪尔.普通语言学教程[M].高名凯,译.北京:商务印书馆,1980.

[31] 费尔迪南·德·索绪尔.索绪尔第三次普通语言学教程[M].屠友祥,译.上海:上海人民出版社,2007.

[32] 王德春.语言学概论[M].上海:上海外语教育出版社,2007.

[33] 王红旗.语言学概论[M].北京:北京大学出版社,2008.

[34] 王力.汉语史稿[M].北京:中华书局,1980.

[35] 伍谦光.语义学导论[M].2版.长沙:湖南教育出版社,1995.

[36] 徐烈炯.语义学(修订本)[M].北京:语文出版社,1995.

[37] 徐通锵.历史语言学[M].北京:商务印书馆,1991.

[38] 许慎.说文解字[M].北京:中华书局,1963.

[39] 杨达复,谭志明.语言学名著选读[M].兰州:西北工业大学出版社,2002.

[40] 叶蜚声,徐通锵.语言学纲要[M].北京:北京大学出版,1991.

[41] B.A.伊斯特林.文字的历史[M].左少兴,译.北京:中国国际广播出版社,2018.

[42] 俞如珍,金顺德.当代西方语法理论[M].上海:上海外语教育出版社,1994.

[43] 赵元任.赵元任语言学论文集[M].北京:商务印书馆,2006.

[44] 詹人凤.现代汉语语义学[M].北京:商务印书馆,1997.

[45] 张登岐.现代汉语[M].北京:高等教育出版,2005.

[46] 张觉.荀子译注[M].上海:上海古籍出版社,1995.

[47] 郑超.当代语言学导论[M].重庆:重庆大学出版社,2006.

[48] 周有光.世界文字发展史[M].上海:上海教育出版社,1997.

[49] Barthes, Roland. The Rustle of Language [M]. Trans. By Richar Howard. New York: Hill and Wang. 1986.

[50] Batterink, L. & Neville, H. J. The Human Brain Processes Syntax in the Absence of Conscious Awareness[J]. J Neurosci, 2013(33): 8528-8533.

[51] Bloomfield, Leonard. Language[M]. London: George Allen &: Unwin Ltd, 1955.

[52] Chomsky, Noam. Language and Mind[J]. Harcourt Brace Jovanovich, Inc., 1968.

[53] Chomsky, Noam. Syntactic structures[M]. Berlin;Hawthorne, N.Y. ;Mouton de Gruyter,2002.

[54] Chomsky, Noam. On nature and language[M]. Beijing:Peking University Press,2004.

[55] Cook, Vivian James. Chomsky's Universal Grammar: An Introduction [M]. Malden, MA; Oxford: Blackwell Pub,2007.

[56] Dehaene, S. & Cohen, L. The Unique Role of the Viual Word Form Area in Reading[J]. Trends Cogn Sci, 2011(15): 254-62.

[57] Dwight Bolinger. Aspects of Language[M]. New York/Chicago/San Francisco/Atlanta: Harcourt, Brace and World, Inc., 1968.

[58] Frawley,William. Linguistic semantics[M]. Hillsdale, NY: Lawrence Erlbaum Associates, 1992.

[59] Halliday, M.A.K. An Introduction to Functional Grammar[M]. London:Arnold, 2004.

[60] Halliday, M.A.K. On Language and Linguistics[M]. By Jonathan J. Webster. 北京大学出版社,2007.

[61] Halliday, M. A. K. Language and Education [M]. by Jonathan J. Webster. London; New York : Continuum, 2007.

[62] Hjelmslev, Louis. Prolegomena to a Theory of Language[M]. Trans. By Francis J. Whitfield. Baltimore: Waverly Press, INC, 1953.

[63] Hockett, F. A Course in Modern Linguistics[M]. New York: Macmillan Publishing co.,Inc, 1958.

[64] Horrocks, G. C. Generative Grammar[M]. London: Longman Publishing Group, 1987.

[65] Hudson, R. A. Sociolingustics[M]. Combridge university Press, 1980.

[66] Humboldt, Wilhelm von. On Language: On the Diversity of Human Language Construction and its Influence on the Mental Development of the Human Species[M]. 北京:世界图书出版公司,2008.

[67] Katz, Jerrold J. The philosophy of Linguistics[M]. New York: Oxford University Press, 1985.

[68] Krashen, Stephen D. The Input Hypothesis: Issues and Implications[M]. London: Longman Group Limited, 1985.

[69] Kutas, M. & Federmeier, K. D. Thirty Years and Counting: finding meaning in the N400 component of the event-related brain potential(ERP)[J]. Annu Rev Psychol. 2011, 62: 621-47.

[70] Leech, G. Semantics: The Study of Meaning (2nd edn.)[M]. Penguin Books Ltd, 1981.

[71] Lyons,John. Semantics. Cambridge[M]. New York: Cambridge University Press, 1977,1978.

[72] Martinich, A. P. The Philosophy of Language[M]. Oxford University Press, 1985.

[73] Payne, Thomas E. Describing morphosyntax[M]. Cambridge University Press, 1997.

[74] Robins, R.H. 普通语言学概论(General Linguistics)(英文)[M].北京:外语教学与研究出版社,2000.

[75] Ryle, G. 'Introduction', in The Revolution in Philosophy[J]. Macmillan & Co. Ltd., London, 1960:8.

[76] Saeed, John I. Semantics. 1997. Blackwell Publishers Ltd. Reprinted by 外语教学与研究出版社, 2000.

[77] Sapir. Language: an introduction to the study of speech[M]. New York: Harcourt, brace and company, INC.

[78] Saussure, F. de, Course in General Linguistics[M]. Eds. By Charles Bally & Albert Seshehaye, etc. trans. By Roy Harris. London: G. Duckworth, 1983.

[79] Taylor, John R. Linguistic Categorization: Prototypes in Linguistic Theory (second edition)[M]. Foreign Language Teaching and Research Press, Oxford Unviersity Press, 2001.

[80] Tzeng. O. J. & Hung. D. L., Cotton, B. Visual Lateralisation Effect in Reading Chinese Characters[J]. Nature. 1979, 282: 499-501.

[81] Wittgenstein, Ludwig. Philosophical Investigations[M]. Trans. By G. E. M. Anscombe. Blackwell Publishers Ltd, 2002.